1966

Jon Savage is a bestselling author, broadcaster and journalist. His books include *England's Dreaming: The Sex Pistols and Punk Rock*; *Teenage: The Creation of Youth, 1875–1945*; and *1966: The Year the Decade Exploded*. He has written sleeve notes for Wire, Saint Etienne and the Pet Shop Boys, among others, and his compilations include *Meridian 1970* (Heavenly/EMI, 2005), *Queer Noises: From the Closet to the Charts 1961–1976* (Trikont, 2006) and *Dreams Come True: Classic Electro 1982–87* (Domino, 2008). His previous book was the top-ten bestselling *This Searing Light, the Sun and Everything Else: Joy Division: The Oral History*.

Further praise for *1966*:

'Savage's best and most vital book since *England's Dreaming*. An intoxicating, cross-cultural survey that uniquely conveys the pure excitement and power of pop as a weapon for change. As always, after reading, you have learnt something new which subtly shifts your pop-consciousness.' Nicky Wire, of the Manic Street Preachers

'The book is a marvel, easily the match of Savage's celebrated punk chronicle *England's Dreaming* . . . Pleasantly dense and beautifully textured, *1966* is like an album by a great band not often enough heard from, with all filler removed. It belongs on the shelf not just with the rock chronicles of Greil Marcus but between David Kynaston's social history, *Austerity Britain*, and Eric Hobsbawm's peerless quarter on the nineteenth and twentieth centuries.' Scott Timberg, *Los Angeles Review of Books*

'*1966* upturns history . . . *1966* is an absorbing and extremely easy read because Savage is a pop writer in the truest sense. He is quick and to the point, he doesn't waste words, bottling an over-familiar song with maximum thrill and minimum fuss . . . This is not only fine pop writing, but social history of a high order.' Bob Stanley, *Guardian*

'A sprawling tour de force about the pop music of 1966 and the seismic events in the world that helped shape it . . . Vast in detail, breathtaking in scope and ambition . . . Savage's book is a timely reminder of when things were very different.' Richard Whitehead, *The Times*

'Erudite and imaginative . . . [Savage] plots a zigzag course through a turbulent and pivotal year.' Richard Williams, *Guardian* (Best Music Books of 2015)

'It is a tribute to the breadth of vision that these twelve chapters could easily have spawned a dozen books . . . Glorious . . . insightful and authoritative.' Johnny Rogan, *Irish Times*

'[*1966* has] everything you always wanted know about sixties pop – and more . . . [Savage captures] the excitement of the music or the speed, by turns thrilling and alarming, of the social change . . . Reading the book often has the arresting effect of making us realise what it must have felt like to hear these songs for the first time.' James Walton, *The Spectator*

'This was 1966; nobody quite knew what was going on. Now, thanks to this exceptional slice of pop culture history, we do.' Mark Paytress, *Mojo*

'[1966] was somewhere beyond exciting and Savage brilliantly captures the thrill of it all.' Allan Jones, *Uncut*

'It's a strength of this project that Savage opts out of the most told stories . . . The selection here of the unexpected, as a means to weave multiple contradictory strands together without losing clarity, is one of the book's pleasures.' Mark Sinker, *The Wire*

'From Haight-Ashbury to pirate radio, via the prosecution of the Rolling Stones and the arrival of the first double-album by a major artist (Bob Dylan's *Blonde on Blonde*), *1966* represents both a watershed and a high watermark in post-war culture, a delineating moment the author documents in twelve chapters, each of which focuses on a scene-setting forty-five, while using primary sources to relay first-hand just how a single year turned into an epoch.' Bill Prince, *GQ* (Recommended Read of the Month)

'Exquisitely written, stuffed full of great ideas and crackling with music, this is not only a great book about pop culture but about the sixties themselves and is a riveting and thrilling can't-put-down read.' *Louder Than War*

'Superbly produced.' Alannah Hopkin, *Irish Examiner*

'From pop to politics, *1966* brilliantly explores how one pivotal year changed our culture.' *Stylist*

'Jon Savage, in his erudite new book, remembers the year through its seminal pop music and the influence it had upon a rapidly changing world . . . The case is expressively made that the era's wild soul, pop and R 'n' B rollercoaster informed the challenges to political outlooks and fuelled revolutions in art, literature, film and fashion.' Miranda Collinge and Jacob Stolworthy, *Esquire*

'Savage is to be congratulated for confounding the preconceptions of the there's-nothing-new-you-can-tell-me-about-this brigade once again. Having achieved the same in his now seminal punk text, *England's Dreaming*, and surpassing it via the pages of the extraordinary and revelatory *Teenage*, *1966* sets a new benchmark in cultural storytelling.' Craig Austin, *Wales Arts Review*

'A detailed and compelling chronicle of the year that delivered *Pet Sounds*, *Revolver* and *Blonde on Blonde*, by the astute bestselling author of the punk bible *England's Dreaming*.' Mark Ellen, *Saga*

1966

THE YEAR THE DECADE
EXPLODED

JON SAVAGE

faber

First published in the UK in 2015
by Faber & Faber Limited
Bloomsbury House
74–77 Great Russell Street
London WC1B 3DA

This paperback edition published in 2021

Typeset by Ian Bahrami
Printed and bound by CPI Group (UK) Ltd, Croydon CR0 4YY

A CIP record for this book is available from the British Library

ISBN 978-0-571-36855-6

FSC
www.fsc.org
MIX
Paper from
responsible sources
FSC® C020471

2 4 6 8 10 9 7 5 3 1

CONTENTS

CONTENTS

viii

FOREWORD

by David Mitchell

Jon Savage has a gift for finding original angles of approach to his subjects and revealing new twists and turns behind the dominant narrative. *1966*, his biography of 'the year the decade exploded', is a fine example of Savage at his most original. To repurpose a Cees Nooteboom quote, all decades are different, but the sixties were differently different. The decade's very name is a synonym for dissent, freedom, social upheavals and clichés about love, peace and understanding. An evergreen curiosity about the era is serviced by a steady flow of histories of the 1960s. Savage sets his book apart, however, by studying the decade through the lens of a single year. The obvious choice would be 1968, a year 'pre-illustrated' with images of demonstrations and riots from Prague to Paris to Chicago and beyond, when – the dominant story goes – sixties idealism ran smack into tear gas, bullets, drug busts and commercialisation, and did not emerge victorious. All of which is, I suspect, one factor for Savage's eschewing 1968 in favour of 1966, when the revolutions – partial, doomed and counter – that defined the rest of the decade were first germinating underground. Having settled on his year, Savage dedicates each chapter to a calendar month and pairs each month with a topic – drugs and LSD; the bomb and peace movements; the effect of black music; the birth of second-wave feminism. This is masterful curating. It gives the book structure and propulsion. *1966* feels, and is, fresh.

Jon Savage has a perceptive eye for changes in the zeitgeist or, more accurately, the plural micro-zeitgeists over half a century after they happened. This clarity of vision is enabled by a deep knowledge of the films, books, drama, sport, political movements and media of the era – and, most of all, the music. Savage was a music journalist for three decades and his bibliography includes definitive studies of punk and Joy Division. *1966* explores how, by the mid-sixties, popular music was becoming a weathervane of social change – and, on occasion, the wind as well. Pro-Vietnam War factions of American society, for example, sent anthems like Sergeant Barry Sadler's 'The Ballad of the Green Berets' and Jan Berry's 'The Universal Coward' up the hit parade, while anti-war youth favoured anti-war songs such as Barry McGuire's 'Eve of Destruction' and Country Joe and the Fish's 'I Feel Like I'm Fixin' to Die'. (The author's analyses of these songs – and countless others – are one of the joys of the book and have me repeatedly opening up my laptop to track down the music.) The music charts were becoming an arena of what we now call the culture wars. Savage's knowledge of musicians' biographies, memoirs and interviews also allows him to cite them directly as evidence for the zeitgeist shifts he identifies. Pop stars stroll through *1966*'s months and pages like an ensemble cast. Not every bassist in a black turtleneck or singer in a miniskirt was an astute social commentator – though the brightest were – but right or wrong, perceptive or naive, they spoke for the youth who idolised them. Savage deploys the Beatles, the Rolling Stones, the Who, the Kinks et al to give voice to the zeitgeist they helped shape and were shaped by. Additionally, Savage conducted over a dozen interviews for the book. *1966* is, in part, an oral history.

Jon Savage possesses an outsider's eye. Historical methodology is rigorous throughout his work, and facts, drawn from fifty pages of sources cited at the end of *1966*, trump conjecture. The prose is lucid, focused and does not take sides or invite us to judge. Yet Savage spent his youth in music venues among misfits and rejects, not in academia, and it shows – as an asset. He writes with a kind of 'underground' sensibility wholly appropriate for a book about a year when the underground was going overground and when outsider groups – African Americans, gay men and lesbians, peaceniks and 'freaks', anarchists and commune dwellers – were forcing the establishment(s) to concede ground, to change or fight back. Savage's outsider's eye affords insights that a purely scholarly writer might struggle to access. In a passage on Brian Epstein, who is usually elusive to Beatles biographers, Savage discusses the strain of hiding one's sexuality on a generation of gay men:

> In many cases, the result was alcoholism, drug addiction, crippling guilt, an inability to form lasting relationships – a monstrous waste of lives. But out of this adversity came an incredible drive – the syndrome of gay overachievement . . . *Right, if you think I'm a piece of dirt, I'm going to fucking show you that I'm not . . . I'm going to ram the fact that I'm better than you right down your throat. In public. So you have to see the fact that I'm richer, cleverer, prettier than you every day, in the newspapers, in the magazines, on the television.*

Such passages are subjective from a scholarly perspective, but when they smack so authentically of earned truth, they let light in.

Jon Savage is a singular and gifted cultural historian. *1966* distils and bottles a decade whose ideas, art and politics continue to influence, haunt and recur in the world of the 2020s. Drink up.

January 2021

INTRODUCTION

'You see, there's something else I'm going to do, something I must do – only I don't know what it is. That's why I go round painting and taping and drawing and writing and that, because it may be one of them. All I know is, this isn't it for me.'

JOHN LENNON, interviewed by Maureen Cleave, 'How Does a Beatle Live? John Lennon Lives Like This', *Evening Standard*, 4 March 1966

In December 1966, an unusual multimedia magazine published its third issue. Created by former *Women's Wear Daily* editor Phyllis Johnson, *Aspen* was constructed as a sequence of stand-alone artefacts, each curated by a well-known artist or communicator and including anything from flexidiscs to Super 8 films, old newspapers and jigsaw puzzles. It was designed, in the vaunting spirit of the time, to break down the boundaries between disciplines, to transcend the bound-magazine format and, ultimately, to push through into another dimension.

The 'Fab' issue was designed by Andy Warhol and David Dalton. The cover resembled a packet of detergent, and inside were plenty of inserts to wipe clean your mind: a 'Ten-Trip Ticket Book'; a flip book with images from films by Jack Smith and Warhol; twelve postcard reproductions of pop art paintings; an *Exploding Plastic Inevitable* underground newspaper, with writing by John Wilcock, Jonas Mekas and several others; as well as a report on the recent 'Berkeley Conference on LSD'.

One of the inserts was an A4 folder entitled 'Music, Man, That's Where It's At', which contained essays by the Velvet Underground's Lou Reed, the sculptor John Chamberlain and Robert Shelton. All sought to describe the new condition of pop music in 1966. It was no longer simple commerce, teen romance or good times but something else: a total immersive experience, the popular form that, out of all the arts, truly reflected contemporary life. It was, in Reed's words, 'the only live, living thing'.

Robert Shelton developed this theme in his essay, 'Orpheus Plugs In', which, by placing Bob Dylan at the forefront, discussed how poetry and poets were taking over the charts. 'The age of space is moving us outward,' he began, 'the age of drugs is moving us inward. And the age of the new mass arts is moving us upward, inward, outward and forward. In this era of exploration, there are many breeds of navigators, but few more daring than the poet-musicians who are leading our pop music in new directions.

'Where was pop music 20 years ago?' he continued. 'Dinah Shore sang "Buttons and Bows". Helen Forrest sang "I've Heard That Song Before". Kay Kyser played "I've Got Spurs That Jingle Jangle Jingle" and "Ole Buttermilk Sky". The level of our pop music has changed profoundly in 20 years, no in five years, from pop art to juke-box poetry. Today's music is talking about unvarnished reality, not about the fantasy that the commercial pop-song-writers were so deeply mired in.'

Citing the fusion of music, poetry, dance, lights and film that could be experienced in the Avalon ballroom in San Francisco or at the Exploding Plastic Inevitable residency at the Dom in New York, Shelton called it 'a new, total art form'. He concluded that 'the 1966 trend is shifting toward a non-political, non-society oriented philosophy as the songs speak of alienation and anti-convention. Paradoxically, they are expressing an avant-garde, underground philosophy to a mass audience, deepening the thinking of masses of young people.'

One might expect Lou Reed to be rhapsodic about pop's possibilities – he was, after all, a young practitioner anxious to make his mark – but Shelton was no youthquaker. Aged forty in late June 1966, he had served in the US Army during the Second World War. In 1955, he was among the thirty *New York Times* staffers subpoenaed by the Senate Internal Security Subcommittee during its investigations into Communist Party infiltration. When he refused to give evidence, he was given six months in prison, but the decision was reversed on appeal.

While his case passed back and forth through the courts, Shelton was reassigned from the news desk to entertainment. He began covering the late-1950s folk revival – most notably the various Newport Folk Festivals – and, in 1961, he wrote the first favourable review of a twenty-year-old singer, presenting him as an apprentice alchemist of time and space: thus launching Bob Dylan's career. In March 1966, he conducted an extraordinary interview with Dylan high above the Earth, on a flight between Nebraska and Colorado.

Shelton wasn't the only one to remark on this flowering of mass art. Other experienced commentators like Nat Hentoff, Ralph Gleason, Kenneth Allsop, Reyner Banham and the sociologist Orlando Patterson all recognised that something extraordinary was happening in popular youth culture during 1966. Their fascinating and thoughtful observations were echoed, in a rawer and less distanced form, by the younger writers in the UK and US pop press: Richard Goldstein, Paul Williams, Tony Hall, Penny Valentine and many others.

It was a time of enormous ambition and serious engagement. Music was no longer commenting on life but had become indivisible from life. It had become the focus not just of youth consumerism but a way of seeing, the prism through which the world was interpreted. 'This isn't it for me': that simple, defiant cry, delivered by John Lennon, the most famous young person on the planet, echoed throughout 1966. Success wasn't the be-all and end-all; it was possible to conceive of an alternative future, to believe that things could be different, that people could be free.

1966 began in pop and ended with rock. Along with the increased ambition to be heard in the music, it was a year of rapid change and development in the various liberation movements: not just civil rights – the engine of dissent in the mid-sixties – but women's rights and the emerging homophile movement. It was also a year in which, triggered by the escalation of the war in Vietnam, the right wing began to organise and, indeed gain power. 1966 began in the Great Society and ended with the Republican Resurgence.

The folk memory of 1966 is contained in songs like 'These Boots Are Made for Walking', 'Sunny Afternoon', 'Reach Out I'll Be There', 'Yellow Submarine', 'Good Vibrations' and so many others, powerful nostalgia triggers that hark back to what appears as a simpler, sunnier time. In Britain, there is the high point of England winning the World Cup and 'Swinging London', two national events that were revived thirty years later during the simulacrum of 'Cool Britannia'.

Everyone thinks they know about the sixties. It was a golden pop age; it was the moment when everything started going downhill. It was the start of the alternative society; it was only a couple of hundred people in London, while 'real life' – whatever that is – went on elsewhere. Even the clichés have become politicised: it should be noted that the sixties have been attacked by successive waves of cultural conservatives – the New Right, the neo-cons and the neo-liberals – over the past thirty years.

This book contains twelve essays, one per month, based on one record and then expanding out into the themes and events of that month in America and Britain. The choice of the single is deliberate: 1966 was the last year when the 45 was the principal pop music form, before the full advent of the album as a creative and a commercial force was heralded by *Sgt Pepper's Lonely Hearts Club Band* in summer 1967. The early chapters are constructed around a single theme: for instance, Chapter 3 is devoted to 'The Ballad of the Green Berets' and the Vietnam war in America.

After Chapter 9, however, there are multiple themes in each chapter, reflecting the fragmentation of modernist time and the breakdown in the unitary pop narrative that occurred at that point in the year with the disappearance of the Beatles. Primary sources have been used where possible in order to eradicate hindsight and to reconstruct the mood of the time by highlighting the way that people thought at the time, the way that they talked and the language that they used, and what they felt was important.

The premise throughout is that music did reflect the world during 1966; that it was connected to events outside the pop culture bubble and was understood to do so by many of its listeners; that there was something more than image and sales at stake. It was a year when audacious ideas and experiments were at a premium in the mass market and in youth culture, with a corresponding backlash from those for whom the rate of change was too quick. The resulting tension was terrific. 1966 was the sixties peak, the year when the decade exploded.

* * *

I was attracted to 1966 because of the music and what I hear in it: ambition, acceleration and compression. So much is packed into the 45s from this period: ideas, attitudes, lyrics and musical experimentation that in the more indulgent years to come would be stretched out into thirty-five- to forty-minute albums. Condensed within the two- to three-minute format, the possibilities of 1966 are expressed with an extraordinary electricity and intensity. They still sound explosive today, fifty years later.

To begin researching the story, I listened to the records, on 45 where possible. Then I went back to the music press of the time. In the US, this was more problematic: most of the pop magazines, like *16* or *TeenSet*, were monthlies, and thus unable to always react with the speed that the developments of the year required. A more accurate mapping of the rate of change was the weekly *KRLA Beat*, published out of Los Angeles during the year that the city became the international pop mecca.

Nothing in America compared to the four British weeklies – the *New Musical Express*, *Melody Maker*, *Record Mirror* and *Disc and Music Echo*. Between them, they covered this extraordinary year in almost complete detail; along with *Rave*, they represent a fertile historical resource. In those yellowing pages, I found the most extraordinary statements and ideas, not just from the writers who defined the year – Penny Valentine, Tony Hall and Derek

Taylor – but from the interviewees, the musicians themselves.

People think that a critical and rebellious youth culture began with hippies and the underground press in 1967. In the music press from 1966, along with Ralph J. Gleason's *San Francisco Chronicle* columns and the new magazines that started that year – *Crawdaddy!*, *Mojo Navigator*, the *Oracle*, *Heatwave*, *International Times* – almost all the ideas and attitudes that would define the remaining years of the decade are in place: the Love Generation, opposition to the Vietnam war, critiques of youth consumerism, an alternative society, a new world as yet unmade.

As a series of essays, the book is not and does not claim to be definitive. As it happens, the only major pop figure of the year who is not discussed at some length is Bob Dylan, who is nevertheless a hooded presence throughout. His travails and extraordinary achievements of 1966 have been well covered by writers like Sean Wilentz, Robert Shelton, Clinton Heylin and C. P. Lee, and I direct you to their books. Even so, if you want to experience 1966 in the raw, just listen to any of Dylan's acoustic concerts from April/May that year.

There are other areas that I would have loved to explore: free jazz, the beginnings of downtown minimalism and the spread of Far Eastern music; ska; Happenings; and the Situationist International's intervention at Strasbourg University, to name but a few. But they are for another book. For reasons of space, sense and fidelity to the material, I decided to restrict the musical coverage to 45s and, in particular, although not exclusively, those that made the charts – *Billboard* in the US and *Record Retailer* in the UK – that year.

I turned thirteen in late summer 1966, and spent much of the year bathed in the music that I saw on television and tuned into on Radio Caroline South. The 45s that I heard went very deep and, in many ways, that mixture of mainstream pop, hard mod pop, West Coast, soul and Motown has stayed with me as an ideal. Those singles are written about in the following pages, and it is to their resounding and unquenchable spirit of freedom that this book is dedicated.

PART 1

ACCELERATION

JOHN LENNON

John Lennon knew all about the MM's Pop Think-in when he was approached to sit in the "hot seat". "Yeah, it'll be a laugh," he said, settling himself down in his chair and waiting for the first question, "but I hope I don't get rotten questions like I get rotten records in Blind Date."

VIETNAM
P. F. Sloan. I don't like what's happening there.

MONEY
Nice. Great.

PLAYBOY
The magazine of the man? The magazine. It's nice.

LITTLE ANNIE FANNY (Playboy cartoon).
I don't read the cartoon. I hardly read the book. I have seen it though. Imagine what the bloke who draws it thinks about!

GUITARS
Guitars are great. Part of life.

AEROPLANES
I don't like them. At first they were a nice adventure. I like flying less the more we do. We can get to most places well enough by road. We've flown so much, something could happen the more we do.

EPPY
He's great, you know. When people talk about him, they say he's harsh and hard and I expect he can be a bit of a bastard at times. He's a businessman, so he has to be. He's never a businessman with us though. We only talk business about twice a year. He sometimes has a go at us, then we have a go back and it's forgotten.

MILK
It's great. It goes on corn flakes, on your porridge or in tea. It does everything. I always drink a pint before going out on the booze. Or I drink it when I come back. It keeps you going, too. Two Aspros and a glass of milk can keep you going for days.

TOURS
Great—if they're great tours. There was only one I didn't enjoy and I can't remember which one that was now.

NEGROES
I always think of music when I hear someone say Negro. I suppose I should think about anti-apartheid and all that. I don't agree with apartheid. But Negroes mean music to me.

BABIES
I'm not keen on any ex-

● No more punch-ups. It all happened at 18 and 19 ●

cept my own. I'm typical of most men in this respect, I suppose. I think he does marvellous things which no other baby ever does. For instance, if he pounds on the piano I think, look at that, it's marvellous, when any kid would do the same in time if there was a piano in the house.

LIVERPOOL
It's still home. Even though my aunt has moved away and I have to stay with Paul if I go there. If I'm in London, home is Weybridge, but if I say I'm going home, I mean Liverpool. It'd be the same if I was from Paris and lived in Marseilles. Paris would always be home.

PUNCH-UPS
They aren't there any more with me. It all happened when I was 18 and 19.

PUBS
I've never gone much on pubs. There have been very few pubs I've had much to do with and they were in Liverpool, like the Grapes near the Cavern, which was the one we used to use.

SKETCHING
I don't sketch. I occasionally draw things but I don't sketch.

WHISKY
I go on it and off it. At the moment, I'm off it. I've been drinking solidly for three years.

JOURNALISTS
On the whole they are all right. There's a horrible nasty element in a few, the same as any job. Usually though the bastards are famous for being bastards.

It's the ones who seem nice and prove to be bastards later that I can't stand. They're all part of the machine after all. If they were no journalists there'd be no us.

SNOW
I liked it in Austria and Switzerland. I liked Austria when I was there.

CHRISTMAS CARDS
I never think about them if I do it's usually too late

ROLLS ROYCES
Great, but even they are not perfect.

SHORT HAIR
Okay if you've a short head. Some people suit their hair long and some suit it short.

AMERICA
Some of it's great and some is awful. Good and bad.

TV POP SHOWS
They could be better or worse. I'd sooner have a bad pop show on TV than none at all.

RHODESIA
I dunno what they're up to. I can't like that Smith bloke. I don't really know enough about it.

BOOTS
They keep me warm. I don't always wear them though.

GOYA
Some of it's all right. Doesn't he paint ballet pictures? No? Oh well ● ● ● ● if there!

COMBS
I only like the kind my aunt gets me from Woolworths in Liverpool.

THE LADDER
A LESBIAN REVIEW

Adults Only .50
Jan. 1966

1 : JANUARY

A Quiet Explosion: CND, Protest and
the Conspiracy of Silence

'"THE SOUND OF SILENCE": "Take my arms that I may
reach you" across the silence that divides the heart, the neon that
burns cold and stabs the night and "formulates on the end of a
pin" all that lives in its light and shadow.'
JUDITH PIEPE, sleeve notes for *The Paul Simon Songbook*, 1965

1966 was a year of noise and tumult, of brightly coloured patterns
clashing with black and white politics, of furious forward motion
and an outraged, awakening reaction. There was a sense that
anything was possible to those who dared, a willingness to strive
towards the seemingly unattainable. There remains an overwhelming urgency that marks the music and movies of that year, counter-
balanced by traces of loss, disconnection and deep melancholy.

But underneath all the sound and fury – and the moments of
regret – lies a profound silence. This is not the silence of peace,
of solitude, of sought withdrawal – or even meditation, although
all of these states would be examined during that year. It's not a
silence that exists within itself; it is a rupture, a prelude to something that is barely conceivable. This silence is an artificially created vacuum – a few instants of bone-shaking terror – that turns
the world inside out.

You can hear traces of that silence throughout the year, among
the many thousands of records released by a rapidly expanding
music industry. Pop was everything in 1966. It wasn't just the life-
blood of youth culture, it was a way of looking at the world and,
as such, it couldn't help but express the thoughts, feeling and values of a generation that was beginning to test its social, political
and perceptual power. But for the young, born in the 1940s and
early 1950s, there were nightmares in their heads that they couldn't
shake off.

The year's first US #1 was Simon & Garfunkel's 'The Sound of

Silence'. The record had both a paradoxical title and a convoluted history. It had already been released in two acoustic versions – on the 1964 Simon & Garfunkel LP *Wednesday Morning, 3 A.M.* and Paul Simon's 1965 solo album – before this autumn 1965 single release. It was produced by Tom Wilson, who had presided over Bob Dylan's unprecedented smash 'Like a Rolling Stone'. After being ousted as Dylan's producer, he took the same electric instrumentation and overdubbed it onto the acoustic original.

The impulse might have been opportunist but the song was highly effective, with its memorable opening line – 'Hello darkness, my old friend, I've come to talk to you again' – and its explicit address to the lost, the marginal and the desperate. Taking over the top slot from the Beatles' 'We Can Work It Out', it seemed to herald a year in which the mass market would not be afraid of depth, in which the bizarre and the as yet unheralded would become commonplace.

'The Sound of Silence' also introduced the year's secret stillness. Throughout 1966 there would be sudden, fleeting lacunae within the unstoppable momentum of songs like the Who's 'Substitute' or the Beatles' 'Rain'. Time accelerated, stopped and began to loop. There would also emerge a strange stasis – the death drive inherent in repetition – within the sudden fashion for monochordal Eastern tones. These were harsh mutations, forged under extreme pressure.

It wasn't just about dropping all the instruments out to create excitement. It was the sense of impending catastrophe that arrived at the end of the second single by Love, a mixed-race group who were, for a few seasons, the toast of Los Angeles' Sunset Strip. '7 And 7 Is' may well be the most extreme record ever to hit the US Top 40: an incandescent burst of reverb guitar, galloping drums and bizarre lyrics that ended with a loud, rumbling explosion – the period's atomic terror made manifest.

However, the most accurate enacting of that silence would appear not on record, but on the screen. Filmed the previous year, Peter Watkins's *The War Game* was shown in a small number of cinemas and art houses throughout 1966. Commissioned by the BBC, it was suppressed on completion because it told a terrifying and unpalatable truth. Despite the best efforts of the Establishment, it became a kind of celluloid samizdat, exhibited as a matter of faith and protest.

The silence comes around a third of the way through the film. The previous fifteen minutes have shown matters escalating: triggered by a flashpoint in Berlin, the Third World War between East and West is depicted by an onslaught of facts, figures and a rising panic signalled by the constant sound of sirens. It's only milliseconds, but suddenly the film's momentum ceases. The screen fills with white, and then the image turns negative; all you hear is the scuffling of limbs and the whimpering of humans in distress.

This silence is the sound of life being sucked out of the world. It does not last, as the dispassionate voiceover returns: 'At this distance, the heat is enough to cause melting of the eyeball, third-degree burning of the skin and ignition of furniture.' It dissolves into the noise of screaming, but the voiceover soon continues – 'Twelve seconds later, the shock front arrives' – and then you hear the deep roar of mass destruction as the camera shakes and the terraced house begins to dissolve.

So this is the lacuna at the heart of this extraordinary year: the sound of nuclear explosion. For the previous twenty-one years, ever since the hecatombs of Hiroshima and Nagasaki, it had invaded the consciousness of the world. The effects were fundamental and, as yet, ill understood, but they poisoned everything. Even so, there were those who continued to think in the old way: the Cold War, the arms race, Mutually Assured Destruction. They were in charge of the weapons, and they clung to the certainties of 1945.

The Second World War ushered in an age of mass consumerism. But, just as the sixties began to unpick the buried doubts of the previous decade, so did the psychic cost of permanent conflict begin to surface with great force in 1965 and 1966. The teenager had been conceived at the Second World War's end, an American invention that spread, with the victor's culture, throughout a shattered Europe. But teenagers had to bear a deeply embedded, barely acknowledged psychic weight.

7

They were the first generation in history to have grown up in this insane world of A- and H-bombs. They had had to face a potentially blasted future from the very beginning. Pop was their culture, and the huge amounts of money flowing into the music industry engendered a confidence that propelled many ever further and deeper, as they began to explore this and other fears. From 1965 on, pop culture offered, as the pioneering critic Paul Williams observed, 'a huge new playground to create and communicate and be perverse in'.

There was also a subtle maths at work in 1966, two-thirds of the way through the twentieth century. The First World War had ended in 1918 and the Second began in 1939. Twenty-one years. The Second World War ended in 1945, so, if history was going to repeat itself – and many wilfully refused to understand its lessons – the next conflict, the Third World War, would begin in 1966. The pressures for another conflict were ever-present and, confronted with this situation, many teenagers decided to act as though life and death itself was at stake.

* * *

'At the end of a four minute count-down the lights went out and a false ceiling made of paper came down on people's heads, to the most deafening noise we could devise. The cloakroom girls screamed and hid under the counter. In the darkness and confusion, strange mutant figures moved.'
ADRIAN HENRI, describing 'Bomb Event', a Happening held at the Cavern Club in Liverpool during 1964

A seven-inch 45 rpm record, copyright 1966, with a generic company bag and a deep pink label. It's on Pye Records, one of the four majors that dominated the British music industry in the mid-sixties. At the beginning of 1966, Pye had a couple of major groups, the Kinks and the Searchers, and an excellent roster of US licensees, but it lagged behind EMI and Decca and was notorious for its unsympathetic handling of artists and contracts that were poor even by the day's shabby standards. From the very beginning, the record stood little chance.

Run by the formidable show-business veteran Louis Benjamin, Pye had had enormous success in the late 1950s with the King of Skiffle, Lonnie Donegan. In the early 1960s, it licensed a good deal of American blues and R&B, before investing heavily in the nationwide pool of talent that emerged in the wake of the Beatles' 1963 breakthrough. Like all the others, Pye's A&R approach was scattershot: sign acts on the cheap and see which one sticks.

The Ugly's were one such group, from Birmingham – very much the third city, after Liverpool and Manchester, in the methodical raiding of the provinces' pool of young talent. They had come together in the late 1950s, during the skiffle boom that gave so many young musicians their first chance to play in public. After changing their name from the Dominettes, the Ugly's played a major part in their city's thriving beat scene, as well as enduring the then obligatory ritual of playing the German clubs.

In such a crowded market, the Ugly's tried to distinguish themselves with their rather perverse name and socially conscious material. 'All of us were socially aware,' says lead singer Steve Gibbons. 'We were striving to be different to the other groups. They'd play American pop, R&B, a bit of Tamla, but we'd have quirky things, coming from within ourselves. The urge came from the Beatles: they'd shown the way. You had to write your own material. That was an essential part of the band's make-up.'

Signed in early 1965, the Ugly's first single was released in June. 'Wake Up My Mind' was an assured Dylan-esque number that protested the rising tide of conformity. Their second record, 'It's Alright', had thoughtful lyrics and an unusual, harpsichord-driven arrangement. Like the first, it went nowhere in the British charts, despite heavy play on the pirate radio stations and an appearance on *Ready Steady Go!*. For the A-side of the group's third 45, the label chose 'A Good Idea' – a bitty dirge that failed to live up to its title.

The flip side was something quite different. 'A Quiet Explosion' begins with the reedy, eerie sound of a Vox Continental organ. It then adds a subtle rolling drum pattern underpinned by a strange, echoing riff reminiscent of the musique concrète electronics pioneered by Delia Derbyshire on 1964's 'Dr Who Theme'. 'That was our bassist John Hustwayte,' says Gibbons. 'He played that riff with a plectrum and our producer, Alan A. Freeman, put echo on it. The falling bass run at the end, well, that's the falling bomb.'

Complementing a sound picture that is sombre and futuristic, even slightly sinister, the lyrics are foregrounded. Principally written by drummer Jim Holden and persuasively sung by Gibbons, they attempt to grapple with serious themes in the spirit of late 1965, a time of caustic comment and pop protest. They touch on world hunger, the nature of peace in a seemingly permanent Cold War and, indeed, the lunacies of MAD: 'The quiet explosion / Bomb's about to fall.'

'I remember recording it very well,' says Gibbons. 'It was an adventure just to get into the studio. I really like the way that I sing it: my vocals weren't always right but that was a good song. And it's what we felt. All the band were obviously aware of the futility of any war. I was born during the war, and I remember the bomb sites as a kid. In Birmingham there were bomb sites everywhere. I had uncles in my family who had been killed. And they were still playing at it – with the Cold War.

'At school we had a great maths teacher. He'd been in Bomber Command and it was easy to get him talking. He was obviously Labour through and through. He never talked about the war – which I'd love to have talked to him about – but he talked about McCarthyism, that witch-hunt, and what the future would be like. The war had a massive impact on my generation because of the way it shaped everything. All of that had a bearing on me as a musician.'

Gibbons also witnessed the exercising of a social conscience within his family, prompted by the period's leading Christian evangelist: 'I have a brother, six years older than me, who became a conscientious objector. He went to see Billy Graham in the late 1950s. When the call-up came for national service, he refused to go. He had to face a tribunal, and it was on the front page of the *Birmingham Mail* for everyone to see. My mother was furious, but I was proud of him: what a great thing to do.'

Like many sixties teenagers, Gibbons would be liberated by the ending of national service: the cut-off age for the last entry was 1 September 1939, and he was born in mid-July 1941. He didn't see it that way at the time, though: 'I just missed conscription, but if I'd been called up, I'd have gone like a shot. It was the travel. I know it's selfish. I'd see guys come back from their national service in Aden, Cyprus, and they'd have suntans and tattoos, they were full of stories. They were men. I did the next best thing and formed a band.'

'A Good Idea' was released on 21 January 1966, one of several Pye singles that week. It got a down-page review in the following day's *Record Mirror*: 'Strong lead voice on this beater – good idea, lyrically, too. Nice sense of rhythm and fair commercial appeal.' Summarised in two words – 'good flip' – 'A Quiet Explosion' quickly disappeared along with its A-side, one of the many barely heard songs in a period of massive, heedless overproduction.

Yet it remains a strange, haunting record. It's not a total success – the lyrics are on occasion garbled – but in its very awkwardness it has the ring of authenticity. It has the sense of thoughtful young men groping towards some understanding of the world in which they live and their place within it: 'but we must unite and all fight with one cause'. It may not be truly psychedelic, but it pushes forward towards that definition: in its experimental fusion of sound, mood and sense, it is imaginative and holistic.

The effectiveness of the song hinges on the word 'quiet'. The sound of war is usually thought of as a monstrous assault on the senses: the constant, whining sirens, the pulverising noise of bombs and shells. But this is describing another, new kind of deadly conflict. It's quiet, if not silent, insinuating. You won't know it's there until it's too late. 'Silence like a cancer grows': like all of their cohort, the members of the Ugly's had grown up with atomic warfare as a fact of life.

The bomb had become integrally woven into Western life. Life could be good in the new Mass Age, but there was a conspiracy of silence at the heart of government about the true nature of nuclear deterrence and the doctrine of Mutually Assured Destruction: the brake put on the use of nuclear weapons through the sure knowledge that their use would result in Armageddon. Everyone knew that the bomb was there, but it was not talked about. The alarms of the 1950s were, by 1966, calming into a dull ache.

In his polemical survey of post-war youth, *Bomb Culture*, Jeff Nuttall marks Hiroshima and Nagasaki as the moment when everything changed: 'In the new world, the light was harsh, a perpetual noon of decisions, every action crucial. No man was certain any more of anything but his own volition so the only value was pragmatic. Moral values, thought absolute, were now seen to be comparative, for all social entities around which morality had revolved were now called into doubt and nothing of morality remained.'

Nuttall sees 1945 as the moment when 'the generations became divided in a very crucial way'. While the pre-bomb generation attempted to continue as normal, 'the people who had not yet reached puberty at the time of the bomb were incapable of conceiving of life with a future. They might not have had any direct preoccupation with the bomb. That depended on their sophistication. But they never knew a sense of future.' Trying to find a way through that impasse would become a major preoccupation in the years that followed.

This generation gap played out in the first musical responses to the nuclear world. The earliest atomic songs were gung-ho, regarding the bomb as a God-given agent of American power, but Sam Hinton's 'Old Man Atom' in 1950 was a witty talking blues ('all men may be cremated equal') that ended with an explicit call to action: 'The people of this world must pick out a thesis / "Peace in the world, or the world in pieces!"' 'Old Man Atom' was not inflammatory, simply critical, but – in the anti-communist hysteria of the early 1950s – it was banned.

A climate of censorship and denial cloaked the acceleration of the arms race during the 1950s. As more states joined the nuclear 'club', in particular France and Britain, there was a massive spike in hydrogen-bomb tests: around thirty-five in 1956, around fifty-five in 1957 and over a hundred in 1958. By that time, those who had not reached puberty in 1945 were beginning to come into their late teens and, unlike the previous generation, they were going to do something about the perilous world in which they found themselves. It was time for a thesis.

The Campaign for Nuclear Disarmament was launched at a public meeting on 17 February 1958, when 5,000 people filled a hastily booked hall in the centre of London to hear speakers like Bertrand Russell, the radical Labour politician Michael Foot and the historian A. J. P. Taylor. 'The size of the response had its effect on the speakers,' Peggy Duff noted in her autobiography, *Left Left Left*; 'one and all came out with a militant denunciation of nuclear weapons, and Britain's in particular.'

Born in 1910, Duff was a journalist and an experienced activist. Indomitable and, despite an air of chaos, a ferocious organiser, she became the organising secretary of the new movement, its unwieldy name abbreviated to CND. The first show of strength occurred a few weeks after the launch, with the march from Trafalgar Square to the Atomic Weapons Research Establishment at Aldermaston, just over fifty miles from the capital. The march took four days and was attended by 10,000 people at the finale.

It set the tone for years to come. CND was a broad church. As Duff remembered, it included 'Members of Parliament, professors and students, teachers and schoolchildren, librarians and nurses, actors and printers, entomologists and engineers, philosophers and plumbers, doctors and draughtsmen, firemen and farmers, every possible profession and trade. It was a community, but it was a community for which no vows were required. All you had to do to belong was to step off the pavement and join it.'

CND's inclusiveness was embodied by the logo designed for the first Aldermaston march. Charged with the task of promoting the movement, Gerald Holton began with the British naval semaphore signals for the letters 'N' and 'D', standing for 'nuclear disarmament'. He placed these within a circle, ending up with a cross that had its horizontal arms pointing downwards at 45 degrees, strong white against a background of black. The peace sign gave CND a potent and instantly identifiable brand.

CND was 'absolutist and compulsive', as Peggy Duff wrote. 'It wanted to get rid of nuclear weapons, all of them. It wanted to do it very quickly.' As such it crossed traditional party lines: radical pacifists marched alongside Labour Party members, communists with anarchists. After the Aldermaston march turned into an annual event and anti-nuclear marches began nationwide, CND became a non-commercial, nationwide bohemian youth culture that crossed geographical and class lines.

The flavour of these times is captured by Pat Arrowsmith's novel *Jericho*, which is situated at a late-1950s/early-1960s peace camp. Among the cast is an ascetic organiser with a martyr complex, a pacifist gay man, a young tearaway, a middle-aged Quaker, a young female student and a forty-year-old agent provocateur. Picketing a nuclear establishment, the protestors succeed in bringing the workers out on strike, but that is only a small victory, as they half expect at 'any moment to be blinded by the first dazzling bomb flash'.

That sense of extreme urgency – that it all might already be too late – gave the movement massive momentum. During the late fifties, a number of films and books examined the possibility of nuclear destruction: Nevil Shute's *On the Beach* (1957) and its relentlessly apocalyptic film adaptation by Stanley Kramer (1959); Helen Clarkson's *The Last Day* (1959); and Alain Resnais's groundbreaking *nouvelle vague* document *Hiroshima Mon Amour* (1959).

Apart from a few isolated instances – the most famous antinuclear song of that period was Tom Lehrer's satirical 'We'll All Go Together When We Go' – the mainstream music industry did not address the topic, but music was vitally important to the Aldermaston marches and CND events in general. It was the era of folk, skiffle and trad jazz, music that could easily be played without

14

amplification and was within the grassroots, non-commercial tradition of the Left. The first CND anthem was written for the 1958 Aldermaston march. The science-fiction writer and skiffle enthusiast John Brunner adapted an old gospel hymn with new lyrics: 'Don't you hear the H-bomb's thunder / Echo like the crack of doom?' At the same time, Ken Colyer's Omega Brass Band gave the gathering a musical focus. Dressed up in a British approximation of a New Orleans funeral band, they lifted spirits with their rousing rags and marches.

In *March to Aldermaston*, the short film produced by Lindsay Anderson and Karel Reisz, among others, trad jazz bands – including the Omega Brass Brand – predominate. A photograph from the Jeff Nuttall archive captures the moment: a motley crew of strangely dressed characters playing trumpets, cornets and clarinets in front of a drummer, dressed in a kilt and bashing a snare. It's a ragged bohemianism, unlike anything else at the time.

The musicians included Dougie and Tony Grey from the Alberts, as well as Jeff Nuttall. A constant presence during these years, the Alberts would be extremely influential, even though they have left little recorded trace. They were quintessentially British: an art-school, *Goon Show* fusion of trad with surrealism, kinetic art and borderline lunacy. The Grey brothers, according to Nuttall, 'owned an extensive collection of Edwardian clothes and redundant wind instruments, all of which they could play with disarming skill'.

The Alberts twisted the guts of trad's New Orleans revivalism into a truly absurd, anarchic stage act, with an edge of deliberate provocation. They were joined by proto-performance artist and sculptor Bruce Lacey, who, Nuttall recorded, 'made his magnificent hominoids, sick, urinating, stuttering machines constructed of the debris of the century, always with pointed socialist/pacifist overtones but with a profound sense of anger, disgust and gaiety that goes far beyond any political standpoint'.

This was a sick response to a sick world. As the Aldermaston marches grew bigger – 20,000 in 1959, 100,000 in 1960 – this renegade element became highly visible. As Nuttall later wrote, 'The

Colyer fans, by now dubbed beatniks, appeared from nowhere in their grime and tatters, with their slogan daubed crazy hats and streaming filthy hair, hammering their banjos, strumming aggressively on their guitars, blowing their antiquated cornets and sousaphones, capering in front of the march.'

Rather than mainstream pop, which was still stuck in a purely romantic mode, this combination of music, clothes and politics became the first widespread movement in Britain to banish the straitjacket of 1950s culture. CND's great strength, as the movement's historian John Charlton writes, was that at a time when travel was still restricted, 'it brought large numbers of Britain's youth together: interacting with older people as well, they were exposed to a wide range of ideas, books, and music'.

Barry Miles became involved with the movement when he started at art college. 'Cheltenham had a youth CND group, which was run by a guy called Nigel Young, sometimes known as Fred Young, who later became Professor Young and ran the Bradford Centre for Peace Studies. I met him because he was going out with one of the girls in my class at art college, who I then later went out with. Then he become the regional organiser for YCND, and he made me the Cheltenham representative. So I got involved with paperwork and distributing posters.

'I remember the Cheltenham Literary Festival of 1961. Arnold Wesker was there, and Harold Pinter and John Berger, and they were all wearing CND badges. You would see this little badge wherever you went. Whoever it was, it was somebody you could relate to. No matter how straight they were or how old, you had something in common. It broke down barriers. I would never have dreamt, at the age of seventeen or whatever I was, approaching someone like Harold Pinter, yet one felt able to, because he was wearing the badge.'

On 17 September that year, there was a major disturbance in the heart of London when the police cordoned off Trafalgar Square before a planned CND meeting. Peggy Duff remembered that 'in the square below there were many thousands. It was impossible to tell how many. And all around it there was a thick queue of people perambulating around, because the police would not permit anyone to stop. So round and round we went. There was a feeling around the square that day – a feeling of revolution, of real challenge.'

Captured by Granada Television in a stirring documentary, *A Sunday in September*, the Trafalgar Square protest ended in chaos: provoked by the sit-down tactics, the police started beating and kicking the protestors, eventually arresting 1,134 people. This was a watershed moment for the movement. Jeff Nuttall recalled drinking with a group of young CND members after the Trafalgar Square demo, 'cynical, sophisticated' teenagers who were becoming hardened. 'They have sacrificed a lot, have come out of viral shells of isolation. They have walked three days and risked arrest again and again. They have been ignored again, snubbed. In the half lit pub I can see profound hatred for the organised world instil itself in their very flesh like poison.'

Indeed, in the face of the government's refusal to discuss the issue, the first cracks in CND began to appear. The fact that it was not a membership organisation resulted in splits between the various factions: between the communists and the socialists; between the organising committee and groups like Spies for Peace who advocated more direct action; between the non-violent adherents to the Gandhian approach and the anarchists who weren't averse to a spot of hooliganism.

International tensions continued to escalate. During the summer and early autumn of 1961, the Berlin crisis developed into a highly dangerous stand-off. Alarmed by the seemingly unstoppable haemorrhage of East German citizens fleeing to the West, President Walter Ulbricht erected, overnight on 13 August, a wall that cut right through the heart of the German capital, a city that had already been parcelled up between the superpowers after the end of the Second World War.

This was seen as an unconscionable act of aggression. As images of the divided city and its inhabitants – cut off from each other through an accident of geography, street by street, house by house

– flooded the international media, Western outrage grew. From then on, matters escalated, until late October – five weeks after the Trafalgar Square riot – when US and Soviet tanks faced each other on the border at Checkpoint Charlie. One mistake and a nuclear strike could well have ensued.

The heat was being turned up on the Cold War. Just under a year later, there was another perilous episode, after the Russians were discovered to have placed ballistic missiles in Cuba, only a hundred or so miles from the US mainland and a fierce Soviet ally. This was in response to the US deployment of missiles in Italy and Turkey, within range of Moscow. For nearly two weeks in the second half of October 1962, matters remained on a knife edge.

On 22 October, President Kennedy broadcast a special message to a panicked nation from the White House, in which he outlined the nuclear capability of the Russian missiles situated in Cuba and stated that the US would initiate a blockade of any Russian ships attempting to deliver materials to the island. On the 27th, an American U2 spy plane was shot down over Cuba. Soviet ships attempted to run the US blockade in a thermonuclear game of chicken. Who would blink first?

Thankfully for the world, saner counsel prevailed, but the Cuban Missile Crisis was a defining moment. All the dystopian visions that had swirled around the world since 1945 were revealed not as the paranoid nightmares of science fiction, but as prophecies. As Norman Moss wrote in his account of the post-war nuclear age, *Men Who Play God*, 'To millions of people all over the world, the crisis made thermonuclear war, with giant fireballs burning up the cities, possible for the first time. It actually seemed that it could really happen.'

Moss observed that 'in Britain there was a widespread sense that the end might be at hand'. He told the story of a young fourteen-year-old at a school in London who, when asked to pipe down and mind her table manners at lunchtime, retorted, 'What does it matter how we eat? This may be the last meal we'll ever have!' Deciding that protest in this instance was futile, CND's Pat Arrowsmith hitch-hiked to a village in western Ireland which she thought might be a refuge if the prevailing western winds held.

Still only twenty-one, Steve Gibbons was playing coffee bars with his group the Dominettes, as skiffle shaded into early R&B. Like teenagers everywhere, he could only watch as events began to spiral out of control: 'That was scary. Nobody thought we were going to come out of it alive. It was real brinkmanship. We were young and having a great time, but the whole time there was this fear that America and Russia would go to war. Most kids of my age didn't expect to make it through the sixties.'

Something snapped at that moment. It would take a little while to make itself manifest in the wider culture, but the feeling that had already bonded the members of CND together – the ever-present fear of nuclear annihilation, the inconceivability of 'life with a future' – became more widespread among the young in the West. If there was no future, then the moment became all-important – the all-consuming NOW. What was there to lose?

Two snapshots from that season of brinkmanship. In early October, Parlophone Records – a subsidiary of EMI – released the first single by the Beatles, a new signing. They were stars in their native Liverpool but, such was the London-centric state of the media and music industries in the early 1960s, they were not well known elsewhere. On 11 October, a few days before the beginning of the Cuban Missile Crisis, 'Love Me Do' entered the charts, where it stayed for a couple of months, eventually reaching #17.

In late 1962, a twenty-two-year-old CND organiser called Mike Down was exploring London's left-wing culture. 'I went to Brendan Behan's *The Hostage*, Joan Littlewood's *Oh What a Lovely War* and to a pub in King's Cross where Bert Lloyd, Ewan MacColl and Peggy Seeger had their Singers Club every weekend. When I moved to London at the end of '62, a skinny American turned up and sang about guns and sharp swords in the hands of small children, and about hard rain.'

The Beatles and Bob Dylan: they would epitomise the at first disparate, then intertwined responses to the threat of no future for the generation born during the 1940s and early 1950s. In 1963, the Beatles became the objects of unprecedented mass female hysteria. With single after single they broke sales record after sales record. They would break through the barriers of 1950s deference and then, for a brief period, they cracked open the class system.

This was a revolution conducted with a tuneful song, a floppy-fringed haircut and a positive 'yeah yeah yeah'. In early 1964, it was exported to the US, where, in the week of 4 April, the Beatles held the top five positions in the *Billboard* singles chart. They initiated a huge boost in the production of singles (nearly 73 million units in 1964, as opposed to 55 million in 1962) and rebranded Britain as Pop Island, a fantasy youth utopia of music and fashion.

Dylan included that song about guns and sharp swords on his second album. 'A Hard Rain's Gonna Fall' encoded the compression of the times. 'Every line in it is actually the start of a whole new song,' Dylan wrote in the sleeve notes. 'But when I wrote it, I thought I wouldn't have enough time alive to write all those songs so I put all I could into this one.' Released in the US in May 1963, *The Freewheelin' Bob Dylan* reached #22 in the album chart, while Peter, Paul and Mary took Dylan's 'Blowin' in the Wind' to #2.

Pop and folk were drawing closer. Pop groups wanted depth. Folkies wanted exposure and fame: for the most part they were musicians, not ideologues, although the tensions between the two impulses would run deep. In many ways, commercial youth culture was beginning to take up the slack of organised politics, for despite greater public awareness of the possibility of nuclear war, stimulated further by Stanley Kubrick's absurdist *Dr Strangelove*, CND was beginning to falter – and there was no equivalent mass movement in the US.

'CND peaked in about '64–'65,' remembers John Hopkins, a freelance photographer who shot the Rolling Stones for the *Melody Maker* and the Aldermaston marches for *Sanity*, the CND magazine. He had worked at the Atomic Energy Authority before being seduced by the beatnik underground. 'It was Wilson who did it. He pretended to be anti-nuclear. He was elected in '64, and as soon as he got elected, he turned pro-nuclear, and that was part of my political education.'

In May 1964, *The Freewheelin' Bob Dylan* entered the British album charts, where it stayed for nearly a year. Pop stars still preferred not to deal directly with the issues of the day, but that was changing: in December 1964, the Searchers – one of the most innovative Merseybeat groups – took a smooth cover of Malvina Reynolds's 'The Rain', retitled as 'What Have They Done to the Rain', into the British Top 20. They showed that it was possible to take lyrics about nuclear fallout and make them accessible to a wider audience.

Even so, at the beginning of 1965, folk was still considered separate from pop. The young musicians and fans who flocked to the latest all-night club in central London, Les Cousins, thought themselves apart from the world of uniformed, besuited, cheeky/cheery pop groups like the Searchers or the Hollies. That was mainstream, commercial stuff; in contrast, they told things as they were, without pulling punches or making compromises. They were the younger brothers and sisters of the beats.

The British folk scene was in transition. In the late 1950s/early 1960s, its revival had been sponsored and shaped by archivists and activists like Ewan MacColl (b.1908) and A. L. (Bert) Lloyd (b.1915). Coming from a hard-left background – both were Communist Party members – they saw folk music as the authentic expression of the working class, a forgotten and precious heritage that, once it had been exhumed through painstaking research, was graven in stone, severe scriptures of solidarity and protest. But the new generation were all born during or just after the war, a generation or two after the folk purists. They were living the life: travelling and squatting, playing in the network of small clubs that were burgeoning throughout the UK. The biggest single influence – and the major transitional figure – was the mixed-race guitarist and composer Davy Graham (b.1940), whose instrumental 'Angi' was a favourite even before its release on record in April 1962: it quickly became a standard, a benchmark for young acoustic guitarists.

In 1964, Graham introduced what is best known as the DADGAD tuning – his attempt to reproduce and complement the tones of the oud music that he had been transfixed by during a visit to Morocco. Enabling both improvisation and rhythmic stability, it quickly became a standard tuning in the British folk scene. This approximation of Near Eastern tones introduced a new, modal element to acoustic guitar music: a hint of exoticism and a sense of critical distance, if not transcendence, that fitted the lifestyles of the new generation.

The folkies found a home at Les Cousins, which opened on 16 April 1965 in Greek Street, at the centre of London's Soho. This was still an interzone in the heart of the capital, a district for dissipation, excess and desperation – all the facets of bohemianism. Whether intentionally or not, the club, as the folk historian Colin Harper notes, marked 'the line in the sand between the old order of folk song epitomised by Ewan MacColl and his left-wing agenda and the new dis-order of individual folk singers'.

As an all-nighter, the club was an instant success: it became a refuge for folk fans, runaways, suburban teenagers, the curious and the homeless. It was also the seed bed for a whole new generation of singers, writers and guitar-players, all born between 1941 and 1947: Bert Jansch, Paul Simon, Jackson C. Frank, Roy Harper, Donovan, Sandy Denny, Mick Softley and Anne Briggs, among many others. In their late teens and early twenties, all had grown up with the bomb.

There remains a record of this world, thanks to a BBC documentary called *Meeting Point: Outcasts and Outsiders*, which covered Soho low life and the pastoral work in that area. It focused on the scene around Les Cousins. The club is clean and the audience is full of fairly fresh-faced teens. Even so, the mood is *maudit*. The pastor Kenneth Leach remembered that songs about 'loneliness, rejection, brotherhood, inhumanity were sung around the Soho folk cellars in 1965 and 1966'. This folk scene 'mirrored the problems of the world'.

This was a new kind of romanticism: anti-pop although soon to become pop, weighed down with the cares of the world yet soon to trip into inner space. No subject was taboo in the repertoire of the Les Cousins regulars: there were songs about male prostitution (Al Stewart's 'Pretty Golden Hair'), drug addiction (Bert Jansch's 'Needle of Death'), isolation (Paul Simon's 'I Am a Rock'), mental-health policy (Roy Harper's 'Committed'), as well as the haunting visions of Jackson C. Frank's 'Carnival' and 'Blues Run the Game'.

It was a small, intimate scene. A generation older than most of the clientele, the outworker Judith Piepe befriended many of the Les Cousins crowd: her flat in Cable Street was open house for anyone who wanted to crash. Among those who stayed there were Sandy Denny, Al Stewart and the transplanted Americans Paul Simon and Jackson C. Frank. The interconnections would result in a couple of extraordinary 1965 albums: *The Paul Simon Songbook* and *Jackson C. Frank*, which was produced by Simon with Al Stewart on second guitar.

It is Piepe's voice who introduces the BBC clip of Stewart performing 'Pretty Golden Hair': 'These troubadours of the 1960s sing to win your love for the unloved, the despised, the rejected. The outsider speaks for the outcast who cannot speak for himself.' This was the sound of silence, a mood and a mode captured by Simon's song of the same name, a track that appeared on *The Paul Simon Songbook*, for which Piepe wrote impassioned sleeve notes that capture the flavour of the time.

The popularity of Les Cousins and its doom-laden yet exploratory aesthetic coincided with the moment when the British folk scene fully intersected with youth culture and transatlantic influences, just at the point when, thanks to Bob Dylan, the wider marketplace was ready for something new, something deeper. Dylan's April 1965 tour was brilliantly captured by D. A. Pennebaker's camera, which showed the acoustic performer just at the moment when he became a pop star, not with bland stylings, but with highly personal yet visionary songs.

Promoted by a *Top of the Pops* video that showed Dylan arriving at London Heathrow, as powerful a potentate as any head of state, the single 'Subterranean Homesick Blues' made the Top 10 that spring. It was preceded by an even bigger pop folk hit, 'Catch the Wind', by the eighteen-year-old Donovan, who, plucked from obscurity by a couple of sharp managers, Geoff Stephens and Peter Eden, was being heavily promoted on the weekly pop show *Ready Steady Go!*. Folk was becoming big business.

In July, the Byrds' perfectly pitched version of 'Mr Tambourine Man' made #1, and it was open season on Dylan and folk rock. Groups queued to cover Dylan songs – the Turtles, Manfred Mann, Sonny and Cher – and, by the autumn, 'Pop Protest' was in danger of becoming a fad: as the *Melody Maker* trumpeted in bold type in its 11 September issue, 'Songs with a message are becoming more and more common in the Pop 50.' The editorial cited singles by Bob Dylan, Manfred Mann, Joan Baez and Donovan.

Banned by the BBC, Barry McGuire's splenetic 'Eve of Destruction' was the commercial zenith and, for many, the artistic nadir of this trend. Mick Jagger and Paul McCartney both dismissed it, but the record went to #3 in the UK and #1 in the US. Written by the nineteen-year-old P. F. Sloan, the song offered a superheated teenage view of the world, geopolitics as apocalypse. It was at once kitsch and sincere: 'If the button is pushed, there's no runnin' away / There'll be no one to save, with the world in a grave.'

CND might have peaked but the political activism of the early decade had transmuted into a wider youth culture of inquiry, exploration and increasingly explicit and pointed dissent. The anti-nuclear songs recorded that autumn were a mixture of the opportunistic, the confused and the dread: 'It's Good News Week' by Hedgehoppers Anonymous; 'Too Many People' by the Hollies; Barry St John's cover of Tim Rose's 'Come Away Melinda'. The most powerful song in that vein was written by Les Cousins regular Mick Softley. There were two versions of 'The War Drags On' that early autumn: the first was by his friend Donovan, on the *Universal Soldier* EP; a couple of months later, Softley performed it on his debut album, *Songs for Swinging Survivors*, the cover of which showed him standing behind a burning pile of rubble. By his own admission, he was a troubled soul during this period, and his song reflects an inner turmoil projected outwards onto an uncertain world.

The music of 'The War Drags On' is relentless: the bottom string is held to a D chord, providing a sombre drone that, in its obdurate stasis, commands the attention. This was partly a matter of practicality. In folk clubs, a solo performer with an acoustic guitar had to find a way of filling out the sound. Holding a drone chord enabled the player to make chord changes on the other strings and thus effectively do the job of two musicians. It also said, 'I am resolute. I am not trying to please.'

Softley's album was hardcore, with compositions like 'After the 3rd World War Is Over' and a cover of 'Strange Fruit'. The visionary lyrics of 'The War Drags On' take some of their apocalyptic flavour from 'Nottamun Town', an old mummers song that travelled to the Appalachian mountains sometime in the eighteenth century. Recast by Jean Ritchie's haunting, crystalline reading, it had became part of the folk repertoire in the early 1960s – and was freely plundered by Bob Dylan for 'Masters of War'.

'The War Drags On' is unremittingly grim. It tells the story of a Vietnam soldier called Dan, who finds himself 'in a sea of blood and bones'. Softley points out the paradox of fighting for peace and liberty while making 'dust out of bones'. The modal drone burrows its way into your skull. The gruff voice does not let up, cracking only in the last verse: 'And right there overhead a great orange mushrooming cloud / And there's no, no more war / For there's no, no more world.'

Right at that moment, a film-maker was fighting hard to put these nightmare visions on national television. After the success of *Culloden* – an inspired account of the 1746 battle that ended the Jacobite uprising – Peter Watkins had been commissioned by the BBC to make a film about the effect of a nuclear attack on Britain. Believing that there was 'a conspiracy of silence', the twenty-nine-year-old director set out to blow the whole subject wide open with the film, which was originally called *After the Bomb*.

Shooting on the by now retitled *The War Game* began in early 1965. Centring the action in Kent, in the towns of Chatham, Dover and Gravesend, Watkins used a variety of techniques – hand-held camera work, captions with carefully researched statistics, vox pop interviews about the ethics and effect of nuclear weapons, pompous statements by Establishment figures and carefully neutral voice-overs, all the tricks of what he called 'the "you-are-there" style of newsreel immediacy' – to take the viewer right into the experience. His ambition was to break 'the illusion of media-produced "reality". My question was – "Where is 'reality'?"'. . . in the madness of statements by artificially-lit establishment figures quoting the official doctrine of the day, or in the madness of the staged and fictional scenes from the rest of my film, which presented the consequences of their utterances?' His prime concern was that the film should 'help people break the silence in the media on the nuclear arms race'.

The War Game lasts for only forty-seven minutes but seems to go on for days. It remains a profoundly disturbing experience, indelibly etched on the sixties teenagers who saw it in art houses or in cinema clubs, who watched their certainties explode on the screen as quickly as nitrate film. The action builds slowly, from international tension – such as existed in Europe at that time – to the use of nuclear weapons. As soon as this occurs, the unthinkable and the barely imaginable is visualised on screen.

Dr Strangelove had made the point that the doctrine of MAD had created a barely resistible momentum of its own, which would override human intention and assure destruction whether by accident or system failure. *The War Game* amplifies the theme, showing that the use of nuclear weapons, once triggered, can proliferate out of control. The effects of just a single one-kiloton H-bomb – just one out of the many thousands stockpiled by 1965 – is shown as fundamentally destructive to human society.

The images burst into your head and lodge there: the fritzing of the screen after an H-bomb airburst; the unceasing screams of a boy who has looked in the bomb's direction as it falls and finds his eyeballs have melted; or the dirty, catatonic faces of the survivors doomed to die a lingering death from the fallout. In two of the most controversial scenes, squads of soldiers are shown shooting those near death to put them out of their misery, while a firing squad executes two looters. Throughout this barely conceivable mayhem the calm voice recites the details of a firestorm, of radiation's effects, of the proportion of British citizens that will likely be killed in such an event: between a third and a half. The bomb's shock wave resembles an 'enormous door, slamming in the depths of hell'. The explosion results in the mass burning of corpses, appalling physical and psychological misery, starvation, civil warfare and social breakdown.

At the film's end, near-catatonic children express their hopes for the future, over and over, in a double negative: 'I don't want to be nothing.' The voiceover continues: 'About the entire subject of thermonuclear weapons, on the problems of their possession, on the effect of their use, there is now practically a total silence in the press, in official publications and on television. There is hope in any unresolved and unpredictable situation. But is there real hope to be found in this silence?'

This is the flip side of the decade. Looked at five decades later, what is shocking is the comparative poverty and greyness of life in non-metropolitan Britain during the mid-sixties. The expressions on the faces of the film's interviewees, their clothes, the sparsely furnished interiors, the 1930s wallpaper, the lack of gadgets – these are not the main point of the film, but they show a country still struggling to climb out of wartime rationing and psychic privation.

The War Game quickly fell victim to the very thing it was designed to oppose: the conspiracy of silence. Subsequent research has revealed that, right from the very beginning, the film aroused anxiety among the BBC top brass: Head of Music and Documentary Programmes Huw Wheldon, BBC Director General Sir Hugh Carleton-Greene, and Lord Normanbrook, the chairman of the BBC Board of Governors. They quickly took soundings from the Home Office.

The first cut was completed by the end of June 1965. Wheldon suggested some cuts, which Watkins agreed to. When the second edit was viewed by the BBC bosses in early September, they decided that the responsibility of showing it was too great for the BBC to bear. They held a secret screening for the cabinet secretary and other government officials, while Mary Whitehouse, the secretary of the Viewers' and Listeners' Association, wrote to the Home Secretary demanding that the Home Office ban the film.

The press had a field day. 'Brilliant, but it must stay banned,' opined the *Daily Sketch*. 'I object to this film because it is propagandistic and negative in its approach.' The *Daily Mirror* thought that this was 'one ban the BBC need not have defended. The real horror is the stark documentary quality of the film. It reproduces with sickening realism charred limbs, crushed faces and eyes melting in their sockets. This, as the BBC rightly decided, could not have been borne by the millions of viewers sitting at home.'

Watkins was no match for the Establishment. As Dr John Cook states in his documentary about the film, 'There was a deliberate, secret move to suppress the film by Harold Wilson's precarious Labour government because of its "serious political implications".' The Home Office took the decision to ban it and informed the BBC of their decision, and in late November it was announced that the film would not be shown. Watkins also alleges that the Corporation made attempts to 'blacken' his professional standing as a film-maker.

Into this climate of censorship and denial dropped the Ugly's' 'A Quiet Explosion', a swirling circus of sour with its dark carnival organ and death-rattle bass that, in its own awkward way, was both insightful and timely. The spread of nuclear weapons and the state-sponsored blackout that surrounded this proliferation was nothing less than a creeping, insidious poison. To a small but vociferous minority, this was the true sound of silence, the quiet corruption that infected every aspect of Western life.

Four days before the record was released, the US suffered its most serious nuclear accident to date. On 17 January 1966, a B-52 bomber collided with a Boeing KC-135 Stratotanker off the coast of Spain, killing seven crew members in the two planes. The bomber was carrying four hydrogen bombs, three of which crashed to earth near Palomares, on the southern coast of Spain. The non-nuclear explosives detonated, spreading plutonium and uranium over several acres.

In a twist that could have come from the fourth James Bond film, *Thunderball*, then in the cinemas, the fourth hydrogen bomb was lost at sea. Around twenty-five US vessels were directed to the area, but it would not be fully recovered until early April. Apart from the dangers of nuclear leakage, the incident was a major embarrassment for the US, making international headlines and focusing attention on a key danger of any nuclear policy: human error.

Just over a week later, Love gathered in Sunset Sound Studios in Hollywood for the third session of their first Elektra Records album. On the agenda was the taping of an all-acoustic song – a change of pace from the raucous, uptempo, Byrds/Stones ready-mades that had made them the toast of the Sunset Strip. Written by Arthur Lee, the lyrics of 'Mushroom Clouds' were brutally direct: 'Mushroom clouds are forming / And the sky is dark and grey.' The nightmares wouldn't go away.

In February 1966, *The War Game* had a screening at the British Film Institute in London for a specially invited audience of politicians, civil servants, military personnel and selected defence correspondents. As Watkins noted, 'Film journalists were not allowed into the cinema. Also not allowed were the public, who were denied entry by a phalanx of BBC security guards standing elbow to elbow in a long line in front of the cinema.' Nevertheless, this was cited as having fulfilled the Corporation's 'obligation to show the film'.

This attempt at censorship backfired when the *Observer*'s Kenneth Tynan went public with his reaction: 'We are always being told that works of art cannot change the course of history. I believe this one might. *The War Game* stirred me at a level deeper than panic or grief . . . It precisely communicates one man's vision of disaster, and I cannot think that it is diminished as art because the vision happens to correspond with the facts. Like Michelangelo's *Last Judgement*, it proposes itself as an authentic documentary image of the wrath to come.'

There was a groundswell of opinion that the film should be shown. Eventually it was given an X certificate – the British Board of Film Censors' 'over-18' category – and went on release in March 1966. Shortly afterwards, the *Record Mirror* columnist Tony Hall urged readers of his weekly pop column to see *The War Game*. 'It's the most devastating, disturbing thing I have ever seen. But you owe it to yourself to see it. And hear the facts and see the effects. Then tell others to see it too.'

Despite the continued urgency of the topic, the organised politics of nuclear protest were shading into something different in early 1966. The suppression of *The War Game* had effectively blocked it from a mass audience, and CND, although still active and popular, was losing its effectiveness. There was a new, more conventional war to protest against – Vietnam – and CND's lack of success in changing government policy engendered the factional in-fighting and apathy that tore the movement apart.

At the same time, the influence of nuclear-derived existentialism quickened in 1966. On 1 January, the US Top 3 comprised 'The Sound of Silence', the Beatles' 'We Can Work It Out' and James Brown's 'I Got You (I Feel Good)', futuristic records all. To be sure, there was a lot of schlock in the Top 20, but that was business as usual. What was interesting was what was not business as usual. 1965 had opened things out, and there were many poised to boldly go where no one had gone before.

The UK chart was similarly burdened with seasonal sentimentality, but the Top 10 was leavened by three tough records: the Beatles' 'Day Tripper', the Kinks' 'Till the End of the Day' and the Spencer Davis Group's 'Keep on Running' – one of the first convincing UK marriages of soul and white mod pop. By the end of the month, Otis Redding was approaching the Top 10 with his cover of the Temptations' 'My Girl' and Bob Dylan's decidedly bizarre 'Can You Please Crawl Out Your Window?' had entered the Top 20.

The stylistic foundations of the beat and R&B booms were pushed to the limit, as if under enormous compression. The week after the release of 'A Quiet Explosion', the US trade magazine *Cashbox* reviewed a 45 by Belfast group the Wheel-A-Ways and gave it a B+: a 'slow raunchy infectious side'. The Wheels – as they were better known – were contemporaries of Them, the group that Van Morrison fronted, and they also specialised in tough R&B. They'd already covered Them's 'Gloria', but 'Bad Little Woman' was something else.

The reviews of the day completely failed to describe what is occurring on this record. It begins slowly, a tortured blues of jealousy and obsession. After two verses, the chorus arrives, and guitarist Rod Demick torques into overdrive, as singer Brian Rossi rants and raves. After a third verse, they do the same thing again, except that Demick keeps on accelerating and doesn't stop. The velocity is so vicious yet controlled that it's like a plunging roller coaster.

Another record released that January captured the heightened momentum. 'Baby Don't You Do It' was the fifth single by the Poets, the baroque Glasgow group managed by Andrew Loog Oldham. Their version of Marvin Gaye's 1963 standard pushes everything off kilter with its trebly sound, strange twelve-string breaks and hysterical George Gallagher vocal. In its extremity of sound and emotion, it breaks the bounds of R&B and beat to enter unknown territory.

The pace of life quickened in the mid-sixties, and the fear of nuclear annihilation was the rocket fuel. During 1965, the topic was broached, however crudely, as part of a folk rock and protest movement, and this, coupled with ever-increasing production on the part of the youth industries and the growing self-confidence of youth itself, pushed the sound and feel of pop into a highly volatile compound that would express anger, frustration and hostility at an unprecedented pitch. The dragon's seeds had been sown.

By 1966, the silence was everywhere: a stealthy psychic radiation, a living death. At once awoken and energised, some of the young began to deal with the fact that it affected every aspect of their lives. It had engendered a kind of forced existentialism, of having to live for and in the moment. So they would make noise, desperately assert life. Some would even begin to think about other ways of living. It was a MAD, mad, mad world. Bathed since childhood in this lunacy, it's no accident that they began to act up.

America's Largest Teen NEWSpaper

KRLA BEAT

Batman: 'I'm the World's Greatest Put-On' . . . Page 2

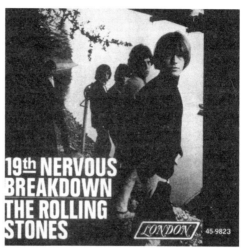

19th NERVOUS BREAKDOWN
THE ROLLING STONES

LONDON 45-9823

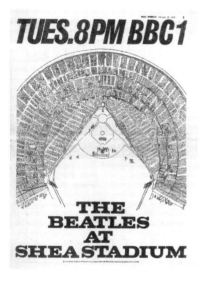

TUES.8PM BBC1

THE
BEATLES
AT
SHEA STADIUM

'Dedicated Follower of Fashion'
THE KINKS

2 : FEBRUARY

19th Nervous Breakdown: British Teen Culture
and the Madness of Swinging London

'Today's Princes of Pop – The Rolling Stones. Now the emphasis is less on majesty and more on frenzy . . .'
'10 YEARS OF POP', *Boyfriend Book 1966*

On 4 February 1966, the Rolling Stones released their tenth UK single, '19th Nervous Breakdown'; in the US, where the band's 'As Tears Go By' was still in the Top 20, it was issued a week later. The group were coming off an extraordinary run – five consecutive #1s in the UK, four Top 10 hits in the US – that saw them rivalling the Beatles in terms of perceived cultural importance, if not actual sales. This was the first big pop statement of 1966.

At the start of the year, the Rolling Stones were white-hot fan fodder. Their latest US album, *December's Children (And Everybody's)* – a cobbled-together selection of recent singles and album off-cuts – had been promoted with a Times Square billboard. It was rising up the American charts, as was their version of 'As Tears Go By' – a hit in the UK for Marianne Faithfull. In Britain, their most recent album, *Out of Our Heads*, was still in the Top 10 after three months.

The 8 January 1966 issue of *KRLA Beat* had a report on the Rolling Stones' recent Los Angeles press conference, held while the group were in town for recording sessions. They were in fine bad-boy mood, tackling questions about a new film – the mooted *Back, Behind and in Front* – their UK arraignment on obscenity charges and their new American LP – 'an album of rejects'. When asked why the Stones disliked the older generation, Keith Richards* replied, 'They dislike me.'

* For a few years in the mid-1960s and the early 1970s Keith Richards was known as Keith Richard, and this is the name used on

Another reporter enquired whether they expected to receive MBEs, like the Beatles. 'No,' they chorused together. 'We've already been convicted of obscenity charges in England,' added Keith, 'so we couldn't get any MBEs.' Another reporter brought up the fact that it was different for the Stones to be wearing long hair. After all, they were performers, but what about the ordinary kids? 'If they like it, they should wear it,' answered Keith, 'and anyway, we're ordinary kids.'

'19th Nervous Breakdown' was the lead single from the Los Angeles sessions, and it caught the careening momentum of superstardom – lives stepped up a gear. Recorded at the end of a six-week, forty-date American tour, there is something volatile and barely controlled about its tempo: the group have forsaken the contemporary soul influence of their previous two singles for a manic rockabilly beat, the country origins of which are reinforced by Keith Richards's high, keening harmonies.

It begins with two metallic guitars interlocking in counterpoint, Richards and Brian Jones weaving together for one last time on a 45. Jagger comes in with a first verse that mixes, in equal measure, contempt, boredom and empathy. The chorus is a blare, with Jagger's upward inflection on the repeated 'here it comes' underscored with foghorn guitar.

Developing the theme of the previous year's 'Play with Fire', the scenario plays out amid the upper class, or nouveau riche, with a neglectful mother who owes a million dollars in tax and a father who's 'still perfecting ways of making sealing wax' – note the pressure of the twelve-week deadline in that terrible rhyme. As the protagonist, Jagger actually tries to get involved: 'Well, nothing I do don't seem to work / It only seems to make matters worse.'

This reasonably nuanced, psychologically acute portrait of a poor little rich girl lasted nearly four minutes – still a long time for a single in early 1966. It ends with a repeat of the twin guitar

---

songwriting credits, magazine articles etc. from that period. For the sake of clarity, I've decided to stick to his given name throughout.

breakdown, then plunges into a repeat of the chorus, underscored by Bill Wyman's dive-bombing bass. The whirling, whirring stasis between verse, chorus, instrumental breakdown and chorus makes the point that there is no hope: the privileged subject of the song is locked in the consequences of her upbringing.

It was met with some confusion. *Record Mirror* noted 'a specially heavy beat, Mick's voice is there, good and strong, but it also tends to get a bit obscured . . . one of our reviewers doesn't dig this at all – but a million fans will'. In *Music Echo*, Penny Valentine praised its 'fabulous, neurotic sound', while *Rave* was on the inside track: 'According to Mick, the words could be directed at a deb. It's a send up and it's very good. And Mick is quite unconcerned whether you take it as a piece of social comment or a load of nonsense.'

On the day that the single was released, the *Evening Standard* published an article about Mick Jagger by Maureen Cleave, the doyenne of sixties pop writers. Cleave had done the first-ever London newspaper interview with the Beatles, way back in February 1963, and had decided to brook no nonsense from this upstart: 'For some unaccountable reason, Mick Jagger is considered the most fashionable, modish young man in London. We are told he is the voice of today, a today person, symptomatic of our society.

'Cecil Beaton paints him, says he is reminded of Nijinsky, of Renaissance angels; magazines report that Mick Jagger is a friend of Princess Margaret; gossip columns tell us what parties he failed to turn up at . . . Mr Jagger himself, as far as I can make out, has lifted not a finger to further his own social advancement. He has said nothing – apart from a few words on the new single – to suggest he is of today, yesterday or any other day. He remains uncommunicative, unforthcoming, uncooperative.'

Cleave would soon be interviewing the Beatles again, and would find in some of them the same vacancy and closed circuitry that Jagger identified in his pop-star status: 'We're earning all this money just to come to these places and be bored.' She reported that his favourite song was 'Satisfaction'. 'It's not about sex at all,' Jagger said. 'People are never bright enough to see where songs really are dirty. When the chap says: "I can't get no satisfaction" he just means he's fed up. I am a cynical person because I don't see any kind of end to anything.'

This was strange: a pop star at the zenith of his fame expressing boredom and anomie. Yet it tied Jagger and the Rolling Stones into how many of their audience felt and how they perceived the world. While they were fantasy figures living a life of opulence and fame, they were also subject to the same boredom, the same frustrations and the same curious dissatisfaction in the midst of comparative plenty. To that extent they were still, just about, able to be seen as 'ordinary kids'.

'19th Nervous Breakdown' set a tone for the year, the advances and perversities of 1965 shooting forward without a brake. It was a recording full of harsh tones, instruments pushed to the limit, with allusive, Dylanesque lyrics that went beneath the surface of a pop culture still in its first flush of expansion and excitement. Just like '(I Can't Get No) Satisfaction' and 'Get Off of My Cloud', it expressed an almost cosmic dissatisfaction with the very consumerism that had thrown the Rolling Stones into prominence.

It was a high-wire act that was doomed to fail, but in the short term their regular bulletins on the culture – released every three months or so – would hit hard. Extrapolating from the personal to the general, '19th Nervous Breakdown' hinted at the psychological disturbance that lay beneath the shiny, brightly coloured new teen world, at the same time as it sought to push those extremes wherever they might go. There was no deliberate programme, at this stage, no 'movement', more an individual sense of what if? Why not?

The problem with the pop culture of the 1960s – exciting and innovative though it was – was that it set up expectations and desires that could never be satisfied. Teens were valued not for themselves, but for the cash in their pocket. Yet the musicians of the day began to delve further into the recesses of the teenage psyche. The resulting tensions would throw up all manner of strange and twisted forms.

* * *

'Now this ain't a very fine song
But lucky for you, it ain't too long
(Sit still or I'll smash your face in!)'
CHAD AND JEREMY, 'Teenage Failure',
January 1966

In early 1966, the single was still king. The previous year, over 60 million 45s had been produced: although down from the all-time peak of 1964 (nearly 73 million), that was still just above the figure for 1963, and double the number of albums manufactured in 1965. The music industry remained in thrall to the post-Beatles world order. This was not just a matter of musical style or taste, but of demographics: the year of the Beatles' breakthrough, 1963, had coincided with the full impact of the post-war baby boom in the UK.

Youth had a significant impact on Western society. Adults preferred to see this in terms of consumerism: as the editorial to the March 1966 *Newsweek* special issue on America's 18 million 'Teen-Agers' observed, 'Most studies estimate that rising allowances and swelling incomes from part-time and summer jobs this year will put a whopping $12 billion into the jean jackets of the nation's high-school boys and girls. That about equals the total output of South Africa and adds up to an income of $670 per teen per year.'

As the sixties progressed, this purchasing power led to wider social consequences. Youth became an ideal that began to percolate through British and American society. It wasn't just about consumerism any more but something else – an ideology, almost, or at least an obsession. The world was changing fast, and music was at the centre of this change. As Peter Laurie noted in his 1965 survey *The Teenage Revolution*, 'Music is the pulse and flow of teenage life: without it perhaps we would have no teenage revolution.'

Within this still centralised economy, the weekly singles charts were the dominant narrative. Albums were becoming more important, but at an average price of 32s/6d, as opposed to 6s/8d for a single ($3.99 as opposed to 99c in the US), they were still predominantly bought by adults – a situation reflected in the UK album chart, where the soundtrack to *The Sound of Music* persisted at the top throughout the latter half of 1965 and most of 1966, ceding only to the Beatles and the Rolling Stones.

Adults also bought a lot of singles, which accounted for the schizophrenic nature of the British chart in 1965, when the Rolling Stones and the Beatles vied at the top of the charts with what teenagers of the time called 'mums-and-dads music': records like 'Tears' by Ken Dodd, and the Seekers' 'The Carnival Is Over'. This had been a constant even in the Beatles' breakthrough period, with acts like the Bachelors and Jim Reeves having huge hits during 1964 with sentimental, almost light-operatic tunes and country-and-western material.

In December 1965, *Record Mirror* published a list of the 'discs which were most successful chart-wise throughout the year'. Of the top ten singles, only two – the Beatles' 'Help!' and the Hollies' 'I'm Alive' – were specifically teen-oriented. At #1 and #4 were the Seekers, with Roger Miller, Cliff Richard, Ken Dodd and Elvis Presley rounding off the list. In the LP chart, the Beatles, the Rolling Stones and Bob Dylan vied with *The Sound of Music*, *Mary Poppins* and Val Doonican.

By 1966, there were already signs of the divisions to come. Longer and longer hair, drugs and abrasive noises marked the change and would deepen the split. The generation that had come up with the Beatles was beginning to either move out of the teenage – still thought, in the mid-sixties, to end at eighteen – or to seek something deeper. At the same time, younger teens found new heroes like the Walker Brothers: melodramatic, Spectorian balladeers emoting from behind a wall of long hair.

The pop charts were becoming a complex ecosystem of micro-generations and micro-tribes: the early teens, the bohemians, the soul freaks, the mums and dads, the vast number of unaffiliated young. In the week that ' 19th Nervous Breakdown' was released, the UK and US Top 50s – still fairly similar at that point – included Tony Bennett, Frank Sinatra, Herb Alpert, the Walker Brothers,

Herman's Hermits, the Kinks, the Beatles, Otis Redding, Fontella Bass, Lee Dorsey and Bob Dylan.

This was a consequence of success and aspiration. Sixties teens had greater mobility and freedom than their forebears, but in the mid-decade the amount of disposable income for each individual was still fairly low: in the UK, teenagers in 1964/5 spent on average £150 a year, much of which went on essentials. At the same time, 75 per cent of the 16–24 age group claimed to save £70 a year. But it was the idea of youth and novelty that was important, and in the short term that swamped all other considerations.

The burgeoning music and media industries successfully conveyed a picture of London – and various other urban centres in Britain and America – as thrown open to the young, indeed transformed by their energy and zest. This was built on a foundation of actuality: a small inner circle of pop stars, designers, photographers and metropolitan *flâneurs* rippling outwards who, rendered as an ideal, inspired imitation and emulation among a wider teen phalanx that was receptive to these ideas and images.

By early 1966, the British youth media had expanded into a sophisticated, comprehensive and fast-moving economy. On the one hand, there were the teen magazines aimed at young women – *Mirabelle*, *Boyfriend*, *Jackie* and *Fabulous 208*; on the other, there was the weekly music press – *Melody Maker*, *New Musical Express*, *Disc Weekly*, *Music Echo* and *Record Mirror*. The key monthly was *Rave*, which appealed to both sexes with a sharp mixture of fashions, self-help features and pop-star interviews.

The depth and reach of these publications was unprecedented. To varying age groups within their target teenage market they pumped out the ideas and the sounds of the British music and media industries, which were still concentrated in London at that point. Although in most cases they shied away from conceptualising the rapid pace of change, they nevertheless faithfully reported the thoughts and attitudes of the pop stars – like the Rolling Stones, the Who and the Yardbirds – who were driving that change.

This was the moment just before any 'serious' writing about pop music, and the general tone was breezy yet informed, of and in the moment. The best writers, such as Penny Valentine, knew their readers because they were like them, or, in the case of people like *Record Mirror*'s Tony Hall, they were so on the ball about future trends that they predicted what was going to occur in the charts weeks before it happened. At the beginning of 1966, that meant Tamla Motown, Atlantic and West Coast.

In early 1966, there were three TV programmes devoted to pop music. Aired on Thursday evenings at the peak time of 7.30 p.m., BBC1's *Top of the Pops* presented a fairly straightforward selection from the weekly chart run-down, with very occasional newcomers. On 3 February, for instance, it showed the Rolling Stones and the Spencer Davis Group, along with Herb Alpert, Petula Clark, Nancy Sinatra, Crispian St Peters and Eddy Arnold, whose 'Make the World Go Away' was a new release. *Top of the Pops* was aimed at a wide audience: there would be no filleting of the charts for the new and exciting, or even the teenage – Eddy Arnold was forty-seven in February 1966. With the limited access to pop music available through BBC TV or radio, the high-sixties pop experience usually meant sitting through several records that you absolutely hated before you got to the one you really liked. That gave the one you liked a terrific charge: in this episode, the Rolling Stones positively exploded out of the box.

In January, BBC2 premiered a new series about pop, *A Whole Scene Going*. Presented by the artist Barry Fantoni and the actress Wendy Varnals, it was more thoughtful and exciting, offering interviews with the likes of Pete Townshend, Michael Caine and David McCallum – then super-hot as Illya Kuryakin in *The Man from U.N.C.L.E.* – as well as videos set to current records (for instance, the Kinks' 'Dedicated Follower of Fashion') and studio performances, such as the Spencer Davis Group's 'Somebody Help Me'.

The best show of all was *Ready Steady Go!*, a sharply conceived, fast-running weekly programme that aimed to translate the excitement of pop and the pace of youth culture directly through the screen, as Jack Good's *Oh Boy!* had in the late 1950s. Beginning in

August 1963 and continuing through into 1966, it featured all the major groups of the day, along with significant American visitors – most notably soul and Tamla acts – as well as promoting women as presenters, producers and artists.

Vicki Wickham worked on *Ready Steady Go!* from the start. 'I was always programme editor,' she states, 'but Francis Hitching and Elkan Allan, our executive producers, both came from Fleet Street, so used "journalist" language and credits. What I did do was book the show, do the running order, organise and arrange call times – nearly everything.'

With exciting credits – fast cut to hip records like 'Wipe Out' and '5–4–3–2–1' – and innovative staging that had the acts placed within the audience, *Ready Steady Go!* emphasised the immersive experience of 1960s pop culture, even more so when the show went 'live' in April 1965. It wasn't just about passively adoring the stars, it was about dances, fashions and attitudes. It was forward-looking, beamed into the future, and over its long run it began to offer a vision of how life could be.

This was deliberate, as Wickham explains: '*Top of the Pops* had much bigger ratings than we did, and *RSG!*, with musicians, singers, equipment, etc., was expensive. *Top of the Pops* had an unbeatable – and very straightforward – concept: chart records. Lip-sync/mime. *RSG!* was irreverent, unexpected, sexy and thought-provoking. We tended to go with new, up-and-coming, exciting artists and bands. Music you mostly heard in the clubs or in select record shops. Not in the charts!'

By 1965, the show was expanding the language of pop television, with camera zooms, freeze frames and the full merging of act and audience. This is best seen in a surviving clip of the Rolling Stones, playing live in late August 1965: the group are playing on a small stage, raised just a few feet above a barely controllable audience. They run through two soul covers from their soon to be released third British album, *Out of Our Heads*: Don Covay's 'Mercy Mercy' and Solomon Burke's 'Cry to Me'. Things start to come unstuck as the group slam into their new single, '(I Can't Get

No) Satisfaction': a mass of young women surge against the studio technicians who are trying to keep them off the stage. The whole stance of the group oozes aloofness, which fuses with the aggressive nihilism of the song's lyrics – all those repeated 'no's – to incite the crowd even more. As Jagger slaps the air with his contemptuous hand gestures, the audience overruns the stage and the group run for their lives.

'Michael Lindsay-Hogg was the director who made *RSG!*' says Wickham. 'He knew that the audience wanted to see Mick as close as the camera could get him. Not a guitarist's hands. His shots of the young mod dancers with short skirts were pretty explicit, and this is how the scene was set. SEXY, shocking, and that's what music was to our parents! He came from theatre and understood lighting, which had really not been used before. He came up with techniques used to "freeze" shots in games like football and applied them to music.'

The other big influence in early 1966 was the pirate radio stations, which had grown from their tentative, chaotic beginnings to become a major force within the British music industry. The idea had started in March 1964, when the Irish entrepreneur Ronan O'Rahilly began transmitting Radio Caroline from aboard a former Danish ferry. As the boat was moored several miles off the British coast at Felixstowe, the station was able to evade the British broadcasting laws because it was broadcasting from international waters. Its impact was immediate. Quite apart from the excitement of the fast-moving, American-style twenty-four-hour pop format, it regularly featured records that you could not hear on the BBC's tightly restricted pop playlist. It was a little slice of America – pop nirvana – coming out of the transistor.

The launch of Caroline was quickly followed by other stations: Radio City in May, Radio Invicta in June and, in December, its closest competitor, Radio London. In July, Caroline had split into two stations, Radio Caroline North and South. Within a year, Radio London and Radio Caroline South had nearly a million listeners daily, not up to the figures for the BBC's Light Programme, but a significant force nevertheless. The stations were strictly commercial enterprises but, with so much airtime to fill, they could not help but play records that were ignored by the BBC and, in general, the more teen-oriented stations like London and Caroline South tended to go lightly on the mums-and-dads records and promote the noisy and new.

Radio London's chart was called the Big L Fab Forty, and it was different to the BBC's: more random, quicker moving, faster on the uptake. On 6 February, records that were not 'official' hits were in the Top 10, such as the Lovin' Spoonful's 'You Didn't Have to Be So Nice' (#5) and the Pretty Things' 'Midnight to Six Man' (#10). There were also dubious placings (David Ballantyne (#9), Paul and Barry Ryan (#12) – the pirates were porous to payola), as well as new releases by the Poets (#35), David Bowie (#26) and Chad and Jeremy (#38).

Pirate radio DJs like Kenny Everett, Johnnie Walker and Emperor Rosko became celebrities. *Music Echo* had a weekly feature called 'The Pirate's Den', and in the 12 February issue Tom Lodge wrote about a record that had been banned by TV but was on heavy rotation on Radio Caroline South, Chad and Jeremy's 'Teenage Failure': 'This rather kinky song was written by Jeremy Clyde and has the condemning line: "Smash your face in". It was this that caused it to be banned by *Thank Your Lucky Stars*.'

The pirates were popular because they would play banned records, new records, hyped records, more and more records in general. Their playlists were a spicy soup of the sacred and the profane, the inspired and the dreary, guided by payola, expedience and genuine enthusiasm for the form. They also gave the drop on new American releases, which would often be released one or two months later in the UK: from early 1966 on, Caroline broadcast a US Top 40 show recorded in New York by WMCA 'Good Guy' DJ Jack Spector.

The pirate stations helped to open out British pop into a confident, experimental culture that fulfilled the logical premise of the teenage ideal. Throughout the sixties, much pop music was as it always had been: emotion as commerce, youth as product. But what made this period different was the extent to which the truly popular was also truly innovative and full of content. Three years after the Beatles' breakthrough, it had become possible to gain mass success with sounds, attitudes and lyrics unthinkable even a couple of years before.

Part of this was down to the increased confidence of mid-sixties teens. In 1965, Peter Laurie had contrasted three generations of teenagers: those born between 1931 and 1936; those born in the early 1940s; and the post-war babies. The first had opted for 'a greedy, resentful conformity'; the second oscillated between spasmodic violence – epitomised by the rock 'n' roll-loving Teds – or the embryonic social organisation of what Laurie called 'Beats, Bohemianism, Trad Jazz Clubs' and CND. In the fifties rock 'n' roll explosion, rebellion was conveyed by sound, attitude and racial integration, in musical styles if not in deed. 'Teenage' was a very popular buzzword, but principally as a marketing hook, epitomised by records like Tommy Sands's 'Teenage Crush' or Gale Storm's 'Teen Age Prayer'. The favoured media definition of youth was in terms of consumerism and romance, with adults very much in control of the media and the music industry. As far as the white mainstream was concerned, pop meant the quiddities of love.

It was the third generation, the post-war babies, who fuelled the 1960s pop explosion, and by 1965 they were finally squaring the circle between high and low art, between mass entertainment and aesthetic expression. As Laurie observed, 'The pop business has many of the features of the commercial culture, most obviously the importance of large audiences and big gates as a measure of success. But by some miracle of adjustment the young have been able to reconcile this fundamental measure with their own intuitive, creative best.'

Summer 1965 had belonged to the Beatles' 'Help!', a multimedia campaign that included the single, the soundtrack album and the film itself, a glossy pop art pastiche that presented the group as sleek, global demigods at the same time as it rehearsed, like a stress nightmare, all the violence that was beginning to swirl around them. The Beatles did not seek to promote chaos – indeed, during 1965, their image was still calculated to appeal across the generations and the various teen types – but their nearest competitors did.

In early September 1965, the Rolling Stones were in Ireland. During their short tour, Peter Whitehead shot the bulk of a documentary, later titled *Charlie Is My Darling*, that – like Pennebaker's *Don't Look Back* – captured a moment of breakthrough. The concert footage is explosive. The group's whole purpose is to create frenzy, and the crowd is barely contained throughout: in Dublin, they scream, yell, throw anything they can get their hands on, rush the stage and assault the musicians, bringing the show to a rapid halt. Whitehead's film intersperses these wild scenes with fly-on-the-wall reportage of their down time and interviews with all the group members except Keith Richards. While posed, these are nevertheless revealing.

By September 1965, the Rolling Stones were two years into their careers as hit-makers. The group's seventh single, '(I Can't Get No) Satisfaction', had stormed to #1 in the UK by the end of the first week, following its success in the US, where it had stayed at the top for four weeks in the high summer. They had begun in the wake of Merseybeat, but, thanks to inspired positioning by their teenage Svengali, Andrew Loog Oldham, they were soon enshrined as the anti-Beatles, opposites yet competitors to the throne. Where the Beatles were styled as polite, charming and acceptable to adults, the Rolling Stones were, to some extent against their class and inclination, moulded into rude and divisive louts.

There is a wonderful photo of the Rolling Stones in 1964, at a Hyde Park press call. It's taken from behind the group, so all you can see is their collar-length hair – long and shaggy for the day. In front of them is a line of photographers, including the veteran Dezo Hoffman, and to one side is Andrew Loog Oldham, resplendent in waistcoat and wraparound sunglasses, gesticulating to the group, his face twisted into a sneer, showing by direct example exactly how to be offensive and disgusting in every way.

By summer 1965, the campaign was in full flight. A trivial incident in March that year, when one of the group, Bill Wyman, had been caught urinating against a garage wall, resulted in a very public court case. In late July, the *Daily Mirror* reported that 'three of the Rolling Stones were fined £5 each for insulting behaviour and were rebuked for not setting a higher moral standard for their fans'. Jagger was cited as saying, when challenged by a mechanic, 'We will piss anywhere, man.'

It was a defining moment. 'Fleet Street went ballistic over the story,' Andrew Loog Oldham remembered in his memoir, *2Stoned*, 'so I moved Mick into the headline and the band's image as long-haired monsters from the teenage Id was enhanced. I say "I moved" – it probably involved nothing more than me lying in the affirmative when some optimistic scribe asked whether Mick was in the front line.' This was a new kind of showbiz: building up anti-heroes, with their worst characteristics amplified.

And yet, at this point, the image was not the person. In Whitehead's interview, Mick Jagger is poised, studied and very eloquent for a young man dismissed as a mindless yob. Drawing on a cigarette and punctuating his words with hand gestures, he discusses the difference between pop now and then, when it 'wasn't a real thing at all. It was very, very romantic . . . in so far as every song was about boy/girl relationships, which is romantic in one sense. Every song was just like romantic lyrics, all about things that don't really happen.'

He developed his theme: 'If you listen to all popular songs ten years ago, very few of them actually mean anything, or have any relation to what people are doing. The songs didn't have any relation to what people actually spend their lives doing, like getting up, washing, going to work, coming back and feeling very screwed up about certain things.'

'Feeling very screwed up': that was the key. There was another side to teendom. For every newspaper article about the young as idealised consumers, there were others about violence, gang behaviour, drug-taking and promiscuous sexuality. The 1959 publication of Mark Abrams's influential report, *The Teenage Consumer* – the real beginning of teenage marketing in the UK – had coexisted with headlines about Teddy Boy violence. This continued with the first flush of the Beatles' international fame.

The mod/rocker battles in spring 1964 led to lurid headlines and outraged quotes from the authorities, 'long-haired, mentally unstable little sawdust Caesars' being the most memorable. A sensationally packaged book of interviews with real-time teenagers soon appeared. Pegged on the disturbances and the then current fashions, Charles Hamblett and Jane Deverson's *Generation X* nevertheless sought to uncover the reality that lay between the polarities of delinquent and consumer, star and fan. As Peter Laurie observed, 'Over the average teenager hovers the appalling consciousness of being average, of being totally undistinguished in anything that matters. Neither schooling nor further education nor industry make much attempt to draw him into the real productive life that can establish him as a member of our society. Without even this dubious accolade they are nothing, and they know they are nothing.'

In his ghost-written autobiography published in March 1966, *Just Me and Nobody Else*, the beatnik Neale Pharaoh went even further: 'Materially, the young person is relatively well off and there are aspects of his wealth and his apparent freedom that no one but a fanatic would want to abolish. But this is all we have; the underlying moral codes are no different . . . young people are suffering from an enforced schizophrenia. The glossy package of the pop world and the hard realities beneath conflict.'

It was this dissatisfaction – along with more general complaints about the state of the world – that many white songwriters and performers began to explore during 1965: the new generation of folkies, tough R&B groups like the Animals, and above all Bob Dylan, whose songs oscillated between industrial-strength vitriol and visionary explorations of a new world, one turned so upside down that it seemed to offer the possibility of a discrete youth universe.

On the West Coast, *KRLA Beat* contributor Eden explained Dylan's almost messianic allure in early 1966: 'Many people, both young and old, have adopted Bob Dylan as their spokesman, their leader, the man who represents the ultimate and final truth in the universe for them. But Bob will take no credit for this, will disengage from this position entirely. He writes entirely for himself, and offers it to anyone who will listen and can find a meaning for themselves within his work.'

The Rolling Stones also assumed this mantle on both sides of the Atlantic with '(I Can't Get No) Satisfaction' – a brilliantly made pop record: chunky, metallic, clear, with a firm yet supple rhythmic base that betrays its origin in contemporary soul music. And then there's the fuzz guitar, slicing through everything. The lyrics send Morse code flashes from a mediascape that promises satiation but totally fails to deliver. It ends with a cluster of repeated 'no's: I and you and we are nothing.

It changed the Rolling Stones' lives and pushed the pop culture of the time further towards harsh truth-telling. Romance was dead in the fast lane. The outsiders were inside, and they embodied change. The effect was to ramp up the demands on the performers. Each new 45 had to be a statement: they had just twelve weeks or so to come up with another hit, one that not only went further than the previous record or two but surpassed all other developments in between. The pace accelerated to a barely sustainable level.

In the early days, the Rolling Stones' position as rivals and co-evals to the Beatles had been, to some considerable degree, built on hype. But in early 1966, it was beginning to become true. In the fourth year of their success, the Beatles were weary, inward-looking and increasingly remote. After 'Day Tripper' and 'We Can Work It Out' went to #1 in Britain and America, they disappeared, and would not resurface in public until June.

To be sure, in January the charts were full of Beatles records: 'Day Tripper', *Rubber Soul* and various Top 30 covers of that album's songs by David and Jonathan, St Louis Union and the Overlanders, whose version of 'Michelle' went to #1 in late January. But these were mainstream pop songs, accentuating the very Beatles balladry that put off many hardcore fans. After the group collected their MBEs at Buckingham Palace in late October 1965, they were – temporarily at least – seen as part of the Establishment.

The Stones were definitely not. Even so, the anti-system that Andrew Loog Oldham had set up back in 1964 flattered to deceive. The Beatles were global superstars, sleek and indivisible, protected by the sophisticated guidance of Brian Epstein. Despite any intra-group tensions, they presented a monolithic, unified front, best exemplified by the famous scene in *Help!* where they pass through four separate front doors in suburban Twickenham to enter a vast communal living space undetectable from the outside. In contrast, the Rolling Stones were all niggles, and any existing edges were constantly sharpened by Oldham. There was a hierarchy that became ever more pronounced: the front man and chief guitarist – and later co-writers – Mick Jagger and Keith Richards, and then the rhythm section of Bill Wyman and Charlie Watts. Orbiting erratically like an already burnt-out star was Brian Jones, at once the group's irritant, pariah and fashion plate.

In late 1965, the Rolling Stones were still fresh to global fame, and they were moving very fast indeed. During their tours in Europe and the US, they met several people who would shape their future: the model Anita Pallenberg, the writer and film-maker Donald Cammell, the cutting-edge gallerist Robert Fraser and the designer/aesthete Christopher Gibbs. They'd begun as lower-middle-class bohemians, but now, as pills shaded into pot and LSD, they were mixing with the social and artistic elite.

They represented a new kind of pop star. 'Rather earlier I hung out with Larry Parnes and a lot of rough boys in this rather nice flat in the Gloucester Road,' Gibbs remembers. 'The Stones were much more sophisticated and subtle and enjoyable and on one's wavelength. I don't know why that was – I was that much older. It was very nice for me, cos they were a bit younger than me, and tuned me into all sorts of things that I didn't know about, so it was a fair exchange of energies and aspirations.

'They were very accepting and tolerant of one's sexuality, they were completely cool about all that. Unlike many of my contemporaries. Like most people of that age, I had a strong sex drive and rather a romantic view of possibilities . . . then drugs came along. Drugs lift one above, and if you smoke enough dope, you can actually find that you haven't got laid or got worried about it. This coincided with me coming into touch with all these young folk and hanging out with them. It all fitted in nicely.'

At the same time as they were becoming chic, the Rolling Stones were finally breaking the US – with two #1 singles and a #1 album in the second half of 1965. After a six-week tour, they ended up in Los Angeles in December, where they stayed in the exclusive Beverly Wilshire, gave a press conference and sequestered themselves in RCA Studios, Hollywood, for a concentrated burst of recording. They also had a shoot with Guy Webster, who snapped a couple of moody rolls up at the Franklin Canyon reservoir.

This was a defining session, providing the attitudinal cover for *Big Hits (High Tide and Green Grass)*, the greatest hits compilation released in different forms on both sides of the Atlantic. London Records also used a variant of the US sleeve for '19th Nervous Breakdown': the colour image was printed in black and white and showed the Stones glowering by the waterside, sullen, threatening and – if you looked closely at the bags under Brian Jones's eyes – quite possibly the subject of the song. It was a haunting, psychological freeze frame.

On 12 February, *Record Mirror* carried large colour photos of Mick Jagger, Keith Richards and Charlie Watts on the back and front pages, together with a banner advert for the new single. Inside were more pictures and interviews. Jagger observed a new kind of fan: 'Recently, in America especially, we seem to have been appealing to the same sort of audiences that turn out for Bob Dylan. Some of the more intellectual types of audiences go for very pretentious analyses of our style.'

In contrast to the always poised Jagger and Richards, Brian Jones revealed more than perhaps he would have wished: 'Life is a paradox for me. I'm so contradictory. I have this need for expression, but I'm not certain what it is I want to do. I'm not personally insecure, just unsure. I would like to write, but I lack confidence. I need encouragement. If someone told me I could write and egged me on, I suppose I could do it. It's like jumping in at the deep end and not knowing which way you are coming up.'

Despite its uncompromising harshness and unusual length, by 24 February '19th Nervous Breakdown' had zoomed up the UK charts to #2. That week, the Kinks released their new single, 'Dedicated Follower of Fashion'. While not at the same level as the Beatles and the Stones, they were serious contenders who had not quite regained the momentum of their first three smashes in late 1964 and early 1965. 'Till the End of the Day', their most recent hit, had only struggled into the Top 10.

The fan magazines and the public found the Kinks hard to pin down. They had tried hard to vary their signature hard-riffing style – most notably with the haunting, modal 'See My Friends' – while developing a reputation for truculence and worse. When the group played Copenhagen in March 1965, an overenthusiastic audience fought with the police and smashed up the Tivoli Hall. 'We had the Rolling Stones here last week,' the group was told. 'They were nice boys but you're horrible.'

At Cardiff's Capitol Theatre in May 1965, drummer Mick Avory climaxed a long-festering row with guitarist Dave Davies by walloping him onstage with a hi-hat. This was patched up just in time for the group to embark on their first US tour, a rancorous and badly organised affair that ended in recriminations between the group and their warring managers, Larry Page, Robert Wace and Grenville Collins, and a US musicians' union ban.

Singer and writer Ray Davies was tricksy, complex and elusive: he took great pains to keep himself apart while playing the pop game with an extremely keen sense of competitiveness. He knew that he was hampered by a poor record deal and inconsistent management. 'I think Oldham gave the Stones a real image,' he reflected. 'Without Oldham I don't think they would have been as good. I saw Brian Epstein starting with the Beatles, it was like another member and I felt we hadn't got that guidance.'

Davies always felt apart from the sixties elite. He nursed this resentment, becoming adept at turning negative energy into inspiration. Released in September 1965, 'A Well Respected Man' was an acid portrait of upper-middle-class hypocrisy and arrogance masked by a jaunty, almost music-hall rhythm. He continued in this fertile vein. The flip of 'Till the End of the Day' was 'Where Have All the Good Times Gone', a moody meditation on what had been gained and what had been lost in the social upheaval of the 1960s.

The Kinks' next single came from the same critical impulse. 'I remember I threw a party,' Davies recalled. 'There was a guy who was a designer and he was on about some style, and I got pissed off with him always going on about fashion and I was just saying you don't have to be anything; you decide what you wanna be and you just walk down the street, and if you're good the world will change as you walk past. I just wanted it to be up to the individual to create his own fashion.'

'Dedicated Follower of Fashion' is a Swinging London song by sarcastic, cynical young Londoners. The Kinks were close enough to the Carnabetian army to know whereof they spoke: 'One week he's in polka dots, the next week he's in stripes.' Bassist Pete Quaife and Dave Davies were well-known fashion plates, the latter outrageous in his shoulder-length long hair, stripy pullovers, Rupert Bear checked hipsters and – to promote the song – thigh-length rubber waders.

It begins with a reverb-saturated fanfare on acoustic guitar, segueing into another knees-up music-hall rhythm. Precisely enunciated by Ray Davies, who is clearly having enormous fun with assuming a variety of voices, the lyrics paint a detailed picture of a 'pleasure-seeking individual', a fickle butterfly who flits from boutiques to discotheques and parties. Here is a hermetically sealed youth world, seen and dissected from within, with its emptiness implicit.

The song's accuracy can be seen in the popular *Rave* column, 'Just Dennis – A Boy's Angle on Fashion'. In early 1966, Dennis was busy writing about polo-neck sweaters, 'ever popular' 1930s-style retro suits, op art ties ('looks great in a discotheque'), thick, bold, checked trousers, jumbo cords, candy-striped shirts and tinted eye specs. This was a flowering of men's fashion, the subterranean gay styles of 1950s Carnaby Street turned admass for teens throughout the country.

With lyrics about 'frilly nylon panties', 'Dedicated Follower of Fashion' was aware of the gay implications. 'That was the first time anybody told me I was camp,' Davies says. 'I remember this guy called Jimmy O'Day, who worked for our agency, came to see us at *Top of the Pops*. I was singing "Dedicated" – I could see him in the audience when I did certain things like [demonstrates camp gesture], he would purse his lips and shrivel up. He thought we were very, very camp, really near the knuckle for straight blokes.'

The publicity accentuated the obvious angle. The photographer Chris Walter took the Kinks around Soho, lining them up in a boutique. Quaife and Dave Davies riffled through a selection of floral and op art ties, while Ray looked on with wry amusement. In another shot from the session, the group loafed outside the Baron J Boutique, Dave to the front with his wide leather belt and cutaway jacket; in the nearby record-shop window was an ad for the new single by David Bowie.

During the mid-sixties, the *NME* featured advertisements on its front page. In the first week of March, Pye promoted 'Dedicated Follower of Fashion' with a drawing by Ray Davies that, again, might have revealed more than intended. The rhythm section are at the back, Quaife posing, Mick Avory trying not to be there. Dave Davies is slumped front right, dandyish and dissipated, while Ray holds himself erect, prim and paranoid, with huge lines around his eyes and disgust curdling his expression.

A March 1966 *Rave* interview with Ray confirmed this malaise: 'We used to like being asked questions but now we are sick of it. Why should we be leaders of fashions, or trendsetters? It makes us out to be different, but we are not, we are like everybody else. When people meet us they are brought down.' He added, 'I've got a quick temper. Once I picked up my guitar and smashed it at the audience. This life makes you all pent up, and you have to smash something.'

By mid-March, 'Dedicated Follower of Fashion' was slugging it out in the Top 10 with another defining new year's statement: the Yardbirds' 'Shapes of Things'. In contrast to the Kinks, the Yardbirds were still coming up fast. It was under a year since their first hit, 'For Your Love', and each of their following two UK singles – 'Heart Full of Soul' and the double A-side 'Evil Hearted You'/'Still I'm Sad' – had been artistic and commercial successes.

The Yardbirds had started out in the same west London blues scene – centred around Ealing, Twickenham and Richmond – as the Rolling Stones, taking over their slot at the Crawdaddy club in autumn 1963. They had struggled with the same problems of authenticity as the Stones: whether to stick with the ever-diminishing repertoire of purist R&B or to go pop. Their lead guitarist, Eric Clapton, knew which side he was on, and quit just as they had their first hit.

Replacing him with the taciturn but wildly inventive Jeff Beck, the Yardbirds struck out for pastures new. 'Heart Full of Soul' was one of the very first Western pop records to integrate Indian modes: the first version was attempted with sitar, until Beck simply simulated the drone with his electric guitar. 'Still I'm Sad' was based on a Gregorian chant, while their surging version of Bo Diddley's 'I'm a Man' climaxed with Beck chicken-plucking the neck of his guitar.

Most histories cite the Yardbirds as the group that included three famous guitarists, but in 1966 they were seen as fashion plates and progressive, exploratory musicians. They were extremely popular in the US, especially in California. 'They have developed a new sound – they call it a "Rave Up",' wrote *KRLA Beat* in January 1966. 'As each new record climbs steadily to the top of all the charts they are rapidly becoming one of the most popular and most successful groups in the world. Also, one of the most respected.'

They were a strange bunch: gothic, moody, volatile. Vocalist

Keith Relf cut a dash with his Brian Jones fringe and sunglasses – diverting attention from his droning, everyman tones – while Jeff Beck alternated between sullen non-communication and the brief moments when he'd come alive, grinning like a droog from *A Clockwork Orange*. The rave-up was their signature: blues figures accelerated and boosted into a climax, or series of climaxes, that reflected the hormonal surges of teenage nervous systems.

They also gave interviews that introduced a new way of talking about pop, one that pointed forward to a merging of the senses. 'Pop music is like abstract painting,' Relf told *Rave*. 'It is somehow easier to paint a sunset like a picture, than to paint it in an abstract mass of colour. People have to feel what the artist is getting at. When we record we don't necessarily sing of mists and sunsets, but put together a sound that puts thoughts of them into the minds of the listeners.'

After their American success, life accelerated for the Yardbirds. In September 1965, they played a private party for the Hollywood elite, before recording a couple of songs – including an explosive version of the Johnny Burnette Trio's 'The Train Kept A-Rollin'' – at Sam Phillips's Sun Studio in Memphis. Restricted by reciprocal visa problems, they returned in December for a six-week tour, during which they taped their new single at Chess in Chicago and Columbia Studios in Hollywood.

Like '19th Nervous Breakdown', 'Shapes of Things' – released on 24 February – is the product of pressure and frantic forward motion: pop modernism at its height. Beginning with a warning rumble, it settles into a stiff, martial rhythm. Keith Relf intones the philosophical lyrics – 'Shapes of things before my eyes / Just teach me to despise / Will time make man more wise?' – while Jeff Beck lets off constant feedback drones. The chorus ponders the future: 'Come tomorrow, will I be older? / Come tomorrow, maybe a soldier?'

The song is a complex, contradictory mixture of idealism, contempt and shame. The lyrics touch on ecology and the nature of perception itself. The message is conveyed through Jeff Beck's

Indian-toned guitar, which rumbles, sizzles and soars in the brief instrumental break; the song fades out on sitar-like fizzes that match the Near Eastern harmonies of the final chorus.

On the flip of the British 45 was another groundbreaking song. Written by Manfred Mann drummer Mike Hugg, and recorded at Sun Studios, 'You're a Better Man Than I' was a finger-pointing classic, tackling racism, militarism and intolerance in three short verses. 'Can you judge a man / By the way he wears his hair?' intoned Relf, before Beck cut the song in half with a raga-like solo.

Rave's review of the new single perfectly captured the pop scene's transition from one era to another: 'Keith Relf's marriage to April Liversedge last month came as a pretty stiff blow to Yardbirds fans. But still, the Yardbirds have been established as a top group for too long for this to affect their popularity. Proof enough is the high placing of their latest, "Shapes of Things", which, say Keith and Jeff, is meant to conjure up mental pictures in the minds of whoever hears it.'

'Shapes of Things' was an outrageous but highly successful record – it eventually reached #3 in the *Record Retailer* chart – that tapped into the new kind of audience that Mick Jagger had already observed. Primed by folk in general and Bob Dylan in particular, a section of the teenage market was now ready for thoughtful, open-ended songs that reflected a new and critical – if not transcendent – perception. Not for nothing did the Yardbirds typify their songs as 'images in sound'.

As both 'Shapes of Things' and 'Dedicated Follower of Fashion' entered the British charts, the fourth big pop statement of early 1966 was released. Like the Yardbirds, the Who had only been chart contenders for a year or so, and were coming up fast. They also came from west London, but there the similarities ended. While the Yardbirds took from the blues, the Who were inspired by Motown and James Brown. They weren't from Richmond and Twickenham, but Acton and Shepherd's Bush; not bohemian but mod.

In early 1966, the Who were still basking in the glow of an unprecedented success with 'My Generation', a Jimmy Reed blues riff with surfing harmonies and Motown hand-claps, that had been twisted and bent into aural violence. Everything in the song was off-kilter. There was no middle eight, just a bass solo; the verses and choruses were repeated until, at around two and a half minutes, the song accelerated and – underpinned by Keith Moon's manic drums – broke apart in a riot of feedback.

Using the keyword 'generation' – a youth-politics term going right back to the early 1920s – indicated the song's divisive and polemical intent. Pete Townshend had written the song as an attempt to get into the heads of the teenagers that flocked to their shows – the mods. He was casting for his role as a songwriter, and found his audience by observing the crowds at the dances the group played during the first half of 1964.

The Who were not mods but had been positioned as such by their then manager, Peter Meaden, a hustler and impresario with his ear close to the ground. In early 1964, Meaden had observed that the growing mod movement lacked any home-grown heroes and performers; it was all American pop and R&B, with a smattering of Jamaican ska. He renamed the Who the High Numbers – the term for the mod elite – and rewrote a couple of R&B tunes tailored for that market: 'Zoot Suit' and 'I'm the Face'.

Townshend had first encountered mod while at Ealing Art School in the early 1960s. 'I have this memory of walking home in a PVC coat, trying to be mod,' he told me in 2011. 'And how torn I was, because I was at art school, and the de rigueur outfit at art school was, you wore Levi's, but not in the mod style. I had a period of wondering how I'm going to fit in and this was overwhelmed when we finally did make it as a "mod band". We were the Who again, we were playing at the Railway hotel in Harrow.'

The Who were a new kind of group, not for the traditional female audience, but for a new constituency of disenfranchised and often volatile young men. For Townshend thought that mod was 'an entirely male system. And what's interesting is that this was running concurrently with Beatles gigs, Wayne Fontana and the Mindbenders gigs and Rolling Stones gigs, at which you would have a few mod girls and loads of silly women screaming their heads off. Who next week would be screaming about somebody else.

'So the tone of the times was one of, not so much experimentation but . . . we are talking about a generational cusp here, there's no question. What's interesting is why at that point pop culture and everything else changed. The first manifestation of it was kids who were born in 1945 and getting to that age, and deciding that they want to enter manhood using a different set of semiotics. You grow up with people that have a fixed way of looking at their lives, and if it doesn't work for you, you have no option but to redraw.'

The Who's inspiration came from Tamla and early soul. 'What happened with post-Beatles R&B was that we made a direct connection with urban black music. The disaffection, disenfranchisement, all of the things that we had about our condition as young people seemed to match what they felt in Detroit at the time. We felt we were in a majority, else we wouldn't have got away with it. Baby boomers. That feeling of being disregarded, in a sense. "I'm over here!" Nobody would listen.

'There was a great Establishment energy, a negative energy that tried to contain us,' Townshend continues. 'Adults thought, "This shouldn't be allowed, young long-haired fellows with make-up and taking pills." They were completely impotent. And we were dealing in the language of impotence, with disenfranchisement. You had these two disenfranchised bodies that were the post-war, previous generation, who were just worn out and fucked up, and us, looking for our next opportunity.'

By 1964/5, the mods had become a major cult, the most identifiable British youth subculture. They weren't the majority of teenagers who liked the Beatles and mainstream pop, but rather a subgroup who set the styles and spent the money – on clothes, records, scooters and their accoutrements, and pills. In an era of reasonably low youth unemployment – the figures for early 1966 showed boys and girls under eighteen at around 5 per cent of the total – the turnover of styles was manic and obsessive.

Peter Laurie went hunting for the type in its natural habitat during late 1964. At around 5 a.m. on a summer Sunday morning in Soho, he 'met a rather gaudy Mod in stripes coming the other way – I wanted him for the picture, but was rather diffident about asking him in case this offended the *esprit de corps* of my companions. "Stranger – this way, man, the feller wants your picture." They yelled cheerfully and made him welcome. The stripey boy said: "I'm hopelessly out of date – these went out three weeks ago."'

Laurie thought that the mods were a seamless product of the new mass-media age: they were 'only comprehensible if one sees them as one-man broadcasting stations distributing wholesale non-verbal messages about themselves and their rejection of the rest of the world. They are the first generation to cope consciously with a world that depends more on mass communications than personal relationships, and they have adapted themselves with striking success to life as they find it.'

The pace was frantic and, indeed, the mods' manic consumerism reflected and amplified wider trends in Britain: the rapid turnover of pop stars and styles; the slow but steady move from a collectivist society towards materialistic individualism. And yet, as epitomised by the very public youth tribe battles that rumbled through the spring and early summer of 1964, there was a downside: alienation, selfishness, heedless violence, drug psychosis, unresolved wartime damage.

In the mid-sixties, Britain was still living in the shadow of the Second World War, pitted by scars both physical and psychological. The stiff upper lip that had served the country so well in wartime had become a straitjacket for those too young to experience privation, rationing, sudden death and constant danger. Their parents had – quite understandably – locked away the awful memories, but now they threatened to erupt. After the state funeral of Winston Churchill in January 1965, something was released. Almost subconsciously – and in a raw and barely controlled manner – a few groups began to open the Pandora's box of repressed experience. Townshend recalled that in late 1965, he felt that 'he had a function, and my role as an artist was very clear. I wrote my best songs then, when I was absolutely clear what my audience wanted me to write. How to explain, how to express, how to dig deep, how to talk about what was unspeakable.'

During the first couple of months of 1966, the Who embodied this sense of disturbance. It was as though they were at war. They fought adults in general, the music industry, their producer and themselves. In the February 1966 issue of *Rave*, Alan Freedman called them 'desperate individualists' and, thanks to their violent stage show, the 'most unpopular group in pop'. He quotes Townshend: 'I got this idea of auto-destructive music. A group which destroys itself on stage playing quite valid music.'

On 5 January, Townshend appeared on BBC TV's *A Whole Scene Going* with the artist Barry Fantoni. Resplendent in a white jacket and characteristically articulate, Townshend talked about drugs: 'We're blocked up all the time.' The audience laughs, nervously. 'It just means that there are certain levels of perception opened up by certain drugs which people in the group don't mind resorting to.' This was extremely shocking for the time. No other pop star had talked so freely about their drug use.

Dawn James took Townshend to task about this in the March issue of *Rave*: 'He looked across the table with pale face and shaking hands, and said defiantly, "Drugs don't harm you. I know. I take them. I'm not saying I use opium or heroin, but hashish is harmless and everyone takes it." He is wrong, of course, everyone doesn't. I don't. Cliff Richard doesn't. Twinkle my sister doesn't. Lulu doesn't. Paul Jones doesn't. Dozens of people involved in pop lead normal lives. But to the world of the Who drugs are a normal thing.'

This was definitely not the bright and breezy type of pop-star interview standard for the time. James caustically observed how 'the Who don't have a great deal of enthusiasm about work. They enjoy being a successful group because of the money they earn, but many of their attitudes are destructive ones. They enjoy battering their instruments to pieces while onstage.' She concluded that they were 'four youthful figures, followed by many, but representative of very few'.

'Substitute' was forged in this fractious climate. Townshend took the riff from an obscure record by Robb Storme and the Whispers, 'Where Is My Girl', the spirit from '19th Nervous Breakdown' and the title from a club favourite by the Miracles, 'Tracks of My Tears'. 'I played that over and over,' Townshend says. 'And then the woman downstairs is saying, "What is it with you? One day you play the national anthem forty-four times in a row, next day you play the word 'substitute' a hundred times. What's the matter with you?"'

It erupts like a thunderclap. Townshend's acoustic guitar establishes the riff and holds down the rhythm, while Keith Moon's drums skitter all over the place: the kick drum keeps a constant, accelerated heartbeat while he ranges all over the snares and the cymbals. At the start of the instrumental break – which, against type, features only John Entwistle's bass guitar – Moon wallops the hell out of the floor toms in a performance so manic, or drug-deranged, that he had no memory of it after the event.

As Moon's drums punctuate the rhythm like jabs to the chest, Roger Daltrey's voice carries the lyric, which – sung to an imaginary girlfriend – is a sophisticated and thorough portrait of teenage insecurity, frustration and confusion, reported from within. Everything is up for grabs: racial identity, physical appearance, the nature of identity itself. Nothing is what it seems: 'I was born with a plastic spoon in my mouth'; 'The simple things you see are all complicated'.

Townshend was determined to go deeper into the realms of the subconscious, and on 'Substitute' it took him into uncharted territory with the conflation of girlfriend and mother in the final verse. Nearing four minutes, 'Substitute' was, like '19th Nervous Breakdown', both long and complex for the time, and in its construction and lyrics it mirrored the stuck psychology of the Rolling Stones' song: 'It's a genuine problem but you won't try / To work it out at all, you just pass it by.'

Unlike 'My Generation', the production and arrangement is disciplined: the violence, embodied by the drums, is there, just under the surface. To some degree, it was understood that anger and frustration were both a part of the Who's image and mod culture in general. But 'Substitute' went further, into the profound sexual confusion hinted at in the song, a taboo topic that Townshend would explore in greater detail in the months and years to come.

'The sexual identity stuff was really important,' he says now. 'We didn't look at the difficulties faced by young people growing up in the aftermath of the war and in the last days of the war, when, to put it bluntly, everything was up for grabs. Nothing was certain. It's in a retreat that the worst rapes happen. It's then that the really abhorrent behaviour happens in war. What was happening in the UK was that in the evacuations, some of the worst treatment happened.

'I remember growing up with boys that were four or five years old, and it would be them that wouldn't talk about what had happened. You'd know that something dreadful, strange or bizarre had happened to them. It might have been simply that they felt abandoned by their parents. Whatever it was, they were scarred. And if you said the wrong thing, you got a smack in the face. Out of all proportion. "Why do you comb your hair back like that?" Boom!'

The record's release was chaotic. The Who and their management were in serious dispute with their record company, Brunswick, and their first producer, Shel Talmy. 'Substitute' was to be issued on a new label called Reaction, with the flip another song about confusion, 'Circles', which they'd already recorded as 'Instant Party'. Talmy sued, and Brunswick released an old song, 'A Legal Matter', as a spoiler. Reaction had to stop production and issue a new B-side.

But 'Substitute' was both well-reviewed – 'some excellent modernistic lyrics', 'a sense of urgency' – and unstoppable, as were the group, almost despite themselves. As it slowly went up the charts, the Who were pictured on the front of the *Observer*'s colour supplement – an unusual occurrence at the time – accompanying an article about the nature of a pop business saturated in speed, violence and cynicism. John Heilpern quoted at length the group's managers, one working-class, one posh – the period's ideal mix embodied.

'I like the blatantness of pop, the speed, the urgency,' said Chris Stamp. 'There's either success or failure – it's no use bollockin' about.' Kit Lambert thought that the Who's 'rootlessness appeals to the kids. They're really a new form of crime, armed against the bourgeois . . . The point is, we're not saying, Here are four nice, clean-cut lads come to entertain you. We're saying, Here is something outrageous – go wild!'

The photographer Colin Jones remembered that he'd 'never met a band that was so antagonistic', but the resulting image freezes a moment. Posing in front of a Union Jack stolen from a hotel flagpole by Keith Moon, the four men glower at the camera. They are living pop art, a riot of clashing stripes, lozenges and Bridget Riley-style optical patterns. Placed front centre, Pete Townshend wears a Union Jack jacket as if to say, 'This is what the country is now, this is what you have become. What are you looking at me for? Boom!'

* * *

'LONDON, the most with-it, exciting city in the world. The pace-setting city; the most watched city. What will London do next, what will London wear next?'
'A RAVER'S POP GUIDE TO LONDON', *Rave*, April 1966

The sense that the young were moving into a more demanding, if not self-involved, phase was reflected in a book published in Britain that March. Collated by Wilfred De'Ath from a series of conversations with an anonymous young man, *Just Me and Nobody Else* was published with a cover blurb that proclaimed it to be 'a vivid and vital clue to the understanding of a generation now on the threshold of manhood. The world will soon be in their hands. The effort to understand them must be made – and now.'

The book was promoted and received as 'a vivid and vital portrait of a Teenager: his world and opinions'. Like *Generation X* and *The Teenage Revolution*, it offered a snapshot of young life seen from within: this time from the perspective of a teenage runaway, beatnik and petty criminal who had come to prominence in the media when, after a spell in a detention centre, he had been wheeled out to offer the youth's point of view on crime and punishment for government committees and the serious weeklies.

The anonymous youth was called Neale Pharaoh. Raised by a domineering and 'emotionally shut down' father, he was in constant trouble at school. His war with his parents had escalated when he started going to jazz clubs: 'Beatniks were all the rage then, with C.N.D. badges chalked on their sweaters and rough denim jeans.' One evening, his father followed him and dragged him out of a club. After a climactic argument, he was thrown out of the parental home.

Pharaoh quickly adapted, finding a place in a hostel and immersing himself in the beatnik culture of the time: jazz clubs, coffee bars, Benzedrine tablets, tenement flats. He was perceptive about the nature of outsider culture, telling De'Ath: 'If there is a break in your experience, like the clash with my parents, you begin to cut yourself off emotionally; if you have any intelligence in the first place you form your own sub-culture. You can't feel a part of the parent culture and your experiences and values become broader.'

He elaborated: 'In the fifties there were a lot of people who never had it so good and a large number had a very disturbed family background as a result of the war and the increase in the gap between the commercial "teenage" identity and the adult world aggravated this. Our whole system, including education, was so rigid that these sub-cultures formed themselves and were pushed further away instead of being absorbed. So the process crystallised into beatniks at the intelligent end of the scale and juvenile delinquents at the other.'

Just Me and Nobody Else is a strange book, caught in the contradictions of Pharaoh's character and his voice, which fluctuates in tone between clarity, honesty, self-justification and pompousness. Like many people who are given a platform, he can grow fond of the sound of his own thoughts. But it's also a valuable and undersourced historical document, giving a genuine insight into a forgotten area of British youth culture. For, freed from parental constraint, Pharaoh went on Aldermaston marches, attended the infamously rowdy Beaulieu Jazz Festival of July 1960 and haunted the youth spots in Soho: 'coffee bars like the Gyre & Gymble in Villiers Street or the Nucleus', or Colyer's all-night jazz club. This was beatnik central: 'By midnight, when the session began, the floor at Colyer's would be packed with people carrying rucksacks and sleeping bags. The night went on from there.'

These sessions were fuelled by Benzedrine: 'Once the kick builds up there is no need to stop moving. More pills and you don't need to sleep or eat the whole weekend . . . you roar into Soho for the all-night sessions, talking and twitching because you can't stop moving. Must move. Dance all night . . . Then you come down, and the lights switch off one by one. You're left sick, grey, shattered, walking down the Charing Cross Road in the Sunday-morning drizzle.'

Despite all the wild parties and the envy of weekend 'ravers', Pharaoh began to feel that he 'was living in a dream in which I didn't feel I was actually taking part'. This disconnection worsened: 'you float above yourself and it's not really you down there'. He started to get in trouble with the law and, after being caught stealing a second time, was sent to a detention centre in Sussex on a three-month sentence. From that point on, the book operates as a report and an exposé on this punitive regime.

On his release in early 1963, Pharaoh returned to the west London beatnik circuit: the Auberge coffee club in Richmond and the Eel Pie Island Jazz Club. At the latter, Arthur Chisnall – an outreach worker in all but name, with a special interest in the problems of youth – presided over a benevolent regime that provided a haven for successive waves of disaffected teens. From 1956 on, the club had hosted trad bands like Ken Colyer's, visiting blues musicians and the new wave of British R&B groups.

Chisnall suggested to the young man that he write about his experiences of the detention centre for *New Society*. The article, entitled 'The Long Blunt Shock', was published in September

1963. Pharaoh wrote a follow-up about the purple hearts 'menace', 'He Gets Out of It', in February 1964, and then, after attending a few meetings of the 1964 Home Office Committee for Juvenile Delinquency, relapsed into a semi-obscurity not reversed by the anonymous publication of his memoirs.

Pharaoh closes the book on a rather sour note about the youth culture of the mid-sixties: 'The "Mod" has been diverted to purely material channels and soon the process is going to begin again. Underneath the new morality and the dress revolution, there is nothing. The priority of the beatniks, a sense of community, an emphasis on coffee-bar intellectualism, on trying to understand, has been supplanted by the mass pseudo-event that young people have created for themselves.'

However, in the time lag between the book's writing, delivery and publication, beatnik culture had evolved and had begun to occupy centre stage in British and American youth culture. Although it wasn't mentioned in the text, Pharaoh had come from the same milieu as the new wave of British pop bands – the coffee bars and church halls in Richmond, and the Eel Pie Island Hotel, where the Stones played fourteen times in 1963. He had even shared a flat for a while with Yardbirds' guitarist Eric Clapton.

The music and the clothes were different, but in many ways the experiments of the early sixties were becoming more and more popular amongst Britain's youth. When Pharaoh returned to art school, he found it strange: 'The students, especially the art students, were beginning to do what I had done three years ago. They were taking drugs, calling themselves existentialists, and doing all the other things that they thought set them apart. It certainly set them apart. From me.'

The outsiders were becoming insiders. The mods had simply taken over the beats' pill-popping, all-nighter habit, with contemporary black American dance music instead of trad, while the mix of sexual freedom, drug experimentation and overt anti-Establishment values that had been rehearsed by those early-1960s pioneers had been assumed by the hit-makers of 1965 and early

1966: the Yardbirds, the Who, the Rolling Stones, all of whom were still in their early to mid-twenties.

By mid-March, these cultural leaders – if not Pied Pipers – were all in the Top 20. Early that month, the Rolling Stones had returned to Hollywood, where they spent another week recording in RCA Studios. *KRLA Beat* reported that unusual instruments were being used: 'a dulcimer, a sitar – there will be a heavy Indian accent on this album . . . some vibes, piano, an organ, a harpsichord, a fuzz organ, and the oddest collection of guitars ever seen'. In the pictures, the group look exhausted. But there would be no rest.

Next up was a short European tour: Holland, Belgium, France. On 30 March, at a date in Marseilles, the violence got out of hand. As *Disc Weekly* reported, 'In a brawl which started at the end of their act Mick was hospitalised by a seat tossed onto the stage by rioting teenagers. "They were ripping the seats apart and beating up the gendarmes," he said. "It all seems to have become part of the performance over there. The kids were going bonkers. Even hitting the police with their own truncheons."'

The second of April saw the American release of *Big Hits (High Tide and Green Grass)*, a good-value package that came with six Top 10 US hits and a lavish sleeve with eight pages of colour pictures. Two weeks later, while the pop papers were full of an apparent feud between Mick Jagger and Scott Walker, the Rolling Stones issued their fourth British album. This had been first trailed in late January under the title of *Could You Walk on Water?* – an implicitly blasphemous Andrew Loog Oldham idea inspired by the Guy Webster reservoir shoot.

The retitled *Aftermath* was another major statement, a very long – at just over fifty minutes, it was cut very quiet – and entirely self-penned album. The group's days of R&B covers were over, on record at least. This was a varied collection of songs that ranged from modern madrigals ('Lady Jane'), music-hall ragas ('Mother's Little Helper'), strange, curse-like dirges ('I Am Waiting') and uptempo pop ('Think') to several bone-dry blues mutations ('High and Dry', 'Flight 505', the eleven-minute 'Going Home'). It got rave reviews.

Richard Green of *Record Mirror* thought *Aftermath* was 'the smash LP of the year', and his prediction was accurate. It went to #1 a week after its release and stayed there for eight weeks, defining the year. For London School of Economics student Pete Fowler, writing in his memoir, 'The Stones had been on a roll since "Satisfaction", and some of the material on *Aftermath* caught the moment of 1966 far more accurately than, say, the contemporary Beatles tracks.'

Fowler was from the first generation in his family to go to university, and he was acutely aware of being caught between two worlds. When he returned to his home town to work in a frozen-food factory in between terms at the LSE, he was surprised by the hostility of his workmates: 'we were pooves, we were idlers, we'd never done a day's work'. Searching for an explanation, he realised that by his very presence, he was 'anathema to the young workers in this Cleethorpes factory. We had a freedom that was now forever denied to the lads working full-time on the factory floor. And they knew, as we knew, that the world was on the cusp of a change – and that they were going to miss out on that change. It hadn't impacted on Grimsby and Cleethorpes yet, but they could see the changes as they watched *Ready Steady Go!* and *The Avengers* on television. Everything seemed looser, it must be different living in London.'

With what Fowler decribes as its 'very singular attitude', *Aftermath* encapsulated that distance and that freedom. It embodied detachment and superiority: 'Life was, basically, one long sneer. It was for us, looking around in a Grimsby pub feeling sorry for the young people there; it was looking back on old friends and knowing that you had moved on so much more than them. It was not only derisory of your parents and their generation, it was scathing of most people of your own age.'

On *Aftermath*, persona becomes person: the nastiness of the Rolling Stones' constructed image spills over into the lyrics of 'Stupid Girl', 'Under My Thumb' and 'Out of Time'. Jagger's difficulties with his then partner, Chrissie Shrimpton – a feisty upper-middle-class girl who gave as good as she got – translate into a high level of contempt towards women that received zero comment from the male reviewers of the album and, indeed, does not seem to have troubled many of the group's female fans at the time.

On the same day that *Aftermath* came out, *Time* magazine published their cover story on 'London: The Swinging City'. This was the culmination of the process that had begun with the unprecedented success of the Beatles three years or so earlier. The idea that London was swinging had been a popular trope in the British pop papers for a while – *Fabulous* had an issue on the topic in 1964 – and it was still current, as *Rave*'s April 1966 issue proclaimed, 'London Swings'. For *Time* to pick it up was big news.

These were features disguised as advertising copy. 'In a decade dominated by youth, London has burst into bloom,' Piri Halasz opined in *Time*. 'It swings; it is the scene. This spring, as never before in modern time, London is switched on. Ancient elegance and new opulence are all tangled up in a dazzling blur of op and pop. The city is alive with birds (girls) and beetles, buzzing with mini cars and telly stars, pulsing with half a dozen separate veins of excitement.'

Halasz had visited London in 1949 and remembered the bomb sites and the terrible food. The city had been transformed, and in preparation for that piece she immersed herself in four days of 'the most concentrated swinging – discotheques, restaurants, art gallery and private parties, gambling, pub crawling'. She noted the distance between then and now: 'In a once sedate world of faded splendour, everything new uninhibited and kinky is blooming at the top of London life.'

There were naysayers, of course, mutterings about decadence and frivolity, but Halasz observed 'a bloodless revolution', quoting Richard Hoggart: 'A new group of people is emerging into society, creating a kind of classlessness and verve that has not been seen before.' There were famous cockneys – Michael Caine, Terence Stamp – but many came from the Midlands, Yorkshire, Manchester and Birmingham: Peter O'Toole, Shelagh Delaney, Albert Finney, Rita Tushingham, the Beatles.

The article took a breathless tour through *Ready Steady Go!*, a lunch with Caine and Stamp, an opening at Robert Fraser's gallery, Carnaby Street, John Aspinall's Clermont Club and various discotheques – Dolly's, Annabel's, the Scotch of St James. The Rolling Stones hover as kings of the scene: 'Lady Jane' is cited as part of a tradition that goes back to Shakespeare, while Mick Jagger is spotted at the Guys and Dolls coffee house with *Ready Steady Go!*'s Cathy McGowan.

Britain was rebranded as Pop Island, with London at its heart. The capital, in turn, had become a city of youth – all 2,400,000 of them, as estimated by *Time*. London's effervescence was 'the result of the simple friction of a young population on an old seasoned culture that has lost its drive. Youth is the word indeed in London – and well it should be: nearly 30% of its population is in the 15–34 age bracket, far more than the rest of the country as a whole.'

This was a seductive and well-presented fantasy that had some basis in truth. Even if the swinging lifestyle was not available to the mass of British teenagers, it was there as an ideal, propagated by a sophisticated national media, and it could be seen and bought in cities around the country – Manchester, Liverpool, Newcastle, Birmingham, Carlisle and so on – each with their own youth enclaves: boutiques, coffee bars, clubs.

The degree to which it was still a fantasy was exposed – just as it was being constructed for an international audience – by cynical young Londoners like the Kinks and the Rolling Stones, who were smart enough to see the emptiness that lay beneath the hype. A key song on *Aftermath* was the slide blues 'Doncha Bother Me': 'All the clubs and the bars / And the little red cars / Not knowing why, but trying to get high,' sang Mick Jagger, before tartly announcing that 'the lines around my eyes are protected by copyright law'.

The truth was that by April 1966 Swinging London was pretty much over. The wave of energy and creativity that had followed the Beatles' first breakthrough was nearly spent. The pop press was full of negative stories during the early months of 1966: the surliness and unavailability of established stars no longer willing to play the cheeky, chirpy game; the American fightback ('The British Boom – Is It Over?', asked *Rave* in February); the sense that things were slipping away from the capital and Britain.

Psychological leakage was spilling over into major pop hits, a reaction to sheer tiredness and the killing pace of international success. In the *Rolling Stones Monthly*, Mick Jagger recalled that the first part of '19th Nervous Breakdown' to arrive was the title: 'We had just done five weeks' hectic work in the States and I said, "Dunno about you blokes, but I feel about ready for my nineteenth nervous breakdown."' It wasn't just a catchy hook but an accurate, if self-mocking, description of his mental state. His nervous collapse was not far off.

March 1966 saw a couple of well-reported crack-ups. The leader of the Searchers, Chris Curtis, had a breakdown during an Australian tour with the Rolling Stones in late March. Details about this event are unclear – Curtis was secretive and never spoke about the episode – but pills were almost certainly involved. Andrew Loog Oldham alleges some impropriety on a naval base: Curtis had 'gone out at night after a show, a Gladstone doctor's bag in his hand, trying to pass himself off as a doctor to all the young conscripts'.

On 17 March, Ray Davies had a major episode that involved him attacking his publicist Brian Somerville: 'It was like *Morgan: A Suitable Case for Treatment* when I look back on it, but at the time it was deadly serious.' As 'Dedicated Follower of Fashion' rose in the charts, he was tormented by people coming up to him in the street and repeating his words: 'Oh yes he is, oh yes he is.' When he saw himself performing the song on *Top of the Pops*, he put the TV set in the oven and then went to bed for a week.

Just as 'Dedicated Follower of Fashion' peaked in the charts at #4, a major new British film was released. Starring David Warner, Vanessa Redgrave and Robert Stephens, *Morgan: A Suitable Case for Treatment* had every appearance of being a fashionable comedy of manners, if not a farce, but quickly revealed itself to be a case study of madness – as defined and used as a method of social control

– and a serious disquisition on the construction of reality. The film was written by the radical playwright David Mercer and directed by Karel Reisz, a founder member of the Free Cinema documentary movement. His 1959 *We Are the Lambeth Boys* was a groundbreaking look at working-class teenage life, while 1960's *Saturday Night and Sunday Morning* showed how naturalism could be big box office. But *Morgan* marks the moment when British social realism moved successfully into a surrealistic, if not absurdist depiction of inner psychological states.

In the film, Morgan – as played by David Warner – is an artist with longish hair and fashionable clothes. He has been living the dream. The grittiness of inner-city life in the original play has been replaced by the luxuries of upper-middle-class London. His wife's Campden Hill flat is full of consumer goodies, while Morgan himself is recast from the original as a painter rather than a writer. His nemesis Charles Napier has a fashionable West End gallery full of mobiles and action sculptures.

Morgan has made it. But the gulf between his hardcore Stalinist upbringing and the new, apparently classless metropolitan consumer culture is beginning to tear him apart. And so a comedy of manners begins to tip into something darker. Morgan appears to be a bumbling fool, but he is also the fool in an older, deeper sense: the jester who strips away the veils of illusion to reveal an unpalatable truth just as his sanity is stripped away. As he admits at one point, 'I've lost the thread.'

To depict this disintegration Reisz begins to intercut natural-history footage into Morgan's reveries. In a famous scene, he is ascending an escalator in the Tube. A dolly bird comes down on the other side. Morgan leans on the moving handrail and, as the young girl flutters her mascaraed eyelashes, envisions a peacock fluffing its feathers – an ornamental but useless creature. Civilisation is a thin veneer in the urban jungle, and Morgan imagines himself as a gorilla, the big beast, King Kong atop the Empire State Building.

His dreams are becoming nightmares – as he admits, 'Nothing in this world seems to live up to my best fantasies' – as they begin to overtake his sense of reality. After disrupting the wedding between Charles and Leonie, Morgan, dressed up in a gorilla suit, spurred on by intercut clips from the original 1933 version of *King Kong*, speeds off on a purloined motorbike, his suit smouldering, along a Park Lane that is still in the throes of redevelopment: a wonderful, iconic shot.

Morgan: A Suitable Case for Treatment appeared designed to cash in on the cachet of Swinging London, but it was a polemic, uncovering the deeper psychological impulses that were cloaked by – but could not be eradicated through – the illusion of youth, fashion and money. Exhaustion had set in among the pop elite: during 1966, almost all the major players of the previous two to three years would withdraw, change shape or actively self-destruct. That's how fast and fundamentally things moved in the high sixties.

With the first wave retreating or going strange, a vacancy had been created. There was a distinct sense of regime change in early 1966. But the previous three years, with their huge influx of money and media attention, had felt like something totally new. It wasn't just business as usual; things weren't going to go back to the way they had been before. Disturbance and breakdown in all their forms would no longer be denied, but would become part of pop's palette.

It was too late to stop. As the period's momentum increased, it was time to strike out for uncharted territory. All this energy, creativity and power had to mean something, but what? It wasn't just about money and chart positions, but a new way of looking at the world, as attitudes became politics, as personal breakdown pointed to social crisis. In the spring of 1966, this was still inchoate, but under the escalating demands of youth and their culture the fantasy of a consumerist teen utopia like Swinging London would crack for ever.

THE WHO
The prediction business (2)

Carpets in Bri-Nylon for the soft, soft life
and the hard wear

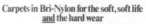

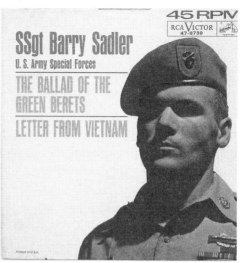

3 : MARCH

The Ballad of the Green Berets:
The Vietnam War in America

'Senators, the Congress and the politician man
Well, they all got me in the mess I'm in.'
BOBBY JAMESON, 'Vietnam', October 1965

There was a war, of course. It hadn't been formally declared – or, indeed, ratified by Congress – but it was understood as such by the vast majority of Americans. It was a war in anything but name, one that had been escalating rapidly during 1965 and that by the end of that year was beginning to dominate American media and politics. In the course of that escalation, it revealed deep fault lines in Lyndon Baines Johnson's Great Society.

There had been rumblings since the early sixties, but 1966 was the year when Vietnam fully impacted upon America. In his third State of the Union address, on 12 January, President Johnson put the war high on the agenda: 'Our nation tonight is engaged in a brutal and bitter conflict in Vietnam,' he stated after his introductory remarks. 'It just must be the centre of our concerns.'

The conflict was beginning to suck in more and more young Americans. In January 1966, there were 185,000 US troops in Vietnam; by the end of December, there would be 385,000 – the biggest single increase in any year of the war's duration. For Americans born in 1947 or earlier – slap bang in the early baby-boomer demographic – this would become the central issue in their lives: whether to evade the draft or do your duty, whether to go or not to go.

These were fundamental but as yet barely understood questions. At the start of 1966, the Vietnam war was still in its infancy. Most Americans supported it: in late 1965, the president had an approval rating of 64 per cent, even if there was unease. The casualty lists were escalating, with an estimated 1,863 deaths during 1965. There was little desire for a prolonged war, and 43 per cent of those polled thought LBJ was not doing enough to bring a peaceful resolution to the conflict.

The majority of Americans were patriotic: in times of war that, quite rightly, meant unquestioning support of the flag. But there was a small, defiant protest movement that grew during 1965. A few adults vocally opposed the war – on ethical and procedural grounds – but it was the young, as ever, who would have to fight. A mixture of moral outrage and sheer defiance informed the actions of a minority whose well-publicised actions infuriated the president. It was 'America: love it or leave it' versus 'We won't go!' In early 1966, this polarisation was just beginning to seep into American society: between, on the one hand, the generation who had fought, with great distinction, during the Second World War and saved the world from fascism; and on the other, their children, born into boom time, who were being called on to fight another war. But this time the theatre and the motivation were quite different.

Johnson was in his late fifties, having been born in 1908, but this would be a teenagers' war. The average age of a soldier serving in the Second World War was twenty-six; in Vietnam, it was nineteen. Young men were eligible for the draft just days after their eighteenth birthday. The parable of Abraham and Isaac was happening all over again. The son was being sacrificed by the father and, just as had happened in Europe during the years immediately after the First World War, this opened up the generation gap.

The president and his advisers had the expectation that the US involvement in Indochina would be limited but, as 1966 went on, the Vietnam war came home. It was a contagious disease, exacerbating divisions throughout the country: between rich and poor, between black and white, between patriots and resisters, between non-draftees and combatants. But none would be quite so bitter as the schism between young and old.

* * *

'Why do you kill all those kids over there in Vietnam?
Mad Viet Cong.
My brother died in Vietnam!'
THE MONKS, 'Monk Time', 1966

On 5 March 1966, there was a new American #1. Staff Sergeant
Barry Sadler's 'The Ballad of the Green Berets' was the first single
by the army serviceman. Released in mid-January, the record shot
up the charts after an airing on the 30 January *Ed Sullivan Show*
– from #51 to #10 in the week ending 19 February – and by early
March it was at the top. And there it stayed for five weeks, keeping
out both the Rolling Stones ('19th Nervous Breakdown') and the
Beatles ('Nowhere Man').

'The Ballad of the Green Berets' would be the biggest American
hit of the year. It was sung by a member of the Special Service
who had fought in Vietnam, and it was an authentic expression
of the patriotic and nationalist mindset: one that had no doubt
about America's involvement in South-East Asia; one that held
the deaths of US servicemen to be a worthy sacrifice; and one that
chimed with a large section of the American public.

It begins with military drum rolls. The pace is slow, ballad speed,
and Sadler's baritone is high in the mix: unlike the muddy vituper-
ations of the Rolling Stones or the convoluted riddles of Bob Dylan,
there is no room for complexity or ambiguity. He is one of those
men 'who mean just what they say'. There are four verses and no
middle eight. Apart from extra instrumentation – a swelling organ,
a military trumpet – there is no variation or escape from the song's
message.

The lyrics celebrate the brave men of the Green Berets, 'fearless
men who jump and die'. This is an elite force and they are expected
to endure extreme hardships and fight 'hand to hand', 'night and
day'. The ending is inevitable: the Green Beret 'has died for those
oppressed' but entreats his wife to 'put silver wings on my son's
chest / Make him one of America's best'.

It's a closed circle, a repeating cycle that brooks no dissent. 'The

Ballad of the Green Berets' was a monolith, in its deliberate pace and four-square approach quite different to the prevailing styles of the day. It seemed hewn from the very rock of the nation, a heroic paean to bravery, patriotism and sacrifice, as obdurate as the qualities that it sought to invoke. As an expression of the martial mindset, it is without peer.

It was also, in the context of the time, extremely effective propaganda. While the single does not explicitly mention Vietnam, there was no doubt about its meaning, and the accompanying album, *Ballads of the Green Berets*, was basically a concept record about the conflict, with songs about the serving soldier's experience like 'Letter from Vietnam', 'Trooper's Lament' and 'Saigon'. This hit #1 in the album charts a week after the single, and also stayed there for five weeks.

Sadler knew of what he sang. Born in 1940, he was the child of divorced parents. After an itinerant upbringing, he enlisted in the US Air Force at the age of seventeen. On his discharge, he enlisted in the army and, after passing the rigorous testing procedure, became a member of the US Army Special Forces – the Green Berets. Sent to Vietnam as a medic, he was injured by a poisoned punji stick (a booby-trapped stake) in May 1965 and shipped home to the US.

It was during his stay in military hospital that Sadler began writing songs. A long, twelve-verse version of 'Ballad of the Green Berets' found its way to the author Robin Moore, who had just published the best-selling *The Green Berets* – a lightly fictionalised account of the elite special forces unit's activities in Vietnam. Moore worked with Sadler on the song and received a co-writer's credit; his book would later be turned into a movie featuring John Wayne.

Sadler disavowed overt politics but his position and intent was crystal clear. In an interview with *KRLA Beat*, he stated that 'the draft card burning and dissent by American youth' had prompted the song. As the magazine editorialised, 'We've heard a lot in the last year or so of protests against the war but now we hear from a man who knows what war is, a man who's been actively engaged in it, and a man who's proud of his part in it, a man who's proud to fight for America.'

'The Ballad of the Green Berets' came at a crucial point in the Vietnam war. Support for it was beginning to erode: by March 1966, the president had an approval rating of 46 per cent – down by 18 per cent from the end of 1965 – with 34 per cent disapproving of his policies. It was necessary to win hearts and minds. Up until that point, comment about Vietnam in pop music and youth culture had been skewed towards the antis – although there was already a healthy dialogue back and forth by the end of 1965.

The loudest noise had been made by Barry McGuire's 'Eve of Destruction', the record that both defined and killed 'Protest' as a short-lived genre. Hitting #1 at the end of September, it polarised the country. There were plenty of hooks in the song to upset the public: lines that linked Red China to Selma, Alabama; that pointed out the paradox whereby a young man could serve in the armed forces (at the age of eighteen) but could not vote (until the age of twenty-one).

Vietnam hangs heavy over the song. 'Eve of Destruction' was relentlessly negative: the lyrics pile up on top of each other as the music grinds through its folk-rock changes. This was seen as unpatriotic in the extreme, and there was a slew of answer records. 'The Dawn of Correction' by the Spokesmen opened with the lyrics: 'The Western world has a common dedication / To keep free people from Red domination.' The group followed it up in late 1965 with 'Have Courage, Be Careful', addressed to soldiers in Vietnam.

Sonny Bono – then a major pop star with Cher – put his oar in with the late-1965 single 'The Revolution Kind': 'We got a land and the land is free / And no one loves it more than me.' There was another answer record by Billy Carr, 'What's Come Over This World', which followed the folk-rock template of 'Eve of Destruction' but with a diametrically opposed lyric: 'There's an army of cowards, see them marching in line / While the country's in danger, they just carry a sign.'

Donovan's cover of Buffy Sainte-Marie's 'Universal Soldier' was released as a single during September 1965. The biting lyric commented on the cycle of violence: 'He's all of thirty-one and he's only seventeen / Been a soldier for a thousand years.' Within a month, it attracted an answer record, Jan Berry's 'The Universal Coward': 'He just can't get it through his thick skull why the mighty USA / Has got to be the watchdog of the world.' Berry got one thing right, though: 'He joins the pickets at Berkeley and he burns his draft card'.

The campus at the University of California at Berkeley had become a centre for anti-war protest after the events of September 1964, when the authorities had tried to ban civil rights meetings and speeches on campus. In response, the Berkeley students held a sit-in. As the stand-offs with the authorities reached a peak, they were inspired by the ringing rhetoric of civil rights activist Mario Savio to turn this spontaneous protest into a movement of freedom.

Savio's words would ring loud and clear throughout the rest of the 1960s: 'There's a time when the operation of the machine becomes so odious, makes you so sick at heart, that you can't take part! You can't even passively take part! And you've got to put your bodies upon the gears and upon the wheels . . . upon the levers, upon all the apparatus, and you've got to make it stop! And you've got to indicate to the people who run it, to the people who own it, that unless you're free, the machine will be prevented from working at all!'

Energised by the Free Speech Movement, student activists began to turn from civil rights to Vietnam. In May 1965, the Vietnam Day Committee (VDC) – founded by Jerry Rubin and Abbie Hoffman, among others – was formed to expand the peace movement and raise public awareness of the war by civil disobedience and community action. In August, with slogans like 'Make Love Not War', activists from the VDC picketed troop trains carrying soldiers from the nearby Oakland Army Base who were bound for Vietnam.

Out of this ferment came one of the most pointed musical protests against the war. Released in October 1965 on the Berkeley Rag Baby label, 'I Feel Like I'm Fixin' to Die Rag' begins with the sound of gunfire before Country Joe McDonald offers the invitation: 'Well, come on, all of you big strong men / Uncle Sam needs your help again.' Over four blackly humorous verses, McDonald apportions blame for Vietnam, castigating generals, Wall Street and unthinking parents who buy the propaganda.

'I Feel Like I'm Fixin' to Die' was a simple ragtime song – perfect for marches – written by McDonald in the summer of 1965 after he had been 'discharged from the US Navy for several years. It just popped into my head one day and I finished it in about 30 minutes.' Raised in a family of American communists, McDonald used the song 'to put blame for the war upon the politicians and leaders of the US military and upon the industry that makes its money from war but not upon those who had to fight the war . . . the soldiers'.

During 1965, protests against the war had grown in size and visibility. In April, the Students for a Democratic Society (SDS) and the Student Nonviolent Coordinating Committee (SNCC) organised an anti-war march on Washington DC, attended by about 25,000 people. At the same time, the practice of protestors burning their draft cards increased in number and intensity. In late August, the president passed a law criminalising the activity: the penalties were up to five years in prison and a $1,000 fine.

The 15th of October saw large protests held in four cities, including New York and Berkeley, the latter attended by around 15,000. Footage from the Berkeley event shows protestors with placards that say 'Bring the Boys Home', 'Stop the Bombing', 'Vietnam for the Vietnamese' and – a fair point, this – 'Did You Vote for War?' On the second day, the police had to intervene when marchers were attacked by pro-war groups: a portent of disturbances to come.

A late-November Berkeley leaflet, 'Why We March Against the War in Vietnam', returned, yet again, to the whole question of the war's legitimacy: 'A year ago, most Americans voted for Lyndon Johnson because he said he would be cautious in Vietnam. But Johnson thought that the American people had given him a blank check on election day; and since then he has gone on a wild spending spree of blood and money – our blood and money.'

It wasn't all one way. In late October 1965, there was a large pro-Vietnam march in Washington DC, attended by about 25,000 people. There were serried ranks of veterans in uniform, bearing billowing flags; other marchers carried signs saying, 'Die, Don't Cry for Peace', 'Guess What Cong Will Bury You' and 'We Shall Overcome the V.C.' An early-1966 poll showed that 47 per cent of American students supported the president's conduct of the war.

Outside of the faux-folk rock of 'The Universal Coward' and 'The Revolution Kind', the clearest examination of the patriotic mindset was to be found in country music. There were many examples: Jack Sanders's mid-1965 single 'The Viet Nam Blues'; Dave Dudley's 'What We're Fighting For' from November 1965; or country veteran Ernest Tubbs's 'It's for God, and Country, and You Mum (The Ballad of Vietnam)' – a title that pithily summarised the hierarchy of many serving soldiers' motivations.

Marty Robbins's January 1966 single 'Private Wilson White' was the story of a Vietnam hero who died to save his comrades: 'As he yelled, "I died for freedom," he threw the hand grenade'. From February 1966, Stonewall Jackson's 'The Minute Men (Are Turning in Their Graves)' took a swipe at the protestors: 'They march in lines and carry signs, protestors one and all / They'd rather go to prison than to heed their country's call.'

The success of 'The Ballad of the Green Berets' was the apotheosis of this country music groundswell. It seems strange that one particular genre of music should have been so associated with the patriotic viewpoint, but there were firm reasons for the link. Country hadn't always been reactionary, but from the mid-1960s onwards it became so: a bulwark against the rapid changes in American life and a safe haven from an increasingly incomprehensible youth culture.

The pace, style and subject matter of country music expressed a deep continuum rather than the radical break espoused by pop's cutting edge. That continuum included Christian values, the importance of everyday experience and an unquestioning patriotism. The southern segregationist George Wallace had attempted to capitalise on that conservatism by using country music in his 1964 election campaign.

There was a class element to this. Country was not a metropolitan, sophisticated style; it was plain-speaking, predominantly white, rooted in the small-town ethos and associated with the lower middle class and the white working class. These were the sections of the population most affected by the Vietnam war, and their resentment of protestors, draft dodgers and draft-card burners was informed by a white-hot class rage just as much as patriotism.

In the Second World War, combatants had been drawn from all levels of society, but Vietnam was different. Part of the problem was the piecemeal escalation of the war: without a formal declaration, draftees were shipped out to the combat zone in dribs and drabs, and there was little consistent planning. Because it was a limited conflict, the authorities hoped to keep the disruption to civilian life at a minimum.

The rules were simple. Within five days of his eighteenth birthday, each American male had to present himself at his local draft board. He would then have to fill in a registration card, with questions pertaining to identification, occupation and marital status. Each board would then send out a classification questionnaire that had to be filled in and returned within ten days: this determined whether you were eligible to serve. There were many categories, but the one that counted was I-A: eligible for military service.

Vietnam was not popular from the off. It was a war by stealth that had not been fully explained to the American public. Avoidance seemed like a reasonable course of action. In their survey of the Vietnam-era draft, Lawrence Baskir and William Strauss estimated that during the conflict 60 per cent of men at draft age took active steps not to see combat. The system was weighted towards more privileged youths, who could claim student exemptions or who had the confidence and financial back-up to work the system. During 1965–6, college graduates made up only 2 per cent of all draftees. In 1966, graduate schools were 'besieged with draft-motivated requests for admission', while the numbers applying to university also increased by 6–7 per cent. Some principled youths announced themselves to be conscientious objectors. These and other options were considered when the registrant went before his local draft board – there were 4,000 around the country – which met once or twice a month.

At these meetings, the fate of hundreds, if not thousands of young men was decided. An analysis of draft board members revealed that they were 'predominantly older, white middle-class men with military backgrounds from World Wars I and II'. Already there was an age and class gap between the boards and many of the young men who appeared before them. Their decisions reflected tradition and patriotic beliefs and were used to penalise registrants who did not conform to those values.

The next step after the declaration of I-A status was induction at the nearest military base. This was the last opportunity to reverse this categorisation, and the drama was usually played out at the pre-induction physical. Pop histories are full of musicians who avoided the draft by pretending to be 'queer' (Iggy Pop) or by exaggerating any mental instability (Lou Reed). Other methods included the artificial inducements of a medical condition, self-harm or the various ailments suggested by Phil Ochs in 'The Draft Dodger Rag'.

These cases were in a distinct minority, however, and the great bulk of I-A registrants were inducted into the army. The next stage was basic training, designed to eradicate any trace of civilian conditioning. At this point, these young men passed out of youth culture. Their teenage years were over: as it had been for centuries past, service in the armed forces was the *rite de passage* into adulthood. Even if they remained young in body, many would never fully recover from their combat experience.

As Christian Appy notes in *Working Class War*, 80 per cent of all those serving in Vietnam came from working-class or poor backgrounds. Despite the illusion of a cross-class, vibrant sixties youth culture, US unemployment in the 16–19 age group averaged 12.5

per cent between 1965 and 1970 (12 per cent for whites, 27 per cent for blacks) – millions of young men. Many high-school graduates found that their prospects were cut short because prospective employers thought that they would be sent to Vietnam and were not worth hiring.

Vietnam was a war fought not only by young working-class whites but also by young black Americans. Although only 10 per cent of their overall cohort, they formed 31 per cent of all combat troops at the start of the war and, during 1965, comprised 24 per cent of all deaths in Vietnam. The armed forces had always been a method of advancement for young blacks – there had been a prolonged struggle for 'the right to fight' during the Second World War – but Vietnam was totally different.

It came at a crucial stage in the fight for civil rights, with the passing of the Civil Rights Act in 1964 and the Voting Rights Act in 1965. These were major gains but there was still discrimination, poverty and anger. Many prominent African American leaders were against the war – Malcolm X, Martin Luther King, Adam Clayton Powell – and were perceiving an unjust bias against blacks in the conduct of the war and a leaking of funds away from improvement programmes.

On 6 January 1966, the principal youth civil rights organisation, the Student Nonviolent Coordinating Committee, issued a 'Statement on Vietnam' that publicly condemned the war and supported draft refusal: 'We are in sympathy with, and support, the men in this country who are unwilling to respond to a military draft which would compel them to contribute their lives to United States aggression in Vietnam in the name of the "freedom" we find so false in this country.'

In February 1966, the world heavyweight boxing champion Muhammad Ali was reclassified as I-A; his previous draft status had been I-Y, qualified for military service only in the event of national emergency. Ali announced that he would refuse to serve in the US Army and that, as a member of the Nation of Islam, he would seek conscientious objector status on religious grounds.

'Man, I ain't got no quarrel with them Vietcong,' he told a reporter, and the media exploded.

Vietnam was becoming a hornet's nest of competing loyalties and clashing world views: the young hated their gung-ho elders; the working class hated draft resisters, while they suffered the worst losses; the hawks provided a vision of war that was unrealistic, while the doves attacked the servicemen who were bearing the brunt of the fighting instead of the policymakers who created the mess.

'The Ballad of the Green Berets' appeared to offer certainty in a changing world but, just like its apparent polar opposite, 'Eve of Destruction', it merely presented abstractions and generalisations. Both sides of the divide claimed right and morality in their attitudes to the war – and both were correct, according to their beliefs – but the reality for many young Americans was something different: a morass of fear, confusion, resignation, hopelessness and anger.

This fury can be found in an early protest record that captured a deeper emotional response to the possibility of being drawn into the conflict. Issued in mid-October 1965 on a small Los Angeles label, Mira – and almost instantly withdrawn because of its controversial approach – Bobby Jameson's 'Vietnam' was a raw and brutal blast, a true *cri de coeur* from a young man facing the abyss.

A fanfare of slow church-organ chords – straight out of a horror film – resolves into a brutal Bo Diddley beat. A few blasts of harmonica carry the riff, and then a full-throated voice begins to testify. It's a stitch-up he's complaining about: 'Fire chief, police chief, district attorney / They're all trying to send me on a long-time journey.' This is a horror movie, only for real, and the singer knows what he's facing. No appeal – whether to President Johnson, the district attorney or 'the lawyer man' – is going to help. The music churns on and Jameson begins to moan and chant and wail, locked in his nightmare. There is no prospect of release, no hope.

In late 1965, Bobby Jameson was a young white man of twenty on the fringes of the LA music industry. He'd started making records in 1963: sharing a house with the musicians who would later form

Crazy Horse, he was picked by manager Tony Alamo and groomed for a stardom that never quite came. In 1964, Jameson travelled to London and recorded a couple of very early Jagger/Richards songs, 'All I Want Is My Baby' and 'Each and Every Day'. By late 1965, he was one of the many hundreds of hopefuls auditioning for the future *Monkees* TV series. He had also received a letter from the draft board and, as a non-student, was in the firing line: he was classified as I-A. He wrote a song about his feelings and recorded it with members of the Leaves – a local band who had released a killer single, 'Too Many People' – and Love's first drummer, Don Conka.

What they concocted was a vehement, swirling statement that captures the moment when the Vietnam war seemed to be spiralling out of control. Although it was quickly buried, footage of the song found its way into Robert Carl Cohen's film *Mondo Hollywood*. It begins at the studio mixing desk: wearing extremely long hair and a three-day-old beard, Jameson dominates the screen, performing the song with unrestrained intensity, bellowing the lyrics from the bottom of his soul. Like Love, the band are interracial – a provocative statement in itself for Los Angeles, a highly segregated city. Shot in a murky half-light, the recording has the feeling of a blues session, and that's what 'Vietnam' is: a white man's blues.

Soon after the record's release, Jameson was arrested for drugs. During 1965, he had taken his first LSD trip, with Danny Hutton, the close friend of Brian Wilson and Van Dyke Parks – 'When it was over, I was different,' he reported – and, by his own admission, became a regular user of both acid and downers. After spending three days in jail, he was released without charge. It was an unpleasant event that would have unforeseen consequences.

Jameson was scheduled to be drafted into the army and, in autumn 1965, the blow fell:

> I was ordered to show up at the draft board to be inducted into
> the military. I had no choice and I hadn't come up with any
> way to get out of it, so I just went there on the date specified.

I stood out like a sore thumb and attracted negative attention from the wrong people as soon as I walked through the door.

'Well who the hell are you bright eyes, one of the Goddamn Beatles?' This was a question hurled at me, amongst others, as soon as I arrived. I tried to lose myself in the crowd, which was large, and not get noticed so much. I looked around at all these young guys of every colour and description and it was not a pretty picture. Each one seemed to be terrified on the inside but trying hard to put the brave face on the outside.

I knew I was scared. Hell I didn't want to go to Vietnam, period. I thought I'd get shot or shoot someone on our side for ordering me around. I was as piss poor at following directions as anyone you've ever met. We were told to remove our clothes down to our underwear, and then got put through a bunch of arbitrary jumping-jacks for what purpose I don't know, maybe just humiliation.

It was real similar to what they'd done when I was arrested and booked for drugs. There didn't seem to be a lot of difference. I stood in line while some drill instructor screamed at us. I tried desperately to think up some way to get my ass out of this situation. I heard the guy who was doing all the yelling say, 'Has anyone here been arrested in the last 6 months for narcotics?' I looked around the room and up and down the lines of some 300 or so guys and didn't see a single hand go up.

The whole room was silent and everybody else was doing the same thing I was. Looking around to see if anyone was stupid enough to raise their hand. 'Me,' I said, 'I was arrested for drugs.' All eyes turned toward me. 'You what?' the D. I. screamed. 'What the fuck makes you stupid enough to raise your Goddamned hand and admit to a chicken shit thing like that you asshole?' I was scared but said, 'You asked if anyone had been arrested and I had, so I told you.'

The Drill Instructor looked at me in utter disbelief. The whole room was completely silent. 'Why you cowardly little shit. Do you see this yellow line on the floor asshole?' he screamed. 'Yes Sir I do,' I said. 'Well I want you to follow that yellow line wherever it goes until you can't go any further, do you understand me?' he yelled. 'Yes Sir,' I said. 'Well then move your ass and get out of my sight you goddamned little coward.'

I pulled on my pants and hauled ass along the route of the yellow line. It went on for a long way and it was a big building in the crappy part of L.A. I went down halls and up a flight of stairs and down some more halls until it stopped outside the door of an office. I figured I was supposed to knock on the door so I did. A voice yelled from inside for me to enter. I opened the door slowly and looked in. It was a tiny dark office with a desk and chair and that's about it.

Behind the desk was another guy in uniform who ordered me inside. He had a similar personality to the guy who'd sent me there. This schmuck wanted every detail about my arrest I could give him and was just plain pissed off at me. I filled him in on the details of my arrest and then he basically kicked my ass out and said I'd be notified by mail of the decision regarding my military status. That was it! I left the building and I was the only one who did as far as I know.

Many were not so lucky: as Jameson reminisces about his fellow draftees, 'Every one of those other guys was still there when I left. I have always wondered about it. Why I was out and they were in? I didn't know whether to be grateful or feel guilty.' For the young men who went into the army, the experience was abrupt and brutal: added to the fear of active service, there was the sense of being taken away from everything you'd known – loved ones, family, neighbourhood.

Released a few months later, in February 1966, the Monitors' 'Greetings (This Is Uncle Sam)' caught this feeling. Like countless others, the protagonist in the lyric has had the letter: 'Greetings, this is Uncle Sam / I want to take you to a far-off land.' After this bald introduction, it resolves into a doo-wop song with a sophisticated treatment that oscillates between the increasingly obnoxious voice of the army and a reluctant draftee. As the music fades, the drill sergeant lapses into a relentless left/right drill pattern.

The song had originally been written and recorded in 1961 by one of Motown's few white signings, the Valadiers. In the middle of 1965, just as the war began to hit home, the Monitors dusted it off and gave it a full makeover in a smooth yet soulful style. When it was finally released seven months later, the escalation of the war gave it extra impetus: the single went to #21 in the R&B charts and just scraped into the pop Hot 100.

'Greetings (This Is Uncle Sam)' was one of the first major records to deal directly with the black American experience of the war. 'It was our biggest record, because the Vietnam War jumped off,' remembered lead singer Richard Street. 'The soldiers and the guys who got drafted loved that song because they did not want to go over there and fight. When we'd sing that in a nightclub, they would just stand up and applaud forever. We went all over the world with that one song.'

Anger, terror, total confusion: the most extreme Vietnam song from this period runs through the gamut of emotions. Recorded in late 1965, by a group of expatriate US ex-servicemen in Germany called the Monks, 'Monk Time' was an aural and verbal assault, a howl of incoherent feeling. 'The images of napalm, race riots, and corruption of flesh were beginning to take over our minds,' wrote Monks' bassist Eddie Shaw. 'Without realising it, we were beginning to react.'

All of the Monks had served as GIs in West Germany, a divided country that was still on high alert against its Communist neighbour. It was only four years since the Berlin Wall had gone up. The five members had begun playing together while in service and, once they had returned to civilian life, decided to stay in West Germany, playing Beatles covers and rock 'n' roll in the beat clubs of Heidelberg, Stuttgart and Hamburg as the Torquays.

The German charts of the period included many British and American records, but the home-grown material was full of novelties and syrupy ballad tunes (called *Schlager*), often with child-like English lyrics – in many ways the forerunners of today's Euro records. The club scene offered a space for foreign beat groups – most famously, the Beatles, whose trajectory from Hamburg to global success haunted all the musicians who followed in their wake.

The Torquays fit right in, but during 1965 things changed. As Shaw wrote, 'The world was no longer a place for fifties-type guys wearing funny glasses and clown outfits . . . We had taken on the grime of gritty night life – trying to be the dark angels everyone wanted us to be. There was a dark pall under our eyes. Our minds were preoccupied with noise as we read American newspapers and magazines, telling us about the Vietnam War and race riots.'

In late 1965, they underwent a name change and a radical make-over: instead of the standard beat group uniform of longish hair and mod clothes, they decided to all dress the same, with monks' habits and tonsures – extremely short hair cropped close to the scalp on top of the head. The effect was electrifying: they looked threatening, intense, fanatical – a perfect complement to the harsh new musical style that they had developed, by trial and error, in almost total isolation.

Playing around with feedback, the Monks began to try to integrate an 'aural hallucination' into a new sound. The drummer Roger Johnston began to play without cymbals, while the organist, Larry Clark, played one-note clusters. Lead guitarist Gary Burger explored the use of fuzzboxes. Everything got simpler, more stream-lined, less funky, more like a stiff German two-step, overdriven by Dave Day's counter-rhythmic banjo.

'We got rid of melody,' remembered Eddie Shaw. 'We substituted dissonance and clashing harmonics. Everything was rhythmically oriented. Bam, bam, bam. We concentrated on over-beat.' The new material was abrasive, with the group singing and playing against each other. The songs ranged from vituperative minimalism – 'I Hate You', 'Shut Up' – through Euro chants – 'Higgle-dy Piggle-dy' – to stream-of-consciousness rants like 'Complication'.

'Monk Time' was the first track on the Monks' first album, *Black*

Monk Time, released by Polydor Records in Germany in March 1966. This was their big statement, the relentless harshness of the music – an upchuck of dissonant organ, fuzz guitar and almost martial rhythms – belying the raw and confused lyrics. A sequence of lightning-fast statements and questions, it reads 'like deranged free verse' or, more accurately, an argument against the war.

In his memoir *Black Monk Time*, Eddie Shaw remembers the song's genesis. The group were talking about the Vietnam war, feeling 'the scrutiny of the Germans, watching our reaction to what was happening in the world. "I'm loyal to my country," Dave said. "The war is wrong," Gary said. "So then, it's all the more reason to say something about it."' The frank disagreement that ensued went, with a minimum of editing, straight into the lyric.

'Monk Time' was an ambiguous song that, allied with the Monks' musical ferocity, aroused strong emotions. Audiences didn't know whether the group were protesting or supporting the war. Their short hair and military background made their performance even more threatening. Shaw remembers being told by one of their managers to 'try looking angry. Try to stand perfectly still as you play. It will enhance your appearance. The music of the future will not be happy.'

The Monks soon found themselves hoist by their own petard. A couple of months after the album's release, they were playing a bar in Mannheim popular with American servicemen. They were playing their signature song when a GI charged the stage, with 'tears in his eyes': 'I just got back from Vietnam you assholes! What do you mean, why do we kill those kids? They're the ones shooting at us!' The Monks stopped playing and the club went quiet. 'The song doesn't mean what it sounds like,' Shaw tried to reason with the GI, while feeling 'very small. How could we possibly criticise our own comrades-in-arms?' The argument continued. 'We were GIs ourselves,' Gary Burger explained. 'We know what it's about. I'm not singing about bad GIs. I'm talking about politicians and old people who send American kids to Vietnam to get killed by Vietnamese kids.'

The GI turned on the singer. 'Did you say that your brother died in Vietnam?'

'Yes,' answered Burger.

'You really had a brother get killed in Vietnam?'

'Figuratively speaking, yes . . .'

'Figuratively speaking? What the hell does that mean? How can you know what it's like to lose a brother over there?'

It was a dreadful encounter. The suspension of disbelief necessary for any successful performance had gone. The Monks were stripped of all their stagecraft. 'The soldier had actually cried for a moment, while we awkwardly stood on stage, waiting for some sign of miserable forgiveness.' After a brief and frank discussion, the GI left. 'None of us felt good about that scene,' Shaw grimly observed. The group had come up against the gap between metaphor and reality.

* * *

'I believe it's all going to end in a nuclear war, the way we're going now, anyway . . . I imagine the only way to get all this stopped is to use the H-bomb. Russia and China don't know as much about it as we do. I figure we could win it.'
    BRUCE CURTIS, thirteen, interviewed in 'Six Faces of Youth', *Newsweek*, 21 March 1966

While 'The Ballad of the Green Berets' was enjoying its third week at the top of the charts, *Newsweek* devoted a whole issue to 'The Teen-Agers – a survey of what they're really like'. This was prompted by a demographic surge: 'The American population has found the fountain of youth and, swimming in it, grows younger. The nation's official median age is 27.9 and declining. There are some 17.9 million Americans between 13 and 17, the high school years.'

As befitted a centrist, adult-oriented publication, *Newsweek* was anxious to present the young as 'docile' and consumerist, cosseted due to a flourishing economy. But there was 'a troubled minority', exemplified by a 14 per cent rise in juvenile delinquency from 1963 to 1965. There were questions about teen fitness, an increasingly important issue for the draft. 'Political apathy' was the rule among adolescents, who had 'a generally hawkish stance in their attitude towards Vietnam', but 'tiny pockets' of revolt were visible.

Newsweek found that the issues of long hair and politics were 'intertwined': 'increasing numbers of teenagers sense the immediacy of the war in Vietnam. Boys are faced with the draft, which worries not only them but the girls they may marry.' Six teens were given about a page each: they ranged from a farmer's son to a fifteen-year-old Negro from Chicago's South Side. These young men were presented as thoughtful, well-adjusted and, despite 'pessimism about Vietnam', attuned to mainstream American values.

Two young women were less certain. Sixteen-year-old Jan Smithers of Woodland Hills in Los Angeles was an habitué of Malibu Beach and the thriving scene on the Sunset Strip. 'Sometimes when I'm sitting in my room I just feel like screaming and pounding my pillow,' she told *Newsweek*. 'I'm so confused about this world and everything that's happening. My friends just sit back and say, "Wow, it's happening." But,' added the *Newsweek* writer, 'she wants to understand why.'

Pictured under a large 'Peace Now' sign, seventeen-year-old Laura Hausman from Berkeley exemplified the district's critical, bohemian spirit. 'All her friends talk about five subjects – the Bomb, Vietnam, civil rights, marijuana and sex.' Hausman was an activist and an idealist, bent on social change. 'I could never join the mainstream of society,' she concludes. 'If you've been made aware, then you can't just suddenly bury yourself. So society is just going to have to accept us.'

In March 1966, the war was beginning to permeate almost every aspect of American life. 'The Ballad of the Green Berets' marked the moment when it became inescapable. It was there, right between the ears and the eyes, on the television and on the radio, recruitment as entertainment. Staff Sergeant Barry Sadler was thrust into the life of a pop star, using his fame to recruit on behalf of the forces and to explain the draft to its potential victims.

In Britain, the record went into the Top 30 but had nothing like the same impact, principally because the British government, under the Labour Prime Minister Harold Wilson, refused President Johnson's repeated requests to send UK troops to Vietnam. Public opinion was against involvement, and the Labour Party was hostile to the war. There was no conscription: national service had ended in 1960. Britain's young would not be required to fight.

There were protests in the UK. In October 1965, thousands turned out for the 'International Days of Protest' in London. Vietnam was a rallying point for the developing counter-culture but, without direct involvement, it would lack the visceral flavour of its American counterpart. In this climate, attitudes to 'The Ballad of the Green Berets' could be more openly hostile than they were in the US. As the British music journalist Ray Coleman wrote, 'Most clear-thinking people must have been sick and horrified at the [song's] exultation of war.'

In early April, the cream of British pop music lined up to take pot shots at the record in *Melody Maker*. 'A terribly sick song,' opined Mick Jagger, while the four Beatles offered comments like 'terrible', 'crap' and 'propaganda. We don't need stuff like that in the Top 50.' Paul Jones got to the heart of the matter: 'The main point is that the American State Department is clearly annoyed because they cannot get people to volunteer to fight in Vietnam.'

The success in America of 'The Ballad of the Green Berets' was partly due to the fact that it was a declaration by the record-buying public in support of American involvement in Vietnam. But this would not be repeated. Along with favourable war news, the song helped to push President Johnson's approval ratings up to 67 per cent in April 1966, but that was the peak: by June, after another escalation, they had gone back down to 46 per cent.

Sadler's song coincided with the zenith of the war's popularity in America. Heard in context with other hits of the time, it feels like a brick wall – as though pop music has suddenly come right up against a hard, immutable reality. Which, of course, many young

Americans just had, or were about to in greater and greater numbers. As draft levels increased during 1966, attitudes towards the war hardened on either side.

Attempting to create a patriotic unity of thought, 'The Ballad of the Green Berets' only increased the divisions in the country. In style and content, it was a polarising force. Although none would reproduce its success, several aggressively patriotic songs would make the charts over the next few months, such as Johnny Sea's interminable 'Day for Decision' and 'Gallant Men' by the seventy-year-old Republican senator Everett Dirksen.

The New Right was on the march. Stimulated by editorials that described the Berkeley protests as a 'nightmarish carnival', the Republican politician Ronald Reagan moved to make student unrest a central plank of his campaign for the governorship of California. In the January 1966 announcement of his candidacy, Reagan posed a question that concealed a threat: 'Will we allow a great university to be brought to its knees by a noisy, dissident minority?'

Under the pressure of war, the middle ground was eroding. During 1965 and early 1966, American youth culture had experienced an increasing confidence and an incipient generational hostility, but this was nothing compared to what was to come. With life and death at stake, it became harder-edged, more confrontational, more radical. In turn, adults and conservatives began to push back with all their might.

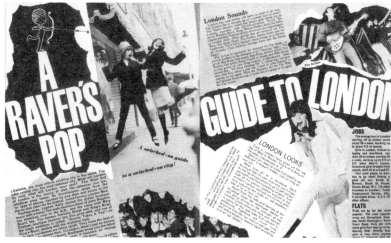

4 : APRIL

The Third Eye: LSD and Its Discontents

'I began to turn into myself, to loop through my own flesh. I swirled and involuted and squirmed and tried to keep from screaming at the glory and the terror of it all. Then the eye appeared, a great shining eye suspended in space. The eye pulsated and shot rays of burning, sweet-sounding light through my body. But it wasn't my body. Suddenly I was the great eye and I saw everything there is to see. It was ecstasy and it was horrible and I saw it all and understood it all . . .'
  STUDENT under the influence of LSD, quoted in John Cashman, *The LSD Story*, 1966

It begins with a rising, Eastern-tinged guitar fanfare, Ravi Shankar drones against a sliding bass. As the last note rings out, there's a quick tap and a roll on the snare, and the ride begins – with raga twelve-strings, deep bass and clattering drums chasing each other down the rabbit hole. A young voice sings in the soon-to-be-standard punk mystical style, with each syllable drawn out and stretched against the rhythm. The melody and harmonies are horizontal, without the chord changes standard in Western pop. The words speak of nothing less than a fundamental transformation:

> Unlocked by the key
> And now I am free
> Magic curtains of green and blue lights pass by
> Moon and sky.

The fanfare returns: the guitar spirals upwards in ever-ascending scales – underpinned by a high-pitched drone – while the drums splash and clatter. It's a brief passage, only twenty-five seconds, but it's almost out of control, grounded only by the rumbling, minatory bass. The group crunch out of this brief improvisation into the song's tricky central riff, a jump-cut so jarring that it feels as though they've leapt out of their skins. The voice returns from high on the mountaintop: 'Understanding the secrets of space and time / The third eye.'

The frantic spiral returns, with even greater intensity, resolving into a growl of guitar amplification. The song only lasts for 135 seconds, but it's so compressed that it feels much longer: a seven- or eight-hour experience concentrated into a recognisable pop format. It's a sincere attempt to capture something shattering, if not fundamental; all the musicians are working at the limit of their capabilities in an attempt to explain the inexplicable.

Released in April 1966, the Dovers' 'The Third Eye' is one of the earliest attempts at reproducing the LSD experience on record; it's also one of the most accurate expressions of how this extraordinarily powerful drug impacted on the consciousness of those teens who took it in late 1965 and early 1966. Like many early acid records, it is not beatific – that would be a later gloss – but raw, wild and threatening.

LSD opened a window into another world, but it was so strong that it easily derailed the fragile and the unwary. This is the contradiction that 'The Third Eye' encodes. Lyrically and vocally, it captures a moment of visionary transcendence. The rational mind seeks to define the experience in positive, if awestruck terms. But if the words speak of premature maturity, the explosive, chaotic intensity of the performance tells you that the whole experience is all too much. The listener is left with a disturbed aftertaste, a growl of chemical electricity that is anything but resolved or peaceful.

'The Third Eye' was a lightning strike. Based in Santa Barbara, about ninety miles from Hollywood, the Dovers had formed as a high-school group inspired by frat rock and the British invasion. They recorded a couple of superior folk rock records at Gold Star Studios during 1965 – the teen janglers 'Your Love' and 'I Could Be Happy' – which were released on the small Hollywood Miramar label. 'I Could Be Happy' was quickly picked up by Reprise Records, but that didn't break the group nationally.

The Dovers were one of a thousand groups living through

108

the rapid changes of the time. They'd hooked up with their own Svengali figure, a producer and sometime singer called Tony Cary, who had Hollywood connections: in 1965, he produced a single by famed guitarist James Burton, then working with Rick Nelson and part of the house band for the nationally syndicated pop show *Shindig*. With his friend, Dovers' bassist Robbie Ladewig, Cary immersed himself in the psychedelic scene that was developing at Los Angeles' teen central, the Sunset Strip.

This precipitated a crisis. Two of the group left, wanting nothing to do with drugs or the police attention they brought in their wake. The Dovers recombined in early 1966 with a definite purpose: according to Mike Markesich, Ladewig 'encouraged everyone to trip on out for the good of the band'. Lead guitarist Bruce Clawson followed his instructions and had an overwhelming experience. Directly inspired by a Ravi Shankar record, he sought to render his sense of wonder – and an underlying, barely acknowledged terror – within the two-minute pop format of the day.

In its barely filtered state, 'The Third Eye' reflects some of the ideas and influences in this early period of LSD expansion, when teens, academics, writers, artists and bohemians were attempting to translate acid for pop culture and Western society. This was something so new that there were few rules: some groups embraced chaos and chance, while others attempted to tame the untameable through religious concepts and doctrines. Underlying all these different attempts was a messianic drive, a desire to proselytise, as personal revelation pointed towards powerful social change.

The song's central concept came from a controversial book first published in the mid-1950s. Written as an autobiography by a Tibetan lama called Tuesday Lobsang Rampa, *The Third Eye* told the story of a young neophyte who, taken away from his family at the age of eight, undergoes various initiation ceremonies before becoming a lama at the age of twelve. The book was a best-seller, and revealed to a Western readership for the first time the depth and breadth of Buddhist beliefs and spiritual practices: levitation, astral projection, meditation and yoga.

The crucial part of Lobsang Rampa's initiation was the opening of the Third Eye, an operation that would allow him 'to see people as they are, and not as they pretend to be'. This involved what is now known as trepanation: a small hole was opened in the centre of his forehead by a specially designed steel instrument, which was pressed down until it penetrated the bone. After the operation, Rampa realised that he could see people's auras as colours swirling around their physical form; he could determine the state of their health or know whether they were speaking the truth.

This was not merely a spiritual metaphor. The Third Eye is generally held to correspond to a little known organ called the pineal gland, which is located near the centre of the brain and is in charge of regulating the production of both serotonin and melatonin – powerful mood triggers in the human psyche. It is often thought to reside in the front of the forehead, between the eyes, and was described, by Madame H. P. Blavatsky in her monumental 1888 survey of the occult, *The Secret Doctrine*, as the organ most closely associated with 'the more highly evolved, or spiritual man'.

It's clear that Lopsang Rampa had read *The Secret Doctrine*, as had most travellers down the byways of esoteric thought during the first half of the twentieth century. Like Blavatsky, Rampa was held to be a fraud, especially after it was revealed in the late 1950s that the author of *The Third Eye* was one Cyril Henry Hoskin from Devon. When confronted by the British press, Hoskin did not deny his identity but claimed that the soul of Rampa had transmigrated into his body. This controversy barely harmed the popularity of the book one whit.

Rampa's book had its first US paperback edition in 1964, and the phrase had quickly passed into the language of pop. In late 1965, Dylan used 'the Third Eye' in the splenetic lyric of 'Can You Please Crawl Out Your Window?' while the 13th Floor Elevators – a young group from Austin, Texas, explicitly formed to broadcast LSD consciousness – picked up on it as a central motif. Designed by John Cleveland, their business card had the image of a single eye, placed upon a plinth, with the legend 'psychedelic rock'.

The Third Eye was a wonderful metaphor for LSD. After taking it, one saw the world anew, as if for the first time. The experience was so overwhelming that it was often seen in religious terms: like the ancients described by Madame Blavatsky or the young Tibetan child in Hoskin's lamasery, LSD adepts felt that they had attained another level of consciousness. To many this awakening had spiritual overtones, the drug providing a short cut to the state attained only by the application of rigorous spiritual discipline.

At the very least, the LSD experience was inimical to the mainstream values of Western society. Competition and materialism seemed ludicrous to the cosmically attuned mind. Things and stuff suddenly weren't enough. LSD had first been synthesised during the development of the atom bomb, and to some teens these events seemed to fuse into some bizarre symmetry. 'Acid can be a beautiful reaction lighting up cities,' one user told the photojournalist Lawrence Schiller in March 1966, 'or it can be Hiroshima, an event you must live with forever.'

'Soldiers, take orders only from the rainbow alliance! Peace to the world,' the poet George Andrews wrote in early 1966. 'LSD is the only answer to the atom bomb.' Acid took the existentialism that seemed like the only viable response to a world where instant atomisation was possible, if not likely, and transformed it into an eternal present for which there was barely a language yet outside the furthest reaches of Eastern thought. Along with the bomb, it was the single most powerful dissolving agent in sixties culture. After its arrival, nothing would ever be the same.

LSD had been in the public domain for several years, at least since the early 1960s, but the first few months of 1966 saw the drug move to centre stage. Pandora's box had been opened. The already hyperventilated teenage psyche was bombarded with sensations and revelations beyond the ken of most humans. This was an instant satori, the result of a single ampoule or sugar cube, often sourced on the black market and taken in unstructured circumstances. It wasn't like pot or pills; it was fundamental.

In its troubled mysticism, the Dovers' song exemplifies the

drug's power. For a young man in his early twenties to be writing about 'understanding the secrets of space and time' was something barely imaginable. But Bruce Clawson was not alone as, in the first few months of 1966, young musicians and writers – including Bob Dylan, the Byrds, the Rolling Stones and the Beatles – recorded and released LSD-saturated material. Many of these songs, like 'The Third Eye', helped to open up the pop audience to a whole range of forbidden, forgotten knowledge.

Despite its raw power and existential force, 'The Third Eye' dropped into a vacuum. Without major-label back-up, it was doomed to obscurity. To add insult to injury, Clawson heard a record on the radio that thoroughly trumped their effort at the same time as it validated their approach. 'We had already worked on the tune and everything. A few weeks later I'm in the car and "Eight Miles High" came on. I was crushed – I thought I had something unique.'

Released a few weeks before 'The Third Eye', the Byrds' 'Eight Miles High' took a similar approach: a transcendental experience translated through Indian drones. The mood is similar, but the Byrds were better musicians and established hit-makers. Skilled communicators, the group knew that an overt LSD lyric would cause trouble, so they cloaked their visions within an account of their August 1965 visit to London: 'Eight miles high / And when you touch down / You'll find that / It's stranger than known.'

Mixing drones, free jazz harmolodics and hard rock dynamics, the record was new, startling, original and irresistible. It moved up the *Cashbox* charts throughout April, from the lower regions to the Top 40 by the middle of the month. On the 30th, it was at #22 in the *Billboard* Top 100, marked with a red star for 'registering greatest proportionate upwards progress this week'. At #15 were the Yardbirds with 'Shapes of Things'; the Lovin' Spoonful's 'Daydream' was at #9 and the Rolling Stones' '19th Nervous Breakdown' at #27. Drug culture was going mass market.

* * *

'Q: What is your concept of the Teenage Revolution?
David Crosby: 'It definitely is a revolution and it definitely
involves the teenagers and a great many more people than the
teenagers. Over half the people in this country are under 25. The
country isn't being run as they know and feel it should be. The
discrepancies are too obvious. The wrongness and the corruption
disturbs and upsets them. And then the uncertainty of the nuclear
thing, which is something we've lived with since we were born.
They definitely want to change this and a lot of other things.'
  BOB FEIGEL, '"Real" Teen Revolt – Byrds', *KRLA Beat*, 27
  November 1965

LSD had been percolating into youth culture since the early sixties.
Its earliest appearance on record had occurred in the title of a May
1960 single called 'LSD-25' on the Los Angeles World Pacific label,
by a West Coast group called the Gamblers – a bunch of session
musicians including future members of the Mothers of Invention,
Canned Heat and the Beach Boys. The title had very little to do
with the song, which was a standard surfing instrumental: the guitarist saw the phrase in a book and thought it looked good.

The first major pop cultural figure to take LSD was Bob Dylan,
at a party to celebrate his successful solo show at the Royal Festival
Hall in May 1964. Soon afterwards, as part of his move away from
overt social and political comment, he recorded several new songs
that seemed to reflect the hallucinogenic experience. One of them
hinted at synaesthesia, music as a cosmic force. 'Take me for a trip
/ Upon your magic swirling ship,' Dylan sang on 'Mr Tambourine
Man'. 'My senses have been stripped / And I can't feel to grip.'

In late August 1964, Dylan turned the Beatles on to marijuana
at the end of their first major US tour. By their unanimous account,
it was an epiphany. From then on the group began to experiment
with sound: you can hear the result in subsequently recorded songs
like 'What You're Doing', 'I Feel Fine', with its feedback opening, and the droning 'Ticket to Ride'. By the time that the Beatles
were making the film *Help!* they were – in John Lennon's words –
'smoking marijuana for breakfast'.

Lennon and George Harrison were first exposed to LSD in late March 1965, while they were busy with the production of their second film. They went out for dinner at the Bayswater flat of their dentist, Dr John Riley, who laced the coffee with LSD-drenched sugar cubes – at that point, the drug was not available in tablet form but had to be titrated. Upset at being dosed – even though they had said they wanted to try the drug – the Beatles and their wives hurriedly left Riley's flat and, ignoring set and setting, travelled through the centre of London to the Pickwick Club, off Charing Cross Road.

The effect was shattering. 'We went up into the nightclub,' Lennon remembered, 'and it felt as though the elevator was on fire and we were going into hell (and it was and we were).' When the nightclub closed, the Beatles were still sitting there, transfixed. To Harrison 'it felt as if a bomb had made a direct hit on the nightclub and the roof had been blown off'. Once it wore off, the Beatles began to process what had happened. Always the first of the group to jump into any fire, Lennon thought it 'was terrifying but it was fantastic'.

Within a couple of weeks, the Beatles were back in the studio recording what would be the title track of their new film. Masked by a fast, punchy, effervescent treatment, 'Help!' was what Lennon proclaimed it was from the very first word: a cry from the heart. Although not necessarily totally autobiographical, it felt that way: sung in the first person, the lyric touched on deep psychological themes – vulnerability, the need for others, growing into adulthood. An immediate talking point among adults and fans, 'Help!' was the first major crack in Lennon's impenetrable facade.

In Britain, 'Help!' hit the top of the charts in the first week of August, replacing the Byrds' version of Bob Dylan's 'Mr Tambourine Man', which, although it wasn't designed as such, was the first major drug-culture hit. Having programmed his voice to come out as a blend of Lennon and Dylan, Jim McGuinn hit just the right note of ecstatic passivity, while the record's keynote sound, a twelve-string Rickenbacker, merged with the group's lush harmonies to create an underlying, hypnotic drone.

The group were explicitly tied into the new consciousness. That summer, Paul Jay Robbins summed up the group's impact in the *Los Angeles Free Press*: 'What the Byrds evoke is an Enlightenment in the full psychedelic sense of the word . . . the modes of dancing that the Byrds incite is a thing of open loveliness to behold and a state of ecstasy to involve yourself in.' Lennon and Harrison used one of their rare days off during their second, full US tour to take LSD again – this time by choice, with the Byrds' Jim McGuinn and Dave Crosby.

By mid-September Dylan's first major hit single, 'Like a Rolling Stone', was at #2 to the Beatles' 'Help!'. This was an all-out truth attack performed with a full band treatment and dominated by Al Kooper's untutored carnival organ. At just over six minutes, 'Like a Rolling Stone' shattered pop's time barrier: hit singles were usually less than half that length, but the song's relentless, seemingly endless churning motion both reproduced acid's time expansion and pulled the trigger on a new age of pop ambition. The Great Race had begun.

In autumn 1965, LSD was still legal in both the US and the UK. Thanks to the activities of acid evangelists like Timothy Leary and Ken Kesey, what older or less dazzled psychiatrists had long feared was beginning to occur: the drug was leaking ever faster out of the clinics and the hands of psy-ops spooks, whence it had begun. Supplies were no longer controlled from just one source, Sandoz, but were flooding in from bootleggers in both Britain and America. As it always would have been if anyone had thought through the implications, acid was out of control.

In Britain, LSD was spreading through a similar kind of demographic as in the US: art students, hipsters, bohemians, artists, poets, many of whom had come through CND. They didn't as yet have a name, but they appear in glimpses: the hard-faced young men, old before their time, with extremely long hair pictured in Jürgen Seuss's 1965 photo book *Beat in Liverpool*; the lost beatniks, squatting and taking drugs in the deserted village of Imber, on Salisbury Plain, depicted in John Boorman's *Catch Us If You Can*.

The first major gathering of this subculture was the June 1965 International Poetry Incarnation at the Albert Hall, where an audience of several thousand witnessed performances by Allen Ginsberg, Alex Trocchi, William Burroughs, Christopher Logue, Gregory Corso and many others. Harry Fainlight prevailed through several hecklers to finish his mescaline nightmare 'The Spider', while Adrian Mitchell brought the house down with 'To Whom It May Concern', with its refrain, 'Tell me lies about Vietnam'.

The New Zealand poet and film-maker John Esam organised the Poetry Incarnation and assisted director Peter Whitehead with the film of the event, later released as *Wholly Communion*. Then living at 101 Cromwell Road, not too far away from the BEA air terminal, Esam was one of the major conduits for LSD that autumn and beyond. Among the visitors was Donovan, who later wrote about this 'LSD ashram' in the song 'Sunny South Kensington': Come loon soon down Cromwell Road, man / You got to spread your wings.'

Like almost all of the early LSD distributors, Esam was a trickster-like figure. Barry Miles remembers him as 'a frightening character, but I quite liked him. He used to come and hang out at my flat all the time. He used to have his hair plastered down, almost like an insect. Absolutely jet-black hair, shiny and brushed forward and flat. Like a skull cap, almost. All the girls used to call him the Spider. He moved into 101, but there wasn't a room there, so he set up a sort of shack in the corridor.'

In October 1965, the acid proselytiser Michael Hollingshead arrived back in the UK with instructions to set up a British equivalent of Millbrook, Timothy Leary's acid ashram in upstate New York. Armed with enough LSD for 5,000 sessions, he found a flat at Pont Street in Mayfair and, together with Lloyd's underwriter Desmond O'Brien, founded the World Psychedelic Centre. 'We believed that London would indeed become the centre for a world psychedelic movement.'

The WPC quickly attracted a roster of 'aristocrats and artists and musicians and writers'. They included Victor Lownes, who co-founded the *Playboy* empire, Alex Trocchi, Julie Felix, Roman Polanski, George Andrews, R. D. Laing, William Burroughs, John Esam and Christopher Gibbs. The WPC vice-president was an old Etonian called Joey Mellen, who soon became infamous as an early exponent of trepanation – the attempt, as per Lobsang Rampa, to forcibly open up the Third Eye.

'It was very fancy,' Miles remembers, 'but even then there was something wrong with the place. I did quite like Michael, but there was something I didn't trust about him. It's all very well, there's this guy who's running the Playboy club sitting there, and Ronnie Laing . . . It started off very laudably. There were talks at the ICA about psychedelics. It was taken very seriously, and it was still legal then, of course. But I didn't find the atmosphere there very conducive. It all seemed kind of phoney to me.'

In the autumn and early winter of 1965, there was a cluster of frankly hallucinogenic records. Donovan's 'Sunny Goodge Street' mentioned 'a violent hash-smoker', while his 'Hey Gyp (Dig the Slowness)' – released as the flip of 'Turquoise' in late October – went even further. Taking the wonderful 1930 blues 'Can I Do It for You?' by Kansas Joe and Memphis Minnie, Donovan souped up the call-and-response banter with an intense acoustic riff, off-kilter handclaps and a lyric that offered a 'sugar cube' as a courting ploy.

Kim Fowley's 'The Trip' was even more explicit, with a phantasmagoric lyric barked out in the producer's customary hoarse style: 'A world of frost and clean fountains / And flying dolls and silver cats / And emerald rats and purple clouds.' Another Los Angeles act, the boy/girl duo Gypsy Trips, documented the spread of LSD into the wider world on 'Ain't It Hard', a 45 released on World Pacific. Taking its title from the opening lyric of Bob Dylan's 'Outlaw Blues', the song recast teen confusion and anomie – 'You go to bed at night wonderin' who you are' – for the acid era.

While Dylan continued his explorations of time, space and the oppressive nature of everyday perception and power politics on the ten-minute-plus epic 'Desolation Row', the Beatles delivered their most explicit statement yet on *Rubber Soul*. On a record filled with acerbic textures, 'The Word' didn't seem that radical, but its off-kilter Stax rhythm belied a lyric ('In the good and bad books that I have read') that echoed Huxley's realisation that 'Love is the One', with sweet–sour harmonies that increasingly teetered on the edge of dissonance as the song progressed.

During that autumn, Timothy Leary was out on the road as the LSD High Priest of America. He was preaching nothing less than a revolution in values: the mass use of LSD in a vast social experiment of reconditioning, in order to overcome 'the games' that Western society forced its populations to play. Leary regarded all behaviour patterns as resulting from these socially imprinted roles. To change the world, man would have to change himself. As one university paper reported, 'He envisions a society in which LSD is administered to an infant once a week.'

At the same time, Ken Kesey's acid gang, the Merry Pranksters, stepped up their activities. They had the idea of an initiation ceremony, and with typical machismo designed a flyer that demanded: 'Can You Pass the Acid Test?' Held at Prankster Ken Babbs's house, the party was 'slightly formless'. The second test, held in San Jose on 4 December 1965, was different. The challenge was passed around in handbills distributed outside a Rolling Stones show, and this time the Pranksters got closer to their intended maelstrom: lights, film, swirling sound recorded and instantly played back.

By the beginning of 1966, there were psychedelic districts in several major cities – London, Los Angeles and San Francisco, in particular – all of which had their own venues, their own groups and their own subcultures based around clothes, print, music and drugs. The traditional youthful artistic desire to create one's own world was heightened by LSD. No drug before or since has driven such a wedge between those who partook and those who did not.

In late January, John Hopkins organised a night at London's Marquee club together with Steve Stollman, whose brother Bernard owned the New York label ESP Disk, home of the Fugs, Albert Ayler and Sun Ra. This 'Giant Mystery Happening' featured Donovan, Mose Allison and Graham Bond, along with ad hoc theatre pieces and poetry readings. 'Who will be there?' wrote the *Sunday Times* in a preview. 'Poets, painters, pop singers, hoods, Americans, homosexuals (because they make up 10 per cent of the population).' This was an attempt, like the Acid Tests held by the Merry Pranksters on the West Coast, to create an environment that approached the perceptual disruption experienced under LSD, as well as the desire to explore the furthest possibilities of artistic endeavour and fuse them in a kind of synaesthesia. The so-called Spontaneous Underground quickly became, as Miles writes, 'the village pump of the underground. It had something of the atmosphere of the Albert Hall reading, except that it was weekly and there was a lot of pot and acid about.'

During February, Miles opened up Indica in partnership with the art dealer John Dunbar, right next to the Scotch of St James club in Mason's Yard. The idea was to pull together the various strands of experimental art and literature in one place, to reflect the new consciousness. The shop stocked a selection of records (ESP-Disk material and the spoken-word album *Call Me Burroughs*), the latest poetry magazines and a wide selection of books – from Nietzsche, Burroughs, Timothy Leary and beyond to Antonin Artaud, Aleister Crowley, George Gurdjieff and Madame Blavatsky – a treasure trove of arcana.

On 13 March, Stollman advertised the latest Spontaneous Underground event as 'The Trip'. It would feature the avant-garde improv group AMM, along with the Marquee debut of a young group called the Pink Floyd, who were morphing from R&B covers into something less formalised. The girlie magazine *Titbits* covered the event: 'What a rave! A man crawling naked through jelly. Girls stripped to the waist. Off-beat poetry. Weird music. It all adds up to Raving London. For the capital no longer swings. It goes berserk!'

The word was spreading. On the West Coast, the Merry Pranksters held a series of nine Acid Tests in the first three months of 1966. There were five in Los Angeles, dotted around the city in Northridge, Hollywood and, bizarrely, Watts – still highly unsettled after the disastrous riots. At the same time, teen nightspots began to mushroom out from the traditional Sunset Strip base: as well as Elmer Valentine's The Trip (opened in late 1965), the new clubs had psychedelic, Huxleyan names like the Brave New World or the Doors of Perception.

Three Acid Tests were held in San Francisco, where there had long been a burgeoning bohemia centred around the University of California at Berkeley. In the city, the hardcore beats had moved from North Beach into the Haight-Ashbury district, hard by Golden Gate Park, taking advantage of low rents, spacious Victorian housing and a few businesses that provided the germ of an alternative community. When Dylan arrived in San Francisco for a show in early December, he gave a televised press conference for KQED TV that was full of stoned insider jokes.

And, as ever, the Beatles showed the way. Haight historian Charles Perry wrote how they were 'the soundtrack of Haight-Ashbury, Berkeley and the rest of the circuit. You could party hop all night and hear nothing but *Rubber Soul*.' San Francisco quickly gained a cohesive psychedelic identity. In January, the Thelin brothers opened up the Psychedelic Shop on Haight Street, which stocked everything an acid head might find interesting or necessary. Later that month, the Pranksters combined with local activist Stewart Brand to hold the Trips Festival: 6,000 people attended over three nights.

With such a rapid expansion in the number of those being exposed to LSD and its culture, it was becoming clear to both friends and foes alike that things were getting chaotic. Leary's sensible requirement to take care about 'set and setting' was being challenged by the chaos of the Acid Tests. There was a particularly unpleasant event during the February 1966 Watts Test, when Ken Babbs found a young woman freaking out: rather than helping her, he held a microphone close to broadcast her cries of distress throughout the venue.

Ecstatic visions were matched by horrors. LSD was powerful and extremely volatile, rendering anyone who took it highly sensitive to external influences and internal vulnerabilities. Even in these early days there was an atmosphere of one-upmanship, if not bravado, and a lack of responsibility towards those who would be subjected to the most powerful experience of their lives. In this climate, the age of free exploration could not last.

While LSD was still legal, marijuana was not. As they often went together, the authorities had the perfect method of harassment. Ken Kesey had been arrested for possession in April 1965; when his case came to court in January 1966, just before the Trips Festival, he was sentenced to six months on a work farm. Just over two days later, he was arrested again, in Texas, for the same offence. Timothy Leary was on his way back into America from Mexico in December 1965 when his daughter Susan was arrested for a small amount of marijuana. Leary took the rap. When the charge came to court in March 1966, he was sentenced to a maximum of thirty years in prison and fined $30,000. He was let out on appeal, but his wings were effectively clipped.

These official moves to shut down LSD culture were echoed in the UK. In January, the inevitable happened when the police raided the World Psychedelic Centre. Things at Pont Street had quickly gone downhill: Miles remembers how 'they used to spike stuff all the time. That irritated me.' The flat had been under surveillance for some weeks, and plain-clothes officers had been dosed at a party. Michael Hollingshead was charged with possession of cannabis, heroin and morphine, and with allowing his property to be used for the smoking of cannabis.

That the authorities – in particular the interconnected duo of the police and the tabloid press – were acting in concert to prepare the ground for legislation against LSD was confirmed in mid-March, when there were three major UK exposés. *London Life* magazine interviewed the WPC's Desmond O'Brien, who freely admitted the centre's Huxley-like plan to distribute the drug among 'intellectuals, writers, artists and other creative people in London'. The article was trailed by television ads, exposing a wider audience to LSD's very existence.

More damaging were the sensationalist articles in the *News of the World* ('Menace of the Vision of Hell') and the *People*, the latter of which gained entry to the WPC's Pont Street base: 'There were used hypodermic syringes, empty drug ampoules and a variety of pills.' John Esam was also arrested by the Flying Squad after another surveillance operation. They found a syringe used to titrate the drug and enough LSD to make the desired charge of dealing stick: although possession was still legal in early 1966, distribution was not.

On 25 March, a few days after the British exposés, *Life* magazine came out with its LSD cover story. Based around photos taken by Lawrence Schiller at the 25 February Acid Test in Hollywood, the anonymous text amplified the horrors: 'The colorless, odorless, tasteless substance called LSD can be made in any college chemistry lab. A black market dose costs only $3 to $5. But that is enough to send a person on a 10-hour "trip" – sometimes into a world of beatific serenity and shimmering insight, sometimes to frenzy and terror.'

Nowhere in America was immune from this new science-fiction drug. 'LSD has been taken up by a large, underground cult,' the article continued. 'Starting in artistic, bohemian and intellectual circles, the cult has now become a dangerous fad on college campuses. At least one million doses of LSD . . . will be taken in the US this year. Hospitals and doctors are suddenly treating scores of panic-stricken young patients who have "taken a trip" on LSD with disastrous psychological effects. Some have been hospitalised for weeks.'

This was not strictly true. There *was* psychological damage caused by LSD, but in early 1966 it was still rare: contemporary researchers estimated that out of every thousand people who took the drug, seven would have an adverse reaction. That was sobering, but nothing like the rampant epidemic predicted by *Time* and *Life*. The real message came a few lines further down in the *Life* story: 'Now the federal Food and Drug Administration is moving in with new laws which will outlaw LSD's illegal manufacture, sale or transportation.'

It was into this polarised climate that the Byrds released 'Eight Miles High', on 14 March. Begun by Gene Clark after the group's alienating visit to the UK, the song had been honed and perfected during a long American tour in the autumn. The group travelled in a motorhome, which allowed them the freedom to travel when they wanted and to create their own soundtrack for the journey. They reprogrammed themselves with frequent applications of Ravi Shankar and John Coltrane, in particular the latter's *Impressions* and *Africa/Brass*.

The song had first been attempted right at RCA Studios right at the end of 1965, only weeks after the completion of their second album, *Turn Turn Turn*. Fine as that record was, it had merely refined standard pop, folk and country modes, but 'Eight Miles High' was something completely new: a masterpiece of tension and release based on ascending chords, with the Byrds distanced, almost remote harmonies gliding above a bubbling lava of metallic twelve-string guitar and Far Eastern harmonics.

Forced by Columbia to recut the song at the company studio, the Byrds tightened everything up, with more low end and sharper solos. The song began with a fanfare and an introductory solo – played in unrestrained Coltrane style – before launching into Clark's allusive lyrics, which told of 'sidewalk scenes / And black limousines'. The location was easily identifiable as London but the feeling was harder to pin down, at once ecstatic and profoundly adrift.

The song's Elvin Jones-style drums, Coltrane convulsions and time-stretching Shankar drones fused two staples of sixties minority taste: free jazz and Indian classical music. Both had been the period's secret soundtrack – the preserve of beats and hipsters – and 'Eight Miles High' brought them into the mainstream pop market. It was an indication, shared by all involved in the Great Race – the Beatles, Bob Dylan, the Byrds, the Yardbirds, the Rolling Stones – that beat and blues were no longer enough.

Miles remembers that 'Indica imported a big load of ESP records: *The Heliocentric Worlds of Sun Ra, Volumes 1 and 2*;

Albert Ayler's *Ghosts* and *Spirits Rejoice*; Eric Dolphy, *Live at the Village Vanguard, Vol. 2*, I think. We just liked the music. It was an extension from Charlie Parker and Freddie Hubbard, Sonny Stitt and those people. Then Charles Mingus, of course. "Oh Lord, Don't Let Them Drop That Atomic Bomb on Me", all these kind of songs. It went right across the culture.'

The Indian influence had already begun to percolate through pop's mainstream, with the Kinks' 'See My Friends' and the Yardbirds' 'Heart Full of Soul'. The first truly mass exposure came in summer 1965, with the Beatles' *Help!*, the soundtrack of which contained a couple of instrumentals – 'The Chase', in particular – that placed the sitar centre stage. The Beatles had heard the instrument during the filming of *Help!*, shortly after Lennon and Harrison and been dosed, and found that music from the Indian subcontinent was the perfect soundtrack for the drug's overwhelming effects.

Both the drone of the sitar and the length of the pieces paralleled LSD's time dislocation, while the timbre of the instrument reverberated right through the body. The music's spiritual overtones also matched strong religious impulses freshly awakened by the drug. Most of all, it seemed to Western ears to contain no ego, nor any constriction into pop-friendly two- or three-minute formats. Like free jazz, it was the sound of true and untrammelled expression, which was highly attractive to musicians who were exploring their new freedoms.

The Byrds had been immersed in Ravi Shankar through their co-manager, Jim Dickson. He had strong affiliations with World Pacific Records, who recorded several Shankar albums during the mid-sixties – most notably *Portrait of a Genius* (1965) and *Sound of the Sitar* (1966). Both were issued in the UK, reflecting the emerging interest in the subcontinent's music. 'You can even dig Indian music,' wrote Tony Hall in his *Record Mirror* column during January 1966, after seeing a Shankar concert. 'Try buying one of his albums sometime. And live with it. He's something else.'

Indian music was shaping up as the central aural metaphor

for LSD and the wider hallucinogenic experience. In early 1966, records by The Great!! Society!! ('Free Advice') and the Yardbirds ('Shapes of Things') explored these tonalities. These jagged, abrasive early LSD records totally lacked any blissful gleam. The drug unlocked feelings and attitudes buried deep in the subconscious, tapping into the roiling teenage id that had been awakened by consumerism's fresh freedoms and the fraught relationship between the 1920s generation and their children.

'Eight Miles High' was a quantum leap, and the Byrds knew it. The reviews came in quickly: *Record World* thought it was 'eerie', while *Cashbox* praised its 'inventive riffs'. *Billboard* only gave it a Top 60 tip, however, perhaps put off by the failure of the group's last single, 'Set You Free This Time'. On 28 March, the by now four-man group – founder member Gene Clark had left at the beginning of the month – gave a press conference in New York, shepherded by the urbane former Beatles PR man, Derek Taylor. Taking pride of place on the table in front of the musicians was a sitar.

In between fielding tricky questions about Gene Clark, Crosby and McGuinn traced the Indian influence on pop, playing taped extracts of Shankar and Coltrane and citing the Beatles and the Yardbirds as their only peers in this field. Asked about psychedelic music, Crosby observed that Archie Shepp and Albert Ayler's work fitted the description, and criticised the superficiality of the media term, which existed 'in order to package it. Rather than in the genuine meaning of psychedelic awareness: being involved with the music.'

Whatever the Byrds' intention, the journalists came away with two ideas in their mind: the linkage of hallucinogenic drugs with music, and the concept of 'raga rock', fostered by the brandishing of an instrument, the sitar, that did not appear on 'Eight Miles High'. The ebullient Crosby was also incautious in talking publicly about acid: 'The only way we could perform [psychedelic music] would be to have all the musicians on LSD! I don't think we've ever managed to play any jobs on LSD.'

On 25 March – the publication date of *Life*'s LSD exposé – the

Beatles gathered together in Bob Whitaker's studio in Chelsea for a photo shoot and a series of interviews. It was their first public appearance as a quartet since the end of 1965, a gap of nearly four months – the longest time off they'd had since the onset of fame. Early 1966 had been allotted for shooting their new film, the third under their United Artists contract, but no script had been agreed. Once that had fallen through, the group took the time as their own.

Fans had to make do with the 1 March screening of *The Beatles at Shea Stadium* on BBC1, but, during the hiatus, the group had metamorphosed into entirely different creatures. Each of the four had had time to reflect on their situation and to explore their own interests, instincts and inclinations – maybe even to conceive of that heretical concept, what if I wasn't a Beatle? These changes were marked by a series of individual interviews conducted by Maureen Cleave of the *Evening Standard* and published weekly, as a series called 'How Does a Beatle Live?' during March 1966.

Ensconced in suburban bliss with wife Maureen and baby Zak, Ringo seemed the least affected, 'mature', 'sensible' and 'contented'. Recently married to Pattie Boyd, George was the 'youngest' and 'least well-known' Beatle. Cleave found him 'a strong-willed and uncompromising character, with a strict regard for what he considers to be the truth, and an even stricter regard for his own rights. "I asked to be successful," he said. "I never asked to be *famous*; I can tell you I got more famous than I wanted to be."'

The 'curiously elegant' George played Cleave a new composition, with the 'not beautiful' words: 'Love me while you can; before I'm a dead old man'. He expounded on his passion for the sitar, recently awakened by seeing Ravi Shankar play at the Festival Hall. 'I couldn't believe it,' he said. 'It was just like everything you have ever thought of as great all coming out at once.' He concluded with a rant against organised religion, the Vietnam war and anybody 'in authority, religious or secular'.

Paul McCartney was 'self-conscious, nervy, restless and on the go: he will surprise us all in the end'. He was the only Beatle to live in the centre of London, having bought a detached Regency town house in Cavendish Avenue, St John's Wood. Unlike the others in outer suburbia, he had access to all that London had to offer, and immersed himself in everything esoteric and avant-garde. One of the few sightings of him at this time came when he was, much to his displeasure, snapped at a 21 February lecture given by Luciano Berio, the Italian electronic composer.

Through his friend Barry Miles, McCartney got involved in the Indica bookshop, designing wrapping paper and flyers, helping with the renovations and buying the stock. 'He would sometimes go down to the basement at night,' Miles remembers, 'and browse among the piles of books to find something to read.' After meeting William Burroughs and his collaborator Ian Sommerville, McCartney also developed a fascination for tape loops, cut-ups and sound manipulation, and started making his own experimental recordings.

Cleave captured this moment: 'He is fascinated by composers like Stockhausen and Luciano Berio; he is most anxious to write electronic music himself, lacks only the machines. He is fascinated by the work of the French playwright Alfred Jarry (*Ubu Cocu*, *Ubu Roi*) and keeps urging Brian Epstein to stage them here. He would like to paint, he would like to write. Indeed, heaven knows what he is painting and writing and in what disguise at this very moment. He sees no limit to his own possibilities.'

John Lennon was the most complex. Along with George Harrison, he was the most enthusiastic drug-taker of the group and, as the leader, bore the psychic burden of the Beatles' almost overwhelming global fame. He was the one that always changed the most in photographs and television appearances, and, during the latter half of 1965, he appeared ill at ease: long-haired, overweight and sweaty, oscillating between zany humour and profound discontent. Stunned by his LSD experiences the previous year, he dedicated his time off to a thorough exploration of inner space.

Cleave described a modern emperor, a bundle of contradictions, simultaneously spoiled – swamped by all manner of expensive, useless objects – yet dissatisfied and questing. 'He looks more like Henry VIII than ever now that his face has filled out – he is just as imperious, just as unpredictable, indolent, disorganised, childish, vague, charming and quick-witted.' Lennon expounded on his fascination with Indian music and his compulsive reading. 'I've read millions of books,' he said, 'that's why I seem to know things.'

The journalist looked at his bulging bookshelves. In early 1966, Lennon was 'reading extensively about religion', and Cleave quoted his thoughts on Hugh J. Schonfield's 1965 best-seller, *The Passover Plot*. 'Christianity will go,' he said. 'It will vanish and shrink. I needn't argue about that; I'm right and I will be proved right. We're more popular than Jesus now; I don't know which will go first – rock 'n' roll or Christianity. Jesus was all right but his disciples were thick and ordinary. It's them twisting it that ruins it for me.'

'ON A HILL IN SURREY. . .', ran the standfirst at the top of the article when it was published on 4 March, 'A YOUNG MAN FAMOUS, LOADED, AND WAITING FOR SOMETHING'. For Lennon, Weybridge was like a waiting room on the way to somewhere else. 'Bankers and stockbrokers live there; they can add figures and Weybridge is what they live in and they think it's the end, they really do. I think of it every day – me in my Hansel and Gretel house. I'll take my time; I'll get my real house when I know what I want.'

Towards the end of March, Lennon visited Indica. This was McCartney's territory, which made him suspicious, and his innate anti-intellectualism made his initial encounter with Barry Miles spiky. 'He was looking for a book by someone called "Nits Ga". It took me a minute to figure out he was talking about Nietzsche, which was just long enough to make John uptight.' Once he'd relaxed, he became 'extremely friendly' and curled up on the shop sofa with a copy of Leary, Metzner and Alpert's *The Psychedelic Experience*.

On 25 March, the Beatles arrived at Robert Whitaker's Chelsea studio brimful of forbidden knowledge. They didn't look that different – still smart in polo necks and tailored jackets – but they had gone through a profound change, and they didn't care to disguise the fact. Their first job was to record an interview with Radio Caroline DJ Tom Lodge for a flexidisc, *Sound of the Stars*, that would mark the merger in April of two music papers, *Disc Weekly* and *Music Echo*,* into a new colour weekly.

Lodge found it an uphill task. Despite the Epstein connection, the Beatles were sarcastic and unhelpful. The razor-sharp timing and wish to accommodate that had marked their initial media exposure had disappeared along with their mop-top innocence. Any dialogue was stilted and short-lived. There were many pauses and a lot of off-mike laughter and in-joking, very much like the stoned sniggers that peppered Bob Dylan's televised December 1965 press conference. Nobody seemed to know what they were doing.

Even so, there was plenty of leakage. The Beatles couldn't help but slip into drug talk and what was then, for pop groups, radical esoterica. Lennon mentioned 'hallucinations', while McCartney talked about 'you know, purple hearts, all them pop groups take them'. When Lodge asked John and Paul if they had ghostwriters to write their songs, Lennon replied that they had 'Gershwin and Trotsky', while McCartney added, 'And Lenin and Blavatsky writing the lyrics.'

The Beatles were more focused on the photos. Robert Whitaker remembered that their PR man, Tony Barrow, 'hated the session basically, because he had six other journalists, all wanting to do interviews, and I was taking a long time. The Beatles were highly amused by what I was up to. And when the interviews started with the most inane questions, they answered with stupid replies. Consequently, Tony didn't get the interviews that he thought were of vital importance to the world.'

The Beatles tended to have the favoured photographer of the moment, and Whitaker's time was 1966. They knew him well: he'd

---

* *Music Echo* was formerly called *Merseybeat* and was owned by Brian Epstein.

been part of the group's circle for at least a year. He was especially close to John Lennon – they shared a similar artistic sensibility which tended towards the sick and the surreal. The group
had never been that easy to photograph and, three years into their
global fame, they were, in Lennon's later words, 'really beginning
to hate it – a photo session was a big ordeal and you had to try and
look normal and you didn't feel it'.

Whitaker had come up with a complicated idea, which was meant
to be displayed on a gatefold LP sleeve. Called 'A Somnabulant
Adventure', it was inspired by *Un Chien Andalou* – the film collaboration between Salvador Dalí and Luis Buñuel – as well as
the work of the German Hans Bellmer, who was infamous for his
queasy doll assemblages. That afternoon, he posed the Beatles in a
series of tableaux that were meant to comment on the arbitrary and
toxic nature of their global fame.

As Whitaker told me, 'I'd got fed up with taking squeaky-clean
pictures of the Beatles, and I thought I'd revolutionise what pop
idols are. I asked for some dolls. I'd gone to Barley Mow Passage,
where there was a doll factory, and they said, "Oh, we've only got
bits." They threw them in a box, which I emptied out in front of the
Beatles. They then fiddled around with them – George has got an
arm on his shoulder, Ringo's got a spare leg. The group were OK
with it, right up until the point where I started bringing trays of
meat onto the set. George wasn't overly impressed.'

Whitaker shot several reels. In one image, George is hammering nails through a blissful John's skull – hints of trepanation. As
Whitaker told me shortly before his death in 2013, 'My thinking
was that they were human beings, but I had to show that, rather
than them being idols. So I was going to cover John's face with
wood grain, so his head would have been a block of wood, and the
nails and the hammer would have been made of fur. The reason I
was doing this, I'd seen little girls absolutely idolising the Beatles.
I've always thought these screaming, knicker-wetting girls, if they
ever got hold of the people, they'd have torn them apart.'

In other shots for the inside of the album, John is holding a box that frames Ringo's head – on the front is written '2,000,000' – while George is seen from within a birdcage. 'There's a picture of Ringo being unpacked from a box, actually the box from the doll factory. John was going to open the box and there was going to be a head, made of alabaster, in the manner of Chopin or Mozart, in an edition of two million. Then the birdcage, which was my own budgerigar's cage. There was nothing more to it, apart from the effrontery of putting a Beatle in a birdcage.'

In the projected front-cover image, a young woman – symbolic of a million fans – kneels in worship before the four young men, while Lennon brandishes a string of sausages. 'It would have been drawn into the womb of a woman,' Whitaker says of that particular image, 'and there would have been a breast in the top right-hand corner, and the sausages are meant to be an umbilical cord, which in those days I thought was perhaps too much to show.'

This was Beatles dream time, the group distorted through a prism. The level of fame that they experienced had become all-devouring. They were, quite literally, in danger of being dismembered – physically by their fans, and psychically by their celebrity. The photos are awkward, half-formed and, as Whitaker always claimed, unfinished, but they tell a truth. Stumbling around in the dark, the photographer enacted what the Beatles felt: that what had begun in innocence and excitement was turning dark and dangerous, that it was all getting far too much.

The starkest image features the four sitting on a low table. The Beatles are wearing white laboratory/butcher's smocks over their fashionable polo necks, their cleanliness forever polluted by a series of dismembered doll parts and red, raw chunks of meat. Every member of the group is giving a sick leer, mouths wide open, pot-slitted eyes staring into the camera. Ringo doesn't look totally present and George barely manages to conceal his disgust, but both Paul and John – sitting in the front row – are totally in the moment, endorsing the idea in triumphant rebellion.

Just under two weeks later, on 6 April, the Beatles convened at Abbey Road for their first session since mid-November 1965.

They began with a song that would be variously called 'The Void', 'Mark One' and 'Tomorrow Never Knows'. It started as a one-chord drone – an extrapolation from the sitar's tonality – over which John Lennon sang lyrics taken directly from the general introduction to *The Psychedelic Experience*: 'whenever in doubt, turn off your mind, relax, float downstream'.

Filtered through a Leslie speaker, Lennon aimed to redact these extracts from *The Tibetan Book of the Dead* by simulating the sound of a Buddhist monk: 'Turn off your mind, relax and float downstream / It is not dying, it is not dying.' Over two more days, the basic idea was tightened up: Ringo Starr's thunderous, threatening drum pattern was looped and accelerated, while McCartney overlaid a sequence of tape loops – sped-up laughter, backwards guitar, treated orchestral music – that, set against the unyielding rhythm, stretched time and spun it into a new consciousness.

'Tomorrow Never Knows' *was* acid. Swerving and swooping through the sound mix, the overdubs captured the ebbs and flows, zaps and zings of LSD's perceptual overload, while the overall drone – established on the final version by the opening tambour – harmonised with the synaesthetic lyrics: 'Listen to the colour of your dreams'. This was the drug as interpreted by Leary and Aldous Huxley: 'Love is all and love is everyone.' In its final version, completed on 22 April and released just under four months later, the song sounded like the jet stream, marking a change in the weather.

Just over three years previously, the Beatles had been recording 'From Me to You' and 'Thank You Girl'. They were now a million miles away from writing simple songs about love and courtship, with a definite beginning, middle and end. In 1963, John Lennon had been a young bull ready to take on and take over the world. In 1966, he was recording a song that shattered pop's linear time. He already sounded like an old man, and he was only twenty-five: 'So play the game "Existence" to the end / Of the beginning, of the beginning.' The last phrase looped ad infinitum, into eternity.

* * *

'The hedonistic cults take over, the dance gets wilder, everything goes, the music is louder, the strobe lights flash faster, every stimulus maximises. The capsules which two years ago contained 250 mcg of LSD now have been fortified to 700 mcg. More. Longer. Forever.'

SIDNEY COHEN, in Richard Alpert, Sidney Cohen and Lawrence Schiller, *LSD*, 1966

Once the biggest group in the world had become adepts, LSD's spread throughout pop culture was inevitable. What had previously been a trickle of acid songs would soon become a rushing torrent. Naturally, the authorities were horrified. The whole thing was like a paranoid 1950s science-fiction movie, a laboratory experiment gone disastrously wrong. LSD sent existing concerns about illegal drug use and youth lifestyles – primarily focused on amphetamines, marijuana and hair length at this stage – spiralling off into the stratosphere.

It wasn't just LSD. 1966 was a year of panic about drugs in general. Alan Bestic's sensationalist tract *Turn Me On, Man* covered the whole pharmacopeia: heroin, purple hearts, marijuana, amphetamines. He thought that the mystique of LSD made it 'particularly attractive to students. They are drawn by the propaganda which describes how it enlarges the mind, the perception, and the understanding of life; and excellent student bait too, heady stuff indeed, is its intellectual snob value as something to be appreciated by writers, artists and serious thinkers, but not by the masses.'

In an April 1966 pamphlet, the sociologist Anne Gillie noted how 'the widespread use of LSD represents a new force in the United States. In the past, drug users have always been members of the lowest classes; the poorly educated and the slum dwellers, but LSD users are the "cream of today's youth"; college and high school students, as well as advertising men, housewives, and ministers. These people take LSD for religious and aesthetic experience, for insight into themselves, and a view of the world as it could be rather than as it is.'

This wasn't mere teen obnoxiousness but the advance guard of a full-blown youth revolution. Where 'the cream of today's youth' led, the masses might follow – and then what would happen within a society full of critical and questing individuals? That question gave the authorities' attempts to dampen down the threat particular urgency, and during April 1966 the campaign against the most visible LSD adepts gained momentum – in a series of arrests, court cases and hostile press.

On 6 April, John Esam's case came up for trial. It was, as John Hopkins observes, 'the first police attempt to make LSD illegal. LSD itself was legal, so they busted him under the Poisons Act, for being in possession of ergotamine, which was a constituent of LSD.' Esam fought the case, which, thanks to the prosecution's confusion about which substances were involved and which were or were not illegal, would drag on through several court sittings throughout the year and end in his acquittal.

Five days later, the annual CND march ended with the usual meeting at Trafalgar Square. An estimated 20,000 turned up for the final rally, where Barry Miles and John Hopkins distributed issues of their new magazine, *THE Global moon-edition Long Hair TIMES* – a few pages of montages and concepts, with a fake competition penned by Paul McCartney. 'I remember going out with an armful of this stuff, going round and round Trafalgar Square,' Hopkins remembers. 'I'd just printed them on my little litho press that I'd had for a year or two, because I'd wanted to learn about printing.'

On 16 April, the BBC filmed an acid party at Christopher Gibbs's flat for their daily late-evening news programme *Twenty-Four Hours*. The *People* got wind of this and splashed the event across its front page the next day: 'BBC in a Wild "Drug Party" Sensation'. In their prurient tabloid account, full of the usual sensationalised quotes – 'Look at me, I'm high on LSD. I'm a baby again' – about the worst thing was that 'men danced with men – women danced with women'. The BBC pulled the item at the last minute.

In America, the acid evangelists were undergoing their own

travails. Ken Kesey was on the run in Mexico after his second arrest for marijuana, and the Pranksters were in disarray. On 16 April, state troopers burst into Millbrook. Timothy Leary was arrested but nothing stuck. With a thirty-year stretch already hanging over his head, he was busy backtracking on his previous evangelism. As he informed a thousand-strong audience at New York's Town Hall on 21 April, 'I propose for one year a moratorium on the taking of LSD and marijuana. I'm going to stop and I'm asking you to stop.'

This was reported the next day in a long *New York Times* article, which summarised the increase in hospital admissions due to LSD and the then current media scare story of Stephen Kessler, 'a 30-year-old former medical student with a hospital record as a user of LSD' who had stabbed his mother-in-law with a kitchen knife. It also reported the sudden cessation of the drug's supply. Appalled by the controversy surrounding the drug, Sandoz – 'the country's only legal distributor of LSD' – decided to terminate all research contracts in the US that month.

On 23 April, Mick Jagger, Brian Jones and Keith Richards took a quick trip to Ireland during the first proper break they had had that year. They were the guests of Tara Browne, the son of the 4th Baron Oranmore and Browne and Oonagh Guinness. It was his twenty-first birthday party at Luggala, an exquisite Gothic Revival house nestled in the Wicklow mountains, and the Lovin' Spoonful (taking a break from their first visit to the UK) and the Peter B's – a group formed by former Them organist Peter Bardens – were due to perform.

There is an extraordinary picture by Michael Cooper, a young photographer who had just joined the Stones' circle, that freezes the moment: an ambiguous and not entirely well-starred collision of worlds. On top of the windswept Wicklow moor are six people, including Brian Jones, Browne's wife Nicky, the designer Bill Willis and Anita Pallenberg. All are displaying signs of drug-induced incapacity, most obviously John Paul Getty III and his wife Talitha, who are collapsing to the ground in the photo's centre.

There's something disturbing about the image: the bleakness of the landscape, the softness of the ground on top of the moor. It's all focused on Brian Jones's face, which is locked into a manic, rictus grin, caught between hilarity and disturbance. Jagger took LSD for the first time on this visit and did not exactly enjoy the experience. Anita Pallenberg remembered 'feeling awful' during the whole time she was in Ireland – 'it was all pretty heavy' – while Marianne Faithfull later pointed to Luggala as a turning point: 'the start of a quest for decadence among these people'.

That same day, the journalist Mary Campbell's report on the Byrds' press conference almost a month earlier was syndicated in newspapers around the country, some of which included Crosby's LSD comments. The linkage was there: 'Eight Miles High' sounded so strange and so new that it was easy to think, as did the student newspaper *The Tech*, that the song 'was a description of the condition brought about by drugs, and seems particularly appropriate to hallucinogens'.

On 29 April, the *Gavin Report* – the most influential publication in the radio industry – announced that it had dropped Bob Dylan's 'Rainy Day Women #12 and 35' and 'Eight Miles High' from its recommended playlist. 'In our opinion, these records imply encouragement and/or approval of the use of marijuana or LSD. We cannot conscientiously recommend such records for airplay, despite their acknowledged sales. We reserve the future right to distinguish between records that simply mention such drugs and those that imply approval of their use.'

The Byrds cried foul, but the damage was done: 'Eight Miles High' was immediately banned in several cities and its chart momentum slowed in the first few weeks of May. Despite getting a partial retraction in the *Gavin Report* a month later – under the threat of litigation – the charge that this was a drug song stuck. There was even controversy in the UK, where the record made the Top 30: a Birmingham city councillor asked Home Secretary Roy Jenkins to have 'Eight Miles High' and 'Rainy Day Women #12 and 35' banned by the BBC.

Stalling at #14 in the *Billboard* chart, 'Eight Miles High' marked the zenith of the Byrds' career. Derek Taylor blamed the *Gavin Report* for the record's comparative failure, but 'Rainy Day Women #12 and 35' made #2 in the US. The fuss didn't seem to harm Dylan's record at all and, in fact, the Byrds' single was already faltering on the radio. The record was too complex for crossover appeal and the group were seen as too difficult. Columbia's resources were diverted to the more pliable Paul Revere and the Raiders, whose anti-drug tune 'Kicks' eventually rose to #4.

On 19 May, just as 'Eight Miles High' peaked in the charts, the Berkeley university newspaper the *Daily Californian* published a long article called 'The Future of Psychedelics'. The pseudonymous Mr Jones observed the polarising effect of the drug, which had become a 'national obsession': 'LSD-users want no part of today's social structure. It's not just Vietnam and Alabama, for these are merely first level atrocities. These things are manifestations for a culture for which we don't care and we won't support. The culture itself permits such atrocities.'

He wrote as the Rolling Stones' latest single was surging up the charts on both sides of the Atlantic. 'Paint It, Black' was the most extreme thus far in the group's malign mid-sixties run. Signalled by Brian Jones's distorting sitar and driven by Bill Wyman's rumba rhythms and Charlie Watts's slamming beats, the song expressed a grief so overwhelming that it spilled over into an angry, almost apocalyptic nihilism. Not that that was picked up by contemporary reviewers. On 14 May, *Record Mirror* pronounced it 'a sad old theme' but 'immediately commercial'.

In the same issue Tony Hall trailed the new Beatles LP: 'SOME OF THE TRACKS . . . ARE THE MOST REVOLUTIONARY EVER MADE BY A POP GROUP!' He singled out a track called 'The Void', which 'has the weirdest, wildest electronic effects I've ever heard. Sound-wise, it's like a hypnotically horrific journey through the dark never-ending jungle of someone's mind. Indian instruments are cleverly utilised. And the effect is of shapes and sounds and colours looming over and above one and zooming in and out of a monotonous drone.'

During the week that 'Paint It, Black' hit the top of the UK charts, the Beatles released their first single for six months. Saturated in clanging guitar and Indian textures, the two songs reflected both sides of the psychedelic coin. McCartney's 'Paperback Writer' was a tricksy, fast, Swinging London satire, performed with an engaging humour, while Lennon's 'Rain' was deeper and darker, the backing track slowed down for a song that evoked an enlightened or narcotic acceptance.

'Paperback Writer'/'Rain' was trailed, in the 11 June issue of *Disc and Music Echo*, by the first appearance of any image from Robert Whitaker's March session. On the publication date of this, the 'most controversial shot ever', the first major pop-star drugs bust occurred. At 1.30 a.m., Donovan was woken by the arrival of nine police officers at his Maida Vale flat. Looking for LSD, they found a large lump of hashish. All the controversies and sonic extremities of the previous few months had alerted the authorities to the fact that pop musicians were vanguard agents of the psyche-delic revolution, openly pumping acid propaganda into the mass media. It was time to prick the pop-star bubble.

Under the soon-to-be-notorious Sergeant Norman Pilcher, the London Drug Squad were becoming much more assertive about policing illegal drugs. Donovan had come to the attention of the authorities after his January 1966 TV documentary, *A Boy Called Donovan*, featured a wild party sequence during which his smart/beatnik friends smoked marijuana and sipped from a suspicious-looking wine jug. The Rediffusion film had also shown Donovan singing 'Hey Gyp (Dig the Slowness)' – with its 'sugar cube' line – to a rapt teen audience on *Ready Steady Go!*.

Donovan was represented by the Beatles' lawyer, David Jacobs. He avoided jail but received a hefty fine of £250. Nevertheless, his well-publicised arrest and trial was intended to send a warning. Sentencing Donovan, the magistrate remarked on 'his great influence on young people'. The British authorities meant to serve notice on the pop world: no musician, however big, would be exempt from the inten-sifying scrutiny concerning drugs – in particular, the psychedelics.

That month, the governors of California and Nevada signed bills that imposed fines of up to $1,000 and prison sentences of up to a year for the possession of LSD. The arguments about LSD had entered a new, even more polarised phase: as the *San Francisco Chronicle* observed, 'The boundaries between rational social control and punitive laws pose a central dilemma for the whole LSD question.' The drug had become the focus of a battle between young and old, as 'Mr Jones' observed, and the legislation further divided 'the two generations here at conflict'.

The first skirmishes in the LSD battle had been won, decisively, by the authorities. But it was too late: the genie was out of the bottle. LSD was an extremely powerful dissolving agent, with a great ability to shape-shift and mutate, and its ability to transcend social and legal structures had already been observed. The siren call of self-discovery and instant transcendence – as broadcast by the sequence of extraordinary records in early 1966 – would not be silenced. The messages had been well heard.

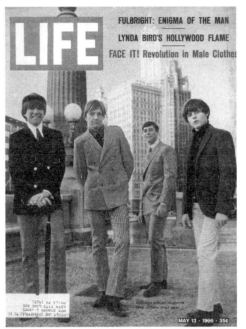

Op art, mad rags and a dazzle of changing color

5 : MAY

Walkin' My Cat Named Dog: The Feminine
Mystique and Female Independence

Amidst all the turmoil, it was spring, and with the change of season came hit records that captured a feeling of openness, like the long exhalation of breath when winter is finally done. The New Orleans whorehouse rhythms of Bob Dylan's 'Rainy Day Women #12 and 35', the ecstatic harmonies of the Beach Boys' 'Sloop John B.', the footloose funk of Junior Walker and the All Stars' 'Road Runner' – all spoke of a new confidence and freedom, that you could try anything and it might work.

Two records epitomised this mood. Both came from New York, which was but one of the several American cities attempting to claim the title of World Pop Capital just as London passed its peak. By spring 1966, the Lovin' Spoonful were the hot new group, feted by the Beatles and the Rolling Stones, trendsetters in both image and music with John Sebastian's granny glasses, Zal Yanovsky's fur coats and their inspired updates of American folk blues styles. 'Daydream' delivered on its promise. The Lovin' Spoonful presented themselves as goofy, bohemian, warm. They also had a coded message. In 1966, 'dream' no longer meant the swoon of teen love, but signalled initiation into the still secret world of psychedelics. 'I'm blowing the day to take a walk in the sun,' Sebastian sang, and 'Daydream' was a footloose anthem beautifully sold by the relaxed performance of a group at the very top of their game.

Norma Tanega's 'Walkin' My Cat Named Dog' had the same feeling: mooching down the city streets, kicking at the cobbled stones, feeling good for no particular reason. It expressed the simple joy of being alive. Released in America during February 1966, it followed 'Daydream' into the charts, eventually peaking at #22 in the *Billboard* chart and #25 in *Cashbox* in mid-April. In Britain, it was a pirate radio favourite, peaking at #14 on Radio Caroline's *Countdown of Sound* near the end of April.

'Walkin' My Cat Named Dog' had an impact beyond its chart placings: it was one of those records that made people sit up and take notice. Norma became a star with her first single. Invited onto nationwide television, she initially came across like Joan Baez, a severe folk singer, but she played an electric guitar and shook a pair of big earrings designed by Kenneth Jay Lane. On her face was a look of amusement and total surprise. 'It was shock. And awe,' she says now about her unexpected fame.

In sound and appearance, Norma Tanega represented something new and fresh. In their 14 May issue, *Record Mirror* printed a large picture of her to accompany a reader's letter. 'I never thought I'd see the day when this happened,' wrote Tony Grinham, 'but the most imaginative and innovative records around today happen to be by girl singers.' He cited current hits by Nancy Sinatra, Cher and the 'weird folknik tinged "Walkin' My Cat Named Dog"' as part of this trend.

The record bears this out. It begins with a simple harmonica and guitar duet. An electric bass introduces the vocal, which is both relaxed and distinctive. The lyrics are hip, terse, positive: 'Me and my cat named Dog / Are walkin' high against the fog.' As was the custom in many sixties records, which operated on the principle of a constant build, each verse added something new – in the case of the second verse, a contrapuntal guitar figure.

The chorus opens the song out: 'Happy, sad and crazy wonder / Chokin' up my mind with perpetual dreamin'.' The third and fourth verses add a female chorus, a flute and a more prominent, danceable rhythm – what Norma calls 'the Motown bass'. A quick instrumental break for harmonica and bass leads into the pay-off: 'Dog is a good old cat / People, what you think of that?' All the elements of the arrangement reappear at full pelt, and then it's over and out.

'Walkin' My Cat Named Dog' came out of nowhere. Tanega's first choice of career had been to be an artist, and to that end she graduated from Scripps College in California with a BA in painting, and then took a Masters at Claremont College. In the early sixties, she moved to New York and got a job at Random House publishers. 'Because I was educated and smart, they let me answer the phone and talk to people. I became Mr Knopf's personal secretary, and I'm a crappy secretary. But I did it, because that was how I earned my living. I had to eat. And they did let me advance and learn things, and they let me go to the camp in the Catskills, and that's where I met Norma Kutzer. It was a Jewish camp, for Jewish kids, and I was the camp counsellor who sang all the folk songs that I learned – 'In the Pines', 'We Shall Overcome'. The students loved it.'

Music and culture was in the family. Tanega studied classical piano for twelve years, while developing skills as a poet, singer and painter. In between her studies, she travelled around Europe, living the life of a free spirit. As she told *KRLA Beat*, 'I sang on the road and in youth hostels. Most of the American folk singers go for the lines outside of the theatres but I didn't do that. I just sang for people wherever they were. It was great! One suitcase and a guitar – I learned how to hitchhike.'

Her entry into the pop world came by accident. One of the other Catskills camp counsellors taught at a Brooklyn high school and introduced her to Herb Bernstein, a part-time record producer. When he heard Norma's songs, he signed her up to a production deal with Bob Crewe, the Four Seasons' producer, who had his finger on the pulse with recent hits by the Toys ('A Lover's Concerto') and Mitch Ryder and the Detroit Wheels ('Jenny Take a Ride').

Tanega was bewildered by the whole process. 'After I met Bob Crewe and signed all that stuff, I thought, "Well, at least I have a job." But I didn't know anything. They had a guy in playing harmonica, and I thought they must have pulled him in off the street. I didn't know about session musicians.' Bernstein was just starting out as a producer, but he constructed a contemporary sound picture for Tanega's first single.

'Walkin' My Cat Named Dog' was a sophisticated creation. Just as the music fused folk and Motown and set philosophy to a go-go beat, the lyrics were a mixture of autobiography and wish fulfilment. 'I did have a cat named Dog,' Norma says, 'and I would stick my head out the window and call, "Dog!" And this cat would come running up three flights of stairs. I always wanted a dog, but my mother was allergic. So I had to have a cat instead. But you can't walk a cat in New York.'

Tanega presented the city as a playground, a place of possibility that a young woman could still pass through without fear. As she remembers, 'I walked through Central Park, alone. I'm just here, like everybody else.' She presented a new kind of femininity. With its street slang and paradoxes, 'Walkin' My Cat Named Dog' showed that women could be just as hip and allusive as Bob Dylan, whom Norma had met the year before. 'He was kind to me, very kind,' she says.

The song's deceptive and subtle confidence struck a chord with the public. After it entered the charts on both sides of the Atlantic, Tanega found that she was part of the music industry. She was quickly added to a six-week package tour with Gene Pitney, the McCoys, Len Barry and others. 'Oh, that was an eye-opener. It was such an education to learn about pop. How can you be prepared for what goes on? But if you can live through a tour, you can live through anything, I thought.

'The first place we played, I went and called my manager in New York and just cried. It was awful. And when I first went on in a stadium, in front of 20,000 people, grabbing at my guitar, I thought, "My god, what is going on?" It felt like two years, but it was only a month and a half on the road, on a bus, with all the guys gambling. I just sat there, looked out the window and dreamt. I was the only woman on the tour. Also, they only had dressing rooms for the guys. So I would change . . . in a stable, in one place.'

In late June, Norma was flown over to the UK to capitalise on her success. Arriving in Swinging London was like a dream: 'Lionel Bart came onto the tarmac to pick me up! I guess I'd spoken to somebody and they knew what I wanted. I'd been talking about the last thing that had struck me, which was I'd just seen *Marat/ Sade* in New York, with the original players, and I was stunned. And EMI had them at the studio when they picked me up. I was flabbergasted.'

She was plunged into the usual round of PR, doing interviews with the pop weeklies and appearing on *Ready Steady Go!* and *Thank Your Lucky Stars*, where she met Dusty Springfield for the first time. A chance encounter in an unglamorous TV studio led to a long friendship. 'I lived with her right after that. I moved everything over, about two tons of stuff, and I expected to be there for ever.'

Tanega was a different kind of female pop star. Discussing her collaboration with songwriter Norma Kutzer, she told *Record Mirror*, 'It's like sharing the same philosophy. I think I'm Nietzsche.' In *KRLA Beat*, she cited as her heroes Van Gogh, Robespierre, Kafka, Isadora Duncan, Dostoyevsky and Greta Garbo. As the magazine reported, 'She writes about the beauty of the ordinary things in life and raises them to a level of importance seldom seen by the average person.'

The language of pop was expanding, and women were the beneficiaries as well as men. At the time, Tanega did not ally herself with any overt women's politics. 'I was a creator,' she retorts when the word 'feminism' is mentioned. 'That was never a question for me. It didn't matter.' Yet 'Walkin' My Cat Named Dog' and its follow-up, 'A Street That Rhymes at 6 A.M.', were but two of several pop records that, during the first half of 1966, broke the mould of what women could sing about, and indeed could be.

In America, 'Walkin' My Cat Named Dog' shared chart space with Nancy Sinatra's massive first hit, 'These Boots Are Made for Walkin'', an extraordinary mixture of Las Vegas and Los Angeles, of S&M fantasy and feminine revenge, produced by her Svengali and long-time collaborator, Lee Hazelwood. The follow-up was the soundalike 'How Does That Grab You Darlin'?', another tough tale of tables turned, with more than a small seasoning of camp.

In the UK, the chart for May included Tanega's single, along with Cilla Black's 'Alfie' and Sandie Shaw's astonishingly down-beat 'Nothing Comes Easy', the story of a hunter who is captured by the game. Dusty Springfield's signature tune 'You Don't Have to Say You Love Me' was the #1 record at the start of the month, an extraordinary vocal performance – showing enormous technical skill and emotional empathy – that turned her into a superstar.

None of these singers set out with the intention of redefining femininity, but the rules were beginning to change. For various reasons, women had taken second place in the beat boom that followed the Beatles' success: the charts seemed to be, as the *Radio Caroline Annual* for 1965 noted, 'invariably dominated by male singers'. As if to confirm this, the pop 'zines of the time routinely observed that things were 'tough on girl singers', lumping all the female pop stars (Cilla, Sandie, Dusty, Kathy Kirby) into one round-up article.

In spring 1966, the second wave of feminism had not yet fully begun, although the ideas and the structures were beginning to fall into place. Like their counterparts in the outside world, women pop singers were caught between the old and the new, between acceptance of the status quo and the free, questing spirit caught by Norma Tanega's curiously insinuating song about her counter-intuitively named cat. Something was in the air: a new kind of independence.

* * *

'The freedom to lead and plan your life is frightening if you have never faced it before. It is frightening when a woman finally realises that there is no answer to the question "Who am I?" except the voice inside herself.'
BETTY FRIEDAN, 'A New Life Plan for Women', *The Feminine Mystique*, 1963

In January 1966, the author Richard Mabey began his survey of the pop scene with 'a fairy tale for our time': the story of a seventeen-year-old called Kathy, who has a relationship with a pop star called Mick and runs her own boutique. 'The clothes she designs are so successful that she too is invited to America. She celebrates her eighteenth birthday with Mick at the New York Hilton.' She has arrived on her own terms, needing 'no miraculous help in her rise to the rooftop bar'.

Mabey's story illustrated how things had evolved since the mid-1950s. 'The pop music scene has become an arena in which the old lodestar divisions of class, age, sex, status and geography have been challenged and uprooted. The marks of this economic, social and cultural upheaval are everywhere around us.' These were big claims but, clearly, things were changing in the youth culture of the mid-1960s, and some of that change had to do with gender.

In 1966, women were still treated as second-class citizens. Both in America and the UK, there were stringent laws about divorce and abortion. In the UK, family law still allowed husbands considerable control over their wives: for instance, a woman could not open a bank account without the approval of her spouse. Women were subject to inequalities in employment, both in pay and the nature of the jobs available. They also bore the brunt of the social disapproval resulting from any sexual activity outside marriage.

'Imagine a world – or summon it back into memory – in which the Help Wanted columns were divided into Male for the jobs with the future and Female for the Dead End positions,' the activist Susan Brownmiller later wrote of that period, 'when a husband was required to countersign a wife's application for a credit card, a bank loan, or automobile insurance . . . when rape was the woman's fault, when nobody dared talk about the battery that went on behind closed doors, or could file a complaint about sexual harassment.'

However, this inequality was under attack from a variety of sources. By the mid-1960s, employment was plentiful and on both sides of the Atlantic more women were able to go out to work. In late March 1966, a BBC programme called *Six Sides of a Square: A Woman's Place* followed three women in Gibson Square, Islington, who had gone back to work after several years at home with young children. As the commentary stated, 'Their opportunities would have been unthinkable a generation earlier.'

One of these was a spirited mother-of-three called Jeannie Read, who had taken work in a 'joke shop'. Her opinions were forthright and sharp. 'I think it's very boring to stay at home,' she stated. 'I'd sooner be at work myself: I don't get so fed up. I was very irritable before, when I was at home, but all that's finished with now. I just come and go as I like.' She relished the fact that she earned her own money. 'Oh yes,' she beamed, 'I'm very independent now.'

The reasons given for this included the partial availability of contraception since 1961, smaller family sizes, labour-saving devices and the proven ability of women to tackle most industrial tasks – the fact, as the narration concluded, that women 'were also able to do things long thought to be the preserve of men'. There was a realisation that the traditional role of stay-at-home mother was obsolete: the nature of marriage and, indeed, the relations between the sexes were up for negotiation.

These and other questions were explored by Nell Dunn in *Talking to Women*, a book which featured nine interviews that ranged from the artist Pauline Boty to the model Suna Portman, the novelist Edna O'Brien and a working-class Battersea resident, Kathy Collier. Dunn wrote that 'if these girls have anything in common it is a belief in personal fulfilment – that a woman's life should not solely be the struggle to make men happy but more than that a progress towards the development of one's own body and soul'.

Marriage, abortion, contraception, moral codes and the struggle to find a new way of life dominated the discussions. A young mother called Frances Chadwicke told Dunn that 'there seem to be very few practical reasons for sexual fidelity in marriage – now that there's no danger of putting a cuckoo in the nest. And more than that, it's a cumulative thing when the old laws break down, of people wishing to be independent, seeking desperately for their new identity.'

Many of the ideas and attitudes in *Talking to Women* could have come straight out of Betty Friedan's *The Feminine Mystique*. Published in 1963, this groundbreaking polemic had a huge impact at the time, focusing its ideas with enough clarity and force to start a political movement. Much of Friedan's book reads like the theoretical underpinning for the first three series of *Mad Men*, set in the early sixties, with Betty Draper as the listless suburban wife driven mad by an all-pervading yet nameless anomie.

As Friedan wrote in her preface, 'The problem lay buried, unspoken for many years in the minds of American women. It was a strange stirring, a sense of dissatisfaction, a yearning that women suffered in the middle of the twentieth century in the United States.' Friedan had experienced this in her own life. Having graduated *summa cum laude* from the all-female Smith College, she was persuaded to curtail her academic career, becoming a freelance journalist for *Cosmopolitan*, among others.

The Feminine Mystique came out of a survey of Friedan's Smith College contemporaries. Sifting the responses, she realised that they 'simply did not fit the image of the modern American woman as she was written about in women's magazines. There was a strange discrepancy between our lives as women and the image to which we were trying to conform, the image that I came to call the feminine mystique. I wondered if other women faced this schizophrenic split, and what it meant.'

Over several hundred pages, Friedan collected data from women's magazines, interviews with advertising men and psychological works to construct an impassioned polemic against what she argued was the concerted attempt by male experts of all hues to reverse the professional and economic gains of women throughout the 1930s and the Second World War. This was not just a climate but a hegemonic conspiracy that had disastrous effects on the female psyche. She quoted some young wives:

'I feel as though I don't exist.'

'I'm desperate. I begin to feel I have no personality. I'm a server of food and a putter-on of pants and a bedmaker, somebody who can be called upon when you want something. But who am I?'

'I just don't feel alive.'

What Friedan gave evidence of was more than just a malaise; this was the tip of a widespread depression, a 'hunger that food cannot fill'. Women were twisted and warped by the societal expectation that they should stay at home. The result was that they felt awful, but didn't know why. Some turned to the tranquillisers that doctors handed out like candy – 'because it makes you not care so much that it's pointless'.

The social pressure to conform was a constant in American life but, in the 1950s Cold War era, dissident voices had been silenced. The roll-back of women's rights and the curtailment of their potential was part of this climate but, in the mid-1960s, this was about to break. In giving a comprehensive and well-argued critique of the position of women in American society, Friedan helped to give the push for women's rights and independence a fresh boost.

The ground had already been prepared by Simone de Beauvoir's 1949 book *The Second Sex*, an impassioned survey of the way that women, defined by men, are robbed of their potential. Extraordinarily wide-ranging, the book covered topics as diverse as the female orgasm, prostitution, abortion, education, child-rearing and the tyranny of fashion. The book had an epic sweep that, like Friedan's book, collected a wealth of data into an unstoppable argument.

De Beauvoir's book became a touchstone for young British women in the late 1950s and early 1960s. As the feminist writer Sheila Rowbotham remembers, 'Like many others of my generation, I began reading Beauvoir, along with the works of Sartre, when I was at school.' She constructed her own world based on existentialism: 'A compilation of Simon de Beauvoir, Juliette Gréco singing "Je suis comme je suis", Edith Piaf's wail "Non, je ne regrette rien" and Bessie Smith's earthy blues.'

This discovery was shared by many others. Jenny Diski was 'thirteen and fourteen' when, in the early sixties, she 'became aware of the Beats, jazz, poetry, cool'. In her memoir of the period, she remembers how she 'muddled them properly with the existentialism of Sartre and Camus' fiction while I was at boarding school, mixing with the wrong crowd from the local town who had designated a corporation bench near a roundabout just outside the centre the "Beat Seat"'.

'We appeared to have no history, no culture, certainly no movement,' Rowbotham wrote about that period, 'just snatches of suggestion to ponder.' But other voices began to clamour. In 1960, Lynne Reid Banks published *The L-Shaped Room*, a best-selling novel about a young unmarried mother who attempts to control her own destiny. Moving into a Fulham boarding house, she encounters not the standard narrative of disaster, but self-determination and respect. It was turned into a successful film in 1962.

A grittier version of the same topic was delivered by the eighteen-year-old Shelagh Delaney in her 1958 play *A Taste of Honey*, which was filmed in 1961. These films reinforced the point that, in the early sixties, young women bore the brunt of any sexual mishap. Starting from a position of weakness and ignorance, they were all too often forced to steer 'without a compass between the dreaded Scylla of frigidity and the humiliating Charybdis branded "nymphomania"'. They were damned if they did, and damned if they didn't.

American and British writers began offering advice, information and polemics on this and other vexed topics. In May 1962, Helen Gurley Brown published the sensational *Sex and the Single Girl*, which stated that a young women didn't need 'to be married to enjoy a satisfying life'. In spring 1963, Gloria Steinem published a long article about her experiences as an undercover Playboy Bunny – an exposé that nailed the lie that the Bunny was 'the most envied girl in America'.

By the middle of the decade, the move towards greater equality was becoming law. In America, Congress passed the 1963 Equal Pay Act. Title VII of the 1964 Civil Rights Act barred discrimination on the basis of sex or race. In the UK, the Married Women's Property Act entitled a woman to keep half of any savings from the allowance granted to her by her husband. In 1965, Barbara Castle was made minister for transport, the first female ministerial appointee.

That same year, Margaret Mead co-edited a book called *American Women*, which published the findings of the president's Commission on the Status of Women, set up by John F. Kennedy in 1961. The report was nothing less than an invitation to action: as the editors observed, 'The human and national costs are heavy; for the most part, they are avoidable. That is why we urge changes, many of them long overdue, in the conditions of women's opportunity in the United States.'

But it was an uphill struggle, even in the most progressive enclaves. One of the most famous early women's rights documents was written by two civil rights workers, Casey Hayden and Mary King. As volunteers in the Student Nonviolent Coordinating Committee, they had worked on 1964's gruelling – and hazardous – Freedom Summer campaign in Mississippi. Despite the camaraderie, the shared dangers and their belief in the movement's work, both women felt slighted and short-changed.

Steeped in their readings of *The Second Sex*, they wrote a discussion document called 'A Kind of Memo', which exposed the fact that women were second-class citizens even within a movement for social justice and equality. Observing that 'all the problems between men and women and all the problems of women functioning in society as equal human beings are among the most basic that people face', they used the phrase 'a caste system' to describe their subordinate status in the movement and in society at large.

As Mary King admitted in her autobiography, terminology was a problem: 'Since the term liberation was not then widely used pertaining to women, the word sexism had not been coined, feminism was rarely heard, and other now familiar argot of the women's movement did not exist, we searched for the best term to use to describe the condition of women. We liked the concept of a caste system because it suggested an arbitrarily imposed method of valuation . . . based on involuntary status at birth.'

When Hayden and King wrote and revised the document, from late 1964 to late 1965, they felt that the chances seemed 'nil that we could start a movement based on anything as distant to general

American thought as a sex caste system'. They sent out the manifesto to forty women activists who were 'involved across the spectrum of progressive organising' – in Students for a Democratic Society and the National Student Association, as well as the SNCC.

The response was immediate. In December 1965, inspired by the memo, female attendees of a Students for a Democratic Society convention in Illinois walked out and held a separate meeting of what they called 'A Women's Caucus'. A few months later, in April 1966, the War Resisters League magazine, *Liberation*, printed the manifesto in full – a publication that, according to King, 'increased by a quantum leap the number of people circulating it'. This was an idea that had found its time.

* * *

'The real dynamo behind the teenage revolution is the anonymous adolescent girl from twelve to sixteen, nameless but irresistible.'
PETER LAURIE, *The Teenage Revolution*, 1965

The general feeling that things had to change was prompted by a profound shift in what women expected from life. As Jenny Diski pithily observes about the generation that came of age in the sixties, 'The higher education our parents were so proud to have achieved for us gave us time to wonder why we had to recreate the desired world of our parents. And those who did not go to university wondered why they had to spend their lives in factories replicating the passive acceptance of the status quo.'

This feeling was highlighted by the new pop culture in Britain. When Sheila Rowbotham moved to Hackney in autumn 1964, 'East London was in the midst of a style revolution. Working-class women of my age still sported elaborate beehive hairdos as they pushed their prams from the housing estate and flats to the small shops on Amhurst Road. But the teenage girls' hair was now straight and they wore the dark-coloured, three-quarter-length leather jackets made in the local East End sweat shops.'

This was the new cohort scrutinised in depth by pop sociology books like *Generation X*. Jane Deverson and Charles Hamblett interviewed a cross-section of young women, including a debutante, a high-class vice girl, a model, a young Christian and 'a nice middle class girl'. They related the anguished tale of an illegal abortion: 'It was agony, as though my whole inside was being ripped out.' A young Soho dancer thought that 'the present generation is going to be all right. There's a lot less hypocrisy these days.'

Generation X captured the new, discrete youth world. Films were still important as fantasy vehicles – 'most teenage girls think of themselves as Samantha Eggar or Julie Christie or young Brigitte Bardot' – but public life was acted out in terms of mod clothes, blue beat music, Soho clubs. Peter Laurie observed the teenagers' emergence as a 'solidly integrated social bloc': 'a fifteen-year-old girl in a Devon village has more in common with her contemporaries on Tyneside, than with her own parents and neighbours'.

The trigger for this generation's youth culture was the success of the Beatles, which in turn had been graphically signalled by the mass public fervour of their young female fans. From late 1963 on, a sophisticated youth media – including magazines, TV and pop songs – propagated fashions and sounds with incredible speed. Reflecting the importance of young women in the youth market, it began to broadcast fresh images and ideas of femininity.

As the co-host of *Ready Steady Go!,* Cathy McGowan was a key icon. When she began appearing on the show, she was in her very early twenties, near enough in age to her viewership to be one of them, yet media-savvy thanks to her experience in the fashion department at *Woman's Own*. Having answered an advert for 'a typical teenager', McGowan's presenting style was fresh and enthusiastic. Compared to her older and squarer colleague, Keith Fordyce, she was amateurish, but totally of the moment.

'Cathy was the face of the 1960s,' remembers Vicki Wickham. 'She was perfect, with the shiny straight hair and fringe, her clothes and fashion. She loved music too and was much more "mainstream" than I was. She was the *perfect* mod, and we had her on telly every week.' Wickham and McGowan didn't necessarily see what they were doing as political; they were just having fun. They were inspired by other women: not by Gloria Steinem or Betty Friedan, but by designers Barbara Hulanicki and Mary Quant.

The feeling was mutual. In her memoir *From A to Biba and Back Again*, Barbara Hulanicki remembered McGowan's impact. 'The lift door opened and this lovely leggy creature stepped out. She had long straight luminous hair with a fringe that hid her eyes. Her clothes were simple but immaculate. I thought it must be Miss McGowan's secretary. I was twenty-four and she only looked about eighteen. I was amazed how cosmopolitan her style was. Her taste was impeccable for someone so young.'

Hulanicki began designing for the presenter, and the effect on her new boutique, Biba, was immediate. 'With Cathy MacGowan endorsing our clothes by wearing them nearly every week on TV, there was a sort of underground grapevine which was growing daily. As soon as there was a new style the tom-toms would beat out a message throughout the clubs and the offices and the shop would be full again. Every girl could buy a new dress for her evening date.

'The girls aped Cathy's long hair and eye-covering fringe,' she wrote. 'Soon their little white faces were growing heavier with stage make-up, lids weighed down with doll-like thick fake lashes. Their matchstick legs were encased in pale tights and low-cut patent pumps. Miniskirts led to the adoption of tights. They seldom needed to wear roll-ons or bras. Their bosoms and tummies were so tiny there was no need for the heavy upholstery.'

Biba had begun with an idea born out of rebellion. Hulanicki wanted to break the straitjacket of women's clothing. Having been called 'heavy boned' by her mother, she wanted to make 'skinny looking clothes' for herself. 'I wanted clothes cut with armholes so high up the body that your torso looked long and skinny.' This fitted the needs and aspirations of her young clientele. 'In the buoyant mid-sixties they all had jobs and were not used to eating massive meals.'

This was the generation who had grown up with rationing, 'the

157

postwar babies who had been deprived of nourishing protein in childhood and grew up into beautiful skinny people. A designer's dream. It didn't take much for them to look outstanding. The simpler the better, the shorter the better. Their legs seemed to be never-ending. Suddenly London was filled with long-legged girls and boys.'

Another important transmission route for clothes was young women's magazines – a huge market. In the mid-sixties, there were several well-established romance weeklies, magazines that ran illustrated stories about love and romance with pin-ups of pop stars and adverts for clothes and cosmetics. Titles like *Boyfriend*, *Marilyn*, *Valentine*, *Roxy* and *Mirabelle* all shifted around half a million copies every week, while *Fabulous*, which relied on a heavier colour pop content, sold nearly a million.

Monthlies like *Honey* and *Rave* were aimed at a slightly older age group. Issues of both magazines during 1966 reflected the changes in young women's roles and expectations. *Honey*'s February issue contained adverts for 'Modern Wedding Etiquette' – and even a feature that enshrined the 'Bride of the Month' – but at the same time there were appeals to join the Women's Royal Air Force ('Let yourself GO GO GO') and a long feature about 'jobs for the girls' that announced, 'Anyone Can Do Anything Anywhere'.

Rave was aimed at both sexes, with adverts for cosmetics and guitars as well as for records and bras. Among the pop gossip and record reviews were women's style pages that, by spring 1966, were proclaiming 'Fashions for the Jet Set', with young models posing by BEA aircraft and wearing two-piece 'go-anywhere' suits by Biba, among others. It also included a regular, serious feature under the rubric of 'This Is Your Life', which covered topics like 'Drugs: Yes or No?' and 'When a Girl Gets Into Trouble'.

The single most vexed question in this booming economy was the one that bore down hardest on women: sex and its consequences. As far as adults were concerned, the new cultural openness seemed to confirm all their worst fears. The popular image of the giddy sex-crazed teenager wasn't borne out by the facts: a 1965 survey,

'Sexual Behaviour of Young People', revealed that of their UK sample only a third of boys between seventeen and nineteen and a sixth of girls in the same age group had ever had sex.

But sex was an explosive issue. Peter Laurie thought that 'the present unsatisfactory state of affairs is due perhaps to the collision or overlapping of two contradictory ideas of sexual morality'. In *Generation X*, a 'middle class girl' talked about how she was torn between her mother and her friends. While her mother had told her 'never to give in to a boy because he won't respect you', among her peers there was a 'mystique' about sex. 'You feel you're missing something and you're not a real woman until you've slept with a boy.'

There was a sense of flux, and one obvious sign could be found in mod androgyny. 'Both sexes looked identical,' Richard Mabey noticed. 'At times this amounted to near transvestism. Mod girls had always been inclined to masculinity in their fashions, and not only did they copy the boys' clothes and crop their hair short, but the whole pattern of their mannerisms and behaviour seemed to be an elaborate structure designed to disguise their femininity.'

Some observers, including Laurie, thought that the balance was beginning to tip away from traditional male privilege, 'from a gross inequality of the sexes which prescribed a double standard of morality for men, complete chastity for women'. The old system of sexual morality appeared to be obsolete – although a careful look at the lyrics of the androgynous Rolling Stones might have given pause for thought – but even so, Barbara Hulanicki felt concerned about the young women who flocked to her shop. 'We worried about the girls and their fast life,' she wrote. She watched the ebb and flow of their relationships closely, the way that they navigated the treacherous rapids between directness, freedom and loneliness. 'I don't think our girls were promiscuous; they picked and chose. If they fancied someone they went right out and got what they wanted instead of weaving webs and hypocritical traps, as we had to in the fifties. In their flats and bedsits they had no mother waiting for them to see if they came home in a crumpled dress.'

The L-Shaped Room was based on a social fact: in the early to mid-sixties, it was possible to rent cheaply rooms or flats in the capital. London was still scarred by bomb damage, insanitary housing and a general air of greyness against which the multicoloured, vital appearance of the young appeared in even greater relief. This was the backdrop against which the clash of generations was played out, with many young women having to work out the answers for themselves.

In May 1966, *Rave*'s problem-page dilemma was 'Leaving Home?', in which a girl of seventeen has to decide whether or not to leave her home town for the capital. Her friend talks about 'going to parties every night and eating in sleazy coffee bars full of beatniks and sharing a flat so you can stay out all night. But strangely, you hesitate. Is there something holding you back beyond the magic idea of freedom?' What did the magazine and its star experts advise?

The answers were realistic and sensible. Both Ian McLagan (the Small Faces) and Wendy Varnals (*A Whole Scene Going*) advised against leaving home: 'It doesn't all happen in London, it happens where you want to make it happen'; 'London swallows you up. It is madness to come here without a job and a home.' 'There would be long, dull, lonely evenings in a dingy bedsitter,' *Rave* warned. 'There are a lot of lonely girls in London, still-on-the-outside-looking-in.'

Guidance had always been an important part of young women's magazines, expressed in 'how to' stories, problem pages and etiquette manuals. The advice given depended on the nature of the publication and the age of the intended readership. Many young women, like the writer Janice Winship (who in 1987 would publish the standard text on the topic, *Inside Women's Magazines*), began with the romance magazines and worked up to more sophisticated products like *Rave*, *Honey* or *Nova*, which was launched in 1965 as 'the new magazine for a new kind of woman'.

A major function of these magazines was to make women buy things. In her 1964 memoir *Millions Made My Story*, Mary Grieve, the long-standing editor of *Woman's World*, wrote that 'an immense amount of a woman's personality is engaged in her function as a selector of goods, and in this she endures many anxieties, many fears. Success in this function is as cheering and vitalising to her as it is to a man in his chosen career, failure as humiliating.'

In 1966, Grieve edited *Fifteen*, 'a book for girls who want to do something positive to help themselves into that magical but disconcerting world of grown-ups'. The large-format annual recognised that 'young people today seem confident – even over-confident: ready to carve their own world and discard much that their elders value'. Aimed at younger teens, the book covered all aspects of young life: clothes, parents, money, party planning, hair and skin care. Featuring a young Pattie Boyd on the cover, *Fifteen* talked a lot of sense: one piece, called 'Odd One Out', warned against stigmatisation and bullying. The format followed a pattern: a short article presenting a problem or dilemma, a picture-strip dramatisation, a discussion group and then a quiz. There was nothing about boys or sex. There is an acknowledgement that 'Independence is coming . . .' but nothing about jobs or careers.

The *Boyfriend Book 1966* was an obviously more commercial product, with 'sizzling colour portraits' of pop stars (Elvis, the Rolling Stones, Manfred Mann), 'moving text stories' and 'romantic picture strips'. Articles about astrology, hair and make-up vied with advice on how to deal with the boy who is a 'wolf'. One feature, 'Can You Be a Star and Human Too?', directly addressed the nature of fame, talking to 'three girls on the crest of show-business, turning to look back at the things show-business has taken away'. Dusty, Cilla and Sandie, the copy asked, were they all 'really happy? Don't they miss the old days when they could just walk down a street without an awareness that people are staring at them?' Cilla and Sandie missed their parents and 'Mum's home cooking', while Dusty paid a different kind of price for her success: 'Even shopping, which I love doing, I can't be bothered with because there are always people staring – I don't mind them so much, it's just that they make me nervous.'

The female mystique still held sway in much of the mid-sixties pop media. Young men were not asked whether they missed their mums, nor about their secret sorrows. They were asked about their music, their fights, their ideas about the world. A woman's place was still, largely, in the private sphere. Whether plucked out of obscurity by a chance encounter or having determined from a young age to be a professional musician, the female stars of the mid-1960s contradicted this idea simply by their actions. They were all, in one way or another, pioneers. In 1966, women still did not have the same advantages as men, but this entrenched privilege was now under attack. From being consumers they became producers – out there, in the wider world.

* * *

'Our own personal top girls choice for 1966 are Dusty, Cilla and Brenda Lee. They were the ones to bring the girls back on the pop scene, crashing through all male barriers.'
'PICK OF THE POPSIES: OUR STAR CHOICES FOR 1966',
Boyfriend Book 1966

Nevertheless, women faced a quandary. The Beatles had tilted the balance even more towards male performers. Just as their masculine counterparts from the previous era – the solo singers, the Bobbies and the Frankies – had had to adjust, so female performers were forced to develop their own strategies to deal with the beat groups. This was compounded by the fact that young women formed the audience for these almost exclusively male musicians, and were not automatically expected to transfer their affections to their own gender.

In the years immediately before the beat boom, the girl group style had dominated the American charts. After the Shirelles hit #1 with 'Will You Still Love Me Tomorrow' in early 1961, a stream of female groups followed them into the charts. At their best – the Shirelles' 'Boys', the Chiffons' 'He's So Fine' and 'My Boyfriend's Back' by the Angels – they were the top records of their era: sharp, danceable, well-observed expressions of youth and vitality.

The biggest British female star of the early 1960s was Helen Shapiro, who was fourteen when she had a hit with 'Don't Treat Me Like a Child', a declaration of independence backed up by her soulful voice. Yet her recordings were controlled by producer Norrie Paramor, who swamped the chart-topping 'Walkin' Back to Happiness' with a fussy arrangement that featured chirruping female singers and saccharine strings. Despite touring with the Beatles in early 1963, Shapiro didn't survive the chart onslaught of Merseybeat.

The new era demanded a new kind of female star, one that broke with the old showbiz type, women who could be seen as representatives of the female audience itself. The truth was rather more complicated. Cilla Black came up with the first Merseybeat wave: her first record was a Lennon/McCartney cast-off, 'Love of the Loved', and she was managed by Brian Epstein. Accentuating a certain gawky charm, she had been performing on and off for three years before her first hit.

Black usually covered American material. Her first #1 was 'Anyone Who Had a Heart', a huge US hit by prime Burt Bacharach/ Hal David interpreter Dionne Warwick. Although she had a tendency to bellow like a foghorn during a song's climax, Cilla released several fine singles, including an early cover of Randy Newman's 'I've Been Wrong Before' and, in early 1966, the melodramatic yet highly effective 'Love's Just a Broken Heart'.

Sandie Shaw was even more one of the audience, a Biba girl stepping out from the street onto the stage. She was seventeen when she had her first #1, 'There's Always Something There to Remind Me', another Bacharach/David cover. Ably guided by Adam Faith's manager Eve Taylor, she enjoyed a sequence of big hits throughout 1964/5: 'Message Understood', 'I'll Stop at Nothing' and her second #1, 'Long Live Love'.

Less declamatory than Cilla Black, she tended to understate in her vocal and onstage performance – a highly effective tactic. Her finest moment, 'Girl Don't Come', was an unusual twist on teen romance, with the girl doing the standing up, not the boy. Shaw performed it on *Ready Steady Go!*: with her Mary Quant fringe, long slim dress and her signature bare feet she radiated a new kind of femininity, one that was cool, calm, collected and in control of her image and emotions.

Her second single of 1966 accentuated this idea of control. Released in mid-May, 'Nothing Comes Easy' was the bitter tale of a female stalker: 'Each place he'd go, there I'd be / I made each move so carefully.' Women weren't supposed to admit to that sort of thing, and Shaw ran the gamut from irritation to desperation when she snared her man, only to find the tables turned: 'Now he won't leave me alone / He follows me each place I go.'

Marianne Faithfull was elevated by accident. Discovered at a party by Andrew Loog Oldham, she was the perfect fit for his ambitions to become both a manager and a producer, an unholy mix of Brian Epstein and Phil Spector. Selected purely for her looks, Faithfull was given one of the first songs written by Mick Jagger and Keith Richards, 'As Tears Go By', which was a Top 10 hit for her in early autumn 1964. The life of a pop star beckoned.

Within the context of the time, Faithfull was seen as a bit posh, even if her upbringing, which involved divorce and genteel poverty, had been difficult. Her first hit set the style, as did her static performances: angelic, almost virginal, with a deep husky voice. She was presented, as she remembers in her autobiography *Faithfull*, 'as an eerie fusion of haughty aristocrat and folky bohemian child-woman. It was a tantalising ready-made fantasy. Unfortunately it wasn't me.'

Unlike her contemporaries, Faithfull had almost no singing experience. She was only seventeen when she had her first hit, and she struggled to reconcile leaving home, marriage and the vagaries of her 'Mad Hatter' manager. Faithfull felt cast to the wolves. Like Norma Tanega, she was plunged into the male-dominated life of a sixties package tour. 'I was thrown into this freakish half-life. The tours were brutal and there seemed to be no end to them . . . The loneliness of life on the road was awful.'

In America, similar conditions pertained after the Beatles' take-over in early 1964. The girl group sound slowly passed from the charts but was developed, for a couple of years at least, by the Shangri-Las. Signed to Red Bird Records in 1964 as teenagers, guided and shaped by the producer and Brill Building habitué George 'Shadow' Morton, they had five Top 30 hits, including the #1 'Leader of the Pack'. During 1964 and 1965, they became the leading white female group in the US.

Morton regarded the group as a blank canvas onto which he could project his ideas about drama and sound. He produced the Shangri-Las' singles using all manner of tricks, adding effects like the beach ambience of surf and seagulls to 'Remember (Walkin' in the Sand)' or a revving motorcycle to 'Leader of the Pack'. Most of the songs featured recitation by lead singer Mary Weiss or a sassy back and forwards exchange between the Ganser twins, Marguerite and Mary Ann, that caught the idioms of New York teen speak.

These were 45 rpm pop symphonies, hormone-enhanced slices of melodrama that were method-acted out on stage. The Searchers' Chris Curtis saw the Shangri-Las in their pomp and commented on their 'weird presentation': 'The lead singer stands right over on one side of the stage while the other three stand in the middle. When they sing "remember" she sings "walkin' in the sand", then turns her head away and looks away despondently. They wave their arms around and do all sorts of weird actions.'

Morton might have been their Svengali, but he allowed the group the freedom to be who they were: real teens from deep sub-urbia – Cambria Heights in Queens – who had been thrust onstage and given a chance to act out the highs and lows of adolescence. 'You can find kids like them under the el in Rockaway, under the lamppost on Broadway,' wrote the founding rock critic Richard Goldstein at the time. 'On street corners anywhere and everywhere in New York. Their look and sound are the city'.

Their songwriter, Ellie Greenwich, remembered them as 'street-classy'. 'They were kind of crude. Having to deal with them on a daily basis used to get me very uptight. We had a really big blow-out

in the ladies room of the Brill Building one night. We were screaming and yelling and ranting and raving. I cried and it was horrible.
But after that it was wonderful. They were on time, they wouldn't
chew the gum so much and they controlled their language to a reasonable level. They were tough girls, they really, really were.'

In the early 1960s, songs by female artists tended to be about
boys and affairs of the heart. In this climate the Angels' vengeful 'My Boyfriend's Back' and Lesley Gore's declaration of independence 'You Don't Own Me' were shocking declarations. The
Shangri-Las pushed these themes into more realistic scenarios. 'I
Can Never Go Home Anymore', for instance, spoke of a daughter's
regret that, after she left home in a temper, her mother died without
her ever managing to apologise. It ended on a downbeat 'and that's
called . . . sad'.

The group's songs took the listener into a teen world of doomed
romance, street survival and serious parental problems. Goldstein
observed how 'there is something eternal about the Shangri-Las,
something mythic. Talk about the suffering teenager. Their her-
oines are the victims of high parental tragedy. But they remain
loyal and passionate. They persevere. The kids in these songs have
never heard of the Cool Generation. They are actively, hopelessly
involved.'

'We try to stay real close to our audience,' lead singer Mary
Weiss told him. 'Most kids have a hang-up with their parents, and
a lot of girls want to be the centre of attention the way the girl in
"Leader of the Pack" is. These are the kids that listen to us.' 'They
may buy the Supremes,' her colleague Mary Ann Ganser added,
'but they listen to us. Because the Supremes come on very feminine
and chic, but we come on like the average girl, who just isn't slinky
and sexy.'

In May 1966, the Shangri-Las released their final single on Red
Bird. Set to the strains of Beethoven's 'Moonlight Sonata', 'Past,
Present and Future' is a bleak examination of the long-term damage done by a disastrous love affair. The piano-led melody moves
up and down the scales and goes precisely nowhere, just as the

narrator is stuck in psychological shut-down. 'At the moment it doesn't look good,' Mary Weiss sings, 'at the moment it will never happen again.'

The Shangri-Las were so preternaturally tuned into teenage angst that their records – particularly 'Past, Present and Future' and their previous 1966 single, 'He Cried' – cut very deep. Their songs were heightened for effect but they held an emotional truth. 'Our lines are realistic and frank,' Mary Ann Ganser told Richard Goldstein while discussing 'Past, Present and Future'. 'Take our latest single. The girl who's talking in it has one tragic affair, right, and she is obviously hung up on it. Well, we don't put her down for it.'

Much of the slack created by the demise of the girl groups had been taken up by the Tamla/Motown artists. Berry Gordy had a roster of powerful female vocalists and groups in the mid-sixties: Gladys Knight and the Pips, the Marvellettes, the Velvelettes, Brenda Holloway, and Martha and the Vandellas, whose tough, soaring, surging 1963–5 Top 10 hits – 'Heat Wave', 'Quicksand', 'Dancing in the Street', 'Nowhere to Run' – remain without peer. But the biggest of them all – and the most successful American pop group of the period – were the Supremes. By May 1966, they had racked up eight Top 20 hits, including six #1s, in just under two years – an astonishing achievement. Their latest record was 'Love Is Like an Itching in My Heart', a fairly straightforward lyrical riff on the idea of a 'love bug' set to the usual compulsively propulsive Motown template. By mid-month, it was in the Top 20.

The Supremes had worked hard to get there. Formed as the Primettes in 1959, they were three friends from the Brewster-Douglass housing project in Detroit: Diana Ross, Mary Wilson and Florence Ballard. They were all self-motivated teens, working in department stores and taking professional courses. Having set their sights on a recording contract at Motown Records, they haunted the lobby of the label's West Grand Boulevard building until Berry Gordy succumbed to the pressure.

Renamed the Supremes, the group recorded seven singles in just over three years. Nothing clicked, and they became known as the 'no-hit Supremes'. However, their first collaboration with the writers Eddie Holland, Lamont Dozier and Brian Holland, 'When the Lovelight Starts Shining Through His Eyes', was a Top 30 hit in late 1963, but it wasn't until their eighth record, 'Where Did Our Love Go?', that they finally broke through, taking it to #1 in the US and #3 in the UK.

Motown had already tasted significant pop success with the Miracles, the Marvelettes and Mary Wells, but Gordy saw something more malleable in the Supremes: they would be the Trojan Horse for Motown's assimilation into the white mainstream. The team was there: the musicians, the Funk Brothers; the writers, Holland–Dozier–Holland; and now the group. The Supremes would become a hit machine, and 'Where Did Our Love Go?' was the template.

It begins with a break, just handclaps and footsteps, cut loud and high, before the bass comes in with Diana Ross's first line: 'Baby, baby, baby don't leave me.' The backing track had already been cut for the Marvelettes, who rejected it, so Ross had to work in a lower register than usual. The result is a totally individual sound, as her voice cuts through the percussion with a seductive catch that gives weight to the lyrical pleas.

While the production retains the space of Mary Wells's summer #1, 'My Guy', the effect is bluesier – a deceptive toughness that belies the apparently submissive lyrics. Berry Gordy called Eddie Holland a 'psychological writer': he told the lyricist that 'you write things that gnaw on people's emotions'. For the next three years or so, almost all the Holland–Dozier–Holland songs for the Supremes would feature female-oriented playlets on the ins and outs of love.

'Now that I've surrendered, so helplessly,' Ross sings on 'Where Did Our Love Go?', and the listener has entered a world of emotional power plays. Each verse has the pleasure/pain duality: 'You came into my life, so tenderly / With a burning love, that stings like a bee.' This was not the feisty backchat of the girl groups, but a complex, passive/aggressive stance further explored on songs like

'Stop! In the Name of Love' and 'Nothing but Heartaches'.

The music worked against the lyrics. Diana Ross sang of waiting by the telephone, looking at 'these four walls', of crying in her sleep. Love is presented as an addiction, an illness or a deep yearning that can only be fulfilled by a man, however unfaithful he may be. In this, Holland–Dozier–Holland were writing for their audience, who were described by Eddie Holland as 'mostly females': 'I felt that females in that teenage group were always in love with some guy or someone in the neighbourhood. It's just a common feeling, girls having crushes.'

Ross's voice wasn't as gospel as Martha Reeves or Gladys Knight, but her high, keening style perfectly suited the material. As Eddie Holland remembered, 'I felt that teenage girls go through this romanticising of relationships more than males at that time, and it was just fortunate that Diana's voice could sell it. It was a combination of the rhythm, the music, the tone of the vocals of the Supremes. I looked upon them as capturing a mood, a feeling that expressed an emotional situation.'

But the music was sensational – tough, upbeat, sophisticated: the vibes in 'Stop! In the Name of Love', the insistent bass and exploding drums at the beginning of their first hit of 1966, 'My World Is Empty Without You'. The group was filmed recording the song in the Motown studio for a major ABC special, *Anatomy of Pop: The Music Explosion*: the Supremes are smart, styled and totally poised in their wigs, slacks and matching ribbed sweaters and houndstooth coats.

By then they were at the top of their game: regulars on the *Ed Sullivan Show*, opening for a second season at the upscale Copacabana Club in New York, cover stars of *Ebony* and *Time*. Self-improvement had been the Supremes' motto, and in this they were assisted in every single way by Motown's Artist Development department, which was modelled on the 'charm schools' of the Hollywood studios. They were chaperoned until 1965, when they turned twenty-one.

Wilson remembered how 'Mrs. Maxine Powell was in charge of

etiquette and grooming. She spoke and carried herself very properly. "Young ladies always . . ." was the stock opening for Mrs. Powell's directions. Hats and gloves were mandatory attire for the girls around Motown, and she often lectured us about clothes. Since Flo, Diane, and I had already devoted years to creating our own unique and sophisticated style, we quickly became Mrs. Powell's star pupils.'

With tailor-made songs, the finest back-up musicians, chaperones and dance steps worked out in detail with the experienced dancer and choreographer Cholly Atkins, the Supremes were totally styled. Wigs, false eyelashes and a huge array of stage costumes all went into constructing a 'sexy but wholesome' image. 'Contrary to what some people think it wasn't foisted upon us,' Wilson remembered. 'We really were those girls.'

Compared to the West Coast beatnik look sported in early 1966 by Cher and the Mamas and the Papas, however, the Supremes definitely looked showbiz. Integration with the white media establishment was part of Berry Gordy's goal, but occasionally all the hair and cosmetics piled up into a construction of femininity that just looked bizarre, if not camp – not too far away from the drag queens of the Jewel Box Revue that the Supremes followed onstage one 1964 night in Philadelphia.

This was in contrast to the new rock bohemianism. When the Supremes finally met the Beatles in August 1965, it was an awkward affair. 'We wore smart, elegant day dresses, hats, gloves, high heels and jewellery, as well as fur jackets – Flo in chinchilla, me in red fox, and Diane in mink.' When they got into the Beatles' suite, 'perfectly poised', Wilson noticed 'that the room reeked of marijuana smoke, but we kept smiling through our introductions'.

Neither party could believe their eyes. 'It was difficult to be gracious and friendly in the face of what we could only see as the coolest reception we'd ever received. Every once in a while Paul, George, or Ringo would ask us about the Motown sound, or working with Holland–Dozier–Holland, then there would be silence again. Someone might crack a little joke, but we never knew what they were laughing about. John Lennon just sat in the corner and stared. After a few moments, we wanted out.'

The pull of show business was much stronger for female artists. Aligning with more traditional industry mores offered a chance of integration and another, more lucrative career path in night-clubs and cabaret work. The Supremes weren't forced into doing the Copacabana; it was a mark of pride. Even so, there was a gap between their records and their image. Singles like 'My World Is Empty Without You' might have pointed forward, but their stage presentation sometimes harked back to the early 1960s.

In May 1966, the Supremes were profiled in *Look* magazine, with a cover strap and five pages of pictures and text. The introduction cited their extraordinary run of #1 hits and quoted Berry Gordy on the genesis of the Motown sound: 'We thought of the neighbour-hoods we were raised in and came up with a six word definition: "Rats, roaches, struggle, talent, guts, love."' Even so, some of the answers echoed the reality of being a woman in the music industry. 'It's pretty hard for a woman to be an entertainer,' Florence Ballard said. 'It's murder for a woman – the work, the rehearsing, the buses and planes, the interviews, the questions, always walking in heels. Her stomach aches, her back aches, but I still love it, because what else would I be doing, not married?' Mary Wilson also talked about the downside: 'What we have now is what other girls want to have, fame and money. But we don't have fellas. I guess there's time for that stuff later, when it slows down. But I'm so tired.'

In contrast, Diana Ross was a scorch of anger and pride: 'We've had six number-one hits in a row, but we're still treated like some ordinary rock 'n' roll group. On TV shows like Ed Sullivan's, we're pushed on and off the stage fast, as if we were nothin', and there are the Supremes, cryin' behind the wings . . . I see all these phonies who never even had one number-one hit runnin' around actin' like big stars. I've got something they don't have, and the kids know it.'

The biggest female stars of the mid-sixties would probably have made it in any period, but their particular struggles were sympto-matic of the time. Like the Supremes, Dusty Springfield had been performing for several years before true fame struck; she also had strong show-business affiliations at the same time as she broke new ground with the intensity and depth of her music. Like the Supremes, she turned these tensions into a sequence of outstanding hit records.

Born in 1939, Dusty was brought up in Ealing, west London. After a job at her local department store Bentalls, she began performing in 1958 with the Lana Sisters. In 1960, she formed the Springfields with her brother Tom and Mike Field, performing a mix of folk, country and world music. 'We got TV exposure very quickly,' she told me in 1989, 'and we discovered that if you sang loud and fast everybody was impressed. We were terribly cheerful. It was extremely important to be cheerful.'

A BBC TV clip still exists of the Springfields mugging through a version of the Zulu song 'Wimoweh'. They are better heard on 1962 singles like 'Island of Dreams' and 'Silver Threads and Golden Needles', which contain a quality of yearning unusual in British pop at the time. When the latter was a surprise American Top 20 hit, in early 1963 the group flew to Nashville to record, and Dusty found the country and the music of her dreams. 'It was love at first sight. I remember this quite clearly, because you always remember the First Time. I was sitting in the Capitol Motel in Nashville when I heard "Don't Make Me Over" by Dionne Warwick. I actually sat down very hard because it was different to anything I had heard before. The other record was "Tell Him" by the Exciters, which I heard in New York. The pure power of "Tell Him" was more important because I could approximate the voices. I wanted that crispness, the ballsiness in the voice, which we hadn't had in England.'

Soon after that US trip, the Springfields broke up – 'We were all smart enough to see what was coming. That was the Beatles. We'd seen them play at the Cavern' – and Dusty had the chance to put her ideas into practice. 'I was going for the Phil Spector sound,' she said of her first single, a smash hit in the Beatles winter of 1963. 'I Only Want to Be with You' captured all the giddy excitement of first-time infatuation, with a strong vocal that soared above the studio orchestra.

It launched Dusty as the first of the new generation of female singers. Her friend Vicki Wickham was the editor of *Ready Steady Go!*, so Dusty was regularly featured on the programme, acting as commère, swapping barbs with the Beatles, miming with Gene Pitney to a sped-up version of '24 Hours from Tulsa' and singing 'I Only Want to Be with You', as well as her cover of Arthur Alexander's 'Every Day I Have to Cry Some'. She was a part of the new London.

As Wickham and Penny Valentine observed in their authorised biography, Dusty had 'The Look'. It was constructed from a variety of parts, principally the eyes, which were surrounded in thick, black 'panda' eyeliner to counter what she saw as the heaviness of her face. Along with the dramatic make-up worn by Juliette Gréco, she admired sophisticated Continental stars like Monica Vitti and Catherine Deneuve, whose 'black velvet bow, catching her smooth blonde hair, was a look copied directly by Dusty'.

In all, Dusty was a complex, fascinating figure, oscillating between confidence and deep shyness, sharp wit and total commitment to her singing. While her appearance was as solidly armoured as the Supremes', her spirit was constantly mobile, the fluttering of her hands giving away the tensions and the driven ambition beneath the surface. 'I want to sing songs that are real, human, with deep emotional appeal,' she told an American interviewer in 1964, 'this is my hard fight.'

Despite her drive for success and musical perfection, Dusty found fame perplexing at first. 'I was very sheltered,' she remembered, 'and suddenly we were taken out to these little clubs off Sloane Street, and I didn't know what the people I was with were talking about, and I didn't know about the food they were serving. I was raised on meat and potatoes. So I developed this front so they wouldn't know. Because if they knew the real me, they wouldn't like me.'

Indeed, the artificiality of her appearance – the hair, the sequinned clothes and the panda eyes – was a kind of mask. 'It was a good thing to hide behind. Without the face I was a quivering wreck. I was terribly shy. So the more eyes I put on, the less shy I had to feel. And once you put that eye make-up on, it was such a hell getting it off that you would just leave it on. And put more on top of it, for three weeks at a time. By that time it was really solid.'

Unlike many female singers, Dusty was determined to take control of her career. Her manager, Vic Billings, was an adviser and guide rather than a Svengali. His cautious, long-term approach bore dividends. He let Dusty focus on the music, while building her up as an international performer: during the next two years, she would visit South Africa, Australia and America, where she had a Top 10 hit in summer 1964 with her cover of 'Wishin' and Hopin''.

From the beginning, Dusty presented herself as a musician. The November 1963 *Melody Maker* cover that announced the success of 'I Only Want to Be with You' ran a photo of her in the studio with a guitar, looking as though she meant business. She was also pictured in another magazine playing the drums. This was at a time when female musicians in pop groups were unusual. The Honeycombs would make great play of their drummer, Honey Lantree, almost as a gimmick.

On her records, Dusty worked closely with her producer at Philips, Johnny Franz. He dealt with the music, she dealt with the vocal arrangements. This unusual level of involvement raised hackles. 'There was a lot of angst concerned because it wasn't easy to get those sounds onto four-track,' Dusty recalled. 'I was breaking a lot of new ground and asking musicians to play things they had never heard before because I had been to the States and they hadn't. So I scowled a lot. I got a reputation as a great scowler.'

Neither a dolly bird nor a teenage mod, Dusty prevailed through the quality of her records, which built up into a long-running narrative informed by emotional, if not tragic scenarios like 'I Just Don't Know What to Do with Myself', 'My Colouring Book' or 'Losing You'. As is often the case with charismatic performers, Dusty's material appeared to run in parallel with her life – acting almost as a real-life soap opera – and during 1964 and 1965, triumph was matched with controversy and collapse.

Dusty began by singing a mixture of R&B, Motown, showbiz ballads and girl group records like Lesley Gore's 'You Don't Own Me'. In 1964, she focused on songs by Burt Bacharach and Hal David. Her first cover was of 'Wishin' and Hopin'' – a Dionne Warwick flipside in early 1963. Both Cilla Black and Sandie Shaw had hits with covers of Warwick-sung Bacharach–David songs that year, so Dusty decided to get ahead of the game by visiting the writers themselves in New York.

She came away with her first masterpiece, 'I Just Don't Know What to Do with Myself'. First recorded by Tommy Hunt in 1962, the song was a controlled soul ballad of loss and desperation, with a declamatory bridge. Dusty's version was pitched higher. The arrangement is all ebb and swell, building through the second verse to the climactic bridge. It ended with a restatement of the third verse, at the end of which Dusty let rip on the fade-out. This was almost like method-acting, and it came at a cost.

Dusty had already fallen ill with laryngitis in early 1964 – the first of several very public collapses. She had another attack in August, and there was another major collapse in Tulsa a month later, during her first major US tour. 'Suddenly it's all too much,' she told *Woman's Own*. 'The walls start spinning. I can't go on any longer. It's being hungry and stopping in a roadside cafe to eat and having everyone staring at you. "Click" go their eyes to your plate and then back to your mouth.'

The pressure was relentless. 'Girls don't have automatic hits,' Dusty told an interviewer in 1964, 'it's much tougher for them than it is for the boys . . . their follow-ups to previous hits usually walk, or run, straight into the charts.' She felt that a female singer had 'to work a whole lot harder at being an artist. If she doesn't push her latest record – supporting it with as many live performances as possible on TV and radio – she has very little chance of getting a hit.'

Her life was becoming like the switchback changes of mood and pace in a Bacharach/David song. She got into trouble later that year during her December visit to South Africa: having insisted in her contract that she would not play to segregated audiences, Dusty was harassed by government agents trying to make her do that very thing. She refused. The tour was cut short, and she was escorted out of the country under armed guard. While she was away, she'd been voted British Female Singer in the *NME* Awards.

Dusty was always promoting black American music. In early autumn 1964, she raved to the *Melody Maker* about playing on a bill with the Supremes, the Temptations, the Shangri-Las, Martha and the Vandellas, the Miracles and Marvin Gaye: 'I'm playing on a bill of artists whom everyone raves about. It is just terrific. Rhythm-and-blues stuff is still very strong, not the kind of R&B they have cottoned on to in England – as far as I'm concerned, that's the wrong kind. Tamla-Motown is R&B as far as I'm concerned.'

She was also plugged into the gay taste of the period. Although Dusty was not at all public about the matter – and could barely be so in the climate of the time, when male homosexuality was still illegal – she was a gay icon. This accorded with her predilections, her friends – there is a fabulous picture of her dancing with Michael Aldred, Polly Perkins and Peppi Borza – and the music that she both liked and played: her albums and Motown singles were very popular in the still subterranean queer clubs.

In compensation, she presented herself as wedded to her career. In the candid series of interviews that she did with *Woman's Own* in 1965, Dusty talked about her upbringing, her time with the Springfields and her difficult reputation. 'Naturally I don't like the idea of people thinking I'm cantankerous, but I can't help it. I hate it when things don't go as well as they should. That's why I spend hours working on the arrangements for a record, why I snap sometimes when the musicians don't do it exactly the way I see it.'

She was asked about her attitudes to marriage: 'I'm a little afraid of marriage. Maybe it's all tied up with my personal fear of failure.' Male musicians weren't asked these kinds of questions, but then, in 1965, having a wife was still seen as alienating female fans. As she concluded, 'Success, as I've told you, has brought me some wonderful times, but it seems as though you must always pay a high price for it. And perhaps the highest price of all is when it comes to love.'

The pressures of conventional morality bore down heavier on female performers in the mid-1960s. Dusty was typified as a 'bachelor girl': code for someone who did not fulfil woman's highest destiny as it was then interpreted – love and marriage. She was caught between the mores of the time and her own desires. The impossibility of telling the truth about herself conflicted with the emotional authenticity she brought to the material she sang. Nothing quite fitted.

During 1965, she went from success to success, from collapse to cancellations. She had three hits, including two Top 10s – 'In the Middle of Nowhere' and 'Some of Your Lovin''. In July, she was ordered to rest by her doctor and took several weeks off. In December, she won a major award, taking the prize of World's Best Female Singer in the *NME*'s Annual Popularity Poll. This was the first time that a British singer had ever done so, and it made national news, with headlines like 'Dusty Sweeps to the Top of the Pop World'.

In late January 1966, she released 'Little by Little'. Dusty regarded it as a pot-boiler, but it was a great R&B stomper with a skip beat. As it hit the Top 20 in mid-February, she sat down for a revealing interview with *Disc Weekly*'s Penny Valentine, who wrote, 'Dusty Springfield is a warm, intelligent and complex person. More than any other star, there is an aura of mystery about her personality that people apparently find hard to penetrate.'

In March, came Dusty's ninth UK single. 'You Don't Have to Say You Love Me' began as a full-blown Italian ballad. Sung by Pino Donaggio, 'Io Che Non Vivo (Senza Te)' had been premiered at the 1965 San Remo Festival, which is where Dusty, sitting in the audience, heard it first. Moved to tears, she cast around for an English writer, before Vicki Wickham and Simon Napier-Bell wrote what began as a rushed compromise but ended up, almost despite their intentions, as a complex text.

It begins slow, but sure. Befitting a big, melodramatic ballad, the scenario is a classic double bind: 'When I said I needed you / You said you would always stay / It wasn't me who changed but you / And now you've gone away.' What she is pleading for is not love but any kind of contact, any closeness at all. Singing in the stairwell at the Philips studio at Stanhope Place, Dusty gave her voice extra resonance as it really took off during the repeated chorus. The last minute or so is one constant build as she goes up a key, and the track ends on the repeated plea 'Believe me', stretched out and sung at the very top of her register.

Ending in a bleak loneliness, the song could have been kitsch, but Dusty's totally committed performance – she dreaded singing 'You Don't Have to Say You Love Me' live as it strained her voice – gave the song total authenticity. It went to #1 in the UK right at the end of April, just as Dusty played the *NME* Poll Winners Concert: the only woman on the bill, she had a great time romping through three songs with her band, the Echoes, and her backing singers, Lesley Duncan and Madeleine Bell.

This was a career-defining moment. Dusty was now an acknowledged star. 'She is recognised wherever she goes,' wrote Penny Valentine in April, 'people respect her as an artist, she has money and success.' Dusty underplayed the song's melodramatic message – 'It's just a nice, corny old song, when you take away the trappings and the *Ben Hur* sound,' she told the *Daily Express* – but 'You Don't Have to Say You Love Me' cemented her in the public eye as a tragic diva.

While Dusty recorded episodes of her forthcoming BBC series, 'You Don't Have to Say You Love Me' entered the *Billboard* Top 30 in the first week of June 1966. That same week, James Brown was at #4 with 'It's a Man's Man's Man's World'. This was an extraordinary record: from the title, you would expect braggadocio, if not male dominance, but the song was a tortured, sweat-drenched ballad that delivered on the desperation hinted at by the repetition of the male gender in the title.

The same basic phrase had already been explored from the other side of the gender divide by the British pop art painter Pauline

Boty. Dating from 1964 and 1965, *It's a Man's World I* and *It's a Man's World II* examine the implications of that simple statement. Both are striking paintings that exhibit the artist's background in, and love of, collage; both contain complex grids that build up to an image that is both satirical and unsettling.

The first version is high pop. At the top of the painting there is an American B-52 bomber, the epitome of masculine aggression. Beneath this image are pictorial renderings of various heroes – Elvis, Marcel Proust, Lenin, Einstein, Muhammad Ali, the Beatles – but at the bottom centre is the blurred rendering of Abraham Zapruder's 8mm film of the Kennedy assassination, with Jackie comforting the dying president. At the heart is a red rose, Boty's symbol for female potential and sexuality.

The second is more elliptical. In this case, the collaged imagery is collected into a vertical band, either side of which is an idealised painting of a neoclassical landscape. There are ten images of naked women. These are dominated by the figure of a headless women, all legs and sexual parts – the female as object. But the figures around her, draped though they are to please and titillate, have a life and a vigour of their own: you feel that they could have an existence beyond the male gaze.

In her late twenties when she completed these paintings, Pauline Boty had long been saturated in pop art and pop culture. Brought up in an apparently conventional middle-class family – the youngest child – she had to fight to hold her own with her brothers and had a fractious relationship with her 'Victorian' father. Against his wishes, she insisted on going to art school – first Wimbledon, and then the Royal College of Art, where she found her feet.

Boty was determined and sophisticated. She had travelled to America in 1954, a time when very few British people had been to the fountainhead of pop. In the late fifties, she visited Paris several times and assumed the existentialist ideas and look propagated by Juliette Gréco and Simone de Beauvoir. In 1958, she helped to found the Anti-Ugly Action group, designed to protest against the 'fake' new architecture being hastily erected on London's bomb sites.

In 1960, Boty moved into the Notting Hill Gate area, then still a working-class area with a great street market, which would prove a bountiful source of the Victoriana that permeated her early work. She began to find her style in a sequence of striking collages and stained-glass images that mixed found elements – mainly taken from women's magazines, high and low – with almost symbolist depictions of dream imagery, all from a firmly feminine perspective.

During the next couple of years, Boty successfully aligned herself with the upcoming wave of British pop art. Many of her collages were based on pop songs with titles like 'Target for Twisters', 'Goodbye Cruel World' and 'Darn That Dream'. These last two songs – plus Chubby Checker's 'Let's Twist Again' – formed the soundtrack to her most famous appearance: the BBC *Monitor* programme, directed by Ken Russell and transmitted in March 1962, called 'Pop Goes the Easel'.

Featuring four pop artists – Peter Blake, Derek Boshier, Peter Phillips and Boty – the film weaved their source material into their everyday lives. In the opening shots, Boty is seen in her Notting Hill Gate room with her huge wall collages, featuring images of Elvis, Marilyn and nineteenth-century ads. She appears totally at ease in the company of her fellow artists – explaining her work to Blake, twisting with gusto to Chubby Checker at a group party.

But there was another side. Much of Boty's work from this period expressed, as she described it, 'a kind of premonition' where 'you are suspended in time'. In her solo scene, she acted out the part of a victim in a disturbing stress dream, as she is chased by a ruthless force – in this case, a sinister woman in a wheelchair (an uncanny prefiguring of Lotte Lenya's role in *From Russia with Love* the following year). It's quite unlike anything else in the film, and it hints at a deeper anxiety.

Around this time, Boty moved from abstract painting into more figurative pop pieces, usually sourced from photographs. The result was an extraordinary run of images, a secret history of the 1960s. The subjects were wide-ranging, pop culture from a feminine perspective. They included Monica Vitti – the Italian actress who was also Dusty's inspiration – Jean-Paul Belmondo and Marilyn Monroe, who had just died in mysterious circumstances.

1963's *My Colouring Book* was sourced from the 1962 Kitty Kallen song. In the picture, Boty takes you into a private, feminine world: a pristine, chintzy bedroom surrounded by hearts, sunglasses, snatches of the song's lyric and a blurred image of a young woman holding an erased image of her lover. At bottom right, a young man, dressed all in leather, holds the blue mood with an arrogant, uncaring expression.

5–4–3–2–1 was the flipside to this melancholy. Boty was a *Ready Steady Go!* regular – credited as a 'dancer' in the first episode – and the title echoed the programme's future Manfred Mann theme tune. Under a carnivalesque rendering of the numerals, a young woman gazes out from bottom left with an ecstatic grin on her face. To the right is the legend, picked out in pink on a yellow background: 'OH FOR A FU . . .' The last two letters are out of frame.

Her pictures began to move out of the interior landscape of fandom and emotion into a wider, more contested arena. *Scandal 1963* was an ambitious, highly coloured piece that placed the famous Lewis Morley photograph of Christine Keeler centre stage. The artist's depiction makes her look even more threatening and, if possible, more sexual. At the top of the frame are images of the men who sought to shape and manipulate her: Lucky Gordon, Johnny Edgecombe, John Profumo, Stephen Ward.

Boty was highly aware of sexual politics. In the winter of 1963/4, she contributed to a BBC radio programme called *The Public Ear*. She flayed the feminine mystique: 'The golden climax of life, a young girl's dream. Yes, yes, the stories say, marry, marry, marry as soon as you can. Get him and nab him, hook him and grab him.' In another broadcast, she excoriated the traditional, upper-middle-class Englishman: 'Your ideal woman is a kind of faithful adoring slave.'

Nell Dunn made her the star interviewee of *Talking to Women*. Boty was extremely forthright about her sexuality, stating that it was 'really important'. She thought of 'the present. Not much about the future. Well only in terms of sort of like I found myself sort of living my life as though I'd probably only got a few more years to live – because the bomb was going to drop and I found this terribly exciting – not the bomb but living for today . . . I think the threat of it makes you much more aware of now.'

Boty was also highly aware of being seen as a 'dumb blonde'. She told Nell Dunn, 'There are lots of women who are intellectually cleverer than lots of men but it's difficult for lots of men to ever accept this idea and they often feel "Well, anyway, I'm a man and being a man is a lot better than being a woman."' But she also thought 'women are much better off in some way because they haven't been told "You've got to go out and get a job and you've got to be masterful."'

In 1964, she did get married, to the writer and left-wing activist Clive Goodwin. But she was living on borrowed time. During the medical tests for her pregnancy, a malignant lump was discovered. Boty was offered an abortion so that she could have radiation treatment but refused. She decided that the life of her child was more important and died, five months after her daughter's birth, on 1 July 1966 – the week that Dusty Springfield's 'You Don't Have to Say You Love Me' entered the American Top 10.

The two had much in common, despite the singer being much better known. Quite apart from sharing space at *Ready Steady Go!* and inhabiting 'My Colouring Book', both women were pioneers who were as much ahead of their time as they were of it. Despite her success, Dusty still struggled to get respect as a musician and to integrate her public and private lives. Pauline Boty was, in turn, a fascinating pop artist who failed to get any kind of recognition at the time.

In the first few months of 1966, however, London was still swinging, and the capital needed a new It girl. None of the pop singers were quite right: most of the successful ones were the wrong side of twenty and had been around long enough to approach overfamiliarity. No, what was needed was a dolly bird specifically adapted to the demands of the moment, and the way it happened was as though Richard Mabey's fantasy of the 'seventeen-year-old Kathy' and her apotheosis had came to life.

In February 1966, Lesley Hornby was only sixteen. Born and raised in Neasden, north-west London, she had a close relationship with her parents and was happy at home. By 1964, she was already a confirmed mod: she remembered going out for the first time, to the Kingsbury Ritz, wearing 'a grey pin-stripe pinafore dress, down to mid-calf, at a time when normal skirts stopped at the knee. It was A-line with a big V to the waist and crossover straps over a white milky blouse with a big pointed collar.'

Lesley was one of the teenagers whose antennae were totally attuned to the new youth culture. She took her cues from *Ready Steady Go!* and Cathy McGowan, wore her hair long like Jean Shrimpton, parted in the centre, and was inspired by Mary Quant and Barbara Hulanicki, who sated 'the new hunger for clothes that were different, not just cut-down versions of their parents". She wore long plastic macs, chiffon blouses and ankle-length skirts.

By the time she was fourteen, Lesley had a Saturday job in a Bayswater hairdressing salon. With her wages and proximity to central London, 'life was beginning to open up'. As soon as she could, she began to visit Biba every week and managed to get onto *Ready Steady Go!*. 'Oh the excitement! The great hope was the Beatles would be on, but they weren't. I wore a white pleated knee-length skirt and a mustard and grey two-ply jumper and a string of pearls.'

Despite having a place at grammar school, Lesley quit in 1965 at the age of fifteen. Swimming in the world of Swinging London, she was determined to make her own clothes. 'Biba's was the tip of a very big fashion iceberg,' she wrote. 'Boutiques were opening up by the day. Clothes were everything and there was money to be made.' She knew she had to seize the moment: 'Who knew when the youth bubble would burst? If I was to go into business it had to be now.'

A few months previously, Lesley had met the twenty-five-year-old Justin de Villeneuve, who was running a stall in Chelsea antiques market. De Villeneuve did two crucial things: he insisted that the young Lesley begin modelling and gave her the name that would accompany her future fame, Twiggy. For Twigs, as he called her in private, was extremely thin, so much so that, as Hornby remembered, 'At school they'd laughed about what I looked like. I was known as Olive Oyl, because of my stick legs and Mod uniform of Hush Puppies and plastic mac flapping round my ankles.'

In 1965, her bust measured 30½ inches and her hips 32 inches, way under the norm, but this apparent disadvantage would be turned into a unique selling point once the miniskirt came in. 'To wear these skimpy fashions you had to be . . . young and thin.' In February 1966, Twiggy got a modelling contract at *Women's Mirror*. As part of the grooming process, she was sent to a top hairdresser's of the time, Mr Leonard, who agreed to restyle her long hair in a radical new cut.

'It took seven hours,' Hornby remembered. It was a work of art: the sides and back were cut close to the skull, sweeping down from the crown, with a little tail of longer hair at the back, while a vestigial fringe hung down just over the eyebrows, creating a geometric drape. The effect was elfin, timeless and totally original. 'From the moment I got up from the chair . . . my life changed.'

The next day, Barry Lategan took some photographs of the young model, which were seen by the highly influential fashion editor of the *Daily Express*, Deirdre McSharry. Within days, Twiggy was being interviewed and photographed wearing 'a skinny rib polo neck and a pair of bell-bottoms I had made'. It all happened very fast and, on 23 February, McSharry ran the Lategan picture, together with a *Daily Express* shot of the model in her own clothes.

'THIS IS THE FACE OF '66', proclaimed the headline, while McSharry described Twiggy as 'the Cockney Kid with the face to launch a thousand shapes . . . THIS IS THE NAME, Twiggy (yes really) because she is branch slim, bends to every shape in fashion, and has her hair cut like a cap made of leaves. THIS IS THE LOOK that from this moment will launch thousands of clothes, a craze for freckles, dozens of hairpieces, and will cause a sell out in eye pencils.'

The sixteen-year-old 'went from total obscurity to full-time working model in a matter of days', as Twiggy remembered in her autobiography. Shoots for *Honey*, *Petticoat*, *Look*, *Brides* and *Fabulous* were followed by an appearance on *A Whole Scene Going*. In April, she featured in British *Vogue*. In those few months of 1966, Twiggy had shot to the top of the world. 'It was like being in love,' she wrote. 'In front of a camera I seemed to get an extra burst of energy, like the feel of the sun on your face in spring.'

DISC
and MUSIC ECHO 9d
JUNE 11, 1966   USA 25¢

MERSEY UPROAR
after 'Whole Scene' attack
SEE PAGE 6

SANDIE
TV miming no CRIME!
Page 7

MERSEYS
jealous of the Hollies!
Page 6

CILLA
I just can't stop myself GIGGLING!
Page 8

BEATLES: WHAT A CARVE-UP!

FIFTEEN
clothes friends parties parents health make up food money leisure

6 : JUNE

I'll Be Your Mirror: The Velvet Underground
and Warhol's America

'A Pop person is like a vacuum that eats up everything, he's made up from what he's seen. Television has done it. You don't have to read anymore. Books will go out, television will stay. Movies will go out, television will stay. And that's why people are really becoming plastic, they are just fed things and are formed and the people who can give things back are considered very talented.'

ANDY WARHOL, quoted by John L. Wasserman in 'Conjurer's Dream from Pop World', *San Francisco Chronicle*, 23 May 1966

There was a new Pop Girl in spring 1966, but she was no seasoned professional, nor a sample teen elevated into instant fame. She was European, cool, uncommunicative; speaking slowly and existing in her own time. Her every move spoke of her membership of haute bohemia, just as her icy beauty disguised a certain innocence. She was an odd, contradictory presence, but nevertheless she was there, in the media glare, together with her Svengali, Andy Warhol.

On 1 June, Nico travelled to Boston with Ingrid Superstar and Andy Warhol and what the city's WNAC-TV station hailed as 'other glamazons from his underground movie entourage'. They had just returned from a less than successful Exploding Plastic Inevitable tour of the West Coast that had been marked by venue problems and a hostile press. Clearly, Los Angeles and San Francisco were not ready for the latest effusion from the underbelly of New York.

The reviews from San Francisco were hot off the press. 'If this is what we are waiting for, we are going to die of boredom,' wrote the *Chronicle*'s Ralph J. Gleason, who, rather unkindly, called Nico 'the whip girl who looks like Mick Jagger in drag'. Another reviewer observed that 'the audience was at least as interesting as what was happening on stage', and that 'Andy's Girl of the Year', Nico, 'delivered the songs in a monotone'.

Still on the news-stands was the 27 May edition of *Life*, with its front-cover story 'New Madness at the Discotheque'. Subtitled 'Op art, mad rags and a dazzle of changing color controlled by music', the five-page spread led with a picture of the Exploding Plastic Inevitable during their Los Angeles residency at the Trip, with Mary Woronov and Lou Reed onstage, and film of Mo Tucker and Edie Sedgwick projected onto screens behind them.

The new condition of pop was moving towards an op/pop art/ Happenings environment of lights, music, dancers, films. *Life* called it 'total recreation': 'a touring unit, created by Pop Artist Andy Warhol and equipped with movie projectors and musicians, has been playing Los Angeles before moving on to San Francisco. Unexpectedly, the clubs report that liquor is less than in conventional spots, mainly because the pandemonium takes the place of stimulants.'

This was an extraordinary level of media attention, and Nico was at the heart of it. To all intents and purposes, she was the Velvet Underground's front person, the featured singer and the most striking presence. She tackled a 23 May *Chronicle* interview in a double act with Warhol, who 'said that he wasn't bothered by being called a phoney, while Nico said, with a half-smile, that she was in fact a total phoney. "It's my defense," she explained.'

Warhol, Nico and the others went to Boston to record links and introductions to a film season called 'Pop Art Theater' – a grand title for a season of old movies including *Dick Tracy*, *Tarzan the Ape Man*, *White Savage* and *King Kong*. WNAC-TV's press release pushed all the buzzwords, describing its season as going 'Camp with Pop Art Movies for the In Group'. Nico was pictured with Warhol at her most crystalline, captioned as 'Miss Pop-Off of 1966'.

After recording the links, the New Yorkers attended a 'Pop Art–Las Vegas Gambol party for ad agency people, press and clients'. This was 'Pop all the way with four things going on at once from a Discotheque with a Bat Girl in the Cage, dancing, Guessing who's In and Out on three giant rear projection screens, Gambling, Dining and watching the characters just waking around the huge armoury in costume of Batman, Superman, Lil Orphan Annie and many more.'

Nothing could have been more transcendently, transparently of the moment in June 1966.

A fragment of Nico's presentation has survived. It begins with a station announcer: 'Now here she is, Miss Pop Art of 1966, and your hostess for Channel 7's "Pop Art Theater", Nic-o!' A huge swirling 'POP ART' logo fades into Nico's face, as a record plays underneath. 'That tune is called "All Tomorrow's Parties". I'm Nico and I sang it,' she says in her somnambulist style, 'with the Velvet Underground, the new – uh – exciting rock 'n' roll group of tomorrow.'

The Boston visit wasn't just to cement Warhol's status as 'the Peter Pan of the current art scene'. It was also to promote the Velvet Underground, who were preparing the release of their first single. This was not the standard way that pop groups went about things, but then the Velvet Underground occupied a very unusual position, being managed by Warhol and his assistant Paul Morrissey, who knew about art, film and media rather than the specifics of the music industry.

At this point, the Velvet Underground were an adjunct to Warhol's ambitious new art project. Having announced his decision to give up fine art the year before, he had decided to concentrate on film and the coming new form, total environments. 'I'm not doing paintings any more,' he told interviewer Bob Reilly in spring 1966. 'But I think I'll glue together some of the parts of old studies I did and sell them as whole paintings to get the money.'

The Exploding Plastic Inevitable was a synthesis of film, interpretative dancing and drone-based instrumental explorations, a barrage of lights and backdrop films, 'Screen Tests' shot, in close-up, at the Factory, and projected many times life size. 'Andy's movies are the parts of a giant hypnotic machine,' the writer Jim Paltridge observed at the time. 'This machine spins an endless cable of steel sound.'

Deliberately provocative, an assault on the senses, the Warhol multimedia show got an enormous amount of column inches right from the off. Alerted by the publicity, and the existence of a

nine-song recording session held with Norman Dolph, record companies quickly began evaluating the Velvet Underground that early
spring. Some, like Atlantic, were put off by the drug songs, but Tom
Wilson of Verve Records held out for a deal.

Wilson was a big name in 1966. With a background in avant-
garde jazz (Sun Ra and Cecil Taylor), he was hot, with recent hits by
Bob Dylan and Simon & Garfunkel. Having moved over to Verve,
he was overseeing a label revamp, with a new roster that included
the Mothers of Invention, the Animals and the Blues Project. A 21
May *Billboard* article noted his ambition to 'build up an LP operation and establish artists with consistent LP value'.

There are accounts stating that Wilson only signed the Velvet
Underground because he liked Nico. Certainly, the two had met
during Bob Dylan's May 1965 tour of the UK, having been caught
by D. A. Pennebaker's camera when Nico was unsuccessfully trying to hustle Dylan's manager, Albert Grossman. Whatever the
reason, it was a quick deal. Contracts were issued and dated 2 May,
the day before the band's first Californian date.

That month, the Velvet Underground went into TTG Studios
in Hollywood to rework several numbers from the Dolph session. Verve was already thinking about a single, and decided to
go with two of the four Nico songs. After re-recording 'Heroin',
'I'm Waiting for the Man' and 'Venus in Furs', the group double-
tracked the voice on 'All Tomorrow's Parties' and added a new
Nico vocal to 'I'll Be Your Mirror'. The single was ready.

Nobody was out of their minds in preparing these two songs for
release. 'All Tomorrow's Parties' begins with a short guitar intro,
before resolving into a Spectorian sound picture – all booming drum
and foregrounded tambourine – exploded by John Cale's repeated,
droning clusters of piano notes. Nico gives an icy detachment to
Lou Reed's pitiless dissection of party culture: 'And where will she
go, what will she do / When midnight comes around?'

'I'll Be Your Mirror' starts off folk-rock sweet, with two guitars intertwining in counterpoint. Nico's voice is right up front, soft
and lightly accented, slightly shaky on the longer notes. Compared

to many Velvet Underground songs, the production is muted: the only hint of rock 'n' roll is in the short guitar riffs that punctuate the verses. The mood is tender and intimate: 'I'll be your mirror / Reflect what you are / In case you don't know.'

Soon after Nico joined the Velvet Underground – as a featured vocalist, not part of the group – she had a brief affair with Lou Reed. This song celebrates that moment, with Reed's customary sharpness, and alludes to Nico's chronic insecurity with the line 'when the night has seen your mind'. One contemporary account has her lost in her reflection in the mirror, trying to decide whether or not she is beautiful.

There was another song about mirrors in early 1966, by a British group called Pinkerton's Assorted Colours, but the lyric was standard romantic fare. 'I'll Be Your Mirror' was something quite different, cutting deeper than most contemporary pop songs. It takes you right into the intimacies of a love affair – the intertwining of two individual psychologies and the way that two people can fill in each other's weaknesses.

'I'll Be Your Mirror' was written during the very first few months of the Velvet Underground's involvement at the Factory, and it reflected the febrile atmosphere. Warhol was very taken with the song and suggested that, when it was cut as a single, the last phrase should be repeated as a locked groove. Clearly, it was an idea that resonated with him: 'I'll be your mirror / Reflect what you are / In case you don't know.'

Reed and Warhol were fascinated by each other. In the beginning, it was an intense and creative friendship, and it's possible to see 'I'll Be Your Mirror' as a comment on Warhol's extraordinary position in American life during 1966. Certainly, mirrors thread through the Velvet Underground's time at the Factory: the huge mirror ball in the studio; the silver foil with which Billy Name covered the walls; the song itself, played live at the EPI dates.

Mirrors were also an integral part of the EPI's sensory overload. Underground press journalist John Wilcock observed how, at the Dom during April 1966, 'a colored spotlight onstage focused onto the mirror ball that revolved in the ceiling, sending pinpoints of light on predictable circuits around the room'. This revival of the 1920s nightclub/ballroom staple was not just campy fun; it was a reflection of amphetamine's ability to send consciousness shooting off into hundreds of tiny shards.

The mirror is a highly ambiguous and powerful portal. The man-made version is polymorphous: the flat household surface; the fragmented shapes of the mirror ball scattering light like fragments of thought; or the spherical witches' ball, so favoured by M. C. Escher, that warps the veil of everyday consciousness. It has long been used in fine art – by Velázquez, Van Dyck and Magritte, among many others – to suggest other worlds, to throw the image back at the viewer. It can be hard and precise, silvery and sibylline. It can reflect the harsh reality of the morning after or offer a window into an alternative reality, life through the looking glass – quite literally, in the case of Jean Cocteau's *Orphée*, where the flat surface dissolves into ripples that allow Jean Marais to pass through to the Other Side. It can offer an affirmation of identity or be the receptacle of human vanity. It can lead the unwitting into madness – the hall of mirrors fleetingly inhabited by Orson Welles in *The Lady from Shanghai*.

The mirror also casts its blank gaze on the Velvet Underground's most notorious song from the period, 'Heroin'. The lyric does not seek to convince, proselytise or condemn; it simply reflects what it is to dice with death. The blank facade of the Velvet Underground as they played – wearing sunglasses to protect themselves against the barrage of lights – was deliberately obtuse. 'I might be dumb, I might be smart, but you'll never know.'

The group were abrasive and provocative, a mirror to their audiences. They quickly evoked a high level of hostility, which they used as fuel. 'The worst that you can say about me – "sick", "trash", "garbage" – I most certainly am. So fuck you.' This emanated in part from the master himself. Jim Paltridge caught this dynamic in an exchange between Warhol and 'Clark Kent':

Clark: Andy, did you ever get a copy of the review in the
Sunday Times?
Andy: Oh, that terrible one?
Clark: I thought you'd like a really terrible review like that.
Andy: Oh, sometimes I do. I think people will come if there is a
really terrible one.

Like the Wizard of Oz, Andy Warhol stood behind a dazzling
array of effects – 'It's all done with mirrors' – but his projections
hooked into the barely expressed desires of the wider society. John
Richmond observed in July 1966 that 'Warhol is an artist in the
purest and simplest manner. He sees the world for what it is: a
nut-hatchery. He records the garish and the tinsel. He satirises
romantic delusion by portraying the instinct as manifested in the
Campbell's Soup label.'

But, unlike the Wizard, Warhol did not claim to be what he was
not. His interviews were gossipy, confrontational or completely
blank. In *Andy Warhol's Index (Book)*, one of the three total art-
works that Warhol would produce from his activity during 1966
– the other two being the December 1966 'Fab' issue of *Aspen* magazine and *The Velvet Underground and Nico* album – the last two
pages contain just the simple, crudely silk-screened word 'blank'.

Behind Warhol's impenetrable facade lurked an outsider's fury.
As a working-class gay man from the deepest Rust Belt, he had an
incredible drive to assimilate – to crash the glamour world of metropolitan society, inherited wealth and artistic fame. Suffering serial
humiliations and setbacks, he played the game until the point, sometime in the early sixties, when he began to achieve his goal. Then, for
a brief period, he rewrote the rules. His underlying rage came out.

From 1964 onwards, the East 47th Street Factory became a mirror image of New York society, and all the more so when Warhol's
retinue was asked to smart parties – a tiny ritual of sadomasochism. Warhol's world worked through magical inversion. What
society regarded as a deficit became a benefit; no became yes. Drag
acts; drug addicts; hustlers; the disturbed, destitute, desperate and

degenerate; the obverse, inverse, reverse and perverse – all could become superstars.

Warhol's high 1960s paintings and silk screens reflected the country's dominant values back at America: sex, death, crime, celebrity, media, money, mass production. Just as the mirror works with psychology, the response to these works changed with the individual gaze. Contemporary critics were divided, if not actively hostile. Were they a put-on? Were they a critique? Were they a wish fulfilment? Or were they just there?

Warhol worked out of intuition and instinct. He was a true receptor and reflector at a crucial time in American history. He worked hard to disclaim all meaning. 'If you want to know all about Andy Warhol,' he told Gretchen Berg in spring 1966, 'just look at the surface of my paintings and films and me, and there I am. There's nothing behind it.' But it was all there. The mirror can tell uncomfortable truths. It can show blemishes, wounds, scars – disfigurement even – to a level that it needs courage to confront.

In 1967, Jean Clay wrote about Warhol in terms of the photographic process. He was 'a sensitive plate' on which America recorded 'its real face'. 'After assimilating all the outward manifestations and mental images of American society, after wallowing in it all, he turns on us and says: "Here, this is YOU. I am just the visible product of this world: my image is YOU." He throws back at us our own brand products, our idols, our habits – but fossilised and isolated so that we see in them a morbidity, a death which we had never expected was there.'

Like the mirror, Warhol was plastic and multiphrenic, deceptively seductive yet icily dispassionate. As he told Gretchen Berg, 'The artificial fascinates me, the bright and shiny.' During 1966, he was in tune with the times – their profound confusion, escalating violence and sheer mediated frenzy – in a way that he never had been before and never would be again. This was his peak. Almost unconsciously, certainly without stated intent, he *became* America.

* * *

'Pop is trying to give people instant psychic distance. It takes whatever things are and turns them around to give them a mirror reflection.'

RICHARD GOLDSTEIN, quoted in 'Before or Beyond the Slick?', *New York*, February 1967

Warhol was an inveterate media scanner. Jim Paltridge's account of the EPI's May 1966 visit to California opens at 'this big Hollywood-Spanish Castle' where the troupe stayed. 'Andy goes into the bedroom and takes a black leather motorcycle jacket and a copy of *Vogue* off the bed. Andy Warhol's bed is very messy. Fashion magazines, *Los Angeles Times*, *Variety*, photographs are under and in it, taking their rightful place in Andy's sleeping and waking hours.'

He was also a life-long hoarder, regularly throwing whatever was to hand – magazines, business letters, all kinds of ephemera – into the box of the moment. On his death, these archive boxes – hundreds and hundreds of them – were handed over to the Andy Warhol Museum in Pittsburgh. Named Time Capsules, they were catalogued and made available for researchers, representing as they do an extraordinary week to week, month to month, year to year diary of materials.

Three boxes in particular covered the year during which Warhol worked most closely with the Velvet Underground: 1966. When I went through them, they were like a complicated puzzle that had just been left where it lay. But a pattern began to emerge. There was, inevitably, a lot of material relating to the VU and the EPI: contracts, typescript interviews with Warhol and dozens of press clippings that ranged from bemused to celebratory to extremely critical.

There were multiple issues of *Time*, *Newsweek* and *Life*, which covered Warhol and the EPI in amongst their standard news fare, a litany of crime, murder, war and cultural confusion. The cumulative effect is of a country moving at breakneck speed into random violence, environmental degradation, materialism and its multiple discontents. In the centre of it all, bathed in the sensory overload of the EPI, stands Andy Warhol in shades, his finger touching his chin.

Warhol had been moving very fast since his arrival as an Artist in spring 1962. His life thus far had been in preparation for this moment. During the next three years, he expanded into sculpture, environmental art and film-making. He became the master of the East 47th St. Factory, an old warehouse that encompassed a variety of functions: the industrial production of silk-screen images, a set for filmed scenarios and, within limits, an open stage.

During this period, his imagery shifted from the deceptively simple reproduction of everyday objects – the Campbell's Soup can, a dollar bill, a Coca-Cola bottle – into repeated images of mass production: not just inanimate objects like Green Shield stamps but human icons – reified demigods like Liz Taylor, Elvis Presley, Jackie Kennedy and Marilyn Monroe. Warhol understood how fame abstracted a person's humanity and rendered them into an industrial process.

At the same time, there was always a darker undertow. Beginning with 1962's *129 Die in Jet (Plane Crash)*, Warhol investigated the media's ghoulish delight in death and disaster. Pictures like *Suicide (Fallen Body)*, *Orange Car Crash Fourteen Times*, *Tunafish Disaster* and *Mustard Race Riot* made multiple copies of horrific images. The whole process was taken to its apogee in the *Disaster* series, which depicted an electric chair in various colour washes.

It was all there, in front of him. In *Popism*, Warhol describes a moment of revelation during a cross-country trip in autumn 1963: 'The farther west we drove, the more Pop everything looked on the highways. Suddenly we all felt like insiders because even though Pop was everywhere – that was the thing about it, most people took it for granted, whereas we were dazzled by it – to us, it was the new Art. Once you "got" Pop, you could never see a sign the same way again. And once you thought Pop, you could never see America the same way again.

'The moment you label something,' he continued, 'you take a step – I mean, you can never go back to seeing it unlabelled. We were seeing the future and we knew it for sure. We saw people walking around in it without knowing it because they were all thinking in the past, in the references of the past. But all you had to do was KNOW you were in the future, and that's what put you there. The mystery was gone, but the amazement was just starting.'

In another respect, Warhol mirrored the speed of the times. The sixties were a period of openness and free experiment in art and music, and those who were able to match the acceleration of life – funded by a booming economy and a burgeoning mass media, peopled by a generation becoming aware of an international youth culture – were able to set the killing pace. The fact that he felt himself beamed into the future gave him enormous momentum.

By 1965, the immigrant boy from Pittsburgh had made it. Warhol was expanding into video and scripted films like *Vinyl* and *Kitchen*. He'd got the glamour and was beginning to shape the culture. He presided over a revolution in style and society. At the April 1965 'Fifty Most Beautiful People Party', Judy Garland, Tennessee Williams and Montgomery Clift were not the true attractions; they were outshone by the new superstar, Edie Sedgwick.

In May 1965, Warhol announced that he was retiring from painting. 'Art just wasn't fun for me any more; it was people who were fascinating and I wanted to spend all my time being around them, listening to them, and making movies of them.' Warhol felt that 'the basic Pop statements had already been made'. He didn't stop painting or making silk-screens – they were a basic money-earner – but his announcement marked a shift in his focus into movies and beyond.

His most famous event of 1965 was an unplanned Happening. In early October, Warhol travelled to Philadelphia for a major retrospective. Curator Sam Green worked on an intense publicity campaign, which included TV coverage and invitations that reproduced a Campbell's Mushroom Soup label. He also sent out six thousand invites for a 400-capacity space. Norman Dolph was hired as DJ, while Green removed most of the art from the walls to ensure its safety.

The blank space was more like a discotheque than an art gallery. It quickly became overcrowded. To the amplified sounds of the Rolling Stones' 'It's All Over Now' and Ian Whitcomb's campy 'You Turn Me On', the crowd of about a thousand people slowly boiled over. Chanting 'We want Andy and Edie', they chased Warhol and Edie Sedgwick up a staircase and cornered them against a closed-off ceiling, which had to be prised open to assist their escape.

Warhol was both terrified and thrilled. He had become a rock star. 'I'd seen kids scream over Elvis and the Beatles and the Stones – rock idols and movie stars – but it was incredible to think of it happening at an ART opening. Even a Pop Art opening. But then, we weren't just AT the art exhibit – we WERE the art exhibit, we were the art incarnate and the sixties were really about people, not about what they did; "the singer/not the song" etc.

'I would have felt like a public relations genius if I'd thought all that out in advance. As near as I could figure, why it was all happening was because we were really interested in everything that was going on. The Pop idea, after all, was that anybody could do anything, so naturally we were all trying to do it all. Nobody wanted to stay in one category; we all wanted to branch out into every creative thing we could.'

In August 1965, *Life* had published Gloria Steinem's article on 'The Ins and Outs of Pop Culture'. 'Do you sometimes wonder what Pop and Op Art are all about?' she began. 'Are you a wall-flower when they play a Frug? Are you confused when you hear statements like "He's in that Warhol bag" or "The Jerk is fab" or "The royal family's gone kinky at last"? . . . Do you wonder why our foreign policy has been called Unconscious High Camp?' Steinem's piece was so wide-ranging and reference-saturated that it made a simple point: pop was the condition of contemporary life, and Warhol was at the very centre of this trend. One spread was made up of Warhol's Campbell's Soup cans adapted to reflect classic pop culture figures: F. Scott Fitzgerald, Marlene Dietrich, Liz Taylor, Groucho Marx. Another pictured a wheel of current media figures: Elvis, Robert F. Kennedy, Ringo and Andy Warhol.

She observed the accelerating turnover of styles: 'If there is one thing that threatens to take the fun out of Pop Culture, it is this continuing speed-up. How fast can it get? Already it has created an odd problem for artists, who used to struggle a lifetime to find acceptance. Now their problem is to keep from being absorbed into Pop Culture before they have a chance to experiment and mature: to keep from being Out before they are even ready to be On-The-Way-In.'

Because of this warp speed, there was a blurring of boundaries, as previously discrete forms came together: 'Theatre, art and literature have been combined in something called the New Environment, and that in itself requires some new definitions.' Steinem went on to itemise the 'Happening', the 'Unaltered Found Object', 'Junk Art' and the 'Underground Movie'. 'Movies will be the next paintings,' she predicted, citing 'such epics as *Sleep*, by Andy Warhol'.

Within this climate of fusion and sense blurring, Warhol's hook-up with an underground pop group was almost inevitable – although, in the spirit of the time, it was also an inspired shot in the dark. By 1965, pop culture was broad enough to include and exalt the avant-garde. It was also, as Steinem hinted, voracious: the constant and ever-escalating demands for new sounds, new images and new styles meant that all contemporary art was there to be plundered.

Nor was Warhol ignorant of pop music: he was well aware of the iconic and sexual appeal of its stars. His time capsules are full of early-sixties teen magazines like *Stardom* ('Fabian Tells All') and *Favorite* ('Huge Super Pinup: Ricky Nelson'), in which some of the stars look not too dissimilar from the male models to be seen in his favourite porno 'zines: fly-by-night publications like *Wonderboy*, *Mannlich: The Big Boys*, *Male Swinger* and *Teen Nude*.

Popism is peppered with references to individual 45s: as a flavour of a memory, an artistic moment or to mark a particular point in time. From 1963, Warhol cites 'songs like "Sugar Shack" or "Blue Velvet" or "Louie Louie"' as forming part of the Factory soundtrack, along with Billy Name's opera records. The next year, he remembers working at the Factory to Lesley Gore singing 'You Don't Own Me' and Dionne Warwick's 'A House Is Not a Home'.

This formed an aural collage, a clashing sound environment. Remembering his routine for 1964, Warhol remarked how after a long night he would get into 'the Factory by early afternoon. As I walked in, the radio and the record player would both be blasting – "Don't Let the Sun Catch You Crying" mixed with *Turandot*, "Where Did Our Love Go?" with Donizetti or Bellini, or the Stones doing "Not Fade Away" while Maria Callas did *Norma*.'

The Velvet Underground were not the first musicians with whom Warhol had sought to collaborate. From mid-1965 on, he attempted to involve various New York players in his work. The Greenwich Village folk singer Eric Andersen appeared in at least one film, *Space*, while two hardcore downtown groups, the Holy Modal Rounders and the Fugs, were filmed and photographed performing in the Factory during July 1965. But, for some reason, none jelled.

The Velvets came from the same Lower East Side milieu but they were younger, better looking and part of the same film milieu that Warhol inhabited. As John Cale writes in *What's Welsh for Zen*, the Velvet Underground's first performances saw them extemporising 'soundtracks, playing in front, beside or behind screens on which silent black and white movies by Jack Smith, Piero Heliczer, Barbara Rubin, Andy Warhol and many others were shown'.

Most accounts have Warhol and the group meeting up right at the end of 1965 – at the Cafe Bizarre – but there is enough evidence to suggest that Warhol was aware of the group earlier. Both parties were heavily involved with Jonas Mekas's Cinematheque. The group played live during mid- and late 1965, being first shown as the Velvet Underground on a Cinematheque bill for 1 November, soundtracking Angus MacLise's film *Rites of the Dream Weapon I*. They were also featured in a CBS news segment entitled 'The Making of an Underground Film', which showed John Cale, Lou

Reed, Sterling Morrison and new drummer Maureen Tucker impro-
vising a soundtrack to Piero Heliczer's *Venus in Furs*. The musicians all had their faces painted, according to Morrison. 'Maureen
Tucker wore a bridal dress . . . The rest of us had on more conventional clothing, but I suppose it looked weird enough to outsiders.'

However it happened – and both Paul Morrissey and Barbara
Rubin claimed the credit – the Velvet Underground were taken
under Warhol's wing by the end of the year. It was a good deal
for them: management, new guitars and amps, possible shows and
record-label involvement, and freedom of the Factory, where they
would become the house band. It wasn't as though they were inundated with other offers.

The Velvet Underground performed pretty songs of anomie;
they experimented with feedback; they reflected alternative states
of consciousness. So far, so 1965. Even though the group saw themselves as creatures of their time – checking out peers like the Small
Faces, the Kinks, the Who, even Bob Dylan – there were a few
stones in their pathway. They might have reflected the emerging
drug culture, but they sang about the wrong drugs.

One of their earliest, and strongest, songs was 'Heroin', a dispassionate description of using the drug and what the drug took from
the user. But the group was greeted with what Sterling Morrison
remembered as a 'mighty howl of outrage and bewilderment' during the song's first live outing, at Summit High School auditorium,
New Jersey, in November. Although William Burroughs had written about it at length in several published novels, this was not a
proper topic for pop music.

But Lou Reed was a reflector, a facet that he shared with Warhol.
He was inspired by the outcast writers of the 1950s: Burroughs,
James Purdy and Hubert Selby were right off the map, over the
edge of the respectable world, but they were describing – often in
deadpan, demotic prose – a recognisable, empirical reality: drug
addiction, male prostitution, transvestite and gay life, at a time
when all were illegal and completely marginalised and despised.

At the same time, Reed was a music obsessive, his tastes ranging from deep R&B – songs like Eddie and Ernie's 'Outcast' – to free jazz – Cecil Taylor in particular – and the dreamy romanticism of doo-wop. He and Warhol bonded on their love of early-sixties chart music. Both cited as a lodestar the Jaynetts' autumn 1963 US hit 'Sally Go Round the Roses', an elliptical girl group hymn that rises and falls in never-ending, cyclical waves of sadness and regret.

Reed's project was to match the unflinching attitude of the outcast writers to pop music. This was an inspired idea for, by 1965, the rules of the game had changed. It was no longer possible to recapture the innocence of Alicia and the Rockaways' 'Why Can't I Be Loved?' The Beatles had ushered in a new mass culture, while Bob Dylan had taken a literary, beat language to the top of the charts. The serpent of self-consciousness had entered the paradise of superpop.

Pop had become more than just teen product. The music industry had usurped Hollywood's place as the modern Olympus. Reed knew that this was *the* arena for his generation. In 1966, he wrote an essay, 'The View from the Bandstand', which stood as a credo and a statement of intent: 'But meanwhile everything was dead. Writing was dead, movies were dead. Everybody sat like an unpeeled orange. But the music was so beautiful.'

The piece was peppered with superpop lyrics from 'Sally Go Round the Roses', Lee Dorsey's 'Ya Ya' and Ritchie Valens's 'Donna'. Reed went back to his adolescence: 'When Johnny Ace died, everyone was sad. Black arm bands in school. The early fifties, the first race music to make it to N.Y. white station. Alan Freed, the great father, clipped, fast speech and table pounding. The Jesters, Diablos, Coney Island Kids, Elica and the Rockaways [*sic*].'

He attacked the existing hierarchy of literary value: 'Through all those years were these beautiful rock groups, tweeting and chirping like mesmerised sparrows, and if you weren't dead, you psyched in now, because no one had made a good book, a good movie, just bullshit over and over. Only the music, and now Robert Lowell, up for a poetry prize without a decent word ever written. The only decent poetry of this century was that recorded on rock-and-roll records.'

Reed regarded music as the only positive force in American life, the only thing that made any sense to the young. 'The colleges are meant to kill. Four years in which to kill you. And if you don't extend your stay, the draft, by and for old people, waits to kill you. Kill your instincts, your love, the music. The music is the only live, living thing. Draft only those over forty. It's their war, let them kill each other.'

It wasn't just the Velvet Underground's lyrics and attitude that polarised audiences. It was the way they sounded. Viola player John Cale had had a thorough schooling in the Dream Syndicate, an improv group that comprised La Monte Young, Tony Conrad and Marian Zazeela. 'Motivated by a scientific and mystical fascination with sound,' as Cale later wrote, they 'spent long hours in rehearsals learning to provide sustained meditative drones and chants'.

Born in South Wales, Cale had moved to America in 1963 to take up a scholarship at Tanglewood, where he worked with Aaron Copeland and John Cage. A chance meeting with Lou Reed in early 1965 sidetracked him into pop music. 'I was terrifically excited by the possibility of combining what I had been doing with La Monte with what I was doing with Lou and finding a commercial outlet.'

Reed had already released a record in December 1964, on Pickwick Records, a fly-by-night cheap label specialising in facsimiles of current styles. Working on Merseybeat, surfing and hot rod knock-offs, he got industry experience at ground level. The single that he recorded with the Primitives, 'The Ostrich' – a spoof dance number – is a masterpiece of one-note drone and vocal attitude. Cale observed its proximity to the tenets of the Dream Syndicate.

Both Reed and Cale shared a steely core of determination and a deep confrontational streak. 'Lou and I both had high aims,' Cale remembered. 'We wanted to be the best band in the world and we thought we could be. We began to formulate a list of basic precepts. Lou's lyrical and melodic ability would be combined with my musical ideas to create performances where we wouldn't ever repeat ourselves.

'As people our image was that we were weird, sadistic, aloof, unfriendly and nasty: that was how we always came across and how people expected us to be. We hated everybody and everything. We did not consider ourselves to be entertainers and would not relate to our audience . . . we never smiled and would turn our backs on the audience or give them the finger. Our aim was to upset people, make them feel uncomfortable, make them vomit.'

This chimed with both Warhol's sense of mischief and outsider rage and the prevailing mood at the Factory. By 1965, there was a much sharper edge, as methamphetamine permeated Warhol's entourage. Baby Jane Holzer told Jean Stein, Edie Sedgwick's biographer, that 'it was getting very scary at the Factory. There were too many crazy people around who were stoned and using too many drugs . . . the whole thing freaked me out . . . I couldn't take it.'

A key early Velvet Underground song was 'Venus in Furs' – Reed's lyrical synthesis of the famous novel by Leopold von Sacher-Masoch. During 1965, Warhol had explored similar territory with *Vinyl*, an adaptation of Anthony Burgess's *A Clockwork Orange* that featured Gerard Malanga – as 'a juvenile delinquent in leather' – being tortured by professional sadists to a soundtrack of singles by the Kinks, the Rolling Stones and Martha and the Vandellas.

Vinyl also saw the first appearance of Edie Sedgwick in a Warhol film. During summer 1965, Warhol shot several more with her, including *Kitchen* and *Beauty #2*, in which Sedgwick, visibly wilting under the attacks of the off-camera Chuck Wein, finally snaps, 'I wish you'd SHUT UP.' This was celluloid gold for Warhol: those moments when his 'actors', placed under undue pressure, revealed more than they were prepared to and allowed a moment of reality.

This was a kind of sadomasochism, and certainly that mood was prevalent in the Factory of late 1965. Warhol's papers include a catalogue from The Leather Man in Christopher Street, which offered high-collared jackets, wristbands, chaps, etc. for the gay market. Malanga was in the habit of going out with a whip, and it was his spontaneous dancing to 'Venus in Furs' at the Cafe Bizarre that helped to seal the collaboration between the group and Warhol.

In January 1966, the Velvet Underground showed up at the Factory, to be presented with their new singer. Paul Morrissey had serious doubts about Lou Reed's ability to front a hit band, and decided to parachute in one of his contacts. Warhol always had Girls of the Year: in 1964, it had been Baby Jane Holzer; in 1965, Edie Sedgwick. As Edie was on the way out – being courted by Albert Grossman and Dylan's entourage – Nico was the perfect candidate.

Nico had visited the Factory in autumn 1965, with a copy of her one single as a calling card. 'I'm Not Sayin'' was the product of her London visit earlier in the year, a sweet but slight folk rock song released on Andrew Loog Oldham's label, Immediate. The flip was something else: 'The Last Mile' contained much darker overtones, a companion piece to the haunting, Oldham-produced 'Some Things Just Stick in Your Mind' by Vashti Bunyan.

In retrospect, it was an inspired if bizarre move. The group were not happy, but quickly adapted. Nico broadened their visual appeal: her background as a model and actress – with a short but impactful appearance in Fellini's *La Dolce Vita* – made her a striking presence. As John Cale remembered, 'Nico had a style that she picked up from Elia Kazan, who taught her at the Actors Studio: "Take your time. Create your own time." And she did with a vengeance.'

With Nico added to up their pop quotient, the Velvet Underground began working immediately. On 3 January, they had their first rehearsal with their new singer. It was recorded, and reveals a group doing what most groups do in rehearsal: play old favourites ('Green Onions' and Buddy Holly tunes), while tinkering around with contemporary hits ('Day Tripper') and making serious attempts at new songs ('There She Goes Again'). The pressure was on.

Warhol's foray into pop music was prompted not only by his recognition of its cultural power, but by the possibility that this could be the key to his next artistic stage. His celebrity had resulted in an offer of a large discotheque space in Long Island, and this could be a good way to fill it. Thus the Velvet Underground were seen not just as a group but as a part of a total experience that would encompass performance – dance, mime and, most importantly, film.

During January and February, all five members of the group sat for Screen Tests at the Factory. The format was well-established: beginning in 1964, Warhol put friends, business associates, lovers and Factory visitors in front of a camera. Every subject had three minutes or so to fill, the length of a reel. Facing the blank lens was another kind of pressure, and many people found the experience discomforting. However, it could be revelatory.

Nearly five hundred Tests were shot between 1964 and 1966. The subjects included gallerists (Ivan Karp, Henry Geldzahler), poets (Harry Fainlight, Charles Henri Ford), Factory denizens (Baby Jane Holzer, Edie Sedgwick, Ondine, Billy Name, Chuck Wein) and various attractive young men, including Warhol's lovers, such as Richard Rheem. Warhol also shot pop stars, including Donovan and Bob Dylan, who made his distaste perfectly obvious by sulking furiously at the camera.

The group's Screen Tests were conceived from the off as background material for their forthcoming shows. They featured all five members in close-up, sometimes with everyday consumer items, like a Hershey Bar or a bottle of Coca-Cola: pop art props – or perhaps Warhol was hoping for commercial sponsorship. These were augmented by other reels showing featured dancers Mary Woronov and Gerard Malanga: see them live on stage, then see them multi-lifesize on screen. As Callie Angel observes, these pieces 'contain notably frenetic camerawork, with rapid zooms and pans, single-framing, and deliberate jigglings and blurrings that approximated the avant-garde "noise" of the Velvets' music and added still more layers of visual disorientation to the choreographed chaos of loud music, flashing lights, and wildly dancing bodies that constituted the EPI'.

One assembly includes a dual portrait of Malanga and Woronov – as well as the pair indulging in whip play – along with close-ups of John Cale's eye and mouth and portraits of Reed, Cale, Tucker and Morrison. Others include Screen Tests of Salvador Dalí,

Marcel Duchamp, Jane Holzer, Ivy Nicholson, Marisa Berenson, Edie Sedgwick and Susan Sontag. This was the lineage and the feel that Warhol sought.

The Velvet Underground went public during the first month of 1966. Attached to an artist at the height of his media fame, they would, during that year, play large venues, sign to a major label, record an album and release two singles. The myth is that they were despised outsiders, but the Velvet Underground were initially envisioned as a pop group. Their association with Warhol guaranteed publicity, even if wasn't always favourable.

They played their first major date within two weeks of hooking up with Warhol. It was a bizarre event: the annual dinner of the New York Society for Clinical Psychiatry on 13 January. Warhol was invited to give a speech but opted instead to provide entertainment for the 350 or so psychiatrists and their wives, bringing along the Velvet Underground and Nico, plus a couple of dancers, and billing it as 'The Chic Mystique of Andy Warhol'.

In Adam Ritchie's photos from the event, you can see the group playing while the diners tuck into their 'roast beef with string beans and small potatoes' against the ornate decor of the Delmonico hotel, without any visual backdrop except Malanga and Edie Sedgwick – her last major Warhol appearance. Given Lou Reed's less-than-happy experience of psychologists, one can only imagine his glee at facing his former tormentors.

Seymour Krim's review in the *New York Herald Tribune* called the show 'an electric shock treatment' the 'head doctors would never forget'. In the *New York Times*, Grace Glueck quoted several ruffled audience members: 'a short-lived torture of cacophony'; 'it seemed like a whole prison ward had escaped'; 'a spontaneous eruption of the Id'. Krim quoted the Freudian Dr Marcel Helman as he left in a huff: 'I'm ready to vomit.'

Warhol's total environment started small. An early film of the Velvet Underground, shot by Danny Williams, shows a fresh-faced group with a minimal backdrop. The idea developed over the next month or so. Paul Morrissey and Danny Williams handled the film projections and the lights – which included patterned op art slides and strobes – while Malanga was augmented onstage by, first, Edie Sedgwick and then Mary Woronov.

In the second week of February, from the 8th to the 13th, the troupe began its first residency as a multimedia package at the Film-Makers' Cinematheque, under the name of Uptight. Unlike Stevie Wonder's exultant 45 (#3 in the US during March 1966), the word did not denote everything copacetic, joyous or 'all right': this was a feel-bad experience. In Factory slang, 'uptight' denoted nervousness, uneasiness, the near-the-knuckle jangle of amphetamine.

In the *New York Post*, Archer Winsten observed how the Velvet Underground, 'prodigiously amplified, prepares itself in a tuning session, then produces a rhythmic beat proving that the session may not have been necessary'. What emerged for him was 'a sense of climactic noise, exhibitionist movements, and the devil take the audience. The devil did get quite a few numbers, for they left at regular intervals before the two hour show finished.'

The Velvet Underground fit Warhol's world like a glove. Playing in front of projections was second nature to them after the Cinematheque: as Lou Reed told John Wilcock, 'we worked with lights and stuff behind us before we met Andy'. Their modus operandi and their attitudes to the public were the same: neither made any concessions to the audience, with the group declining to reveal their motives, preferring instead to deliver an unexplained assault.

Yet Warhol's troupe was playing with a loaded gun. They were reflecting what was already there – the madness of America in 1966 – but the danger was that it was without a filter. This was a real-life experiment with no safety net. It was as though, in reflecting the psychic mood of the times, the Velvet Underground and the EPI were drawing all the poison, all the aggression, onto themselves. They were out to provoke, and provocation almost always brings a reaction.

When the troupe (including Barbara Rubin and Ingrid Superstar) visited Rutgers College – as invitees of the film society – they were called Andy Warhol's Underground or Rutgers Uptight. John

Wilcock was there, and recorded how they got into trouble in the college cafeteria and were nearly thrown off campus: 'There's something about authoritarian creeps which is triggered instantly by the tiniest glimmering of anarchistic freedom.' He described the Rutgers show in terms of sound as environment: the Velvet Underground's 'most notable attribute is a repetitive, howling lamentation which conjures up images of a schooner breaking on the rocks. Their sound, punctuated with whatever screeches, whines, whistles and wails can be coaxed out of the amplifier, envelops the audience with disploding decibels – a sound two-and-a-half times as loud as anybody thought they could stand.'

At this point, the Velvet Underground were fused with the troupe. Bathed in lights and films, they were almost anonymous. Sterling Morrison remembered that at Rutgers, 'We were all dressed in white; the effect, with all the films and lights projected on us, was invisibility.' Like Warhol, they cultivated a blank facade: one of their forte numbers was called 'The Nothing Song', which 'was just noise and feedback and screeches and groans from the amplifiers'.

Nothing, nil, *nada*. Like a mirror, the Velvet Underground and Warhol were showing America a truth that it did not want to face. Although they did not start the war in Vietnam, although they did not produce or sell heroin, although they did not create cultural alienation, they got the blame. 'One of his constant themes has been boredom, ennui, stagnation,' John Wilcock wrote of Warhol. 'It is a subject he has endlessly explored, exploited, exploded.'

The polarisation continued during March and April. Ingrid Superstar remembered how 'part of the audience went berserk' during the 12 March show at the University of Michigan, in Ann Arbor: 'There were a few hecklers. They're all a bunch of immature punks.' Two weeks later, they played the upscale 20th Anniversary Party for the *Paris Review*. Frank Sinatra walked out, while – as Mo Tucker remembered – the comedian Dick Gregory called 'us either "trash" or "garbage".'

The Exploding Plastic Inevitable was launched with a month-long stint at the Polish Cultural Institute in St Mark's Place. This was perhaps the only time that the Velvet Underground and the troupe would have a secure environment. 'The Dom was an unused, huge hall with a nice high stage, nice high ceilings and a balcony,' Sterling Morrison told Ignacio Juliá. 'A wonderful location, perfect. When we opened the place, there was no East Village.'

What's usually called 'the Dom' was in fact the hall above the Dom Bar, which was run as the Open Stage. In *What's Welsh for Zen*, John Cale remembered the venue's unpromising nature: 'You trudged upstairs to this place that smelled of urine. It was filthy and had no lights in it, but Andy took it over and turned it into something totally different. He projected films all over the wall behind us and we had slides projected onto another wall shown through gauze.'

After three months, Warhol's multimedia environment finally found its full expression. As the ad in the *East Village Other* stated, it included 'Superstars Gerard Malanga And Mary Woronov On Film On Stage On Vinyl: Live music, dancing, ultra sounds, visions, lightworks by Daniel Williams; color slides by Jackie Cassen, discotheque, refreshments, Ingrid Superstar, food, celebrities, and movies, including: Vinyl, Sleep, Eat, Kiss, Empire, Whips, Faces, Harlot, Hedy, Couch, Banana, Blow Job, etc., etc., etc. all in the same place at the same time.'

At the Open Stage, the Velvet Underground attracted a sympathetic audience from the off. Seven hundred and fifty people attended the opening night, while the takings for the first week totalled $18,000. As Lou Reed told Bruce Pollock in 1975, it was a show 'by and for freaks, of which there turned out to be many more than anyone had expected, who finally had a place to go where they wouldn't be hassled and where they could have a good time'.

The residency was well covered by the *Village Voice*, the *New York Times* and the *East Village Other*. John Wilcock thought that 'Art has come to the discotheque and it will never be the same again.' Clearly, this was something totally radical, the Velvet Underground's drones and feedback combining with the lights' sensory assault to create an atmosphere described by *The Exemplar* as 'everything occurring simultaneously'.

Long-time supporter and collaborator Jonas Mekas was the most fulsome and lucid: the Velvet Underground performances at the Open Stage 'provided the most violent, loudest and dramatic exploration platform for this new art', he wrote. 'Theirs remains the most dramatic expression of the contemporary generation. The place where its needs and desperations are most dramatically split open ... At the Plastic Inevitable it is all Here and Now and the Future.'

The same week that the Norman Dolph acetate was cut, *Newsweek* published its 25 April cover story on 'Pop', which ticked all the contemporary boxes: Batman, camp, Dadaism, mod fashions, while highlighting Warhol and the EPI. 'What's happening now is happenings – where music, dancing, movies, everything happens at once and assaults all the senses.' Nico was captioned 'Pop girl of '66?'

A few days after the end of the season at the Dom, the Velvet Underground, Warhol and members of the troupe flew out to California for a two-week residency at the Trip, on the Sunset Strip. By then, the EPI had developed into a full-on barrage of flashing lights, multiscreened films, sadomasochistic mime and music amplified to the point of pain. This was total envelopment. As Warhol stated in *Newsweek*, 'I guess it'll all get so simple that everything will be art.'

The EPI was the most fully worked-out staging, up to this time, of the inexorable high-sixties pop drive towards the dissolution of hierarchies, linear perception and overt meaning. By 1966, many strands of art, music and entertainment were all coming to the same point by different means: the total focus on the instant that is the hallmark of many Eastern religions; the Happening; the drug experience; the ecstasy of dancing.

Only the multimedia pop extravaganza could convey this dissolution and, in early 1966, the idea was developing in Los Angeles, San Francisco and London. The EPI was way ahead of anyone, not only in terms of sophistication but also press attention. This resulted in some plain old regional hostility, as different cities vied to become the new international centre of pop, and the Velvet Underground walked straight into the centre of the storm.

'The first time we went out to the West Coast was an amazing experience,' Sterling Morrison told Ignacio Juliá. 'We liked it a lot, but it was very intimidating also, because musically the West Coast was an organised force trying to predominate in the pop scene. I remember we were in a rented car going back from the airport and when I turned on the radio the first song that came out was "Monday Monday". I thought: "I don't know, maybe we're not ready for that sort of thing yet, to be taking these people on, right in their own backyard."'

The first night at the Trip was packed with celebrities and the curious. *KRLA Beat* covered the event with an innovative montage of shots from the show and copy that accentuated the freak angle: 'The Velvet Underground should go back underground and practice' (Barry McGuire); 'It's like eating a banana-nut Brillo pad' (David Crosby, the Byrds); 'It will replace nothing, except maybe suicide' (Cher). It was, ran the headline, 'A Happening!'

Two nights later, the Exploding Plastic Inevitable received its first major setback. On 17 May, *Variety* ran a story on the closing of the Trip due to a legal dispute relating to the wife of one of the operators, who sued for $21,000 'allegedly overdue on a promissory note'. Caught in the middle was 'Andy Warhol's Velvet Underground', who in turn sued the Trip's owners for the balance of their contract: $3,000.

This incident has been presented as an example of West Coast hostility to the VU, but, quite apart from the actual dispute between the Trip's operators, there was another possible factor. In his book *Riot on Sunset Strip: Rock'n'Roll's Last Stand in Hollywood*, Domenic Priore speculates that the EPI were an early victim of the concerted city and police campaign to clear the Sunset Strip of clubs and teens, an operation that would explode later in the year.

Whatever the reason, the EPI were forced to remain in Los Angeles for the duration of their original contract in order to receive the money due. Jim Paltridge visited the group at the Castle, the Hollywood Hills mansion inhabited by Lisa Law, Severn Darden and others, where Dylan had stayed in January. The VU are 'passing the time, listening to electronic music, writing poems, reading, bopping. There is plenty of time to pass.'

Warhol, meantime, goes to the Ferus Gallery, where they have an installation of his helium balloons, and reads EPI press, arranges the WNAC-TV contract and handles interviews:

> TV reporter: Andy, what kind of following do you and your friends have?
> Andy: (looking at Nico, his thin bubble-gum fingers caressing his lips)
> Gerard [Malanga]: You mean who is following us?
> Andy: (softly, amused) The FBI?

The real hostility began in San Francisco, where the EPI arrived on 27 May for three nights at Bill Graham's Fillmore Auditorium. The first signs were encouraging. The *San Francisco Chronicle* ran a favourable interview on the 23rd. On the 27th, the paper printed another interview by columnist Merla Zellerbach, who faithfully reproduced bons mots like, 'We're pop people, formed by television.' Asked to explain the EPI, Warhol simply said, 'It's a totality.'

That same day, *Life* published its cover story, 'New Madness at the Discotheque', but the EPI did not go down well with the cheerleaders of the San Francisco scene. On the 30th, the *Chronicle* published two critical pieces about the Fillmore engagement. Joan Chatfield-Taylor wrote a gossipy account of the audience, while Ralph J. Gleason laid the hostility bare: 'It was all very campy and very Greenwich Village sick.' Warhol's films were 'the triumph of monotony into boredom', and the EPI was 'the same principle applied to a rock 'n' roll dance'. The Velvet Underground were 'dull, behind at least a dozen local groups in interest'. The whole Barnumesque con was 'nothing more than a bad condensation of all the bum trips of the Trips Festival of last January ... Camp plus con equals nothing. You may sell the sizzle, but you can't eat it, only the steak will do for that.'

And here was the rub. It was the traditional civic distrust of New York placed into a new context. Gleason was a passionate writer about music and a booster of the new and exciting, but it was vital for him to put the EPI down to elevate the whole San Francisco scene. And this pattern would be repeated with the VU's nearest competitors: the Mothers of Invention, signed to the same label, Verve, and who opened for the EPI at the Trip.

In some ways, the Velvet Underground and the EPI asked for it: they were not operating by the rules of the arena that they had chosen to work in. The music industry and its commentators valued sincerity. Neither they nor Warhol were in the business of explaining their ideas. This in turn led to misinterpretation and reflexive hostility. Certainly, the EPI felt unwelcome in San Francisco and reflected that back at the section of the audience who were predisposed that way.

Mary Woronov caught the utter lack of comprehension between the two cities: 'We spoke two completely different languages. We were on amphetamine and they were on acid.' Yet there was a problem with this amphetamine acceleration. Gloria Steinem had already observed the dangers of pop culture's 'continuing speed-up' in the wider culture. The VU were ahead of the pack, but, just as their first single was readied for release, their momentum was beginning to slip.

* * *

'TV reporter: Andy, as a leader of youth (Andy smiles), do you feel any responsibility toward them?
Andy: Oh . . . I . . .'
    JIM PALTRIDGE, 'Andy Out West', *Daily Californian*, 10 October 1967

In the spring of 1966, Andy Warhol was the most famous artist in America, but he wasn't making art in the traditional sense of the word. The Factory was an atelier: it functioned both as an assembly line of large-edition silk-screened artefacts and an arena, a meeting place where the unexpected could occur. Warhol was not a tortured, lone genius like Jackson Pollock; he had become an impresario, a wizard, a creator of worlds.

His 'retirement' from painting officially sealed the process, although in fact Warhol would continue to quietly produce individual portraits to raise money. 1965 had been principally taken up with the production of silk-screens, a sequence of films and the achievement and maintenance of celebrity. From the beginning of 1966, Warhol's principal focus would be the Velvet Underground and his total environment discotheque.

In April, Warhol held his first major art show of 1966 at the Leo Castelli Gallery. Called 'Cow Wallpaper and Silver Clouds', it contained just that: a wall of brightly coloured wallpaper with a magenta maternal image of a cow printed on yellow, together with another room of silver helium-filled balloons that floated around the space depending on the air flow. Encouraging play and involvement, the reflecting surfaces mirrored the EPI's constant shifting of light and image.

In commercial terms, the show was a flop: all that there was to buy were slices of cow wallpaper and slowly deflating silver balloons. Reviewers called it 'an embarrassment' or an example of 'banality', but the show generated enormous publicity. The 'Pop!' issue of *Newsweek* quoted Castelli's director, Ivan Karp, talking about the wallpaper – on sale at $75 a cow – as 'an example of repetition in its most vicious form'.

It also furthered Warhol's celebrity: he was all over the *Newsweek* 'Pop!' article, in photographs, in copy about his various activities and in quotes like 'Intellectuals hate Pop. Average people like it. It's easier to understand.' Indeed, the cow wallpaper marked the final stage of Warhol's 1963 revelation: art had become indistinguishable from a factory process, from everyday, useful consumer products. It had become the environment.

In spring 1966, Warhol was thirty-seven: middle-aged. But he was curiously ageless in his silver wigs, striped turtlenecks and heavy boots. Indeed, that very look was an attempt to defy time and gender. 'When I was young I always wanted to look older,' he told Bob Reilly, 'and now I'm looking older I want to look younger. So, uh . . . Edie's hair was dyed silver, and therefore I copied my hair because I wanted to look like Edie because I always wanted to be a girl.'

Being gay liberated Warhol from the traditional ways of growing older. He was, after all, the 'Peter Pan of the current art scene'. In the Factory, he surrounded himself with younger people and acted younger than his years. He became part of the gang he never had during his isolated adolescence in Pittsburgh. But that isolation had stunted him. His relationship to his protégés would never be equal: Warhol functioned as a king disposing favours on his court.

As most of those drawn into the Factory would discover, involvement with Warhol was complicated and, although exciting and in some cases empowering, not always benign. If you wanted to make art, dance, perform, make films, write pop songs or just be yourself in a flagrant manner, then here was your opportunity. But you might or might not get paid, and you would struggle to get credit.

The Factory was a hothouse of forced development, with every tic and foible mirrored by the blank eye of the camera lens. Warhol was firmly at the centre of this world and he ruled by the giving and withholding of affection. Desiring and receiving love and attention in the widest sense, he did not always reciprocate, and the arbitrarily flickering current of his gaze dominated the Factory as surely as any heavy-handed imposition of control.

This was not a place for the sensitive or the open-hearted. The increased use of amphetamine made people more paranoid and quick-tempered. Those who thrived in this atmosphere were tough and had a function: the Velvet Underground were the house pop group; Billy Name was the manager of the Factory building; Paul Morrissey was Warhol's principal collaborator on the films; and Gerard Malanga was the silk-screen assistant, sexual bait and EPI dancer.

Woe betide you if you were unsure of yourself or failed to find a role. The Factory crowd could be merciless, as cinema-goers witnessed later on in the year when Ondine – in his role as the Pope

– exploded at Jonas Mekas's friend Ronna Page. Warhol gave no moral guidance in these matters; everything was to be recorded, the more humiliating the better. Because it was a slice of real life, not something staged. But then, a mirror does not intervene; all it does is reflect.

Elenore Lester described Warhol's emotional blankness that year in a major *New York Times* profile: 'Andy's boys and girls find their way to him, the neglected, rejected, overpsychoanalysed children of the rich, and the runaways from jobs as supermarket check-out clerks in the bleak suburbs of New Jersey. They find their way to the enchanted silver playroom on East 47th in Manhattan, to Mother Andy – neutral, cool and withdrawn in goggles and leather jacket . . . He listens to each one, watches each one, an open shutter.'

Warhol's interest in teenagers was multifaceted: he was fascinated by the teenage market as an exemplar of the Now; he was fascinated by the appeal of pop stars as the sixties equivalent of the Hollywood icons he had idolised in his own teens; he enjoyed and exploited the energy of youth in his workplace; he was interested in their problems; he was also fascinated by sexual images of younger men and took some real-life examples – usually men in their early twenties – as his partners.

At the beginning of 1966, his lover was Danny Williams. A film editor who had worked on the Maysles brothers' first feature, *Anastasia*, Williams was sensitive and talented. Warhol gave him a Bolex, with which he shot films: portraits of Billy Name and the artist Harold Stevenson, as well as a startling sequence of orgiastic dancing. From early 1966, his visual and spatial awareness was invaluable in creating the lighting effects for the Exploding Plastic Inevitable.

For the mass media, Warhol signalled Youth. In early 1965, *Time* hired him to design the cover for their latest youth survey – a mass-market magazine staple. 'Today's Teen-Agers' is a classic design, a grid of seven young men and women, each marked out in a different colour, all caught in a moving sequence of eight photo-booth poses. There are three women and four men, one of whom is African American. All are in motion – playful, happy, sad, signifying.

Having experienced a kind of mini *A Hard Day's Night* at the October 1965 Philadelphia Happening, Warhol wanted further access to this new teenage world. Hooking up with the Velvet Underground seemed the perfect way to achieve this. Indeed, Jim Paltridge's fly-on-the-wall account of the Exploding Plastic Inevitable in California captures Warhol's delight at being bathed in youth. At the Fillmore, the crowd included a cross-section of current teen types: 'Lots of teenyboppers; hairdressers-on-leave and their dates, smart hippies and sloppy hippies; Junior League members, looking uncomfortable in their phosphorescent all-vinyl pants suits are all milling about in the lobby.' Paltridge concludes with a vivid snapshot: 'On the balcony a crowd forms around Andy. Four boys in electric paisley shirts and tight red pants are seeking his favour.'

Warhol was also, literally, on sale to teens. Gloria Steinem noted the lightning-fast crossover between fine art and the mass market, exemplified by the feeding frenzy that surrounded Bridget Riley's first New York show in March 1965. A serious, thoughtful artist, Riley was appalled when she 'was driven from the airport down Madison Avenue and to my amazement I saw windows full of my paintings on dresses, in window displays, everywhere. My heart sank.'

In high summer 1965, the American Greetings Gallery had held an exhibition of 'Posters by Painters'. The catalogue cover showed 'Liz by Andy Warhol', while the essay inside talked of the fine art/commercial poster lineage established by Toulouse Lautrec, and the opportunities for the poster as 'a mass communication device'. The artists included Fernand Léger, Roy Lichtenstein, Henri Matisse, Mucha, Joan Miró, Picasso and, last but not least, Andy Warhol.

In the spring 1966 issue of *Datebook*, there was a feature entitled 'Decorate with Art Posters'. The copy noted how the fad for posters had spread to the high school: 'On the walls of rooms of the most aware teenagers all over New York you'll find gallery and museum posters announcing exhibitions of such leaders in the op and pop art world as Lichtenstein, Warhol, Rauschenberg and Riley.' On sale for $5 were two Warhol posters, *Liz* and *Flowers*.

Images and stories about teens percolate through the clippings in Warhol's 1966 boxes, partly because he and Morrissey were seeking to promote the VU and the EPI within a teen context. Whether intentionally or not, the clips reflect a shift in youth culture that mirrored the news: Vietnam, Black Power and race riots, James Bond-type spy weapons, ecological pollution and bizarre crimes of violence ('Murder on LSD?').

If *Time* had asked Warhol to create his 'Today's Teen-Agers' cover a year later, his subjects would have looked like the sullen kids featured in 'Children's Village', a *Newsweek* story from 23 May 1966: 'lank-haired Mods from Mineola and leather-jacketed Rockers from Rockaway, a covey of Byrds, several dozen Rolling Stones, and a multitude of Sonny and Cher's. They appear, on the average, to be about 16 but a disconcerting percentage are scarcely 12 years old.'

The report noted how the Greenwich Village kids managed, in the midst of one of the world's greatest cities, to be exquisitely bored: 'For the teen-agers, the 2-square-mile area loosely bounded by the Hudson River, Broadway, Spring and Fourteenth streets serves as one big corner drugstore. Surprisingly enough, they come because there is no place else to go. "For a kid under 18," says 14-year-old Patti Meyers of Queens, "New York is the draggiest city in the world."'

In Greenwich Village, in Chicago's Old Town, in Los Angeles's Sunset Strip, in San Francisco's Haight-Ashbury the kids were taking over the streets. The innocent joy of superpop had gone. The blank and provocative facade of the Velvet Underground was mirrored and amplified by the Rolling Stones' raging 'Paint It, Black' and the sullen, suspicious glares of the teens caught in the light of the mainstream media.

The miasma of violence that permeated the Factory and the Exploding Plastic Inevitable was mirrored in the wider culture's fascination with teen violence. In April 1966, a *Village Voice* profile of the writer Anthony Burgess zeroed in on *A Clockwork Orange*, which offered, in the interviewer's words, 'an hilarious and somber prophecy of a world dominated by teenage gangs, a kind of comic cross between *1984* and *The Wild Ones*'.

During 1966, fiction became fact, and Warhol clipped it. In a 6 May article entitled 'Addenda to De Sade', *Time* reported on the trial of a middle-aged woman, Gertrude Baniszewski, together with three of her children and two neighbouring 'teen-age' boys. They were accused of causing the death of a sixteen-year-old girl, Sylvia Likens – 'a pretty lass who liked the Beatles and roller skating' – who had been left in their care while her parents 'traveled the Midwest fair circuit'. The torture started when Paula Baniszewski hit Sylvia on the jaw. Gertrude began slapping her and, when the girl did not complain, the two neighbours and son John began 'the laceration game': burning Sylvia with matches and cigarettes, whipping her with a heavy leather belt. The family treated her like a slave, and she was reduced to picking scraps from a garbage can. At her death, her body 'bore an estimated 150 burns, cuts, bruises and other lesions'.

Warhol became obsessed by a sensational teen murder case, the Tucson Murders. When Charles Howard Schmid, Jr went on trial in March 1966, he became a new kind of creature from the id, a psycho-killer prowling boom-town teenage anomie: 'Among the odd collection of restless, thrill-hungry teenagers who hang out in the garish juke joints and drive-ins along Tucson's East Speedway Boulevard, swarthy blue-eyed "Smitty" commanded adoration and terror.' Quoting a then popular song by the Changin' Times, 'The Pied Piper' (co-written by Artie Kornfeld, the future promoter of Woodstock), *Time*'s Robert Moser posed Schmid as the narcissistic, charismatic hero to a section of the city's bored, restless, disenfranchised youth. At twenty-three, he was a bit older than his followers, a fine athlete who had never quite adapted to the world outside high school and who cultivated a bizarre image.

This was Leopold and Loeb projected forward into the pop age. Schmid had 'idly wondered if [he] could kill someone and get away with it'. Like a Warhol superstar, he made himself over, stuffing three or four inches of rags and tin cans into his boots to make him taller. 'He dyed his hair raven black, wore pancake make-up, pale cream lipstick and mascara.' Most curiously, he wore a large beauty spot on his cheek, marked with grease.

Dominating a group of younger and impressionable teens was not enough. Schmid's power games led to not one murder but three, as Aileen Rowe and sisters Wendy and Gretchen Fritz were taken out into the desert and bludgeoned to death. It took a while for their disappearance to be taken seriously, as at least fifty teen runaways a month were reported to the Tucson police. The case was cracked when one of Schmid's helpers, Richie Bruns, confessed.

The arrest and court pictures of Schmid were genuinely weird and haunting. After reading Robert Moser's long article about the boredom in Tucson, Warhol commissioned Ronald Tavel to write a script based on the case, called *Their Town*. As Tavel later recalled, Warhol's 'attention was nailed from the start with the fact that "the townspeople", as he put it, "knew about the murders and never said anything"'.

The maelstrom was beginning to swirl around Warhol. The S&M flavour of the Exploding Plastic Inevitable was seen as part of the whole 'campy' and 'sick' pop trend that had been kick-started in January 1966 by ABC's *Batman*, a cartoon-slick serial with pop art violence – sudden on-screen captions stating 'Zap!', 'Pow!' and 'Zok!' – and villains like Catwoman, who in her leather outfit was an amped-up version of Emma Peel in *The Avengers*.

Camp itself, thanks to Susan Sontag's famous *Partisan Review* essay, had become a major mid-sixties obsession. Gloria Steinem had noted just how important it was 'as a kind of early-warning system for Pop'. Adding a sidebar called 'A Vest Pocket Guide to CAMP', she also brought out the gay influence: 'Homosexuals, who always have a vested interest in knocking down bourgeois standards, are in the vanguard of camp, although no longer its sole custodians.'

Steinem was cool and knowing, but middle America was not. Within a society where homosexuality was still illegal, the linking of camp and pop was enough to engender a backlash. Many of the hostile articles on the EPI contain hints of prejudice, but the most extreme was an April *Village Voice* piece by Vivian Gornick that accused the Velvet Underground and Warhol of being part of a homosexual conspiracy to control US culture.

Several readers retorted. Gregory Battcock called her response 'prejudicial in the extreme and insulting to any cultured person'. Harriet Zwerling noted that 'camp is sweet and sugary . . . but Selby, "Flaming Creatures," and "Scorpio Rising" are not. They are not camp, anymore than is *The Story of O*. They are children of the violent and the dark, like the high black boots we are wearing and the shiny vinyl trench coats. Watch for the leather underwear next.'

Warhol's campily violent miasma was in sync with these times, something that was noted by an article in the May 1966 issue of society magazine *Town & Country*. In the feature 'Selective Panel Casts "In Cold Blood"', several 'leading columnists and one pop artist' chose various public figures to play the leading characters in a potential film of the real-life murder story made famous by Truman Capote's infamous book – an immediate best-seller on its publication in January 1966.

To be cast were the two killers, Dick Hickock and Perry Smith; the four victims, Mr and Mrs Clutter, Nancy and Kenyon Clutter; and the investigator, Al Dewey. Alan Pryce-Jones chose Warhol to play Dick Hickock, while Warhol himself entered the joke. As the two killers, he chose John Cale and Maria Montez. As for the victims, the Clutter family, he picked Gerard Malanga, Mary Pitt, Ingrid Superstar and Lou Reed.

A couple of months later, the July issue of *Mademoiselle* magazine featured a discussion that aimed to 'shed light on the present murkiness that surrounds the hero image in 1966'. Among the guests were comparative mythologist Joseph Campbell, reactionary

commentator and L'il Abner creator Al Capp, *New Yorker* staff
writer Renata Adler and David Newman, co-author of 'the new
Broadway hit "It's a Bird . . . It's A Plane . . . It's SUPERMAN".'
Campbell identified the 'negative hero' as a person who 'takes
pride in failure'. This very contemporary type formed 'a growing
minority that may presently be a majority. The survival-of-the-
fittest law no longer operates.'

Newman: Who are those negative heroes?
Campbell: Herzog, Kafka's heroes.
Adler: The perennial loser. The Andy Warhol cult. The slip-
shod, ugly, talentless . . .
Capp: Warhol a hero? To whom?
Adler: It's the American success story in reverse. In high school
the class president was everything. Then at a given moment,
all the losers, all the people who had elected the president, the
prom queen, suddenly noticed there were more of them than
anybody else. All the complete wallflowers – the camp crowd –
whom nobody ever danced with, found each other!
Newman: Andy Warhol is not a hero; he's a celebrity.
Adler: You're right. But celebrities are heroes to some people.

During 1966, the demands of the oppressed became more and
more strident. Already riven by the civil rights movement and the
Vietnam war, America had to deal with a wave of generational
assertion such as it had never experienced before. It was not only
black Americans and women who wanted more but teenagers as
a class and, behind them, the losers, and, behind them, the biggest
outcasts of all – the queers.

Things were being turned upside down, and the most visible symbol of this disturbing change was a wig-wearing, middle-aged artist who barely spoke in public. In summer 1966, Warhol was both
channelling and reflecting America's violent spasms, just as hostile
critics like Archer Winsten had intuited: 'It is even possible that the
more Andy kicks his audience in the teeth, the more he shovels nonsense into its hanging-open mouth, the more they like it.

'This is a strange taste,' Winsten concluded, 'but we live in strange times.'

* * *

(Background audio: Factory atmosphere, *The Velvet Underground and Nico* album plays – 'I'm Waiting for the Man' followed by 'Femme Fatale')
Alan Rinzler: We wanted to talk about the book. Did you look at it?
Nico: The product of the – aaah – underground, is that it?
Alan Rinzler: It's supposed to be emblematic of the world of Andy Warhol. It's Andy's book. For the rest of the world.
Nico: For the rest of the world?
Alan Rinzler: Outside of New York.
Nico: The beginning of the world. Because I think that the rest of the world is us.
  Transcribed audio from the flexidisc contained in the *Index* book, 1967

On 6 July 1966, Nico wrote to Andy Warhol from Ibiza. 'Dear Andy,' she begins, 'I had a long dream about you last night & that got me kind of worried – maybe you're thinking that I'm not coming back at all.' She complained about 'being extremely nervous these days' and having 'nothing important to do'. All she could think about was 'coming back over' as soon as she could: 'maybe next week???' But what was she returning to?

Written entirely in capitals, her letter is filled with exactly the kind of demands from which Warhol would have shrunk: 'When does this job start & where exactly? Has the record come out yet? I still have not received the M.G.M. contract. Is everything dissolving? Lou sounded rather positive about everything – he said that he was looking for a place for me to stay – I hope he is not into these Placidyl pills again in order to survive his ego.'

During the spring, the Velvet Underground and Nico and the Exploding Plastic Inevitable had been way ahead of the pack but, from early June, their momentum stalled. The troupe's hostile reception during their Californian stay had cast a malign spell. After appearing on WNAC-TV, 1966's 'Pop-Off' girl had departed for Ibiza, while Lou Reed – after shooting up some bad speed in San Francisco – went into hospital for six weeks with a severe case of hepatitis.

Warhol readjusted his focus. From June onwards, he and Paul Morrissey began a renewed burst of filming. Among the material shot over the summer was the *Hanoi Hannah* segment, scripted by Ronnie Tavel and featuring Mary Woronov as a hardcore politico dominatrix; *Their Town*, featuring new Warhol discovery Eric Emerson, along with Woronov, Ingrid Superstar and International Velvet; and *The Pope Ondine Story*, with its explosive denouement.

The Velvet Underground and the EPI were left in limbo for much of June. On the 21st, the troupe travelled to Chicago to play a residency at Poor Richard's. They were without their featured singer, their lead singer and their famous impresario. Forced to improvise, they took original drummer Angus MacLise back into the fold, switched Maureen Tucker to bass and showcased John Cale as lead vocalist: 'No one knew the difference.'

The shows were, in a quiet way, a triumph. The Velvet Underground used Reed's absence as an opportunity to try something new. A set list from the residency, written by John Cale and amended by Sterling Morrison, shows familiar material interspersed with new songs like 'Foggy Notion', 'Mr Rain', 'Story of My Life' and 'Pale Blue Eyes'. The group played their soul instrumental, 'Booker T'. Also on the list is 'Searching' – the first incarnation of 'Sister Ray'.

The EPI was held over for an extra week, and recordings from the residency exhibit a different side to the group. John Cale had already featured as a vocalist on the summer 1965 demos of 'Venus in Furs' and 'Wrap Your Troubles in Dreams', and his droning, Welsh-inflected voice combined with MacLise's tribal drumming to replace Reed's street-wise confrontation with an insinuating sense of unease.

In the *Chicago Daily News*, Michaela Williams reviewed the Poor Richard's residency as 'Warhol's brutal assemblage – non-stop horror show . . . It is an assemblage that actually vibrates with menace, cynicism and perversion. To experience it is to be brutalised, helpless – you're in any kind of horror you want to imagine, from police state to mad house. Eventually the reverberations in your ears stop. But what do you do with what you still hear in your brain?'

The Poor Richard's residency was significant for three reasons. Firstly, as Cale was not slow to point out, neither Reed nor Nico were indispensable. Nobody had commented on their absence. Secondly, the tensions between the EPI's crew reached boiling point. As Cale remembered, 'Paul Morrissey and Danny Williams had different visions of what the light show should be like and one night I looked up to see them fighting, hitting each other in the middle of a song.'

1966 had not been kind to Danny Williams. His relationship with Warhol had ended earlier in the year and, deeply hurt, he got further and further into drugs. As Cale told Robert Greenfield, 'He used to carry this strobe around with him all the time and no one could figure out why till we found out he kept his amphetamine in it.' Unable to break away, he began living in the Factory. His appearance deteriorated from a handsome preppy to a skinny speed freak.

Without Warhol's protection, Williams lost his place in the Factory pecking order and was subjected to serial indignities. Things came to a head during the Poor Richard's residency. Apart from the fist fight with Morrissey, there was the not insignificant matter of a major review in *Variety*, on 29 June, which gave Williams full credit as 'the mastermind of the Exploding Plastic Inevitable'.

That did not go down well, and in the hiatus before the next EPI date – at the end of August – Williams was ousted. At the end of July, he returned to his parents' house near Gloucester, Massachusetts. After a family dinner, he declared he needed some air, drove away and never came back. His car was found above the cliffs by the sea at Cape Ann. His body was never discovered. He left some lighting diagrams, journals and a shaving bag full of amphetamine.

Poor Richard's was also the venue for the only film ever recorded of the Exploding Plastic Inevitable. It seems strange that no one in the Factory filmed any of the shows. Maybe they were so busy creating an environment that they didn't feel the need to record it. The challenge was taken up by a young Chicagoan film-maker called Ronald Nameth, who, having been alerted by press reports about the EPI, got permission to film the concerts.

Working with a 16mm Bolex camera, Nameth shot in three-minute bursts over several nights, capturing principally the lead dancers – Gerard Malanga and Ingrid Superstar in her reflective silver costume. He also caught the back projections, the patterned slides and the shards of mirrored light cast by the strobe. He then overlaid layer upon layer of these images – sometimes looped, freeze-framed or shown in negative – to create a thirteen-minute sensorium.

Grainy, underlit and claustrophobically close up, *Andy Warhol's Exploding Plastic Inevitable* takes the viewer right into the experience: the hypnotic lights, the frantically gyrating dancers, the dream-like self-absorption of Ingrid and Gerard as they enact their S&M dumb show. Most of all, it captures the overload that the event was designed to create, the sense that everything was happening at once, far too fast to catch fully, leaving impressions and sensations of frenzy, violence, chaos and a strange beauty.

On 8 July, Nico's pre-recorded introductions for the 'Pop Art Movies' series began airing on WNAC-TV. A week or so later, Verve released the Velvet Underground's first single, 'All Tomorrow's Parties', backed with 'I'll Be Your Mirror'. The first promo copies came with a picture sleeve depicting the group in a narrow band of light: a window into another world peopled by strange, blank-looking young men and androgynous women.

Sung by Nico, 'All Tomorrow's Parties' was a bulletin direct from Warhol's world. The lyric was 'a very apt description of certain people at the Factory at the time', Lou Reed later told David Fricke. 'I kept notes of what people said, what went on, and those notes would go directly into songs.' This was a snapshot of the

Factory at its height: the parties, the ragged costumes, the ego peeled open like a banana once the speed had worn off.

Although on the surface it sounded like a slightly twisted folk rock song, the music was avant-garde in the extreme. 'All Tomorrow's Parties' was one of the first pop songs to use prepared piano (where the instrument has its sound altered by placing external objects on the strings) and a kind of prepared guitar (all of the strings on Reed's 'Ostrich' guitar were tuned to D). It was then edited down from the full six-minute version and sonically boosted into a 2:52 single mix.

Backed up with 'I'll Be Your Mirror', this was an information-packed, content-rich 45 – a total pop art product. Nothing could have been more Now. Everything had built up to this point, but, despite all the press, all the TV, all the attention, nothing happened. There were no reviews. There was a substantial DJ mail-out – maybe several thousand copies – but, as one, the radio stations baulked.

The record did not make the charts. It might have been pop art *in excelsis*, but it was not pop. There are several possible reasons for its almost complete disappearance. The first can be put down to the A-side's radical sound. It might have been wiser to go for the more accessible 'I'll Be Your Mirror', but then Warhol and the Velvet Underground were locked into a cycle of confrontation. Affecting to despise the audience, they wore their art as a baffle and a banner.

Even so, there were other strange, tough-sounding records making the American Top 10 at that time: the Association's drug-saturated 'Along Comes Mary', the Troggs' 'Wild Thing', the Standells' 'Dirty Water'. But all had sweeteners – the Association's harmonies, for instance – or extremely simple, powerful hooks. 'All Tomorrow's Parties' came at the listener strong but sideways; it engendered an unspecific unease that was hard to pin down.

It was also clear that Verve, still new to the pop arena, had absolutely no idea of what to do with the record. The Mothers of Invention also released a Verve single that July, 'How Could I Be Such a Fool?', which barely made it into stock copies. The label was happiest with the organist Jimmy Smith, who made a series of tough, danceable crossover singles like 'Got My Mojo Workin'" and 'Who Do You Love Pts 1 & 2'.

Both groups were doing something entirely new. It would soon be called rock, but in mid-1966 it did not yet have a name. Whatever it was, it needed careful handling, and that was exactly what Warhol could not provide. Unlike the Mothers of Invention, who had the wily Herb Cohen, or their New York rival Bob Dylan, with the brutal Albert Grossman, the Velvet Underground did not have a manager versed in the complexities and pitfalls of the music industry.

Andy Warhol was an artist, not a mogul, and he had many other irons in the fire. Paul Morrissey was a film-maker, not a record man. The group's involvement with Warhol was, in fact, a double-edged sword: his generosity had given them a home, money, a record deal and press attention, but in return their unique character and their futuristic contribution were, like their appearances at the EPI, left in the shadows.

During the first half of 1966, Warhol's fame drew all the light to himself. The Velvet Underground had got a lot of press – more than most new groups – but it wasn't in the places that sold records. It was mainstream news outlets or art critics who had written about the group, mostly in dismissive or disparaging terms. The emerging underground press oscillated between confusion, awe and under-standing. The teen magazines basically held off. Even when they were mentioned, it was always in the context of Andy Warhol. The Velvet Underground had taken a short cut to a pop career but, as they would slowly realise, it would prove to be a dead end. Warhol was not built for the long haul in these matters: if something didn't work, he'd move on to the next thing – in this case, the spate of filming that would eventually be packaged as *Chelsea Girl*, his smash success of late 1966.

But there was perhaps another reason. There was something deeply unsettling about the Velvet Underground, something that went beyond their Warhol association and sadomasochistic miasma. They were, like Warhol, a mirror of America in 1966, and they aimed to tell hard truths to anyone who wanted to hear – an offer that, in that mid-sixties peak before the second wave of assassinations and the full onset of the Vietnam war, was almost universally refused.

The Velvet Underground were truly a product of their time in that they reflected America as it was, not how they wished it to be. Schooled in the exposé writers of the late fifties and early sixties – reports from the outcast and the damned that existed right in plain sight – Reed constructed a sequence of demotic, desperate scenarios that depicted the rat run of New York life and the dream-like states that people constructed as their escape. With the EPI, the group were plugged directly into the deeper currents of American life. A Stephen Shore picture from their residency at the Trip would be used, a few months later, in *The Medium Is the Massage*, the fourth book by the Canadian academic Marshall McLuhan. With a montage of faces – including two separate images of Nico – coming up on the screens, the VU are seen as shadows in the dark. They have become their environment.

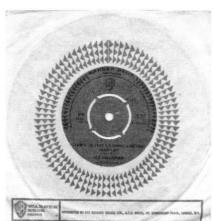

7 : JULY

Land of 1000 Dances: Tamla, Soul and
the March Against Fear

'To enjoy the latest new thing in discotheques, you had better wear ear plugs, dark glasses and shin guards. Otherwise you might be deafened, blinded and bruised in an electronic earthquake that engulfs you completely in an experience called "total recreation".'

Life magazine, 'Wild New Flashy Bedlam of the Discotheque', 27 May 1966

'One, two, *three*', '*one*, two, three': two countdowns, punctuated by horns, act as a brake. But what's to come cannot be stopped. There's a fast bass run; Wilson Pickett lets loose a little scream – just as a foretaste – and the full track comes in at breakneck speed. There's no time to think, no time to hesitate. The ride has begun. 'All right!' Pickett yells, before hitting the list of dances that comprise the first verse: the Pony, the Mashed Potato, the Alligator, the Watusi.

Nothing quite like 'Land of 1000 Dances' had been heard before. The music licks along at an incredible pace, the cyclical guitar riff counterpointed against the explosive horns. Pickett drives this instrumental intensity with vocal interjections and gospel exhortations: he grunts, he screams, and hits at top speed the first 'na, na-ne-na-na' section that was the song's hook. His voice is there not so much to convey the lyric – a series of dance-floor attitudes – but to be an integral part of the rhythm.

The guitar and brass drop out, leaving just the pounding drums and Pickett himself, augmented this second time round ('Need somebody to help me say it one time') by a large chorus. He lets rip another scream – in tune, one of his trademark skills – and the full band returns for a long sax solo. Pickett screams again, then riffs, as the drums pound, 'You know I feel all right, feel pretty good, y'all'.

At his prompting the massed chorus come back in for the 'na, na-ne-na-na' hook, before Pickett rips through the second verse

– 'Do the jerk / Watch me work, y'all' – riding the song out with a selection of instructions and screams: 'Ahh do it! Watch me do it! Oh, help me! Oh, help me!' This is not an ending but an early climax. The performance feels like a section from a live show that could go on for hours, rising and falling and rising again.

In July 1966, Wilson Pickett was twenty-five, a complex mixture of abrasiveness, kindness and swagger. Dubbed 'the wicked' by his record company, he lived up to the image, with sharp suits, slicked-back hair and a volatile demeanour. The owner of Fame Studios, Rick Hall, told Peter Guralnick that when he first met Pickett in spring 1966, 'He was such a good-looking black man, muscular – he reminded me of a black leopard, you know, look but don't touch, he might bite your hand.'

By that summer, Pickett was moving very fast. After years in the music industry – his first brush with fame was in the Falcons, whose 'You're So Fine' went Top 20 in 1959 – he signed to Atlantic. Beginning in summer 1965, he hit a consistent run with big sellers in the R&B chart – 'Don't Fight It', 'Ninety-Nine and a Half (Won't Do)' – and two pop crossover records, 'In the Midnight Hour' (#21) and '634-5789 (Soulsville, U.S.A.)' (#13) – all recorded at Stax. The collaboration had begun with an inspired, intuitive decision by Atlantic's Jerry Wexler, who brought Pickett down to Memphis to work with the studio and the house band responsible for successes by Carla and Rufus Thomas, Booker T. & the M.G.'s and, most recently, their breakthrough with Otis Redding, 'I've Been Loving You Too Long (To Stop Now')' – #21 in the *Billboard* Pop chart in early June.

Stax was a small, family-owned business operating from an old cinema in downtown Memphis. The old lobby was a record shop, Satellite, and the main hall was converted into a small studio that was open day and night. Although owned by whites – Jim Stewart and his sister, Estelle Axton – Stax ran an integrated house band – which featured, among others, Steve Cropper, Isaac Hayes, Al Jackson, Duck Dunn and Booker T. – and promoted exclusively black American performers.

Jim Stewart detailed the company's rationale in a June 1965 feature on 'The Memphis Sound'. 'All our artists at Stax are Negroes,' he told *Billboard*. 'Naturally our sound is directly oriented in that direction. The sound is hard to describe. It has a heavy back beat . . . That beat – a hard rhythm section – is an integral part of our sound. The combination of horns, instead of a smooth sound, produces a rough, growly, rasping sound, which carries into the melody.'

Atlantic had signed Pickett the previous year, but couldn't get the right sound in New York. Wexler decided to try something else. 'I couldn't get over the way they recorded in Memphis,' he told Stax historian Rob Bowman. 'It was really inspirational. The idea of coming to a place where four guys come to work like four cabinetmakers and plumbers and hang up their coats and start playing music in the morning, and then the beautifully crafted records that came out of this!'

The Stax band were sensitive to new dance rhythms – they'd seen different dances as they began to tour the country – and they responded to the New York visitor. To get the right feeling on 'In the Midnight Hour', Wexler performed his version of the dance of the moment, the Jerk, encouraging the band to play a slightly delayed two and four beat, a device that, by slowing the track down infinitesimally, created torque and tension. Yet, despite this creative flow, Stax barred Pickett from the studio after the third session. There has been some controversy as to exactly why, but it seems likely that Jim Stewart didn't want anyone else having hits with his studio's trademark sound. By late 1965, Stax was the label to watch, but this cult status had not yet fully translated into record sales. Establishing and preserving the brand name had become all-important.

The result was that, in spring 1966, Pickett travelled to Muscle Shoals, Alabama, to record at Rick Hall's FAME studios. Set up in 1962, FAME had been responsible for Joe Tex's early-1965 hit 'Hold What You've Got' (#5 *Billboard* Pop), one of the first soul records to break through into the mainstream, and at the time of Pickett's visit the studio had the hottest soul record in the US, Percy Sledge's wracked, gospel-drenched 'When a Man Loves a Woman'.

Pickett was appalled when, flying back to his home state of Alabama after many years, he looked out of the plane window and saw 'people picking cotton. I said to myself, "I ain't getting off this plane, take me back North." This big Southern guy was at the airport, really big guy, looks like a sheriff. He says he's looking for me. I said, "I don't want to get off here, they still got black people picking cotton." The man looked at me and said, "Fuck that. Come on, Pickett, let's go make some fucking hit records."'

There's a picture of Pickett at FAME in 1966 with two members of the predominantly white house band. The keyboard player, Spooner Oldham, is thin, bearded, beatnik, all angles, with a studio pallor and a bright white shirt. Pickett, dressed in high-waisted, light grey pants, a black shirt and a short black leather jacket, looms above him, driving both him and the other musicians on. This unlikely combination hit pay dirt with their first song. 'Land of 1000 Dances' was a strange choice for a studio and a singer wanting to push things forward: it was nearly four years old and had hit the Top 30 the year before. By spring 1966, there were well over a dozen versions, by black and white artists alike. Yet both Pickett and the FAME musicians heard something in it, and they stripped and boosted this contemporary standard into the definitive version.

'Land of 1000 Dances' had first been recorded by its writer, Chris Kenner, in a rolling New Orleans style, with odd, turned-around rhythmic accents. Released in October 1962, in the middle of the novelty-dance craze that followed the Twist, it was just a riff, with a lyric that itemised the various dances of the past and the present: the Pony, the Twist, the Stroll, the Mashed Potato, the Watusi, the Fly, the Hand Jive, the Tango.

Kenner's record had begun with the feeling of an old southern spiritual, but as it developed over the next three years it became a dance favourite. The most important retooling was by east LA group Cannibal and the Headhunters, who added crowd noises and the 'na na-ne-na-na' chant. After their version hit #30 in the *Billboard* Pop chart in spring 1965, it was open season on the song, with covers by Round Robin, Sandy Nelson, the Walker Brothers, Johnny Rivers and the Action. It remained current well into 1966, with strong versions by Nino Tempo and April Stevens and by Earl Cosby, a cool, vibes-led 45 on the Mirwood label out of Los Angeles. Nevertheless, Wilson Pickett and Rick Hall felt confident enough to make the song their top priority in their first FAME session. With a band that included Jimmy Johnson on guitar, Spooner Oldham, Tommy Cogbill on bass and Roger Hawkins on drums, they produced a masterpiece.

Pickett was known as the most exciting of the rising black singers, so he had to pull something out of the bag. Previous covers of the song had upped the excitement by including audience effects, but that was becoming a cliché. All concerned knew they had to trump that artificial hysteria, and they did so through an attack so feral – the combination of Pickett's unleashed energy with the pill-popping musicians – that it rendered all other versions obsolete.

Explosive, compressed, ecstatic, Pickett's 'Land of 1000 Dances' was faster than any other dance tune of the time. Bucking and leaping like a wild mustang, it had an immediate impact upon its release in mid-July 1966, hitting radio playlists and the *Billboard* Top 60 by the end of the month. It was one of those records that, through its very force, pulled the culture along with it, ratcheting up the intensity, matching and pushing the changing rhythms of the dances.

It resonated beyond the charts. 'Land of 1000 Dances' was startlingly new, but at the same time it was part of a continuum of black music and black culture that went back through the twentieth century and beyond. As the dancer, choreographer and scholar Naomi Elizabeth Bragin writes, 'Dance crazes have always been a way of creating lineage, kinship and counter-memory within black communities by recycling and transmitting embodied knowledge.'

Ahmet Ertegün reflected on this to the writer Gerri Hirshey. He felt that black music was 'all part of a continuum. Black audiences aren't fickle, but they're not nostalgic either . . . They not only make the records but they make the music. They buy it; they dance to it. Black music evolves. It's a living thing.' Jerry Wexler confirmed this, telling Hirshey, 'You could cut a record in one or two takes, with just a head arrangement, but it might have a resonance that took in generations.'

This is how it worked with 'Land of 1000 Dances'. Chris Kenner's original sourced an old southern spiritual and retooled it for an accelerated, more volatile moment in American history. At the same time, it referenced many dances that had originated within the black community over the previous decade, dances that had already offered a measure of visibility and chart success. Pickett's version was for all time: it was a mixture of past, present and future.

Until the mid-1960s, this kind of lineage had operated under the radar of white America. Apart from very specific areas – music, dancing – black culture was part of another, alien world, kept separate by segregationist laws, vicious prejudice and institutionalised apartheid. But this system was under concerted attack. The gains of the civil rights movement, together with the new visibility of unapologetic, proud black American pop stars, seemed to herald a new era.

By summer 1966, black American music was crossing over more and more from the R&B into the pop charts, as artists like the Supremes, James Brown, Stevie Wonder and Percy Sledge had Top 10 hits. At the same time, the civil rights movement was facing a crucial moment, as all the marches and even affirmative government legislation failed to counter the deep, fundamental prejudice that existed throughout America. Hope was being replaced by frustration and anger.

Wilson Pickett's 'Land of 1000 Dances' is poised between these twin movements and the feelings that they encompass: between assertiveness and anger, pride and defiance. The fact that Pickett felt confident enough to completely overhaul a four-year-old song about a dozen dances showed just how steeped he was in his black heritage and how, with his new-found crossover success, he sought to transmit that knowledge to white America and then the world.

* * *

'The dance floor was swaying. The bombastic drive of the rock 'n' roll music had the dancers pounding the floor in unison, and under the impact the sturdy dance floor bent, but fortunately did not give. On display was the twist and a large group of dances derived from the twist – the Frug, the wobble, the surf, the Hully-Gully, the uncle willy, the Jamaican ska, the mashed potato, and the smashed banana.'
ROBERT ALDEN, '1,000 Twisters and One Floor Swing at Venerable Palladium', *New York Times*, 4 June 1964

In the modern era, it all began with the Twist – the pop sensation of 1960, 1961 and 1962 and the great liberator of social dancing. It had taken about three years for the style to pass from a small group of young black Americans to a worldwide phenomenon, and, in the early to mid-sixties, other dances rushed in to fill the frantic need for more novelty – new beats, new steps, new names – that the Twist had created through its unexpected success.

Some of these new dances were showcased on the first, 1960 album by Twist maven Chubby Checker: the Hucklebuck, the Strand, the Slop, the Stroll, the Madison, the Pony, the Shimmy. Most of these followed the Twist in that they did not necessarily require a partner, were freestyle and involved minimal footwork and what dance historian Ralph Giordano called 'pantomime' arm movements. Many were made up on the spot. The point was accessibility and rapid turnover.

'They're some of the most enjoyable – certainly the most do-able – dances ever to come along,' explained the *Hullabaloo Discotheque Dance Book* in 1966. 'Sure, there are movements to learn, sometimes even patterns for your feet; but almost anything goes in these dances, so long as you keep loose, and keep the beat.'

The introduction reinforced the centrality of rhythm: 'You can't help hearing the beat, really *feeling* it, and that's what you move to – not to the melody.'

'Keep loose', 'really *feeling* it': these were powerful instructions to the white Americans targeted by the booklet. Most of the new dances originated among teenage blacks and were popularised by black musicians. Indeed, dance records would provide their entry into the pop charts. In turn, young whites were exposed to black culture as they rarely had been before. The Twist represented nothing less than the return of the body within mainstream American popular culture.

By 1963 and 1964, the charts were full of the post-Twist dances. The Watusi, the Mashed Potato, the Frug and the Monkey all made hits for a variety of artists, including the Vibrations, Major Lance, the Miracles and James Brown. The initial hit, which always included the name of the dance in the title, announced the style, and this then passed into the general repertoire, to be performed as part of an increasingly complex and improvised mix.

This eclectic, fast-moving economy was institutionalised by the spread of the discotheque as a new concept in entertainment. Following the lead of Twist clubs like the Peppermint Lounge and Peppermint West, Elmer Valentine, the former owner of another successful Twist club, P.J.'s, opened the Whisky a Go Go on the Sunset Strip during January 1964. It was an instant success, a venue whose time had come.

The new dances were promoted by a new generation of pop TV shows: ABC's *Shindig!* (first broadcast in September 1964), *The Lloyd Thaxton Show*, *Hullabaloo*, *Hollywood a Go Go*, *Shivaree* and Dick Clark's *Where the Action Is*. These all featured high-voltage pop, with enthusiastic audience settings that often featured a Whisky innovation: young women dancing the Frug, the Swim and other permutations from within a cage – go-go dancers.

Dance styles continued to evolve. 1964 saw the popularity of the Jerk, described in the *Hullabaloo Discotheque Dance Book* as 'basically the Monkey – but with your arms and hands moving as if you were leading a band'. The snap forward of the upper body, combined with a slight hesitation, was the rhythm that Jerry Wexler demonstrated to the Stax house band as the correct tempo for 'In the Midnight Hour'.

1964 was a breakthrough year for black music. Between November 1963 and January 1965, *Billboard* didn't run their R&B charts – an index of increasing musical integration. The end-of-year charts bear this out: there are five British songs in the top twenty singles of the year (three by the Beatles) but four Motown hits: two by the Supremes and one each from Mary Wells and Martha and the Vandellas, whose 'Dancing in the Street' went to #2 in October 1964.

'Dancing in the Street' was a call-to-arms of such power and ambition that it still sweeps all before it: 'Callin' out around the world, are you ready for a brand new beat? / Summer's here and the time is right for dancin' in the street.' The lyric pulls the old city-by-city trick, but the music is so transcendent that it feels inclusive rather than rote. The tambourine hits the snare, the bass hits the solar plexus, and Martha Reeves sings her heart out in a joyous ecstasy.

From being a novelty, dance music was becoming *the* sound of the times, true contemporary art. The Beatles and the Rolling Stones got all the mainstream media attention, but the Supremes, Martha and the Vandellas and James Brown were easily their equals, if not superiors. Nowhere was this better seen than in the *T.A.M.I. Show*, a concert film shot over two days at the end of October 1964 in which James Brown shredded the Rolling Stones.

Brown finishes a storming set with a super-fast 'Night Train'. He stops, does some a cappella call-and-response with the audience, before executing some insane dance steps, doing the splits, shimmying and shaking like a man possessed. His eighteen minutes is a masterclass of tension and release, of the most dazzling, gravity-defying footwork designed to make life difficult for the upstart headliners. As he understated, 'It was hard for the Rolling Stones to follow us.'

The T.A.M.I. Show was released on 29 December. Two days before, the Supremes had made their debut appearance on that conduit to the American mainstream, *The Ed Sullivan Show*, singing 'Come See about Me'. Introduced by Sullivan as 'three youngsters from Detroit', the Supremes are highlighted on an empty stage. They present a unified front, confident and proud, effortlessly overcoming the house band.

This was a new version of black culture for America's heartlands. The Supremes were sophisticated, poised and urban contemporary. Sullivan signed off by warmly greeting each member of the group, inviting them into millions of American homes. It was a pivotal moment: as the historian Suzanne Smith writes, 'a landmark in the history of the record company, of black cultural production in Detroit, and of the promotion of "Negro Life" in America'.

By the first week of 1965, the Supremes were at #2 in the American charts. The year would be dominated by Motown: with a gross income of around $8 million, it was America's top seller of singles. As well as six #1s, the various Berry Gordy labels – Motown, Gordy, Tamla – had Top 10s by Marvin Gaye, Junior Walker and Martha Reeves and the Vandellas.

Berry Gordy's integrationist policy was working, with huge hits in both the pop and the R&B charts. Reflecting Detroit's core industry and Gordy's own working experience at the Lincoln-Mercury plant, Motown was run on the basis of an auto assembly line: songs were often constructed out of interchangeable parts, to be assembled at a later date and assigned to whichever artist Gordy and his team felt would suit.

Motown's success was based on several factors. One was songs with repeated hooks and first-person lyrics that established a scenario and ended in some kind of denouement, even if there was rarely any complete resolution. Holland–Dozier–Holland's material for the Supremes was a perfect example: the situations were usually downbeat, with Diana Ross calling out for a love that the arrangement told you she would never regain. She was stuck in a loop.

It was that very loop that made people play the records again and again, a hypnotic pull. Above all, Motown was dance music, not imposed from 'above' by cynical record companies – like it had been with some of the post-Twist dance crazes – but developed and performed by audiences. Saxophonist Junior Walker described how he wrote the Top 10 pop hit 'Shotgun' after watching a boy and a girl try out a new step:

> I said, 'What are you doing now? What kind of junk is this?'
> The girl looked at me and said, 'Man, that's the Shotgun!'
> I said, 'The Shotgun?'
> They said, 'You'd better write a tune to that! That's what's happening!'

The basis of the Tamla sound was the heavy bass and the sharp, simultaneous crack of the tambourine and the snare drum, driving the rhythm home and reinforcing the material's dance-floor imperative. It had another effect: allied to a fairly unvarying 4/4 beat, this created another kind of loop that, together with the songs' often light and airy melodies and powerful emotional hooks, made Motown 'the ideal accompaniment for driving'.

Conceived and run as a brand, Motown had a strong claim not just to being the sound of black America but the sound of young America. On 21 May 1965, *Time* magazine ran a pop cover feature entitled 'Rock'n'Roll: Everybody's Turned On'. The cover montage showed a line of go-go dancers, Trini Lopez, the Beach Boys, the Righteous Brothers, Herman, Petula Clark and, in the bottom right corner, the only black act – the Supremes.

Motown's success triggered an explosion of black music production in the US, as myriad labels each tried to capture that identifiable but hard-to-reproduce sound: Okeh, Mirwood, Cadet/Checker, New Voice, Wand and literally hundreds of others. The most authentic soundalikes came from the Detroit label Ric-Tic, which tended to use moonlighting Motown musicians wherever possible.

Ric-Tic's fourth release was Edwin Starr's 'Agent Double-O-Soul', which hit a peak of #21 in early October 1965. 'I dig rock and roll music,' Starr sang over a fast, 4/4 rhythm. 'I can do the Twine and the Jerk / I wear strictly continental suits / And high-collared shirts.' A riff on the very popular James Bond films, the song was the first of several spy-themed dancers, a major obsession that would continue throughout 1966.

Starr wasn't licensed to kill, but to thrill; he wasn't 007 but 00 Soul. By 1965, with hits like the Impressions' 'Woman's Got Soul' and the name of Gordy's earthy subsidiary label Soul, the word was beginning to solidify as the term of choice for the new wave of black American music, one that was dance-oriented but not fly-by-night, one that was increasingly popular in the mainstream American charts and increasingly assertive about black culture.

The meaning would become hotly contested in the years to come, but in the mid-sixties it served as a catch-all term for everything that made black music different, that recognised its emotional and kinetic power and its intimate relation to a people's life just as things appeared to be changing for the better. Soul meant Not Blues. It was urban, confident, two generations away from the plantations. It symbolised moving on up.

Soul didn't happen just because of one person. It was a com-bination of Ray Charles, Solomon Burke, Motown, Atlantic, the Impressions, Sam Cooke, Stax all coming together to the same point. It came from gospel music – the church being, historically, one of the very few places where blacks could congregate, organise and, indeed, be themselves – but was highly secular: as one defini-tion offers, with 'girl' replacing 'God'.

Soul put the black back in America, slowly at first but with increasing force. Black American music was replacing the British invasion as the pop style to watch, and it was taking with it the hopes of millions. LeRoi Jones identified this: 'The hard, driving shouting of James Brown identifies place and image in America. A people and an energy, harnessed and not harnessed by America. JB is straight out, open and speaking from the most religious people on this continent.'

'Agent Double-O-Soul' entered *Billboard*'s Pop 30 on 4 September

1965. The same week, James Brown's 'Papa's Got a Brand New Bag Pt. 1' rose to its peak Pop position, #8. This was a stunning return from an artist who was about to reach the height of his powers. Short, stocky yet wiry, with the body of the boxer he had once been, Brown rolled with the punches and came out even stronger, with a sequence of huge hits that would change music for ever.

During 1965, Brown returned to King Records after a debilitating dispute with owner Syd Nathan. In autumn 1964, Brown had released the futuristic 'Out of Sight' – with its extended vamp – on Smash Records. It went to #24 Pop. Nathan slapped him with a suit, and the gloves were off. King proceeded to release substandard, old JB material, while the man himself issued instrumental recordings under a couple of different names.

After Nathan capitulated, Brown returned with a brand-new song that he had been playing live and was itching to record. Spread over two sides of a single, 'Papa's Got a Brand New Bag' was a deconstruction of dance music, with all the different parts – the horns, the lyrics, the scat interjections, Jimmy Nolen's scratching guitar – taken apart, looped and reassembled into something that, dispensing with traditional song structure, accentuated feel and groove. It continued the devices premiered on 'Out of Sight'. As Peter Guralnick writes, 'All the grunts, groans, screams, clicks and screeches that had been lurking in the background, the daringly modal approach to melody (soon there would be virtually no chord changes in a James Brown song, with forward motion dependent entirely on rhythm) were – without anyone's fully realising it in 1965 – intimations of African roots, declarations of black pride.' But this was also a dance song, with a lyric that went back to the history of dance fads in looking to the future, citing as it did the Jerk, the Fly, the Monkey, the Mashed Potato. As the bass leaped and looped like the Boomerang, 'Papa's Got a Brand New Bag' took on a life of its own. 'It's a little beyond me,' Brown admitted to disc jockey Alan Leeds in 1965. 'I'm actually fightin' the future. It's – it's – it's just out there.'

'Papa's Got a Brand New Bag' was that rare beast: a huge hit that fused commercial appeal with innovation. This was Brown's first *Billboard* Pop Top 10 record, and he was determined to make his success stick. As he played to increasingly integrated audiences during the second half of 1965, he prepared his next single: a re-recording of a tune he had already recorded for the hit movie *Ski Party*, but this time stripped and revved for the kids who were doing the Jerk.

'I Got You (I Feel Good)' was more traditional in structure than his previous record, with verses, choruses and a middle eight. Even so, it continued Brown's radical retooling of dance music, with a light, sharp drum sound, a complex bass pattern, a jazzy breakbeat just before the middle eight, a stuttering final section repeating like a stuck groove, and a liberal application of the singer's trademark screams. It went into the Pop Top 10 at the end of November.

By this time, Stax were beginning to feel a little left behind. They had the sound, they had the identity, they had the respect of musicians and industry insiders alike, but they weren't able to translate this into big pop hits, unlike Tamla, King or even Chess. The label had only two *Billboard* Top 30 hits that year, and one was by an Atlantic artist, Wilson Pickett – hence the prickliness about who exactly should have access to the Memphis studio.

Their biggest artist was Otis Redding. After Sam Cooke's murder in December 1964, some of that great crossover artist's mantle seemed to fall on Redding, a gentle man and a genuine vocal artist who, as 1965 progressed, was increasingly driven and prolific. He was on a mission: on the one hand, to pare down words to an essence – a sequence of rhythmic, percussive ticks; and, on the other, to bring the testifying gospel approach of deep soul to a wider audience.

'I've Been Loving You Too Long' was the breakthrough. The song hinges on a dilemma: 'I've been loving you too long – *to stop now*'. The more the woman wants to leave, the more the man loves her: 'My love is growing stronger as our affair grows old'. This wracked examination of love's exquisite tortures is given total authority by Redding's vocal, intense and measured in the verses, soaring on the phrase 'you are tired' and obsessively vamping over the extended fade.

This was a different kind of intensity: shamelessly emotional, if not confessional, and admitting adult complexities. Redding quickly followed its success with the album *Otis Blue: Otis Redding Sings Soul*, a definitive statement of Stax in mid-1965. Beginning with a stinging Steve Cropper fanfare on 'Ole Man Trouble', the eleven songs include the hit and its follow-up, the original version of 'Respect', which, surprisingly, only reached #35 in November.

Otis Blue offered material as diverse and as inclusive as B. B. King's 'Rock Me Baby', the Temptations' 'My Girl' and the traditional 'Down in the Valley'. Redding ripped through 'Satisfaction' – the soul-influenced riff returning to source – but his true intentions were served by his dignified inhabitation of Sam Cooke's 'A Change Is Gonna Come', retitled 'Change Gonna Come'. But, although the album helped to cement 'soul' as the word of the moment, it didn't make the US pop chart.

In an attempt to address the gap between influence and sales – indeed, to find another way of breaking through – Jim Stewart and his partner Estelle Axton hired Al Bell as Stax's promotions man. A black American who had been involved with Martin Luther King's Southern Christian Leadership Conference in the early 1960s, Bell used his DJ contacts to spread the word, in an attempt to turn a still small southern record company into a national force.

Much of the word-of-mouth groundwork had already been done. In the 31 December 1965 edition of *Record Mirror*, Tony Hall ran a feature entitled 'George Harrison's Fab Forty'. Based on the contents of the Beatle's jukebox, the list is worth reproducing in full:

1. 'Harlem Shuffle' – Bob and Earl
2. 'Good Things Come to Those Who Wait' – Chuck Jackson
3. 'Be My Lady'/'Red Beans and Rice' – Booker T and the M.G.'s
4. 'Please Crawl Out Your Window' – Bob Dylan
5. 'Baby, You're My Everything' – Little Jerry Williams

6. 'Back Street' – Edwin Starr

7. 'Work, Work, Work' – Lee Dorsey

8. 'The Little Girl I Once Knew' – The Beach Boys

9. 'My Girl Has Gone' – The Miracles

10. 'I Don't Know What You've Got (But It's Got Me)' – Little Richard

11. 'I Can't Turn You Loose' – Otis Redding

12. 'My Girl' – Otis Redding

13. 'I Believe I'll Love On' – Jackie Wilson

14. 'Plum Nellie' – Booker T and the M.G.'s

15. 'Everything Is Gonna Be Alright' – Willie Mitchell

16. 'A Sweet Woman Like You' – Joe Tex

17. 'Something About You' – The Four Tops

18. 'I Got You' – James Brown

19. 'Ain't That Peculiar' – Marvin Gaye

20. 'Turn, Turn, Turn' – The Byrds

21. 'See Saw' – Don Covay

22. 'I'm Comin' Through' – Sounds Incorporated

23. 'Don't Fight It' – Wilson Pickett

24. 'Bootleg' – Booker T and the M.G.'s

25. 'I Ain't Gonna Eat Out My Heart Anymore' – The Young Rascals

26. 'Respect' – Otis Redding

27. 'Try Me'/'Papa's Got a Brand New Bag' – James Brown (instrumentals)

28. 'I've Been Loving You Too Long' – Otis Redding

29. 'All Or Nothing' – Patti Labelle and her Belles

30. 'Pretty Little Baby' – Marvin Gaye

31. 'Oowee Baby I Love You' – Fred Hughes

32. 'The Tracks of My Tears' – The Miracles

33. 'Yum Yum' – Joe Tex

34. 'Agent oo Soul' – Edwin Starr

35. 'Money' – Barrett Strong

36. 'Some Other Guy' – Richie Barrett

37. 'It Wasn't Me' – Chuck Berry

38. 'Mohair Sam' – Charlie Rich
39. 'Let Him Run Wild' – The Beach Boys
40. 'Do You Believe in Magic' – The Lovin' Spoonful

Thirty-four out of the forty-two songs listed are black American records: two from Ric-Tic, three by James Brown, six Motown singles and ten Stax productions. The sound of Stax – in particular the slower, chopped rhythms and biting Steve Cropper guitar – was all over the Beatles' new LP, *Rubber Soul*. Both 'Drive My Car' and 'The Word' adapted the label's sound into abrasive, contemporary rockers, one humorous, the other confrontational.

Indeed, the Beatles were such Stax fans that, in March 1966, their manager, Brian Epstein, made enquiries about recording sessions at the Memphis studio. The *Memphis Press Scimitar* reported that they were arriving on 9 April to record an album there, but that Estelle Axton was having problems finding somewhere for them to stay. It never happened: word got out and, in the still fervid climate surrounding the Beatles, that was enough to nix the idea.

The Beatles weren't the only white culture leaders to pick up on Stax. The Rolling Stones had always taken black music as their principal source, and the British release of *Out of Our Heads* was filled with covers of Marvin Gaye, O. V. Wright, Solomon Burke, Larry Williams and Barbara Lynn. They tried out a cover of 'I've Been Loving You Too Long', just weeks after its release, on the same day that they recorded 'Satisfaction'.

In May 1965, Solomon Burke released his version of Dylan's 'Maggie's Farm' on a single. From early 1966 on, this interaction would increasingly become a two-way street: a recognition of Dylan, the Beatles and the Rolling Stones, but also an assertion of pop equality – 'We're just as good as you.' Otis Redding recorded both 'Satisfaction' and 'Day Tripper', replaying the Stax influence, while J. J. Barnes released a stomping version of the latter on Ric-Tic.

1966 began with James Brown's 'I Got You (I Feel Good)' at #3. On 12 February, there were five black records in the US top eleven:

Stevie Wonder's 'Uptight', Ray Charles's 'Crying Time', 'My World Is Empty Without You' by the Supremes, the Marvelettes' 'Don't Mess with Bill' and the Miracles' ecstatic 'Going to a Go-Go' – a hymn to the discotheque as social leveller, with its pounding tom-toms and Smokey Robinson's wide-eyed, high vocals.

Motown continued the punishing pace into 1966, the year in which it would rack up twenty-two Top 10 Pop hits. Top 30 entrants in the first few months included Martha and the Vandellas' 'My Baby Loves Me', the Temptations' 'Get Ready' and Marvin Gaye's extraordinary 'One More Heartache' – a Smokey Robinson song with an addictive Marv Tarplin riff and an odd Eastern tinge, a portent of things to come.

Stax was also shifting gears. Otis Redding had missed with the breakneck 'I Can't Turn You Loose' but had a hit with 'Satis-faction' in early April. The crossover was happening: on 2 April, Redding played the Hollywood Bowl on a bill with Sonny and Cher, Donovan and the Mamas and the Papas. The next week he played four days at the Whisky a Go Go, right in the heart of white Sunset Strip.

But the Stax breakthrough came with Sam and Dave's 'Hold On! I'm Coming'. Writers Dave Porter and Isaac Hayes studied the Motown narrative template – in particular, Smokey Robinson's lyric for the Temptations' 'Don't Look Back' – and decided to throw in a bit of James Brown and Lee Dorsey. It reached #21 in mid-June. 'That's when the thought processes really started work-ing,' Porter told Rob Bowman, 'and an identity started taking place.'

There was another new dance craze in 1966: the Boo-Ga-Loo. This was popularised by a comedy/singing act called Tom and Jerrio, who saw kids performing the dance at a Chicago record hop. Released in March 1965, their single 'Boo-Ga-Loo' welded a fast Motown rhythm to a Latin feel and James Brown-style interjec-tions. The record went to #11 in *Billboard*'s R&B charts, prompt-ing a quick follow-up, '(Papa Chew) Do the Boo-Ga-Loo Part 1'.

So far, so much a novelty, but the Boo-Ga-Loo stuck around. It followed the trend of integrating Latin dances and rhythms into black music and the pop mainstream that had begun with Chris Montez's 'Let's Dance' and followed through in the east LA versions of 'Land of 1000 Dances'. The biggest selling 45 of 1965 was 'Woolly Bully' by the Mexican American Sam the Sham and his Pharaohs, which began with the countdown *'Uno, dos*, one, two, *tres, quatro'*.

Boo-Ga-Loo records flourished in early 1966. In January, veteran R&B group the Flamingos released the storming 'Boogaloo Party', while James Brown released two quick-cash instrumentals on Smash: 'New Breed (Part 1) (The Boo-Ga-Loo)' in March and 'James Brown's Boo-Ga-Loo' in June. J. J. Jackson dropped the storming 'Do the Boogaloo' – with a horn riff a hair away from the Rolling Stones' 'Satisfaction' – during July.

Motown might have made all the running in 1964 and 1965, but early 1966 belonged to James Brown – despite, it seemed, the best efforts of his record company. On 1 January, while 'I Got You (I Feel Good)' was in the Top 3, King slapped out an album of the same name which collected old 45s from 1959–64 – an eminently playable record, but not where the singer was at in that new year.

The real follow-up to 'I Got You (I Feel Good)' was 'Ain't That a Groove Part 1'. It only made #42, but the momentum of his two more recent hits meant that it hardly mattered. In March, Brown visited Europe for the first time: Paris and London, where he played a couple of ballroom dates (one at the Walthamstow Granada on the 12th) to audience pandemonium and took over *Ready Steady Go!* for an entire show.

During his UK visit, Brown was interviewed by Dave Godin, the long-standing booster of black American music. Godin duly noted 'the dubious image that rumour and gossip had created of him before his arrival, but perhaps I was luckier than most in being able to spend a whole hour with him between shows, and I'm happy to be able to say that he is no ogre – nor a superman, he's a very warm and affable person who is highly intelligent, supercool and hip'. Godin's enthusiasm and knowledge broke through

Brown's habitual reserve: 'I asked him what was his favourite song out of all his repertoire, and he said it was "Please, Please, Please". I had to disagree on this point and said that I personally preferred "Lost Someone" and "The Bells". He looked at me for a second, and then a large smile crept over his face – "Man," he said, "now you're really talking soul," and so we got to talking about the soul trend.'

James Brown had become a unique figure, which is what he had intended all along: 'He said that when he was starting his career in show business, he was in no way influenced by other performers – "What I set out to do was to create James Brown – a new and original singer who would not be a copy of someone else. I imagined my act and my image how I wanted it to be and never looked back."'

Brown was a phenomenon. He didn't need a machine like the Motown artists, he was his own machine. When he returned to America in mid-March, he was greeted at JFK airport by hundreds of fans. A few days later, he headlined the 15,000-capacity Eighth Avenue Madison Square Garden, supported by Len Barry, Lou Christie, Slim Harpo and the Shangri-Las. It was a sell-out: as Brown remembered, 'Things were just getting bigger and bigger real fast.'

The Garden show was witnessed by the legendary tap dancer Buster Brown and the documentary film-maker Mura Dehn. Both thought that Brown was a performer totally in sync with his times. Dehn recognised his 'genius and madness': 'James Brown is unprecedented. A man touched by divine power. He absorbs. He stuns. And yet you don't feel enriched. You cannot live on what he reveals. You simply experience him, and he is fabulous.'

Time reported that 'for one frenetic hour, Brown commanded the stage like a one-man riot'. It noted the rising graph of his live performances ('on the road 340 days last year, he grossed more than $1,000,000') and his singles sales ('over 1,000,000 copies each'), and concluded by observing that 'on *Billboard*'s campus popularity poll he ranks just behind Bob Dylan. His rise in the mass market gives a sign that "race music" is perhaps at last becoming interracial.'

That month, Brown released the tortured ballad 'It's a Man's

Man's Man's World'. It entered the *Billboard* Top 100 (at #70) on 30 April 1966. The next evening, he appeared on the *Ed Sullivan Show* with the Supremes. It was his first time: the invitation had been extended several times before, but Brown had held out until he could bring his own band into the television studios – a wise move considering the mangling customarily dished out by the show's orchestra.

Introduced to the American mainstream by the stony-faced Sullivan, Brown performed a rapid-fire, intense medley of 'Papa's Got a Brand New Bag' and 'I Got You (I Feel Good)', as well as 'Ain't That a Groove?', 'It's a Man's Man's Man's World' and 'Please, Please, Please'. Doing the Slide, the Boo-Ga-Loo and the James Brown with pin-drop timing and precision, Brown epitomised black artistry and black pride, with no quarter given to the mass audience.

The next week, Brown broke his own house record at the Harlem Apollo and, on 4 June, 'It's a Man's Man's Man's World' reached its peak of #8 in the *Billboard* chart. Percy Sledge was at #1 with 'When a Man Loves a Woman', the Supremes at #11 with 'Love Is Like an Itching in My Heart', Robert Parker at #12 with 'Barefootin'', the Chiffons at #13 with 'Sweet Talking Guy' and the Capitols at #17 with the snappy 'Cool Jerk'.

It seemed as though the bastions of white America were falling to the soul onslaught. The force of black music in 1965 and 1966 was unstoppable, a peak of artistry equal, if not superior, to anything produced by the white culture leaders, who were smart enough to pay their respects. When asked by reporters who was America's greatest poet, Bob Dylan cited Smokey Robinson along with Rimbaud, Allen Ginsberg and W.C. Fields, and the pop elite welcomed black Americans into their orbit.

In the wider society, however, things were not so rosy. The performers knew it. How could they not, when every time they stepped outside their bubble it was made very clear to them that they were just another black person, low-caste, low-grade, still a second-class citizen, if not worse? For all the media attention and record sales, they were still human beings like all the others who were not onstage. They were part of the great struggle of the day, whether they liked it or not. Sometimes it was obvious, even in the very avenues that seductively promised integration. In the issue of *Look* that had featured the Supremes, they shared the cover strap-line with a picture of men in hoods: 'The KU KLUX KLAN'. In this context, it's hard to read Diana Ross's explosive rant inside except in terms of personal frustration and racial pride.

James Brown knew exactly what he was doing, as did Otis Redding and Berry Gordy: they were walking the tightrope between public silence on the burning issues of the day and the presentation of black culture to the mass market in an undiluted form. It was a cultural putsch – with aims that were still largely unstated – that co-existed with an organised mass political movement. The two had been running on parallel tracks, but that would soon change.

Things were hotting up. On 5 June, while Percy Sledge, James Brown and the Supremes rode high in the charts, James Meredith began his 'March Against Fear' in Memphis. It began slowly – Meredith was only joined by four other people on that first day – but the events that ensued posed a huge question for that movement at the same time as they demanded a renewed, if not greater commitment.

* * *

'The Impressions' "Keep on Pushing" or Martha and the Vandellas' "Dancing in the Street" (especially re: summer riots, i.e., "Summer's here . . .") provided a core of legitimate social feeling, though mainly metaphorical and allegorical for black people.'
    LEROI JONES, *The Changing Same (R&B and New Black Music)*, 1966

A long trail of 600 predominantly black marchers are trying to leave Selma, Alabama. They are walking to the state capital, Montgomery, to raise attention for a black-voter registration drive. They proceed in line along the sidewalk of the Edmund Pettus

Bridge. The slight slope propels them down towards serried ranks of state troopers bearing billy clubs, bull-whips and gas masks. The front few rows of the suddenly halted march look very fragile.

A cop with a megaphone issues the warning, 'This is an unlawful assembly, you are to disperse.' A rank of troopers march menacingly to the front of the gathering. When they meet the front few rows, they push them down like nine-pins. Accelerating in pace, they drive a wedge through the static, unarmed marchers, men and women alike. Backed up by horses and tear gas, the police lash out with their billy clubs, consigning seventeen marchers to hospital.

The flickering television images still make the blood boil. But, in early March 1965, they were even more shocking. The events in Selma made national news and quickly gained their own term – 'Bloody Sunday'. The Student Nonviolent Coordinating Committee's leader, John Lewis, at the very front of the march, was hospitalised with a fractured skull, while fifty-four-year-old Amelia Boynton, a long-standing and well-respected civil rights activist, was gassed and beaten unconscious.

Newsreels of the violence were shown on that evening's national news, galvanising opinion in America. President Johnson seized his moment. Just over a week later, he went to Congress and argued persuasively and passionately for the Voting Rights Act, in a keynote speech that referred explicitly to events in Selma. The Act proposed to end racial discrimination in voting – a direct counter to the endemic intimidation that faced black voters in the south.

Johnson was a Texan who combined crudity with a sharp intelligence, slippery pragmatism with passionate beliefs. His stated commitment to civil rights came from his own experience as a teacher in a Mexican American school: 'My students were poor and they often came to class without breakfast, hungry. They knew even in their youth the pain of prejudice. They never seemed to know why people disliked them. But they knew it was so, because I saw it in their eyes.'

Near the speech's end, he used the keynote civil rights slogan: 'What happened in Selma is part of a far larger movement which reaches into every section and State of America. It is the effort of American Negroes to secure for themselves the full blessings of American life. Their cause must be our cause too. Because it is not just Negroes, but really it is all of us, who must overcome the crippling legacy of bigotry and injustice. *And we shall overcome.*'

This was a ringing endorsement of the civil rights movement and a major step in black American life. But there was an undertow to Johnson's words. It had taken violence – blind, stupid, ugly hatred – to push public opinion towards equality, and the most terrible thing about the Pettus Bridge footage is how that violence was not an isolated event, but had been endemic through every stage of the civil rights struggle.

For every gain, it seemed, there were beatings, murders, faces screaming hatred. Many of the confrontations had been filmed: the white faces shouting abuse at the Little Rock Nine in 1957; the young men and women attacked at luncheon counters in the deep south during 1961; the Freedom Riders' bus being burnt at Anniston, Alabama, in 1961; the young men and women blasted by water cannon and savaged by dogs in Birmingham, Alabama, in 1963.

It was terrifying, even more so because under the inspired leadership of Martin Luther King, the various civil rights groups were passionately committed to non-violence, to Gandhian passive resistance. Watching the young protestors refusing to defend themselves as they are viciously attacked is both upsetting and very powerful: they have a dignity under pressure that is designed to appeal to a nation's conscience, even if they have the broken bones to show for it.

In this footage a thin veil of civility has been lifted to show the deep, atavistic ugliness underneath. The whites committing this violence are positively driven to do so, often by forces that they do not fully understand. It's elemental and visceral, impervious to any reason and legislation. Many photos show large white cops stuffed into their uniforms, smirking at the lens: they think they'll get away with it and, in the short term, most of them did.

The flashing images of violence built up to a picture of a country being torn apart by irreconcilable forces. The real war is being fought not in Vietnam but in the southern states, and it's on TV. There was a wildness, a mania, that shrieked through America in the mid-1960s. Like the high whine of a wire twisting in the wind, it was always there in the background, a constant backdrop that frazzled thought and fostered a mood of public hysteria.

Despite all the gains, the hate only continued and, if anything, deepened. In July 1964, the Civil Rights Act had been passed, which outlawed discrimination in voting, public accommodations and employment. Ten days previously, three civil rights workers involved in the Freedom Summer campaign – James Chaney, Andrew Goodman and Michael Schwerner – disappeared in Mississippi. Their bodies were found in early August.

In Selma, the voting drive had been initiated the previous year by the SNCC, but the group was weary. In January, the campaign was given a boost by the involvement of Martin Luther King and his Southern Christian Leadership Conference. Cracks were already appearing in the relationship between the two key civil rights bodies: the SCLC was the officially recognised group, while the SNCC was younger in constitution, committed to local activism and more radical.

The campaign was met by brute force. The city sheriff, Jim Clark, was implacably opposed to integration and was not afraid to be violent, brutally driving men and women down the stairs of the courthouse with his billy club. When, on 15 February, SCLC organiser the Reverend C. T. Vivian provoked Clark and his henchmen – 'You're racist in the same way that Hitler was a racist' – the sheriff lost his temper and smashed the preacher in the face. On camera.

It was a defining incident in one of the most vicious and hotly contested campaigns in the south. In one particular incident, all the 300 students who were engaging in a silent protest were rounded up and driven with cattle prods to a detention centre. On 18 February, a march in the town of Marion, near Selma, ended in the death of a twenty-six-year-old protestor, Jimmie Lee Jackson, who was shot in the stomach by a highway patrol officer.

Three days later, the charismatic black leader Malcolm X was shot at the Audubon Ballroom in New York. This was a brazen assassination in front of a 400-strong audience, carried out by members of the Nation of Islam, the separatist organisation which he had assiduously supported until a bitter schism in March 1964. In breaking with the NoI, Malcolm X was freed to refine his thinking and seek new alliances, particularly with the civil rights leaders.

On 12 April 1964, he gave a keynote speech, 'The Ballot or the Bullet', in which he posited the development of black-owned and black-run businesses as the basic building block for liberation: 'Once you can create some employment in the community where you live it will eliminate the necessity of you and me having to act ignorantly and disgracefully, boycotting and picketing some [white man] some place else trying to beg him for a job.'

After travelling to Mecca and Britain, where he took part in a televised debate at the Oxford Union – the motion was 'Extremism in the Defense of Liberty is No Vice; Moderation in the Pursuit of Justice is No Virtue' – Malcolm X returned to America a marked man. During 1964, he received regular death threats, which finally became manifest in the very early hours of 14 February 1965, when his Queens house was fire-bombed and rendered uninhabitable.

Without pause he travelled to Detroit to deliver a keynote speech at the First Annual Dignity Projection and Scholarship Awards Night, an event aimed at honouring 'those persons and firms who have contributed most . . . to the projections of the Afro-American as a being with hope of the future'. One of the winners was Motown Records, 'for consistent presentation of Afro-American music without apology, by Afro-American artists who project vibrant DIGNITY'.

That evening, various dignitaries, including Berry Gordy, heard a 'jittery and distracted' Malcolm X strike right at the heart of non-violence as an organising principle. 'If a man speaks the language of brute force, you can't come to him with peace,' he observed. 'So, we only mean vigorous action in self-defence, and that vigorous action we feel we're justified in initiating by any means necessary.' He then delivered a prophecy: '1965 will be the longest and hottest and bloodiest year of them all.' Exactly a week after delivering those words, he was dead. Two weeks later, his comments about the limits of non-violence appeared to ring true with the savage, undefended beatings at the Pettus Bridge. But the SCLC knew what they were doing: it was a high-risk strategy of provocation and martyrdom, but it was still very effective.

The situation was still unresolved when King led the second march on 9 March. Instead of proceeding beyond the point where the march had been stopped two days before, he led a mass prayer and then turned back into Selma. That evening, a young white minister and father of four called James Reeb, who had attended the march, was attacked and murdered by a number of white assailants, none of whom were ever convicted.

Sheriff Clark might have felt justified in unleashing his troopers – some of whom, it was alleged, were KKK members – in a 'police riot', but his loss of control made the march from Selma to Montgomery a national issue that rumbled on for a couple of weeks, until 21 March – four days after President Johnson submitted voting-rights legislation to Congress – when the march was finally allowed to go ahead.

The events at Selma drove a split between the SCLC and the SNCC. The two organisations, along with the NAACP and CORE (the Congress of Racial Equality), had worked well together in previous years; indeed, the SNCC had begun as the student arm of the SCLC in 1960. Both were committed to the principle of non-violence, which, as Daniel W. Wynn observes, 'was not a method for cowards . . . the nonviolent method resisted and was aggressive'. The control exercised by the protestors were designed to provide moral leadership, if not superiority. 'The nonviolent resister was passive in the sense that he was not physically aggressive to his opponent. Spiritually and morally, however, he was extremely aggressive. While a truly nonviolent resister would refuse to physically strike an opponent, his mind and his motions were always active, seeking to persuade his opponent that he was wrong.'

At the centre of the campaign was Martin Luther King, the Baptist minister who had taken up the civil rights struggle as far back as the 1955 Montgomery Bus Boycott. His charisma, courage, moral authority and clear thought made him a national figure. King made the ideal of non-violence the central part of his 10 December 1964 Nobel Prize acceptance speech, making it clear that he was part of a civil rights movement involving 22 million Negroes. He argued that non-violence was 'a powerful moral force which makes for social transformation', but this ideal was becoming frayed in the face of blind, unthinking hatred. Non-violence presumed a moral conscience on the part of America, and it was becoming quite clear that many of its citizens had had that particular organ extracted at birth. Younger SNCC activists like Stokely Carmichael were beginning to question the principle, and that schism would deepen.

It's always useful in pressure politics to have two contrasting organisations: one can play off the other in dealing with the authorities. The SCLC were the establishment, raising funds, talking to the media, meeting with the president. They were the adults. The SNCC were the upstarts: many had bonded during the 1964 Freedom Summer in Mississippi. That long and tough campaign would be the seed bed for much subsequent student activism.

The SNCC were also angry about King's rejection of confrontation at the Pettus Bridge. Some activists decided to try another approach: on the march to Montgomery, Stokely Carmichael slipped away to talk to the residents of Lowndes County, one of the poorest districts in Alabama and one with extremely low rates of black voter registration. Along with his colleagues, he began an experiment in the possibilities of local democracy, encouraging residents to vote.

In the short term, the integrationists were reaping enormous rewards. Martin Luther King was present when President Johnson signed the Voting Rights Act on 6 August 1965. Referring back to the 'outrage of Selma', Johnson called the right to vote 'the most powerful instrument ever devised by man for breaking down injustice and destroying the terrible walls which imprison men because they are different from other men'. This was a stunning victory.

Within days, however, triumph was answered by terror. On 11 August, a twenty-one-year-old black man, Marquette Frye, was arrested for drunk driving on the edge of the Watts district. Frye accepted his arrest but, when his mother arrived, they began arguing with each other, and then the police. A struggle ensued and a crowd gathered. As he was led away, Frye heard some of his friends saying, 'Don't worry, we're going to burn this mother down.'

Things quickly escalated. When two patrolmen tried to arrest a young woman for allegedly spitting at them, the crowd erupted and chased them as they tried to flee. One of the patrolmen remembered 'people running after us – yelling, screaming, They began throwing anything they could get their hands on. Bottles and rocks were bouncing off the back of the station wagon.' Reports had rioters shouting the phrase, 'Burn, baby, burn!'

Watts was a tinderbox, an undistinguished district in the flatlands of South Central Los Angeles that, with the constant sunlight and low-density housing, could pass for a liveable suburb. But it was zoned for poverty, the product of a rigid planning policy that restricted opportunity and blighted life. Los Angeles was, beneath the shiny surface, a conurbation built on racist lines, segregation by any other name, rammed home by a vicious and deeply unpopular police force.

Rumours flew, crowds gathered, and Watts went up on that Wednesday night. Over the next six days, a 3,000-square-metre area became a battlefield. It began with residents stoning cars and beating up white people in the neighbourhood, but spread to full-blown rioting. The police were greeted with stones, bricks and bottles, while rioters engaged in a concentrated programme of arson and looting – usually white-owned businesses.

Watts was a war zone. Dramatic pictures of fire billowing above the Los Angeles streets shocked a nation, but the riots didn't stop. After two days of intensifying disturbances, the National Guard was called in. It took another three days for an uneasy calm to settle over the ravaged district, by which time an estimated $40 million worth of damage had been caused and thirty-four black citizens killed.

It was an explosive, defining event. The anger and frustration of decades, if not centuries, had burst out in what *Life* called 'the most destructive race riot in US history'. Watts was not unique – there had been riots the previous year in Rochester, north Philadelphia and Harlem – but it was infinitely larger in scale and impact, the culmination of years, if not decades, of ill-treatment, deprivation and discrimination.

It shocked and divided America, at the same time as it drove a wedge into the civil rights campaign. Mainstream America was encouraged to view the riot as a direct attack. 'Get Whitey! The War Cry that Terrorized Los Angeles', thundered *Life*. In its opinion, the riot 'did nothing to ease the poisonous hatred in Negro districts everywhere; rather it fed the fear that grows between white and black Americans'.

Many black Americans thought differently. Watts was not a riot but a rebellion, an outraged, spontaneous outburst against their 'lower-class' conditions of life. As Bayard Rustin wrote in March 1966, 'The whole point of the outbreak in Watts was that it marked the first major rebellion of Negroes against their own masochism and was carried on with the express purpose of asserting that they would no longer quietly submit to the deprivation of slum life.'

The civil rights movement had made huge gains, but Watts derailed its positive forward motion. As King later wrote, 'We maintained the hope while transforming the hate of traditional revolutions into positive nonviolent power. As long as the hope was fulfilled there was little questioning of nonviolence. But when the hopes were blasted, when people came to see that in spite of progress their conditions were still insufferable . . . despair began to set in.'

The riot drew in the Stax musicians, who were in town to play a series of dates at the 5/4 Ballroom, at 54th and Broadway, in the centre of Watts. With a roster featuring Carla Thomas, Rufus Thomas, the Mad Lads, the Mar-Keys and Booker T. & the M.G.'s, this was Stax's major push on the Los Angeles market. Members of the revue did press and television, performed on the Sunset Strip and played two nights at the 700-capacity club, one of which was recorded.

The shows were promoted by Magnificent Montague, the morning DJ at Los Angeles' top R&B station, KGFJ. Montague's catchphrase was 'Burn, burn, burn' – a hipster greeting among young black Angelenos. As the MC at the Stax Revue, he is to be heard yelling the phrase like a gospel preacher, as he segues between William Bell and Carla Thomas. For Montague, it was an expression of excitement: 'Everything is up, up, up! And that's when you "burn, baby, burn".'

The phrase took on more sinister overtones a few days after the Stax residency. Some of the Stax musicians saw the flames from the riots as they flew out, while others – like Estelle Axton and William Bell – were stuck in a war zone. Booker T. was in a recording session in Los Angeles. 'So I walk outside the studio and there are National Guardsmen on the corner,' he told Rob Bowman. 'It happened so quickly and it was so devastating.'

For the Stax artists, Watts was a dose of reality. They weren't activists; they were entertainers and artists whose purpose was to make an audience dance and feel. The realpolitik of civil rights and black everyday life was scary; the musicians didn't want to invoke hatred and violence, but joy, togetherness and release. They saw music as an escape from the privations caused by prejudice and segregation, and sought to rise above it until they found out that they couldn't.

For many, Watts was the start of that process. Marvin Gaye was one. 'I remember when I was listening to a tune of mine playing on the radio, "Pretty Little Baby",' he told biographer David Ritz, 'when the announcer erupted with news about the Watts riot. My stomach got real tight and my heart started beating like crazy. I wanted to throw the radio down and burn all the bullshit songs

I'd been singing and get out there and kick ass with the rest of the brothers.'

The simple fact was that, in all this turmoil, black R&B and pop had struggled to make overt statements. The music and the movement were inextricable, but it's startling just how few mid-sixties black American R&B and pop records directly addressed civil rights: the most obvious were Sam Cooke's hymnal 'A Change Is Gonna Come', a Top 40 hit in early 1965 before its revival later that year by Otis Redding; and the Impressions' 1964 'Keep on Pushing' and 'People Get Ready'.

It seems extraordinary that there were not more rabble-rousing pop tunes, but it's not so surprising within the context of the times. In the mid-sixties, black popular music was still R&B, a dance music that was only just emerging out of the fad period into a new kind of confidence. Even so, that confidence did not extend to making explicit statements: to do so would vitiate the imperative of the day, which was to sell records and gain economic status.

Black artists and record labels wanted to get their records heard. It was tough enough to get access to the mainstream without potentially alienating a big section of their audience. The most successful black businessman, Berry Gordy, was insistent on keeping politics out of Motown products. Although he had released a Martin Luther King album during the summer of 1965, he was occupied in getting the Supremes into that bastion of white nightclub life, the Copacabana.

Marvin Gaye felt frustrated by Gordy's refusal to engage, but also realised his own complicity in refusing to make any comment about the Watts rioters: 'I knew they were going about it wrong, I knew what they were thinking, but I understood an anger that builds up over years – shit, over centuries – and I felt myself exploding. Wasn't music supposed to express feelings? No, according to [Berry Gordy], music's supposed to sell. That's his trip, and it was mine.'

Speaking out was problematic. There was one single that did explicitly address civil rights, and that was Nina Simone's

'Mississippi Goddam'. If the second word of the title wasn't offensive enough to delicate sensibilities, the sentiments of the song were an excoriating blast of rage triggered by the murder of Medgar Evers and the Birmingham church bombing of September 1963, which resulted in the deaths of four black children.

Simone attacked the slow rate of change and caught the atmosphere of spiralling violence and intensity: 'Alabama's gotten me so upset / Tennessee made me lose my rest / And everybody knows about Mississippi Goddam.' Simone's bitter, sarcastic response expressed the 'fury, hatred and determination' that she felt after the bombing.

The song was controversial in the extreme. It was banned in four southern states and subjected to national TV censorship. Simone later felt that 'Mississippi Goddam' did her enormous damage. 'I wouldn't change being part of the civil rights movement, but some of the songs I sang, I would have changed because they hurt my career,' she told *Jet* magazine years later. 'The industry decided to punish me and they put a boycott on those records.'

But there was another way in which black R&B and pop illustrated and supported civil rights, and that was in the context of time and place. During the Selma violence, the new record by Junior Walker was rising up the *Billboard* Pop charts. 'Shotgun' began with what Suzanne Smith calls 'an opening gunshot crack' that 'lost its novelty in that instant. The real violence of the historical moment transfigured the playful violence in the song.'

Black Americans heard messages in songs like 'Shotgun', 'Dancing in the Street' and 'Nowhere to Run' that mirrored what they were thinking and feeling. As Marvin Gaye later observed, they 'captured a spirit that felt political to me'. They were metaphors that filled the gap left by the absence of any overt statements; they were a kind of meta-commentary on the feelings, frustrations and anger that still could not be freely expressed.

In this mindset, 'Dancing in the Street' seemed to both predict and mirror the events in Watts. A couple of months after the riot, a young black author, Roland Snellings, explored the link of music and rebellion in his ecstatic prose poem 'Rhythm and Blues as a Weapon':

> We sing in our young hearts, we sing in our angry Black
> Souls: WE ARE COMING UP! WE ARE COMING UP!
> And it's reflected in the Riot-song that symbolised Harlem,
> Philly, Brooklyn, Rochester, Patterson, Elizabeth: this song,
> of course, 'Dancing In The Street' – making Martha and the
> Vandellas legendary. Then FLASH! it surges up again: 'We're
> Gonna' Make It' (to the tune of Medgar Evers gunned down
> in Mississippi: POW! POW! POW! POW!) 'Keep on Trying'
> (to the tune of James Powell gunned down in Harlem: POW!
> POW! POW! POW!) 'Nowhere To Run, Nowhere To Hide',
> 'Change is Gonna' Come' (to the tune of brother Malcolm
> shot down in the Audubon: POW! POW! POW! POW! POW!
> POW! POW! POW!) . . . OUR songs are turning from 'love',
> turning from being 'songs', turning into WAYS, into WAYS,
> into 'THINGS'.

Anger and assertive racial pride were beginning to overtake non-violence. During the autumn and winter of 1965, the divisions in the civil rights movement deepened. As far as the SCLC were concerned, it was time to make further inroads into the political establishment. President Johnson was eager to push forward on a variety of fronts, including school segregation and tackling urban poverty. It was time to move into the cities of the north.

On 7 January 1966, Martin Luther King announced plans for the Chicago Freedom Movement, which aimed to tackle the economic and social problems faced by blacks in that city – housing, unemployment, zoning, the 'vicious system which seeks to further colonize thousands of Negroes within a slum environment'. In late January, he moved into the Chicago slums to organise from within.

In the meantime, the SNCC had been making inroads into the Alabama grassroots. In late 1965, Stokely Carmichael and his colleagues formed the Lowndes County Freedom Organisation as a party to promote voter registration and contest the upcoming

Democratic primary in Alabama. Casting around for a symbol, they began commenting upon the local Democrat symbol: a proudly strutting white rooster with the slogans 'White Supremacy' and 'For the Right'.

The head of the Democratic Party in Alabama at the time was George Wallace, an avowed segregationist. As Stokely Carmichael remembered years later, 'Well of course when the Black panther came everybody was happy and laughed. Oh, this Black panther will eat up this White cock tomorrow. But unfortunately we had not thought really at that time about the press, media would create such a confusion over the symbol of a Black panther.'

The Black Panther symbol marked a new aggression. The SNCC were no longer practising non-violence. 'By Lowndes County we were carrying guns,' Carmichael recalled. 'It would create problems for some SNCC people who were claiming to be conscientious objectors, so their problem was if they were conscientious objectors, they can't be found with a gun. But those of us who were not clean and claiming conscientious objections, it made no difference.'

In early 1966, Vietnam became an unavoidable issue within the civil rights movement. King had declared his disagreement with the president's policy, but he tempered his criticism. However, on 6 January 1966, the SNCC published a policy statement which averred its 'right and responsibility to dissent with U.S. foreign policy concerning Vietnam' and explicitly supported those who refused the draft.

The SNCC's increasing radicalism was confirmed by the election of Stokely Carmichael as chairman in May 1966. When the civil rights leadership attended the 1 June 'To Fulfill These Rights' conference in Washington DC, the SNCC refused to participate, picketing delegates with placards that read, 'UNCLE TOMS!' King was heckled by the protestors and withdrew to his hotel room. The conference itself was tense and marked by bitter disagreements about Vietnam.

Three days later, James Meredith began his 'March Against Fear'. A USAAF veteran, Meredith had been national news in

1962, when he became the first black American student to be admitted into the segregated University of Mississippi. After weeks of rebuffs and legal arguments, Meredith actually entered the campus on 1 October, triggering a riot that involved US marshals, snipers and US Army troops. Two people died and over two hundred were injured.

At thirty-two, Meredith was courageous, obdurate and independent. After his transfer to law school in New York during early 1966, he planned to walk the 220 miles from Memphis to the state capital of Tennessee, Jackson, to encourage voter registration. 'Nothing can be more enslaving than fear,' he told reporters. He said that he wanted 'to drive despair from the frustrated mind of a teenage Negro boy who had only just begun to feel the consequences of being inferior'.

Meredith was acting alone, without any organised support. On the afternoon of the march's second day, he was shot three times by a stocky, middle-aged white man in full view of the police and the FBI. The violence was shocking enough, as inevitable as it was quick. Meredith's plight suddenly focused the minds of America's civil rights leaders, who flew in from all over America. While Meredith was stabilising in hospital, a major march was up and running.

On the afternoon of 7 June, leaders and activists from the SCLC, SNCC, CORE and other groups resumed the march from the point where Meredith had been shot. This was one last show of unity. Martin Luther King marched with Stokely Carmichael: despite the splits and sneers promoted in the media, the two shared a long history of activism and friendship, as well as many of the same principles.

They were walking into a situation just as fraught as any civil rights campaign thus far. Legislation hadn't guaranteed advancement. Enforcement was still patchy, and the problems went way beyond simple voter registration. White racists were digging in, and many young blacks were frustrated as the promises and the rhetoric didn't seem to be achieving results on the ground. It was all roiling away, and this high-profile march began in a fraught climate.

In late May 1966, the mainstream black American magazine *Jet* had printed a warning. 'Negroes in South To Be Violent if Whites Continue', the headline ran, reporting that 'ten killings and "uncounted" beatings, burnings, bombings and shootings were recorded in the South during a six-month period' after the start of 'peaceful desegregation of the region'. There was a possibility of 'answering anger' and 'retaliatory violence'.

The move towards self-determination was already moving into a new phase. It was all coalescing around two words: 'Black Power'. The phrase was not new – the famed author Richard Wright had written a book with that title back in 1954 – but it was definitely in the air. In their 16 June issue *Jet* featured a report about SNCC policy in Lowndes County entitled 'Carmichael's Stand on Mobilising Black Power Is Unequivocal'.

That evening, Carmichael addressed a crowd in Greenwood, Mississippi, a long-standing site of struggle in the civil rights movement. In the early hours of that morning, Carmichael had been arrested for trespassing when he tried to raise some tents in the grounds of an all-black school. It was his twenty-seventh arrest. When he finally got out several hours later, he was seething. By the time he got onstage, he was in storming form, weaving and bobbing like an infuriated cobra.

Beginning by protesting over his arrest, Carmichael continued by asserting the Malcolm X-derived tenet of black self-determination: 'Everybody owns our neighbourhood except us. We outnumber the whites in this country, we want black power. That's what we want – black power!' He continued, 'We been saying freedom for six years and we ain't got nuthin'. What we got to start saying now is Black Power!'

Carmichael began repeating the phrase over and over again, whipping the crowd up in a call-and-response frenzy: 'What do you want?' 'BLACK POWER!' 'What do you want?' 'BLACK POWER!' 'What do you want?' 'BLACK POWER!' 'What do you want?' 'BLACK POWER!' Despite the raw emotion, Carmichael knew what he was doing. Martin Luther King would not have approved of the action, but he was temporarily absent from the march in Chicago. The way was clear.

Even so, the young activist felt overtaken by events. 'I didn't expect that enthusiastic response,' he told interviewer Judy Richardson, 'and the enthusiastic response, obviously, not only shocked me but gave me more energy to carry it on further.' But there was no time for Carmichael, in the heat of the march, to fully articulate what Black Power meant, and many commentators confused 'power' with violence instead of self-determination.

Carmichael expected hostile press attention, and he got it. The March Against Fear had begun to drop out of the news, but Black Power refocused mainstream media attention. Much was cast in terms of black violence. Part of this seemed to come from a surprise that black people were no longer grateful for whatever crumbs they were granted, but there was also the fact that Black Power was an expression of a frustration and anger that was threatening to explode. The pressure on Carmichael was enormous. He was not a white-hating ogre but a passionate activist who was seizing his moment. He knew that his message would be twisted. 'Whites get nervous when we don't keep talking about brotherly love,' he observed. 'They need reassurance.' But he was not prepared to cede to this pressure.

There is a snapshot of him at this moment. A young white woman from Memphis was caught up in the march. As the activists swirled around her car, she felt panicky but found herself looking at Carmichael through her window. She remembered 'his sad, angry eyes', but also his 'feeling of invulnerability'. Something transmitted: 'I let go of my own fear. We were within the corona of Stokely Carmichael's fortuna, the mantle of fate that falls upon the shoulders of kings and warriors, and were safe.'

Black Power was an honest attempt to push black politics forward, but it became trapped within an accelerating spiral: the violence directed by whites against blacks caused anger and frustration;

this anger and frustration resulted in the abandonment of non-violence as a policy; the abandonment of non-violence opened up the gates to black violence, which then created more reactive white violence, which created more anger and frustration . . . and so on.

Within a week of Carmichael's speech, there was a riot in Pompano Beach, Florida, caused by a white store owner slapping a black boy. On 21 June, Martin Luther King took a detour from the march to the town where Andrew Goodman, James Chaney and Michael Schwerner had been killed. Surrounded by a hostile mob, King barely escaped with his life. 'This is a terrible town, the worst I've seen,' he said. 'There is a complete reign of terror here.'

So far the main section of the march had been trouble-free, but on the evening of the 23rd that all changed. The flashpoint occurred when marchers attempted to pitch their tents in the grounds of an all-black school in Canton. When permission was refused by the local authorities, the marchers went ahead anyway, and were met by a fusillade of tear-gas canisters. This was not simple crowd clearance but a punitive, brutal attack.

State troopers fired tear gas at close range and beat up the helpless, choking marchers. The school grounds had become another war zone – 'a scene from hell', as a reporter from *Time* magazine put it – and another twist was added to the spiral. The writer Adam Goudsouzian quotes the reaction of an SCLC minister called Andrew Young: '"If I had a machine gun," he thought, "I'd show those motherfuckers!"'

Two days later, on the 25th, a major event was held at Tougaloo College, as celebrities performed to raise morale and thank the participants for their travails. *Jet* cited 'Sammy Davis Jnr, movie stars Anthony Franciosa, Marlon Brando, Burt Lancaster . . . and comedian Dick Gregory, who emceed the show'. James Meredith, who had rejoined the march, came onstage to the strains of 'Happy Birthday' – both he and Carmichael were born in the last week of June.

But the star attraction was James Brown, who arrived with his band in 'his $713,000 Lear Jet'. It had been a long and hard road that brought him to Tougaloo, to testify and to affirm. He had attempted to sidestep segregation and white violence but, in May 1961, it came to haunt him when, on a stop in Birmingham, Alabama, he became involved in a Freedom Riders protest and got chased by 'white folks waving axe handles and baseball bats'.

Upset at Meredith's shooting, Brown flew to Memphis and visited him in the hospital. 'It was the first time I'd ever met him,' he wrote in his autobiography. 'I told him I supported him and admired what he was doing.' He was aware of the tensions on the march: 'Black Power meant different things to different people. To some people it meant having black pride and black people owning businesses and having a voice in politics. That's what it meant to me.'

By 1966, Brown was starting to get involved in public issues. 'It really went back to the "White Water" and "Colored Water" signs I saw when I was little. I wanted to be more than just a person who screams and hollers on stage, and I wanted to say something about the country I lived in.' Having become involved in the civil rights movement thanks to his contact with the SNCC's programme director, Cleveland Sellers, Brown readily agreed to perform at Tougaloo.

He took the crowded, rudimentary stage in the evening in front of a 10,000-strong crowd and 'wheedled, shouted, moaned, screamed his way through several tunes, including Try Me, I Feel Good and A Man's World, and left the stage and the audience as dripping wet with perspiration and exhaustion as he was'. It was the first time that he publicly affiliated with the movement and, indeed, the first time that a star of his magnitude had put himself on the line in this way.

The march ended in Jackson the next day. Jet ran a picture of the state capitol grounds thronged by thousands of marchers. The event was presented as a huge success, but even the black press noted that the civil rights leaders were 'divided on tactics'. Martin Luther King thought that the march put extra pressure on Congress to pass the 1966 Civil Rights Bill, but he also felt that the Black Power slogan was negative. The twin polarities were set.

There's an ominous clip from the march: a chaotic street scene, shot from within the crowd. A young man, dressed in a military-style cap, begins to rap rhythmically, 'Freedom got a shotgun,' and the crowd yells, 'Oh yeah,' in response. The chant breaks into a call-and-response routine: 'You know freedom gonna shoot it' – 'Oh yeah!' – 'Freedom got a shotgun.' The rapper breaks into the 'na na-ne-na-na' chant from 'Land of 1000 Dances', and the crowd join him all the way.

King had been outflanked, and it was almost as though the magic halo that had surrounded him and protected him had been punctured. But there was no time to rest. After the march, he returned to Chicago, where he inaugurated the Freedom Movement campaign with a huge rally on Sunday 10 July. Mahalia Jackson, Peter, Paul and Mary, and Stevie Wonder appeared. After the event he posted a list of demands on the door of Chicago City Hall.

The next day, King met with the Machiavellian mayor of Chicago, Richard Daley, who was not prepared for one instant to see his machine subverted. It was not a success, with the mayor stonewalling at every point and insisting that the programmes suggested by the Chicago Freedom Movement were already in place. But King could taste the air. 'We cannot wait,' he warned the obdurate, obstructive Daley. 'Young people are not going to wait.'

During July, the weather in Illinois was 'quite intolerable, with average daily temperatures ranging between 30 and 40°C. 'Across the nation', wrote *Newsweek*, 'the cities baked in the record heat until it seemed they would crack open.' The hot spell peaked on 12 July. That day, the West Side erupted in violence.

It all began, as ever, with a trivial event, when two policemen tried to shut down a fire hydrant being used by young blacks to cool off. Push turned to shove, shove turned to full-blown fights, arrests and brick-throwing, and the riot started. King tried to calm the situation, but the disturbances raged for three nights, resulting in $2 million worth of damage, two deaths and four hundred arrests. It seemed like Watts again.

A furious Mayor Daley blamed the SCLC incomers for the violence. This was a blatant misrepresentation. King was appalled by

Watts and the spate of black violence. 'What did it profit the Negro to burn down the stores and factories in which he sought employment?' he asked a Chicago audience in March 1966. 'The way of riots is not a way of progress, but a blind alley of death and destruction which wreaks its havoc hardest against the rioters themselves.'

But it was too late. The civil rights leaders thought they were in the driving seat, but they were hostage to forces that they could not control. While King was struggling in Chicago, Stokely Carmichael began a national speaking tour, preaching the message of black self-empowerment and lashing government policy on the Vietnam war. He was cool, sharp, a new-generation black hero and role model, walking on the tightrope that Black Power had created.

The national news magazines were full of Black Power and black riot. On 11 July, *Newsweek* had a keynote piece about the 'Politics of Frustration', singling out Stokely Carmichael and describing the SNCC's 'new style' – 'which seeks patently to chill whites with visions of black revenge'. This was 'a very real crisis for the Movement . . . a crisis of confidence among Negroes and of confidence among sympathetic whites'.

The media atmosphere was divisive and poisonous. On 15 July, *Life* had a front-cover story on Watts one year on entitled 'Still Seething', with a photo of militants carrying out drills. As the police and scared whites stocked up on guns and ammunition, and extremist groups 'multiplied' in this blighted zone, the ghetto was 'close to flashpoint'. '"We know it don't do no good to burn Watts again," a young Negro says. "Maybe next time we'll go up to Beverly Hills."'

Two weeks after the West Side riot, Carmichael visited Chicago. He was on a roll. 'This is 1966 and it seems to me that it's "time out" for nice words. It's time black people got together,' he began, before ramming home his message: 'We have got to get us some Black Power. We don't control anything but what white people say we can control. We have to be able to smash any political machine in the country that's oppressing us and bring it to its knees.'

On 30 July, Carmichael gave a major speech to an enthusiastic audience at the Cobo Auditorium in Detroit. 'I'm going to try to speak the truth,' he began. 'That's very hard to do in this country, you know. A country which was founded on racism and lies. It's very hard to speak the truth. But we're going to try to do that tonight.'

Criticising the press for creating a false image of him as 'a ba-a-a-d nigger', Carmichael restated his position: 'All I said is that I'm just a poor old black boy, and I think it's time black people stop begging and take what belongs to them . . . And I said that because I learned that from America. They take what belongs to them. And what don't belong to them, if they can't get it, they destroy it. We going to take what belongs to us. Because it's been taken away from us.'

On the same day that Carmichael spoke in Detroit, Wilson Pickett's 'Land of 1000 Dances' entered the *Billboard* Top 100 at #76 – the start of an eleven-week stay that would last well into the autumn. Thirty-six places above it, at #40, was Stevie Wonder's new record, 'Blowin' in the Wind', a soulful cover of the Bob Dylan song, a civil rights favourite when it was first released three years earlier, both as Dylan's original and Peter, Paul and Mary's #2 hit.

Releasing this record was a deliberate statement on Wonder's part, the first time that a Motown artist had broken Gordy's 'no politics' rule. In another metaphorical comment on the state of the civil rights movement, its message was hopeful, yet realistic and resigned: the battle was far from being won, but if we stand together, we might still reach the mountain top.

'Blowin' in the Wind' was a huge hit, reaching #9 in early September. The ban against speaking out would slowly be loosened. Like Pickett's 'Land of 1000 Dances', 'Blowin' in the Wind' spiralled back to 1962, when Dylan had premiered the song, as the past informed the present. Both songs were part of a continuum that showed what had been gained and what had been lost, just how far things had come and how far there was to go.

BEATLES USA '66

From JERRY LEIGHTON
chief dj Caroline North

* Rain-spattered Beat[le]
on their adventurous t[...]

A CHRISTIAN knows John Lennon is right: The Beatles ARE more popular than Jesus Christ.

That comment comes from neither Cynthia, Satan nor NEMS Enterprises. It's the observation of Ross Reardon, who addresses himself "cordially" to "Disc and Music Echo" as "dj—WPEG radio, Winston Salem, North Carolina."

With "Just A Closer Walk With Thee" whining away in the background, Mr. Reardon addressed his American radio [...]

CLEVELAND, Ohio, Tuesday. — "We STILL love [...] a holiday soon and I hope I succeed. They look as if they need [...]

Bible-thumper's message to John

is right: The Beatles ARE more popular than Jesus Christ.

"Seven days a week Beatle records are broadcast and adored; Beatle concert attendances overflow.

"One day a week Jesus asks to be adored—Church attendance is off 40 per cent less than it was.

Mr. Reardon continues i[...] chest-thumping fashion abo[...] Nazis burning bibles i[...] World War II and likenes[...] to Beatle-burning in '6[...]

He ends: "A Christian wi[...] thank John Lennon fo[...] shocking him into prope[...] perspective: John is a ver[...] perceptive student of huma[...]

HIT PARADER

Los Angeles' TROUBADOUR Pg.

NEW STARS OF TOMORROW Pg.
4 DJs ANSWER YOUR QUESTIONS Pg. 44

FROM LONDON...MEMPHIS...NEW YORK, COMES THE ANSWER TO DO THE
ROLLING STONES HATE THEIR FANS?

MEET SIMON AND GARFUNKEL

THE TURTLES

JAN AND DEAN

SENSATIONAL NEW LOVIN' SPOONFUL BABY PIX CONTEST!

JERRY LEWIS' LITTLE BOY
PAGE 13

A Loud and Quiet Look AT THE POP SCENE

TOP TUNES song lyrics
I'M HUNGRY • ME
NEIGHBOR, NEIGHBOR
GIRL IN LOVE
BETTER USE YOUR HEAD
I KNOW YOU BETTER
YOU DON'T HAVE TO
SAY YOU LOVE ME
TAKE THIS HEART OF MINE
AIN'T TOO PROUD TO BEG
MY LITTLE RED BOOK
GOOD TIME CHARLIE
SWEET TALKING GUY
S.Y.S.L.J.F.M.

SPOONFUL SUMMER IN THE CITY
OPUS 17
CLOUDY SUMMER AFTERNOON
RED RUBBER BALL
I'LL LOVE YOU FOREVER
OFF AND RUNNING
POPSICLE • CRYING
TAKE SOME TIME OUT FOR LOVE
I LOVE ONIONS
BREAK OUT • 99 1/2
LET'S GO GET STONED
THE LAST WORD IN LONESOME IS ME
OH HOW HAPPY

TOP TUNES song lyrics
LOVING YOU IS SWEETER THAN EVER
STRANGERS IN THE NIGHT
BAREFOOTIN' • MAMA
HOLD ON I'M COMING
COME ON LET'S GO
DEDICATED FOLLOWER OF FASHION
PAINT IT BLACK
IT'S A MAN'S MAN'S WORLD
SO MUCH LOVE
COOL JERK

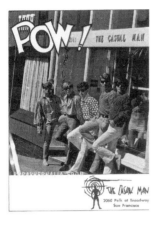

including and Eleanor Rigby

8 : AUGUST

Do You Come Here Often? Joe Meek,
Gay Rights and a Summer of Violence

'Johnny's radio is on: pouring out its mad, maddening cacophony, sounds ripped from the frayed edges of contemporary despair, often the slurred despair of those who are, emotionally, eternally children: who feel savagely but don't understand. Now the Rolling Stones are conveying the sound of Johnny's anguish, speaking of the lonely blackness inside; and convoluted bastard sounds spawn convoluted bastard sounds, not finished, leading to others, also unfinished.'
JOHN RECHY, *Numbers*, 1967

It was summer, and the time was right. In New York, temperatures were down slightly from the almost unbearable 39°C peaks of June and July. On 1 August, the city was boiling again as the temperature soared once again to over 30°C. In Britain, the heatwave that had occurred at the end of June had dissolved into a more familiar pattern: changeable weather, with frequent rain and the occasional hot day.

The charts favoured songs that caught the summer mood of relaxation, escape, some kind of surcease. On 1 August, the top two US singles were throwbacks, basic party records: Tommy James and the Shondells' 'Hanky Panky' and the Troggs' 'Wild Thing'. Coming up fast were Bobby Hebb's 'Sunny', a hang-loose, vibes-driven tune that became an almost instant standard, and Billy Stewart's funky bebop reworking of 'Summertime'.

The fastest riser was 'Summer in the City', the fifth single by the Lovin' Spoonful, which went from #21 to #7 in the *Billboard* chart of 30 July. This would be the American song of the summer, reaching #1 on 13 August and staying there for three weeks. By the end of the month, there would be four sunny summer songs – 'Summer in the City' at #1, 'Sunny' at #2, Donovan's 'Sunshine Superman' at #5 and 'Summertime' at #10 – in the US Top 10, just as the temperature reached 32°C in New York.

'Summer in the City' offered momentary relief from the unbearable heat. From the opening two-note lick, it was tougher than anything the Lovin' Spoonful had yet recorded, with an insistent riff, ringing guitars and pounding drums. In the breaks, all the instruments faded out; while dancers paused in mid-spin, they heard electric drills and a variety of car horns – the inescapable sounds of the city.

In the UK, the beginning of the month saw the afterglow of England winning the FIFA World Cup for the first and, so far, only time, as the host country. While the celebrations continued, the Who marked the occasion in their own way. Headlining the Sixth National Jazz and Blues Festival at Windsor, they kicked in the footlights and threw microphones around; the show ended in utter chaos. Was this, as one pop paper put it, 'the ultimate in pop violence'?

In Britain, the #1 record on that day was Chris Farlowe's 'Out of Time', the first major hit for the R&B pioneer. Written by Mick Jagger and Keith Richards and released on Andrew Loog Oldham's Immediate Records, the song was a putdown cloaked in a sweet, string-enhanced melody. 'You're obsolete, my baby,' Farlowe sang: in the modernist demand for perpetual novelty, even personal relationships were rendered throwaway. At #4 was the previous #1, Georgie Fame's 'Get Away', a hymn to holiday escapism with a novelty horn curlicue that betrayed the song's origin in an advertising jingle. Even Fame's smoky voice and deep immersion in soul and jazz – with a multiracial band and his residency at the Flamingo Club he was a major interpreter and populariser – couldn't rescue the song's slightness. Much more substantial was the Kinks' 'Sunny Afternoon', still at #5.

This was the fourth and the greatest in the Kinks' contemporary run of social commentary songs, preceded by 'A Well Respected Man', 'Where Have All the Good Times Gone?' and 'Dedicated Follower of Fashion'. It wasn't a raver but a mid-paced, almost music-hall piece, as the Kinks developed the descending riff into a devastating portrait of an upper-class waster in his stately home

– a summer anthem with dark presentiments of decay.

Ray Davies had already turned his sharp eye on the class system and the absurdities of Swinging London. After his breakdown in March 1966, the songs had poured out. 'I tried not to write,' he told me, 'then I came out of it and wrote "End of the Season", "Sunny Afternoon" and "I'm Not Like Everybody Else". I was very clear afterwards because my mind had been rested, and I went into "Sunny Afternoon", which was like magic.'

'It was a strange time,' he remembered later. 'At the time I wrote "Sunny Afternoon" I couldn't listen to anything. I was only playing the *Greatest Hits of Frank Sinatra* and Dylan's "Maggie's Farm". I just liked its whole presence.' Partly inspired by his upper-middle-class managers, Robert Wace and Grenville Collins, Davies constructed a lyric that caught a person, a class and a lifestyle on the point of dissolution.

As effective as the song's lyric was Davies's vocal performance, a deliberately world-weary croon. 'I didn't want to sound American,' he said. 'I was very conscious of sounding English.' And yet, after everything, it was a summer song, as Davies, trapped as ever within his own ambiguities, managed to make decadence sound like fun: 'I love to live life so pleasantly / Live this life of luxury / On a sunny afternoon.'

On the flip was something entirely different. 'I'm Not Like Everybody Else' was a snarling rocker with a minatory opening guitar figure and an extraordinary vocal by the still teenage Dave Davies that oscillated between quiet menace and barely restrained fury. This was a brutally direct statement of outsider alienation and aggression: 'I won't take all that they hand me down / And make out a smile, though I wear a frown.'

Both 'Sunny Afternoon' and 'Summer in the City' had a wider resonance that neither writer could have foreseen. The Kinks' song caught the mood in Britain after Prime Minister Harold Wilson announced a major freeze on prices and wages on 20 July. A prolonged seamen's strike had resulted in a poor balance of payments and a run on the overvalued pound. During the previous three years, wages had risen ahead of retail prices, and this was an attempt to jam on the brakes.

With immediate effect, hire purchase rates, purchase tax and petrol duty were increased, while there was an immediate six-month wage freeze. The full effect of this was obscured by World Cup euphoria, but it marked the end of the British high sixties. 'The Age of Pop' seemed to be swinging 'to a stop', observed the *Sunday Times* that August, and 'Sunny Afternoon' caught the sighing exhalation of a deflating boom.

With its jagged edges and rampaging beat, 'Summer in the City' reflected a season not of relaxation, but of riot and disturbance. The 2 July *Billboard* advert for the single showed three young Negro boys, in silhouette, playing with a fire hydrant, with the copy: 'The Lovin' Spoonful captures the feel, the heartbeat of Summer in the City.' The promise that this would be the 'single of the season' was fulfilled by the fire-hydrant riot in Chicago's West Side.

As it climbed the charts in the first week of August, America was shocked by a series of violent events. On 1 August, a twenty-five-year-old engineering student called Charles Whitman broke into the observation platform of the Main Building on the University of Texas campus and shot forty-four people in just over an hour and a half. Sixteen were killed outright. Whitman was shot dead at the scene, but that was not the end of it, as America struggled to adjust to a new kind of crime.

On 5 August, Martin Luther King led a march through the Marquette Park district in Chicago's South Side. This was part of the campaign to protest against the effective zoning by realtors of blacks into inner-city ghettos. The march was well represented by about seven hundred people, but no one had expected the local response, as the white residents of Marquette Park and nearby Gage Park turned out en masse to oppose the demonstration.

The civil rights activists had never faced a hostile crowd of this size: a mob of at least 5,000. The mood was electric with hatred, with shouts of 'We want King, kill him, kill him'. As Dr King arrived and got out of his car, he was struck on the head by a rock 'the size of a fist'. This was the cue for the hail of bottles, rocks and firecrackers that 'rained down' on the march.

Two days later, a race riot erupted in East Lansing, Michigan, when two to three hundred black American youths went on the rampage for a couple of days. Three days later, on 10 August, George Rockwell, the head of the American Nazi Party, held a rally in Marquette Park, attended by up to 3,000 people. Almost immediately afterwards, white demonstrators began to display placards with swastikas and White Power slogans.

On 12 August, the Tornados released their last-ever record with Joe Meek. Beginning with the sound of waves and seagulls, 'Is That a Ship I Hear?' bore all its producer's hallmarks: the boot-stomping drums, the extraterrestrial keyboard sound and fierce, fierce compression. It was constructed around a gimmick: Meek hoped that the title and the ocean effects would convince the DJs on the pirate radio stations to put his new record on heavy rotation.

Just when the pirates' influence on the British charts was at its height, it seemed like a good angle. However, this was neither the Tornados' nor Joe Meek's time. Dylan's *Blonde on Blonde* was released that week. The music papers were full of this landmark album, but the Tornados got short shrift: 'Good of its kind and doubtless a hit three years ago, but not for today's market'; 'Somebody must be joking.'

The unkindest cuts came in the *Melody Maker*. The singles reviewer praised the seagulls rather than the group, while in the 'Blind Date' feature – where artists were played new records without being told who they were by – Billy Fury guessed it was the Tornados. 'It's about time they changed the sound,' he sniffed. 'There's none of the original members of the group in it now anyway so they shouldn't be playing this sort of gear. It's about five years out of date.'

There was a bit of needle here from 1962, when the Tornados had been Fury's backing band, a relationship sundered by the bickering between Joe Meek and Fury's manager Larry Parnes. But the singer was correct: it had been a long slow fall since 'Telstar', through seven flop singles. By 1966, the Tornados had shed all the original members, so Meek simply found another group, called the Saxons, and renamed them.

Despite a rhythm stolen from Dave Dee, Dozy, Beaky, Mick and Tich's smash hit 'Hold Tight', the Tornados' rinky-dink instrumental had no chance. The pirate stations played it a few times: it struggled to #48 in the Radio Caroline chart for one week, and then sank without trace. Meek must have had a deal with Caroline: his previous release, The Millionaires' 'Wishing Well', was at #49 the same week – another suspiciously low and short-lived chart placing.

Although 'Is That a Ship I Hear?' was a novelty, the flip was something quite different. 'Do You Come Here Often?' begins as an organ-drenched instrumental – with its burlesque sashay, similar to David Bowie's contemporaneous 'I Dig Everything' – and stays that way for over two minutes. By that time, most people would have switched off. Had they persisted they would have heard two sibilant, camp voices bitching.

The corrosive lines were voiced by Dave Watts and Robb Huxley of the Tornados. 'Joe thought that we should put some funny talking on the track,' Huxley remembered. 'We all bounced ideas around and finally decided that Dave and I should carry on a conversation together as if we were in a club somewhere. We would talk about fashion and chatting up birds, and be sure to mention something about the pirate radio stations.

'We put on these real camp voices and by running through it a few times we got the idea of where we were going. Joe suggested that I should ask Dave "Do you come here often?" And that Dave should answer by saying "Only when the pirate ships go off the air." Dave came up with the bit about the pajama style shirts being "In". Joe . . . really got excited when he told me that my reply would be that "Pajamas are out as far as I'm concerned anyway."

'Dave and I presumed that we would be on the lookout for women so Dave said "Here's two girls coming now, what do you think?" Joe immediately told Dave not to say "girls" and just say

"Here's two coming now, what do you think?" I of course replied with the corny line "Mine's alright, but I don't like the look of yours."

'Throughout the whole session and particularly during the recording of the talking parts Joe was totally happy, excited and smiling. We were not really aware at the time but Joe must have felt that he was in some way making a Gay statement by the way that he had Dave and I put on those camp voices and carry on that conversation. We had a ball doing it also. It was really like having fun, the pressure was off and we all had chances to be creative.'

The result was a masterpiece. The scenario is a London club, quite possibly the Apollo or Le Duce. The organist is still pumping away, as he has done for the last two minutes, but that's only background as the sound dims and the bar atmosphere comes in. The two run through their brief but diverting exchange, ending with the kiss-off:

'Well I must be off.'
'Yes, you're not looking so good.'
'Cheerio. I'll see you down the "Dilly".'
'Not if I see you first, you won't.'

Exeunt, to swelling organ.

Meek was determined to deliver an authentic slice of gay life. As Huxley writes, 'Any time that he could creep out of his closet and create something like "Do You Come Here Often?" . . . probably brought him a great deal of satisfaction and release.' The track's incessant bickering is not just beastliness but the most important component of the camping, which, as historian Richard Dyer writes, is 'the only style, language and culture that is distinctively and unambiguously gay male'.

Partly a form of aggression, partly a form of self-mockery, partly a form of self-defence, in its social mode camp privileges a caustic wit, best expressed by the quick-fire verbal retort. It's an insider code that completely baffles the heterosexual majority, as it's meant to. Its poisoned psychological arrows can help to control and neutralise the threat of homophobic violence: many bullies are right to fear the queen's forked tongue.

Like the famous Negro 'dirty dozens', the cut-and-thrust spotlighted on 'Do You Come Here Often?' represents a complicated response to an explicitly hostile world. Camping can provide a kind of bulwark from which the gay man can sally forth into the world at large. It freezes the simplistic typecasting of homosexuals as effeminate, internalises it and then throws it back in the face of the straight world as a kind of revenge.

Watts and Huxley really inhabited their roles in that late-spring recording session. Enjoying the play, they portray a pair of queen bitches briefly united by an unstable mixture of camaraderie and competitiveness. Ever hopeful, ever alert, the gay man in cruising mode is relentless in pursuit of cock. The usual social rules go right out of the window. Sex drives the gay scene, its iconography, its economy, its inner and outer life.

Meek's scenario highlights that heart-stopping instant, that high-wire walk between acceptance and rejection that every gay man knows. The extraordinary thing was that he managed to involve two blokeish musicians in such an authentic-sounding insider joke. 'Dave and I never thought that we were portraying a couple of gay guys,' Huxley remembered, 'but at the same time if it came across that way it was OK, it was fun and we thought we were being cute.'

'Do You Come Here Often?' was the first record on a UK major label – Columbia – to deliver a slice of homosexual life so accurate that it's possible to hear its cut-and-thrust in any gay bar today. And, although Meek wasn't aware of the wider implications, the hints of violence and the subcultural assertiveness contained within the track chimed exactly with both the public mood and the underlying trends of that troubled, heightened high summer.

* * *

'We are undergoing presently what I have called in the title of this book a homosexual revolution. To date it has been a rather quiet revolution, though a very busy and far-reaching one. It is too soon to say whether the revolt of the homosexuals will become a truly dramatic uprising – like, say, the revolt of the American Negroes.'

   R. E. L. MASTERS, *The Homosexual Revolution*, 1962

Before 1966, homosexuality had been merely hinted at in mainstream records like the Kinks' 'See My Friends'. Although it saturated Meek melodramas like John Leyton's 'Johnny Remember Me', the allusions had been veiled. None of these songs offered an insider viewpoint, just a mood or a stray word that seemed to briefly open a door usually locked and barred. It all depended, as so much to do with the gay world did then, on interpretation.

In the mid-1960s, an American label called Camp Records produced ten singles and two albums directly aimed at the gay market. Promoted in homophile publications like *ONE*, *Butch* and *Vagabond*, they offered a number of insider-code scenarios and stereotypes: the butch/femme duality of the single 'I'd Rather Fight Than Swish'/'I'd Rather Swish Than Fight', as well as 'Leather Jacket Lovers', 'Rough Trade' and 'Stanley the Manly Transvestite'. All ten 45s were released with eye-catching covers, a couple of them using the same tightly dressed model. Of the two albums, *The Queen Is in the Closet* featured a few of the 45 songs, as well as tunes like 'Florence of Arabia' and 'Down on the River Drive' (a parable about the dangers of cruising), while *mad . . . about the boy* consisted of camped-up show tunes like 'He Needs Me' and 'The Gentleman Is a Dope'.

There was no thought that these records would sell outside the ghetto. In both the US and the UK, the physical expression of homosexuality was totally illegal. The author and researcher Patrick Higgins points to at least eight specific charges that could be brought against practising homosexuals in the UK. The situation was similar in the US, although the exact restrictions varied from state to state. Quite apart from legal sanctions, public opinion was hostile.

In a January 1966 essay, *Time* magazine observed how 'homosexuality is more in evidence in the U.S. than ever before', before charging that 'homosexual ethics and esthetics are staging a vengeful, derisive counterattack on what deviates call the "straight" world. This is evident in "pop", which insists on reducing art to the trivial, and in the "camp" movement, which pretends that the ugly and banal are fun.' It concluded that homosexuality was 'a pernicious sickness'.

In late 1965, the activist Randy Wicker quoted a poll which stated that 82 per cent of American males and 58 per cent of American females felt that homosexuals were 'harmful to American life'. There was public support in the US for an arsenal of punitive measures, which included entrapment, prison sentences and – because homosexuality was seen in terms of mental illness – asylum committals. Underlying it all was the ever-present threat of exposure and blackmail.

The psychological impact on the generation who, like Joe Meek, came of age in the 1950s was considerable, as the external homophobia was internalised to fuel low self-esteem. Donald Webster Cory's groundbreaking 1951 survey *The Homosexual in America* had clearly identified poor self-image as the greatest threat to gay men's mental health, but it was difficult, given society's attitudes, to break the cycle of prejudice and self-hatred.

Born in April 1929, Meek was sensitive, almost clairvoyant, but highly volatile. His native temper was exacerbated by his father, who suffered violent fits after experiencing shell shock in the First World War. Dressed as a girl by his mother until the age of four, Joe was called a sissy and left alone by most of his peers. This difference, coupled with his hair-trigger temper, led to the start of the persecution (both real and imagined) that lasted for the rest of his life.

As soon as he could, Meek fled rural England for London. With a growing reputation as a top sound engineer/producer, Meek struck out on his own – a pioneer in the closed world of the British music industry. He was completely self-contained in the production of his records, working out of an upstairs maisonette on Holloway Road in north London. After his Triumph label folded in 1960, he tried to place his RGM Sound productions with all the majors.

He arrived as the period's foremost independent with John Leyton's summer 1961 chart-topper, 'Johnny Remember Me', an eldritch spasm that embodied the heightened teenage emotional state. Addressed to and sung by a man, the song also acted as a metaphor for the sense of loss and disassociation felt by Meek and many others. The follow-up, 'Wild Wind', was even more hysterical, with its boosted middle eight of wild vocals and wind sounds.

Meek's moment of triumph came with the Tornados' 'Telstar', which stayed at #1 for three weeks in the US and five in the UK. It remains as haunting and as evocative as it was over forty years ago, a triumph of technological optimism. But success did not alter his life; if anything, it compounded the pressures. Despite his freedoms, Meek had all the worries of an independent producer: without a regular outlet, each record had to be placed individually.

He was only as good as his last hit and, after the advent of the Beatles, they were slower in coming. The organic group sounds of the beat boom made his compressed productions sound passé. And, as ever in the music industry, success brought litigation: in this case, by a French music publisher who held that 'Telstar' had a similar melody to one of his copyrights. While the matter was decided, all the royalties from his biggest hit were frozen. He was in limbo.

In November 1963, Meek was arrested for importuning in a public toilet just off the Holloway Road. His conviction made the front page of the *London Evening News*. His friends were amazed: Meek could have had all the young men he wanted, as they were queuing up to be recorded by him and he was not averse to using this power for sexual purposes. They concluded that he liked the frisson of danger. But, after the conviction, the danger became real, as Meek was harassed by would-be blackmailers. Nor did he help himself, popping the amphetamine pills that accentuated his natural tendency towards paranoia. He was obsessed with the possibility that he was being bugged, that people were stealing his ideas by using electronic listening devices. He was spooky: obsessed with other worlds, with graveyards, with spiritualism and the occult.

The negativity that he experienced clung to him like worn-out, not-yet-shed skin. Charles Blackwell, the arranger of 'Johnny Remember Me', remembered Joe 'as a split personality. He believed he was possessed, but had another side that was very polite with a good sense of humor.' Meek terrified the usually fearless Andrew Loog Oldham when he visited him on a professional matter: 'He looked like a real mean-queen Teddy Boy and his eyes were riveting.'

Meek pulled off a huge coup with the success of the Honeycombs' 'Have I the Right?', #1 in the UK in August 1964 and an oblique comment on his own blocked right to emotional fulfilment. This was his last chart-topper, but he continued to adapt to the time with records like the Syndicats' September 1965 'Crawdaddy Simone', an R&B record with a guitar break so frenzied that it put the Yardbirds' rave-ups to shame.

Although Meek put out forty-four records during 1965, only two hit the Top 40. Both were by the Honeycombs, whose 'That's the Way' went to #12 in the summer. The pace of his releases began to slow down. In March 1966, he scored his last-ever hit with Liverpool group the Cryin' Shames' 'Please Stay' (#26), an overwrought version of the Burt Bacharach song.

Meek's continued fascination with the possibilities of sound meant that he was far from a spent force even in early 1966. He remained a player in the British music industry's gay mafia. The success of 'Please Stay' resulted in conversations with Brian Epstein about the possibility of NEMS managing the Cryin' Shames. During the brief *entente cordiale* that followed, Meek accompanied Epstein to watch Bob Dylan's Royal Albert Hall concert in the Beatles' box.

But there were signs of his worsening mental state. 1966 productions like 'You're Holding Me Down' by the Buzz and Jason Eddie and the Centermen's cover of 'Singin' the Blues' – a bizarre arrangement that transformed the old chestnut into a repeated burble of reverbed electric squeals – both sounded fragmented, the elements of his one-time winning formula dissolving into seemingly random static. Meek's increasing disturbance was not helped by the feeling that his sexuality made him an outcast. However, he was unusually privileged, as the music industry was one of the few places where homosexual men could be themselves. If only he had been able to take some comfort from that realisation.

As Andrew Loog Oldham and Simon Napier-Bell both relate in their memoirs, the British music scene of the sixties was saturated in homosexuality. This was a natural consequence of its roots in show business and theatre, but even more basic was the way in which the sexual/social aesthetic of innovators like Larry Parnes – the biggest player in British rock 'n' roll – alchemised the raw material of working-class adolescents into hit-parade gold. Spurred on by witnessing the frenzied fan scenes that surrounded Johnnie Ray on his 1953 visit to Britain, Parnes transformed all the young Reginalds and Ronalds into a new Olympus peopled by deities-cum-archetypes like Billy Fury, Dickie Pride and Vince Eager, who were named according to their emotional and amatory possibilities. His sensibility transmuted homosexual attraction into an erotic climate that excited the young women who made these idols stars.

Parnes was born in 1929, the same year as Joe Meek. The Beatles' manager, Brian Epstein, was born five years later, in September 1934, but was still old enough to feel the full force of society's proscriptions. Until he found success with the Beatles at the age of twenty-eight, his life was full of false starts and hopes only partially fulfilled and, underneath, the sense that he never had, and never would, fit in.

Born into a prosperous Liverpool merchant family, Epstein had a fitful education at a number of schools. His stint doing national service – still compulsory for young men of his cohort – ended prematurely in mutual incomprehension. Expected to join the family's retail business, he shocked his parents by applying to, and being accepted by, RADA, but this too ended inconclusively. He seemed unable to settle into anything.

In April 1957, Epstein was entrapped for 'persistently importuning' in a public lavatory in north-west London. When he arrived at the police station, the one abortive encounter was amplified by the police into 'persistently importuning seven men'. In Marylebone Magistrates Court the next morning he pleaded guilty. The experience left him 'stunned' at the 'lying criminal methods of the police'.

In the late 1950s, Epstein returned to the family firm, NEMS, and opened a separate records department. He quickly showed that he had a nose for a hit, ordering hundreds of copies of John Leyton's 'Johnny Remember Me' as soon as it was released. The heightened melodrama of the song – plus the fact it was featured on television – piqued Epstein's interest, and his judgement was proved sound when the song shot to #1.

When he signed them in late 1961, the Beatles were going nowhere. In Liverpool they were regarded as untrustworthy and unmanageable, but Epstein had faith in the group when they were at their lowest ebb. He told Decca Records executives in early 1962 that the Beatles 'would be bigger than Elvis', a statement that got him laughed at until it actually happened. He grounded them and shaped them into the show-business mores of the day, and they flourished under his faith.

Epstein was a new kind of manager: neither manipulative nor authoritarian, but sympathetic. The Beatles were not wide-eyed teenagers, but worldly-wise musicians in their early twenties. They worked with Epstein on their public presentation, while fiercely guarding their musical output. Unlike Larry Parnes or Joe Meek, who regarded their artists as pegs to be put into whatever hole suited, Epstein left them space to develop artistically.

They were all in it together, five outcasts and misfits against the world. 'This was what bound Brian and the boys together,' remembered Derek Taylor. 'They all did think big. Very high notions of themselves, and very high expectations. George [Harrison] says . . . we were very cocky, we didn't know what we were going to do, but we knew we didn't have to get any fucking "O" levels for what we wanted to do. In other words, they always felt they were going to be OK.'

For the next couple of years, Epstein was flying as the Beatles racked up success after success. In 1964, he was well-known enough to be offered a book contract for his autobiography. He chose Derek Taylor, an urbane journalist from the Wirral, to be his ghost. Taylor had met him in June 1963, when he wrote a profile on Epstein for the *Daily Express*. He found Epstein nervy but extremely well dressed: 'he was undoubtedly very impressive'.

They collaborated on *A Cellarful of Noise*, a best-seller when published later in 1964. The book is full of sharp self-revelation unusual in showbiz biographies of the period. There was one area, however, that Taylor found off-limits. While Epstein was frank on a one-to-one basis, he refused to 'have had anything in there that implied or hinted at homosexuality, because of the dangers of jail. After the Lord Montague witch hunt, which was only ten years before.'

While the Beatles slogged around the US in summer 1964, Epstein discovered a new world. As his American colleague and confidant Nat Weiss remembers, 'When I first met him, there was really a mental block to him. He still saw homosexuality as something you do in back alleys and out of the side of the pub and something you just didn't talk about. When he started going to bars in New York and meeting people he became notoriously open about the whole thing.

'There was a bar, called Kelly's Bar, on 45th Street between 6th Avenue and Broadway which originally was very famous as a servicemen's bar, but then began to attract all kinds of people. We used to go there a lot because a lot of male hustlers used to hang out there with the servicemen and the girls that were around. What these hustlers used to do was pick up someone gay, make their money, and then take out a girl. Like the food chain, so to speak.'

During the Beatles' second US tour, Epstein fell in love. Weiss remembers that 'Dizz Gillespie was a young man that Brian had met in New York. He was a rather good-looking, sophisticated male hustler, and Brian got to like him. He was from the Midwest and obviously he seduced Brian into thinking that he really cared about him. Brian had never really been seduced that way before and he really fell for it.'

Epstein oscillated between enjoying his freedoms as an extremely rich, unattached gay man and succumbing to his own compulsions. As Derek Taylor observed, 'He was much more optimistic and cheerful and happy than sad, lonely, isolated, and a lot of his troubles with being mucked about and blackmailed . . . were a pattern repeat, which he brought on by living dangerously, and drinking too much probably, and there were quite a few pills knocking about then.'

Both Epstein and Meek had come of age when the harshness of public opinion and the police harassment of homosexuals were both at their peak, but, by the mid-1960s, things were progressing, partly as a result of the changes that they both helped to inaugurate. To the upcoming generation of twenty-year-olds, born towards the end of the Second World War, the law was an anachronistic irrelevance, as were all the thunderings from press and pulpit.

For a younger man like Peter Burton, born in 1945, things were different. Fortunate enough to be born in London and to find a 'vaguely arty' job at the age of sixteen, his homosexuality was never a problem. 'I never worried about whether my homosexuality was "right" or "wrong",' he wrote in his memoir *Parallel Lives*, 'because it seemed perfectly natural to me and by the time I had become aware of society and the law's attitudes, it was too late for me to change mine.'

At some point between Winston Churchill's death and the granting of the Beatles' MBEs, the old Britain began to dissolve. While the country's new-found concentration on youth was, in part, a chimera, it nevertheless went hand in hand with two Labour governments that were determined to counter the vestiges of Victorian Britain with progressive social legislation on homosexuality, divorce and abortion. It was a time of greater openness and greater democracy.

Indeed, 'Do You Come Here Often?' emerged into a more expansive cultural climate. Joe Orton had already used camp's caustic cadences in his West End success *Entertaining Mr Sloane* – a key weapon in his desired 'mixture of comedy and menace'. Orton was a new kind of playwright: working-class and intentionally confrontational. He deliberately rejected the stigma that still surrounded homosexuality, preferring to ram his outsider rage in the public's face.

Beginning in 1965, the extremely popular BBC radio serial *Round the Horne* featured two flagrant queens talking in the gay argot of the time. Executed by Hugh Paddick and Kenneth Williams, Julian and Sandy's double entendres and quick-fire Polari – that mixture of gypsy language, cockney backward slang and thieves' cant used as a queer insider code – slotted right into the verbal surrealism that the Goons had pioneered during the previous decade.

At the beginning of the 1960s, Meek had entitled his stillborn space concept album *I Hear a New World*. Music is always ahead of social institutions, and the new world that Meek had dreamed of became tangible in the mid-sixties, when the agitation for social and sexual liberation gathered pace throughout the Western world. The long years of stasis and repression had banked up the flood, and it was ready to burst.

One obvious sign of these new freedoms, for the young in particular, was the hothouse flowering of teen fashions, as young women went op and pop, and young men squeezed themselves into striped hip-huggers and polka-dot shirts, topped off with Prince Valiant fringes. Just as 1966 had seen full media recognition of Swinging London, so its associated fashion, mod, crossed the Atlantic.

Trumpeting the 'revolution in men's clothes', *Life* magazine's 13 May 1966 cover showed four young men aping the Rolling Stones. It was an arresting image: with a backdrop of the downtown Chicago skyline, a local group called the Del-Vetts were captured squeezing their Midwestern frames into light blue double-breasted jackets, teal corduroy jackets, matelot shirts and Rupert Bear check trousers, topped off with Dutch Boy caps and Brian Jones fringes.

This was not standard male gear, and the copy played up the freakish angle: 'The Guys Go All Out to Get Gawked At'. But mod's hint of mint was not entirely in the heads of hostile observers. *Life* singled out John Stephen as the 'man who led the young clothes revolution in England' and who was 'fomenting it now in the US', running a picture of the young entrepreneur posing in front of his Cadillac in Carnaby Street, super-sharp in a waisted check jacket.

Born within three weeks of Brian Epstein in 1934, Stephen was a similarly driven and obsessive individual. He had built up an empire out of nothing, with a personal wealth estimated by *Life* at $15 million. His clothes were on sale in Stern Brothers in New York, while copies of the styles he popularised were being sold throughout the US by McGregor-Doniger, 'one of the biggest American clothes makers'.

The man who sold mod to America had begun his career at the mainstream tailor Moss Bros, before working at Vince, the boutique opened up by Bill Green in Newburgh Street, Soho. This pioneering shop featured items from the gay subculture – leather posing pouches and leather caps – in the window, and inside it sold polo necks and shirts in bright colours. Vince quickly attracted a clientele of rent boys, actors and pop stars like Cliff Richard.

Opening up in Carnaby Street during 1956, John Stephen and his partner Bill Franks aimed for a wider market. They adapted Vince's vivid colours and form-fitting shapes for a new kind of teenager: the modernists that were beginning to appear in central London. Ten years later, they owned nine shops in Carnaby Street. Predicting and driving the super-fast turnover of styles, the John Stephen brand was the hottest thing in mass-market teen fashion.

The crossover between the Carnabetian army and younger gay men was observed by Peter Burton: 'Both groups paid the same attention to clothes; both groups looked much alike. Not surprising really, as their clothes came from the same shops – initially Vince in Carnaby Street and eventually from the John Stephen shops in the same street. Both groups took the same drug – basically "speed", alternatively known as "purple hearts", "blues", "doobs" or "uppers".'

Despite the spread of peacock finery among the young of Britain and America, most gay clubs were stuck in the 1950s, an era of frequent police raids and enforced seclusion. As Burton writes, most were 'hidden away in obscure streets and in the nether regions of unobtrusive buildings'. He cites, 'with varying degrees of affection', period venues like 'the Calabash, the Festival, A&B, the Apollo, as well as coffee bars like the Coffee House and As You Like It'.

Inspired by a short-lived coffee bar called the Lounge, Burton teamed up with the bar's co-owner, Bill Bryant, to open a new club. Located in D'Arblay Street, Soho, Le Duce was conceived as a gay version of the premier mod venue, the Scene. Opened in 1966, it was a club for dancing, fuelled by the uppers that kept you going all night. 'They gave you confidence. You felt you could talk to anyone; you could dance all night.'

The playlist at Le Duce reflected hardcore mod taste: Tamla Motown in all its hues, soul, and ska records by Prince Buster and Desmond Dekker. More than anything else, Le Duce aimed to banish the guilt. 'By the mid-sixties, everything was changing,' Burton remembers. 'Those of us from the immediate post-war generation were developing our own tastes and inventing our own styles. We were evolving our own look and we had adopted our own music.'

* * *

'Ten years in the community have proven that we are not quitters, nor are we "kooks". We will not shut up and go away until we receive a hearing and see the conditions we protest corrected. Our grievances are valid and we will not watch injustice, discrimination, prejudice and inequality in silence. We will not stand by and watch homosexuals mistreated, we will not permit them to be excluded from the community. We have begun the fight, and we will continue it with determination, responsibility and charity.'
DICK LEITSCH, 'We Are Ten', *Eastern Mattachine* magazine, November–December 1965

By 1966, there was a fresh urgency on the part of homophile groups in both the US and the UK. Although these organisations were entirely separate from the world of clothes, drugs, music, clubs and sex – speeding mods tended not to care about the law, until it laid its gnarled hand on their shoulder – they had been touched by the same sense that things had to change and that the time, if it was not right now, had to come soon.

Although the goal was the same – a change in the proscriptive statutes – the situation in the US and the UK was completely different. In America, there was a much wider variety of homophile groups, but there was no nationwide campaign and, indeed, the movement in general showed a distinct tendency towards internecine warfare. At the same time, the expanding gay consumer market had an activist side, as pornography coexisted with sharp calls for freedom.

In the UK, there was a determined campaign to overhaul the laws, particularly the conspiratorial aspect used to ensnare networks of gay men, typified by clauses like the illegal procuring of acts of gross indecency between male persons. The first step had been the formation of the Wolfenden Committee, which published its report in September 1957. This, in short, recommended that private homosexual relations between adults above the age of twenty-one was their own affair, and the police and courts should stay out of their business – a view contrary to public opinion. As late as 1963, the year that the gay civil servant William Vassall was convicted for selling secrets to the Russians – he had been photographed in a compromising situation and blackmailed – a poll of 2,500 people showed that 67 per cent were against the decriminalisation of homosexual behaviour between consenting adults in private.

The combination of prejudiced press coverage, public hostility and a lack of enthusiasm from Parliament resulted in a prolonged lobbying campaign to pave the way for a change in the law. The Homosexual Law Reform Society (HLRS) was part of this consciousness-raising and, under the stewardship of Anthony Grey, by the mid-1960s the tide was turning its way. In September 1965, a national opinion poll showed that 63 per cent were in favour of decriminalisation.

The cause was taken up by Lord Arran, who raised the issue in the House of Lords on 12 May 1965 with the words, 'We are persecuting a minority and we are being unjust.' After a long and tortuous process – peppered by vitriolic speeches on the part of the bill's opponents and interrupted by a general election in March 1966 – Arran succeeded in passing a sexual offences bill through its third reading in June 1966, before it ran out of time.

After this success, the Labour MP Leo Abse introduced his third attempt at a bill on the subject on 5 July. This measure was based on Arran's bill, and it passed its first reading by 244 votes to 100, with an overwhelming amount of Labour MPs constituting those in favour. The countdown to legalisation was on, but campaigners had mixed feelings: the proposals had been considerably watered down as a sop to the more determined antis.

In 1966, there were only three campaigning groups in the UK: Arena Three, a lesbian group; the HLRS; and the North West HLRS set up by Allan Horsfall in 1964. Gay rights were still, largely, a parliamentary affair. During the passage of the various bills, the grassroots activists were kept firmly in the background lest they frighten the horses. They had done much to create a climate in which law reform would occur, but it had come at a cost.

The American experience was almost the mirror opposite: plenty of inspired grassroots activity but little impact on politicians or the legislature. As in England, the small number of homophile activists had to overcome the vast inertia caused by self-hatred and self-concealment. A frequent metaphor in the 1950s was 'the mask', referring to the ability of the non-effeminate gay man to appear as 'normal' as everyone else. Donald Webster Cory thought that this pretence engendered a self-destructive spiral: the fear of openness meant a concealment that served the status quo that had engendered the fear in the first place. Only activism could smash this closed loop: 'Until we are willing to speak out openly in defense of our activities, and to identify ourselves with the millions pursuing these activities, we are unlikely to find the attitudes of the world undergoing any significant change.'

While Cory was preparing his book, the first post-war homophile organisation was formed in Los Angeles. The Mattachine Society's founder members included Harry Hay, Dale Jennings and designer Rudi Gernreich. Their title came from the Société Mattachine, a medieval masque group that travelled around France dramatising injustice. The name was used to emphasise the fact gay men and women were a 'masked people, unknown and anonymous'.

The aims of the society included reaching out to isolated homosexuals, organising 'toward an ethical homosexual culture paralleling the cultures of the Negro, Mexican and Jewish peoples', and assisting men who were victimised. There was plenty of that in 1950s America – this was the time of the McCarthy witch-hunts, the gay spies and the routine use of police entrapment in public spaces. The society gradually spread, with branches around the country – in Chicago, Washington DC, New York and San Francisco. As important as the grassroots activism were the publications issued by the Mattachine Society and its affiliates: *ONE* magazine, founded in 1952 by Dorr Legg and Dale Jennings, the *Mattachine Review*, founded in 1955 by Hal Call, and *The Ladder*, the magazine founded by the first American lesbian activist group, the Daughters of Bilitis.

This was a long, lonely struggle that, over a decade, attempted to combat guilt and hopelessness with startling visions of a possible future: in 1963, *ONE* ran a cover which proclaimed 'Let's Push Homophile Marriage'. But, by 1965, homophile organisations had grown in number and confidence. This was inspired by the success of the civil rights movement, another 'very large minority' that had gained national publicity and public support for its cause.

In September of that year, a group called ECHO – East Coast Homophile Organisations – held a conference in New York City. It was an ambitious attempt to bring together representatives of homophile organisations from all over the US. The theme was 'The Homosexual in the Great Society', a reference to President

Johnson's promise that every American citizen had 'a right to be treated as a man equal in opportunity to all others'. Reporting on the conference in the January 1966 issue of *The Ladder*, Erika Hastings observed how the conference's 'emphasis on the homosexual as a citizen and a social being, not as a psychological subject, is in keeping with the philosophy spun by ECHO, that the fundamental problems facing the homosexual minority are not in essence psychological ones, but social and political ones – problems of prejudice, discrimination, law, and custom'.

It was a rambunctious yet hopeful affair: as Hastings noted, 'the spirited audience also reflected new expectations'. After all the speeches and proposals, what struck her were the popular slogan buttons. One of the favourites being worn was EQUALITY FOR HOMOSEXUALS? – referring to the movement's campaign 'to secure for the homosexual, as a homosexual, complete equality with his or her fellow citizens'.

This increased confidence went hand in hand with the expansion of gay male consumer culture, in particular the physique magazines, which, bought under the counter or by mail order, were for many gay men the only connection with others of their kind. Their spread was huge: in 1965, one title, *Tomorrow's Man*, had a circulation of 100,000 copies – at least twenty times that of *ONE* – while the monthly sales of all titles was around 750,000.

The physique magazines were a hidden organising force in the 1950s and early 1960s. In *Hard to Imagine*, Thomas Waugh called them the 'most significant gay cultural achievement during the formative quarter century after World War II'. This freighted them with an unbidden significance, a fact that many publishers chose to ignore but which others, like Directory Services Incorporated, decided to accommodate in their increasingly frank products.

After the 1962 ruling of *MANual* v. *Day*, which effectively curbed the US Post Office's appetite for the censorship of mail-order material, the physique magazines got bolder and bolder. The old justifications – of the body beautiful or nudism – were jettisoned as more identifiably gay models replaced the idealised body-builders of yore in magazines like *Trim and Vim, Adonis, Body Beautiful* and *Young Physique*.

There was also an explosion in lurid gay paperbacks, a strange half-world of titillation cloaked in consciousness-raising. 1966 saw the publication of new sociological or anthropological titles like *America's Homosexual Underground, The Other Men* or the hysterical *I, Homosexual* ('The Homosexual Reveals Himself In All of the Stark Nakedness of his Inner Torments, Revelations, and Orgiastic Revelries').

Then there were the porn novels, published with lurid covers: *The Dungaree Jungle, The Lavender Elves, Gay Three-Way*. Some of these achieved the status of high art, like Don Holliday's 1966 novel *The Man from C.A.M.P.*, a homosexual spy with his call sign, 'Yoo Hoo! Lover Boy!' But even this parodic froth began with a serious prologue: 'Unorthodox sexual behaviour may itself acquire the tone of a general protest against "things as they are".'

This twinning of exploitation with protest was at its height in the mid-sixties. The editorial page of *BUTCH*, issue no. 1, proclaimed that the publishers 'hold that all of us, every citizen, have a common ground to defend. There is no place in our society for efforts, whether legal or extra-legal, to coerce the taste of others . . . to inhibit the efforts of writers or photographers to achieve artistic expression'. An unsigned editorial called for a world without 'guilt and shame'.

Inside the magazine was the first full-frontal male nude to be commercially published in America – soon to be followed by a flood. Published in 1966, *BUTCH* no. 5 featured a naked model with a semi-erect penis on the cover; inside was an editorial extolling healthy sex and ads for '*Vagabond* – the catalog unusual', which advertised books (*Mr Madam* etc.) and records (*The Queen Is in the Closet* et al.) on the Camp label.

During the first half of 1966, events gathered pace. In February, the National Planning Conference of Homophile Organizations was held in Kansas City. In April, a 'sip-in' was held in New York, dramatising the fact that many city bars refused to serve homosexuals. In May, there was the 'first ever gay motorcade' in Los Angeles to protest against the 'Exclusion of Homosexuals From the Armed Forces'.

In some ways, this was business as usual: the same groups, the same few hundred activists. But, in July, a new kind of group, Vanguard, was set up in San Francisco by members of the Glide Memorial Church, a parish in San Francisco's Tenderloin, a district of poor elderly people, hustlers, transsexuals and teenage runaways. Realising the depth of the social problem right in front of their noses, they consulted with the youths of the area about their troubles and their needs.

These were detailed in a July 1966 handbill called 'WE PROTEST': 'police harassment of youth', 'the endless profit adults are making off youth in the central city', 'the unstopped and seeming unstoppable flow in pills which afflict the area', 'being called "Queer", "Pillhead" and being placed in the position of being outlaws and parasites when we are offered no alternative to this existence in our society'.

It was estimated that there were around a thousand young men and women aged between twelve and twenty-five working in the Tenderloin as 'prostitutes, pimps, jack rollers and pill pushers'. Some of these were runaways trying to survive loneliness and constant police harassment. As one of them, Jean Paul Marat, told the *Berkeley Barb*: 'I was stopped by the police seventeen times in three days. The last time I got a dislocated jaw. That sort of thing happens all the time.'

Vanguard was set up with the help of local hustler/activists like Keith Oliver and Adrian Ravarour, who had already begun attempting to organise their peers 'at the Meat Rack'. 'People were being ground down by their environment, by being called names, by being told they were worthless, by families who threw them out,' Ravarour remembered. 'I saw Vanguard as an opportunity where people could stand their ground.'

A July report noted that 'VANGUARD is an organisation whose membership is drawn right off the streets of the city, with aims of self-improvement of the lot of hair-fairies,* lost kids, hustlers, young adults without family ties, and all the other varied types that frequent Market Street seeking entertainment, money, a meal, a change of clothing, or just kicks.' Members held weekly dances in the church's basement, distributed free food and clothing to their peers and produced a magazine called *Vanguard*. The first issue, published in August 1966, featured an editorial by the elected president, Jean Paul Marat, who, in his *Berkeley Barb* photo portrait, resembled those Chicago youths on the May 1966 *Look* cover with his Beatles cap, mod jacket with epaulettes and Brian Jones bob.

Vanguard #1 featured poetry, instructions on what to do if arrested and an editorial by Mark Forrester that described the denizens of the Tenderloin in terms of the wider society: 'Does the hustler damage anyone but himself? Is his poverty or spirit less than those middle-class whites in Chicago who chant "White Power" in the face of orderly challenges to their security by the long-suppressed "Blacks", who are the REAL derelicts of this society?'

In the same month that this issue of *Vanguard* was published, there was the first gay riot, when about fifty or sixty young queers and drag queens erupted in fury inside an establishment, Gene Compton's Cafeteria, that they felt to be a safe haven. Infuriated by heavy-handed and intrusive policing, a young transvestite threw coffee over an aggressive cop, and the other customers went on the rampage.

This had been building up for a while. Compton's popularity among hustlers and drag queens came from its status as an all-night venue and the fact that the evening manager had been an older effeminate homosexual who created a sympathetic atmosphere. When he died, the management introduced a 25 cents cover charge and hired Pinkerton security guards to harass the clientele. On 18 July, members of Vanguard picketed the venue in protest.

---

* Young men who ratted up their hair into a beehive and wore make-up, along with mohair cardigans, very tight, short trousers and slingbacks.

On that night in August, it exploded. As an eyewitness related, 'With that cups, saucers and trays began flying around the place and all directed at the police. They retreated outside until reinforcements arrived, and the Compton's management ordered the doors closed. With that, the Gays began breaking every window in the place, and as they ran outside to escape the breaking glass, the police tried to grab them and throw them in the paddy wagon.

'They found this no easy task, for Gays began hitting them "below the belt" and drag queens hitting them in the face with their extremely heavy purses. A police car had every window broken, a newspaper shack outside the cafeteria was burned to the ground, and general havoc raised that night in the Tenderloin. The next day, drag queens, hair fairies, conservative Gays and hustlers joined in a picket of the cafeteria, which would not allow the drags back in.'

The fightback against prejudice and harassment began from those who had nothing to lose, the lowest of the low. The Compton's riot did not achieve much on the ground, as the police continued to arrest hustlers 'en masse', but it showed that violence was necessary to make the point to those who would not hear, to make a show of strength and self-worth when that was exactly what the attitude of the city – its businesses and its police – was trying to deny.

As if to clear the air, Vanguard organised a 'clean sweep' by hair fairies in Market Street shortly afterwards, with a press release that stated their position: 'the VANGUARD demonstration indicates the willingness of society's outcasts to work openly for an improvement in their own social-economic power. WE HAVE HEARD TOO MUCH ABOUT "WHITE POWER" AND "BLACK POWER" SO GET READY TO HEAR ABOUT "STREET POWER".'

* * *

'America is not too settled at the moment and I don't think it is any time for the Beatles to be here. There is much violence and the sun is burning out of the hard sky. Psycho, schizo, paranoid are words as familiar in the newspapers here as freeze, crisis and rain are in the British press.'

DEREK TAYLOR, 'But They Shouldn't Be Here . . .', *Disc and Music Echo*, 20 August 1966

A blistering hostility was in the air during August 1966. There was a sense of matters coming to a head, as the pressure rose with the heat and violence became not a random event, but a climate. There were many words expended on causes and reasons, but the purple and black heart of that turbulent season was definitively evoked not by a literary insider or a New Journalist, but by the taboo-busting novelist John Rechy.

His exposé of the late-1950s Los Angeles underworld, *City of Night*, had been written to the pace of rock 'n' roll, and his new novel, *Numbers*, accelerated the action with pop tunes from that summer: 'Dirty Water', 'Hungry', 'Summer in the City', 'Paint It, Black'. These were hard, tough songs – 'hopped up dirges' – that soundtracked Rechy's apocalyptic vision of Los Angeles as a jagged, toxic, harshly lit blare.

There was no escape within this metallic, smog-shrouded nightmare – a fitting backdrop for his protagonist's desperate struggle against age, against time, against the loneliness that threatens to swallow him up. Driving into Los Angeles, Johnny Rio finds that the warped sounds of 1966 uncannily replicate the black hole that threatens to suck out his soul:

Suddenly, with a blast, a rocking L.A. station shatters the static. A male voice groans:

Wild thing, you make my heart sing –
You make everything grooooooveee . . .

The music, by a group called the Troggs, with its persistent beat (like life embedded in the record's groove, to be played over and over – the same; what changes between the beginning and the end?) acts as a catalyst for Johnny's buried despair; and despair flows in a confused mixture of panic and excitement which burrows between his legs; his cock begins to swell.

As insects hit his windshield, he counts them down, fantasising that God is a sniper with 'a roster, with everyone in the world – past, present, future – numbered . . . all listed neatly in long, thin, tight columns. Say that your number is infinite-billion, six million, eight hundred and sixty-six thousand, three hundred and seventy-two. If you could only determine the number of those before you, then you'd know almost to the instant when your own would come up.'

Numbers is an elaborate pun: on the numbers of Johnny's hecatomb imaginings: on the phrase 'your number's up'; on the word 'numb'; on the book of the Bible; and on the use of the word in the gay subculture, where it means 'a casual homosexual partner' or 'a trick'. But Johnny is more than that; he is a butch number, a former hustler who has foresworn that way of life, a still fit and desirable man on the cusp of a maturity that fills him with an overwhelming dread.

For Johnny, violence, sex and death are intricately intertwined. The plot of *Numbers* concerns itself with the great gay unmentionable: the sex-hunting so obsessive and divorced from emotion that it becomes mathematical, an all-consuming tabulation. He only feels alive when he is desired and, as he revisits his recent, barren past in the city, he formulates a plan that he will leave Los Angeles once he has achieved his aim of having sex with thirty men in ten days.

In *Numbers*, autobiography and fiction intertwine like a curlicue of cigarette smoke. It was originally based on a ten-day bender that Rechy underwent in 1966. When it was published the next year, it featured a picture of the author on the cover as Johnny Rio, a confusion heightened by the use of friends like Christopher Isherwood as characters in the narrative. But fiction it is, Rechy's binge redacted into a harsh, taut parable.

By the book's end, the magic number has been reached, but still he does not stop. *Numbers* ends in psychic disintegration, as Johnny Rio is gripped 'by an enormous craving whose demands are already multiplying, squaring themselves, burgeoning geometrically – a craving that expects no surcease'. Satiety is impossible, and Johnny is trapped in his sex loop like a fly in amber. This was not liberation but annihilation.

The month had begun with a terrible crime, and the 12 August cover of *Time* – 'The Psychotic and Society' – featured a snapshot of its perpetrator, Charles Whitman, blank and impenetrable behind his heavy glasses. Inside the issue, on the page before the cover feature, there was a long list of race riots: 'summer is the season of rioting', *Time* opined, before reporting on unrest on Omaha, Minneapolis, Philadelphia, Atlanta and Chicago.

Whitman's rampage in Texas was a shattering event, the sort of crime that, once it has happened, spins the world on its axis. It was graphically stark: the puffs of smoke emanating from the neoclassical tower, white against a blue summer's sky; the lightly dressed students, workers and teachers clustering for cover behind the extravagant chrome tail fins; the photographs of the dead and wounded laid out like tombstone grids.

'The madman in the tower,' *Time* called the perpetrator. Whitman had been 'an exemplary boy', but this compliant face hid family problems – his father was 'an authoritarian, a perfectionist and an unyielding disciplinarian' who beat his wife. After receiving an honourable discharge from the Marines, Whitman enrolled at the University of Texas. He married and took on extra jobs to support himself and his wife.

At the age of twenty-five Whitman was a seething compound of hostility reaching critical mass. He popped Dexedrines and beat his wife. He went to see a psychiatrist at the university, worried that he might explode. On 30 July, he wrote his suicide note: 'I've been having fears and violent impulses. I've had some tremendous headaches. I am prepared to die. After my death, I wish an autopsy on me to be performed to see if there's any mental disorders.'

After killing his mother and his wife, Whitman picked up a bag containing five different guns and, after mortally wounding a receptionist and killing two sightseers, he barricaded himself in the observation tower. Within ninety minutes he had wounded dozens and killed a further eleven people, including two teenage students. One shot hit the eight-months-pregnant Claire Wilson: she survived, but the bullet shattered her baby's skull.

The horror triggered an anguished self-examination. *Time* ran a piece about America as 'A Gun Toting Nation', calling for stricter 'arms licensing'. In another article, called 'The Symptoms of Mass Murder', it linked Whitman's murderous spree to a new kind of threat, a new kind of random irrationality: the lives that were taken 'were victims of the blind fury of the psychotic murderer'. This was a new numbers game. Estimating that there were around 800,000 psychotics in American hospitals, *Time* calculated that 200,000 Americans were potential mass murderers: 'Most, of course, will never carry out their aggressive urges, but enough will so that unsuspecting people will continue to fall victim to their irrationality.' Potential killers were everywhere: 'They are driving their cars, going to church with you, working with you. And you never know it until they snap.'

This was a new stain upon America. Charles Whitman presented himself as an unprecedented kind of enemy within – all the more disturbing because he was so apparently 'a real all-American boy'. Previously unrecognised and still ill-defined, the psychotic was added to the cluster of enemies and subversives that appeared to be threatening the country's way of life: war protestors, assertive Black Power ideologues, homosexuals.

The old certainties were under attack, the nation riven. *Life*'s 12 August issue offered, intentionally or otherwise, a prolonged disquisition on violence, its manifestations, causes and effects. Leading with graphic full-page photos of the University of Texas killings, it continued with a long article about the effect of the Vietnam war on the Midwestern town of Massillon, Ohio: 'A Town's Troubled Mood as . . . A War Comes Home'. The piece reflected a change in the national mood from the uncritical, gung-ho mentality epitomised by 'The Ballad of the Green Berets'. Massillon was split evenly down the middle on the war. The town's principal corporation, Republic Steel, was booming due to the increased demand for military hardware, but this prosperity came at a price. Residents complained about the war, about the new aggression of 'negroes', and placed all the blame at the feet of President Johnson.

A few pages later, *Life* ran a long article by Pamela Hansford Johnson about the deeper implications of the Moors Murders, written after the UK conviction of Ian Brady and Myra Hindley on 6 May 1966. This was, as the judge, Mr Justice Atkinson, observed in his closing remarks, 'a truly horrible case' involving 'two sadistic killers of the utmost depravity' who committed the horrific murders of defenceless children and adolescents, terrifying the city of Manchester.

Hansford Johnson attended the trial and was appalled by both defendants: 'Both, in the witness box, are controlled and quiet; steadily and remorselessly, often stupidly, they lie and lie and lie.' Brady was gaunt, 'a cross between Josef Goebbels and a bird'. He looked ordinary and was impassive in court, but 'under interrogation he displayed a violence and an arrogance terrifying in its intensity, the dirty language spouting out of him like oil from a well'.

Hindley was worse: 'If she has an expression, it is one of sullen hatred. She hates us all – judge, jury, reporters, public: she does not yet seem to hate herself. My initial instinct is to think of her as a concentration camp guard. Later I find that Irma Grese, "Beastess of Belsen", was her heroine. She possessed Grese's photograph and among the literature found in the suitcases were "Mein Kampf" and other Nazi books.'

Profoundly shocked by what she saw in Chester Crown Court, Hansford Johnson saw Hindley and Brady as symptomatic of a much wider and dangerous trend, the seemingly inevitable result of an untrammelled licence. 'We are left with a moral problem as weighty as Everest,' she concluded. 'A boil has burst in the flesh of society and the pus flows. How far are we responsible for that society?'

The violence did not stop. On 12 August, the British press reported on 'the worst crime London has known this century'. At around 3 p.m., three police officers stopped a suspicious-looking van near Wormwood Scrubs prison. All three were gunned down by the vehicle's three occupants. A ten-year-old boy saw the whole thing. 'I saw a man shoot the policemen,' he told the newspapers. 'It was horrible and I was so scared.'

Nothing about the murders could have been further from Swinging London. The location was Braybrook Street, right on the edge of Old Oak Common, a large, open space surrounded by industry and railways. In contemporary news photos, the grim Victorian outline of Wormwood Scrubs looms above the policemen's devastated 'Q-Car', a brand-new Triumph 2000. In contrast, the killers used an old Standard Vanguard, an unlovely, bulbous design.

This was old-style villainy, performed by hardened criminals. It was the worst police shooting for fifty-six years. Cop-killing was a huge taboo, and the nation recoiled. Two of the perpetrators were arrested within a week, but the third, Harry Roberts, remained at large, prompting the biggest manhunt ever in Britain.

On 12 August, the Beatles faced the first concerts of their third annual summer tour in America. Things had changed since August 1965, when the group had played the biggest pop show to date at the 56,000-capacity Shea Stadium. This year the mood was totally different. The continent had replaced love with hate: pulpit denunciations, Ku Klux Klan threats and Beatle-product pyres reminiscent of Nazi book burnings.

It had been a torrid few weeks for the previously inviolable quartet. For the previous three years, the Beatles' success had grown along with their ambitions. They had been in an unassailable position: much of the Western world had fallen at their feet, they had sold millions of records, had been honoured by their country and were indulged and protected as the avatars of a new, vibrant and progressive youth culture. By summer 1966, this had changed.

Orbiting very fast within their private sphere, the Beatles were effectively working in two separate time zones: their own present as increasingly experimental artists, and the past of Beatlemania. 'Our image was only a teeny part of us,' John Lennon later told Hunter Davies. 'Newspapers always get things wrong. Even when bits were true, it was always old. New images would catch on just as we were leaving them.'

This time slip had increased during their early-1966 hiatus. The Maureen Cleave interviews and the Bob Whitaker photo session were indicative of a new attitude within the Beatles. They had tasted freedom and, whether consciously or not, they wanted to smash their previous pop-idol image – to show the public just how much they had changed, to make it clear that it was their prerogative to change. But these words and images would return to haunt them.

The first sign of any public activity had come in mid-May, when the Beatles filmed several clips for both sides of their forthcoming single, 'Paperback Writer' and 'Rain'. The Beatles had decided on a minimum of TV appearances to promote the new record. Hiring Michael Lindsay-Hogg as director, they shot a few differ-ent set-ups in Abbey Road and, the following day, in the grounds of Chiswick House, west London. In all the clips, the Beatles are a self-contained, elite unit, dressed in the latest Carnabetian fash-ions: turtlenecks, floral shirts, brightly coloured sunglasses. If any-one had been of such a mind, drugs were indicated, but the group were still beyond suspicion. There were omens, however. At the start of the studio video for 'Paperback Writer', Paul McCartney holds up a number of large-sized, colour 35mm transparencies, zeroing in on the 'butcher' image.

On 11 June, an image from the Whitaker session was repro-duced on the front cover of *Disc and Music Echo* – partly owned by Brian Epstein – to promote 'Paperback Writer'. Subtitled 'What a Carve-Up!', the cover showed four unsmiling Beatles with white coats and meat, but without the doll parts. 'I wanted to do a real experiment,' Whitaker told the paper. 'And this is the result – the use of the camera as a means of creating situations.'

Inside, Paul McCartney gave Ray Coleman an exclusive interview that trailed the new album and hinted at some kind of end: 'The future could be very interesting – there's so many things to try. We've been lucky, so lucky. We've had some great experiences, and now it's something like a school leaver wondering what career to choose. We can always write music, and still choose something to break into.'

Neither side of the new single gave any indication of pandering to the public. 'Paperback Writer' was an extension of 'Day Tripper', that song's monolithic riff accelerated and broken up into a tumble of words, Beach Boys-in-raga harmonies, and punchy, ringing guitars. This was not a song about love, but about the mass media, performed under fierce compression, as though the images and thoughts were coming in too fast to process.

The sense that the Beatles were determined to pursue their increasingly esoteric preoccupations was heightened when the record was turned over. 'Rain' was a hymn to cosmic acceptance and the primacy of interior states couched in a very strange soundscape: the song was taken down a semitone in the mix, resulting in a slurred, queasy tone; at the fade, the track was reversed, creating a sound that drew you in at the same time as it belied sense.

There was a definite sense of us and them: were you on or off the bus? That was the effect of the hallucinogenic drugs that, despite the much touted ego-loss, had failed to blunt John Lennon's sarcasm. 'If the rain comes they run and hide their heads,' he sang in a raga sneer, 'they might as well be dead.' In the Abbey Road videos, the group are unsmiling and opaque. When the clips were aired live on the 5 June *Ed Sullivan Show*, there was no screaming.

This new aloofness was mirrored by the hard shiny surfaces of the new single, designed to throw off the casual listener. Construed as arrogance and laziness, this lack of willingness to please was immediately spotted by the ever-alert fans, who queued up to give their verdict on both sides of the single in the 4 June *Record Mirror*. Mostly in their late teens, workers rather than bohemians, they had grown up with the group and did not much like what they heard:

Ann Shaw (23), typing pool supervisor: 'not as good as their previous hits'.

Vera Shotton (19), copy typist: 'I couldn't understand a word of what they were singing on "Paperback Writer". They're just not as good as they used to be – there are better groups around these days. As for "Rain", it just dragged on and on. I didn't like it at all.'

Alan Herrick (18), apprentice compositor: 'I didn't like "Paperback Writer" much. It seemed to be too much the same. I preferred "Rain", it has more of a tune to it.'

It fared much better with the professional reviewers. '"Paperback" has a marvellous dance beat,' wrote Penny Valentine in *Disc and Music Echo*. 'It's very striking with break-up drumming and an ethereal surf chorus.' As if to assuage the fans, the Beatles made their only live appearance on *Top of the Pops* on 16 June. Both that and the *Ed Sullivan* appearances had the desired result, as 'Paperback Writer' went to #1 on both sides of the Atlantic.

In mid-June, Capitol Records were preparing to release their ninth album of Beatles music in the US, two more than in the UK at that point. This was achieved by including singles, EP tracks and foreign-language recordings. It was done because American record companies paid royalties by the song rather than by the whole album, so Capitol paid less royalties on an eleven-track LP than they would have done on the fourteen-track version that was pressed in the UK.

The resulting records were pure merchandise, with cheesy covers and short running times, but *Yesterday and Today* was an egregious botch even by Capitol's standards. Including the group's last four US hit singles, it made commercial sense, but it also contained three new John Lennon songs, earmarked for *Revolver*, that were in varying degrees of completion: 'And Your Bird Can Sing', 'Dr Robert' and an early mix of 'I'm Only Sleeping'.

The record was released with Robert Whitaker's doll photo on the cover, overprinted with a canvas-type texture, like a painting. It is a very strange image: nothing about it is right, from the grubby doll parts, to the red, raw chunks of meat, the white butcher's coats and the queasy grey wash. It might be thought that someone at Capitol would have looked hard at the picture and called a halt, but no: the Beatles' magic still held.

Contemporary reports stated that the Beatles chose the cover themselves, but it seems clear that John Lennon pushed the hardest. Having suffered most from the dismemberment of the *Revolver* material, he was infuriated and, indeed, unrepentant, later stating in the press that the cover 'was as relevant as Vietnam' – hardly a phrase likely to pour oil over troubled waters, for the reaction from DJs and retailers was both adverse and instantaneous.

On 14 June, Capitol's manager for press and information services, Ron Tepper, sent a letter out to reviewers stating that 'the original album cover is being discarded and a new jacket is being prepared'. It quoted company president Alan Livingston: 'The original cover, created in England, was intended as "pop art" satire. However a sampling of public opinion in the United States indicates that the cover design is subject to misinterpretation.'

Livingston remembered that 'the word came back very fast that the dealers would not touch it. They would not put the album in the stores . . . I had to call Brian Epstein and tell him that I couldn't put the album out. It was out of my hands. They finally sent us another album cover that we could put out. Brian was there to represent their interests and wanted the Beatles to have the cover they wanted. But he was also concerned about money . . . he eventually gave in.'

The initial run of covers was estimated at 750,000. On 28 June, Jo Sobeck from Capitol's Scranton plant wrote a memo to R. L. Howe, the company's national distribution manager, to inform him that 'the destruction of 50,000 T2553, Beatles jackets, was completed on Monday, June 27, 1966. About 35,000 were destroyed on Friday, June the 24th, and the balance on Monday.

'Destruction was accomplished by having a hole dug by a clam shovel in a swampy part of the Needham Town Dump. By the time the hole was ready for us it had filled with water. The jackets were dumped on the ground as close as possible to the hole and then a bulldozer pushed the jackets into the hole. The hole was then covered with about one to two feet of dirt and will subsequently be covered with garbage which will be well compacted as time goes by.'

This was a determined but incomplete act of erasure that cost Capitol over $200,000. Many of the original covers were pasted over with a photo of the thoroughly fed-up quartet draped around a steamer trunk. In the teen mags of the time, fans discussed the best way of peeling off this dreary substitute to reveal the taboo image. The 'butcher' cover might have been a secret communication for those in the know, but it also marked a turning point.

'The Beatles have turned out the most nauseating album cover ever seen in the US,' opined *KRLA Beat* on 2 July. 'Not even one person who saw the banned album cover liked it. No one found it even slightly amusing. In short, they all felt it was the most sickening spectacle they'd ever seen. Many agreed that it must have been done for shock value. And this poses the question – why do the Beatles feel they must resort to shock to sell an album?

'Personally I think the Beatles are so far from their public that they don't even know what their public wants anymore. Actually, ever since the Beatles first were introduced to America, people have been predicting their downfall. But those wise in the ways of the entertainment business have stuck to the same thought throughout the Beatle reign – "No one can kill the Beatles except themselves". And perhaps they're doing it now.'

In the short term, however, the controversy was moot: *Yesterday and Today* was a big seller, reaching #1 in the US album charts at the end of July. The Beatles had other concerns. After finishing up two months of work on their new album, they set off in the fourth week of June for an ambitious world tour that would take in Germany, Japan, the Philippines and then, after a break, America in August. They had no idea of what faced them.

The first date was held at the Circus-Krone-Bau in Munich,

Germany, on the 23rd, and it was awful. The Beatles had not performed live – except for a brief burst at May's *New Musical Express* Poll Winners Concert – for six months. Locked in the studio working on their futuristic new album, they had given no thought to their live presentation, and Robert Whitaker's photographs show them holding a last-minute rehearsal in their dressing room.

It was a strange set, one that would remain in place, with minimal variation, throughout the tour: 'Rock and Roll Music', 'She's a Woman', 'If I Needed Someone', 'Day Tripper', 'Baby's in Black', 'I Feel Fine', 'Yesterday', 'I Wanna Be Your Man', 'Nowhere Man', 'Paperback Writer' and 'I'm Down'. Rockers were interspersed with slow or mid-paced numbers, preventing any excitement from building. There was only one song from 1966, the new single.

The footage from Hamburg, two days later, shows the group playing in a huge barn, the Ernst Merck Halle, to a large and unruly crowd of 5,600 people. There is an air of mania inside the hall that is not necessarily triggered by the Beatles' performance. At one point a teenage girl is shown, dressed in a hand-made T-shirt with the name of the group scrawled over it. In between her fits of screaming, she throws jelly babies onstage, just like in 1964.

The next day, the Beatles flew back to London, then on to Japan – a route that took them eastwards over the North Pole. On their arrival in Tokyo, they were immediately whisked off and, surrounded by unusually heavy security, driven at high speed to the Hilton Hotel in the centre of the city. There they were effectively under house arrest, forbidden to leave the building except for their performances.

The group bridled under the strict regime: at several points they tried to escape and get a feel for the city, but each time they were brought back like naughty schoolboys. They were not aware of the level of hostility that greeted their visit: various Establishment figures, from the Japanese prime minister down, had criticised the group and stated that they were not fit to play the Budokan Hall. Whipped up by nationalist groups, there was a groundswell of

'Japanese xenophobia', with influential journalists and even the promoter of the Budokan shows ranged against the group. Students at some Tokyo schools were ordered not to attend the concerts, and there was a bid to stop young Japanese from playing electric guitars: the fear was that rock music would turn youths into delinquents and hooligans.

Perhaps mindful of their status as ambassadors, the group were respectful and forthcoming during the ritual press conference. It was notable for a key exchange in which John Lennon finally ignored Brian Epstein's instructions not to venture into controversial territory. Asked about the Vietnam war, he said, 'Well, we think about it every day, and we don't agree with it and we think it's wrong.'

On 3 July, the Beatles flew out to the Philippines. While they were performing two chaotic shows in the Rizal Memorial Football Stadium on the 4th, the local television network showed pictures of the Beatles' non-arrival at a formal reception held by the First Lady of the Philippines, Imelda Marcos. The group hadn't been informed of the event and were asleep when the police came to escort them to the palace. Epstein refused to wake them up.

The next day, the newspapers were full of headlines like 'IMELDA STOOD UP: FIRST FAMILY WAITS IN VAIN FOR MOPHEADS'. It was alleged that the Beatles had 'spit in the eye of the first family'. Brian Epstein was hit by an unexpected tax demand on earnings from the two shows – a piece of naked extortion, backed up by threats and violence – and the touring party were given no assistance in loading their baggage and equipment. At the airport, everyone was subjected to a violent assault. Although the group were shielded from the worst, their assistants came off badly: Epstein was kicked in the groin and punched in the face, while their assistant, Mal Evans, was kicked in the ribs. Even when they had made it onto the plane, it was delayed when two of the party were taken off because of a passport irregularity. When it finally took off, the Beatles' party 'broke into spontaneous applause'.

When the group arrived back in London, they showed their evident relief and anger after the violence in the Philippines. 'I was petrified,' John Lennon told ITN. 'We'll just never go to any nuthouses again.' When George Harrison was asked by a radio reporter what was next on the group's agenda, he replied: 'We're going to have a couple of weeks to recuperate before we go and get beaten up by the Americans.'

The worst affected was Brian Epstein. On his return to the UK, he was immediately rushed to hospital with glandular fever. As he wrote to Derek Taylor on 25 July, he was 'housebound'. He thanked Taylor for his *Disc and Music Echo* column about the 'bloody Philippines', and mentioned that 'I managed to get a copy of "The War Game" to show at home this weekend and cannot say how impressed I was.'

Four days later, the second explosive device from the March lay-off was activated. *Datebook* was not a major player in the teen 'zine market, and editor/publisher Art Unger had obviously decided that controversy boosted sales. On 29 July, he published their September 'Shout-Out' issue. Emblazoned on the cover, along with a photo of Paul McCartney, was a pull-quote from John Lennon: 'I don't know which will go first – rock 'n' roll or Christianity.'

But Lennon's quote was only one of several sensational statements on that cover:

Paul McCartney: 'It's a lousy country where anyone black is a dirty nigger!'

Tim Leary: 'Turn on, tune in, drop out!'

Scott Walker: 'Pop music can warp your sense of values about life!'

Len Barry: 'English groups won't last. There is no longevity in dirt!'

Unger republished the Maureen Cleave interview, contextualising it with the photo caption, 'John Lennon sights controversy and sets sail directly towards it. That's the way he likes to live!' Within a few days, the gauntlet had been taken up, most vocally by a DJ from WAQY in Birmingham, Alabama – Tommy Charles – who announced over the air that he was refusing to play Beatles records because of their comments.

Sales of *Datebook* went through the roof – to a million copies – while Charles escalated his rhetoric, urging listeners to bring their Beatles records and paraphernalia to the studio to be destroyed in a tree shredder. Other stations in the south joined the Beatles boycotts, while KCBN in Reno broadcast an anti-Beatles editorial every hour and announced a rally to burn the group's albums on 6 August.

These demonstrations overshadowed the release of the Beatles' new single and album. Brian Epstein flew to New York and gave a press conference in which he explained that Lennon 'meant to point out that the Beatles' effect appeared to be a more immediate one upon, certainly, the younger generation. John is deeply concerned and regrets that people with certain religious beliefs should have been offended.'

This didn't stop the outpouring of hate: on the 11th, the day that the distinctly nervous quartet flew into Chicago, the Ku Klux Klan held a 'Beatle Bonfire' in Chester, South Carolina, in which they threw records and ephemera into the flames of a burning cross. The group's first performance on American soil was a tense press conference held at the Astor Towers Hotel, in which a visibly agitated John Lennon was captured on nationwide TV tying himself in knots.

In the footage, Lennon is soberly dressed, serious and chastened. His face is pinched, and he incessantly chews gum. He couldn't actually see what he had done wrong. He knew there was a very serious uproar but he didn't understand why it had happened and why it had taken so long to happen: after all, he had done the interview with Maureen Cleave more than five months previously – in Beatles terms, almost another life.

Lennon apologised, not for what he said, but the fuss that it had caused: 'I'm not saying that we're better, or greater, or comparing us with Jesus Christ as a person or God as a thing or whatever it is, you know. I just said what I said and it was wrong, or was taken wrong. And now it's all this.' George Harrison was characteristically blunt: 'Christianity is declining, and everybody knows about that, and that was the fact that was trying to be made.'

It took Paul McCartney to summarise the underlying problem. It wasn't just about the specific comments and the outrage they had caused. It was about the Beatles' simultaneous existence in two time zones, the schizophrenic duality between their public image and their increasingly private existence that was threatening to tear them apart: 'We're just trying to move forwards. And people seem to be trying to just sort of hold us back.'

The Beatles thus began their third US tour – fourteen shows in seventeen days – in a state oscillating between resentment, deep frustration and sheer terror. For three years they had walked the high wire between godlike stardom and ordinary humanity, between public expectation and private fulfilment, between pop stars and pop artists. It had been an extraordinary act of talent and persistence, but now it was threatening to come undone.

The polarity had flipped from positive to negative. The 'butcher' cover had been uncannily predictive of the way that the Beatles were being taken apart. In Japan, Manila and America, they seemed to have become a lightning rod for all sorts of tensions – the penetration of Western culture into previously untouched markets, the decline of religion in the face of pluralistic consumerism – that were an inevitable product of the economy and the times. They were also a target for all those who resisted the pace of change. That August, the writer James Morris declared how 'the Beatles' absolute aloofness to old prejudices and preconceptions, their brand of festive iconoclasm, has developed an attraction for me, as it has for millions more skeptics the world over'. But this iconoclasm had its dangers. Morris quoted an elderly acquaintance: 'I'll tell you what the trouble with the Beatles is: *They've got no respect.*'

Meanwhile, they had dates to play. None had been cancelled,

and one positive result of the Chicago press conference was that Tommy Charles called off his additional threat to burn Beatles records on 19 August. The first two shows were in Chicago on the 12th, where they were backed up by the Ronettes, the Cyrkle (an Epstein-managed group who had a US #2 hit that summer with Paul Simon's 'Red Rubber Ball'), Bobby Hebb, and the Remains, a tough young R&B group from Boston. The group played to around 25,000 fans, in a venue that smelt of the Chicago stockyards. The furore did not seem to have affected their popularity: as one reviewer wrote, 'The reaction to the Beatles' appearance was tumultuous. If this is what happens when the Beatles were banned, what do you think would happen if they were abolished?' The next night, they played two shows to over 30,000 people in Detroit, where the fans 'generally blew their minds'.

Almost every concert on this tour was marked by rabid crowd scenes – stage invasions, objects thrown from the audience, fraught getaways – but always in the back of the Beatles' minds was their 19 August show in Memphis, the heart of the Bible Belt. This would be the flashpoint of the tour. Their PR man Tony Barrow remembered that when the touring party got to Memphis, 'everything seemed to be controlled and calm, but underneath somehow, there was this nasty atmosphere'.

The forces arrayed against the Beatles were highlighted by an ITN crew, sent to America to cover the controversy. Reporter Richard Lindley first talked to Tommy Charles, who thought that 'because of their tremendous popularity throughout the world, especially with the younger set, [they] have been able to say what they wanted to without any regard for judgement, maturity or the meaning of it, and no one has challenged them to any degree'.

Lindley discovered that the DJ was well supported in Birmingham. Conducting vox pops in a record shop, he found many teens expressing anti-Beatles sentiments: 'I think they need to watch what they say'; 'Every time I hear them sing, I can't help but think about what they're saying. I don't know . . . I guess it sort of hurt, it just hurt people's feelings'; 'What have they done for us?'; 'I just don't appreciate it.' The reporter also talked to a Methodist pastor, Alan Montgomerie, who was charm itself until he recalled his phone call with Brian Epstein: 'He said to me, "Do you think it is becoming of anybody in Birmingham to criticise the Beatles? Because Birmingham is known all over Europe as the place where the negro is treated so badly."' Up next was the KKK's Imperial Wizard Robert Shelton, who castigated the group for being communists and supporting civil rights.

The Beatles were interviewed backstage, four furious and seriously displeased musicians who could no longer be bothered to hide their anger and contempt. John Lennon always physically took on the changes that the Beatles went through: in the footage, he is no longer the moon-faced, slightly plump emperor of the 'Paperback Writer' video, but nervous and thin, severe, his hair cut short by George Harrison the day before.

McCartney plays the diplomat. Harrison is particularly terse. Lennon switches between madcap humour, evasion, bravado and blunt honesty. At the interview's end, he fixes the camera with a look and a voice that drips sarcasm: 'It doesn't matter about people not liking our records, or not liking the way we look, or what we say. You know, they're entitled to not like us. And we're entitled not to have anything to do with them if we don't want to, or not to regard them.'

There were KKK pickets outside Memphis's Mid-South Coliseum, and a Christian rally. The first show passed without incident, but during the second some teenagers threw a cherry-bomb onstage during 'If I Needed Someone'. The group didn't stop, but played through the rest of the number in a quicker tempo than usual. They all looked at each other to see who had been shot. 'It was that bad,' Lennon later remembered.

In 1966, the business of pop touring was still in its infancy. The Beatles and their support groups faced dreadful logistics, abysmal sound systems and almost non-existent technical back-up. The day after Memphis, the show at Cincinnati's Crosley Field was cancelled at the last moment because of heavy rain and inadequate stage covering. When Mal Evans was setting up the gear, he received an electrical shock that threw him across the stage.

The next day, 21 August, was a logistical test. The touring party returned to Crosley Field to play the cancelled show, then packed up for the drive from Cincinatti to St Louis, with a flight to New York scheduled afterwards. Busch Stadium was another rainy nightmare: as the Remains' Barry Tashian wrote, 'Our roadie, Ed Freeman, was stationed at the main AC connection to watch the performance and unplug the whole stage if anyone showed signs of an electric shock.' The Beatles had to play through the torrential rain. This was the final straw even for McCartney, the member of the group most committed to live performance: 'It felt like the worst little gig we'd ever played at even before we'd started as a band. We were having to worry about the rain getting in the amps and this took us right back to the Cavern days – it was worse than those early days. And I don't even think the house was full.'

In New York, they played Shea Stadium for the second time. Despite press reports of empty seats, the crowd was still rabid. An intrepid radio reporter called Myles Jackson took a tape recorder to the show. When the group come on, the screaming rises to a frenzied pitch; individual outbursts of hysteria are caught by the microphone against the backdrop of what sounds like a hurricane of female emotion.

The Beatles flew to Los Angeles straight after Shea. The concert at Dodger Stadium was attended by 40,000 people. It ended in chaos. The Beatles' attempted getaway in an armoured car was blocked by hundreds of fans and, after their driver failed to get them out, they were trapped in a dressing room for a couple of hours. After three more attempts, using decoy limousines and an ambulance, the group and their entourage were finally rescued by the police.

On the next day, the 29th, the touring party travelled up to San Francisco for the last show of the tour at Candlestick Park, to the south of the city. It was not an ideal venue, a large sports stadium right by the San Francisco Bay. 'On stage, a wild sea wind was blowing in every direction,' Tashian remembered. 'The audience was about 200 feet away – much farther than usual. It made us feel extremely isolated from the audience.' The Beatles knew this was the last show they would do for some time, if not ever. They did not end on a high: the venue was far from full, the sound was terrible and their performance perfunctory – much of it lost in the wind. The group set up cameras onstage to record the event, and the photographs capture blurry figures in motion, as if they have already left the arena in spirit, as if they are already slipping into history.

On the flight back to Los Angeles, Paul McCartney talked to Judith Sims of *TeenSet* about the group's future plans: 'All four Beatles want to cut down on their performing time so they can concentrate more on recording. "We're not very good performers, actually," he said. "We work better in a recording studio where we can control things and work on it until we are right. With performing there's so much that can go wrong, and you can't go back over it and do it again."'

On the day that the Beatles flew out of America, 30 August, 'Yellow Submarine' was at #8 in the *Billboard* chart, a massive leap from #52 the previous week. The downbeat 'Eleanor Rigby' had just entered the charts at #65. During the overnight flight, George Harrison turned to a reporter and flatly stated, 'Well, that's it, I'm not a Beatle any more.'

* * *

'It yet remains to be seen what the results of a homosexual revolution will be, but most knowledgeable authorities agree that things could hardly change for the worse, because they are so bad.'
REV. RALPH BLAIR, '"Op-Op": 'Open Panel on Problems',
Drum, September 1966

On 2 September 1966, Joe Meek released his fourth-to-last single. Performed by a reconfigured Paul and Ritchie and the Cryin' Shames, 'September in the Rain' was a piece of pop fluff, but the flip, 'Come on Back', was his final masterpiece: beginning and ending with wicked guitar reverb, it was a tough rocker that matched powerful call-and-response vocals with a serpentine electronic figure and a sinuous rhythm, all tension and release.

By autumn that year, Meek's mental state was worsening, as his heyday receded into the past. The Epstein/NEMS connection came to nothing, and the Cryin' Shames' records went nowhere. Almost all his productions were being turned down. Giving free rein to his instincts with 'Do You Come Here Often?' he had gained satisfaction from exposing a reality long suppressed, but this was a transient revenge as the forces ranged against him gathered speed. Jekyll overtook Hyde as money troubles and declining fame caused him to up his pill intake and dabble further in the occult – poltergeist phenomena and past-life guides. Meek's finances were in a 'helluva mess', thanks to his own lack of attention and the freezing of the 'Telstar' royalties. He owed money to the taxman and artists like Screaming Lord Sutch, his debts adding up to about £20,000, with only £1,300 in the bank.

Meek was threatened by gangsters who wanted to take over the Tornados' management. In response to this and other violent events, he kept hold of a shotgun in his flat. He felt that his time was running out. When the Honeycombs' singer Dennis D'Ell asked him about the downward curve of his success, Meek replied: 'If they're artistic enough and they don't achieve success – because not all artistic people achieve the success they deserve – then they die.'

The early autumn was also difficult for Brian Epstein. Upset at the Beatles' decision to stop touring, he did not attend the Candlestick Park show, which left him open to something far worse, for, after some time apart, Dizz Gillespie had turned up in Los Angeles. Despite Nat Weiss's warnings, Epstein had welcomed him back. While Weiss and Epstein went out to dinner on 29 August, Gillespie got into their rooms and stole their briefcases.

Epstein's case, according to his assistant Peter Brown, comprised 'a witches' stew of enormous ramifications'. It contained a large supply of pills, letters from some of his young lovers, compromising photos and $20,000 in brown-paper-bag money 'skimmed from concert funds to be distributed as a bonus'. Brown realised that 'the revelation of any of these items would make John's "Jesus" furore seem like an Easter pageant'.

Epstein received a blackmail note for the return of the briefcase. 'Brian didn't want us to pursue Dizz,' Nat Weiss remembered. 'He felt it would be embarrassing. The briefcase contained things he didn't want people to know about, and Brian was very much afraid of what could happen. I had every right to go against Dizz for my briefcase. Which I did, and Dizz was arrested and the things taken were returned. But that was the beginning of Brian's loss of self-confidence.'

On 26 September, it was reported that Epstein had been hospitalised in a London clinic. It was claimed he had gone in for a check-up, but in fact he had overdosed on prescription drugs. Peter Brown had been at Epstein's house that evening: 'I suddenly realised that Brian had been missing for part of the evening and I found him in a very heavy state of unconsciousness and called his doctor. He took an overdose on purpose. We know that because we found a note.'

For all their achievements, both Meek and Epstein were prone to the insecurities of the music industry and their own poor self-esteem. Both had suffered violence, both had been on the receiving end of the law. Both had been blackmailed and were terrified of being exposed for who they really were. Both had found that success didn't eradicate the deep scars of exile. They had reached the top but it was a barren plateau full of further uncertainty and humiliation.

Both were marked by what they had experienced in their youth, when they had been taught that they were the lowest of the low. 'Hey, you've got to hide your love away,' John Lennon had sung in one of the Beatles' most poignant songs, and the strain of doing so was disastrous for a generation of gay men. In many cases, the result was alcoholism, drug addiction, crippling guilt, an inability to form lasting relationships – a monstrous waste of lives. But out of this adversity came an incredible drive – the syndrome of gay overachievement, exactly analogous to the revenge that drives many pop stars: *Right, if you think I'm a piece of dirt, I'm going to fucking show you that I'm not. In fact, I'm going to do more than show you, I'm going to ram the fact that I'm better than you right down your throat. In public. So you have to see the fact that I'm richer, cleverer, prettier than you every day, in the newspapers, in the magazines, on the television. So you can choke on your dirty words.*

But if there was an underlying message to 1966's careening momentum, it was that satiety could never be achieved by the consumption of drugs and bodies, and that rage – unless channelled and externally directed – could turn inwards and result in self-destruction. At the very point when gay people began to agitate more confidently for their rights, and pop culture began to relax into the new freedoms they had presaged, Meek and Epstein began to slip into the shadows.

PART 2

EXPLOSION

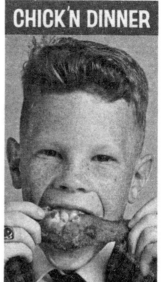

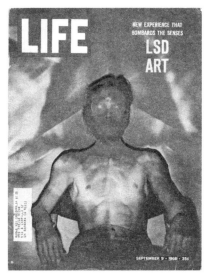

9 : SEPTEMBER

7 And 7 Is: Provocations, Shadows
and a New Language

'One of the basic factors in the rock'n'roll revolution was the shift by the entertainment industry towards the youth sector of the population. Youth-organisation emphasises virility, action, sensationalism, speed and violence.'

ORLANDO PATTERSON, 'The Dance Invasion', *New Society*, 15 September 1966

After a quick photocall at London Heathrow on the morning of 1 September, the Beatles went their own ways, scattering like spores in the wind. The group's future was uncertain. John Lennon's commitment to spend ten weeks filming Richard Lester's new anti-war movie had been publicised the previous month. Apart from that, there was no hint in the press of when the Beatles would reconvene. They had, for all intents and purposes, left the stage.

The British beat boom was over. The Beatles had begun the cycle in early 1963 and, in September 1966, they brought it to a close. Their contemporary interviews reflected this realisation. 'I think we've all got a lot to learn and a lot to do,' George Harrison said during the campaign to promote *Revolver*. 'Songs like "Eight Days a Week" and "She Loves You" sound like big drags to me now,' Lennon told Ray Coleman; 'I turn off the radio if they're ever on.'

At the same time, 1966 was the year when the unrelenting, accelerating pace of sixties pop – three singles a year, one or two albums, hundreds of live dates, television shows, radio commitments, photo shoots, foreign tours – began to catch up with many of its leading protagonists. It wasn't just the constant pressure to come up with hits and enforced intimacy that did for these musicians; it was the unprecedented nature of their global fame, the sense of being propelled far from any familiar shore.

There was an outbreak of surliness and moody behaviour, which was not the way that stars were supposed to behave. Having already commented on the rudeness of the Who and the Rolling Stones, *Rave* ran a feature in August about the withdrawal of Brian Jones from the public eye: 'He hasn't disappeared, his office assured us. Well, where is he then? The fans want him, we want him. Why doesn't he come out of his secret pleasure dome?'

There was a sequence of well-publicised breakdowns and hospitalisations: Mick Jagger's 'exhaustion' in June; Scott Walker's apparent suicide attempt in August. Several major groups split up or shed key members: Paul Jones left Manfred Mann; the Hollies sacked bassist Eric Haydock; Eric Burdon reconstituted the Animals as the New Animals; Georgie Fame dissolved the Blue Flames; while the Yardbirds lost arranger and composer Paul Samwell-Smith. 'Everybody has had enough,' ex-Animal Chas Chandler told the *Melody Maker*. 'In the Animals, we were just getting into a rut and we were just repeating ourselves for the last 18 months. We weren't getting any kicks. We had to go on stage every night and be expected to put on a raving show every time. We didn't always feel like that.'

This sense of exhaustion, if not satiation, was captured by a sensational novel published that September. Thom Keyes's *All Night Stand* told the rags-to-riches story of a north-western beat group called the Rack – from Hamburg to London, from obscurity to British hits and American fame. There were many references to sex and drugs, as well as contemporary obsessions like pirate radio and expensive fast cars – including an Aston Martin DB6, the then current choice of Mick Jagger.

The press cited British instrumental group Sounds Incorporated as the model for Keyes's exposé, but the book was an obvious *roman-à-clef* about the Beatles. Certainly, the denouement captures the air of estrangement already shown by John Lennon in his interview with Maureen Cleave. The book ends with the Rack's Gerry spinning out in his stardust mansion: 'Things got tired. I got tired. I changed a lot. Everybody wants to know me. I don't want to know. Bored. Worst of all, I'm bored with myself.'

The Beatles had suggested a unitary narrative of pop, whereby beat groups occupied the same space as black American dance records and mums-and-dads music. It had been a seductive fantasy but, with their exit, the centrifugal force of pop had disappeared, and in its place came a myriad of symptoms. The most obvious was the resurgence of light entertainment: frothy, catchy songs with simple hook lines or traditional tear-jerkers that referenced music hall, operetta and interwar crooners.

Even during the height of Beatlemania, there had been hits by the Bachelors – an Irish group specialising in deep-throated ballads like the 1927 song 'Diane' – and the comedian Ken Dodd, whose revival of an old Rudy Vallee song, 'Tears', stayed at #1 for five weeks in autumn 1965. In early September, one of the fastest risers in the British charts was 'Distant Drums', a slow, doomy single performed by a middle-aged country singer, Jim Reeves – a cult in the UK after his death in July 1964.

The tide was ebbing away from the UK. This sense of dissolution was a hot topic in the British music press that summer. In July, *Record Mirror* had asked, 'Are our stars finished abroad?' In the *Melody Maker*, Chris Welch noted that the British beat group scene was 'tearing itself to pieces', before simply concluding: 'One thing is certain. An era has ended.'

By August, America was the source of half of the records in the UK Top 50. As well as what the *NME* called 'the sudden Tamla Motown comeback', the new threat came 'from the new school of West Coast groups – the Beach Boys, the Lovin' Spoonful and the Mama's and Papa's'. At that point, West Coast still meant Los Angeles and, as if to seal its position as the centre of the pop universe, the city came up with the next Beatles right on cue.

Pop abhors a vacuum, and just as the originals disappeared, their simulacrum was heavily promoted by a full-page ad in *Billboard*: 'A different sounding new group with a live, infectious feeling demonstrated by a strong rock beat'. 'Last Train to Clarksville' was the first single by the Monkees, the four-man group assembled, after a long period of research and development, to star in a *Hard Day's Night*-type TV series. The timing was perfect. Touted as 'the spirit of 1966', the four good-looking group members reproduced the elements of the Beatles' unified 1964 camaraderie. An infectious acrostic of 'Paperback Writer', 'Last Train to Clarksville' was released four weeks before NBC's premiere of *The Monkees*. With its crackling performance and Vietnam-timely theme of unwilling partings, it entered the Top 40 a week after the series premiered – the start of a three-month run that would top out at #1.

It was a great record, but it also contained a clear message: if the Beatles weren't around, they would be cloned by the industry. And the younger teens would hardly care: 'I luv 'em,' said a reader polled by *KRLA Beat* after the show's premiere. 'Mickey and Mike are so funny and Davy's so cute and Peter's just so . . .' As another commented: 'I thought the show was great. It's kinda like *A Hard Day's Night* but it's even better because it's in color and we can see it every week.'

* * *

'A 20-year-old told me: "The younger generation – it's kind of an explosion of youth – is sick and tired of all the eight-hour-a-day junk and Vietnam and all the rest. And we've got what we were after – recognition – and now we have the power to instigate change. I firmly believe the impossible can now become possible. Nothing is really impossible as long as people are interested in change and looking for something new."'
ROBERT DE ROOS, 'The Lacy Trousered Kids Are in Revolt', *San Francisco Sunday Examiner and Chronicle*, 25 September 1966

It begins like a sudden, violent storm: a clashing, reverbed guitar driven by a hot bass over another, trebly reverbed guitar, splashy cymbal crashes and galloping drumbeats that, in 1966, were the fastest thing that anyone had heard. The tune is carried by the vocalist, who comes in hard and harsh: 'When I was a boy I thought about the times I'd be a man / I'd sit inside a bottle and pretend that I was in a can.'

There is a brief instrumental interlude, lifting off from the singer's headlong 'Yeah!' Kenny Forssi's bass carries the melody and the momentum, while the guitars continue in their reverb loop. The pace does not slacken. The singer returns, to a low hum of feedback: 'If I don't start cryin' it's because that I have got no eyes / My father's in the fireplace and my dog lies hypnotised.' Seventy-five seconds have passed, half the song, and a whole psychodrama has been revealed.

There's another brief instrumental interlude before the singer counts out 'One . . . Two . . . Three . . . Four!' and the group accelerates into a screeching spiral of sound that has no possible exit except catastrophe. There is a final guitar crash and then a deep, earth-quaking explosion that, to many listeners, meant just one thing: the H-bomb. As the noise fades away, there is a fragment of blues guitar left in its wake, like a pottery shard from a long-forgotten civilisation.

Love's second single, '7 And 7 Is' was recorded in Sunset Studios on 17 and 20 June. During the sessions, on the 18th, Love appeared on Dick Clark's *American Bandstand*, playing both sides of their first single, 'My Little Red Book', a Californian radio hit that broke into the *Billboard* charts, rising to its peak of #52 on 25 July, after their TV appearance. The clip is bizarre. The five-man group is integrated: three white musicians, one mixed-race guitarist playing a double-neck and a mixed-race singer wearing smart mod gear and strange rhomboid sunglasses. Love's version of the Bacharach/ David song sheds any sophistication for a brutally simple rhythmic treatment – an aggressive feel enhanced by Arthur Lee's stagecraft, as he constantly weaves in and out of the camera's sight line, banging his tambourine like a weapon.

This aggression translated into the recording of the new single. At the time, almost all of Love were living at The Castle, the 1920s Spanish-style villa in Rancho Los Feliz that was open house in 1966. In the brief interview that follows their lip sync to 'My Little Red Book', Dick Clark tries to get the band to talk about the fact that they live in 'a castle'. Neither Arthur Lee nor Bryan MacLean are remotely interested, giving monosyllabic answers and adopting a combative stance.

Despite being the darlings of small Los Angeles clubs like Bido Lito's and Brave New World, Love were not as their name proclaimed. Insular, moody and unfriendly, they were dominated by singer and writer Arthur Lee, who oscillated between extreme sensitivity and threatening, controlling behaviour. It was a volatile mix, not least because both he and his childhood friend, Johnny Echols, were doing something that had never been done before.

Born in Memphis, Lee and Echols remained in touch after they both moved to Los Angeles, where they started making records in the Booker T. mode before collaborating with an east LA group, Ronnie and the Pomona Casuals, on the local hit 'Everybody Do the Jerk'. Lee also worked with the then unknown Jimi Hendrix on a 1964 single by Rosa Lee Brooks, 'My Diary', and, that same year, recorded a 'Twist and Shout' rewrite called 'Luci Baines'.

During 1965, Lee and Echols swapped soul for the Beatles: wearing Merseybeat wigs, they began playing as the American Four. As Echols told writer Mike Stax, this was quite natural: 'The neighbourhood that we grew up in was totally diverse, and since both Arthur and I are mixed race, we wanted our group to reflect who we were. Our audiences were fantastic. They were more interested in the music than the melatonin content of the band members.'

The huge success of the Byrds had turned the Los Angeles music and teen scene on its head. Arthur Lee saw them during their pivotal March/April 1965 residency at Ciro's Le Disc. 'The Byrds blew me away, their music went right to my heart,' Lee wrote later in a memoir quoted by his biographer John Einarson. 'After I heard them play, and saw the response of the people, I knew exactly what I was going to do. I was going to join in and create a new kind of music.'

While the Byrds were off touring after the success of 'Mr Tambourine Man', new groups vied to fill the gap: the Leaves, the Seeds, the Rising Sons – an integrated group fronted by Taj Mahal – and Love. Lee added Beverly Hills brat and former Byrds roadie Bryan MacLean to the line-up. 'He brought a lot of Byrds groupies with him,' he remembered. 'Bryan had that baby face: he wore pin-stripe pants, a red handkerchief around his neck, and was about as arrogant as they come.'

In early 1966, Love signed with Elektra Records' Jac Holzman, who was seeking to expand out of the label's folk repertoire into the new pop. The group were quickly whipped into Sunset Sound Studios to record their first LP, an inspired, at times sloppy but riveting mesh of the Byrds and the Rolling Stones, with lyrics that dramatised drug addiction ('Signed D.C.'), nuclear paranoia ('Mushroom Clouds') and Lee's own seer status as a 'pop art politician' ('Gazing').

Lee intended Love to be not just a pop group but to have content, to reflect the world around him. 'We had the perfect band,' he later wrote, 'there was nothing else like it in the world. We had the sound, the look, the crowds and the songs that the youth, and the Hollywood scene, wanted. What made us stand out most was our different races. We were so unique and sounded, and looked, so good, it didn't seem to matter what colour we were.'

By luck or design, Love were placed at the epicentre of America's madness in 1966, a time of race riots, youth polarisation and police brutality, the latter a major and increasing problem for teens in Los Angeles in general and the Strip in particular, where LAPD harassment was routine and 'one could be arrested and beaten for "fraternising" outside their race'. As Echols remembered, 'Much of Love's music is actually a newsreel, memorialising the times in which we lived.'

The war was a burning topic for both Lee and Echols, who were conscious that many of their classmates and high-school friends were out there in Vietnam, serving and dying. 'We were at ground zero because of our ages,' Echols remembered. 'Both of us were certain it was only a matter of time before our numbers were called and we would end up dying in some godforsaken jungle.' The friends evaded the draft by being 'the most obnoxious assholes one can imagine'.

By spring 1966, Love had the Hollywood scene sewn up. It was a time to be weird, and Lee acted out the part: wearing only one boot, posing for photos with a cigarette stuck in his ear and sunglasses with one red and one blue lens. 'The Strip would be packed with people, back then,' Lee remembered. 'A lot of them drove by just to see the styles we were wearing. We sure didn't disappoint them. We were as freaked-out looking as you would want to see.'

This surge of confidence propelled '7 And 7 Is'. Echols recalled that the song began as a basic, 'Dylanesque' folk song transformed during a group rehearsal into a fast rocker: 'Without much urging Arthur abandoned the sappy lyrics about his former girlfriend and started to recite these mind-blowing lyrics about his childhood. At the time it appeared that this was spontaneous, and he was in effect "freestyling". I later learned he had been working on a poem for months.

'"7 And 7 Is" is a poem about Arthur's childhood. His father would arrive home from work at precisely 6 p.m. every day. He would plop down in the overstuffed chair, and stare into the fireplace. Flash, the cocker spaniel who adored him, would sit transfixed, watching his every move. As a child, when Arthur mis-behaved, Mrs Lee would give him a time out by banishing him to his room, where he had to sit in the dark, wearing a cone-shaped purple hat.'

The session was fraught with problems. The group were deter-mined to play loud and live, without any separation. The harmon-ics set up by the guitars overloaded their amplifiers and distorted the sound, which was against every rule of recording. Echols told Holzman and studio engineer Bruce Botnick that he wanted the sound to be loud and that he wanted the overload and leakage: 'This is about controlled chaos. The song is all about the sound.'

The vibrato on the guitars made for 'an unyielding electronic metronome': the rhythm was not only fast and ferocious but also required an absolute precision that appeared to be beyond novice drummer Snoopy Pfisterer. In the end, around the seventy-seventh take, Snoopy nailed it once and for all. 'He really played his little heart out on that song,' Echols told Mike Stax, 'and he needs the credit for it. It's the best he ever played.'

There was one final touch. Holzman found an old Elektra sound-effects LP, and slowed the recording of a gunshot right down so that it sounded like a hydrogen bomb. The group then added a brief, descending blues improvisation by Bryan MacLean. When Love played the song live, as Echols told researcher Andrew Sandoval, 'We would end the song with me slapping the reverb on the amp and it would sound like an explosion.'

In early July, just after their appearance as part of KRLA radio's summer spectacular at the Hollywood Bowl, Love were featured in the station's magazine. It was a disaster. When reporter Rochelle Reed travelled out to the Castle, she was met – in her account – by an obnoxious Bryan MacLean and a stoned and surly group. 'It was the first interview I almost walked out on,' she wrote. 'Monosyllables and giggles were their only comments.'

This was a new kind of group, inspired by the Rolling Stones' rebel image and willing to take it further into downright rudeness. In general, the Rolling Stones were prepared to play the teen magazine game, but Love were not. 'Maybe it's because we were so close and rather stand-offish,' Echols reflected, 'outsiders and folks who didn't know us were put off.' Nevertheless, the article added to Love's allure as rebels.

Even by the standards of 1966, '7 And 7 Is' was extreme. On the one hand, it was a trip back to childhood trauma – soon to be a staple concern of LSD-altered consciousness – written by Arthur Lee, whom Echols typified as 'a brilliant, misunderstood young boy crying out to be heard'. On the other, it took the harsh threat and bad attitude of the Rolling Stones and amplified it into an intended holocaust of rage and frustration.

The single was released in mid-July and was reviewed in *Billboard*: 'Raucous rocker that never stops should hit hard and fast.' Entering the Top 100 in late July, two weeks after its release, '7 And 7 Is' rapidly rose up the charts, without any TV plugs. On 3 September, it hit #41, with a star registering 'greatest proportionate upward progress this week'. The next week, it entered the Top 40, eventually rising to a peak of #33 on 24 September.

'7 And 7 Is' wasn't the only tough tune to hit the Top 100 that September. The monstrous impact of 'Paint It, Black' had initiated a mood of snarling negativity that was replicated by songs like Los Bravos' 'Black Is Black', which reached the Top 30 on 10 September. '7 And 7 Is' was at #38 that week; seven places below was another extraordinarily harsh record, one that, like the Love single, would later be seen to define its place and time.

On first hearing, ? and the Mysterians' '96 Tears' is all wrong: the tempo is slow and shaky, the singer is Jaggeresque in a particularly flagrant way, and the predominant organ backing, as Penny Valentine wrote at the time, sounds as if it comes 'from another record'. But it quickly reveals its charms, as the organ transcends relentlessness to become hypnotic, its clusters of repeated notes echoing the lyrical mantra of obsession and revenge: 'You're gonna cry, cry, cry, cry.'

Although it's in the patented teen angst style, it's not a pretty song, but it's authentic in the depth of emotion. In the middle, the song cracks open into an impassioned, arrhythmic and garbled rant: 'And when the sun comes up, I'll be on top / You'll be right down there, looking up.' As numerically incomprehensible as '7 And 7 Is', '96 Tears' draws from the same well of frustration, while at the same time crossing the colour line.

Question Mark was really called Rudy Martinez, and the Mysterians were a group of Mexican Americans from Flint and Saginaw, deep in industrial Michigan. Recorded back in March and originally released on a local label called Pa-Go-Go, '96 Tears' was picked up by Cameo Parkway in August, reviewed in *Billboard* ('Blues rocker with wailing, emotional vocal performance') shortly afterwards, and hit the Top 100 on 3 September.

Like Arthur Lee and Johnny Echols, ? and the Mysterians had something to prove, and their October appearance on *Where the Action Is* is a testament to the power of integration. On a flatbed truck, in the harsh Californian sunlight, the group – all dressed in polka-dot shirts – play to corn-fed white teens and local hipsters. Question Mark is barely able to contain his glee: grinning hugely in wraparound insect shades, he snakes and glides in a delirious, slightly camp version of the James Brown slide.

Eight places down from '96 Tears' was another terse rocker, this time from a group of Los Angeles scufflers. The Standells had been around since the discotheque days of 1964 and Johnny Rivers, cutting one of the many live albums to come out of the Strip, *The Standells in Person at P.J.'s*, for Liberty Records in 1964. After recording for several labels, they ended up at MGM's teen exploitation label, Tower, where they released 'Dirty Water' in December 1965.

Unlike the UK with its centralised media, the American market was large and porous. Records could disappear and reappear months later, building out of one or two key markets and the enthusiasm of individual DJs. There was a randomness as well as a kind of democracy in this process. '96 Tears' was one of those records, as was 'Hanky Panky' by Tommy James and the Shondells, which hit #1 for two weeks during the second half of July. Written by Ellie Greenwich and Jeff Berry, the Shondells' version – a 'Louie Louie'-style rave-up with single-entendre lyrics, mush-mouthed vocals and a cow-pasture rhythm section – was released in January 1964. The record disappeared and James went back to college, breaking up the Shondells. The Snap single was picked out by the inspired Pittsburgh DJ 'Mad Mike' Metrovich, played to death, and became a local smash.

James hurriedly reconvened another version of the Shondells to capitalise on this renewed interest. He then took the record to New York and sold it to Roulette Records, who reissued it as it was in May. Its primitive amateurism hit a chord amid all the musical sophistication of the Beatles, the Rolling Stones, the Beach Boys and Bob Dylan. It was like two separate cloud systems folding over each other.

The similarly basic 'Dirty Water' took over five months to hit the charts, breaking out of Florida, of all places. Entering the Top 40 in mid-June 1966, it climbed all the way to #11 in the *Billboard* chart in July. It was a strange record, elemental yet manufactured, a song about Boston and its polluted River Charles performed by Los Angeles musicians, with a confused narrative that took in the Boston Strangler and 'lovers, muggers and thieves' – with the aside, 'But they're cool people.'

The Standells were masterminded by producer Ed Cobb, the writer of Gloria Jones's June 1965 single 'Tainted Love'. The sound was simple but clear, with a raunchy guitar riff augmented by organ stabs. Singer Dick Dodd pulled out the requisite sneering drawl, but added his own touch with the frequent asides that punctuated the tune. The whole effect was powerful, but any menace was slightly undercut by the group's relentless mugging in front of the TV cameras.

Thirteen places below the Standells was another young group with a harsh, arresting single. On the surface, the 13th Floor Elevators' 'You're Gonna Miss Me' was a revenge song in the teen romance mode, just like '96 Tears'. Yet the performance and the record's whole ambience spoke of something completely different, with its slashing chords, plunging melody and an intense, rasping vocal that broke into testifying screams. The hook was the strange reverberation that resonated through the record, a primitive electronic bubble that was both a signature and a challenge. In the first verse, the singer gives the clue: 'You're gonna look around in your mind, girl / You're gonna find that I'm gone.' In 1966, 'mind' was a keyword that spoke of hallucinogenic drugs, and 'You're Gonna Miss Me' was a Trojan Horse for the psychedelic revolution, a teen romance song that proselytised LSD.

'You're Gonna Miss Me' had been written by singer Roky Erickson in late 1965 for his group the Spades. Still only eighteen, he was poached by Austin musicians Stacy Sutherland and John Ike Walton for a new group that would almost immediately embark on a course of psychedelic evangelism. The 13th Floor Elevators recorded their first single in early January 1966; three weeks later, four of the group were arrested on drugs charges – a serious matter in mid-1960s Texas.

The reverberation on the track came from the electrified jug played by Tommy Hall, a philosophy and psychology major at the University of Texas who had swapped Republican politics for a passionate belief in the beneficial properties of psychedelic drugs. Hall wanted to turn on the world, and in support of this vision he persuaded the Elevators to record and play concerts on LSD. If the group played on acid, they could give the audience a contact high.

The sound of LSD, 'You're Gonna Miss Me' was first released on local label Contact in January 1966, then picked up for wider distribution by Houston's International Artists in June. When it started to take off, another pressing came out on Hollywood's Hanna-Barbera Records – a confusing picture common to many successful independent records of the period. The song entered the Top 100 in August and, by 10 September, reached #66.

Thirteen places below that was a song that showed exactly what was stirring in teen America. All the members of Count Five were eighteen or nineteen. Inspired by the Yardbirds and the Who, they added that rolling American swing and recorded 'Psychotic Reaction' at the time that the P-word came into prominence in the American media. In fact, it was another teen angst song given a contemporary, albeit troubling, hook and a robust, loose but kinetic performance.

'Psychotic Reaction' was an almost direct copy of the Yardbirds' 'I'm a Man', which had replaced Bo Diddley's original slow blues with a harsh, ramped-up performance. The Yardbirds' record made the US Top 20 in early 1966, and the group made an ecstatic live appearance on the pop show *Shivaree*, during which guitarist Jeff Beck threw his guitar around and made chicken noises, high up the neck, at the song's climax. The Count Five song begins with a fuzz-guitar figure and a blast of harmonica, before settling into a circular riff. After the first verse, 'Psychotic Reaction' breaks into a Yardbirds-style rave dominated by harmonica and those clucking noises. In the second verse, John Byrne reveals the song's debt to the Rolling Stones, while adding a disturbing element: 'I can't get your love, I can't get satisfaction / Uh-oh, little girl, psychotic reaction.'

What went unnoticed at the time was just how much these complaints were aimed at women. This was partly the influence of the Rolling Stones and, in turn, their own redaction of blues braggadocio, and partly the development of the teen romance style into more assertive territory. Long hair and androgyny did not preclude misogyny in the mid-1960s, but this mode of attack would soon pass into something much wider and, no doubt, more deserving of the musicians' contempt. At the time, however, these singles spoke of a fresh confidence. America's young musicians were making harsher, more demanding records, and they were popular.

The creative US response to the British Invasion had started in 1965 with the Beau Brummels and the Byrds. The success that year of earthy dance records like 'She's About a Mover' by the Sir Douglas Quintet – Texans mocked up as Englanders – and 'Woolly Bully' by Sam the Sham only added further fuel to the flame. The US Top 40 in spring and summer 1966 was full of these records: the Knickerbockers' 'Lies'; Love's 'My Little Red Book'; the Bobby Fuller Four's 'I Fought the Law'; the Syndicate of Sound's 'Little Girl'; and the Leaves' version of 'Hey Joe'. America's youth saw these groups on TV: they didn't look so different and, encouraged by the simplicity and attack of these songs, teenagers formed their own groups and began the slow process of learning to play together.

This was a white style, tending towards the suburban or exurban, where there were spaces to rehearse – often the family garage – and a variety of venues to play: these included high-school gyms, church halls, fraternity parties, local clubs. If they were lucky, these groups might get to make a record and get it played on local radio; if lightning struck, it might then get picked up by a major and promoted nationwide.

Garage bands, they're called today, but there was no single name for this style in 1966. *Billboard* called most of them 'rockers' in the capsule reviews, and that's what they were: the original wildness, attack and teenage intensity of rock 'n' roll updated ten years on. It's no accident that Tommy James and the Shondells' 'Hanky

Panky' was such a big hit that summer: recorded in 1963, it captured the exact moment when white American music was flourishing, just before the Beatles revolutionised the country's teen taste.

When 'I Want to Hold Your Hand' entered the *Billboard* Top 100 on 18 January 1964, the Kingsmen's 'Louie Louie' was at #2. At #5 was 'Surfin' Bird' by the Trashmen, a hysterical record that fused surf, rock 'n' roll and R&B glossolalia. Drag racing crops up in 'Hey Little Cobra' by the Rip Cords (#6) and 'Drag City' by Jan and Dean (#10). At #9 was the ominous *Twilight Zone*-inspired instrumental 'Out of Limits' by the Marketts.

This American style had been knocked out of the water by the Beatles' takeover. Both the Kingsmen and the Trashmen struggled to reproduce their success. It was as though a whole line of musical development had been forcibly terminated. The prevalence of rocker records in 1966 indicated, to some degree, the return of the repressed and, in the wake of 'Hanky Panky', the Surfaris' summer 1963 hit 'Wipe Out' re-entered the Top 40 in early September.

Many of the garage bands had begun as surf- or Kingsmen-inspired groups before they were twisted by the Byrds and the British wave of R&B, in particular Them, the Yardbirds, the Animals and the Rolling Stones, who by the end of 1965 had god-like status. With its fuzz guitar and cosmic complaint lyrics, 'I Can't Get No Satisfaction' was catnip to American teens, who also copied the group's haircuts and their dishevelled yet styled mod/bohemian fashion sense.

Richard Goldstein captured this allure in the gently satirical short story 'Gear', from summer 1966, in which a fourteen-year-old boy tries to match up reality with teen mag fantasy:

A face that looks like the end of a watermelon, and curly hair – not like the Stones, not at all like Brian Jones – but muddy curls running down his forehead and over his ears. A bump. Smashed by a bat thrown wildly. When he was eight. Hunchback Quasimodo – Igor – Rodan on his head. A bump. Nobody hip has a bump or braces. Or hair like a fucking Frankenstein movie. He licks his braces clean and practices smiling. Hair straight and heavy. Nose full. Lips boiling like bulging frank-furters. Hung. Bell bottoms and boss black boots. He practices his Brian Jones expressions. Fist held close to the jaw. Ready to spring, ready to spit. Evil. His upper brace catches on a lip.

Look at pictures of any young American group from 1966 and you'll see Brian Jones bowl cuts, Mick Jagger's slouch and shaggy mane, striped T-shirts, tailored mod jackets, polka-dot shirts, pointed 'fruit boots' and a general air of surly disdain. They came from all over the country, in their thousands: We the People from Florida; the Del-Vetts from Chicago; Mouse and the Traps from Texas; the Groupies from the New York area; and the Golliwogs from Oakland, to name but a few better known examples.

Most of their records took from their British models and added an American teen attack, winding up the fuzz guitars, rave-ups, choppy chords and rebarbative lyrics into a pure distillation of the teenage Now. Tough post-Brit R&B wasn't the only option: also part of the mix were the minor-chord moods premiered by the Zombies, Byrds jingle-jangle and the first hints of psychedelia, expressed through raga-like overtones and punk-mystical lyrics.

There was one element that distinguished the American rockers from their UK counterparts: the almost ubiquitous use of the electric organ – usually a Farfisa or a Vox Continental – which usually gave a sinuous, if not sinister, undertow to proceedings. In the mid-1960s, the drive-in was a major teen venue in the US, and a constant diet of horror movies satisfied both the needs for sexual experimentation and the perennial teen penchant for living at the extremes.

Typical of these films is *Carnival of Souls*. Filmed in Kansas, Herk Harvey's low-budget 1962 movie is a chilling example of the genre, full of supernatural phenomena that culminate with the appear-ance of dead souls in a deserted amusement park. The score relies on wispy organ motifs to give the sense of the church denied, fuel-ling a whole Satan-referencing subgenre that includes the Satans' 'Making Deals' and 'Speak of the Devil' by Things to Come.

This was a style that synthesised a wide variety of elements in American teen culture, both high and low, both elitist and populist. But things were moving so fast that, by the early autumn of 1966, it was under enormous pressure from the competing demands of psychedelic experimentation and the underlying imperative of directness and simplicity. What to sing about? Inner or outer space, girls or drugs, the parents or the system – the dilemmas were acute.

One record in particular caught that moment of compression. Released in mid-1966, the Roosters' 'One of These Days' was perfectly poised between glistening Byrds twelve-string jangle and surf kinetics, between high Hollies harmonies and punk-mystical lead vocals, between teen yearning and universal protest: 'One of these days when I'm of age / And nobody can tell me what to do.'

The Roosters were a teenage group from Westchester, a neighbourhood hard by Los Angeles airport. They'd started out in surf groups, then had their heads turned by the Beatles and the Byrds. Close to the LA music industry, they quickly found a manager and a record label, Progressive Sounds of America. In a quick four-hour session, the band recorded two tracks: 'One of These Days' and the moody 'You Gotta Run', both sides of a single that quickly disappeared on release.

The Roosters' journey can be seen in the few photos still extant: from pompadours, waistcoats and bum-freezer jackets to beards, corduroy trousers and long, long hair. For 'One of These Days' contained an inchoate threat behind its charm: 'One of these days there's gonna be / A lot of changes that are new.' It has the sense, common to many records in this period, of petty complaints becoming more universal, of undirected grievances beginning to find a focus.

With its endless suburbs, good weather and status as a major media centre, the extended Los Angeles area was the epicentre of this mood, with the teen bands vying for space with already established acts like the Standells, Sons of Adam, and the Turtles, whose fifth single, the terrific, Stones-y 'Outside Chance', was released late that summer. All this activity was funnelled down one particular thoroughfare: the Sunset Strip.

California was coming into its own. Ever since the early sixties, the largest Pacific state had been seen as 'a window into the future', as *Look* magazine proclaimed. California was both utopia and dystopia, 'hope or horror'. To observers like George B. Leonard, writing in 1962, it represented 'the promise and the challenge contained at the very heart of the American dream; here, probably more than at any other place and time, the shackles of the past are broken'.

As the 1960s progressed, Los Angeles showed the state's Janus face: the sun-kissed bliss of the surfers, the vicious urban warfare of Watts. Hollywood's music and media industry, with its globally distributed images of plenty and freedom, was situated in a hot, arid 'moral Kansas' run by a barely restrained police force. In the greater Los Angeles area, extreme conservatism and conformity clashed with free and easy lifestyles, if not eccentricity.

'I think that Hollywood, perhaps more than any other city in the United States, lends itself towards the so-called variant, the deviant,' said the dancer Vito Paulekas, captured in voiceover by Robert Carl Cohen in the movie *Mondo Hollywood*, and he knew of what he spoke. In the mid-sixties, at the age of fifty, he and his band of 'freaks' were associated with the most numinous of the new rock groups: the Byrds, the Mothers of Invention, Love.

Shot on location during 1965 and 1966, *Mondo Hollywood* is a deliberately provocative slice of LA life: the talented are cut against the desperate; topless waitresses share space with effeminate queens; outspoken rebels come up against Ronald Reagan invoking 'law and order' at a Republican fundraiser. Notables like Princess Margaret, Jay Sebring and Richard Alpert appear, while there is a respectful portrait of Estella Scott, an African American woman from South Central LA.

Cohen captured the neon/smog madness of mid-sixties LA, the synapse-frying electricity in the air, but, apart from the electrifying footage of Bobby Jameson singing 'Vietnam', he missed the opportunity to capture the Sunset Strip at its peak. It had been building since spring 1965 and, by early 1966, the district was exploding along the section of Sunset Boulevard between Hollywood and

Beverly Hills that had once been the centre of LA nightlife but had since become a youthtopia.

The writer Mike Fessier Jr described the scene: 'The Strip was suddenly alive with hairy teen hobos and older hippies in nifty belly-button-baring shirts and little girls with mop straight hair and belted hip huggers settled low and cool on their anatomies. The convergence of social types has created a permanent bumper-to-bumper weekend traffic jam in which it now takes some 30 sardine-like minutes to inch along the strip's 1.7 miles.'

Some teens cruised, but many more walked. The Strip was a teen magnet, a total environment of futurism, play, entertainment and chance encounters. In his survey of that time and place, Domenic Priore summarises its 'centrifugal force': 'Modernist architecture added a celestial feeling to the drive-in restaurants, underground theatres, and coffeehouses, not to mention more than 35 psychedelic/ mod nightclubs catering to the scene.' They included Gazzari's, London Fog, the Trip (which had showcased the Exploding Plastic Inevitable in May), the Sea Witch, the Melody Room, Ciro's and, in a triangular plot at the intersection of Crescent Heights and Sunset Boulevard, Pandora's Box. Further along Sunset to the east were more established venues like the Hollywood Palladium and Hullabaloo!. A few blocks south, on North Fairfax south of Melrose, was Canter's Deli – *the* teen meeting place.

The Strip's status as pop culture incubator was promoted nation-wide by the syndicated pop shows taped in the city: *Shindig!*, *Where the Action Is* and *Shivaree*. There were also local shows like the *Lloyd Thaxton Show* and *Hollywood a Go Go*. All of these featured go-go dancers, teens displaying the latest Strip fashions, and sets and lighting that actually enhanced the music – most notably *Shivaree*, with its banks of go-go dancers and its wild audience.

In the first week of September, the #1 record in America was 'Sunshine Superman'; on the flip was Donovan's documentary description of the Strip scene, 'The Trip', with its references to the club and to notables like Bob Dylan – aka 'The Mad Hatter'. There was a double entendre in the song title for the initiated, and

Donovan spelt it out with another Lewis Carroll reference: 'I said, "Girl, you drank a lot of drink-me / But you ain't in a Wonderland."'

There was a dark side to the Strip, explored by the Seeds' insinuating, sinister 'The Other Place', a song about a club which made you feel 'strange, if not disarranged'. During that summer, the Seeds released a very popular album, *The Seeds*, that defined the new teen angst attitude. On songs like 'Nobody Spoil My Fun' and 'No Escape' singer Sky Saxon's adenoidal whine was set against a stiff, almost burlesque backing that exploded into sudden, exhilarating breakouts.

The Seeds had formed in early 1965. With no bassist, it fell to Daryl Hooper to play the low lines on his Wurlitzer keyboard – an arrangement later developed by the Doors. Their simple songs were matched by an image that defined Strip eccentricity: sporting the longest hair imaginable, they assumed costumes, with guitarist Jan Savage kitted out as a Native American and Hooper an eighteenth-century composer. Dressed in full LA mod gear, the slightly older Sky Saxon disported himself like a Pied Piper.

In November 1965, the Seeds reissued a single, 'You're Pushin' Too Hard', that, in the mode of the day, expanded from a boy/girl complaint into a more general frustration. In the summer, they went into the studio to make their second album. As well as the fourteen-minute 'Up in Her Room' – inspired by the Rolling Stones' 'Going Home' – they recorded several songs that directly referenced the drug culture: 'Tripmaker', 'Rollin' Machine' and an instrumental freak-out called 'Acid'.

The Strip was saturated in drugs, and the West Coast musical references became ever more blatant: 'The Trip', 'Tripmaker' and, most outrageous of all, the Other Half's 'Mr Pharmacist', which pleaded with the drug dispenser for sackfuls of his produce. Drugs not only heightened and prolonged the teenage experience, they injected a new level of messianic address into the culture, as musicians and artists felt compelled to share the chimera of chemistry.

It also brought the attention of the police. The LAPD were notorious for being a law unto themselves, and indeed various parts of

Los Angeles were like a police state – a prime cause of the Watts Riots. The massed presence of teens on the Strip's sidewalk and outside Canter's drew attention in an automotive city, and police harassment for loitering, racial mixing and drugs became endemic, a sour undertow to the sense of excitement and freedom.

The only LA group to sing about the Watts Riots were the Mothers of Invention. Written by Frank Zappa, 'Trouble Comin' Every Day' was a prolonged and troubled rumination on August 1965, full of anger at the obvious manipulations of the mass media and the intractable racial situation in America. The worst thing for Zappa was that the riots weren't an isolated incident, but a perfect example of the violence and the stupidity of mid-1960s America.

'Trouble Comin' Every Day' was the standout track from the Mothers' first album, *Freak Out!*, which was released in late June 1966. It was ambitious double set that mixed musique concrète, doo-wop, Latin R&B, Stones-style riffs and Motown, sometimes all in the same song. In the liner notes, Zappa amplified the freak angle: 'We would like to encourage everyone who HEARS this music to join us . . . become a member of the United Mutations . . . FREAK OUT!'

Early editions of *Freak Out!* contained an A2-size fold-out map of teen LA entitled 'Freak Out Hot Spots'. It featured all the major sites, but the grid was peppered with pictures of police brutality – 'from a highly recommended film: BLUE FASCISM' – and red over-printings of atomic explosions, denoting 'a bust . . . by the L.A. heat'. The biggest cluster was around Canter's, 'scene of more blatant Gestapo practices than the peaceful natives care to recollect'.

Things escalated over the summer. In late September, middle-aged writer Robert de Roos travelled to the Strip and found it both titillating and disturbing: 'The Sunset Strip had been seized by the long-hair, bell-bottom, miniskirt, high-boot generation, and the parade that passed was wondrous fair . . . girls in lacy trousers which fell from their knees in cascades of flounces, girls in high squaw boots, girls with their long blonde hair pressed stark and straight.'

De Roos's guide was actor Jeff Cooper, who told him: 'You better look at these kids and listen to them too. Their gods are Bob Dylan and Timothy Leary, the LSD guy. All the groups are singing Dylan's songs and it's the first time the kids – kids from 10 to 15 – have ever been talked to that way, and they're hearing what's been said. Dylan's singing against war and against bigotry, stuff teenagers never dug before. So you've got to listen too. This isn't rebellion – it's what's happening.'

The harsh singles crashing the charts expressed this sense of incipient violence. These were unignorable demands. The August *Hit Parader* satirised the new trend for 'LOUDISSIMO': 'We foresee as the next logical step: The Detonators, a new group with no guitars no amplifiers, and no organs. The Detonators consist of lead pneumatic drill, bass pneumatic drill, air raid siren, steamboat whistle, cannon, TNT and buss saw.'

Kings of the Strip, Love synthesised its swirling currents and funnelled them into a short, two-and-a-half-minute burst. '7 And 7 Is' is full-tilt, compressed, a vortex of gnostic ideas and futuristic musical technology. Its messianic fervour and furious attack presents individual psychology as generational assertion. It encapsulated youth culture as a pressure cooker on the point of explosion, the incredible acceleration of mid-1960s pop hurtling headlong into a cataclysm. The H-bomb sound at the climax hooked the song into the crux of the generational matter: the increasing hostility of some American youths to adults and the system, a critique that was regularly broadcast in the teen media. It wasn't just Vietnam or LSD – or even a sense of entitlement – that was driving this agitation. It was something more: the deep malaise of the modern world, with the nuclear bomb at its apex.

In the sleeve notes to the Rolling Stones' *Out of Our Heads*, Andrew Loog Oldham had written: 'The only message about this new elpee is let's all live to enjoy it. And in the words of my local parson, If the bomb does go off, just make sure you get higher than the bomb.' Reproduced on the sleeve of the American album *December's Children (and Everybody's)*, Oldham's thoughts were relayed to millions of teens in Britain and America, and they struck a chord.

As the young British radical Charles Radcliffe reflected, 'I was beginning to think he might have a point. I had spent the early part of the sixties waiting to die in a nuclear holocaust, perceived then as being almost inevitable. I was determined to spend the rest trying to live life to the full.' Fear of nuclear annihilation remained the rocket fuel of mid-sixties youth culture. It resulted in the feeling that the only way forward was to live in the present.

The Byrds' Roger McGuinn commented on this in *TeenSet* during the early autumn of 1966, describing the group's music as being 'aware of the immediacy of time and the "now" of everything hitting you right in the face. That's what we'd like to get in our music and that's where I think we're going. We're going to where "now" is going.'

In early autumn 1966, 'now' was going faster and harder. The anti-nuclear movement was losing fire, and there would soon be new forms of agitation to dramatise this existential urgency. Facing violence in all its forms – whether it be the war, the police, the bomb – the radicalised young began to act in kind at the same time as they sought to investigate the deep source of that violence. This in turn would lead to further confrontation.

* * *

'California is the centre of radical change in every form, from the space race and automation to a whole new way of life. From political awareness, the FSM (Free Speech Movement), to the sensual awareness in trip dances, and kinetic involvement of the surfer generation.'
EDITORIAL, *San Francisco Oracle*, issue 1, 20 September 1966

It was time for a new way of speaking about pop culture, a new way of conceptualising and asserting the demands of youth. By 1966, pop was becoming self-conscious, a natural response to the vast amounts of money pouring into the music and media industries and a general creative climate of cross-pollination and experimentation. Teenagers already had purchasing power and cultural clout, and they wanted more.

Both the mainstream media and the established music press struggled to cope with these changes. As the jazz critic Nat Hentoff observed in June 1966, 'Grownups hear fragments of the pounding beat and the electronically raw sound making it in popular music and they don't get the message. The words, it's hard to hear the words. And when they do come through, what are they SAYING? . . . There's no one to tell the adults in the language of the adults what's happening.'

1966 had already seen singles of extraordinary density and complexity by the Beatles, the Lovin' Spoonful, James Brown, the Rolling Stones, Wilson Pickett, the Byrds, Love and many others. They weren't just songs about love or individual feelings; they were projecting out into the world as it existed or as it could be. They demanded to be written about in a way that transcended hit picks or the 'toe-tapping'/'rockaballad' formulae of the beat sixties.

Even more to the point, the year had seen the arrival of the pop album as more than just two to three hits and a bunch of filler. Singles were still the principal teen currency, however, and album reviews were usually short and formulaic. In the October *TeenSet*, an anonymous reviewer came to grips with the magazine's shortcomings, observing of *Blonde on Blonde* that 'a full review of this album would require at least a page'.

Young writers were hired to fill this gap. Richard Goldstein's columns in the *Village Voice* and *New York* magazine mixed the immediacy and descriptive detail of what would later be called the New Journalism with sharp, savvy descriptions of hype and fantasy. 'Shango Mick Arrives' eviscerated the Rolling Stones' pretensions at their June 1966 press conference, held on a yacht that sailed the Hudson River: 'You want to touch Mick Jagger? You can't even come close.'

Two new magazines went even further. *Crawdaddy!* was founded in January 1966 by Paul Williams, a seventeen-year-old student at

Swarthmore College in Boston who had published science-fiction fanzines before being struck hard by an encounter with Dylan. 'I met him in Philadelphia last winter,' Williams wrote in 1966. 'He is a friendly and straightforward young man, interested in what others are saying and doing, and quite willing to talk openly about himself.'

Crawdaddy! began slowly as a mimeographed sheet but, by the fourth issue, Williams felt confident enough to issue a mission statement. 'Nobody used to take music very seriously,' he remembered, citing the old days of Elvis, Fabian and 'Surfin' Bird', 'but one thing has changed over the years, one minor detail: The music has gotten better. So much better, in fact, that there are even people who are beginning to take rock 'n' roll very seriously indeed.

'CRAWDADDY! is for those people: for anyone with an interest in discussing the most exciting and alive music in the world today, music that is alive not because of its heavy beat but because of its fantastic inventiveness, its ability to assimilate widely different forms of music, its freshness and awareness of a world other forms of music seem ready to desert. CRAWDADDY! is an experiment; some say it's ahead of its time. I don't think so.'

In a record review entitled 'The New Sounds', Williams made an important distinction between what was pop and what was populist: 'Sometimes the only way to feel better, after looking at the Top 100 charts, is to remember that they have practically nothing to do with rock 'n' roll. Rock 'n' roll, or the big beat, or whatever clumsy term we want to use, is a musical idiom quite apart from what is selling at the moment, i.e., quite apart from pop music.

'Money and popularity serve as important influences on the field, inevitably, but they aren't in control. Barry Sadler is about a significant an influence on r'n'r as Harold Robbins is on American literature. The important influences in this field are not, per se, the people who sell a million records. The important influences are those people who are creative, imaginative, who can change the idiom by introducing a new sound.'

Williams was writing when the sixties charts were at a peak of creativity in terms of content. But his polemic opened up a new kind of criticism, one that was enshrined in *Crawdaddy!*, a magazine that didn't just cover chart music, but that included long articles on blues artists like John Lee Hooker and reviews of non-hit groups like the Blues Project or the Butterfield Blues Band, whose 'East West' was very popular among aficionados in summer 1966.

The pop market had become large enough to support musicians whose records did not make the charts but would still sell in the tens of thousands – whether singles or albums. This in turn encouraged free experimentation and a more demanding attitude on the part of listeners, in particular the college students that had been radicalised by civil rights, the Free Speech Movement and the growing opposition to Vietnam. It amounted to a secret youth code, hiding in plain light. The old gush and PR-driven churn of the teen magazines were beginning to seem old hat. Despite the quality of the charts in 1966, the music that appeared there was only part of the story. For the cutting-edge music writers, value would not be conferred simply by success or money, but by artistic worth – a subjective measure, to be sure, but one that carried huge weight at the dawn of rock criticism.

Williams's argument simplified the old elitist versus populist discourse. But what was extraordinary about 1966 was that the very popular could also be 'vital musicians' like the Beatles, the Rolling Stones, Dylan, the Spoonful, the Byrds, that the charts could be a place where new sounds and new ideas were disseminated weekly to millions of teens. Art and commerce were not mutually exclusive, far from it, and that's what made 1966 so exciting.

This new language drew from the well of critical language that had been used in folk music. In an earlier issue of *Crawdaddy!* Richard Fariña had written about 'Songwriting in the '6os', during the course of which he talked about the 'underground' reaction of topical songwriters to the nuclear paranoias of the early sixties: 'The protest songs lost their earlier occasional subject matter and were ambitious enough to take on concerns like the military–industrial complex.'

Williams was concerned with a new kind of mass art form, one where the effect on the listener was profound and unprecedented. Dylan was at the sharp end of this change, and elsewhere in the August issue of *Crawdaddy!* Williams wrote an extended essay on *Blonde on Blonde*, which he noted as 'one of the best-produced records I've ever heard, and producer Bob Johnston deserves immortality at least. Certainly, Dylan's songs have never been better presented.'

In a 3,700-word article, Williams summarises Dylan's career – 'from the very beginning his desire was to make it in the field of rock and roll' – and delves into the album's deeper currents: 'Helplessness is still the prevalent emotion ("Honey, why are you so hard?"), but chaos has been relegated to the periphery. Love (and sex, love's half-sister) are all-important, and love, as everyone knows, has a certain sense of order about it, rhyme if not reason.'

Williams was helping to define the new condition of pop. In the same issue, he reviewed *Love*: 'a highly unusual album put together with paste and pyrotechnics, a montage of marching rhythms and resilience and subtle silences'. At the review's beginning, he stumbled across one of the terms that would come to mark this two-tier phase of youth culture: '"Underground" is the big word this month, thanks to the *Evergreen* subway ads and the *New York Times* review.'

'Underground': that would do it. Underground film, the Velvet Underground, under the ground, away from the harsh exposure of the light, where new ideas could burrow away like termites. From mid-1966 onwards, a group or performer could have a big impact even if he, she, they or it did not make the charts. As youth culture fragmented into those who valued experiment and those who didn't care either way, the singles charts would begin to slip as true indicators of progress.

In contrast, *Mojo Navigator* was created to crystallise a scene. First published in August 1966 by David Harris and the seventeen-year-old Greg Shaw, another alumnus from the science-fiction fanzine world, it ran record reviews and articles about cult figures like Howlin' Wolf and the instrumentalist Travis Wammack, but its focus was entirely on San Francisco. The contact address was Shaw's flat in McAllister Street, halfway between the Fillmore and the Haight.

In the editorial for their second issue, Shaw and Harris promised to 'have in-depth studies of some of the local r&r groups, or maybe interviews with them. We will also try to keep you posted on everything of interest in the Bay Area.' By summer 1966, the seeds sown by the Acid Tests had begun to bear fruit: San Francisco was a ferment of new groups, new venues and new attitudes, full of people who wanted 'to do things that nobody has done before'.

The first few issues of *Mojo Navigator* were full of gossip, news and concert lists featuring exotic names like Big Brother and the Holding Company, Quicksilver Messenger Service, the Sopwith Camel and the Charlatans – local groups that were not even a blip on the national radar. The New York scene was attacked in the magazine's review of 'I'll Be Your Mirror': 'Andy Warhol produced it, Nico sings (hah-hah) on it. It's the musical equivalent of a painted Brillo box that sells for $400.'

Mojo Navigator had an immediate impact. The writer Gene Sculatti remembers picking it up 'in the summer, at the Psychedelic shop. He [Greg] and David Harris used to have copies they would sell inside the Avalon, and he probably said, come up and see me when you get to the show. I met him that way. I used to go over to where he lived, and published it, there was this wonderful sense of being very hip at that time.'

In 1966, Sculatti was eighteen, a sophomore at the University of California at Davis who had transferred to San Francisco State. 'A guy I knew in Davis and went to school with, we hitch-hiked to San Francisco in March of '66 to the first show. It was Paul Butterfield, supported by Quicksilver. Everything was happening in the Bay area. We were reading Ralph Gleason. I'd been going to shows for a few months, so I wanted to go to San Francisco.'

San Francisco had never had the clout of Los Angeles but, in 1965, it had produced the first serious US response to the British

Invasion, the two Top 20 singles by the Beau Brummels. 'Laugh Laugh' and 'Just a Little' were issued on the local independent Autumn Records, run by KYA DJ Tom Donahue. Autumn also released R&B: co-written and produced by Sylvester 'Sly' Stone, Bobby Freeman's 'C'mon and Swim' went to #5 in late summer 1964.

By 1965, the wider Bay Area was producing its fair share of R&B and rock 'n' roll records: Sly Stone's 'Buttermilk', the Vejtables' 'I Still Love You' and the Brogues' 'Someday'. This continued into 1966 with terrific 45s from the Oxford Circle, Butch Engle and the Styx, the New Breed and the Golliwogs – the hyper-intense, 'Gloria'-inspired 'Fight Fire' – but urgent teenage rock or sly R&B was not what San Francisco would become known for.

The main booster of the local scene was Ralph J. Gleason, then the forty-eight-year-old music columnist for the *San Francisco Chronicle*. In December 1965, he had hosted one of the scene's founding events: Bob Dylan's televised press conference at the studios of the public education broadcaster, KQED. The mercurial pop star was in a generally amenable mood that day, and obligingly held up a poster for a Mime Troupe benefit that featured the Mystery Trend and the Jefferson Airplane.

Gleason was on the ball very early, reporting local developments in his weekly 'On the Town' column. In early March 1966, he noted that 'a kind of dancing madness has taken hold in San Francisco and is spreading to the rest of the country, it appears. Whether or not it will be as strong a thing as it is here only time will tell, but it does seem as if a definite trend to dancing, one which may make the swing era seem tame by comparison, is on the way.'

The San Francisco scene had its roots in the Acid Tests, the Family Dog and the Mime Troupe benefits. Gleason observed how 'there hasn't been a weekend without one and sometimes three dances a night at the Fillmore Auditorium, California Hall, and the Longshore Hall. Many of these dances have been benefits or affairs sponsored by fans of the music and dancing. Even by poets!'

In May, he reported on a new group, the Grateful Dead, praising

Jerry Garcia, their lead guitarist, as 'an interesting soloist with a wild surge of inventiveness'. Steeped in jazz and folk, Gleason was more sympathetic to folk-based or improvisational groups like the Grateful Dead and the Jefferson Airplane than their teen rock 'n' roll contemporaries. His predilections helped to shape the media coverage in the months to come.

By September 1966, Haight-Ashbury was shaping up as another youthtopia. Like the Sunset Strip, the area had been blighted for well over a decade by planned highway development, and it afforded cheap and liveable housing near the centre of the city. The architecture was late-Victorian, and the atmosphere relaxed and spacious: Haight Street stopped at the eastern end of Golden Gate Park, with the Panhandle stretching in parallel for several blocks.

Gleason's columns detailed the narrative: this was a self-starting, localised scene with its own stores, its own fashions, its own style of music and its own sense of community. It favoured long modal improvisations and hallucination-inducing poster art, and was large enough to support local stores – the Psychedelic Shop, Mnasidika – as well as two rival promoters, Chet Helms's Family Dog and Bill Graham at the Fillmore West.

This prelapsarian idyll, fuelled by the city's Wild West history, was as yet untainted by glitz or commerce. 'Los Angeles had the infrastructure,' Gene Sculatti recalls, 'and therefore the tendency for an ambitious act to want to get in and do it right commercially might have been greater. 'Frisco wasn't under any microscope, so it was evolving on its own. Records is ultimately how you're going to do it, but it didn't always seem like that was the main aim.'

Unlike Los Angeles, with its small venues, the San Francisco scene, as Sculatti remembers, 'went right to 400- or 700-capacity places, which allowed them to process people in greater numbers. There's a sound that I identify with San Francisco. I don't know if it's inadvertent or intended reverb. That is what particularly the Fillmore sounded like. Anyone who played there, regardless of the settings on your instruments, you're going to pull some of that in.'

This embryonic sound is best heard on the recordings made by the Great!! Society!! at the Matrix club during summer 1966. Formed by brothers Darby and Jerry Slick in 1965, the group showcased a striking and intense female singer, Jerry's wife Grace. The group had made a flop single early in the year, coupling the acid-tasting rock song 'Someone to Love' with 'Free Advice', in which Grace's scat vocal wove a sarcastic raga around the self-pitying lyric.

Sarcastically named after Lyndon Johnson's flagship policy, the Great!! Society!! drove producer Sly Stone to distraction in the studio. Yet the Matrix recordings are fascinating, spacious, dark and deep songs like 'Grimly Forming' and 'Someone to Love' stretched out with modal overtones. By that time the group were confident enough to master Eden Ahbez's 'Nature Boy' and, on 'White Rabbit', to fuse *Alice in Wonderland* to a bolero beat.

In September 1966, the city had two magazines reporting on the scene: *Mojo Navigator* and the *San Francisco Oracle*, which had launched as *P. O. San Francisco* at the beginning of the month. This was a different kind of publication, much more political and activist-oriented, its first edition leading with a long and serious interview with a Vietnam veteran that laid out the effects of combat service for all to read: 'He's just nothing, just like a zero, a zombie, an actual walking zombie.'

As well as articles about Ron Boise – inventor of a percussion instrument called the Thunder Machine – and LSD, it also included a long and dismissive discussion about the improvisational abilities and raga pretensions of the San Franciscan musicians. Even so, the unnamed writer was forced to recognise the fact that there was 'a tremendous ferment in music' and that San Francisco was witnessing 'the beginning of a new musical world. There is an odor of creativity in the air.'

The variety and strength of the city's music scene was celebrated that September by a glossy publication called the *I.D. 1966 Band Book*. Peppered with pictures of Dylan and the Rolling Stones, the magazine was purely pictorial, with striking images of groups as varied as the Outfit, Thorinshield, Calliope Company, the New

Arrivals, Quicksilver Messenger Service, and Big Brother and the Holding Company, who were showcasing their new female singer, Janis Joplin. Apart from the Charlatans, who were heavily styled in nineteenth-century Wild West costumes that reflected the city's outlaw history, none of the musicians looked mod. Reflecting the city's disdain for commercialism, the early SF look was downbeat, bohemian. As Gene Sculatti remembers: 'We wore blue jeans. I had my father's army coat, a sort of fatigue jacket. Other people wore corduroy coats, some had professors' arm patches on them. Work shirts became a thing.'

By late summer, San Francisco was making waves with the nationwide release of *Jefferson Airplane Takes Off*. One of the first SF groups, Jefferson Airplane had signed a contract with RCA Records in late 1965 and had released a couple of flop folk rock singles, 'It's No Secret' and 'Come Up the Years'. Delayed by RCA, who objected to the use of the word 'trips' in a song called 'Runnin' Around This World', the album was the scene's first coherent statement.

It served as a rallying call for the city's boosters. Gene Sculatti used the record as a hook for the first major piece about the Haight-Ashbury scene, 'San Francisco Bay Rock', in *Crawdaddy!* issue 6. 'This is perhaps the best rock album ever produced,' he wrote, calling it a 'great testimony, and collectively a pop prophecy'. This was a city that continued 'to provide an open, receptive and progressive testing ground to assimilate and perpetuate the new good thing, Rock'. The Word was out.

The San Francisco scene was also defined by its relationship to Berkeley, on the other side of the Bay. Sculatti remembers 'a perceived and very real divide in the Bay area between Garcia types and Berkeley types, who were very activist, you know. The two prongs of the whole thing are like the ecstasy of the whole thing, and also dealing with the realities that are going on there, which is a horrible thing that might get you ground up and killed in a war machine.'

Berkeley was permanently in the news that summer, constantly castigated by Ronald Reagan in his campaign for governor and subject to government scrutiny as opposition to the Vietnam war stepped up a gear. In early August, agents of the House Un-American Activities Committee served subpoenas on various leading radicals, including the chief organiser of the Vietnam Day Committee, Jerry Rubin. But it wasn't the 1950s, and that trick didn't work a second time.

When the three Berkeley VDC members appeared at the HUAC hearing in Washington DC in mid-month, the hearings were held in 'an atmosphere of hostility and absurdity'. Dressed in a Revolutionary War uniform, Rubin heckled and objected so persistently that he was hustled from the room. The committee was largely frustrated in its desire 'to make it a felony for Americans to aid persons engaged in hostilities against the United States' – in other words, to increase the penalties for anti-war protest.

In pointing out the absurdity of the hearings, and in refusing to accept their very framework, Rubin hinted at a new kind of politics. The old certainties of the New Left were being replaced by something else, a fusion of traditional protest, drug-derived playfulness and a renewed generational urgency. As a spokesman for the three told the *Berkeley Daily Gazette*, 'Each day of war has brought close the possibility of a nuclear holocaust.' It was time to change the frame of reference.

* * *

'We denounce capitalism, bureaucracy, militarism, and the inevitable military collapse of World War III. We acclaim resistance, freedom and creativity. In other words, we repudiate the positive and affirm the negative. Hence we love hatred and hate love.'
ROEL VAN DUYN, 'This Is Provo', translated by Hugo le Comte, *Anarchy*, issue 66, 'Provo', August 1966

The Bay Area newspapers were busy reporting on the strange moods of youth that mid-August. In a *Berkeley Daily Gazette* story, Bill C. Haigwood criticised the teenagers that congregated on Berkeley's Telegraph Avenue: 'They pride themselves on their precociousness and their rebellion. Some of them are just young kids who have found a new "scene", some are honestly serious about their rebellion, and some are legitimate runaways, some involved with drugs.'

This scene defied a definition, but its atmosphere was 'a seemingly cynical, leftist intellectuality supported by a fatuous and simplistic view of the world, typical of the most typical of teenagers. They have a language born, they say, out of the "psychedelic revolution". "Freak out", "flip out", "blow my mind", "turned on", "losing cool", "on a trip" are part of a hip mental thesaurus of drug allusions which every "in" hipling shares with the hip establishment.'

The Telegraph kids came from every class, 'from college professors' cosy homes on the hill, to the rich opulence of a businessman's Park Hills residence, to the flatboard stucco of West Berkeley, or the closely crowded tenements of West Oakland. There are no economic sanctions on joining the hipling scene. The premium is pure, unadulterated freedom.' Despite all the rhetoric, however, the reporter observed that the Avenue's real atmosphere was one of 'awful boredom'.

In the same week, the *San Francisco Sunday Examiner and Chronicle* reported on a new kind of youth protest movement. 'Revolution in Amsterdam: Another Kind of Dutchman' chronicled the rise of the Provos, a Dutch anarchist group that had come to international prominence after 'the explosive riots that rocked Amsterdam in June, during which Provos, other idle youths and striking building workers burned cars, broke windows and disrupted the city.'

What distinguished the Provos was their prankster modus operandi. They were, as Joseph Lelyveld wrote, 'Dadaists in Politics', conducting absurd events like this Amsterdam demo: 'The youths start distributing sheets of paper; as at a signal, the police move in with truncheons, evidently unaware that the sheets of paper are blank on both sides. "Make your own pamphlets tonight", the youths shout over their shoulders, laughing, as they scamper off the way they came.'

The Provos fused anarchist provocation and issue-based protest together with artistic ideas and slogans taken from Happenings. They then welded this to a holistic view of protest, with unexpected, apparently bizarre actions that saw them, in June 1966, succeed in getting the twenty-five-year old Bernard de Vries elected to Amsterdam's city council. Their slogans included 'Provoke' and 'Vote Provo for a Laugh', but they also had more considered policies. For instance, there were the five 'white' plans: 'A white zone through the centre of the city where cars would be banned and free white bicycles provided for anyone to ride at will, white chimneys with filters to clean the smoke, a white wives' plan to give girls sex instruction and contraceptive advice whenever they wanted whether at 12 or 30, a white houses campaign to make available empty houses for the homeless, and most important, a white police plan not only to change the hated blue uniforms to white but to have an unarmed police force trained in special work.'

They fused direct action – a sequence of provocative events in the centre of Amsterdam, in the square called the Spui – with the combination of eye-catching graphics and pointed critiques contained in their pamphlets, placards and the monthly magazine, *Provo*. It was a new kind of youth idiom, which made it hard for the authorities to contain. If the police responded to the provocations, which they almost always did, they were falling into the Provos' trap.

Most of all, the Provos sought to bring all the different youth types together. 'WHAT IS THE PROVOTARIAT?' the editorial in *Provo* 8 questioned, and it immediately gave the answer:

Provos, beatniks, pleiners, nozems, teddy boys, blousons noirs, gammler, raggare, stilyagi, mangupi, mods, students, artists, rockers, delinquents, anarchists, ban the bombers, misfits . . . Those who don't want a career, who live irregular lives, who feel like cyclists on a motorway. Here in the carbon-monoxide poisoned asphalt jungles of Amsterdam, London, Stockholm, Tokyo, Moscow, Paris, New York, Berlin, Milan, Warsaw, Chicago . . . The proletariat is the last rebellious grouping in the Welfare State countries. The proletariat has become the slave of the politicians, happy to watch TV. It has joined its traditional enemy, the bourgeoisie, making with it, becoming a bloated grey Arse-People.

The text referred to international youth types: rockers from Holland (*nozems*), France (*blousons noirs*), Sweden (*raggare*); bohemians in Holland (*pleiners*), Germany (*gammler*) and Russia (*stilyagi*); as well as the post-war British tribes. All of these were potential dissidents, bound together by 'a tasteless, monolithic mass society'. The Provos understood that the alienation and boredom so eloquently exhibited by the teens on Berkeley's Telegraph Avenue could be a powerful organising force.

Provo's origins lay in the Dutch avant-garde of the 1950s and early 1960s: the COBRA movement of abstract painters and their link, thanks to Constant Nieuwenhuys, to the Lettrists and early Situationists; the influence of Allan Kaprow's original Happenings; Julian Beck and Judith Molina's Living Theatre, resident in Holland from 1964 onwards; and the frank advocacy of drugs that eventually surfaced in Happenings like 1964's 'Stoned in the Streets'.

The fuse was lit by the artist Robert Jasper Grootveld, who during 1964 ratcheted up his one-man campaign against the evils of smoking, which he thought was a pointless act of self-harm and the way in which the powers-that-be kept people enslaved. In one action, he set alight the Lieverdje, the statue of a small boy situated at one end of the Spui. His rationale was that the statue had been sponsored by the Hunter Tobacco Company. The Spui Happenings became a weekly event.

In early 1965, a young anarchist called Roel van Duyn tried to initiate a new kind of politics. The Ban the Bomb movement had run out of steam, and the typical class-based rhetoric of the left had become bankrupt. With two other radicals, Marijn Lindt and Robert Hartzema, van Duyn published the first Provo leaflet at the end of March. 'We want to renew anarchism and spread the word,' they wrote, 'especially among the younger generation.'

The name Provo came from a dissertation written by Wouter

Buikhuisen concerning the behaviour of the *nozems*, the Dutch rockers. Published in early 1965 to considerable attention, 'Background to Nozem Behaviour' studied the group's random hooliganism, ascribing it to boredom and rootlessness. Buikhuisen called them 'provos' because of their senseless provocations and, wishing to tap into this anomie, van Duyn took the name for his new movement.

Provo was deliberately non-partisan, issuing broadsides that veered from standard anarchist alarmism to sophisticated, mind-twisting paradoxes. The whole movement was galvanised by the announcement of the forthcoming royal wedding, in March 1966, of Princess Beatrix to Claus von Amsberg. The fact that the heir to the Dutch throne was betrothed to a German who had been forcibly conscripted into the Hitler youth was enough to reopen old wounds within a country that had suffered an extremely harsh occupation under the Nazis.

Together with the young pacifist Robert Stolk, the Provos quickly linked up with Robert Grootveld and collaborated in ever larger Saturday Happenings in the Spui, during which the white bicycles mentioned in their five 'white' plans were unveiled. When the police seized the bikes on the basis that, because they were not locked, they could be stolen, and that was a crime against the law, the full absurdity of their actions was unmasked.

Things accelerated after the Provos burnt a TV set festooned with a picture of Queen Juliana in September. There's nothing like a protest against royalty to bring out the underlying authoritarianism of a monarchical democracy and, throughout the rest of 1965, the Provos and the police held a ritual dance in the centre of Amsterdam. The more the Provos tweaked the authorities, the more the police hit back; the more they hit back, the more sympathy and press attention the Provos got.

Initially, this was a mere irritant, but as the March 1966 wedding approached, it came close to a national emergency. The authorities didn't know what to expect next, taking seriously the group's mooted intention to drop LSD into the reservoirs that supplied Amsterdam's drinking water – the 'white explosion' plan. By early

March, police raids on Provo addresses were a daily occurrence, and much of their literature was confiscated. Most of the leaders were in hiding.

On the day of the royal wedding, chants of 'Claus out' and 'Republic, republic, republic' were quickly followed by the explosion of smoke bombs. Meanwhile, a crowd of around 5,000 protestors, made up of Provos, students and *nozems*, slowly travelled towards the Dam. The violence spilled over into the royal progress. A young protestor threw a chicken into the path of the Golden Coach that contained the royal couple, causing the horses to bolt; a few minutes later, a pair of radicals threw smoke bombs that landed right underneath the Golden Coach, swathing it in white smoke and providing the world's media with an extraordinary front-page image. This seemed like a total vindication of the Provos' approach, a dramatic but minimally violent action that, turned into a media spectacle, dramatised a nation and a society in turmoil. After the event, the Provos were subjected to even more police pressure.

This escalating spiral of demonstration and repression exploded in June. The trigger was a seemingly trivial labour dispute: a 2 per cent cut in the holiday allowance of casual construction workers in Amsterdam, ratified by the construction unions. Irritated by this authoritarianism, the workers held a demonstration on the evening of 13 June. When a middle-aged worker called Jan Weggelar died in the ensuing disorder, the stage was set for a furious reaction.

On the morning of the 14th, a crowd of 5,000 workers, Provos and *nozems* massed to the east of Amsterdam's centre. Some protestors made for the offices of *De Telegraaf*, the paper that had reported, in the late-night edition, that the death of Weggelar had been caused by other protestors. They smashed up the offices, causing extensive damage, and burnt the paper's delivery lorries. The disturbances continued for two days, with the *nozems* up front.

The events of 13–16 June thrust the Provos into international prominence. A week after the riots, Charles Radcliffe visited Amsterdam and noticed that it was 'full of kids, police and promenaders'. Wandering through the narrow streets that could have been 'designed for the guerrilla warfare of provocation', he thought the city was 'the capital of youth rebellion'. He talked to 'a long-haired kid wearing the brightest floral suit I have seen', asking him when the next riot would happen. '"When we feel like it. Authority needs time to prepare for us fighting but we just come when we want. We always win. Riots, then, don't cost nothing for us. Authority pays." Did he read PROVO? "Sometimes I see it. I like PROVO and Provo happenings. PROVO gives us cause and we enjoy rioting. There will be more riots."'

Inspired by his visit, Radcliffe rushed out a new magazine called *Heatwave* – named after the Martha and the Vandellas song – which aimed to develop the idea of a youth revolution. It included several pieces about the Provos, as well as articles about drug addiction, the Puerto Rican riots in Chicago during June, random acts of vandalism and a review of Dave Wallis's novel *Only Lovers Left Alive*, pegged on the fact that it was mooted as the forthcoming Rolling Stones film.

The central text was Radcliffe's manifesto, 'The Seeds of Social Destruction': 'One of the most interesting aspects of revolt within the more advanced capitalist states since the war has been the emergence, one after the other, of groupings of disaffected youth. Such groups are not isolated phenomena; they exist wherever Modern, highly bureaucratized consumer societies exist; in the USSR (Stilyagi), France (Blousons Noirs), Britain (Mods and Rockers), in Holland (provos).'

Like the Provos, Radcliffe realised that the previous political affiliations of the Left and of CND were being superseded. He was attempting to articulate a new kind of politics, one that addressed the overwhelming sense that the consumer society, even in its first full flush, was hollow and empty. 'What happens', he asked, 'when everyone discovers that he has everything there is to have and still has nothing, that all objects are impoverished?'

Radcliffe then tabulated the history of Britain's youth types – 'The Teddy Boys', 'The Ton-Up Kids', 'The Beats', 'The Ban the Bombers', 'The Ravers', 'The Mods and Rockers' – delineating their clothing styles, the music they liked and their potential as revolutionaries. In the final section, called 'The Future: Can't Get No Satisfaction', he observed that all these movements could be seen as 'the groping of youth towards explosive self-expression'.

Radcliffe was well placed to construct this new critique. A journalist and former member of the Committee of 100, the radical wing of CND, he had passed through many of the decade's undercurrents, having been immersed in CND, free jazz, deep blues, the early drug culture and the leftist politics of magazines like *Rebel Worker*, for which he produced his first attempt at yoking pop culture to youth revolution: the 'Mods, Rockers and the Revolution' issue of mid-1965. Seen through this filter, pop music wasn't just an industrial process, but a critique. One of the most popular records of 1965, '(I Can't Get No) Satisfaction', was a million-selling consumer item that protested the fact that consumerism created desires that could never be satiated. The dissident teen groups had grasped that idea. Radcliffe argued that the ensuing instinctive youth revolt was 'one of the few things in this society worth serious defence and support. I welcome youth's rage: I share it.'

However, by the time that *Heatwave* issue 1 was published, the Provos began – like the Cheshire Cat – to slowly disappear from view. The events of mid-June had shocked the group. When Radcliffe tracked down Roel van Duyn in Amsterdam, he found the Provo leader furiously backtracking: 'He said they dissociated themselves from the riots because they were caused by blousons noirs from outside town, who had no political consciousness and were violent.' When Radcliffe pointed out, quite reasonably, that 'many Provo statements were inflammatory', Van Duyn replied that 'the more extreme statements were essentially provocative satire more than direct statement'. This was echoed by another leading member, Irene van der Weetering, in a *Guardian* interview: 'It was sad for us to see these youngsters following the methods of the strikers. We thought they might have learned from us, have followed our pacifist ways.'

Soon after the riots, the Provos suspended their weekly Saturday

Happenings. For over a year, they had led the Dutch authorities a merry dance and had provided an influential new framework for youth protest. But they were pinned, like a butterfly to a board, by the violence of June. It was an exquisite irony that they were most famous for riots that they did not originate. After one last big action – at the State Opening of the Dutch Parliament in September – the Provos dissolved themselves.

Violence was a hot topic that high summer and early autumn. The August edition of the avant-garde monthly *Art and Artists* featured a whole issue on the theme of 'Auto Destructive', with statements by Al Hansen, Gustav Metzger, Ralph Ortiz and Tony Cox. 'We have among us a new generation of dissidents,' wrote Kenneth Coutts-Smith in his introduction, 'Violence'; 'the beatniks of yesteryear have grown up and the hard core have turned into serious artists.'

The themed issue aimed to show the response of artists to the 'public violence' of the modern world. It wasn't just the war and riots in the daily press and on the nightly TV news. As Coutts-Smith wrote, 'We are invited daily by the machinery of advertising to live in a manner conditioned by fantasies of violence; James Bond and Modesty Blaise obviously, but also more insidiously, Boysie Oakes, George Smiley and Illya Kuryakin haunt our daydreams.' This avant-garde art was concerned with reality: 'But reality, our reality, also includes the Bomb, Rhodesia, Vietnam and Freedom marchers. The most striking aspect of the artists who organise Happenings and Events is their political and social involvement. For instance, when just recently a group of Dutch Provos, politically active left wing intellectuals, visited England it was quite logical that their host should have been the auto-destructive artist Gustav Metzger.'

Illustrated by his acid nylon pictures, where the chemical destroyed the 'canvas' in random patterns, Metzger's essay amplified this theme: 'Auto-destructive art is intended as a slow time-bomb to be placed in Bond Street and equivalent "centres-de-luxe". Auto-destructive art is public art. We want monuments – to the power of man to destroy all life. Monuments to Hiroshima, where all the material is squirming, writhing, where heat bursts puncture the material.'

This was violence not as a mirror, but as a hammer: 'Auto-destructive monuments contain the brutality, the over-extended power, the nausea and unpredictability of our social systems. But there are other directions in our societies. There are forces that oppose war and work for disarmament. Auto-destructive art contains the contradictions of our situation. It is an instrument for probing the consciousness of masses of people on issues of peace and war.'

During the last week of August, the Who released their second new single of 1966, 'I'm a Boy'. In June, Charles Radcliffe had approvingly noted the 'violence in the Who's music', which he thought was 'symptomatic of discontent. Their appearance and performance alike denounce respectability and conformity.' He believed that they accorded with a rising revolutionary feeling: 'On a good night the Who could turn on a whole regiment of the dispossessed.'

During 1965, the Who had made public statements about 'auto-destructive art' to explain Pete Townshend's regular guitar-smashing at their shows. The guitarist had studied at Ealing Art School under Roy Ascott, and had attended lectures by Gustav Metzger. As he told me in 2011, 'He was saying the artist's duty is not to produce art, because we're just decorating. He was talking about the ice caps melting in 1961. Ridiculous far-sightedness.'

The Who were saturated in violence. The destruction of costly guitars was matched by the group's own propensity for vicious in-fighting. In May 1966, for instance, Roger Daltrey and Pete Townshend were furious at the rhythm section's non-appearance at an out-of-town gig near Newbury. Keith Moon and John Entwistle were busy partying. When they finally arrived, Townshend attacked the drummer with his guitar, and the group nearly broke up.

'I'm a Boy' was a bizarre song which told the tale of a young boy whose mother dressed him up in girl's clothes – Joe Meek's pathology in a nutshell. 'My name is Bill and I'm a head case,' Daltrey threatened over Moon's distorting drums, 'they practice making up on my face.' In the final verse, Townshend writes about self-harm – not that anyone picked up on it at the time – when he declares the child's wish to 'cut myself and see my blood'.

This was a new kind of lyric, as Ray Davies approvingly noted that autumn: 'I don't think the rebellion line has been properly covered yet; I'm just very pleased that people are writing things like "I'm a Boy".' As John Entwistle admitted to *Record Mirror*, 'The songs that we write, especially Pete, are very unromantic and we somehow can't imagine ourselves singing love songs, especially at this stage. I mean, "I'm a Boy" is almost a queer song.'

'I'm a Boy' was an extraordinary record, cut so hot that the needle struggled to keep in the groove. Like 'Substitute', the storyline went straight to the deep disturbance behind high-sixties androgyny. In mod's double bind, dressing up was twinned with messing up, foppishness with violence, subjects that, alone out of his contemporaries, Townshend felt free to tackle. Not that this controversial nature threatened what the pop press called 'an obvious hit' as it entered the UK Top 50 on 3 September.

Earlier that same week, on 31 August, Gustav Metzger held a press conference at St Bride's Institute to announce DIAS – the Destruction in Art Symposium, which was to be held in London during September. 'In the context of the possible wipe-out of civilisation,' he stated to the packed room, 'the study of aggression and the psychological, biological and economic drives to war is possibly the most urgent work facing man.'

The central idea of DIAS was to 'isolate the element of destruction of new art forms, and to discover any links with destruction in society'. A glance at some of the headings of the symposium papers makes this clear. 'ART: Architecture, film, Happenings, language, music, plastic arts, theatre. SOCIETY: Atmospheric pollution, creative vandalism, destruction in protest, planned obsolescence, popular media, urban sprawl/overcrowding, war.' DIAS was an ambitious project, involving a hundred artists and poets from eighteen countries. In the run-up, Metzger had invited Provos Bernard

de Vries and Irene van der Weetering to attend the press announcement in late June, but the actual roster included the American artist Ralph Ortiz, John Latham and Mark Boyle from the UK, Otto
Mühl and Hermann Nitsch from Vienna, and the post-Fluxus performance artist Yoko Ono.

After the introduction, Metzger invited everyone to move to one
of the institute's upstairs rooms, where Ortiz staged a Happening.
In historian Kristine Stiles's account, he approached a man sitting
in a chair reading a newspaper. Ortiz 'said: "You're in my chair."
"How can this be your chair?" the man responded. "It's a club
chair." "No, it's my chair; I own it," said Ortiz. Turning to the club
manager, Ortiz asked, "Will you inform this man that this is my
chair?"'

Ortiz had, in fact, bought the piece of furniture the day before.
Once ownership had been confirmed, the artist systematically
destroyed the chair, kicking it and ripping it apart. As photographers snapped and reporters took notes, he continued his work,
tearing out the springs and pulling out the upholstery, until he was
satisfied. The press went mad, calling it 'sick art', 'hifalutin, organised vandalism'.

The space used for many of the DIAS actions was a bomb site
on Portobello Road, sourced by local activist Michael X in association with the London Free School. This was the location for
the group portrait eventually printed in *Time* magazine's survey
of 'Happenings': eighteen men in a smashed urban environment
dominated by detritus and, at the rear, a monolithic brick wall.
They were described as 'specialists in piano-smashing, car-burning,
street fights'.

This was where the Brazilian artist Pro-Diaz produced *Painting
with Explosion* on 13 September, a work which described itself. On
the same day, Ivor Davies performed 'Robert Mitchum Destruction
Explosion Event' in a derelict house near the Portobello Road site:
this involved constructing a complicated assemblage that comprised an anatomical model, a shop dummy and a picture of Robert
Mitchum, which he then blew up.

On 16 September, Hermann Nitsch enacted his Orgies Mystery Theatre for the first time in the UK. These were brutal *Gesamtkunstwerke* in which Nitsch eviscerated already dead lambs that were attached to white canvases, spattering the viewers' clothes with blood. The action was intended, as the artist wrote, to be poised between 'MEAT' and '(LIGHT) COLOR', with 'anal' and 'sadomasochistic' elements sublimated during the performance into 'the comprehension of colour'.

This performance got the organisers into trouble, after two journalists reported the affair to the police. Metzger and DIAS co-organiser John J. Sharkey were charged with having 'unlawfully caused to be shown a lewd and an indecent exhibition'. Nevertheless, DIAS highlighted the omnipresence of violence, and sought to find a way in which it could be transmuted into positive energy. As Metzger insisted, 'Destruction IN art did not mean the construction OF art.'

Auto-destructive art was part of the post-Happening world, where all the boundaries were blurred. In a spoken-word album released during 1966, Allan Kaprow gave his eleven rules on how to make a Happening, the point being to transcend traditional definitions of art: 'You can steer clear of art by mixing up your Happening by mixing it with life situations. Make it unsure even to yourself if the Happening is life or art.' The ideas contained in the cutting-edge manifestos for Happenings and auto-destructive art pushed forward to a complete fusion of sensory experience, artistic intent and actuality. This was not art but real life, out there in the world as opposed to the gallery or the garret. As Kenneth Coutts-Smith wrote, 'For the artist, the painting or sculpture had also to become something that was experienced, become, in fact, an event.'

The gap between the avant-garde and the mass market closed rapidly during 1966. In early September, *Life* magazine featured the front-cover story 'LSD Art: New Experience that Bombards the Senses'. Here, psychedelic art was a 'bizarre amalgam of painting, sculpture, photography, electronics and engineering . . . aimed at inducing the hallucinatory effects and intensified perceptions that LSD, marijuana, and other psychedelic . . . drugs produce'. The article focused on USCO, the Millbrook collective; their road show, 'We Are All One', simulated 'the psychedelic experience by use of slides, strobes, oscilloscopes, stereo tapes, a dancer and a heart beat'. It also cited 'The World', a sensurround discotheque that featured 'frenzied Op art patterns and 21 screens for simultaneous projection of movies and slides. A closed-circuit TV camera zooms in on the dancers, throwing their magnified images onto the center screen.'

It was all coming together: situations, Happenings, provocations, auto-destruction, riots, explosions – even the perceptual fission caused by LSD and the total immersion environments of the far-out discotheques. These manifestations might well have come from totally different intentions, but the end result was similar: a demand for the total involvement of spectator, listener, passerby. The divisions were down; passivity was no longer an option.

You had to react, because reaction would make something happen. In this, the Beatles' 'butcher' cover was as much of a situation as the Provos burning an effigy of Queen Juliana, the Who's instrument-smashing as much an act of auto-destruction as Gustav Metzger's acid nylon pictures. All were provocations that stepped outside the usual frame of reference. Behind them was the avant-garde utopia, the promise that the world would be seen, and made anew.

* * *

'Greetings and welcome Rolling Stones, our comrades in the desperate battle against the maniacs who hold power. The revolutionary youth of the world hears your music and is inspired to even more deadly acts.'
     'MANIFESTO', a single-page leaflet handed out at the Rolling Stones concert at the Hollywood Bowl, 25 July 1966

On 23 September, the Rolling Stones released their third British single of 1966. In the wake of the Beatles' withdrawal, the Stones had become the top pop group, but the pressure was unrelenting. After Mick Jagger's hospitalisation in June, they undertook a mammoth thirty-two-date North American tour that took them from Cleveland to Sacramento, from Salt Lake City to Winnipeg. After the final date on 28 July, they travelled to Los Angeles for nine days of recording.

'Have You Seen Your Mother, Baby, Standing in the Shadow?' was one of the twenty or so songs sketched out during these sessions. Planned as the next single, it was – at least in the group's eyes – compromised by the haste with which it was recorded and released. In *2Stoned*, Andrew Loog Oldham remembers how the song's opening guitars were under-recorded and lacked impact. The problem was solved by overdubbing some overlapping vocal drones, at once modal and threatening. The end result was two and a half minutes of barely controlled violent sensation. Since the beginning of 1965, with 'The Last Time', the Rolling Stones had accelerated in force and pace, with a sequence of huge hit singles that passed, in the UK at least, from '(I Can't Get No) Satisfaction' through to the minatory rumba of 'Paint It, Black'. All eyes were on them to deliver the ultimate statement, and 'Have You Seen Your Mother, Baby, Standing in the Shadow?' encoded that sudden flash of self-consciousness.

Written on the piano, the song is an out-of-kilter mix of Motown, rockabilly and hard-edged pop. There are jagged edges everywhere. The elements aren't quite synchronised; neither is the lyric, an LSD-informed blurring of lover into mother, of a personal problem – a young man complaining about his girl becoming pregnant – into deep psychological knots: 'Hate in the shadow, love in your shadowy life.' Jagger really seems to be getting somewhere with this, but there is no sure ground here. As the backing thunders on, the lyric then veers into a sideswipe at Swinging London decadence – 'talking about all the people who would try anything twice' – and then climaxes with the warning of a stark choice: 'the brave old world or the slide to the depths of decline'. Keith Richards's distorted guitar unwinds out of Jagger's vocal, drilling down to an end point.

Notoriously unwilling to explain his lyrics, Jagger nevertheless told *KRLA Beat* that the song was 'about a boy and a bird'. 'Some songs I write are just for a laugh. Others are extensions of ideas. This one is both.' Indeed, 'Have You Seen Your Mother, Baby, Standing in the Shadow?' pushes Jagger's allusive, Dylanesque 1966 mix of misogyny and teenage hostility into something more exploratory and uncertain. It's almost like automatic writing.

The song's hook was the final word of the title. The Rolling Stones had always been presented by Oldham as the shadowy side of the sixties, Dionysus to the Beatles' Apollo. They were designed to be disturbing, to go too far, to pour vituperation and discord across the pop charts and the mainstream media – and the idea took off and took on a life of its own. Now they were getting caught in their own shadow, as their own negativity began to collapse in on itself.

'Have You Seen Your Mother, Baby, Standing in the Shadow?' displays a group not entirely in control of what they are trying to do or say. Six months after '19th Nervous Breakdown', the Rolling Stones are running the year's white-line fever right off the rails. This was an amphetamine apocalypse on 45, glossed by Oldham: 'The Shadow is the uncertainty of the future. The uncertainty is whether we slide into a vast depression or universal war.'

The single's release was prefaced with reports about *Only Lovers Left Alive*, which enhanced its frenzied, end-of-days feel. 'Can you imagine Mick Jagger leading an attack on Windsor Castle,' wrote Bill Harry, 'roaring through London streets on a powerful motor bike with an army of teenage marauders; escaping from a pack of wild, mad dogs; being appointed a chief at a huge gathering of Scottish clans. That is exactly how you may see Mick in the Rolling Stones' first film.'

'Have You Seen Your Mother, Baby, Standing in the Shadow?' was being mixed right up until 9 September, the deadline for its *Ed Sullivan Show* premiere. The next day, the group gathered in New York for a photo shoot with Jerrold Schatzberg and the making of a promotional film with Peter Whitehead. This had been a year in which shock and provocation had become part of the product, and the images from these shoots were almost scientifically designed to cause offence.

'We haven't peed in any gas stations lately, so I suppose we've got to do something.' Keith Richards told the *Melody Maker* on the single's release. The paper reported the following exchange: '"I can just see *Newsweek*," said Keith. "'Dragged and drugged. Is '67 the drag and drug year? How low can they stoop for publicity?'" "Actually there's nothing to upset people in the picture or the record," said Mick. "It's just a song and we just got dressed up as 1940[s] women."'

In the photos and video, Jagger, Richards and Charlie Watts are in mufti, all twinsets and fur stoles. Bill Wyman and Brian Jones – the only convincing female – wear wartime uniforms. 'We adopted the names of "Molly" [Richards] and "Sally" [Jagger] for fun,' Richards explained. 'I think Bill must get the "king of the queens" award for his portrayal of the bird in the bath chair in the uniform. I mean, just look at her. I mean, that's the one that pressed the button, right?'

The Rolling Stones had wanted to dress like their mothers, and in Schatzberg's photo they became their mothers. Like 'I'm a Boy', this was an ultimate twist on mod's psychological perplexity: androgyny flipped over into transvestism and possibly further, into the exploration of the Oedipus complex already hinted at by 'Substitute'. There is no indication that the Rolling Stones actually thought this far: drag was another, as yet barely used explosive device from the arsenal of shock.

The two Peter Whitehead films shot that September are perhaps the most remarkable documents of all sixties pop. The first was filmed at the drag shoot and matches the song's pace to a series of jagged, lightning-fast edits: cut on the beat that uses the flicker effect from a car passing over the Triborough Bridge to display – wham! – Jagger in drag – wham! – Bill Wyman – wham! – Charlie Watts. These shots resolve into the full Schatzberg portrait set-up, as the group get into their roles. The film is full of the perceptual touches that heralded psychedelic culture. It begins with a circle of white light, its aurora coming into focus. Brian Jones plays with a trippy puzzle, full of blurring holes. The flicker from the bridge resolves itself into the flutter of Watts's eyelashes, as he gets to grips with the concept of mascara. The group switches from drag to the high-mod clothes of the day. The clip ends with a very stoned Jones laughing hysterically.

Whitehead's first promo film was shown on *Top of the Pops* the day before the record was released. The UK press ads for 'Have You Seen Your Mother, Baby, Standing in the Shadow?', published that week, used one of the non-drag images from the Schatzberg shoot, with the group distorted by a fish-eye lens. *Record Mirror* gave the release feature space: 'a raw-edged, yet melting, sort of tonal effect and there's so much happening behind that it becomes a veritable wall of sound'.

On the 23rd, the group embarked on a short, twelve-date UK tour. Peter Whitehead shot footage at the first show at the Albert Hall, during which fifty girls fainted and the audience, as *Disc and Music Echo* reported, 'came over the top in one gigantic tidal wave. Before the Stones could even set themselves up, they were engulfed by fans. Mick threw off the first girl who got a stranglehold on him and vanished. Keith wasn't so lucky, he went down fighting, clutching his precious guitar.'

Shown on *Top of the Pops* at the end of September, Whitehead's second clip, like the first, opens with a circle of white light. The group are seen preparing for the Albert Hall performance. The live shots are hysterical, with Jagger urging on the crowd like a demonic Pied Piper. Young women try to grab him but are thrown violently off the stage. The camera frame fills with flying bodies. At the end, Brian Jones comes in from frame right, the lord of misrule laughing hysterically.

Nothing illustrated better the turmoil of September 1966 – two-thirds of the way through the year and two-thirds of the way through the twentieth century – as the sexual and social changes of the 1960s accelerated into a frenzy that was impossible to sustain.

Something smashes in these clips: fan mania is seen not as the expression of love, but as a frantic act of possession. The fans are not young women, but Furies, and, in this Dionysian ritual, they are finally devouring the group.

Here, the incredible forward momentum of the Rolling Stones cracks into chaos. The fundamental, subconscious drive shown in these two clips betrays a group and a culture fraying at the edges under a hostile economic climate, audience expectation and sheer burn-out. The single's very musical and lyrical incoherence – together with the fragmented, haunting images with which it was promoted – make it more of a document of place and time than the group could ever have imagined.

'It should be nestling in the number one spot in double-quick time,' *Record Mirror* predicted. Everything had been lined up – sensational photos, promo films, live dates – but, as October drew on, it remained stuck in the lower reaches of the Top 10, ultimately peaking at #5 in the UK and #9 in the US. In mid-October, the *Melody Maker* commented on the 'Stones Slipped Disc': 'very slow' demand, 'little interest' and 'sales not up to the usual standard for the Stones'.

Andrew Loog Oldham fronted it out: 'We're offering no excuses. They are not necessary. In other charts the disc is climbing not falling . . . It is a good disc but a new departure for the Stones. Who wants to stand still, anyway? One cardinal factor is the economic temperature in which the record was released. In the last two months only two records – "Distant Drums" and "Yellow Submarine" – have topped 250,000. In Great Britain "Mother" is close to 200,000 in two weeks.'

However, 'Have You Seen Mother, Baby, Standing in the Shadow?' was not the grand slam that the Rolling Stones and Oldham had expected. It was an ultimate statement that failed. There were several reasons: it wasn't exactly a hummable tune, and many listeners were turned off by the all-embracing sonic murk and uncompromising darkness of tone. Even so, its comparative failure was, as *Disc and Music Echo* put it, 'the most astounding shock of the financial year ending April 1967'. In the paper's post-mortem, the Hollies' drummer Bobby Elliott put his finger on it: 'The record was basically above the fans' heads. It was too hippy and those photos showing the Stones in drag put the youngsters off a bit. The Stones need slowing down.' Manfred Mann singer Mike d'Abo thought that, unlike the Beatles, the Stones had 'not achieved an image of being all-round family entertainers. And the image that brought them to the top now looks a bit played out.'

There was a sense that things had gone too far, far too quickly. The centre had gone. Mod was tearing itself apart and the mainstream audience was turning away from pop art explosions. In the last week of September, the #1 record in the US was 'Cherish' by the Association, a close-harmony tune with a romantic lyric. In the UK, 'Distant Drums' was at its second week at the top. It would remain there for almost all of the next month.

I'M A BOY

By PETER TOWNSHEND

Recorded on Reaction by THE WHO

Fabulous Music Ltd. 3'.

ADVANCE
PROMOTION
COPY

45RPM
7N 25394
P 1966

TELL ME THAT YOU LOVE ME

COLUMBIA

Columbia
45 RPM
DB 8037

RAGA

SMASH! the
**Rolling Stones/Ike &
Tina Turner tour (that's
Tina above) has been
hailed as the wildest
tour ever to hit Britain.
Alan Walsh is with it**

10 : OCTOBER

Winchester Cathedral: Times Past,
Present and Future

'Time, time, time, see what's become of me
While I looked around for my possibilities.'
    SIMON & GARFUNKEL, 'A Hazy Shade of Winter',
    October 1966

'Distant Drums' slowed everything down. With its sparse pro-duction, slow tempo and adult message, this record dominated the UK charts in autumn 1966, a time of youth culture ferment and social uncertainty as, three months into the Labour govern-ment's wage and price freeze – austerity by any other name – unemployment was beginning to rise. It might have infuriated modernist teens and musicians alike, but it was another reminder that British pop no longer had any centre. This time around, there was no Beatles or Rolling Stones record to knock the song off its perch.

This drear, dry, death-haunted hit took the listener into an older, more familiar world, where men were men and women were women, where people knew their place and knew their duty, where music could be a balm rather than a provocation. It could have been made at any time during the previous twenty years, appealing to the generation who had reached adolescence, if not adulthood, before rock 'n' roll, as well as more conservative teenage fans – of whom there were many, as the culture leaders' quest for experi-ment and sensation proved divisive.

It was as though a time tunnel had opened up in the swirls of pop modernism. Six places down from 'Distant Drums' in the 1 October chart was the debut record by a new group, the New Vaudeville Band. Beginning with a prolonged instrumental intro-duction, 'Winchester Cathedral' resolved into a Rudy Vallee-style vocal that cannily mixed the 1920s with the 1960s – nobody said

'You're bringing me down' in the interwar period – before climaxing with a set of vo-do-de-o's.

It was a charming confection put together by Geoff Stephens, the former co-manager of Donovan who had successfully turned his hand to songwriting in 1965 with credits like Herman's Hermits' 'There's a Kind of Hush' and Dave Berry's 'The Crying Game'. As 1966 progressed, Stephens became disenchanted with the state of pop. 'I think the basic job of pop music is to entertain people,' he said at the time. 'But what have we been getting? A deluge of doomy, depressing discs from a scene of poets, messages, freak-outs and psychedelia.'

Stephens's antidote was 'a return to happy-go-lucky, slightly tongue-in-cheek music', the kind of material that he found on his expeditions to street markets and old junk shops. As he told the *Melody Maker* that October, 'I've got a lot of old records from the Twenties and even an old wind-up phonograph. I dig all that scene.' With the beginnings of a vaudevillian melody chasing round his head, he decided to perform a piece of creative recycling – taking the old and discarded and making it into something new.

Playing around with the metre, he circled around the phrase 'Westminster Cathedral'. After some reflection, he alighted on Winchester instead. 'I had America in mind, where Winchester was a very well known word through Winchester rifles,' he recalled, 'and I thought the song would have a wider reach.' In the summer, Stephens recorded a demo with a stronger electric guitar and electric bass groove. For the finished version, the wood instruments were highlighted, while vocalist John Carter sang through his hands to get that authentic 1930s megaphone feel.

Somewhat to Stephens's surprise, the song was a big hit, rising to its eventual UK peak of #4 by mid-October. Much of the publicity surrounding 'Winchester Cathedral' centred on the fact that 1920s records were cheap and plentiful. This was easily accessible nostalgia, if not concentrated camp, bringing into focus and popularising the nostalgic strain within British and American pop music that had been building ever since the Lovin' Spoonful dressed up as

1920s mashers to promote 'Daydream' and Ray Davies channelled Al Bowlly on 'Sunny Afternoon'.

Indeed, a partly affectionate, partly ironic take on the 1920s had been part of art-school/jazz culture ever since the smash success of the Temperance Seven in 1961. The Alberts had used this material as part of their theatre of the absurd: their 1962 single featured a thoroughgoing massacre of the 1929 James Hanley tune 'Sleepy Valley', backed with a slice of rotten trad, 'Morse Code Melody'. In 1965, Spencer's Washboard Kings dressed up in period clothes and released a cover of the 1926 novelty 'Masculine Women and Feminine Men'.

The Bonzo Dog Doo-Dah Band took up the mantle, releasing two singles on Parlophone in April and August 1966. These featured a raucous take on Kim Fowley's 'Alley Oop', alongside covers of interwar songs: 'My Brother Makes the Noises for the Talkies' (1931), 'I'm Gonna Bring a Watermelon to My Girl Tonight' (1924) and 'Button Up Your Overcoat' (1929). Saxophonist Rodney Slater recalled finding Leslie Sarony's song 'Ain't It Grand to Be Bloomin' Well Dead' 'in my mother's record collection – a first lesson in how to wind up adults', while guitarist Neil Innes remembered this material as 'British pop music from '20s and '30s, which was derivative of the proper American jazz, but it was more like sort of bubblegum pop for the Charleston, jitterbugging rich kids at the Savoy Hotel'. The group didn't invent anything that wasn't already there. As drummer Legs Larry Smith wrote, 'As these songs became part of our repertoire, it was a delight to realise that people "once" existed that were just as mad, bad, irreverent and as eccentric as we were. It was comforting in a strange sort of way.'

Fronted by hooligan singer Vivian Stanshall, the Bonzo Dog Doo-Dah Band were an art-school group. Their love of obscure 1920s records was allied to a Dadaist sensibility: their name came from a random word cut-up and their stage shows were augmented by auto-destructive machines (Roger Ruskin Spear had been to Ealing Art School and, like Pete Townshend, had fallen under Gustav Metzger's spell) and surreal props – word balloons, gorilla suits. To top it off, they wore baggy 1920s suits, short haircuts and co-respondent shoes – then the cutting edge of fashion.

Meanwhile, Geoff Stephens was presented with an urgent problem. He had a hit, but no act. Neither he nor John Carter wanted to tour, so he quickly assembled an ensemble from some session musicians, as well as Bob Kerr, recently sacked from the Bonzo Dog Doo-Dah Band. Stephens found the singer in an old contact, Alan Klein, who had pioneered a vernacular English pop style on his 1964 album *At Least It's British*. Renamed Tristram, Seventh Earl of Cricklewood, the working-class Klein was rendered fit for purpose.

The template for the New Vaudeville Band's appearance was Kerr's old group, the Bonzo Dog Doo-Dah Band. Dressed in interwar fashions and displaying word balloons during their TV appearances, the group quickly became a pop talking point as the song rose up the charts. 'What a drag that Vaudeville thing is,' Bob Lang of the Mindbenders told *Disc and Music Echo*. 'It's so monotonous. I know everyone's trying to do something original – but this hasn't come off.' The group hit back in headlines like 'Vaudevilles: Stop all the sneering . . . WE'RE HIP!'

Neil Innes remembered the galvanising effect of their rivals' success: 'The New Vaudeville Band was on television looking exactly like the Bonzos did, with their two-tone shoes and gangster suits and all the props – they stole everything. So everywhere we went, people said, "Oh, you're like that New Vaudeville Band." So it was "Legs" Larry Smith who said, "Right, let's do any kind of music." We said, "Yeah, let's start writing." So, in a way, it did us a favour, because we started writing our own stuff and did any kind of music we fancied.'

In the short term, Geoff Stephens and the New Vaudeville Band had the last laugh. Later in the month, 'Winchester Cathedral' hit the *Billboard* Top 100 as the highest new entry. Under the firm tutelage of road manager Peter Grant, Tristram and the others went to America, where they played Las Vegas and appeared on the *Ed Sullivan Show*. Their success encouraged other musicians to try out versions of the 1920s style that had been the pop music of their parents' youth. It became a mini-vogue. The hype had become real. The past had become the present and the future.

* * *

> 'Happenings ten years time ago
> Situations we really know
> But the knowing is in the mind
> Sinking deep into the well of time.'
>> THE YARDBIRDS, 'Happenings Ten Years
>> Time Ago', released October 1966

Something very strange was happening to time in pop culture during autumn 1966, and 'Winchester Cathedral' was only one manifestation of this warp and woof. The unitary drive of modernism had accelerated beyond the point of sustainability. Under this pressure, time was beginning to fragment, from forward motion into a sequence of loops, into either the perpetual now or the historical periods sourced at will by an overloaded media. It was as though the time travel fictionalised by the film version of H. G. Wells's *The Time Machine* had come to pass.

There had been various songs about time during the year: Chris Farlowe's modernist nightmare 'Out of Time', or the Creation's 'Making Time', a sneer of cynicism so overarching that it verged on disgust. In July, Dusty Springfield had a UK Top 10 hit with Goffin and King's 'Goin' Back', which featured a lyric – written and sung by twenty-somethings – about going back to the innocence and ideals of a youth that had just passed. 'Let everyone debate the true reality,' Springfield sang, 'I'd rather see the world the way it used to be.'

Two extraordinary records blew up linear time in their respective quests for a perpetual present. Placed as the last track on *Revolver*, the Beatles' 'Tomorrow Never Knows' was heard by millions of listeners, a mass market avant-garde artefact that fused radical technology – in particular the use of tape loops, backwards tapes and Leslie speakers – with the most explicit evocation yet in popular culture of mystical transcendence. Its form reflected the circularity of the lyrics, which faded on the end of the beginning.

If 'Tomorrow Never Knows' was a perpetually renewing circle, then James Brown's 'Tell Me That You Love Me' completely deconstructed black music, in a sound field of abrasive and futuristic complexity that predicted the manic, hyper-speed breakbeats of jungle thirty years later. Tucked away on the flip of the activist 'Don't Be a Drop Out', 'Tell Me That You Love Me' serves as the id to the A-side's superego: a manic expression of pride and the power of dance that led the listener into something primal and chaotic. The song – it's almost inaccurate to call it a song, for it's more an elemental force of nature – began in a live version of Junior Walker's 'Shotgun'. It was recorded as part of Brown's set at Tampa, Florida, in April 1966 for a possible live album. Although sound problems prevented that plan, Brown's production manager, Bud Hobgood, was determined to salvage something. Taking the live performance as a base – complete with audience exhortations – Hobgood looped Brown's vocal and added a repetitive guitar figure by Lonnie Mack.

It begins with MC Nat Jones's introduction. A short brass fanfare follows, before a fast tribal beat introduces Mack's guitar loops. The audience squeals and whistles, and the volume suddenly jumps. As Brown's vocal enters, the drums suddenly explode into a direct prefiguring of the 'Funky Drummer' beat. The words are nothing; they don't matter. What does is the way that Brown drives the beat as though everything cannot come fast enough, the otherworldly scream that he unleashes at the end of each verse. It lasts under two minutes, but it sounds like for ever.

The perpetual motion of both these recordings had different sources – the power of spiritual transcendence and the power of dancing as an expression of identity and pride – but they both erased present, past and future in an everlasting Now. As the Byrds sang on that summer's '5D (Fifth Dimension)', 'And I will remember the place that is now / That has ended before the beginning.' The impact of psychedelic drugs was transforming white pop culture, at the same time as the increasing assertion of Black Power was filtering into dance music.

It wasn't just in pop music, either. The second half of 1966 saw a variety of assaults on modernist time, from high and low art, from the avant-garde and the mainstream media. In late September, Pathé News filmed one of Yoko Ono's performances of 'Cut Piece'. She sits, impassively, as a fellow artist cuts away her outer garments until she is in her underclothes. It was a barbed comment about the nature of male violence towards women that echoed Allan Kaprow's fifth admonition on 'How To Make A Happening': 'break up your time and let it be real time'.

Even more so than the efforts of the extreme avant-garde or the spread of LSD, it was the unprecedented and unreckoned effect of the mass media that helped to explode conventional definitions of time. For the increasing pace, penetration and interrelation of the various parts of the media economy – television, film, pop music, magazines, newspapers – were locking people in the West into another kind of perpetual present: not that of transcendence or pride, but of a febrile, destabilised consumerism.

The *Time* issue for 14 October 1966 ran a cover story on television: 'the Electronic Front Page', 'the Most Intimate Medium'. The article was focused on news coverage and the famous news anchor Walter Cronkite – a towering figure. It acknowledged the transformative, if not corrosive, power that the medium had within American life, citing Morley Safer's emotive reports from Vietnam and concluding that 'as a result of its extraordinary impact, TV news has become a powerful force encouraging social ferment'.

That autumn, Marshall McLuhan discussed what he termed 'The Invisible Environment: the Future of Consciousness'. His article observed the impact of the new media totality: 'The young person today is a data processor on a very large scale. Some people have estimated that the young person, the infant and the small child, growing up in our world today works harder than any child ever did in any previous human environment – only the work he has to perform is that of data processing.'

The media were, in effect, creating two tiers of perception, a time slip between past and present, between those born in the time of the mass media and those born before it tightened its grip: 'Growing up has become, in the age of electrically processed information, the major task of mankind. We still have our eyes fixed on the rearview mirror looking fairly and squarely at the job that is receding into the 19th century past . . . the kind of contrast between these situations creates an absurdity.'

One by-product of this was a generation gap, as sixties teenagers surfed a proliferating media with an ease that their elders could only envy: as McLuhan wrote, 'the future of consciousness is already assuming a very different pattern'. Another by-product was the need for more and more content, not just in news, but in features, drama, fantasies. The mass media were all-consuming: not only did they turn the present into the past as soon as it had happened but they began to cannibalise the past through the filters of the moment.

In their voracious need for new material, film and television had already begun to raid outsider subcultures: bohemians, artists, homosexuals. The media sensation of 1964 and 1965, thanks to the surveys by Susan Sontag and Gloria Steinem, camp was all-pervasive in autumn 1966. It had become a fact of life – not just an expression of deviancy or cool or distance but a basic way of processing data, of dealing with an onrush of information from many different times and viewpoints, a method of navigating a schizophrenic consciousness.

In the summer of 1966, two new series had debuted, both concerned with time travel. Launched in early September, NBC's *Time Tunnel* was set in the near future, 1968. The plot concerned the development of a literal time tunnel, which was under the threat of governmental cutbacks. In order to prove its efficacy, two of the scientists on the project enter the vortex and find themselves travelling through various times and places, prevented from returning to the present yet unable to prevent the disasters that, through their historical knowledge, they know will occur.

The treatment was fairly straightforward. The first episode took the two scientists to 1912, where they found themselves on the *Titanic*, with the inevitable results, and left them suspended in a 'time limbo'. In the second episode, they projected ten years into their future, 1978, taking a space flight to Mars. After travelling to 1910 (a mining disaster) and 1941 (Pearl Harbor), the pair alighted in the nineteenth century for the episode of 6 October, 'The Last Patrol', where the action took place during the final battle of the Anglo-American war of 1812–15.

On the same day, the BBC showed the fifteenth episode of *Adam Adamant Lives!*, 'The Village of Evil'. Debuting in late June, the series was designed to take over the audience schooled by *The Avengers* in prime-time surrealism. The central conceit – as shown in the opening episode – was that the titular hero, an Edwardian soldier and spy, has been cryogenically frozen by a masked villain, The Face, and hidden in a derelict building. Disturbed by urban regeneration and discovered in his block of ice, Adam is pitched forward fifty years into the Swinging Sixties.

The six-minute sequence where Adam Adamant attempts to get his bearings in this harsh future is full of soundtrack distortion, echo and oscillating camera focus. It's all about the shock of the new. The difference between then and now is adroitly exploited by the script. 'Is it war?' Adam says as he staggers around a brightly lit Piccadilly Circus. 'What infernal place is this?' Rescued by Georgina, an 'archetypal' Swinging London dolly bird, he is taken to her flat, while all the time marvelling at her 'masculine attire', which is part of 'the madness outside'.

Like *The Avengers*, *Adam Adamant Lives!* dressed up conventional crime plots with a dose of absurdity, an air of apocalyptic threat and a certain sly self-mockery. 'I think it's all a current part of the craze for art nouveau,' says a pompous police inspector as he guards the hero in his Edwardian clothes. This, of course, was part of camp: it was no longer enough to present the play, it had become important for the play to contain historical information and for it to include its own commentary – the lessons of the avant-garde streamlined for the mass market.

In the November 1962 issue of *Scene*, the painter Pauline Boty had talked about the relationship of past and present. As she moved towards pop art, Boty defined her aesthetic as 'Nostalgia for NOW': 'People have this kind of nostalgia for Victoriana and we have a nostalgia for things that are now . . . it's almost like painting mythology, only a present day mythology – film stars etc.' 'Nostalgia for NOW' was a perfect slogan for the mid-sixties: grasp the moment and it had gone.

In the UK, high Victoriana was replaced by the *fin de siècle* as 1966 progressed. Klaus Voormann's cover for *Revolver* reproduced the spidery filigrees of the artist Aubrey Beardsley, who was the subject of a major retrospective at London's Victoria and Albert Museum that summer. Beardsley was also echoed by Nicholas Ferguson in his set design for the Rolling Stones' May appearance on *Thank Your Lucky Stars*, where Mick Jagger crooned 'Lady Jane' in a set that depicted stone-faced, hieratic beauties straight out of the symbolist textbook.

Consistency and fidelity to the original source material was not the point. Like the scientists in *Time Tunnel*, it was becoming possible for designers, musicians, film-makers and artists to travel freely through time and space. It was the time of the 1910s and the 1920s. During 1965, Paul Flora published *Vivat Vamp!*, a collection of found postcards that he assembled into a book in praise of the type, 'from Mae West to Marilyn Monroe, from Marlene Dietrich to Brigitte Bardot'. On the cover was a photograph of the first vamp, Theda Bara, at her most sultry.

In fashionable London, the silver and op designs of high-sixties modernism were already being superseded at their moment of maximum impact. In February 1966, two young entrepreneurs opened a boutique called I Was Lord Kitchener's Valet right at the bottom end of Portobello Road. The shop's stock of nineteenth-century military uniforms soon attracted the cognoscenti – most notably Mick Jagger, who in spring 1966 bought the red Grenadier Guards drummer's jacket that he wore to great effect on his May *Ready Steady Go!* appearance.

The retro style of I Was Lord Kitchener's Valet filtered quickly into Carnaby Street, as well as providing a song title for the New Vaudeville Band. Around the same time, a boutique called Granny Takes a Trip opened at the unfashionable end of the King's Road – at number 488, beyond World's End. This was a time-tripping exercise, that looked back (Granny) at the same time as it looked forward (Trip = LSD). Launched by tailor John Pearse, designer Nigel Waymouth and their partner Sheila Cohen, it sold antique clothes as well as proto-hippie oriental exotica.

Granny Takes a Trip would change its facade many times, in a kind of boutique performance art, but its opening decor used art nouveau graphics in orange on a black background, while in the window was a large image of an Edwardian vamp reclining on a chaise longue. As John Pearse told Max Décharné in his history *King's Road*, 'We were dealing in vintage clothes. What appealed to us was Aubrey Beardsley and the Victorians, "Against Nature" by Huysmans. So we were all doomed Romantics at the time.'

As 1966 wore on, the antique clothing began to dry up and Pearse began making new items out of Liberty fabrics. The Beatles wore some of his shirts and jackets on the back cover of *Revolver*. This was a far cry from the defined shapes and tough attitude of the mods, mirroring two periods (the 1890s and the 1960s) when youth was vigorous. As Nigel Waymouth remembered, 'We started making clothes for men and women. In fact, both hung on the rail, side by side. We were androgynous in that sense. That was part of the look of the time.'

The shop didn't stand still, changing from a futuristic, computer-style facade to a large portrait of Native American chief Low Dog, before shifting again to an idealised 1930s female, loosely based on the blonde bombshell Jean Harlow. Quite apart from the tailoring innovations brought about by Pearse, the shop was, as Waymouth put it, an 'art concept' – a living experiment on the nature and the transience of nostalgia.

In 1966, Granny Takes a Trip was bang up to date. Even so, its flight into the past served time on Swinging London, not that many people truly believed in that any more. Indeed, two singles released that October promoted two separate films that sought to deep-mine the youth revolution that had appeared to grip the capital during the previous two to three years. Of course, the fact that people were making films about Swinging London only reinforced the fact that it was over and, to the extent that it had ever existed, was receding into memory.

Paul Jones's first solo single after leaving Manfred Mann, 'High Time', was released at the end of September. Written by Mike Leander and Chas Mills, it was a commercial number in the mode of the moment, with booming drums, a thin string section and a bouncy melody that modulated nicely into the chorus. The barely coherent lyric punned on the keyword 'time' for all that it was worth, drilling the title phrase into the brain: 'High time, long time / Day time, night time.'

Jones had been a major star with Manfred Mann, and his decision to go solo was big news. He was articulate and thoughtful, and his interviews around the release of 'High Time' were much more interesting than the record. *Rave* put him on the front cover of their September issue, and followed it up with an exclusive piece in October that centred around the shoot for *Privilege*, a new feature film directed by Peter Watkins: his follow-up to *The War Game* was a drama about the harnessing of pop's power in the near future by a clerico-fascist regime. As *Rave*'s Maureen O'Grady wrote, in her explanation of the film's storyline: '"Privilege" is a hard, bitter yet sometimes comic story of a young singer, manipulated to international fame by his manager, agents, the T.V. and Press. The film is set in 1970. "It has to be," says Paul, "because this fellow I play, Stephen Shorter, is someone ten times bigger than the Beatles in popularity. If the film was set in 1966 it would be unbelievable, because everyone knows at the moment that the

Beatles are the biggest thing in the world. Dating it 1970 makes it possible."'

The *Rave* feature begins with one of the film's key scenes. Exploited for the regime's ends, Steve Shorter delivers an explosive, self-loathing rant: 'I'm nothing . . . nothing. I'm a person the same as everyone else. I've got two arms, two legs – I'm a person. I'm not perfect. I've done terrible things. I've slept with girls, and they've meant nothing to me. But you've made me an idol. You've made me this perfect statuette. I'm nothing . . . and that's what you made me. And . . . and . . . I hate you. I hate you. I hate you for what you've done to me!'

On the face of it, *Privilege* was shaping up as an overwrought version of Thom Keyes's *All Night Stand*. The film was based on an interesting idea – pop not as rebellion or youth expression but as a method of social control – but what *Rave* ignored on their brief visit to the set was that Jones was no actor, a fact that would become brutally apparent on the film's eventual release. Still, Peter Watkins was right about one thing: by 1966, pop music had become all-pervasive and powerful enough to warrant governmental scrutiny, if not control.

On 11 October, Major Oliver Smedley was acquitted on a manslaughter charge at Chelmsford Assizes. This was the last act in a complex, violent case that had blown the world of pirate radio wide open. It had begun in spring 1966, when Reg Calvert, the owner of Radio City – based in an offshore wartime fort called Shivering Sands – entered into negotiations with Radio London to relaunch the station. A couple of Radio London disc jockeys went to visit the fort and were appalled by the primitive living conditions and the state of the equipment. The problem for Calvert was that the ownership of the transmitter was disputed. Major Smedley, who had been part of a consortium of rival bidders, believed it was his, and was infuriated by the news that it was going to be sold. A former paratrooper, Smedley took matters into his own hands. Taking along a crew of sailors – there was a seamen's strike at the time – he stormed the fort on the night of 19/20 June and held everyone on board to ransom. The station went off the air and, having posted some guards, Smedley returned to land.

Things escalated at a meeting held later that day in London. The managing director of Radio London refused to negotiate under duress. Calvert was beside himself. Having received no assistance from the police, who thought that the offshore structure was outside UK jurisdiction, he went round to Major Smedley's Essex house on the evening of 21 June to demand the return of his fort. In the ensuing confrontation, the major took a shotgun and shot Calvert dead. It could have been a fantastic plot line from *The Avengers*, but it was real.

Such naked piracy concentrated the minds of the Labour government. The pirate stations had long been a thorn in the authorities' side, offering unrestricted content and threatening the monopoly of the BBC as the state broadcaster. They had a large audience among the nation's youth: in July, the UK National Opinion Poll estimated that Radio Caroline had nearly 9 million listeners, with Radio London not far behind with just over 8 million, and Radio City trailing with 2.5 million. Even so, that was getting on for 20 million British citizens.

Legislation had been on the cards for a while, but the matter had not been a high priority for the government. The shocking violence of the Calvert case and the storming of Shivering Sands was a reminder that, beneath the stations' glossy surface, all was far from well. On 1 July 1966, the Marine, &c., Broadcasting (Offences) Act was brought before Parliament, the first stage in a long process that would see almost all the pirates off the air by the end of 1967. This was not a popular move among musicians, fans and the British music industry in general.

In September, the Yardbirds' former manager Giorgio Gomelsky launched his Marmalade label with a Beach Boys-styled record called 'We Love the Pirates', written by Geoff Stephens and John Carter and performed by a studio group called the Roaring 60s. 'The government wants to close them down,' intoned the singer, 'but we want them to stay [cue sobbing noises].' It was, obviously, a fixture on pirate radio playlists, reaching #24 in the Radio Caroline South countdown in mid-September.

In early October, *Disc and Music Echo* published an article, 'They're Coming to Take Us Away, Yo Ho!', which quoted Simon Dee, a former Radio Caroline DJ: 'All I want and I am sure most people in Britain want is to switch my radio dial to whatever station provides the sort of broadcasting I like.' George Harrison also spoke out: 'The government makes me sick. This is becoming a police state. They should leave the pirates alone. At least they've had a go, which is more than the BBC have done.'

The case of the pirates was an early salvo in the hotly contested battle between free enterprise and state regulation. In 1966, however, it was hard for teens not to see the government as determined to spoil their fun. The squeeze on the pirates marked the death knell of the open culture that had marked Britain's rise to international pop prominence during the previous two years. The charts would soon be full of mums-and-dads records, while innovative singles from America and the UK would be denied radio play and, as often as not, shut out of the Top 20.

Between 12 and 14 October, the Yardbirds were on a set at Elstree Studios, to the north of London, filming a sequence for Michelangelo Antonioni's *Blow-Up*, in which they ran through their version of 'The Train Kept A-Rollin'' – reworked as 'Stroll On' because of copyright problems. The script called for lead guitarist Jeff Beck to smash his instrument. This was not a regular feature of the Yardbirds' performances, but Beck performed the task with a droogish gusto.

The second half of 1966 saw the Yardbirds falter. 'Shapes of Things' was not a stepping stone to greater things, but a peak. The group managed to sustain the momentum with the attitudinal 'Over Under Sideways Down' – 'When I was young people spoke of immorality / All the things they said were wrong are what I want to be' – which scraped into the Top 10 in the UK, but the pop press was full of reports about illness and exhaustion. By September, when they were performing on the Rolling Stones tour, they were seen as – that cardinal sixties sin – old hat.

Bassist Paul Samwell-Smith had quit in June after a particularly drunken performance by Keith Relf at a May Ball in Oxford. At one stroke the Yardbirds had lost their principal composer and musical arranger. They regrouped by adding Jimmy Page, first on bass and then on guitar, and it was this line-up that performed in *Blow-Up*. They were not the director's first choice, but the Yardbirds gave a spirited performance in front of a deliberately static, alienated audience, dressed in the latest fashionable PVC, bright orange and purple.

In the final sequence, the equipment malfunctions about two minutes in: Beck smashes his guitar against the amp. More bashing ensues, before the guitarist throws the instrument on the floor, breaking the neck. After ripping the strings off, Beck throws the neck into the crowd, which, as if at the flick of a switch, transforms from sullen silence into a clawing, hysterical mass. In the fight to get the totemic guitar part, the film's protagonist, David Hemmings, prevails. He leaves the club, chased by fans, before he comes to his senses and quietly drops the item in the street.

This was a graphically illustrated point about the nature of idol worship and the transience of pop objects. Antonioni had come to London a few months earlier to begin shooting *Blow-Up*, with the intention of capturing the feeling of London. 'When I am shooting a film,' he said in September 1966, 'I always try to establish a rapport between characters and landscape. I am most of all enthusiastic about the urban landscape. I like the city. What progress there is goes in the cities, and I want to be a witness.'

According to *Continental Film Review*, the film aimed to capture 'twenty-four hours in the life of a jaded fashion-photographer set against the world of London fashions, dolly-girls, pop groups, beat clubs, models, parties and, above all, the "in" photographers who more than anyone else, have promoted the city's new image . . . and such names as David Bailey, Terry O'Donovan, Brian Duffy, David Montgomery, John Cowan are seldom out of heavy type in the society columns'.

Blow-Up would reveal itself as a carefully wrought parable on the nature of perception, blurring the lines between reality and fantasy in a way that exposed the period's ellipses of communication. David Hemmings is haunted by a murder that he has witnessed in a south London park. He thinks he has caught it on camera, but the film is stolen. He returns to the park, but there is no body. His previous cynicism and laddish certainty evaporates in the face of this mystery, which exposes the limits of mediated reality: if it is not on camera, then does it exist?

Shot between April and October 1966, *Blow-Up* also offered a documentary record of London between the frantic forward motion of Swinging London and something non-linear, blurred, ambiguous. In a sequence near the end of the film, Hemmings visits a drugged party held at a dimly lit, exquisite location – Christopher Gibbs's apartment in Cheyne Walk. Stoned out of his mind, he misses his last chance to tell anyone about the death he witnessed. He is unable to communicate his concern: was the murder real or had he dreamed the whole thing?

The sequence is beautiful and seductive, a door into a gilded life half glimpsed. This was the world that, by the autumn of 1966, the Beatles and the Rolling Stones and the smart end of pop were inhabiting: arty, drugged, closed to the general public. The openness of spirit and class mobility that had characterised the public image of Swinging London were evaporating in the face of an economic downturn. The tide was ebbing away from the capital, and it left a hollow, after-the-party hangover. Had Swinging London ever existed or had it just been a collective fantasy?

The Yardbirds – one-time avatars of all that was progressive and exciting – fell foul of this change in the weather. A week before their appearance in *Blow-Up*, they released their eighth UK single, 'Happenings Ten Years Time Ago'. Recorded in the high summer with the two-guitar line-up, it was a compressed pop art explosion, with a ferocious staccato guitar figure, a massive descending riff, a roiling instrumental break and LSD-inspired lyrics that questioned the construction of reality and the nature of time: 'Was it real, was it in my dreams? / I need to know what it all means.'

'Happenings Ten Years Time Ago' was not well received. The usually benign Penny Valentine savaged it in *Disc and Music Echo*: 'I have had enough of this sort of excuse for music. It is not clever, it is not entertaining, it is not informative. It is boring and pretentious. I am tired of people like the Yardbirds thinking this sort of thing is clever when people like the Spoonful and the Beach Boys are putting real thought into their music. And if I hear the word psychedelic mentioned I will go nuts.'

Like 'Have You Seen Your Mother, Baby, Standing in the Shadow?', the Yardbirds' latest record seemed to sacrifice melody and coherence in favour of sensation and needless obscurantism. The musicians were seen as overreaching themselves; they had lost an influential reviewer and were in danger of losing their audience. Over the next few weeks, 'Happenings Ten Years Time Ago' would flail around in the lower reaches of the Top 50, a major blow for a group who had had five Top 10 singles in a row. The Yardbirds had gone from heroes to bores in eight months.

Where the sharp end of pop led, many teenagers no longer wanted to go. Here was Marshall McLuhan's two-tier consciousness in action within a supposedly transformative popular culture, between those who wanted to forge ahead at the pace set by the previous two years and those who could not, and would not, follow. It was a fact that many listeners could hear in the records: in an attempt to sustain the unsustainable pace of mid-1960s pop, the musicians risked unintelligibility as they sped up and compressed their records to the point of no return.

There was a profound disconnect between the London pop-star elite and many provincial teenagers, who were left feeling high and dry now that the tide was receding. When *Disc and Music Echo*'s Bob Farmer visited Newcastle that autumn, most of the young people he talked to – around 80 per cent – said that they wanted to leave the city. They felt that they were stuck in the north-east and that Britain – thanks to the wages freeze – was no longer a country of opportunity for young people. The Newcastle teens complained about the lack of money, the dullness of TV and the lack of any decent nightlife, and bickered about whether or not John Lennon was right in saying that the Beatles were more popular than Jesus. In the unkindest cut, a couple of interviewees repudiated the whole basis of the country's high profile in the high sixties. 'I'm sick of the British pop scene,' said Bill Rogan, while Bernard Thwaites thought that 'British pop is terrible – the American discs are far better'.

* * *

'The new factor in U.S. race relations and politics that has come to be known as backlash is more than merely the reaction of some white people to Negro rioting or cries of "black power". The attitude of many white Americans is influenced by the belief that the Negro has made great gains in a relatively short time, and that he now would do better to stop agitating and consolidate what he has won. At the same time, much of the new black militancy is a result of frustration over what many Negroes consider their snail's pace of progress.'
Time editorial, 'What the Negro Has – And Has Not – Gained',
28 October 1966

The tensions of the time – between pressing forward and pulling back – were also playing out in America's civil rights movement. For the previous decade, Martin Luther King and the SCLC had succeeded in pulling together all the different strands of radicalism and conservatism, of revolution as well as gradual change, but, after the last show of unity at the March Against Fear, these skeins were unravelling at an alarming rate.

The backdrop for this uncertainty was the flowering of black American dance music. In the *Billboard* chart for 1 October, there were three Motown songs in the Top 10: at #2, the Supremes' 'You Can't Hurry Love'; at #3, the Temptations' 'Beauty Is Only Skin Deep'; and the Four Tops' 'Reach Out I'll Be There' at #7. Motown had two more in the Top 30: Jimmy Ruffin's 'What Becomes of the Brokenhearted' (#19) and Junior Walker and the All Stars' 'How Sweet It Is' (#21).

This was some kind of golden age, but the optimism and strength of these records was not reflected in black politics or black lives. The civil rights movement had shaped and seen itself reflected in the records that Motown and Stax put into the mainstream. Quite apart from consciousness-raising efforts like Brenda Holloway's August single, 'Play It Cool, Stay in School', the lyrics of songs like Stevie Wonder's cover of 'Blowin' in the Wind' or 'Reach Out I'll Be There' offered advice and sustenance to communities and politicians under extreme duress.

James Brown stepped into explicit engagement with his late-September single, 'Don't Be a Drop Out'. His experience on the March Against Fear had stoked his social conscience. Set to a mid-paced groove, the song told a simple story with a simple moral: get an education and get ahead. 'I was a drop-out at 16, but I was forced to,' Brown told *KRLA Beat*'s Rochelle Reed. 'But now the only way to get a decent job is to finish high school, and even that's not enough today. School is your only weapon! If you don't finish, you might as well be dead.'

The record was not a big hit, but it was the start of something for Brown. 'I wanted to build a whole campaign around it. As soon as the record was pressed, I took the first copy to Hubert Humphrey at the White House and told him what I had in mind.' Brown 'visited schools and talked to kids. I told them to stay in school, listen to their teachers, and stay close to their books. They were there to take care of business.' But these positive interventions had a grim counterpoint.

On Saturday 1 October, the riot at Hunters Point, a poor and isolated ghetto south-east of San Francisco, was slowly petering out. It had begun four days previously, when a sixteen-year-old black teenager, Matthew 'Peanut' Johnson, was shot and killed by an SFPD patrolman. He was one of a group of young men who had abandoned a suspect car as the police approached. The weather was muggy, and a large angry crowd gathered immediately at the place of Johnson's death. Tensions quickly escalated.

It was exactly the same situation as Watts: hasty police action triggering an enraged response. While community leaders attempted to calm the situation, the mayor of San Francisco addressed 'an unruly' crowd on the evening of the 27th. Rocks were thrown at him and his entourage. By this time, the disturbances were not so much about the death of a young man but a chance to get back at the white power structure that many young blacks felt was racist and holding them back, patrolled by trigger-happy policemen who gunned them down like animals.

The mutual incomprehension between the police and the young men of Hunters Point was complete. They were all American citizens, but they were living in separate worlds. The riot escalated dramatically after the police opened fire on a community centre: after riddling it with bullets, they stormed the building only to find 'several huddled, cowering children of preteen age'. Full-blown mayhem then ensued, the disturbances spreading to the Fillmore district and resulting in the deployment of 2,000 National Guardsmen and the imposition of an 8 p.m. to 6 a.m. curfew.

This news compounded what had been a dreadful couple of months for the civil rights movement. It was as though some invisible line had been crossed: the movement had seen enormous gains over the last few years, but the continuing violence fuelled a wave of criticism of both the movement and President Johnson's civil rights legislation. In the mass media the idea prevailed that things had gone too far, too fast. Suddenly, the phrase 'white backlash' entered everyday usage.

It had been another long, hot season, with disturbances in the Hough district of Cleveland, Omaha and St Louis. In addition, the situation in Chicago was out of control. On 4 September, an SNCC splinter march passed through Cicero, the blue-collar suburb and one-time Capone stronghold that had seen a major race riot in July 1951. The 250 marchers faced a spitting, howling, brick-throwing mob. The level of hatred was unprecedented, as hundreds of whites came out to protest, holding placards reading 'White Power'.

Two young film-makers from the local Film Group Inc., Mike Shea and Mike Gray, walked among the marchers. Edited into a nine-minute piece, *Cicero March* is an astonishing documentary, taking you right into the madness of 1966. It's a sunny day, but the feel is completely oppressive. Funnelled down streets narrowed by the weight of protestors on the sidewalks, the marchers fight the cops, who fight the protestors. Helicopters buzz low, while National Guardsmen line the top of buildings. Rifles and batons abound: it feels like a war zone.

At the film's beginning, the marchers are quiet and dignified. Middle-aged onlookers openly shout racist remarks, while local youths brandish swastikas and keep up a non-stop barrage of threats. These are not the long-haired, mod-dressed young of the day's pop culture, but greasers with short hair and work clothes, T-shirts – garb little changed since the 1950s. 'Chicago is notorious for its number of greasers,' wrote former resident Mick Rogers that year. 'Dance spots in the aptly-named "Windy City" still feature the old-style rock 'n' roll of 1958 or so.'

The greasers needed no encouragement in bringing trouble down onto the heads of the negroes and whites peopling this alien invasion. The marchers were in the mid-1960s but, to all intents and purposes, they were walking through the 1950s. The police line separating the marchers and the protestors is only one-deep and, towards the end of the film, an imposing gentleman in shades and a pork-pie hat talks back to the jeering whites, making 'come and get it' gestures and exploding in a rash of expletives.

Clearly, the concept of non-violence was fraying at the edges. The man of the moment was not Martin Luther King but Stokely Carmichael, whose national profile had grown and grown since June. While King retreated after the comparative failure of Chicago, Carmichael, on the other hand, was revelling in his new-found fame, spreading the word in a non-stop series of speeches and television appearances. 'No other man,' wrote the historian Lerone Bennett in an *Ebony* profile, 'with the possible exception of Martin Luther King, has risen so far so fast.'

It was a confusing period for the twenty-five-year-old, who was both analytical and impulsive. On the one hand he had become a celebrity, meeting the likes of Muhammad Ali and delivering his vision to enthusiastic audiences. On the other, the attention that he received was drawing him into uncharted territory, where fame elided with notoriety, where provocation was matched by an even stronger reaction. But Carmichael couldn't stop himself either. Sometimes it seemed that he was acting up to his public portrayal.

In August, he urged blacks to refuse military induction in two major speeches – in Detroit and Harvard University – and then went on the nationally syndicated TV show *Meet the Press* to spread the message, stating that America's involvement in the war was immoral. This was heartfelt and very much to the point, as the percentage of black draftees was far higher than their white counterparts, but it was also red rag to a bull, bearing in mind that the majority of Americans still supported the war.

It seemed as though Carmichael's slight, feline frame had become a lightning rod for America's fault lines: white versus black prejudice, urban riot, the Vietnam war – all the violence of a toxic society. On 16 September, he was released on bail, accused of inciting a riot at a demonstration in Atlanta; that same day, the 1966 Civil Rights Bill was defeated in Congress – the victim of a filibuster by the Republican minority leader, Senator Everett Dirksen. It was the first legislation of this nature to fail in nine years.

In early October, *Time* reported on a Gallup poll that logged considerable 'resistance of whites to improving the lot of Negroes': '52% of them think that the Administration is pushing integration "too fast" – as against only 32% when the first survey was conducted in 1962'. As if to confirm this shift of power, the same issue had a cover story on 'California's Governorship Race', with an idealised portrait of Ronald Reagan – the new rising star of the Right.

In autumn 1966, Reagan was on the crest of a wave. He was a sharp, elusive operator, cannily avoiding questions about his right-wing affiliations while promoting a classic laissez-faire agenda. He directly addressed public concerns about the apparently unravelling social fabric, speaking out passionately against rising crime levels, moral turpitude – epitomised by the 'beatniks, radicals and

filthy speech advocates' at the University of California, Berkeley
– and the riots that seemed to be spreading through the cities of
the state. Reagan stood for old-fashioned values: the right of business to be unimpeded, the rule of law and order and, above all,
patriotism. In his eyes, student protestors were, quite simply, un-
American and treasonous. He did not speak for the young but for
their parents, the large number of middle-aged Americans who had
either served or lived through the war, and had participated in the
country's great expansion during the 1950s. This generation could
not understand why a section of their young did not want to offer
themselves as cannon fodder for an undeclared war.

Nor could they understand why, now that blacks were getting
some recognition of their civil rights, they were demanding more
and more. In turn, Reagan was not concerned with the black vote:
a March 1966 debate with black Republicans – supposedly on his
team – was a near disaster, with the candidate storming off stage
after his opponent, George Christopher, invoked against him the
spirit of Barry Goldwater and, by implication, his John Birch
Society affiliations. This was a rare crack in an otherwise seamless
facade.

As the year continued, these positions would become ever more
entrenched. The spiral of escalation was unstoppable: neither side
could understand each other, and the lack of comprehension turned,
on the one hand, to the desire for repression and, on the other, to
the desire for ever greater assertion. The twinned genies of Black
Power and White Backlash were on the loose and, in mid-October,
the pressure was ratcheted up a further notch by the publication
of an extraordinary manifesto called 'What We Want, What We
Believe'.

It was the product of two Oakland natives, Bobby Seale and
Huey Newton. Both were in their late twenties and both had been
involved in black politics since the early sixties, most recently in
the Marxist Soul Students Advisory Council. Both had had a hard-
scrabble upbringing marked by poverty, family violence and confrontations with authority; both had pulled themselves up by their

own efforts and attended college, during which time they developed a theoretical framework to focus their anger at everyday American racism.

Influenced by the Revolutionary Action Movement, which held that the struggle for black American rights was part of the global struggle against imperialism and that black Americans should not serve in the war, they began to protest about Vietnam. At the same time, they were inspired by the activities of two local Oakland activists, Mark Comfort and Curtis Lee Baker, who were advocating the use of militant styles – black berets and black uniforms – to project discipline and counter police brutality.

Newton and Seale's anger was crystallised by the events in Hunters Point and the perennial police pressure in Oakland. Newton was inspired by an August 1966 article in the *Movement*, the West Coast SNCC paper, which reported the activities of a Community Alert Patrol in Watts. The CAP had begun driving round the area to monitor police brutality and, in August, began to display a Black Panther logo on their vehicles. Their mood was not conciliatory: as one CAP member told the *Movement*, 'There's only one way to stop all this, and that's to get out our guns and start shooting.'

Newton and Seale decided to form their own patrols in communities like Richmond, Berkeley and Oakland, but first they needed what Newton called 'a practical course of action'. As he wrote in his autobiography, 'We could go no further without a program, and we resolved to drop everything else, even if it might take a while to come up with something viable. One day, we went to the North Oakland Service Centre to work it out. The Center was an ideal place because of the books and the fact we could work undisturbed.' It took twenty minutes.

'The Black Panther Party Platform and Program' was heavily influenced by Malcolm X and Stokely Carmichael, but it went further than any black activist manifesto had gone before, particularly in the sections that began 'I believe', which cited 'the slaughter of over fifty million Black people' by 'the American racist' and the blanket refusal to fight in the military. But buried in the sixth point was the time bomb, as Newton and Seale wrote: 'We will protect ourselves against the force and violence of the racist police and the racist military, by whatever means necessary.'

* * *

'Amsterdam, London, San Francisco – not Copenhagen – are where the action is.'
DAVE ROTHLOP, letter to *The Psychedelic Oracle* issue 2, October 1966

The Hunters Point disturbances reverberated through San Francisco. The Fillmore district was right at ground zero as the unrest spread to other black communities in the city, and the Haight hippies found themselves in the middle of a riot zone. Gene Sculatti remembers leaving a Muddy Waters/Paul Butterfield/Jefferson Airplane show at the Fillmore at two in the morning to find 'the surrounding neighborhood in flames, cops in cruisers, rioters and panicked neighbors in the streets. We gave a lift to a couple of scared kids.'

The Fillmore Auditorium was an island of sanity amid the turmoil. 'Huge rubber balloons were being bounced round the dance floor like giant basket balls,' Ralph Gleason wrote. Muddy Waters was 'smiling and playing like his heart and his life depended on it. It was beautiful. He was beautiful, and later, when the Butterfield band played, Mike Bloomfield and Elvin Bishop were in the same mood, playing as if possessed by a mission. They all heard the call this weekend. Art vs. force and violence. And they responded.'

It was a crucial time for the San Franciscan 'Youth Quake'. The level of activity from within the subculture was increasing, just at the moment when it was beginning to get national attention. At the same time, many of the participants, who had radical and civil rights backgrounds, were galvanised by the events at Hunters Point and, nearer to home, in the Fillmore district. Quite apart from any interracial solidarity, the police oppression directed at the black community could also be turned against the city's increasing number of alienated young bohemians.

The *Oracle* caught the mood in its favoured beat prose style: 'About five in the afternoon a slowly cruising squad car did an angry u-turn &, with 5 gun barrels pointed out its windows, stopped its swerve abruptly in front of a young long-haired bearded man with yellow boots & a blonde, long-haired girl. "Get off this street, boy – NOW," "git", another voice from within, and a mumbled – "damn niggers," for the boy was brown skinned and he and his fair maid were on Haight & Ashbury on a sunny afternoon.'

With their radical backgrounds and desire for community involvement, members of the Mime Troupe, the Artists Liberation Front and the Diggers got involved in protests against the police action. On Saturday the 29th, while the disturbances were still raging, over ninety people were arrested at a Students for a Democratic Society march against the deployment of the National Guard. Later that night, two members of the Diggers, Billy Murcott and Emmett Grogan, put up posters on Haight Street urging people to defy the curfew but to avoid confrontation.

The next day, the group published one of its very first leaflets. 'A-Political Or, Criminal Or Victim Or Or Or . . .' was a scathing attack on American society, given extra impetus by the fact that areas of inner San Francisco had been turned into a war zone, with an occupying army:

You're born a citizen of a nation.

A citizen of a nation with rulers who legislate rules commanding you to be free.

Free to be conditioned in school until you're sixteen.

Free to be a compulsory soldier.

Free to pay sixty percent of your taxes to the military budget.

Free to get legally married.

Free to work for a minimum wage.

Free to vote when you're twenty-one.

Free to vote for the democratic or republican party of your choice.

Free to buy clothes, food, and property from the 200 corporations which account for 45% of the total U.S. manufacturing in 1966.

Free to obey arbitrary curfews.

Free to have your freedom regulated by officers who are your friends and who protect you.

The Diggers emerged out of the San Franciscan Mime Troupe and the Artists Liberation Front, radical groups that sought to involve the community in their artistic practices and, indeed, to break down the barriers between art and life. The Mime Troupe had been involved in the very beginning of the city's resurgent music scene. In late 1965, the Family Dog held two major shows to raise funds so that the Troupe could fight an obscenity bust; the second was held at the Fillmore Auditorium, and was promoted by the Troupe's business manager, Bill Graham.

During the summer, the Mime Troupe had performed various original productions, including the pointed *Search and Seizure*, a one-act play written by Peter Berg about the police harassment of drug-takers. Featuring Emmett Grogan, Kent Minault and others, it was put on at the Matrix, alongside performances by Country Joe and the Fish. In mid-July, the ALF put on a benefit at the Fillmore Auditorium, during which the Sopwith Camel played and Allen Ginsberg read from his new poem, 'Wichita Vortex Sutra'.

The Diggers emerged out of this ferment. Inspired by the Provos, Grogan, his old friend Billy Murcott, Kent Minault, Peter Berg and others began discussions on how they could affect and shape this new community. As Grogan later wrote in his memoir, *Ringolevio*, 'They decided to get things real by challenging the street people with the conclusions arrived at during these informal Digger sessions. They mimeographed their thoughts, using a different color paper for each set of leaflets, which soon became known as the Digger Papers.'

The name came from the group of British radicals who, led by Gerrard Winstanley, had argued for the redistribution of land affected by the enclosures – Acts of Parliament that, beginning in the early seventeenth century, placed common land into private hands. During 1649–50, they led by example, cultivating the fields thus owned by the rich and issuing pamphlets and broadsides that castigated the unholy power structure of the Church, landowners and 'the sin of property'.

Three centuries later, the nascent San Franciscan group were inspired by this fusion of utopian thought and practical action. Propelled by the Provos, they developed their own harshly sarcastic style, together with a taste for both confrontation and the origination of inspired, out-of-the-box action. Their anger was directed not only at mainstream American society, but at the hip merchants of Haight Street and the 'psychedelic transcendentalism' promoted by Timothy Leary, Richard Alpert and their disciples, which the Diggers thought to be false consciousness.

In early October, under the pressure of riot, curfew and police pressure, all these strands began to wind together: radical politics, street action, utopian visions and new music. On the first day of the month, the Artists Liberation Front held their first Free Fair in the Mission, which featured comedian Dick Gregory, a children's dance troupe and various local rock groups. The next day, the ALF delivered a black coffin to San Francisco's City Hall, with the legend 'Another 16-Year Old', in a protest against the police shooting of Matthew Johnson.

During that weekend, Stewart Brand and others organised the Awareness Festival – also known as 'Whatever It Is' – in the grounds of San Francisco State University. This was a three-day Acid Test by any other name – and, indeed, it featured an unannounced appearance by the fugitive Ken Kesey. Featuring the

Grateful Dead and Ron Boise's Thunder Machines, as well as various audience participation events and Happenings, it climaxed with a *War of the Worlds*-style simulation of a Russian nuclear attack.

On Thursday 6 October, LSD became illegal under Californian law. The Haight celebrated this fact with an event called the 'Love Pageant Rally'. The event was trailed in the eighth issue of *Mojo Navigator* with a new drug-takers' declaration of independence: 'We hold these experiences to be self-evident, that all is equal, that the creation endows us with certain inalienable rights, that amongst these are: the freedom of body, the pursuit of joy, and the expansion of consciousness.'

To combat 'the fear addiction of the general public as symbolised in this law', the organisers urged attendees of the free festival, held in the Panhandle area of Golden Gate Park, to bring 'THE COLOR GOLD', 'PICTURES OF PERSONAL SAINTS AND GURUS AND HEROES OF THE UNDERGROUND', 'CHILDREN . . . BANDS . . . BEADS . . . INCENSE . . . CHIMES . . . GONGS . . . CYMBALS . . . SYMBOLS . . . COSTUMES'. A sound stage was set up, and several groups played, including the Grateful Dead, Big Brother and the Holding Company, and the Wildflower.

The *Oracle* caught the mood of this formative occasion: 'Dancing on the greensward to the Grateful Dead's electronic music. What sort of world is this? Whose world is this? . . . Six hundred to a thousand young souls (an educated guess) dancing with brave banners waving over their looney heads. Posters and placards in evidence. The one I loved best said: THE TRULY INSANE ARE HELPLESS!' The crowd gathered together to 'lay down their gentle message, loud and clear. LOVE.'

Idealism and openness was built into the San Francisco music scene, not just through its close connections to radical action and artistic practice but also from the locations where the music was heard. As the groups played parks and ballrooms, a definite space began to enter their sound, a frontier kind of expansiveness and looseness that can still be heard in early records by the Jefferson Airplane and Big Brother, as well as live tapes from the period by the Grateful Dead and the Oxford Circle.

Sometime during the week of the Love Pageant Rally, the Diggers began their most fondly remembered action: the distribution of Free Food to the young and needy of the Haight-Ashbury district. The exact date is a matter of some dispute, but it is thought to have taken place on or around 6 October. It began when the Diggers produced a leaflet that advised: 'BRING A BOWL AND SPOON TO THE PANHANDLE AT ASHBURY STREET 4PM 4PM 4PM 4PM FREE FOOD EVERYDAY FREE FOOD IT'S FREE BECAUSE IT'S YOURS!' This was an extremely practical solution to the number of young bohemians and runaways who were flocking to the Haight, many of whom had come without any visible means of support. Free Food was a shining example of self-help and commitment to the idea of a self-sustaining community that did things differently to the acquisitive, materialistic American mainstream. The Diggers merely sourced the overflow from markets and food stores; the material was already discarded, and so they turned garbage into sustenance.

It was immediately popular, attracting fifty to a hundred people right from the first day. The Diggers continued the Free Food idea every day, begging out-of-date vegetables and meat off-cuts, collecting day-old bread from local bakers and discreetly pilfering what they were not given. It was, as Charles Perry observed, an updated version of 'the various hustles the Beats had practised', and it also fitted right into the utopian notions that were swirling around San Francisco and that gave the community some moral backbone.

The Diggers compounded this by continuing to issue their broadsides at the same time as they remained anonymous. The point was not to gain kudos in their own patch but to do something that combined practicality with idealism. The idea of Free went against the materialism of high-sixties America, which the Diggers saw reflected even amongst the supposedly enlightened people in the Haight. As they wrote in the pamphlet called 'When Will They All Hear the Death of Lenny Bruce?':

When will TIMOTHY LEARY stand on a streetcorner waiting for no one?

When will the JEFFERSON AIRPLANE and all ROCK-GROUPS quit trying to make it and LOVE?

The week after the Love Pageant Rally and the beginning of Free Food, the ALF held another free festival in the Panhandle. This time, according to *Mojo Navigator*, 'bands appearing were the Quicksilver Messenger Service, the Grateful Dead, Country Joe and the Fish. It was a fine affair on a warm afternoon and a good crowd of people was present.' This was followed by a Family Dog dance at the Avalon, which showcased the Sir Douglas Quintet, the Oxford Circle and the 13th Floor Elevators – 'a really freaky group. They look strange, and sound strange.'

During mid-October, *Newsweek*'s young reporter Hendrik Hertzberg spent time in San Francisco researching an article about the city's music scene. He concluded that it was a coherent community, with its own newspapers, venues, graphics and very particular sound. It wasn't just a way of making money; it was a whole lifestyle. Hertzberg was impressed by its uniqueness: 'It is a sound and a scene that might sweep the country. Or it might not. San Francisco is a very special kind of city, and things happen here that could never happen anywhere else.'

The idea that youth culture should engage with the local community was also a facet of the London underground as it developed during summer 1966. Since its early beginnings in the spring, the London Free School had succeeded in developing contacts in the Ladbroke Grove area, most notably Michael X, a Trinidadian fixer who had a chequered past as one of slum landlord Peter Rachman's henchmen, and the nurse and activist Rhuane Laslett, who lived on Tavistock Gardens, right at the epicentre.

Breaking down the barriers was an explicit part of the London

Free School's utopian mission. As Pink Floyd manager Peter Jenner remembers, it was 'trying to provide an education which would open people's eyes to the realities of the world, and in a broader sense, politicise them. It was about people who had not been given a proper education, by people who had had a proper education, but had also realised how silo-ised it was, and in a sense you weren't allowed to join up the dots. The people in the London Free School were trying to join up some of the dots.'

The idea slowly gained traction over the summer. In May, Muhammad Ali – in London for a heavyweight title bout – visited Rhuane Laslett's home. It was a huge boost for the local youth, who had one of their heroes right on their doorstep. Laslett had been 'a notable figure' in the community since the late 1950s, the era of the Mosley riots, and had helped to set up an adventure playground in the land laid waste by the construction of the Westway. She also established a twenty-four-hour legal-advice service for local residents, the homeless and recent immigrants. Jenner remembers her as 'quite bossy and tough. She was a social worker, trying to stimulate self-respect, self-assertion.' In the mid-sixties, Laslett, who was part Native American, part Russian, had a strange dream: 'I could see the streets thronged with people in brightly coloured costumes, they were dancing and following bands and they were happy, some faces I recognised, but more were crowds, men, women, children, black, white, brown, but all laughing.' This vision was shared by members of the London Free School, who helped to make it happen.

In the *Grove* magazine of 23 June, the announcement was made: 'September 1966 will be a landmark in Notting Hill. For the first time this century . . . Notting Hill will have its own Fair or Fayre.' The whole idea was to bring a poor but diverse community together. As Laslett stated in *Grove*, 'We felt that although West Indians, Africans, Irish and many other nationalities all live in a very congested area, there is very little communication between us. If we can infect them with a desire to participate then this can only have good results.'

In September, things came together quickly. 'Notting Hill in

'66 seemed particularly fertile ground,' says photographer John Hopkins. 'There were a few things that came out of the Free School. The Notting Hill Carnival is one of them, although you can't ever pin it down to one person, or even one group of people. It was more like how the White Nile and the Blue Nile flow side by side and eventually mix. That sort of process. I think the way society is organised induces people to think in a linear, causal way, whereas life is actually a bit more unpredictable than that.'

In the early to mid-month, various DIAS actions were performed in the Portobello Road bomb site found by Michael X. Two musicians affiliated to the LFS, Dave Tomlin and Joe Gannon, also led small processions down the Portobello Road to promote the Fayre – variously known as the Festival and the Carnival – which was scheduled to last from Sunday the 18th to Sunday the 25th. Primarily intended as a children's event, it quickly attracted large crowds of locals, attracted by the sound of Russ Henderson and his steel band combo.

This was the beginning of the Notting Hill Carnival in its present form: a large annual event, full of music and costume, that processes through the stucco of North Kensington in a way that defies English ideas of privacy. 'It was all about the Trinidadians,' says Peter Jenner. 'There were a lot of them in Notting Hill. I think the various islands went to different parts. Over there, it was Trinidadians. Around Powis Square. Michael X was Trinidadian. So, in a sense, Carnival was a manifestation of Trinidadian culture.'

Five days after the Fayre, the LFS held a benefit in a small hall at All Saints Church, a large Gothic edifice close to Portobello Road. As Jenner remembers, 'We needed to raise some money for the new year at London Free School, and whenever you needed to raise a bit of money, you put on a whist drive or a social. So I said, "We should do a social, and we've got this band, they'll do it for us." And we went around to the local vicar, who rented us the church hall. We just passed the word around, and there was probably only about a hundred to a hundred and fifty people there.'

The featured group was the Pink Floyd, and this was their

first show with their new management team, Andrew King and Peter Jenner. The group had played several of Steve Stollman's Spontaneous Underground events at the Marquee and, on 12 June 1966, Jenner saw them and decided to get involved. 'Through the Fugs, which were avant-garde, and the Stollman connection, they put on the thing where I saw the Floyd. It was a Happening at the Marquee. So I thought, "That's great. We had the label, we need some avant-garde pop music."'

In June 1966, John Hopkins and Jenner had recorded an album with the improvisational group AMM. Featuring Keith Rowe on guitar, Lou Gare on saxophone, Lawrence Sheaff on bass and Cornelius Cardew on piano and cello, AMM were rigorous: there were no rehearsals, no discussions; each performance was unique. Every instrument was subordinate to the whole sound, which was further blurred by the use of non-musical objects – coins, knives, a transistor radio. This was a new language.

Two tracks were recorded, named and timed simply so that they would fit on two sides of an album. Despite the lack of traditional hooks – melody, highlighted instrumentation, a regular beat – there is something both delicate and involving about the first side, a prolonged drone. It sounds like an evolving thought process as it percolates and takes shape. 'After Rapidly Circling the Plaza' begins more like a free jazz piece but, even with its sheets of sound, it sounds considered and reflective, not scattered but disciplined – a rare trick in improvisational music.

Part of that had to do with the way the group was set up. As Keith Rowe told Daniel Warburton in 2001, 'The start of AMM was quite a complex chemistry of ideas, ideas deriving from Gurdjieff, Taoism, Buddhism. I studied under a Buddhist monk called Sangharakshita, I studied form, perception, meditation . . . I wanted to be able to walk into a space and immediately comprehend what the space was about. To be able to talk to you now and have part of my brain listening to what that coffee machine is doing or what that person is saying over there.'

'The album was called *Extracts from a Continuous Performance*,' says Jenner, 'which was all about, what was the difference between music and noise. We got a deal from Elektra for AMM which was absolutely appalling, but at least they let it happen and it came out. But there was no way we could even pay recording costs, let alone pay the artists, let alone earn any money, without having huge successful records, like the Beatles. So I had to have a pop band, and that's how I ended up listening to the Floyd and saying, "I now have a pop band for DNA Records."'

By early autumn 1966, the Pink Floyd were in flux. When Peter Jenner approached them about making a record, they told him that they'd talk more once they'd got back from their summer holidays. When they returned, fully expecting to resume their studies, they told him that they didn't want a record deal but a manager. Jenner teamed up with his old friend Andrew King, who had just left his job at British European Airways, where he was 'trying to write a brainwashing programme: his job was to try and get the staff to treat passengers like human beings!'

While the other three members went on their travels, the group's singer and guitarist, Syd Barrett, was writing songs in his flat at Earlham Street, near Cambridge Circus. Jenner remembers encouraging Barrett to write more: 'Syd liked all the avant-garde music. He'd go and listen to Keith Rowe, and he had the relentless, musical, enquiring mind. And he had his book of songs. I'd seen that the really successful bands wrote their own songs. Buddy Holly, Beatles, Stones, Everly Brothers. You don't need another band playing "Dust My Broom" and "Louie Louie".'

On 14 October, the Pink Floyd appeared again at All Saints Hall, playing a mixture of Bo Diddley covers and originals, most of them composed by Barrett, including 'Lucy Leave', 'Stoned Alone', 'Let's Roll Another One' and several that would appear on their first LP: 'Astronomy Domine', 'The Gnome', 'Interstellar Overdrive', 'Snowing' (later known as 'Flaming') and 'Matilda Mother'. Roger Waters contributed 'Take Up Thy Stethoscope and Walk', while the group composed 'Pow R. Toc H.', a reference to army signallers' code.

These songs were a fusion of free jazz, the Byrds and Love. Jenner remembers the impact of the latter's 'My Little Red Book': 'I thought it was a terrific record. I don't think it was available in England then. Maybe Joe Boyd had given it to me. I was talking about it to Syd, and I hummed it to him. I'm not the world's most musical person, and my mishearing of it led to Syd writing "Interstellar Overdrive". That's always remained with me, thinking about all this fucking crap about copyright: the idea that it's all unique flashes of genius. I really do think that musicians channel the culture.

'There was always the connection with America, with the Fugs' people,' he continues, 'but the connection was always with the East Coast. We didn't have the connection with the West Coast. We never heard any San Franciscan music. Love and the Fugs, they were it. I don't think I ever listened to the Fugs' records much, but we liked the fact that it was breaking lots of rules and they put it out themselves. It was a manifestation of our stuff in a way, as subsequently with Warhol, doing it himself. What was important was the fact that the Fugs existed.'

At the 14 October show, the group played long improvisations, during which Syd Barrett, taking a leaf out of Keith Rowe's book, explored the different textures that he could get out of his guitar. In this, he and organist Rick Wright were assisted by the Binson Echorec unit, described by Rob Chapman as 'a pre-pedal echo unit powered by valves and driven by tape heads'. Enhancing tape delay and reverb, it allowed them to echo almost to infinity and then to play against the loop, spiralling off into subtle textures and flights of exploration.

On the flyer for the event, the group were presented as 'London's Furthest Out Group' playing numbers from 'their space age book'. Also billed were 'Light Projection Slides' and 'Liquid Movies', and these were provided by a light show that, for the first two performances, was run by Joel and Toni Brown, two American visitors from Millbrook, Timothy Leary's League for Spiritual Discovery. Very little information had percolated over

429

from the West Coast, but the idea of a synaesthetic environment was in the air.

Even at this stage, the concerns of the British underground were different from those of its American counterpart. In autumn 1966, Emily Young was fifteen. She managed to get into the All Saints Hall show and remembered Syd Barrett having 'a spark that was magnetic. He was incredibly alive, and dripping with that sense of being arty and creative. He was very attractive to be near, a Pan-like character, a creator of the forest. He looked other-worldly, and had this wildness, this quality of not being urban. He had a sense of English wildness.'

None of the Pink Floyd were politically oriented, nor were they particularly enthusiastic drug-takers, except for Barrett, and his experiences had been mainly confined to smoking marijuana. Sometime in spring 1966, he took LSD for the first time, and it had a profound effect on his consciousness, liberating him to write a sequence of songs that, in their mixture of space exploration, nature worship and disturbing psychological undertones, shaped the concerns of the subculture building around the London Free School.

'I think nearly all the songs that Syd is recognised for were written in 1966,' says Peter Jenner. Certainly, Barrett developed quickly from the fairly conventional 'Lucy Leave' to the cosmic flights of 'Interstellar Overdrive'. 'The Gnome' switched from a third-person narrative to a direct address: 'Look at the sky, look at the river, isn't it good?' And, on 'Matilda Mother', he dived deep down into the rabbit hole of childhood fears and feelings, a well-spring opened up by John Lennon's recent declaration on 'She Said She Said': 'When I was a boy, everything was right.'

'He was very into Lewis Carroll, Hilaire Belloc, A. A. Milne,' Jenner says, 'all these traditional English children's stories, often quite weird and bleak, and there's a strong element in there. Even perhaps Beatrix Potter. It's a reversion to childhood, isn't it? Those were the good days, and now it's a bit more complicated somehow. There's a lot of that in Syd's writing. And a lot of tragedy, in terms of parents being killed in the war, certainly Roger's were. Looking back to when things were good and, on the other hand, looking to a cosmic future.

'I think it goes back further to the First World War and the thirties. One's parents came out of a horrible fucking existence. The First World War was a catastrophe, and then the chaos of the twenties and thirties. My mother told me she had been walking down the street when she was pregnant with me and she saw a bus hit by a bomb, and she saw a head rolling down the street. She thought that was why I was born with club feet. She was so traumatised by it, she thinks that was why I had bad feet. I mean, can you imagine? A fucking head rolling down the street.'

At the same time as it began to address buried traumas, the art and politics of the new underground were, in Jenner's words, looking forward to 'building a new Jerusalem. I think we were the last generation, in a way, still hoping to build the new world. Our world was free love and drugs and rock 'n' roll, and alternative societies, being ourselves. It wasn't Marx, particularly, it certainly wasn't the cold war. The nuclear paranoia was huge. The implicit thing was that we had to build a new world before we got blown up.'

On the night after their second All Saints show, the Pink Floyd played at the *International Times* First All-Night Rave, at the Roundhouse, a former British Railways building in Chalk Farm. 'It was filthy,' Jenner remembers. 'The thing was, there was no real power in there, so all through the power kept going out. The trip switches were going, all the way through. The place was absolutely packed. There were no lights, except on the stage. The odd bulb scattered around. And all the hippies were milling around. Everyone who was in the underground at that time was there.'

This was a multimedia event. Films by Kenneth Anger and Antony Balch were projected alongside a light show, while Michelangelo Antonioni, Monica Vitti and Paul McCartney walked around. 'The big thing at the time about everything was, were the Beatles there?' says Jenner. 'Not the Stones. It was always the

Beatles. It was always Lennon and McCartney who were involved in the underground stuff. Possibly Brian Jones was, but he never had the salience of those two.'

Attendees were urged, in the customary spontaneous Happening way, to 'bring your own poison & flowers & gas filled balloons & submarines & rocket ship & candy & striped boxes & ladders & paint & flutes & ladders & locomotives & madness'. Around 2,000 people turned up. They were given sugar cubes at the door: placebos clearly intended to suggest an LSD trip. The Roundhouse was completely unsuited to a crowd of this size. During the evening, the two lavatories flooded out, creating a spreading pool of urine.

While the power flickered on and off, a new group called Soft Machine played, while Yoko Ono got onstage and encouraged the audience to touch each other. The Pink Floyd went on and, as the *International Times* reported, did 'weird things to the feel of the event with their scary feedback sounds, slide projections playing on their skins (drops of paint ran riot on the slides to produce outer-space/prehistoric textures on the skin), spotlights flashing in time with the drums'.

This was the coming-out ball of the underground, held to launch the *International Times*, a new magazine hot off the press. The idea that had begun in the spring with *THE Global moon-edition Long Hair TIMES* had finally come to fruition in a biweekly tabloid that aimed to crystallise the London underground. Barry Miles and John Hopkins were involved, but it was edited by Tom McGrath, who was not sympathetic to the West Coast scene and 'resisted any whole-hearted move in that direction'.

This was apparent in the first issue, which was soberly laid out, in black and white type, without the mandalas and drug-inspired spirals that peppered the pages of the *Oracle*. It looked like what, to a considerable degree, it was: a serious arts magazine with articles about the activities of the Red Guards in China, Peter Brook's anti-Vietnam play *US*, the Warsaw International Festival of Music, Yoko Ono's forthcoming one-woman show at Indica, and the recent DIAS symposium. Closer inspection, however, revealed frivolity and generation-specific concerns. There was an 'Interpot Report' with the latest international updates on busts and drug availability. And a third of the front page was taken up by a large logo, *it*, placed next to a bleached representation of Theda Bara, the famous 1910s vamp. Even in the midst of forward motion, there was time warp; in this case, however, it was inaccurate. As Barry Miles admits, they had wanted to print a picture of the original It girl, Clara Bow, but they got it wrong and used Theda Bara instead.

On the front cover, a long article, marked by the word 'YOU' printed upside down, announced the magazine's break with Swinging London, which 'isn't quite as switched on as our ad-men make out. Things are happening all over the city, but there is a lack of togetherness: if you're on the jazz scene it's unlikely you'll be much in touch with what's going on in the art world, and vice versa. And, whatever scene you're on, with the possible exception of the pop music explosion, you're likely to discover that things aren't happening quite like they should.'

The editorial continued with a call to action and a warning: 'We're not going to make any false claims on London's behalf – although we will boost anything that is moving somewhere and encourage others to move with it. But more than what it tells you about this paper, it brings you up against a basic problem: if you decide you want to change things at base, you are taking on governments, you are deciding to be your own government.' It ended with the ringing phrase 'Change begins with you.'

* * *

'There seem to be many parallels that can be drawn between treatment of Negroes and treatment of women in our society as a whole. But in particular, women we've talked to who work in the movement seem to be caught up in a common-law caste system that operates, sometimes subtly, forcing them to work around or outside hierarchical structures of power which may exclude them. Women seem to be placed in the same position of assumed

subordination in personal situations too. It is a caste system
which, at its worst, uses and exploits women.'
CASEY HAYDEN AND MARY KING, 'Sex and Caste: A Kind of
Memo', *Liberation* magazine, April 1966

In America, that autumn was a time of manifestos, of bold statements and renewed engagements, not just in youth culture but in
the other areas of society transformed by the civil rights movement.
It was as though, dammed up for so long, the demands of minor-
ities were bursting out in a tidal flood that would dominate the
shape of society for decades to come. Freedom was not partial, but
it was slow to arrive, and it was resisted at every stage. In turn,
this required tougher language, better considered programmes and
more accelerated calls to action. 'Forward' was the word.

In this phase, politics ran ahead of pop culture, but in October
there was a symbiosis between radical action and the various ideas
and images that were bubbling up, as if unbidden. Popular music
was, obviously, not designed as a political programme but, in the
mid-sixties, the music industry was not as controlled as Hollywood
or television. Success was still so random that all kinds of messages
were allowed to get through. Some went straight into the mainstream, while others pointed to the future.

The best-selling novel of 1966 was Jacqueline Susann's *Valley
of the Dolls*, which followed three women through the treacherous
rapids of the entertainment and media industries. It was, in part,
a morality tale about female dependency and the warping effect of
living in a man's world, spelt out in graphic descriptions of Seconal
addiction and 'doll' overdoses. The three friends, Anne, Neely and
Jennifer, are dependent on men, whether they like it or not, and
much of the time they bridle at this state of affairs.

The idea that women could be independent was trickling
through into prime-time TV. In September, ABC premiered a new
sitcom called *That Girl*. Starring Marlo Thomas as Anne Marie,
the series followed the adventures of an aspiring actress trying to
make her way in New York. Although she has a boyfriend, Anne

Marie is living on her own, which at the time was something new in television, even if most of the plot lines – like in the fifth episode, 'Anatomy of a Blunder', aired on 6 October – concerned social embarrassment and courtship rituals.

On the 8th, the Supremes were at #8 in the *Billboard* chart with the relentless 'You Can't Hurry Love', a tough, tuneful slice of romantic advice from mother to daughter. Five places down was the first hit from a young southerner, Sandy Posey. Produced by Chips Moman and recorded at American Studios in Memphis, 'Born a Woman' was released in March and, as was often the way with American records at the time, took seven months to reach its peak at #13. It was a strange, ambiguous song, oscillating between feistiness and subjection.

On 16 October, Grace Slick sang her first show with the Jefferson Airplane. It was a baptism of fire: the group's previous vocalist, Signe Toly Anderson, had left the night before and Slick had to plunge straight in. During a year with the Great!! Society!!, however, she had developed her own distinctive style of vocalising, sometimes cool, sometimes high and cutting. But things weren't coming fast enough for her and, when she was offered a place in Jefferson Airplane, she jumped.

Anderson had sung on the just-released album, *Takes Off*, but, as a mother with an infant, was unsuited to the working life of a busy musician. When she joined Jefferson Airplane, Grace was twenty-six, intense, strong-willed, to all intents and purposes unattached, and endowed with a mordant sense of humour and a debutante's confidence. Despite terrible nerves, she imposed her presence on the group that night, matching lead singer Marty Balin on 'Tobacco Road' and 'Bringing Me Down', and bringing an unexpected steely element to the sound.

In mid-October, Big Brother and the Holding Company released their first single, a group composition called 'Blind Man', backed with a version of 'All Is Loneliness' – a round by the blind street composer Louis Hardin, better known as Moondog. Both were recorded hurriedly and cheaply in Chicago that summer. The

A-side was muddy, routine folk rock. 'All Is Loneliness' was something else, however, a circular drone that began with what sounded like a Jew's harp and opened out to feature Janis Joplin's raspy, keening voice riffing on the title word, 'loneliness'.

Joplin was a compelling performer. Her voice sliced through the group's *Sturm und Drang*, while her vulnerability was well hidden under a tough facade. By October, Big Brother were one of the leading groups on the scene. 'The audience is getting bigger and bigger,' bassist David Getz told *Mojo Navigator*, 'there's really no limit to how big this thing could become, in this country.' Joplin was more direct: 'Something's gonna happen. It isn't just gonna go on. Something's gonna happen. Either we're all gonna go broke and split up, or get rich and famous.'

In the middle of the month, Motown released the Supremes' third single of the year. 'You Can't Hurry Love' was still in the Top 10, but 'You Keep Me Hangin' On' was intended as a 'one–two punch'. The track had been recorded in the summer, at the same time as 'You Can't Hurry Love', but was held back: a smart move, because it heightened the intensity that had been building in the Supremes' releases that year. Motown had long had a penchant for melodrama, and 'You Keep Me Hangin' On' winds it up tight and hard. The track begins in alarm: four guitars stacked in a Morse code-like pattern, intended, as Lamont Dozier recalled, to simulate 'the sound of a telegraph that you'd hear in an old movie'. It's bad news all the way, as the guitar riff continues and Ross – in a return to her customary lovelorn role – pleads for her man to let her go: 'Set me free, why don't you, baby / Get out of my life, why don't you, baby.' But what sticks in the mind is not victimhood but the toughness of lines like 'Why don't you get out of my life / And let me make a new start?'

'You Keep Me Hangin' On' entered the *Billboard* chart at #68 on 29 October, but clearly some women had had enough of simply asking for men to give them their freedom. On that day, the National Organisation of Women held a meeting in Washington DC attended by three hundred members, the official launch of an organisation that had begun in late June with the aim of taking 'the actions needed to bring women into the mainstream of American society now, exercising all the privileges and responsibilities thereof, in truly equal partnership with men'.

It was time, as Betty Friedan writes in her memoir *Life So Far*, for 'not just talk'. Despite all the lectures, the articles and even equal rights legislation, what was needed was a new organisation 'to speak on behalf of women'. As she remembered, 'I knew in my gut how important jobs were for all these women who could no longer plan to live an eighty-year life span as "just a housewife". And I knew it would take a revolution to move beyond the feminine mystique.'

On 29 October, the three hundred members of NOW – professionals all – agreed the full Statement of Purpose. It began with a simple statement: 'We believe the time has come to move beyond the abstract argument, discussion and symposia over the status and special nature of women which has raged in America in recent years; the time has come to confront, with concrete action, the conditions that now prevent women from enjoying the equality of opportunity and freedom of choice which is their right, as individual Americans, and as human beings.'

NOW aimed to 'break through the silken curtain of prejudice' against women. 'The actual position of women in the United States has declined, and is declining, to an alarming degree throughout the 1950's and '60s. Although 46.4% of all American women between the ages of 18 and 65 now work outside the home, the overwhelming majority – 75% – are in routine clerical, sales, or factory jobs, or they are household workers, cleaning women, hospital attendants. About two-thirds of Negro women workers are in the lowest paid service occupations.'

The statement criticised the lack of women in 'the executive ranks of industry and government', and bluntly stated that the provisions of the Civil Rights Act and the suggestions contained in 1965's President's Commission on the Status of Women had not been acted upon. 'We will protest, and endeavor to change, the false image of women now prevalent in the mass media, and in the texts, ceremonies, laws, and practices of our major social institutions. Such images perpetuate contempt for women by society and by women for themselves.'

This was a wide-ranging and ambitious programme, which ended with the belief 'that women will do most to create a new image of women by acting now, and by speaking out in behalf of their own equality, freedom, and human dignity – not in pleas for special privilege, nor in enmity toward men, who are also victims of the current, half-equality between the sexes – but in an active, self-respecting partnership with men'. 'I knew there were all these women out there waiting,' Friedan wrote. 'Now, finally, we were going to *act.*'

On the same day that NOW launched in Washington DC, Stokely Carmichael gave a major speech at the University of California, Berkeley. Appearing at a packed-out Greek Theatre, an 8,500-seat campus amphitheatre, he was dressed conservatively, in a suit and tie, and began with a moment of sly humour: 'Thank you very much. It's a privilege and an honor to be in the white intellectual ghetto of the West.' Even so, his address was stringent, as he delivered a blistering attack on the whole basis of American society.

On the 27th, Carmichael had presented himself at a pre-induction facility in New York for a final medical evaluation prior to military service. However, he was determined not to serve, and was prepared to hang the consequences. With this on his mind as he travelled to California, he failed to see that he was walking right into a trap. No doubt even if he had, he still would not have changed one comma of his speech, as the two diametrically opposed stars of American politics charged to meet each other head-on.

Stokely Carmichael and Berkeley: as far as the Reagan campaign team were concerned, it was almost too good to be true, as two of their candidate's bêtes noires combined together just ten days before mid-term polling day. Reagan's advisers prepared a brief that stated 'if the disorders boil into public prominence again, before the election, on balance it would be good for our campaign'. It behoved the candidate, in other words, to exploit the divisions and to ramp up his rhetoric.

On 18 October, Reagan had issued a public plea to Carmichael to cancel the appearance, stating it 'could possibly do damage to both parties'. This was not a request, more of a threat. His Democratic rival, Governor Pat Brown, immediately saw through the tactic, blaming Carmichael 'and his Black Power friends' for helping to elect Reagan: 'They don't want peaceful progress, they want panic in the streets and publicity. And Reagan serves their purposes by helping to give them both.'

Certainly, Carmichael was not one to back down from a challenge, and his Berkeley speech was a rip-snorter. He began by thoroughly trashing the tenets of the civil rights movement thus far: 'We maintain that in the past six years or so, this country has been feeding us a "thalidomide drug of integration".' The central part of his speech urged resistance against the Vietnam war: 'This country will only be able to stop the war in Vietnam when the young men who are made to fight it begin to say, "Hell, no, we ain't going."'

Black people, he concluded, were standing up for their liberation. 'We are tired of trying to explain to white people that we're not going to hurt them. We are concerned with getting the things we want, the things that we have to have to be able to function. The question is, can white people allow for that in this country? The question is, will white people overcome their racism and allow for that to happen in this country? If that does not happen, brothers and sisters, we have no choice but to say very clearly, "Move over, or we're going to move on over you." Thank you.'

Carmichael designed the speech as a major intervention on a big stage, and he succeeded. As his biographer Peniel E. Joseph writes, 'This galvanic address, carried by newspapers across the nation, made him America's leading critic of the Vietnam War.' It spurred on the white activists at Berkeley to resist the war in greater numbers, and gave an extra impetus to Bobby Seale and Huey Newton to put their programme in action and organise the Black Panthers as a viable, radical Black Power group.

After the speech, Carmichael visited Haight-Ashbury and partied with white friends and colleagues. If he had expressly designed it, he could not have woven together more thoroughly all the elements in America that restive middle-aged citizens – the large cohort that Richard Nixon later called 'the silent majority' – loathed and, indeed, blamed for all the country's ills. Ronald Reagan had already pledged 'to get to the bottom of the Berkeley mess', and, thanks in part to the narrative that he had shaped, the voters would soon give him a mandate to do exactly that.

THE SOUL PARADE

JAMES BROWN

WILSON PICKETT

SUPREMES

THE ALAN BOWN SET

FORTY CENTS   NOVEMBER 18, 1966

TIME

ROMNEY

PERCY

REAGAN

ROCKEFELLER

VOL 88 NO. 21

YOU KEEP ME HANGIN' ON
REMOVE THIS DOUBT

THE SUPREMES

SEPIA   LSD
MONSTER OR MIRACLE?

NOVEMBER 1966 35¢

LSD carries its users to a world of fantasies and nightmares

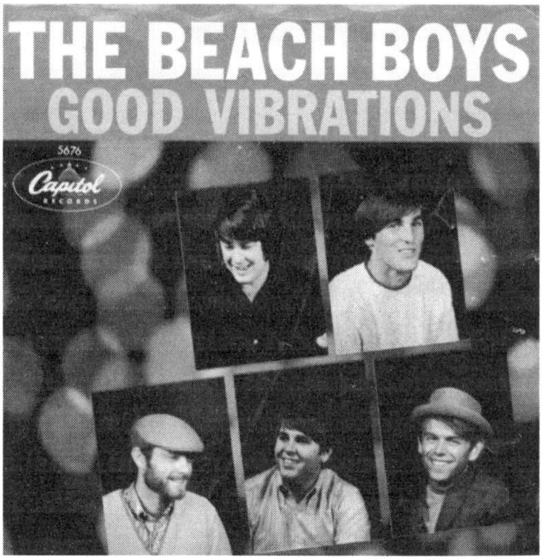

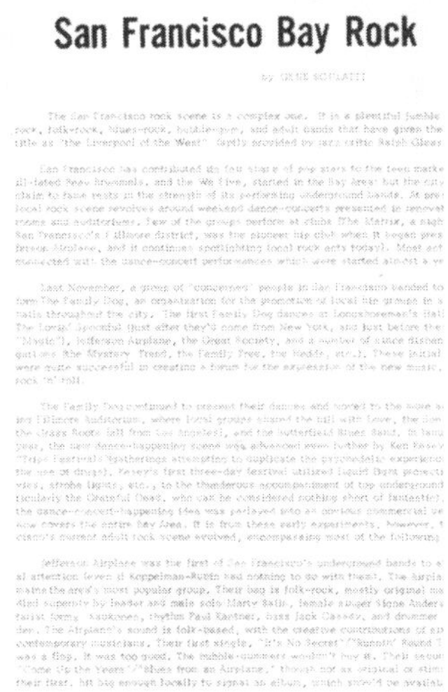
San Francisco Bay Rock

11 : NOVEMBER

Good Vibrations: Motown and Soul in the UK, the Beach Boys and the Sunset Strip

'It is way off beam to say that fans of R and B and Soul say it is the colour of a star's skin that brings the elusive "soul" quality. Anyone who has seen opera performed with sensitivity and skill will agree that the depth of emotion and feeling doesn't particularly hinge on the singer's past suffering, but on his dramatic ability and acting power. We do maintain, however, that because American Negroes can only enter the entertainment field, and are denied opportunities to enter other fields, this pent-up talent will dominate the one area where they are allowed artistic expression.'

DAVE GODIN, letter to *Record Mirror*, 26 November 1966

On 1 November, Britain had a new #1. The morbid miasma of 'Distant Drums' had finally been dispelled, on 26 October, by a record so strong and so unexpected that it hit the country with all the force of a hurricane. The Four Tops' 'Reach Out I'll Be There' had received unprecedented pre-release raves earlier in the month: it was 'a knockout disc', 'the most important record of the year'. Penny Valentine went even further: 'If you have ever been lonely, if you have any soul or any heart at all, you must go and buy this disc now.'

The record begins with a flute fanfare, part ominous, part Near Eastern; a clicking rhythm guitar and rumbling bass set up a fast, syncopated rhythm. Levi Stubbs enters, near the top of his range, singing lyrics that gave the year's dark preoccupations an entirely different spin: 'And your life is filled with much confusion / Until happiness is just an illusion.' Underscored by the Tops' wordless exclamation under the first line, the song has an incredible forward drive, so much so that it dispenses with a middle eight in the headlong quest for resolution.

Poised between negativity (the verses) and reassurance (the chorus), the emotional switch-back of 'Reach Out I'll Be There' demanded a full-blooded vocal and, after a decade of making records, Levi Stubbs delivered the performance of his life. You can hear the strain during the verses, as he drags out the phrasing, before emitting the briefest of exclamations – 'Hah' – as he dives into the chorus: 'I'll be there to love and comfort you.'

Sixties singles were designed for maximum impact. Whether it was a different vocal trick, added instrumentation or a key change, something had to happen in each verse that developed the intensity over two to three minutes. Most Motown artists were experts at ad-libbing, and in 'Reach Out I'll Be There' Stubbs bridges the verse and chorus with an extra 'reach out'. His voice cracks slightly, before he interjects 'Just look over your shoulder!' and the track explodes into the final chorus and fade.

'Reach Out I'll Be There' had the 'wow' factor, not least because it was a radical departure from the usual Motown sound. It wasn't just the lyric but the whole torque of the record. 'Dylan was happening at the time,' co-writer Lamont Dozier told author Marc Weingarten, 'and the phrasing for "I'll Be There" came from the way he sang. He'd do that thing (sings), "Heyy", and "Heyy", and "Heoww", where he'd drag a phrase out, that I liked. The day we wrote it, I just began mumbling: "Now if you feel that you can't go on, because your hope is gone . . ."'

Released in August after some internal disagreements, 'Reach Out I'll Be There' reached #7 in the US charts in early October. The company was hitting an absolute peak, driven on by Berry Gordy's injunction to his staff, issued in early July, that 'we will release nothing less than Top Ten product on any artist. And, because the Supremes' worldwide acceptance is greater than the other artists, on them we will release only #1 records.'

The first demand might have been impossible, but 'You Can't Hurry Love' went to #1 in the US in September. 'Reach Out I'll Be There' then hit the top. In early November, as 'You Keep Me Hangin' On' was waiting in the wings, *KRLA Beat* noted what seemed like a conveyor belt: '1966 will undoubtedly be recorded as "The Year Of The Motown Sound" in pop history, as one after another of the Motown groups takes up residence in the Number One spot in the charts.'

On 15 October, the Four Tops' record entered the UK chart at #15. The week before, Tony Hall had predicted that 'Reach Out I'll Be There' would be the group's 'biggest success in Britain. It's certainly one of the most commercial records they've ever made . . . The whole approach is much more pop-conscious than anything I can remember coming out of Hitsville. In fact, I think there's a subtle change going on there. The Holland–Dozier–Holland team seems to have learned some new lessons. Perhaps from the British sound.'

Boosted by ecstatic reviews and constant pirate radio play, 'Reach Out I'll Be There' hurtled up the UK charts. The Four Tops became bona fide pop stars – a slightly bewildering state of affairs for the group. On the phone to Detroit, *Disc and Music Echo*'s Bob Farmer found them 'lazily swinging golf clubs on a local golf course, quite unconcerned that they have all America and England falling all over the place in ecstasy'. The article emphasised their married maturity: as Levi Stubbs admitted, 'We are an adult act that appeal to a large age-group.'

The Four Tops were overtaken by events. Bowled over by the record, Brian Epstein quickly booked them as the first major pop attraction at the West End theatre he had leased, the Savile. When the group flew in for the 13 November booking, they were interviewed by *Record Mirror*, who found them in an understandably ebullient mood. 'This is the most important record of our career,' they told Norman Jopling. 'We have been aiming for a number one record in Britain, and our writers and producers, Holland and Dozier, have been aiming for us too.'

Mindful of the Epstein connection, they talked about the Beatles: 'They've done a lot for pop music. Before the English sound invaded the American charts, U.S. pop music was very dead-beat. There was no real tuneful music and the whole thing was stagnant. The British groups, and especially the Beatles, brought a big revival to the scene. Some of the Beatle tunes featured real chord changes and were genuinely good musical tunes. Good music became accepted. Would "Michelle" have been a hit before the Beatles? Of course not.'

On 13 November, the atmosphere in the Savile Theatre was

electric. 'Tony Hall introduced the Four Tops to a roar that would not have disgraced a Wembley crowd,' wrote Penny Valentine. 'The ceiling lights nearly jumped out of their sockets, and then there they were, grinning, moving, full of their music – the people we had been waiting for so long to see. Our hearts were theirs before they stepped on stage. By the time they left, our hands, feet and lungs were theirs too.'

From his onstage vantage point, Tony Hall observed that he'd never seen a British audience 'behave in such a traditionally un-British manner. It was simply fantastic! . . . There's something about Motown music that alone evokes such emotion and enjoyment. It's today's sound. Today's spirit. Today's "feel".' After the shows, Brian Epstein held a party at his Belgravia house: the guests included George and Pattie Harrison, John and Cynthia Lennon, Mick Jagger, Charlie Watts, Donovan, Georgie Fame, Vicki Wickham, Tony Hall and Eric Burdon.

With one unstoppable record, the Four Tops had vaulted to the very top. For a short but intense moment, they were the toast of the town. In the continuing vacuum following the disappearance of the Beatles, there was a demand for new culture leaders to take their place in a pop market habituated to a dominant presence. Dusty Springfield commented on this in November: 'There is absolutely no definite trend on the British music scene. But then it is hard to say what constitutes a trend. It's like saying margarine is going to take over the world.

'The Beatles only happen once a lifetime with the sort of force and consistency that the Beatles had,' she continued. 'Things in the music field go full circle, just like fashion. It's rather like keeping a pair of shoes for ten years and finding they've come into fashion again. It's not a question of America having a greater musical talent – although they DO have a greater musical talent both in the creative and the technical production field – it's in the general scene. At the moment, American records are of a better standard than British ones.'

By the last quarter of 1966, the energy had definitely ebbed away from Britain. Between the beginning of October and the end of the year, there would be only four #1 records in the UK; the same period in the US would see nine. The British chart had become stodgy and static. In contrast, the American Top 100 was dynamic and forward-looking, reflecting a resurgence influenced by the great British boom at the same time as it was determined to supersede it with home-grown artists and material.

'Reach Out I'll Be There' was one of those records that pulled the culture along with it. Just as the Four Tops and Holland–Dozier–Holland took from the sharp end of white pop, so the leading white musicians of the day then lined up to pay due homage to a tricksy, complex gospel performance. This was a rare moment of unity, one that was encoded in the song itself, a mature, heartfelt statement that appealed to all ages. Instead of a sneer, it was an admission of darkness and a celebration of its transcendence through warmth, solidarity and empathy.

In that, it represented the very height of black American music, defined by Dave Godin as 'a divergent culture which values other, abstract things like tenderness, generosity of spirit, of love. Why these records have found an echo in so many hearts – and I should also mention that it is mainly male hearts – is that men are brought up in our society to despise the feelings that these records represent. They may be brought up to despise them, but that doesn't eradicate them. And there's a recognition, like coming home, and a realisation that yes, this is how we should interact with one another. Yes, we should put a value on love.'

'Reach Out I'll Be There' was one of three records that winter that foreswore the spring and summer's superheated negativity – that 'fabulous, neurotic sound' – in favour of more humane qualities. It also marked the moment when black American music emerged from the shadows to claim its place in the sun. The British beat boom had been built on the back of R&B and early soul, and November 1966 was the moment when the reverse occurred, when black American music arrived to claim its place at the heart of British youth culture.

* * *

'The "in" crowd always said it would happen . . . and it has!
Everyone's raving about rock'n'soul. And those disciples who
have been singing its praises for years, have been proved right.
Nearly a quarter of the Top Fifty positions are now taken up by
rock'n'soul artistes.'

MAUREEN O'GRADY, 'The Soul Parade', *Rave*, November 1966

It had been a long time coming. The British taste for black
American music had been established from the early years of the
twentieth century on, with the successive popularity of the cake-
walk, ragtime, blues and jazz. But access to the real thing was limited, thanks to the difficulty and expense of transatlantic travel, the
practice of white artists covering black R&B and rock 'n' roll hits,
and the lack of any radio exposure outside the BBC. Even in the
1950s, black American music enthusiasts like Dave Godin found
themselves 'like orphans in a storm'.

Transfixed by early-sixties records like Maxine Brown's 'All
in My Mind' – which he calls 'the first soul record' – and the
Marvelettes' 'Please Mr Postman', Godin became frustrated at
their lack of presence in the UK: 'I actually sat down and wrote a
letter to Berry Gordy, and said it's terrible what happens to black
American music over here, and I'd like to do something to help.
I'd like to start a fan club, for Mary Wells and for all the Motown
artists. I got a nice letter back saying, "Please go ahead."'

Formed in 1963, the Tamla Motown Appreciation Society helped
to fuel the growing groundswell of black American music in the
UK. Apart from Norman Jopling's regular bulletins in *Record
Mirror*, there was a fresh push by British record companies to
release American material. EMI's Stateside label issued singles by
the Isley Brothers, the Shirelles, the Jaynetts and, from October
1963 – beginning with Martha and the Vandellas' 'Heat Wave' –
material from Berry Gordy's various labels.

Most British fans initially heard this music as covers, by the new
beat groups like the Hollies or Brian Poole and the Tremeloes. It
was just like the mid-fifties all over again. The real thing was shut

out: as Dave Godin remembers, 'How can kids be expected to buy the records if they never get the chance to hear them? All the while the BBC dominated the airwaves, the records weren't being sold because people tend to buy that which they hear and decide that they like. Often soul fans would have to buy records blind, on the strength of an artist's name.'

Clubs and ballrooms were the only places where the originals could be heard. By 1963, there were several metropolitan venues that catered to black-music aficionados. Most were in Soho: coffee bars like La Poubelle or hardcore dives like the Roaring Twenties – presided over by the Jamaican sound system operator Count Suckle – or the Flamingo, which began running all-nighters in 1962. At the Lyceum Theatre, Ian Samwell played an eclectic mix of the day's hits, along with R&B and rock 'n' roll records, to a packed venue during his Sunday and Tuesday sessions.

'The Flamingo was probably the most popular with the hard-core crowd,' says Jeff Dexter, 'and if you wanted a bit of colour, you'd go to La Discotheque or La Poubelle, which was a French influence, but you'd also get a few Africans in there as well. But the ballrooms were more important than most people will ever know, because most of the hacks wrote about the clubs. You rarely got a review from a ballroom, except for up north, where you got a few.'

A pop obsessive from south London, in his early teens Dexter befriended the young Mark Feld (later known as Marc Bolan). In September 1961, he talked his way into the Lyceum Theatre ball-room dances, despite the fact that he was only fourteen. Shortly afterwards, he was banned from the Lyceum for doing the Twist and was rewarded with a slot on Pathé News for his pains. The management immediately allowed him back in and hired him as a featured dancer, just at the moment when the strict rules of ball-room dancing were beginning to break down.

The playlist at the Lyceum was an eclectic mix: 'All the pops of the day, along with the small amount of imports that we had, and what was getting released here that had that black influence. But, of course, the pops, the Everly Brothers, Carole King, were all very important in our grounding. "How Can I Meet Her?" or "Cathy's Clown". Or people like Dion, "The Wanderer". That was an exceptional, great jiving record for the mods. It was kind of left over from the rockers, but some of those records just cracked the best jive out of everybody.'

In 1963, the black American influence was boosted by Ray Charles's major spring tour and, as Dexter remembers, 'The Beatles helped a lot as well. When they came back to England from Germany, they were playing things like "Money" and good R&B stuff. They were the first beat band, as people called them back then, that I actually took seriously, because they understood that the off-beat was the important thing to make great dance music. If they hadn't have been screamed at, they would probably have been one of the best dance bands in the country.'

That year, two clubs opened to pursue a strictly black American music policy. Situated in Ham Yard, the Scene was a basement dive that, in May, turned over its dead Monday nights to a twenty-year-old music obsessive, Guy Stevens. Stevens was both fan and educator: he would announce the name of every record on his eclectic playlist, which ranged from contemporary Phil Spector hits to gut-bucket rock 'n' roll – like Wilbert Harrison's 'Let's Stick Together' – as well as blues and the new urban styles.

Stevens was a young man on the run from a troubled adolescence. Having had his head turned by Jerry Lee Lewis on the ill-fated tour of May 1958, he was expelled from school at the age of fifteen. His life 'turned instantly to night', he later wrote. 'There was no in-between period, when I could sow my wild oats and enjoy life without worries.' At twenty, he was married, a parent stuck in a boring job. Playing black American records at the Scene was a lifeline for him, and an inspiration for an increasing number of regulars.

For young punters like Geoff Green, the music at the Scene 'seemed incredible'. 'I was a mod (of sorts, I was an apprentice and didn't have a lot of money), but the main reason we went was that the advert in the *Record Mirror* spoke of records played by artists including Chuck Berry, Bo Diddley, Jimmy Reed, Howlin' Wolf, Jerry Lee Lewis and others. At this time the Merseybeat boom was getting under way, beat groups were beginning to feature cover versions of rhythm and blues songs, and we wanted to hear the originals.'

Guy Stevens was the first person to run a music policy that was reliant entirely on records rather than live bands, and the Scene set the pattern for the next wave of British clubs. Inspired by his example, Roger Eagle started a residency at Manchester's Twisted Wheel club, in Brazenose Street in the city centre. 'The first night I did was an all-nighter,' he remembered. 'I was playing anything. I was playing R&B, I played rock 'n' roll, I played early ska, whatever I could get my hands on . . . 99.9% was black music and that was the difference.'

Eagle began his all-nighters in September 1963, and the Twisted Wheel featured performers from the emerging UK R&B scene and bluesmen like Muddy Waters and John Lee Hooker. 'I had to keep people dancing for seven hours, with a break for the band,' he remembered. 'Seven hours is a long time and there weren't that many soul and R&B records available at the time.' The regulars were 'scruffy kids who had combat jackets with Little Walter stencilled on the back, things like that. This was just as the Stones were getting off the ground.'

By late 1963, Motown songs were being pumped into millions of homes thanks to the Beatles' covers of 'You Really Got a Hold on Me', 'Please Mr Postman' and 'Money'. During that winter, the British music industry began to wake up to the untapped market for black American music. Island Records released a whole slew of early ska records from Jamaica and, in December 1963, the label's owner, Chris Blackwell, diversified into R&B, launching the Sue Records subsidiary with Inez Foxx's 'Mockingbird' – a club favourite.*

* At around the same time, Rita and Benny Isen began issuing hardcore Jamaican records – by Lee Perry, the Maytals and the Wailers – on their R&B label, King, based in Stamford Hill.

Black voices started filtering into the charts: Big Dee Irwin's humorous take on the Dirty Dozens in 'Swinging on a Star'; the Ronettes' 'Be My Baby'; and, in spring 1964, Mary Wells's 'My Guy' and Millie Small's 'My Boy Lollipop'. In April, Guy Stevens joined Sue Records, which began to issue an eclectic mixture of blues, R&B and jazz. Distributed by Island and supported by both regular ads in *Record Mirror* and plays on the brand-new pirate station Radio Caroline, Sue was a major factor in the spread of contemporary R&B in the UK.

In these early days, the idea of soul was not yet codified, barely even named. This was, as soul historian Ady Croasdell writes, 'a time when genres and pigeonholes within soul music were unknown. It was all so new, uncharted and exciting – who knew what twists and turns the path of black music would take, even in the next week? The concept of what was soul then was much more vague, and most of the crowd were eclectic and adventurous enough to enjoy black music in all its forms – R&B, jazz, blues, soul and even West Indian ska and blue beat.'

In spring 1964, Dave Godin went to Detroit. 'Out of the blue I got a five-page telegram, from Motown, inviting me to go there as their guest and meet everyone. I was just gobsmacked. For a start, I never knew five-page telegrams existed! They said, "Please phone to confirm your acceptance," which I had to do from a call box. They said they'd be sending me an airline ticket . . . Looking back on it now, I think it was like an interview, and they offered me a job as their English rep, which I was glad to accept.

'They had this huge reception for me when I got there. Marvin Gaye, Kim Weston, Stevie Wonder, the Marvellettes, Martha and the Vandellas – all the big names at that time, everyone who was everyone. It was like a three-line whip to attend. The Supremes were considered so second-level that they were not even invited to this reception. I was chatting to Berry and said, "Are the Supremes here?" He was very embarrassed and he went off and obviously it was a desperate phone call. And, sure enough, they turned up.

'I remember riding in Berry's car with him and he had one of those things that you posted a 45 in and it played. We were talking about the Supremes again, and he said, "Oh, we've just cut a new side on them, it's on the floor." There was this pile of white-label 45s on the floor, and I picked this one up, and it was "Where Did Our Love Go?" I heard it and I said, "If this one doesn't do anything, there is no justice."

'He gave me some copies to bring back with me, and the pirate stations had just started up then, so I went to see them and said, "Why don't you start playing some records which the BBC will not play. And then if these records get into the charts, you will know that you've got the listeners." There was a saying then that nobody really listens to the pirates, they're marginal. And that really sparked their imagination. So they did this, and this is how we got the most amazing response. "Where Did Our Love Go?" was down to the pirates. They made it a hit record.'

'Where Did Our Love Go?' was a huge UK hit in early autumn 1964, reaching #3. Godin found the tide turning in his favour. 'One of the first recruits was Vicki Wickham, who worked on *Ready Steady Go!*. She said, "Any soul artist who comes to Britain, we'll have them on the show."' In early winter, the black artists were coming thick and fast on *RSG!*: John Lee Hooker, Kim Weston, Rufus Thomas, Marvin Gaye and, in a memorable October appearance, an ecstatic Martha and the Vandellas miming 'Dancing in the Street' and 'Heat Wave'.

In November, Tamla got its first UK #1 with the simplistic but effective 'Baby Love'. The Supremes visited the UK for the first time, doing *Top of the Pops* and a one-off club date. But, for Godin, this was not enough: the successes were still too hit-and-miss. 'It was my idea to go for the label. The reason I thought of that was that here were all these people having hits in America, and who could tell which of these already established American artists might have the first hit over here?

'So my idea was to market this collectively as a sound, as an abstract thing, this Motown family of artists that make records in this identifiable style. Mary Wells had a hit with "My Guy" on

Stateside. This puts us in a very strong negotiating position with EMI. It was a new idea, it was lunatic, but, to their great credit, Berry Gordy and Esther Edwards said they would do it. I wrote all the label names down on bits of paper and jiggled them about – Motown Tamla, Gordy Tamla – but when I got to Tamla Motown it did seem to roll off the tongue pretty well.'

The Tamla Motown label was launched through EMI on 19 March 1965, with six EPs and six singles, three of which made the charts. On the same day, the Tamla Motown Revue held the opening show of its UK tour at the Astoria Finsbury Park: featuring the Supremes, Martha and the Vandellas, the Temptations, Stevie Wonder, and the Miracles, this was the first proper exposure that young Britons had had to the Motown sound, and the initial response, in London at least, was extremely enthusiastic.

The feeling was reciprocal. 'I went to Manchester Square to meet them,' remembers Jeff Dexter of the Revue. 'Oh, they were spellbound by England. Coming to a country where they could walk freely as a black person, and they were treated with respect in coffee bars. To them, it must have been like going to another planet.'

Tamla Motown's status as the 'in' thing was promoted by big articles and event-style advertising in sympathetic magazines like *Record Mirror*, and it was sealed by the *Ready Steady Go! Motown Special* that was filmed during the Revue's visit. Hosted by Dusty Springfield, who could hardly contain her glee, it was a fast-moving, exciting show that featured the Miracles, the Temptations, Martha and the Vandellas and the Supremes. So far so good, but the problems occurred on the eighteen or so dates around the country. In each venue, the pattern was the same: a hardcore of fans in the low hundreds and then a vista of empty seats. 'It was the Motown Revue that caused the break,' says Dave Godin. 'I was adamant that Britain wasn't ready for it. Berry overrode my judgement, which would have been OK, other than I was proved right. It hadn't had long enough to sink through. We were making inroads, but not on any mass scale. It was so disastrous, the Motown Revue, that when they played Cardiff there were more people on stage than there were in the audience.'

In the spring and summer of 1965, soul records continued to percolate into the lower regions of the charts: the Drifters' 'At the Club', Dobie Grey's 'The In Crowd', the Four Tops' 'I Can't Help Myself' and Sue's only hit, Charles and Inez Foxx's 'Hurt by Love'. In July, *Record Mirror* began running the UK's first R&B chart: in the Top 5 were 'I Can't Help Myself', the Sir Douglas Quintet's 'She's About a Mover', Donnie Elbert's 'A Little Piece of Leather', Solomon Burke's 'Maggie's Farm' and 'Mr Pitiful' by Otis Redding.

Stax had not yet broken through in the UK. Atlantic had had its own special imprint in the UK since summer 1964 – distributed by Decca – but, despite issuing peerless records by Rufus Thomas, Solomon Burke and Otis Redding, only the occasional hit. This all changed with Wilson Pickett's 'In the Midnight Hour', which went to #12 in autumn 1965, largely due to the efforts of Tony Hall.

'I was in charge of all Decca group's promotion,' he says, 'but Atlantic became my speciality. I thought it wasn't being given the push it deserved. It ended up with BBC producers like Ron Belcher complaining to their friends at Decca, "Why isn't Tony Hall plugging the Bachelors instead of some black guy called Otis?" I tried with everybody. "In the Midnight Hour" was set for release about the time of my annual holiday, which had been booked. So I asked the rest of my team, in my absence, to take care of it and give it a real good bash. I returned to find that nothing had happened. So I had to start from scratch, which was difficult because there had been loads of other records out since.

'But a friend of mine happened to be doing *Juke Box Jury* here the week I got back, and I went and virtually begged him to include it, even though it was no longer a brand-new release. And he said, "What I can do to help you is put it at number eight on the tape. There's no guarantee you'll get to it, but at least I'm giving you a chance." So I sat and watched it, and chewed my nails, but by a stroke of luck, they did. It was the last record to be played that day. That's what really started it, and then, with the help of Radio London, we made that into a hit.'

Hall also pushed the first major UK hit by Otis Redding. 'With Otis, it was very hard to break him with the kind of singles that Atlantic were putting out. I then discovered "My Girl" – it was on *Otis Blue* – and I remembered that the Temptations' record hadn't been a hit in England. I said to Jerry Wexler, "Why don't you let me go with this as a single?" He thought I was crazy, but he let me go ahead. I think it was Radio London that broke "My Girl" for me, and we ended up getting to #11 in the charts.'

In late 1965, soul was everywhere – the latest American records were covered by the Rolling Stones and the Who; were blatantly sourced by the Beatles on 'Drive My Car' and 'Day Tripper'; were pumped out by the pirates; were danced to by hundreds of teens in the Scene, the Twisted Wheel and newer clubs like the Last Chance Saloon or the Inferno; were assiduously promoted by Tony Hall and Norman Jopling in the *Record Mirror* – but as far as the general public was concerned, the British groups and the balladeers still held sway.

Guy Stevens observed this strange dichotomy in a November 1965 interview. Island had just released *The Sue Story!*, a Stevens compilation that included club favourites like Chris Kenner's original 'Land of 1000 Dances' and Bobby Parker's 'Watch Your Step' – the record that had inspired the Beatles' 'I Feel Fine'. The article began by observing the debt owed by most British groups to black American music and the Sue label: 'George Harrison is on the mailing list, insisting he receives every single and long player that's issued.'

Stevens talked about Sue's lack of success: 'First, the coloured artist has not really been accepted in this country. And virtually all our artists are Negroes. Consequently we get very few plays and little exposure except by hip record producers and in the London clubs, where they go down a bomb because of the profound dancing beat featured on most of them.' Yet both the Rolling Stones and the Who visited Stevens's house 'to keep up-to-date on the new releases. Once upon a time I used to take a batch of Sue releases to the Stones' recording sessions.'

By early 1966, the major groups' reliance on soul covers was waning, and the influence was being transmuted into something indigenous. The Stax influence began to come through strongly. The work done by pioneers like Guy Stevens and Roger Eagle was beginning to bear fruit: new magazines were launched – John Abbey's *Home of the Blues*, Tony Cummings's *Soul*; new clubs opened – the Ram Jam in Brixton, the Nite Owl in Leicester; and Tony Hall promoted almost exclusively black records and black artists in his weekly *Record Mirror* column.

In March 1966, James Brown arrived for his first UK visit. 'I Got You (I Feel Good)' was in the Top 30, and *Ready Steady Go!* devoted a whole episode to his revue. It was mesmerising, but was greeted with uncomprehending and unpleasant reviews. 'If you have a taste for old-fashioned entertainment (primitive screaming and emotional kidology),' wrote one reviewer, 'done every bit as professionally as top-priced African witch doctors and the most famous minstrel shows, then don't miss the Wild Man of Harlem.' Britain just didn't seem ready for America's top black artist.

That same month, a new club opened in central London. Situated at 79–89 Oxford Street, Tiles was an underground pleasure dome, a world unto itself. It was a basement cavern, hollowed out under several ground-floor premises, that included a stage, a dance floor, a record shop and an arcade of boutiques selling clothes, shoes and the like. It was a new concept: as Pathé News asserted in its coverage of the opening night, when the Animals played, 'The music just filters right through, putting everyone in the right mood for buying.'

Tiles was aimed at a new demographic: mass-market mod. Tom Wolfe visited the club in late spring 1966 and found an alternative society – 'an underground at noon'. He observed the mod ideal of total pop immersion, which he called The Life, aspired to by characters like seventeen-year-old Linda McCarthy, an assistant at Tiles' Ravel outlet, or the fifteen-year-old Larry Lynch, an office worker in headlong flight from 'all the straight human mummy-hubbies'.

A sociological shift had made this possible: 'Over the past year thousands of these working-class mods have been moving away from home at 16, 17, or 18, even girls, girls especially in fact, and into flats in London. They go to work, in offices, in shops, department stores, for £8 to £10 a week, but that is enough to get them into The Life. They share flats, three, four, five girls to a flat, in areas like Leicester Square – jaysus, Leicester Square – Charing Cross, Charlotte Street, or they live with their boyfriends, or everyone drifts from place to place.'

Above all, it was their 'style of life' that marked them out from the crowd. They shunned pub life, preferring pills and hash to 'bitter, watercress and old Lardbelly telling you it's time'. But even from his brief immersion that late May, Wolfe was sharp enough to notice the subtle differentiations within a supposedly classless youth culture: between a 'bourgeois' seventeen-year-old photographer's assistant, wearing a suede jacket and Rolling Stones hair, and the working-class mods in their mohair suits.

As economic forces slowly reasserted themselves, this split within British youth culture would deepen. Styles and attitudes were hardening, particularly among black-music aficionados, which was to some degree a sign of success. Although James Brown had puzzled the Brits, there were other tours – by Wilson Pickett, Don Covay, the Vibrations and others – and the early summer saw a couple of huge soul hits that came out of the clubs and pirate radio: Roy C's 'Shotgun Wedding' and Percy Sledge's 'When a Man Loves a Woman'.

For Roger Eagle, the eclecticism of even a couple of years before had been submerged by a rising tide of machine soul. In late August, he left the Twisted Wheel. 'It became boring quite frankly because the music became too similar at the time, it was just a fast dance beat to keep people dancing all night. They were blocked out of their heads on "blues" or whatever they were taking and you were just a human jukebox. You'd put one record after another and if you tried anything different they would yell at you.'

However, for many young mods, this amphetamined tempo was the sound of soul. It can be heard in contemporary Motown records like Chris Clark's driven 'Love's Gone Bad' and in recordings of live shows by Geno Washington and the Ram Jam Band. Fronted by the American-born singer, this group was one of several – Herbie Goins and the Nightimers, Jimmy James and the Vagabonds – that formed in the UK to fill the demand for soul music. Certainly, if Washington's first album was anything to go by, his sets were breakneck affairs.

Even so, the sound was not yet locked down. In Tiles, Jeff Dexter operated an open-ended policy as one of the DJs. 'It was like finding freedom, really,' he says, going back to one of his set lists from the period. 'The Wailers, "Put It On", "Phoenix City", Roland Alphonso. "Al Capone" hit that year, as well. Alvin Cash and the Registers, "Twine Time". A highlight in terms of sharpness and dress sense was *Gettin' Ready*, the Temptations. That was an LP I used to see in the collection of every mod, because it had that sharp cover.

'We had Eddie Floyd, "Knock on Wood". Every nightclub, every ballroom, played that. Otis Redding I remember playing. Probably the toughest, hardest record that made the biggest impression was Rex Garvin and the Mighty Cravers' "Sock It to 'Em J.B.", parts one and two. A fast record, but in a totally different way. I had three copies of it, so I could segue it into fourteen or fifteen minutes. If you did that in those days, and you had a record that was more than two and a half minutes, it was exhilarating for them, it was quite magic, really.

'All the dances were kind of thrown into one. The latecomer mods were doing what they called the Block, which was used in other Soho nightclubs. And, of course, from '63 there had been a lot of influence from ska and blue beat. Moving like you were from the West Indies. Practically anybody could dance to a ska record. Ska at Tiles became dominant, in a way. A lot of the younger boys came from the working class; it was the first time we were getting a good crossover of black youth in the clubs as well.'

By autumn, the wave of black American music had become unstoppable. Dammed up for so long, it flooded a British pop scene floundering in the wake of Swinging London. In September, *Billboard* recorded the fact that Atlantic Records, flourishing under its new UK deal with Polydor, was 'the hottest American label in England right now, with five records dominating the English market'.

At the same time, Atlantic artists like Solomon Burke, Rufus Thomas, Sam and Dave, Percy Sledge and Otis Redding were visiting the UK in person. Perhaps the one with the most impact was Otis Redding, who, apart from 'I Can't Turn You Loose', had two albums released in the UK during 1966 – the Top 10 *Otis Blue* and the Top 30 *The Soul Album*. He arrived in mid-September to the by now standard fanfare: plentiful coverage in the music press and a *Ready Steady Go!* special, where he performed 'Satisfaction', 'My Girl' and 'Respect', among others.

On the 16th, he played Tiles, which became an inferno for the night. Writing in *Soul Monthly*, Bill Millar observed that 'Otis should receive a mention in the *Financial Times* this year. The attendances on his recent tour, especially in the London area, were quite phenomenal. 6,000 people paid ten shillings to see him at Purley and it was later announced that 8,000 had forked out twenty-five shillings a head to see him at Tiles.' The ensuing crush was 'quite absurd and the heat was intense'.

The next day, Tony Hall commented on 'the changing chart scene' in his weekly column. He had been on the ball all year, promoting Ike and Tina Turner's 'River Deep – Mountain High' and James Brown's 'It's a Man's Man's Man's World' before they were hits. 'I could hardly believe my eyes,' he wrote, 'six Tamla Motowns in the Fifty! And about the same number of Atlantics!' Hall commented on the success of the Temptations' 'Ain't Too Proud to Beg': 'Did plays by dance-hall deejays influence sales? If YOU bought it, where did YOU hear it first?'

By the time that 'Reach Out I'll Be There' had been released in early October, the battle was almost won. Aside from the Atlantic and Motown 45 releases, a new EMI label called Soul Supply was launched in 1966, catering to the hardcore. There was also a slew of compilation albums: *The Sue Story Vol. 2*, with sleeve notes from Keith Reid; *Soul 66*, with notes by Dave Godin; and *The Sue Story Vol. 3*, with notes from the popular black-music DJ Mike Raven. Atlantic also issued a few compilations, including *In the Midnight Hour*, *Hit '66* and *Solid Gold Soul*.

The Four Tops weren't the only black Americans to visit the UK that autumn. In early November, the deep New Orleans vocalist Lee Dorsey was promoting his current single, 'Holy Cow', and touring in a package with Jerry Lee Lewis, Paul and Ritchie and the Cryin' Shames, and Cliff Bennett. Quizzed about the buzzword of the moment, he replied, 'Soul is expressing the emotions of the inner self, being able to get people to feel what you are doing. I guess it's something that Negroes inherited a long time ago when picking cotton.'

The integration of black music into the UK pop mainstream wasn't without its difficulties. Racial prejudice was still rife. In the autumn, *Disc and Music Echo*'s Bob Farmer visited various cities around the country for his series on 'Mod Britain '67'. In Birmingham, his interviewees thought that 'Tamla Motown is really getting strong in Britain'. But there was a strange dichotomy: Tamla might have been 'tops' in the city, but the youth weren't 'embarrassed to temper its pleasure in the Mod look of the Midlands capital with a distaste for the droves of coloured immigrants'.

Even so, 'Reach Out I'll Be There' arrived as the galvanising force that pulled everything together. Jeff Dexter remembers its impact: 'It was incredible. It hit every spot that you wanted to hit with a good dance soul record of that time. It had the harmonies, the highlights, the subtlety. It built and built.' Perhaps its greatest achievement, which could not have been predicted, was that it offered – through an accident of timing but not of spirit – solace and comfort to a country reeling from a terrible and totally unexpected event.

* * *

'Aberfan was no longer a disaster. It was on the verge of becoming a national emotion.'

TONY AUSTIN, *Aberfan: The Story of a Disaster*, 1967

It happened at 9.15 a.m. on Friday 21 October. Weakened by weeks of high winds and heavy rain, the slag heap shifted, slid and then rushed down the mountain towards the floor of the valley. It was foggy that morning, and the wave of accumulated debris travelled so quickly that it hit the small town before anyone could sound the warning. Within minutes, Aberfan was submerged by over 40,000 cubic metres of black, toxic waste. The building that bore the brunt was Pantglas Junior School, directly in the path of the spillage.

The young pupils had just returned to their classrooms after assembly. David Davies 'heard a noise like thunder. I saw the railings come towards me and the windows went dark and all the walls came down on top of us.' As Gaylor Minett, then eight, remembered later, 'Everyone just froze in their seats. I just managed to get up and I reached the end of my desk when the sound got louder and nearer, until I could see the black out of the window. I can't remember any more but I woke up to find that a horrible nightmare had just begun in front of my eyes.'

There were 240 boys and girls in the school. Within five minutes, half of them lost their lives – although, in the immediate aftermath of the tragedy, it was impossible to find out how many were missing. The black wave didn't stop there: moving down the hill, it destroyed another twenty or so houses before coming to a halt. The whole toxic stew was further lubricated by a water main that had been broken during the hill slide. After the first impact, there was a shocked silence. It had only taken moments, but the damage was done.

Nowhere could have been further away from mod Britain. Aberfan was a small town, population 3,000, five miles from Merthyr Tydfil in the South Wales Valleys. It had been developed in the later nineteenth century to house the miners working in the nearby Merthyr Vale colliery and, like many Valleys towns, it bore the scars of the raw materials that had made the whole area the industrial powerhouse of Britain. By 1966, the waste products from the colliery occupied seven tips, and it was tip number seven, on the top of Mynydd Merthyr, that failed.

It was the silence and dark tones that reinforced the horror of the news reports, as both the BBC and ITV gave Aberfan blanket coverage. By the early afternoon, viewers nationwide were seeing the black tide, the faces contorted by grief and pain, the crowds of rescuers, the small bodies being carried out under blankets. The rolling reports would continue over the next few days: as Tony Austin later wrote, 'Aberfan showed that TV observation of grief is acceptable to the vast majority, even if it opened eyes to scenes that they would not wish to see.'

It wasn't at the top of people's minds in late October and November 1966, but the pall cast by Aberfan – a national event of the utmost seriousness – had an effect on Britain's pop culture. The most direct assistance came in the form of two big charity concerts, set for December. And, as the media went en masse to the Valleys of South Wales, the nation's attention was wrenched from the capital and its riches towards the forgotten people and forgotten places of a Britain that suddenly did not seem so great.

The creative response to Aberfan would take a while to surface fully, but the disaster did have an immediate impact on a record released in mid-November. The Kinks had been in the studio recording 'Dead End Street' as the news came through on 21 and 22 October. Although the song had been written some time before, the atmosphere of that weekend came through in a performance that was an equal mixture of bitterness and defiance. As Ray Davies repeatedly emphasised, 'People are *dying* in Dead End Street.'

Over the previous year, from autumn 1965 onwards, Davies had satirised the bourgeoisie, the mods of Swinging London and the upper classes. In autumn 1966, he turned his attention to the class that had spawned him and from which, thanks to his talent, luck and drive, he had escaped. 'I wanted to write a modern-day depression song,' he told me, 'because I felt that's what was happening around me. It's about people who've got no way out, saying,

"What's gone wrong? We were promised the good life – what are we living for?'"

It had been a frustrating few months for the Kinks since their summer peak with 'Sunny Afternoon'. Founder member Pete Quaife was badly injured in a car crash just as the record was released in June, and was replaced by John Dalton. Determined to achieve some autonomy, Davies was struggling with the group's ex-managers, former publishers, producer and record label. A protracted contract negotiation with Pye Records, conducted by new business manager Allen Klein, was holding up the release of their new album, *Face to Face*.

It was the first time the Kinks had been in the studio since June, and 'Dead End Street' was up first. It was a difficult session: the group were dissatisfied with Shel Talmy, who had produced all their records to date. On 21 October, they recorded a first version, which featured a faster tempo, less prominent brass and an organ part that 'gave it a whirligig fairground effect'. It failed to capture the emotions that Davies wanted: as he wrote in *X-Ray*, 'It was not bleak enough for my taste.'

Davies remembered this as a crucial moment in his quest for self-determination. When Talmy was injured in a freak accident – his arm was caught in a swing door – Davies quickly re-recorded the song with a trombone player fished out of a nearby pub. 'Shel came in the next day and heard the new version and said, thinking it was his one, "It's great. I don't know what you wanna do!"' With this sleight of hand, Davies had proved to himself that he needed no producer except himself.

His instinct was correct. The trombone saturates 'Dead End Street', creating a desolate atmosphere – at once reminiscent of brass bands, funeral marches – from the start. This quickly leads into the first verse: 'There's a crack up in the ceiling / And the kitchen sink is leaking.' A fresh scenario has been quickly established. 'We are strictly second-class,' Davies sings, as the group punctuate the chorus with raucous shouts. The final chorus resolves into a loose breakdown: the rhythm changes into a groove, punctuated by wordless, percussive vocals, and the defiance of all those shouted 'Dead end!'s breaks into a prolonged trombone solo on the fade-out, a boozy, blowsy knees-up.

'Dead End Street' was deliberately pitched to stand aloof from current trends. As Davies remembered, 'It's all about people who weren't chic enough and who didn't have access to drugs. I wasn't being fooled by all the euphoria that was around: people were taking a lot of drugs because they didn't want to see. I was trying to see things, but people rejected it: even though it was a big hit, people rejected the idea of it.'

It was coupled with an equally remarkable song. 'Big Black Smoke' is a Hogarthian morality tale about a teenage runaway, 'the frailest, purest girl the world has seen', who is seduced by the lures of the Great Wen. 'It's a very London song,' Ray Davies recalled. 'It's about the evils of the big city. I was just fascinated with the line "she put on her pretty coloured clothes", which is about a girl who comes to London and ends up as a prostitute somewhere like Euston. I knew a girl who was like that. She died of junk.'

With its ringing acoustic guitar, rolling swing and pithy lyrics, 'Big Black Smoke' has the feel of an archetypal folk song. Dominated by the descending phrase that accompanies the line 'She put on her pretty coloured clothes', beginning with church bells and ending in the chants of a town crier, it takes in the sounds and the sweep of the city. But this London is the setting for pain rather than peacockery – the dark side of The Life as described by Tom Wolfe, the amphetamine mod world of clothes, music and shared flats.

A few days before 'Dead End Street' was released, on 14 November, the Kinks made a promotional film: as Dave Davies told *Rave*, 'We're sick of going on TV and just standing there like four dummies, miming to a backing track.' Shot in black and white in and around Camden Town, it begins with a long shot of the four Kinks, dressed in Victorian top hats and tailcoats, carrying a coffin through the cobbled streets. It could be the nineteenth century: for the first two minutes, there are no cars, no mods and very few sig-nifiers of the modern era.

They arrive at the front door of a terraced house. A hand knocks, and the next shot is Ray Davies, grim-faced, bearing bad news. The coffin is carried in to lie in state. As the chorus begins, there is a montage of stills depicting the old, the poor and the desperate. Dressed in a badly fitting wig, Dave Davies plays the mourning wife as the corpse is laid out on the bed. The four Kinks look down with an unpitying gaze. There is also a flash of camp humour in the female impersonations undertaken by both Ray and Dave Davies.

During the second chorus, the stills include Jamaican immigrants, bomb sites and other scenes of urban desolation, interspersed with quick individual cuts of the four Kinks yelling 'Dead end!' at the camera. This is a death, but also a rebirth. At the end of the film, the group are carrying the coffin through the backstreets, presum-ably for burial. It's heavy and they take a cigarette break. The apparently dead man jumps up and runs off in his nightshirt, in a sequence reminiscent of the Keystone Cops as refracted through Richard Lester.

The single was released on 18 November. The chart page of that week's issue of *Disc and Music Echo* featured a Pye advert that had the title crudely painted on a dirty, graffitied wall. Penny Valentine described the single as another 'social survey with a pos-itive hit sound. It wins even over other Kink opuses by having a loud, hard chorus line we can all yell with. I like it, but for their next single, I would like to make a small plea for another subject. Please Mr. Davies may we leave social comment and perhaps even get back to love?'

'Dead End Street' didn't sound like anything else in the charts, whether ballads, Tamla and soul, beat, commercial pop or the early shoots of psychedelia. Shortly afterwards, the BBC banned the 'sick' promo film. 'There's nothing funny about old people dying,' *Top of the Pops* producer Stanley Dorfman told *Disc and Music Echo*, 'and the Kinks couldn't make up their minds whether to be funny or serious. The still shots showed dead and poor people and I didn't like it.' Ray Davies had delivered, in a sense, a dose of unwelcome reality.

This kind of reception was only amplified by the furore that greeted the BBC's *Wednesday Play* aired on 16 November. *Cathy Come Home* fused both drama and documentary to highlight the plight of the poor and the homeless. If anything, it hit harder because both the leads, Carol White and Ray Brooks, appeared young and fashionable. This was another kind of truth and, in order to get it on screen, the production team of Tony Garnett, Ken Loach and Jeremy Sandford had to resort to subterfuge, pretending it was a light comedy.

Cathy Come Home broke all the rules of television drama in 1966. It had no surreal Theatre of the Absurd touches, no redemptive moments, not even the assurance that what was on the screen was purely fictional. It was a deliberately confounding mix of kitchen sink realism and investigative documentary, cut quickly so that scenes involving synched speech were intercut with voiceovers that had no correspondence to the on-screen image. It showed a relentless downward spiral, blow upon blow landing on already bruised flesh.

The film was designed to shock people into action. Its underlying moral outrage originated with the researches of Jeremy Sandford, who, in the late 1950s, had married the writer and playwright Nell Dunn. Shortly afterwards, they left their house in Chelsea and moved over the river. 'There was a moment in the early sixties,' remembered Sandford, 'when all the lovely young sirens of Hammersmith, Battersea and Fulham were making that upwardly mobile journey east or north and ending up in the King's Road, at that time probably the most fashionable and chic street in Britain.

'Society was still very stratified but for the first time, as a result of, among others, the Beatles, style was being created from below . . . The King's Road, not a traditional style centre at all, was the location for some of this. From Battersea, young women were making the journey north. Nell and I were going in the opposite direction.' Battersea was only just over the river from Chelsea but a world away. Dunn would explore this working-class district in her 1963 collection of stories, *Up the Junction*.

Cathy Come Home came from Sandford's direct experience: 'One day, a family living a few doors down the street were evicted. Their furniture was thrown into the street, and they disappeared, apparently without trace. I wondered what had become of them. Because, as I understood it, they had nowhere else to go. A few nights later, a friend came to tell me that this neighbouring family had arrived in a terrible place. This was Newington Lodge, an old workhouse to which all homeless families in London were at that time sent. I went to see for myself.'

Newington Lodge was a large, prison-like Victorian building in Camberwell. 'Stacked into an old workhouse were hundreds of mothers and children who had been separated from their husbands and fathers. Some families were in single rooms. In other cases, four, five, or more families had all been shoved into the same room. There were far too few toilets, the ones there were were filthy, and dysentery had broken out. Ambulances called every day, often more than once a day. There was great demoralisation.'

Appalled, Sandford went back to Newington Lodge and made recordings of the terrified residents. These were done entirely without official approval. The results were broadcast in 1960 as a BBC radio programme called *Homeless Families*, but it received a muted reaction. After his next BBC project – a 1963 film about the Savoy, which, much to the outrage of the hotel management, concentrated on the staff rather than the clientele – he returned to the topic of homelessness.

In early 1965, he wrote a first draft of *Cathy Come Home* called 'The Abyss', informed by his research into caravan fires, families living in derelict housing and homelessness in general. It was written as 'the story of a girl who came down to London full of hope, built up a family, and then lost that family through a tragic chain of events'. Cathy was carefully written as blameless to gain the viewer's sympathy: she was the victim, not of her criminality or bad character, but circumstance and a certain youthful carelessness.

470

Cathy Come Home begins with a shot of Carol White, as Cathy, hitch-hiking to London in her smart coat and blonde hair. Soundtracked by Sonny and Cher's '500 Miles', it could almost be a film insert for *Top of the Pops* or the beginning of a Swinging London flick like *The Knack*. She is in flight from a loveless lower-middle-class background, and her dreams of escape come true: she meets the spry lorry driver Reg (Ray Brooks), falls in love and settles down with him in a brand-new flat. So far, so high sixties – a time for youth.

But reality quickly obtrudes. The couple try and fail to buy a property of their own. After eleven minutes the narrative takes a definitive downward turn when Reg has a road accident. Unable to afford their brand-new flat and burdened with children, they are forced to move back in with Reg's mother in her packed house. 'There are two hundred thousand more families in London than there are houses to put them,' runs the voiceover. 'In seven London boroughs one in ten houses are overcrowded.'

It doesn't work out, and the couple are forced to take rooms in a filthy tenement block. When their old landlady dies, Reg and Cathy are summarily thrown out of their flat, and they have no choice but to move into a caravan. This sequence among the travellers is perhaps the last moment of joy, or at least ease, in the film. But the downward spiral continues: after a local councillor makes prejudicial remarks about 'scroungers, layabouts and vagabonds', their caravan is torched and they are lucky to escape with their lives.

In the next scene, Cathy is looking after the children in a reasonable-looking room, but as the camera pans out it is revealed to be in a house without windows, in a vista of waste ground. They sink even further, to living in a tent, and at that point the eternally optimistic Reg gives up: 'I think we've had it,' he says. After being abandoned by her partner, Cathy is forced to move into Newington Lodge. The final scenes of the film were actually filmed on site, and they depict an overcrowded hellhole. But she is evicted even from this place of last resort.

'These are the casualties of the welfare state,' runs the voiceover.

'They are pushed around like so much human litter and nobody will listen.' Cathy has no choice but to go on the run. As she tries to sleep in a railway terminus, she is surrounded by male authority figures, and her children, squealing and shrieking, are taken away from her. In the last image, Cathy is standing by a roadside at night: she has returned to the opening scene, she is in motion, but instead of youthful hope there is despair and, perhaps, even madness.

The impact of these climactic scenes was underscored by the final captions: 'All the events in this film took place in Britain within the last eighteen months'; '4000 children are separated from their parents and taken into care each year because their parents are homeless.' *Cathy Come Home* was presented as fiction but it was based on fact – 'Nearly everything in the film was founded on something which had actually happened,' Sandford later wrote – and the combination of the cold statistics and the harrowing finale left a powerful imprint on the mind.

Cathy Come Home was watched by just over a fifth of the total UK population and had a huge impact. Reviews attested to its power: the *Liverpool Daily Post* thought it was 'just like a punch between the eyes', while in the *Sunday Times* Frank Norman called it 'the most important piece of dramatised documentary ever screened'. Three days later, the campaigning organisation Shelter was launched, as Sandford writes, 'to draw public attention to the position of homeless people in Britain today and provide accommodation for them'.

By this time, there was a new record at the top of the British charts. Like 'Reach Out I'll Be There', it marked the final breakthrough for an experienced American group after a long, slow build. Like 'Reach Out I'll Be There', it was a hugely ambitious and innovative record. Like 'Reach Out I'll Be There', it offered light and positivity to a country beset by darkness. It arrived in grim November as a blast of California sunshine so intense that, while it played, listeners could bask in the heat and the space.

* * *

'People are part of my music. A lot of my songs are the result of emotional experiences, sadness, pain, joy and an exultation in nature and sunshine and so on . . . like "California Girls" which was a hymn to youth. I find empathy for a subject through communication with people.'

BRIAN WILSON, 'This Is Brian Wilson. He Is a Beach Boy. Some Say He Is More. Some Say He Is a Beach Boy and a Genius', *Go!* magazine, July 1966

'I, I love the colourful clothes she wears,' Carl Wilson comes straight in, 'and the way the sunlight plays upon her hair.' Underneath, there is a modulating organ wash. Everything is texture. The voice rises to a falsetto as the full band comes in. There is an edit, a subtle shift in studio tone barely discernible as the song shifts a gear into the chorus: 'I'm picking up good vibrations,' sings Mike Love, 'she's giving me excitations.' A sawing cello and a strange, soaring but keening tone provide the sound bed.

The second verse develops the mood, before the Beach Boys' harmonies deepen in intensity in the chorus. Halfway through, the song opens out into a wordless instrumental section before the bridge. Another cut segues into a quiet organ passage, accompanied simply by soft percussion. The vocal then picks up again, into a soul-style vamp. The organ returns at a higher pitch for several bars, resolving into a brief group-harmonised 'Aaaah'. The cellos come to the fore, and there is another ratcheting up of the mood – a contrapuntal duet between banks of voices, percussively scatting – before the climax: the return of the cellos, frantically pulsating, overridden by the shriek of the electro-theremin – played by inventor Paul Tanner – as it rises and swoops into the fade. In an era when the cut of vinyl privileged every strange sound, 'Good Vibrations' was packed with aural gimmicks and hooks galore.

Although it was released in October (the 10th in the US, the 28th in the UK), the recordings had begun in February. The song was originally slated for the *Pet Sounds* album, but Brian Wilson held it back. Conceived as an R&B tune – Mike Love thought it was 'in the style of James Brown and the Famous Flames' – 'Good

Vibrations' became something else, as Wilson returned to it over and over again in more sessions during April, May, June and, after a hiatus when the writer seemed to lose faith in his creation, early September.

The finished single was a masterpiece of editing. Dennis Wilson described the process to Jim Delehant of *Hit Parader*: 'It took about four months, but we didn't record every day and we didn't put in 90 hours. We went in one day and we recorded the sound track and we didn't like it. So we did it over again in sections. The sound track was in different sections and we wrote it as we were recording it. As we finished one part, we were inspired to do another. It just kept building and building.'

The basic feeling was captured in the first, February version, which also delivered the verses used in the final master. Other sessions took in different versions of the choruses, the bridges and the fade. All sorts of instruments were added and subtracted: piccolos, a tack piano, a Jew's harp, saxophones, a kazoo, sleigh bells and an electric harpsichord. At one point in the summer Brian Wilson became so confused that he abandoned the song. It was only after the intervention of his friend, David Anderle, that he persisted, adding the final vocals on 12 September.

This laborious process became part of the hype. 'The Beach Boys have mislaid the tapes of the vital music track for "Good Vibrations", their long awaited new single,' Derek Taylor wrote. 'It took 60 hours to perfect and it's still missing.' In mid-October, he gave an update: 'Beach Boys have a giant, monster, mountainous, world-topping, vast rolling ocean, mixed metaphor of a hit of hits in "Good Vibrations", a record which, before the first copy is even in the stores, is named with total abandon, by disc jockeys, as a certain number one.'

'Good Vibrations' was the most complicated and most expensive single ever made, topping even Phil Spector's 'River Deep – Mountain High'. In 1966, most artists would still have been expected to knock out a single and a B-side in one strictly regulated three-hour session, but, like the Beatles, the Rolling Stones and Bob Dylan, Brian Wilson had unbounded time in the studio. *Pet Sounds* had cost $70,000 in total, for twelve tracks, but 'Good Vibrations' alone cost $50,000. It was worth every cent.

There was a grandiosity here, of course. Wilson had been obsessed with the Beatles ever since they hit the American charts in early 1964: not only were they on the same label – Capitol – but, with the same first three letters, they were competing directly in the record racks. For two years, the Beach Boys were eclipsed until, at the end of 1965, Wilson felt confident enough to take inspiration from his competitors, being so fired up by *Rubber Soul* that he conceived his next album not as a random collection, but as a carefully constructed mood piece.

'While Lennon and McCartney were exciting everyone with their new sounds,' he told *Go!* magazine in July 1966, 'we were static. That's why I concentrated on giving the group a sound that would have lasting appeal.' Firmly settled in as the group's *éminence grise*, Wilson spent his time recording endlessly in Los Angeles, while the other five Beach Boys went out on tour. 'When I've thought out a theme I go to the piano and sit playing "feels", which are rhythm patterns and fragments of ideas. Then the song starts to blossom and becomes a real thing.'

Pet Sounds created a consistent musical and emotional mood, with every one of the twelve tracks forming a whole. It was, in essence, a concept album about loss, alienation and the end of adolescence. Blending the true sound of Los Angeles – the full range of exotica, surf and lounge music – with the trademark Beach Boys harmonies, Wilson wrote a series of gorgeous, tricksy melodies and contrapuntal harmony parts that perfectly matched lyricist Tony Asher's disquisitions on failure, loneliness and dashed dreams.

'The Beach Boys are lucky,' Wilson said that year. 'We have a high range of voices; Mike can go from bass to the E above middle C; Dennis, Carl and Al progress upwards through C, A and B. I can take the second D in the treble clef. The harmonies we were able to produce gave us a uniqueness, which is the only important thing you can put into records. I love peaks in a song – and enhancing them on the control panel. Most of all, I love the human voice for its own sake. But I can treat it, with some detachment, as another instrument.'

1966 was a year of knowingness and not a little cynicism, but *Pet Sounds* held onto the primacy of innocence at the same time as it was in danger of being lost for ever. At the moment when the Rolling Stones and the groups that they influenced were propagating an icy mod cool, the Beach Boys admitted to tenderness and vulnerability – 'I want to cry' – in songs like 'You Still Believe Me', an exquisite two-and-a-half-minute mood piece that hung suspended between its tender, devotional lead vocal, sophisticated instrumentation and mass harmony swells.

In America, *Pet Sounds* did not sell as well as expected. The record was released in May, after some delay, as Capitol were committed to churning out product to their timetable, not Brian Wilson's. They had scheduled a greatest hits album to come out in August, which, rising to #8, effectively acted as a spoiler to the new album's continued sales. Despite containing two Top 10 singles ('Sloop John B' and 'Wouldn't It Be Nice'), *Pet Sounds* struggled to #10 in the album charts – the group's lowest position for over two years.

In Britain, however, the situation was very different. The Beach Boys' first single of the year, the goofy, raucous 'Barbara Ann', had been a huge Top 3 hit, and it was followed by 'Sloop John B' and 'God Only Knows', both of which went to #2. The floodgates opened, as EMI issued four Beach Boys albums in rapid succession: *Beach Boys Party, The Beach Boys Today!, Pet Sounds* and *Summer Days (and Summer Nights!!)*. Every one reached the Top 10, with *Pet Sounds* just failing to knock the Stones' *Aftermath* off the top spot.

Despite its comparative underperformance in America, *Pet Sounds* was a distinct *succès d'estime*. Brian Wilson was now being taken extremely seriously, and much of this had to do with the Beach Boys' appointment in the spring of the Beatles' former press officer, Derek Taylor. 'I know that in some circles we're not regarded as all that "hip" or "in",' Wilson said that spring, and he hired the Englishman, as Taylor later wrote, 'to help *Pet Sounds* take them "to a new plateau"'.

As a former journalist, Taylor knew how to bewitch other journalists. He wasn't just a PR, more a conceptualiser and propagandist who used his verbal facility and love of pop music to bring things into the light that might otherwise have been ignored. The result of his input can be seen in an article published in the July edition of *Go!*: 'In Hollywood there's one special name on everyone's lips these days, Brian Wilson of the Beach Boys.' The headline called Wilson 'a genius'.

It wasn't all plain sailing. The Beach Boys might have been generous but they were also hard work, Taylor remembered: 'Brian Wilson shared more than just a first name with Epstein; he was just as impossible to please, just as edgy, and, unlike Epstein, he nurtured grudges and didn't write letters of remorse and regret.' As became very clear, Taylor was dealing with a volatile compound: added to layers of family trauma was Wilson's drug consumption and his obsessive desire to beat his competitors, Phil Spector and the Beatles.

During 1966, Wilson showed distinct signs of the pressure. Tony Asher remembered his 'fits of uncontrollable anger'. He showed distinct signs of paranoia, obsessing about the Beatles and his former inspiration, Phil Spector. 'Brian was forever staring into the mirror to see who was fairest,' Taylor recalled. 'As he said, finally, driving around and round the 9000 Building in a maroon Rolls he'd bought from John [Lennon], "It'll always be the Beatles for you, won't it?" "Yes," I said, "it always will" . . . He laughed frighteningly and stared through me.'

'Good Vibrations' was nurtured as Wilson's riposte to *Revolver*, which had been, in part, the Beatles' riposte to *Pet Sounds*. As the Great Race reached peak velocity that autumn, Wilson had the field pretty much to himself and, for a short while, the Beach Boys would be the hottest group in the world, with a new single that was a perfect match of innovative form and positive content. 'The idea is simple and spiritual,' Dennis Wilson told *Rave*: 'good thoughts – good ideas. An idea which is as old as time itself.'

As the months went on and Brian Wilson's ambitions expanded, 'Good Vibrations' was stacking up to be the most forward-looking, most joyous, most expensive record ever made. It was a year for grand statements, and Wilson began to conceive of 'Good Vibrations' as an instant of fusion that could change the course of pop culture. It spanned both R&B and psychedelia – the biggest new trends of the year. It was technological yet emotional, sensual and spiritual, with an immediate physical impact and a deeper, metaphysical meaning.

The phrase began in a childhood memory. At the age of six or seven, as Tony Asher told Domenic Priore, Wilson was frightened by a 'mean, vicious' dog as he was walking down the street with his mother. 'He was really frightened and started to cry, and his mother said, "Hey, you shouldn't let animals know that you are frightened, because they can tell, and it makes them more aggressive. What you really need to do is to let them know that you're not frightened, because they can pick up these vibrations from people." He said that he'd always thought that it would be fun to write a song about vibes and picking them up from other people.'

It was no accident that 'Good Vibrations' was informed by a return to childhood: it was a psychedelic song. Wilson began taking LSD in early 1965 and was totally struck by its effects. 'About a year ago I had what I consider a very religious experience,' he told Tom Nolan in autumn 1966. 'I took LSD, a full dose of LSD, and later, another time, I took a smaller dose. And I learned a lot of things, like patience, understanding. I can't teach you, or tell you, what I learned from taking it. But I consider it a very religious experience.'

'Good Vibrations' is saturated in heightened perception, whether the switchback in mood and texture created by all the edits, or the extremely precise and vivid detail of texture, colour and smell contained in words like 'blossom' and 'perfume' and phrases like 'the way the sunlight plays upon her hair'. Just as the experience of LSD prompted users to begin examining the potential of the brain, so the deeper meaning of the song is actually concerned with non-verbal communication: subtle feelings, even telepathy and ESP.

The extraordinary thing is that such a packed, compressed piece should have become such a huge hit on both sides of the Atlantic. On 5 November, the song stood at #17 in the American charts (after three weeks) and at #15 in the UK. That week, *Disc and Music Echo* put the Beach Boys on the cover in anticipation of their London visit. As well as a couple of features, the magazine ran a half-page EMI ad for the group's record that exhorted fans to 'make a date to meet them at London Airport. Arriving Sunday Nov 6th at 12.30pm. Flight SK 521.'

Like the Four Tops a few weeks before, the Beach Boys arrived as saviours of a flagging British pop scene. Their cumulative success during 1966 propelled them to the #1 World Male Vocal Group in the *Record Mirror* poll published on 5 November, just pipping the Beatles. When they arrived in London, they were met by a thousand rampaging fans, and quickly settled into a whirl of promotional duties: apart from the routine press conference, they were being filmed by Peter Whitehead for a BBC documentary, *The Beach Boys in London.*

The concerts hit the same problem that the Beatles had had earlier in the year: the near impossibility of reproducing increasingly complex recordings on stage. The Beach Boys were still locked into the traditional package-tour type of live experience. The Astoria show only lasted twenty minutes – 'very short rations', observed Ray Coleman in *Disc and Music Echo*. Not everyone agreed. *Melody Maker*'s Nick Jones thought that the show was 'sensational' and 'shattering': 'their happy stage act is as good or better than most British acts'.

After nine dates in six cities, the Beach Boys flew out on 15 November. Their visit had been an extremely successful media event that propelled 'Good Vibrations' to #1 in the UK on 19 November. California had come to London and conquered. It had been building all year, with the American success of the Mamas and the

Papas, the Association, Sonny and Cher, and the Monkees, but, along with the poll results, this was the final recognition that the centre of pop had shifted 5,400 miles westwards, from London to Los Angeles.

Derek Taylor remembered late 1966 LA as 'a glorious, naive and spontaneous coming together of people who in other times couldn't possibly have been so close and harmonious', but, even from his insider perspective, it was a fragile moment. It was ironic that, just at the moment when Los Angeles was being exalted thanks to the international success of 'Good Vibrations', its primacy as a cultural centre would be threatened. Outside the bubble, hostile forces were gathering strength, and they had America's nascent counter-culture right in their crosshairs.

* * *

'They're calling out the sheriff to bring his guns and tanks
The neighbourhood kids are up to the old pranks
And someone spiked the sugar bowls again down at Ben Franks
And this time no one's around to doubt them
The Playboy Club is retching cause someone gave them a tip:
A bomb is going to explode next door inside the Trip
But the bomb turns out to be another Freudian slip
By the folks who thought it'd be better off without them.'
    TANDYN ALMER, 'Sunset Strip Soliloquy', printed *in KRLA Beat*, 22 October 1966

There was trouble in paradise. On 8 November, Ronald Reagan was elected as the governor of California by just under 100,000 votes. The result was a major reversal for the Democrats, who had held the state for eight years, but, even more so, it signified a major shift in American politics. 'Republican Resurgence', trumpeted *Time* magazine: apart from eight governorships – which increased their tally to twenty-five out of fifty in total – the GOP won 700 seats in state legislatures, compared to the party's 529-seat loss just two years previously.

The post-mortems advanced various theories about the Republican revival. Part of it was the backlash – the hostility against Black Power and the fears about urban disorder. The results were also construed as the end of the Johnson sixties, the end of the legislature that had fostered civil rights and the Great Society. As *Newsweek* opined, 'Now the President's popularity seems to have flagged – and so has the public appetite for action. "I've a feeling that the people want a pause," Ronald Reagan allowed – and this time some of LBJ's friends in Congress agreed.'

The 1966 mid-terms marked the beginning of the New Right surge that would dominate the 1980s and beyond. As the political historian Andrew E. Busch writes, 'It is no exaggeration to say that the Great Society era of federal policymaking ended with the elections of 1966, or that the modern era of Republican strength began in 1966.' On his victory, Reagan was immediately seen as a potential presidential candidate, one of the three men whose 'ambitions and interplay will dominate the party's political life for the next two years'.

In California, Reagan had played on white-backlash fears at the same time as he targeted the most visible signs of the emergent counter-culture – the protesting students at Berkeley. In a major May 1966 speech, he castigated the licentious atmosphere – the dim lights, provocative gyrations, drug-taking and 'sexual misconduct' – that he alleged had occurred at a rock 'n' roll dance at Berkeley's Harmon gym the previous month. The young, clearly, were not behaving as they should, and it wasn't just politics, it was lifestyle: drugs, sex, anti-Vietnam protest.

It seemed, therefore, remarkably coincidental that in mid-November there were three separate events that highlighted a distinct chill in the relationship between California's authorities and the state's youth. The first centred around the symbolic figure of Mario Savio. Having withdrawn from Berkeley in 1964, the leader of the Free Speech Movement sought to reapply to the university in December 1965. He was seen as a troublemaker, not the sort of person the authorities wanted, and his application started a wrangle that went on for over a year.

Berkeley's chancellor, Clark Kerr, resisted concerted attempts within the university to ban Savio, but he was also in Reagan's sights.* Although not yet readmitted, Savio got involved in radical activity on campus, leafleting for a 4 November rally aimed at keeping the steps of Sproul Hall – the very place where he had delivered his famous 'bodies upon the gears' speech in December 1964 – as a legitimate site for protest. This was exactly the excuse that the authorities needed: on 7 November, Savio's application to resume his studies was denied.

Four days after Reagan's election, a major disturbance erupted on Sunset Strip. There was a distinct feeling that a confrontation was inevitable, and the spark occurred when two seventeen-year-olds, fed up with what they saw as the oppressive LAPD presence on the Strip, printed up a few leaflets stating 'that there would be a protest against the police on November the 12th at Pandora's Box'. The complaint was of 'Police mistreatment of youth on Sunset Blvd', citing 'Shackling of 14&15 year olds' and 'Arbitrary arrests of youths'.

After a whip-round at the Fifth Estate coffee house, enough money was raised to print another 5,000 copies. 'The button had been pushed,' wrote Art Kunkin in the *Los Angeles Free Press*, 'and the initiators sat back to watch what would happen, not knowing if more than three or four people would come.' By nine o'clock, it was a Happening: between one and three thousand youths were milling around Pandora's Box, at the junction of Sunset Strip and Crescent Heights. Traffic backed up, and trouble ensued.

A couple of buses were caught up in the mill of people, and about twenty or thirty youths began attacking one of them, breaking a window, covering the inside with foam from the bus's fire extinguisher and rocking it until the driver and passengers were forced to get out: 'The windshield wipers were bent and fingers went to work on the clouded windshield scrawling "Free the

* He would be dismissed on 20 January 1967, three weeks after Reagan took office.

15 year olds" and "Closed".' At the same time, fights broke out between teenagers and servicemen at the edge of the crowd.

The initial reaction of the police, who were taken by surprise, was to pacify the crowd. When they later arrived in force, at around 10.30 p.m., they 'formed into groups and began conventional crowd control techniques, sweeping the streets and sidewalks'. At this point, they made a concerted effort to shift everyone off the street, in particular the youths congregated outside Pandora's Box. They surrounded the club and demanded that the innocent patrons inside leave, leading to a stand-off that lasted for several hours.

Los Angeles was a major media centre and the events of that first night received massive coverage. The *San Francisco Chronicle* jumped straight in with headlines like 'A Riot on Sunset Strip' and 'Teen-Agers, GIs on Rampage', with suitably lurid pictures of pro-testors standing on top of a bus and, in one much syndicated photo-graph, a youth in sunglasses, a stripy top and very long hair striking 'a menacing pose'. The *Los Angeles Herald-Examiner* went even further with headlines like 'Teenage Rampage' and 'Bus Burns in Sunset Strip Riot'.

The events of 12 November were the opening salvo in what would become a prolonged battle. It had been developing for a while: as *KRLA Beat* wondered that month, people were talking about how 'the Strip was suffering from over-exposure publicity wise, and if it will become like the Village'. Los Angeles had been all too successful in promoting itself as the latest centre of pop cul-ture, and, as it hit the national news magazines, the Strip scene began to approach critical mass.

During the summer, the teenagers on the Strip had escalated in number at the same time as they decreased in age. Many could not afford to get into the clubs – even those which operated a fifteen-to-eighteen age policy – and so collected on the street, just to catch the action. 'Every weekend the kids pour into the Strip,' wrote Jules Siegel. 'When they get there, they hang around. "I'm famous," says Renee, who has been standing in front of Pandora's Box for a long time, waiting for something to happen. "I'm Superlungs. They wrote that song about me."'

The sheriff's department took action. There were major incidents at Canter's Deli – 276 arrests on two separate occasions in July – and at Ben Frank's – three busloads of teens arrested in late October. Licences permitting under-eighteens to be served anything were revoked in several clubs. Each weekend dozens of underage kids were taken to downtown police stations after the 10 p.m. curfew: 'to get them out, their parents must sign for them'.

The Strip's street scene was interpreted as hostile by local businessmen and LA County supervisor Ernest Debs. The teen throngs were having an adverse effect on property prices, and local trade associations like the Sunset Plaza Merchants Association lobbied for an even more stringent application of the curfew regulations. Set during the wartime Victory Girl* scandals, these prevented anyone under eighteen from loitering in the area after 10 p.m. As the Strip became a promenade as much as an entertainment area, flashpoints were bound to occur.

On 3 November, brothers Francis J. and George Montgomery, the leaders of the Sunset Plaza Merchants Association, gave an interview to the *Los Angeles Times* in which they asked the police to 'enforce the curfew and licensing laws' because of the hordes of teenagers 'causing commotion'. It was, as Art Kunkin wrote, simply 'two groups of businessmen fighting each other': the owners of the teen nightclubs versus the restaurant owners who catered to an older market. But it had serious consequences.

Once the flashpoint had occurred, both sides quickly entrenched. On Sunday the 13th, the LAPD closed off Sunset Boulevard from Crescent Heights to Fairfax Avenue, four blocks in all. About three hundred protestors turned up, some yelling 'Gestapo Gestapo' at the police, who 'seemed to be in a state of panic': they 'used shocking language to the people present, used their billy clubs unnecessarily toward people who were already obeying their instructions to

---

* The name given to teenage girls in America who offered companionship and, often, sex to servicemen during the Second World War.

move out of the area and, generally, with a few notable exceptions, lost their cool'.

It was the Yardbirds' 'You're a Better Man Than I' enacted on the streets of Los Angeles: 'Why should hair length, a beard or sandals be any more a true test of a man than skin colour?' The teenagers had a point, as Kunkin observed: they argued 'that it takes intelligence on their part to make a choice that is different from that of the majority. And those under eighteen say: "shortly we'll be asked to fight in the jungles of Vietnam. Why shouldn't we be allowed to visit the area of our choice in Los Angeles after ten p.m.?"'

The Sunset Strip riots immediately became a litmus test of youth's increasing assertiveness and the reactionary adult response. Writing in the *Village Voice*, Jules Siegel observed a connection between Mario Savio's recent travails and 'a thousand freaks demonstrating in the name of freedom on Sunset Strip Saturday night': 'in a very important way they were both different faces of the same force of change pumping through California and America in a marvellously powerful, however narrow stream – the force of the turned-on people'.

On Tuesday 15 November, a week after Reagan's election, the police took action in San Francisco. At the Acid Test Graduation in late October, Ken Kesey had talked about 'the west coast and how a cosmic intensity has been been gathering here, that the beat in the music was changing from life–death, life–death to death–life, death–life, but at the same time there was a contracting movement, a tensing, a political and cosmic and persona; movement to the right, a right-wing contraction'.

The forces of contraction were embodied that day in two vice squad detectives called Peter Maloney and Sol Weiner. At 2.30 p.m., they entered the Psychedelic Shop on 1535 Haight and bought a copy of the recently published *The Love Book* by Lenore Kandel. Fetching two uniformed officers from the street, they arrested the shop's clerk, Allen Cohen, for selling an obscene work. They closed the shop and began harassing the customers.

Another young man, James Helms, was arrested when he tried to force his way in.

Within an hour, there was a Happening. KRON TV covered the event: the brief clips show a dozen or so young men and women circling outside the Psychedelic Shop, dressed down in sandals, T-shirts and army surplus jackets, and bearing placards that state 'Fascist Police', 'Cops Go Home', 'Police Illegal'. One young man is interviewed: 'They were pushing people around,' he says of the police, 'they were pushing people out of the store.' When the protestors asked what was going on, they were told that it was 'a pornography issue'.

Two days later, the police struck again. This time they targeted the City Lights bookstore, arresting the clerk and removing sixteen copies of the offending item. The *Chronicle* reported that this was part of a concerted drive on the part of the police 'to find obscene material' and quoted the arresting officer's claims that *The Love Book* was 'hard core pornography'. '"I'm not a prude," Inspector Maloney said yesterday. But, with a gesture towards the poems, he asked: "where is the redeeming social importance in this?"'

The Love Book was a strange test case. It was a slim volume, only six pages of text, housed in a poetry-style format and with a striking cover showing Buddha and an ecstatic female. 'God/Love Poem' contained specific sexual references and explicit words, but the overwhelming drift of the poem was to treat sex as an expression of the deep union between two people: 'We are transmuting / We are as soft and warm and trembling / As a new gold butterfly.' Kandel's ideal was 'to fuck with love'.

With such intentions, *The Love Book* couldn't have been further away from the meat rack of conventional pornography. Quite apart from anything else, it was written by a woman. In 1966, Lenore Kandel was thirty-four. Having moved to San Francisco in 1960 to join the beat scene, she befriended Jack Kerouac and appeared as Romana Schwartz in the novel *Big Sur* – 'a big Rumanian monster beauty of some kind with big purple eyes and very tall and big

. . . but also intelligent, well-read, writes poetry, is a Zen student, knows everything'.

By 1966, Kandel was an established poet and, at the same time, was working as a belly-dancer. She was part of the older bohemian group that included some of the Diggers. She was 'amazed' at the police confiscation and threatened prosecution, she told the *Chronicle* in November 1966. 'Perhaps the obscenity is in their minds – there's none in the book,' she claimed. 'Love words have become curse words and that makes love more difficult. I'd like to free love from those words.'

In making a test case of *The Love Book*, the police were breaking a butterfly upon a wheel. But the double bust was part of a wider anti-obscenity drive, as the *Chronicle* noted: 'The Police Department has just doubled its efforts to find obscene material in a campaign it opened last February. This new drive, Police Chief Thomas Cahill said, has become necessary to "hold this in line".' Periodic checks had been 'sufficient in the past', Cahill added, but 'now it takes constant surveillance because of this type of material that has been appearing'.

Clearly, the political climate was behind the seizure, and that was immediately understood by the underground press. 'One week after Ronald Reagan was elected Governor of the state of California and the CLEAN smut-smiting initiative went down to defeat,' wrote Lee Meyerzove in the *Oracle*, 'the San Francisco Police Department decided to enforce the Reagan-morality of his "Creative Society" by assaulting the Psychedelic Shop in the Haight-Ashbury District for selling Lenore Kandel's *The Love Book*.'

There was a wider backlash not just against the nascent counterculture, but against other expressions of sexual and marginal freedoms: topless dancing, the heightened visibility of gay bars and the increasing assertiveness of the homophile movement, and increased co-habitation between young men and women. Beginning in 1963, a former navy chaplain called E. Richard Barnes made it his God-given task to 'clean up' California, forming the CLEAN initiative (California League Enlisting Action Now). By 1966, he had half a million signatures backing a proposition to be voted on in the November mid-terms. Subtitled 'Prohibition on Obscene Materials and Conduct', amongst Proposition 16's provisions was one removing the need to prove that a work had 'to be utterly without redeeming social importance' in order for it to be found obscene. Barnes claimed that California was on the point of being swamped by material that displayed 'whipping, gagging, sex rituals, trans-vestia, sadism, masochism, homosexuality' et al.

Proposition 16 was roundly defeated on 8 November, but it had the effect of creating a hostile framework for police action, hence Inspector Maloney's comment about 'redeeming social impor-tance'. The affair was not only an attack on Kandel and her poetry but also on the Psychedelic Shop and City Lights, two bastions of the city's alternative community. The *Oracle* was published out of the former, and in issue 3 it had contained an extremely clear account of police brutality towards a man who had been arrested while tripping on LSD.

Clearly, the two sides were shaping up for a prolonged conflict – and, indeed, *The Love Book* case would rumble on through the courts for years. Meanwhile, the police and the teens were back on the Sunset Strip for a second weekend on Friday 18 and Saturday 19 November. 'The situation . . . remains tense and unresolved,' wrote Brian Carr in the *Los Angeles Free Press*, which reported the large demonstrations with the headline 'Youth Provoke Police – All Over'.

The *Los Angeles Free Press* captured the mood: 'Some of the dem-onstrators at Pandora's Box last weekend were blowing bubbles, some had flowers in their mouth, and others were holding picket signs protesting what they called discrimination against youth by city authorities.' The police responded by moving people gently along. At 10 p.m. a police sound truck, accompanied by a phalanx of officers, moved up to the Pandora's Box triangle. 'The missing element of excitement had at last been provided. Unfortunately, it was by the police.'

Another stand-off ensued between the serried ranks of police and about five hundred protestors, during which the owner of Pandora's Box, Bill Tilden, was arrested. On Monday, the County Board of Supervisors rescinded the ordinance that allowed teenagers to dance in licensed Sunset Strip clubs, a move that showed the influence of Ernest Debs. 'The premise that closing such establishments will end this problem is absurd,' stated the *Los Angeles Free Press*; 'if anything it will heighten the resolve of young people to force the issue to a conclusion.'

Both sides were digging in. Amid rumours that local businessmen were urging the police to take a tougher line, the protestors announced another gathering for Saturday the 26th. 'YOUTH WILL NOT BE PUSHED OFF THE STRIP!!!' ran the poster. During that week, as the anti-dancing rules began to bite, more and more adults began to show solidarity with the Strip's youth, either by influencing public opinion in the press or by offering on-the-ground support.

Concerned by the escalation, a group of music industry movers and shakers got together on Friday the 25th to form a supportive umbrella organisation. Headed by the Byrds' manager Jim Dickson and supported by his partner Ed Tickner, Al Mitchell from the Fifth Estate, Elmer Valentine from the Whiskey a Go Go and David Anderle from Beach Boys Enterprises, CAFF (Community Action for Facts and Freedom Committee) aimed to send adults – wearing yellow armbands marked 'Volunteer Parents' – into the crowds as witnesses to any trouble.

'CAFF was to subsidise, maybe pay for, the defence and (maybe) fines of kids framed by the law enforcement agencies,' Derek Taylor later wrote, 'to pay for propagandising the innocence of the young who hung out on the strip, and it was the most logical thing in the world that it should have been Dickson who became involved politically, for it was Dickson who had first seen that the Byrds could not be just a rock 'n' roll band, but also the musical representatives of a whole subculture.'

The 26th was a show of strength: while the six hundred or so youths were orderly, the police moved down Sunset Boulevard, 'shoving the protestors into side streets or clubbing them into the pavement. Those arrested were often prodded with nightsticks or repeatedly shoved into the ground before being loaded off on police buses.' The *Los Angeles Free Press* reported that 'there was no plan or purpose evident in the beatings or the subsequent arrests'. Press photographs from the event showed Peter Fonda being arrested. He told the media, 'Man, the kids have had it.'

The whole affair had escalated from being a hardball struggle between two sets of businessmen into a bitter pitched battle between two groups with vastly different ideas of freedom, divided by a gulf in age and attitude. Derek Taylor was there on the 26th as an affiliate of CAFF and saw how 'professional cops can always crush amateur freedomniks if they have a mind to, saw a sheriff's deputy spit on a woman, saw Peter Fonda in handcuffs, saw how bad things could be before they got worse'.

On the 28th, Brian Wilson returned to Gold Star Studios on Santa Monica Boulevard, around two miles from the Strip's epicentre. He was busy recording the Beach Boys' new album with the crack musicians he had used on *Pet Sounds*. *SMiLE* was designed as a vauntingly ambitious record: just as the Beatles would return to their Liverpool childhoods that mid-winter, so Wilson was going back to archetypal Americana – the Founding Fathers, the great drive west and the myths of California, the home of surf culture and the end of all things.

By late November, Wilson had recorded around twelve songs, or segments of songs. His working methods had become more complicated after 'Good Vibrations', with the next epic, 'Heroes and Villains', threatening to dwarf even that groundbreaking record in complexity and hours of studio time. The material for the new album abounded in short 'feels', beautiful fragments that were in varying stages of completion but were not yet assembled, as was intended, into part of a larger whole.

It was only Wilson who knew the design, and there were signs that the complicated patchwork was beginning to unravel. With the Beach Boys away for weeks on end, *SMiLE* basically existed as a collection of instrumentals. Wilson was planning to add the vocals at some point after the touring group's last date on 24 November. On his return from London in mid-November, Derek Taylor arranged for a number of journalists to capture the 'Genius with a very large capital G' in the studio, working on his magnum opus.

It remains ironic that an album that would not be released for forty years should have been so well documented at the time. The longest and most prestigious article was by Jules Siegel, part of Wilson's entourage that autumn. Siegel was present as Wilson returned to the studio on 28 November, and it was clear that something out of the ordinary was going on: Wilson was 'wearing a competition stripe surfer's T-shirt, tight white duck pants, pale green bowling shoes and a red plastic toy fireman's helmet. Everyone was wearing identical red plastic toy fireman's helmets.'

Wilson was completely in control of the studio, teaching each musician their part, which he already had in his head. They began the take: 'A gigantic fire howled out of the massive studio speakers in a pounding crush of pictorial music that summoned up visions of roaring, windstorm flames, falling timbers, mournful sirens and sweating firemen, building into a peak and crackling off into fading embers as a single drum turned into a collapsing wall and the fire-engine cellos dissolved and disappeared.'

After twenty-four takes, Wilson pronounced it finished. '"What do you think?" Brian asked. "It's incredible. Incredible," whispered one of the musicians, a man in his fifties, wearing a Hawaiian shirt and iridescent trousers and pointed black Italian shoes. "Absolutely incredible." "Yeah," said Brian on the way home, an acetate trial copy or "dub" of the tape in his hands, the red plastic fire helmet still on his head. "Yeah, I think I'm going to call this 'Mrs. O'Leary's Fire' and I think it might just scare a whole load of people."'

'Fire' is indeed one of the most frightening pieces of music ever to come out of Los Angeles. Beginning with a circular introduction – half *Looney Tunes*, half nightmare – it quickly settles into a glutinous triple bass riff and a lowering pattern from drummer

Jim Gordon. The fire-engine string instruments – violas, cellos and violins – loop and twist around each other in a dance that does not resolve but slowly crackles out into a blackened aftermath. Nothing could have been more different to the tenderness of *Pet Sounds*.

Clearly, there was something sinister behind the good vibrations. Indeed, part of the PR for 'Good Vibrations' had been the group's use of the electro-theremin, very similar to the instrument used in the soundtrack of Hitchcock's 1945 psychological thriller *Spellbound*. The sound that it made – swooping and other-worldly – evoked sensations of unease and eeriness, if not horror. Very few people caught this undertow, but Jules Siegel was one: 'To some people, "Good Vibrations" was considerably crazier than Gregory Peck had been in the movie.'

With 'Good Vibrations', Brian Wilson gathered together all the threads of popular culture, but they were slipping through his hands. 'Have you ever tried the mirror technique of the sub-conscious?' he had asked in the *Melody Maker* that October. 'I'm reading a book about it – I'm fascinated by the mind and hypnosis and things like that.' By the next month, he was entering the fun house of his own mind: as Derek Taylor later wrote, 'The mirrors into which Brian Wilson looks for reassurance are not always kind. Sometimes there is no reflection at all.'

Perhaps, also, Wilson captured all too well the atmosphere of his city at this critical time. 'Fire' reflected the fear of the LAPD that many Sunset Strip youths felt, and the conflict between young and old, which was drawing in his close friends and colleagues in CAFF, must have seeped into Wilson's consciousness. Certainly, there was an element of automatism in the piece's composition – an opening up of the psyche to bad vibrations – that made him repudiate the performance within days. It was, too obviously, the sound of darkness, if not madness.

Sunset Strip was not over; the police overreaction on the 26th had only made things worse. Suddenly, what had began as a small protest on the part of a couple of irritated teens was in danger of igniting into a conflagration that could 'dwarf Watts to a tea party'.

The pictures of uniformed officers and grimacing teens, caught in their grip, were a pre-echo of things to come in the sixties' next phase. As the *Los Angeles Free Press* observed, 'If this powder keg is ignored, if its nature is oversimplified: it may well explode.'

An American who loves Britain and a Briton
who lives in America offer diagnosis and cure

Shrinking Pains
of Mini-England

"An acknowledged dandy of the new order" is David Mlinaric, a London interior designer.

The Total Revolution

12 : DECEMBER

My Mind's Eye: Dreams of Freedom,
a Prophetic Minority and the Return to Childhood

'It's pretty obvious that contemporary music reflects contemporary life. And vice versa.'

TONY HALL, 'My Scene', *Record Mirror*, 3 December 1966

Seven guitar notes are completed by two more, rising upwards and emphasised by a celeste. The mood is contradictory: raw and sweetened, impatient and contemplative. After a quick restatement of the riff, the full band comes in, with Steve Marriott's vocal: 'I sit here every day / Looking at the sky / Ever wondering why / I dream my dreams away.' Accentuated by grace-note harmonies, the singer communicates a fundamental revelation.

During the bridge, however, the Small Faces reveal the other side of this blissful state. Whatever this experience is, people don't understand it; they're 'laughing behind their hands'. The third verse is a defiant statement of outsider pride: the singer doesn't care about the non-initiated, 'Because they'll never see / All that I can see / With my mind's eye.' For the remaining fifty seconds of this short song, the group harmonise through the changes, weaving around a melody taken from the old Christmas carol 'Angels We Have Heard on High'.

This was quite a change from a few months before, when the nineteen-year old Marriott was bellowing 'picked her up on a Friday night'. 1966 was a frantic year, and the Small Faces rode it with three Top 10 singles and a Top 3 album by November, all of which explored the common ground between commercial pop, Who-style slashed chords, droning rave-ups and Stax grooves. Their increasing skill and maturity bore fruit in 'All or Nothing', a storming, perfectly realised fusion of soul and hard mod pop that went to #1 in mid-September.

497

After 'Sha-La-La-Lee', the Small Faces had been presented – with their connivance – as cheeky cockneys, a mod boy band, happy to be photographed raiding the Carnaby Street boutiques for clothes marked out by clashing patterns: plaid, polka dots, stripes. Rarely off the television, they were toured relentlessly by their manager Don Arden. They were all young – aged between eighteen and twenty-one in autumn 1966 – and could deal with the pressure, but they were also hip Londoners who could see the way that the wind was blowing.

'My Mind's Eye' was clearly a drug song, although it said much for the comparative naivety of the British music press and record-buying public that this wasn't fully realised in late 1966. Like 'dream', the term 'mind' had become a keyword for the psychedelic experience: a gateway into the interior, subjective states brought on by the use of marijuana and LSD. Nothing could have been more different from the pill-fuelled clubbing and frantic consumerism that marked the Small Faces' early career and the whole idea of Swinging London.

The clues were already there, however, in the interviews that the Small Faces did in the early autumn. *Record Mirror* found them talking about their musical experiments with glasses of water, playing around with 'different levels to get the right notes'. *Melody Maker*'s Chris Welch chatted to Steve Marriott in the *Top of the Pops* dressing room: 'We're progressing all the time. Even "All or Nothing" has moved along, which is a gas. "Sha La La" [*sic*] and "Hey Girl" were nursery rhymes. We're now writing lyrics that mean something, and it'll be great.'

Marriott ran through two new songs for the *Melody Maker* reporter, 'That Man' and 'My Mind's Eye', both of which found the soul belter singing very softly. 'It's a much nicer groove,' Marriott stated, mentioning the group's intention to record 'My Mind's Eye' with this new approach. 'Will the new way out gear be above their fans' heads?' Welch asked. 'We do go along with the kids – we're only kids ourselves,' Marriott replied. 'We can drive along and I don't think it'll deter them. We're putting down something we feel strongly about.'

The interviews for 'My Mind's Eye' went further. The Small Faces were at once mod fashion plates and fearless cosmonauts, wearing Caravel sweaters while expounding on the meaning of life. 'I believe we came from the earth and we go back to it when we die,' Marriott told *Rave* in November. 'The earth gives you and the earth takes back, and you become the bark of a tree, or a cluster of grass. That accounts for the desire of people to get close to the earth. Haven't you ever felt such emotion from the scent of a flower that you wanted to crush it in your hand?

'Thinking is a gas,' he pronounced, but the Small Faces' new single wasn't – not for the group at least. They had delivered a demo of 'My Mind's Eye' to Don Arden before they left for a concert tour. Returning from Newcastle after the final date on 6 November, they heard it on the radio, bare and unadorned. The demo had been leaked by Arden without their approval, sparking a huge row between manager and group, who quickly rushed into the studio to add the extra vocal parts and harmonies heard on the more familiar version.

The music press was ignorant of these rapid manoeuvrings. 'My Mind's Eye' was something different, and was received as such on its mid-November release. 'This is going to be the Small Faces' biggest hit,' wrote Penny Valentine. 'I have never really understood the gigantic commercial success their records have had in the past, being, as they were, rather melodiousless. But this is intensely charming with lots of melody line.' It was an instant hit, rising to #8 in the UK charts on 3 December and peaking at #4 over the next two weeks.

There was some controversy about the fact that 'My Mind's Eye' filched the melody from a one-hundred-and-fifty-year-old hymn, but the religious tinge and transcendent sentiments made it a perfect Christmas record. Behind the scenes, however, the Small Faces were in turmoil. The premature release of the single was the final straw for the group, who brought Don Arden's tenure to an end. The no-nonsense manager had already blotted his copybook when, deflecting criticism of his financial arrangements, he told a deputation of Small Faces' parents that their children were drug addicts.

During December, the Small Faces were palmed off onto the Harold Davidson Agency, which already arranged their concert bookings; they later alleged that they were sold off and passed around like pieces of meat. While their business affairs were in a state of confusion, their record deal with Decca – an Arden tie-in – was also in doubt, consigning recent recordings like 'That Man', 'Just Passing', 'Green Circles' and 'Yesterday, Today and Tomorrow' into an instant limbo.

Melody Maker's Nick Jones attended the early December session for 'Green Circles' – a song based on 'a dream' – and found a group advancing at a rapid rate: 'No more "Sha-La-La-Lee". No more "My Mind's Eye". The past is blocked out completely for the moment. There's only one way – forward. Every record is that bit better. Every record becomes that bit more fascinating.' Like all their most recent songs, 'Green Circles' was a softer drone, with a lyric about a visionary, a seer who, like 'That Man', had hidden knowledge that he wished to impart to the world.

The Small Faces were no strangers to drugs, starting on pills before progressing to marijuana: the moody chalk faces on the cover of their first LP were brightened up by several graffitied spliffs. In May 1966, they had been introduced to LSD by Brian Epstein, who visited their communal Pimlico house bearing oranges spiked with the drug. Afterwards, nothing was the same: as Ronnie Lane told Keith Altham, 'There are other things I'm finding out about – they're as old as time. It's just that I'm beginning to see them more clearly.'

In late 1966, LSD was the great divider: between those who were and those who weren't in the know. Pop was becoming a battleground of warring tribes: between the hippies, the teenyboppers and the mums and dads; between those who wanted to progress, those who wanted everything to stay in the present and those who wanted to hark back to the past. Records were becoming indicators of an attitude, even of a world view. Yesterday, today or tomorrow: what was it to be?

This was a new kind of question, and many groups and artists were not sure what to make of these demands. If the past was the choice, then you risked being called 'square' or other, even worse names – consigned, ultimately, to cabaret. If it was the present, then that involved an almost impossible balancing act between the two extremes. If it was tomorrow, then you were sticking your neck out, fostering not only rejection and paranoia – 'laughing behind their hands' – but also a sense of superiority, the revelling in the intrigue of being part of an exclusive club.

The Small Faces had begun as a classic mod group, the only one to step out of the audience onto the stage and into the charts; in contrast, the Who had been styled as mods before Pete Townshend found his role as interpreter for the subculture. They had exemplified the mod penchant for soul, pills and noisy all-nighters but, by December 1966, their personalities and their music had evolved into something different under the overwhelming impact of LSD. Some of their audience would not follow them, but many others would, for it promised to be a hell of a ride.

Steve Marriott nailed his colours to the mast that December. 'I agree the old "groupy" world is tottering,' he told *Rave*, 'and I'm sad for those who have to go.' But he felt that the pop scene had never been more exciting, after *Revolver* and the Beach Boys had spurred everyone on to higher and higher standards. 'I'm very serious about it,' he said. 'It is an art, whether people wish to admit it or not. There is a whole new outlook in sound now, not around the corner but on the corner . . . you must be a musician, and a thinker.

'Sometimes thinking makes me appear melancholy, when really I'm very happy,' he concluded. 'People who come to my place to hear me listening intently to music, or just thinking, instead of chatting and laughing, accuse me of being a misery, but I'm not. From listening to all kinds of music, I get ideas of my own. The sounds I finally produce are nothing like the ones I've been listening to, but somehow along a chain of thought, they made me produce something good. It's a funny old business, living, and producing tomorrow's sounds.'

* * *

'Very few people are ahead of the "progressive" pop group. Well, they go too fast. All those instruments, arrangements, electronics, voices and the noise. Oh the noise! As for the melody, well y'know, you couldn't whistle THAT in the bath. Thus we have a demand for records that are today. This is common knowledge. Even the hippies don't sneer at the records of today – well maybe one or two – because they are aware of their appeal and position in pop. Some harmony, a touch of sentimentality every now and again, and sound that doesn't offend.'

NICK JONES, 'The Folk Flavour of Today', *Melody Maker*, 3 December 1966

The British charts in early December were an eclectic mix. There was a lot of Atlantic and Motown; some straightforward commercial pop of the day – Paul Jones's 'High Time', Manfred Mann's splendidly splenetic 'Semi-Detached Suburban Mr James'; a few beat boom updates – the Troggs, the Easybeats' 'Friday on My Mind'; and some forward-thinkers – the Beach Boys, the Small Faces, the Spencer Davis Group. Old favourites like Roy Orbison and Cliff Richard slugged it out with pirate radio picks by ? and the Mysterians and the Sandpipers.

Dominating everything that month, however, was Tom Jones's 'Green, Green Grass of Home', which went to #1 on 3 December and stayed there for the rest of the year. Like 'Distant Drums', it was a country song – first heard on the Jerry Lee Lewis album *Country Songs for City Folks* – with a death-haunted lyric that offered some surcease within a nation still coming to terms with the events of late October. For, despite its American origins, it remains hard not to see the success of 'Green, Green Grass of Home' as a response to Aberfan.

It was Jones's fourteenth single, and a distinct change from his recent uptempo sides, most of which had failed to enter the Top 20. It had been a long diminuendo since his early-1965 #1 'It's Not Unusual'. Although Jones declared an intent to record with Motown early that winter, the decision had already been made for him to switch to ballads, a perennially popular form well suited to his rich baritone, which sounded strained on tricksier, faster numbers like 'What's New Pussycat?' or 'Not Responsible'.

'Green, Green Grass of Home' is a classic country song of regret and contrition, but it is also cleverly worded and, in Jones's version, sung with both passion and precision. It begins with two verses, during which the protagonist returns to his old home town, where he sees his parents and his childhood sweetheart and indulges in an ecstasy of redemption. The spoken-word finale brutally reveals this as the fantasy of a condemned man on his last night; the only way he will touch the green, green grass of home is in a casket. There is no return home.

It was recorded on 5 October, sixteen days before the tip slide. Tom Jones was a Valleys boy himself, born during June 1940 in Pontypridd, six miles from Aberfan. Only a few months older than John Lennon, he seemed of a different generation: strong, well built, with a powerful voice and shortish hair. Unlike Lennon, he remained happy to identify himself with his place of origin: his September 1966 album *From the Heart* featured an iconic shot of the singer standing above Pontypridd, with its cluster of houses curling around the valley.

As pop's most famous Welshman, Tom Jones was inevitably identified with the disaster; indeed, the very title of his hit song echoed Richard Llewellyn's classic 1939 novel about a South Wales mining community, *How Green Was My Valley*. In December, he headlined an all-star show, filmed as *The Heart of Show Business*, which featured Richard Burton, Shirley Bassey and Sean Connery, among others, and raised funds for the Aberfan Disaster Fund. His record, meanwhile, stayed at the top, reminding everyone of lives cut short and the impossibility of going back.

Other musicians loathed it. On the point of releasing 'Happy Jack' – the third in a string of psychological singles about extreme outsiders – Pete Townshend ripped into 'Green, Green Grass of Home'. 'I hate this new hit of his,' he told *Disc and Music Echo* in early December. 'It's sentimental crap.' The magazine observed that 'he feels he has every right to be boiling. Reeves has just had a huge success with "Distant Drums" and other singers such as Val Doonican, Tom Jones and the Seekers are all set to swamp the charts with more sugar-laden lyrics.'

This prediction was fulfilled when, in the chart of 17 December, Tom Jones was at #1 with 'Green, Green Grass of Home', Val Doonican at #2 with 'What Would I Be' and the Seekers at #3 with 'Morningtown Ride'. The latter was a folk-lite version of Malvina Reynolds's lullaby, while Doonican's song was a folk-inflected, upbeat number – slightly reminiscent of Bob Lind's 'Elusive Butterfly' – written by pop professional Jackie Trent. The lyric hinted at pop's increased stridency: 'The angry voices raised in vain.'

Doonican and the Seekers gave eloquent defences of their position in the pop press. 'If I was a teenager I'd think Val Doonican was a terrible square,' the Irish crooner admitted. Nearly forty, he regarded himself as 'just one very little name in show business but as long as there are people – children, middle-aged mums and dads and the old folk – who like my songs, that's the point. You see, honesty with yourself is the biggest thing I've learned. To be able to sit back, look at yourself, and accept that obviously there are some people who don't like you.'

Both the Seekers and Val Doonican were perennials on mainstream television: the former with their appearances on *Top of the Pops*, as well as light entertainment extravaganzas like *Sunday Night at the London Palladium*; the latter with his BBC series *The Val Doonican Show*, which went out on Saturdays and was watched by 14.5 million people – over a quarter of the total UK population. This was prime exposure denied to the progressives, who resented them accordingly.

'Morningtown Ride' was the Seekers' sixth Top 10 hit since they arrived in the UK from Australia during 1964; two of these, 'I'll Never Find Another You' and 'The Carnival Is Over', reached #1. Talking to Nick Jones in early December 1966, guitarist Keith Potger described the group as comprised of 'four pretty reasonable people' who were determined to cater to 'the developed and mature taste'. The Seekers, he stated, 'will remain as contemporary as we can without getting too involved with tomorrow!'

In the same week, Chris Welch observed that pop was growing 'older and more complex'. He presented four categories, ranging from traditional to avant-garde pop. In the 'traditional' category he placed perennials like Cliff and balladeers like Ken Dodd and the Bachelors; 'mainstream' covered artists such as Tom Jones, Dusty Springfield, the Kinks and the Troggs; 'modern' exponents included the Rolling Stones, the Who, the Small Faces, the Tamla artists and Donovan; while the 'avant-garde' included the Beach Boys, the Move, the Creation, the Pink Floyd, Cream and the Beatles.

Age was becoming a talking point. 'What's the age limit for Pop success? Is it 21 – or 25?' asked the *Melody Maker*, observing that both John Lennon and Ringo Starr had recently turned twenty-six. Most of the pop stars polled felt that twenty-five was too old to start a career in pop music but that crossing that threshold made little difference. The one dissenter was Stevie Wright from the Easybeats, who felt that groups over twenty-five 'should try to mature and appeal to an older audience – perhaps move into cabaret. You shouldn't be in a pop group if you're over 25.'

The traditional view of pop culture was that it was something you grew out of once you'd reached marrying age or entered full-time work, or, if neither, then the mid-twenties, the upper limit of the classic age definition of the teenager – fifteen to twenty-four. But, in late 1966, the whole nature of what pop music was and what it could be was up for grabs. The title of Chris Welch's article was 'Progressive Pop', and it was the first word of that phrase more than any other that marked the disintegration of any mid-sixties consensus.

Swinging London had been predicated on a fragile economic confidence that, by the end of 1966, had completely disappeared. By December, thanks to the more stringently applied wage and price freeze, unemployment in the UK stood at 542,000, double the figure for July. 'Swinging' had got 'out of hand', according to senior *Life* editor Gene Farmer, 'because it is the kind of fun that only a rich nation can afford – and England is no longer a rich nation'.

By the end of 1966, people were kicking the corpse. 'We hate the Swinging London scene,' Keith Moon told *Rave*. Promoting *Blow-Up*, Michelangelo Antonioni offered his thoughts: 'The young people among whom my film is situated are all aimless, without any other drive but to reach that aimless freedom. Freedom that for them means marijuana, sexual perversion, anything . . . It's the conquest of freedom that matters . . . once it's conquered, once all discipline is discarded, then it's decadence. Decadence without any visible future.'

Certainly, there was material for the moralists to get upset about that December as, in the ever-expanding quest for sensation, the Move chopped up pictures of Adolf Hitler onstage and Brian Jones was pictured – for convoluted reasons of his own – in a full SS uniform with swastika armband. The end-of-an-era feeling was enhanced by the increasing number of *Greatest Hits* albums released as the year went on: collections by the Animals, the Beach Boys, Manfred Mann, the Rolling Stones and, on 9 December, *A Collection of Beatles Oldies*.

The structures that had supported Britain's pop boom were crumbling. The pirate radio stations were in disarray; as the Marine Offences Bill wound its way through parliamentary procedure, fort-based stations like Radio 390 and Radio England were effectively silenced. DJs began to look for the lifeboats: as Radio 390's Stuart Henry admitted, 'Being a deejay on a pirate ship is like being in a condemned cell – except that the bloke in the cell is in a better position because they've abolished hanging. At any moment, the pirates can expect a date of execution.'

In mid-November, Rediffusion announced the cancellation of *Ready Steady Go!*, which was seen as too expensive for the ratings it attracted. The weekly programme had been an integral part of the broadcasting and development of Britain's youth music since its inception in early August 1963. As Vicki Wickham reminded the readers of *Disc and Music Echo*, it had featured the Beatles, very early appearances by the Rolling Stones, the Animals and Dusty Springfield, and US visitors like Ike and Tina Turner, 'who came over better than anything else we've done'.

British television executives did not understand pop music and the demise of *Ready Steady Go!* that December left a large hole that would not be filled by *Top of the Pops*. Variety shows would take up some of the slack, but that inevitably skewed the limited viewing time towards the more acceptable. Most of the stars polled by *Disc and Music Echo* expressed their sorrow at seeing the programme go: 'Everything is going anti-pop,' said 'Dave Dee's Mick', while Ronnie Lane went further: 'Pop used to be everything but it got out of hand and now it's levelling down.'

'In one way, it's right that *RSG!* should finish now,' wrote Tony Hall after the news was announced, 'because its musical mission has been accomplished. Own up. If it hadn't been for *RSG!* would American soul sounds be as big here as they are now? Would the Four Tops have shot so swiftly to number one? Would discotheques be flourishing in the way they are at the moment – all over the country? Would guys like Donovan ever have been heard of? Much of the credit for these happenings – and many more – must go to *RSG!*.'

He thought that 'the whole British fashion revolution which has rocked the world on its feet' had begun on the programme. He reported a conversation with editor Vicki Wickham, whom he found 'rather depressed. Partly sad that the show was going to finish. Partly bored by the current scene. "All the excitement's gone. It's just not happening the way it used to," she said. Basically, I agree with her. *RSG!* epitomised an era. And that era is over. Maybe it's right that *RSG!* ends now.'

His comments provoked a lively debate. Hall printed a riposte from reader R. W. Lightup, who castigated 'the existence called "THE LIFE"... wherein teenagers leave school at 15–16, unqualified for anything, and get a £6 a week job. Which is where they stop for years. Spending all their money on mod gear and discotheques. They forget the future and concentrate on the present moment with apparently no cares for tomorrow.' He blamed Hall for encouraging 'easily influenced youngsters to make decisions which can only harm them in later life'.

Identifying himself as 'staid' and 'middle-class', the nineteen-year-old reader criticised the conformity of 'the clique of mods all supposedly rebelling'. He told Hall to 'own up. The teenage set at the moment is rotting. And it's partly due to *RSG!*. So may it long rest in peace and never rise again in any form. *Top of the Pops* is good enough for a look at the hit groups of the moment. It's normal and refreshing for being so. No freak-outs or "happenings". Just pop music and ordinary teenagers dancing. It's really great. And it's not so blasted IN!'

Over the next few weeks, the debate opened out. Hall was inundated with letters, about 60 per cent of which were pro-*Ready Steady Go!* and 40 per cent anti. Many readers expressed their contempt for the crude commercial imperatives of the 'IN?-SCENE' and its followers, but others took a more pragmatic, if not human, viewpoint. 'Come on now,' wrote Dave Lewis of Liverpool, 'be a little lenient. Let the kids splash out on clothes and records once in a while. They'll be tied down soon enough. Let them have a taste of life.'

In the final survey of 'Mod Britain '67', Bob Farmer returned to the place where it had all begun. He found the capital awash in pills: 'Swinging London? No. Drug scene? Yes.' He quoted a sixteen-year-old from Kilburn: 'The kids come into the West End at weekends and won't go home. There's only one way to stay awake then, isn't there?' Farmer thought that the city itself wasn't swinging: 'It's the people who put the swing into it. Anxious to keep up with the crowd. Stand back and it all looks rather stupid. Get involved and you've got to keep going.'

'The Life' was dissected in a new single by David Bowie. 'The London Boys' was the flip of 'Rubber Band', but it would have been, as Penny Valentine observed, 'a much more impressive top-side'. It was a strange record, long and quiet, powerful and heartfelt, Bowie's fourth single of the year and the third to inhabit the gap between the lures of the metropolis and the cold reality. If 'I Dig Everything' had mentioned 'a connection called Paul', then 'The London Boys' went straight to the heart of the matter.

Over a muted brass and wind backing, the nineteen-year-old singer told the cautionary tale of a teenager who has left home for the stews of Soho: 'The first time that you tried a pill / You feel a little queasy, decidedly ill.' This was not a raucous raver but a deliberately alienated and alienating examination of addiction and loneliness. The song climaxes with the speeding teen wishing he had never left home, surrounded by a crowd but all alone.

'The London Boys' exposed the nullity of pill culture as the engine of mod and of Swinging London. It was, as Bob Farmer concluded that December, 'All rather ridiculous. All rather trite. All rather great fun. If you can last the pace. With or without drugs.' Indeed, drugs had become a big talking point by the end of 1966. Even the temperate *Rave* asked Spencer Davis Group singer Stevie Winwood for his opinion: 'I don't object to people taking drugs if they are old enough, and want to,' he told Dawn James. 'It is useless laying down rules for other people to live by.'

That was quite a statement from an eighteen-year-old, one that was indicative of a new assertiveness. Pop culture was beginning to transcend clothes and clubbing. It wasn't just The Life but a way of living – a new youth paradigm that would also reflect new attitudes, new structures, a new kind of politics. This was, to some considerable degree, a demographic shift: the post-Beatles fans and musicians who stuck with pop were now reaching their late teens and wanted something more. Given confidence by money and attention, they were seeking their time.

These feelings were, of course, exacerbated by LSD, which led users to shun amphetamines and question consumerism. It amplified feelings of grandiosity at the same time as it drew back the veil of the mundane world. For young musicians, who apparently had everything that society could offer, it came as a considerable shock: as Ronnie Lane told the *NME*, 'In the last six months I've completely changed my attitude to life. I suddenly realised I had achieved my ambition of playing in a big group and life must hold something more.'

While commentators poked through the entrails of Swinging

London, psychedelia finally hit the UK. It wasn't just the Small Faces but former ravers like Zoot Money, who informed *Melody Maker* readers that 'psychedelic music is not so much a form of music as a piecing together of sounds. Although these sounds and ideas are not normally connected with each other, true exponents of psychedelic music try to use this effect to enable people to gain the benefits that can be obtained from the human mind if left to roam free.'

The word had filtered into the UK in autumn 1966. On 22 October, the *Melody Maker* offered a guide to 'psychedelic – the new in-word'. What it really added up to was 'the great American comeback': 'A wave of powerful new groups, heavily armed with hits, are saturation bombing the American chart front, and threaten to start shooting down British groups on home ground . . . the Association, Monkees, Left Banke, Happenings, Young Rascals, Thirteenth Floor Elevators, McCoys, Positively Thirteen O'Clock, the Fugs, Love . . .

'Make a note of that word because it's going to be scattered around the In Clubs like punches at an Irish wedding,' wrote Chris Welch and Bob Dawbarn. But what did it mean? The British weren't quite sure what it was all about. From November on, 'psychedelia' was applied to all sorts of acts with simple, striking names: the Move, the Creation, the Who and, direct from America, the Misunderstood. Contemporary music writers were confused, but all were agreed that psychedelia was denoted by 'freak-outs', loud volume and a general air of aural assault.

David Griffiths's description of the Misunderstood was a typical example. After relocating to the UK and signing to Fontana Records, the Californian group played a show to promote their first single, 'I Can Take You to the Sun': 'The singer interspersed the weird noises with such assertions as "We are taking a trip to the subconscious . . . we have arrived at the subconscious mind . . . Open a porthole."' The *Record Mirror* writer felt that although the group called their sound 'Love music', it was 'interspersed with their accurate impressions . . . of destruction and dismay'.

It wasn't called that yet in the UK, but late 1966 was the moment when rock began. There was need for a new word to describe pop, which was no longer just an industrial process but the principal expressive form of the new massed youth society, and as such freighted with demands and ideas that would prove impossible to contain within the confines of a Top 40 chart or even a single. It was no longer pure commerce and simple good times, but the sound of a new freedom and a generational confidence.

There was an inflation of form, dexterity and ambition. In America, *Crawdaddy!* writers like Gene Sculatti and Tim Jurgens had begun to use the word 'rock' to describe the new 'experimental' forms, best heard on albums like *Revolver*, *Sunshine Superman* or *Jefferson Airplane Takes Off* and in shows that were 'more than the ridiculous 20 minutes that is standard at big teen concerts'. It was, perhaps, an inevitable process but, as the next few years began to open out in the imagination, the concision of the mid-decade would be lost.

Two sensational new groups released singles that December. Both would be standard-bearers of the new rock; both dispensed with the classic beat group format of two guitarists, bass and drums in favour of just three members; both were concerned with the technical and improvisational virtuosity that had hitherto been associated with jazz; but, at this early stage in their careers, both were subject to the strictures of the charts, and were thus forced to restrain their more indulgent instincts within the confines of the two-to-three-minute single.

The result, as it so often did that year, made for an explosive tension. Cream's 'I Feel Free' begins with contrapuntal vocals – scat singing, moans and the repeated title phrase all circling round each other. After just over half a minute, Ginger Baker taps the drums and the song explodes with Eric Clapton's guitar. It's taken at a very fast lick, with staccato piano figures driving verses that, just like 'My Mind's Eye', oscillate between revelation and estrangement: 'I can drive down the road; my eyes don't see / Though my mind wants to cry out loud.'

Cream had been formed by three veterans of the British R&B and blues scene. Their first single, 'Wrapping Paper', had been released only a couple of months before. It was a curious song, whimsical and good-timey, but 'I Feel Free' – co-written by Jack Bruce and performance poet Pete Brown – was totally different, a record that combined technical virtuosity with a distinct pop sensibility. It had a fierce, unstoppable energy that gave extra force to the final lines: 'You're the sun and as you shine on me / I feel free.'

Freedom was also at issue on both sides of the first Jimi Hendrix Experience single, released that month. 'Hey Joe' took the 1966 teen band staple, slowed it down, and then wrenched it inside out. To Tony Hall, who previewed it in *Record Mirror*, it had 'quite the funkiest rhythm feel I've ever heard in this country. Quite Atlanticish.' That same week, Hendrix gave an interview to the paper. 'We don't want to be classed in any category,' he told Peter Jones. 'If it must have a tag, I'd like it to be called "Free Feeling". It's a mixture of rock, freak-out, blues and rave music.'

Hendrix had arrived nearly three months before, on 23 September, as the protégé of former Animals bassist Chas Chandler. His first few weeks in Europe had been spent forming a three-piece group and playing warm-up dates on the Continent. In America, Hendrix was nothing, despite years of playing back-up to artists as diverse as Little Richard and the Isley Brothers. For Chandler to bring him over was an enormous leap of faith, but the genial Geordie was struck by Hendrix's whole presence, as well as his obvious instrumental virtuosity.

There was a vacuum in the British pop scene and, as if programmed by an early computer, Hendrix tapped into all the obsessions of late 1966: he was black American, thoroughly immersed at source in soul and blues, profoundly inhabited by Bob Dylan and thoroughly psychedelicised. The British groups had cheerfully plundered R&B and soul throughout the mid-decade, and the best had taken these influences and made something of their own. Hendrix arrived in the UK determined to beat the best of British at their own game, for he was the real thing.

Kitted out in the regulation military jacket, Hendrix was

launched at Blaise's club in central London on 25 November. Peter Jones was there and commented on the 'mountain of amplification equipment. Jimi was in full flight. Whirling like a demon, swirling his guitar every which way, this twenty-year-old (looking rather like James Brown) was quite amazing. Visually he grabs the eyeballs with his techniques of playing the guitar with his teeth, elbow, rubbing it across the stage. But he also pleasurably hammers the eardrums with his expert playing.'

'Hey Joe' was not a full-blown freak-out but a carefully constructed pop song. It was chiefly memorable for Hendrix's clear, bluesy guitar solo and the individuality of his voice, pitched somewhere between Dylan and a soul singer, most noticeably in the ad-libs that pepper the last minute of the song. Even more convincing was Hendrix's own composition on the flip, 'Stone Free', a proud, if not defiant, statement of outsider pride and a traveller's braggadocio. Featured on the penultimate *Ready Steady Go!*, the Jimi Hendrix Experience were on their way.

Also making waves that December was Donovan, who had returned to the UK after six months of travelling. It had been a roller-coaster year for the twenty-year-old singer, who had had an American #1 at the same time as he endured a well-publicised drugs bust and underwent an enforced career hiatus while various management and business problems were resolved. In early December, Donovan's first new single of 1966, 'Sunshine Superman', was rush-released in the UK, five months after it had come out in the US and almost a year after it was first recorded.

'Sunshine Superman' unveiled a new Donovan, not the beatnik protest singer but a psychedelic sophisticate full of the strange breezes percolating in from the West Coast that he described on the single's B-side, 'The Trip'. Principally acoustic but laced with distorted electric guitar and a harpsichord, it was a light and limber single, jazzily swinging but with an acid edge, full of hipster slang and nature mysticism. It was received with enthusiasm as a breath of fresh air – another blast of Californian sunshine in a dreary British winter.

Despite the record's rapid success, interviewers struggled to make sense of the newly cosmic singer. 'I've lost a lot of ego and selfishness and gained more humbleness and peaceful thinking,' he told *Disc and Music Echo*. Like the Beach Boys with 'Good Vibrations', Donovan wanted to spread positivity: '"Sunshine Superman" is commercial but we all need our medium to teach through. I want young people to see through me a lot of pretty things around them in the world.'

This seemed like gobbledegook to the paper: 'Donovan in Wonderland is an infinitely more beautiful experience than the horrifying happenings Carroll dreamed up for Alice. Donovan claims reincarnation is a reality and, if you accept that, you have to admit he probably penned "All Things Bright and Beautiful" in a previous existence. He waxes lyrical and loving all the time. If it's a publicity pose, it's pretty convincing.' As the unnamed interviewer concluded, 'We all went home. Except Donovan. He's staying permanently in Wonderland.'

Certainly, the British pop press found it hard to cope with psychedelia, partly because it demanded a new language, partly because it so obviously espoused drugs. In its predictions for 1967, the teen-oriented *Rave* hoped that 'psychedelic music and psychedelic happenings won't happen'. Letters to the weekly papers castigated marijuana as 'evil' and psychedelic music as 'a long word to keep masses interested in a dying scene' or 'a contrived studio sound to hide the inadequacies of many new groups'.

However, the genie would not be put back in the bottle. The culture leaders in British pop embraced the new movement. Speed in itself was no longer enough. LSD changed everything: it stretched time as well as encouraging the blurring of sight and sound in the environment – the definition of synaesthesia in that period – and, by the end of 1966, the twin ideas of psychedelia as a Happening and a drug culture were taking hold in the UK. Rock was just around the corner.

Just at their moment of ubiquity, the mods had been outflanked. In late 1966, the newer adherents – the younger brothers and sisters of the originals – were populating a mass movement, not a collection of elitists. They were no longer leaders but followers. The drugs were getting harder, the music faster, the attitudes more inflexible. For those that would not or could not follow the top faces down the rabbit hole, the future was suddenly static. They were no longer modernist but beginning to recede into history.

Innocence had been replaced by experience and, whether anyone liked it or not, there was no going back. The old cheeky certainties that had permeated the atmosphere of the British music scene from the later 1950s onwards were disappearing. Even in 1965, pop groups had been expected to be, in Ray Davies's words, 'really normal, go-ahead . . . boys – you know, have a pint and piss off'. By late 1966, they were being asked to give their opinions on their position in the marketplace and on the meaning of life, love and death.

It was all very unsettling and, as reports about a new Beatles record began to spread in late November, musicians, fans and writers alike began to wonder how this would shape the culture. Since September, there had only been sporadic sightings of the moustached, serious, short-haired young men. Everyone was agreed that, as Pete Townshend said that mid-December, 'it needs the Beatles . . . to sort things out'. Surely they would have the word, surely they would show the way, surely they would bring everyone back together.

* * *

'Young people are measuring opinion with new yardsticks and it must mean greater individual freedom of expression. Pop music will have its part to play in all this.'
    KEITH RICHARDS interview, 'Not Respectable Now Say Stones', *KRLA Beat*, 5 November 1966

While the British struggled with psychedelia, in America it was the most visible sign of a rapidly coalescing, antinomian youth culture. In style-obsessed Britain it was, initially, just another costume to add to the mad charade, but in America it was much more serious: it wasn't just about Vietnam – although that was a pressing issue – or even civil rights; it was something deeper that went to the heart of American life. As the influential sociologist David Riesman told *Time*, 'The generation gap is as wide as I've ever seen it in my lifetime.'

America's psychedelic subculture was born out of beats, outcasts and elements of the New Left, all of whom were disposed to be critical of American society. This intrinsic rebelliousness was only exacerbated by the authorities' crackdown on marijuana and LSD, as well as the recent events on the Sunset Strip and in Berkeley. It seemed, as John Wilcock wrote that winter, that the opening shots had been fired in 'a civil war that may or may not be bloodless but that will certainly revolutionise the lives and habits of everyone in America and eventually the world'.

In late November 1966, *Newsweek* observed in a survey of drug use on campus that one out of every hundred American college students was using LSD as 'a way of life'. Speaking in San Francisco in mid-December, Timothy Leary asked college students to 'help your professors and your fellow students face social reality. Psychedelic drugs are being used in larger and larger numbers. It's impossible to stop or even check this use of psychedelic drugs. To attempt to stem this tide is a discouraging proposition.'

Even so, the exact definition of psychedelia was still up for grabs. For seasoned observers like BBC reporter Kenneth Allsop, it included the multimedia extravaganzas hosted by the Exploding Plastic Inevitable, which he thought 'an elegant piece of the Theatre of the Absurd, a ruthlessly rehearsed happening. But there are disquieting reminders of primordial Saturday nights at the Locarno: the blue-and-pink spotlights on the waltzing tulle as the saxes mooed Deep Purple . . . should not a psychedelic voyage be more than eye-balls aching? Any sign of Nirvana to starboard?'

As 1966 progressed, the competition to claim supremacy in the total pop environment increased in intensity just as the idea of Happenings crossed over from the art world into the sensoria of the drug culture. No wonder commentators were confused, with huge discotheques like Cheetah, the touring Warhol troupe and the light shows at the Avalon and the Fillmore all vying for attention. But it was the increasing use among the youth of LSD and marijuana that finally tipped the balance towards the 'total experiences' being developed on the West Coast.

For the Exploding Plastic Inevitable, the late autumn saw a trudge around the Midwest, playing to small and barely appreciative crowds. Confronted by the titanic instrumental blasts of the Velvet Underground, the audience at the Valley Dale Ballroom in Columbus, Ohio, on 4 November managed only a few desultory claps and a couple of muted shrieks of recognition when Nico, still the featured performer, came up front to sing her numbers. Two days later, the EPI played Cleveland; the review in the local paper stated, 'What Happened? NOTHING!'

That month, the Velvet Underground also released their second single, a new song recorded at the insistence of producer Tom Wilson, who felt that the delayed album needed something to sweeten the pill. Originally written for Nico but sung by Lou Reed, 'Sunday Morning' was a superficially soft folk rock song that revealed itself as a meticulous statement of paranoia, as icy as the winter wind slicing between the Manhattan skyscrapers. *Cashbox* called it 'a potential filled deck', but it disappeared as quickly as it arrived.

The EPI was not concerned with psychedelia, even though it took on some of its appurtenances: the idea of total immersion in a multimedia environment; the idea that the audience was part of the performance. Having had its publicity peak in the spring, it was in danger of becoming passé. At the same time, the eerie unease of 'Sunday Morning' and the harsh tonalities of 'Loop' – the John Cale recording released in the Warhol-authorised 'Pop' issue of *Aspen* magazine that December – were too confrontational for newly sensitised psyches.

The tide was ebbing away from the EPI and from New York. One of the year's biggest groups was the Lovin' Spoonful, who since January had had four Top 10 singles, with 'Rain on the Roof' entering the Top 30 in early December. When they were arrested for marijuana in San Francisco during May, they were intimidated into fingering their source. After the case came to court in early December, the documents were released to the underground press and their name was mud in San Francisco and the West Coast.

Inter-city rivalry was one small part of this. The centre of American pop had been shifting westwards for much of the year. Partly it was to do with the idea of space that psychedelia was re-asserting, an updating of the free feelings that California's pop had long been broadcasting. Claustrophobia was not an ideal combina-tion with LSD, and the harsh bustle of Manhattan not conducive to heavenly visions. There had also been months of intense lobbying by writers and musicians in San Francisco and Los Angeles to pat-ent the next trend, and that was the drug culture.

In December, there were albums by New York's Blues Magoos (*Psychedelic Lollipop*) and Austin's 13th Floor Elevators (*The Psychedelic Sounds of . . .*). Both were trailed by hit singles: the latter's 'You're Gonna Miss Me' had peaked at #55 in the autumn, while the Blues Magoos' '(We Ain't Got) Nothing Yet' was ris-ing rapidly up the Top 100 that month. *Psychedelic Lollipop* was a hard-edged teen pop album, with covers of songs by James Brown, Big Maceo Merriweather and John D. Loudermilk, whereas *The Psychedelic Sounds of . . .* was the real thing.

With its brilliantly coloured cover – replete with a Third Eye at its centre – and detailed sleeve notes, the Elevators' album was designed to act as an acid guide. 'Recently it has become possible for man to chemically alter his mental state and thus alter his point of view,' wrote the group's Tommy Hall. 'He can then restructure his thinking and change his language so that his thoughts bear more relation to his life and his problems, therefore approaching them more sanely. It is this quest for pure sanity that forms the basis of the songs on this album.'

Although the eleven songs were written at various times – at least a couple before the authors had taken LSD – they formed a remarkably coherent whole. That was partly due to the Elevators' fearsome reputation as a live act – as early as February 1966, they were performing acts of collective levitation with their home-town audiences – while their songs had a bedrock of teen beat snap. With a solid rhythmic base and their experience at getting a crowd dancing, they could layer anything on top.

The 13th Floor Elevators had three unique facets: Stacy Sutherland's ringing guitar – a psychedelicised Buddy Holly; Tommy Hall's jug, which created an almost mechanical, pulsing drone in the background; and Roky Erickson's voice, which could switch from R&B testifying to an other-worldly shriek, as if something had possessed his soul. With this armoury, they inhabited the LSD experience in songs like the wildly bucking 'Roller Coaster', the paranoid 'Reverberation' and the sheer velocity of 'Fire Engine', a drug rush incarnate.

The Psychedelic Sounds of . . . was patchily distributed by an independent label, International Artists. What little press the 13th Floor Elevators had outside their state was due to their brief sojourn in San Francisco that autumn, but, by the time of the LP's release, they had returned to Texas, where they remained marooned due to the legal problems that resulted from their January 1966 arrest for marijuana. Despite capturing the pure essence of LSD, their album went largely unnoticed at the time.

California was the place to be. A *Time* report that winter stated that 50 per cent of high-school students in the state had tried marijuana, and at least 25 per cent were using it once a week. In his memoir of the Sunset Strip, Mick Rogers, a refugee from Chicago who revelled in Californian freedoms, took the reader into the experience: 'If you've held the correct mixture in your lungs, you're stoned, baby! You'll know it all right! That's for sure! And it's a totally groovy experience. Whole new realms of sight and sound – of beauty – seem to be born all about you.'

Rogers described how, under the influence, he focused intently on a simple filament: 'You almost seem to become one entity with that light bulb, as your attention focuses ever sharper on that illuminating curvature of glass. A Byrds album starts playing. The words, the music all take on a new meaning, new beauty as the sounds suddenly become full, whole. Your very skin seems to "hear" and your ears "feel" the Byrds' sounds. You lean back, sitting on the floor, against the wall. You and the music have absorbed each other.'

Fusion was the hallmark of the psychedelic experience and, despite Los Angeles' primacy in the charts, San Francisco was coming up fast in December. The Haight-Ashbury culture was reaching critical mass. 'San Francisco is, as far as I'm concerned, the farthest out community that I know of now,' Richard Alpert said in mid-December, 'either New York, Los Angeles, Chicago or Boston included. It is full of some extraordinarily spiritually advanced people, many of whom are very young.' Contemporary accounts emphasised Haight-Ashbury's holistic nature. The sculptor John Chamberlain, a friend of Warhol, described the scene at the Avalon, the 1930s ballroom that doubled as a psychedelic church: 'mirrors, carpeted lounges, chandeliers, draperies on the ceilings, and a dance floor on springs . . . buzzing buzzing buzzing buzzing electric music buzzing through the airwaves, flickflickflick-flickflickflick strobe light flicking energy quanta into the dancers'.

This was drug music for drugged audiences. Barry Melton, the guitarist in Country Joe and the Fish, told Greg Shaw that 'people come up to us all the time and they're stoned on acid when they watch us play, right? So I figure now that the rock 'n' roll bands are now the psychedelic guides, man.' This togetherness struck outside observers: as one reader wrote to *Mojo Navigator*, 'San Francisco's contribution to the music scene might be the total scene, bands, light shows, posters, auditoriums, the way people look and most of all, the intelligence of the audience.'

Mojo Navigator and the *Oracle* were full of news about new groups like Moby Grape and new singles by the Charlatans ('The Shadow Knows'), the Sopwith Camel ('Hello Hello') and the Oxford Circle ('Foolish Woman'). The first two were in the post-Lovin' Spoonful good-time bag, but the Oxford Circle showed a British mod influence from Them and the Yardbirds, broken down, reconstructed, then taken somewhere different. On the flip of 'Foolish Woman' was 'Mind Destruction', a full-blown, discordant five-minute freak-out.

In early December, Ralph J. Gleason reviewed a Fillmore concert by the Grateful Dead, the Wildflower and the Quicksilver Messenger Service in glowing terms. It was something 'absolutely unique in the world of entertainment': a free concert, open only to regulars, with free food and 'no tension, no trouble and no arguments'. Even the venue's cops were applauded by the audience. Gleason thought that the event dramatised 'the difference between the avant garde of the New Generation (the "Love" generation if you will) and its elders'.

The Love Generation: it was a very powerful idea, and reflective of the mood in San Francisco that winter. It wasn't the full story, however. Haight-Ashbury had started small but was swelling day by day, week by week, and the tensions were growing. The *Oracle* ran a piece about methedrine abuse in the city. Chet Helms at the Avalon was busy arguing with Bill Graham at the Fillmore, who had banned *Mojo Navigator* from the venue. The Diggers hated the *Oracle* as 'an old cunt rag of misinformation, outdated "news", fey psychedelic bullshit art'.

In an enclave where everyone was far out, the Diggers were determined to be furthest. Their events were designed to assert their position as the emerging subculture's public conscience; held on the streets of Haight-Ashbury, they were also calculated to bring them into direct conflict with the authorities. On 17 December, they held a parade to celebrate the death of money and the rebirth of the Haight. After two Hells Angels accompanying the march were arrested by the police, the paraders – around two hundred in number – stormed the police station.

The Diggers also produced a rapid series of broadsides – like late November's 'In Search of a Frame' – that roasted everyone, including Bill Graham, the 'hip' merchants of the Haight and the Jefferson Airplane. 'Love isn't a dance concert with a light show at $3 a head,' they wrote. 'It is free food in the Panhandle where anyone can do anything with the food they bring to each other. It is Love. And when love does its thing it does it for love and separates itself from the false-witness of the Copsuckers and the Gladly Dead.'

A visitor to the Diggers' Page Street garage that autumn got a chilly reception from the organisers. 'All this Love bullshit around here,' a Digger told him, 'they don't know what love is. When that kid got shot at Hunters Point and the cops were firing into the windows of the building where all those kids were lying on the floor . . . Afterward these Love cats wanted to give Mayor Shelley a rose. I'm not gonna lie down in the street. I don't believe in that anymore. If they want riots and Molotov cocktails that's what they'll get. There's THEM and there's US.'

The word was Love but the shadow was Hate. Gleason was determined to present the positive side of the San Francisco scene, but the actuality wasn't always up to the ideal. What with *The Love Book* arrests, the regular problems at Diggers street events and constantly hostile policing, Haight-Ashbury felt under attack. In December, the *Oracle* canvassed its readers for 'written reports with dates, names and badges' for a portfolio on police harassment, illegal searches and the like.

The new psychonauts were also divided among themselves, and were just as prone to violence as previous youth cultures. Like many young people, the hippies of Haight-Ashbury delighted in testing the boundaries and, when they got the desired reaction, they determined to push even further. In turn, the authorities increased their determination to extirpate any manifestations of this critical subculture, not just by arrests for drug-taking and street actions, but by shutting down squats like the Diggers' Page Street garage.

Los Angeles was still the test tube for this chemical compound and, in early December, the Sunset Strip remained highly volatile. A major demonstration was planned for the 10th, and a handbill was printed with pictures of the 'police mistreatment of youth on Sunset Boulevard' and a statement, signed by five clergymen, that read, 'We have come here tonight on the Sunset Strip to stand with you who have gathered here because we believe that they have legitimate grievance with which our society must deal.'

Not that these fine sentiments cut any ice with the LAPD. Organised by Al Mitchell of the Fifth Estate under the name RAMCON (Right of Assembly and Movement Committee), the demonstration began peacefully. The bulk of the 2,000 protestors were of high-school age but there was a smattering of adults: clergymen, members of CAFF and the occasional celebrity, most notably Sonny and Cher. The atmosphere was good-humoured, with only the placards – 'A Better Police Force: A Better Police State' and 'Stop Blue Fascism!' – hinting at any trouble.

As the march dispersed at midnight, the LAPD entered Pandora's Box to check IDs. When the fifty-seven-year-old Eason Monroe, the head of the Southern Chapter of the American Civil Liberties Union, protested that they were acting illegally, he was arrested. This was observed by Michael Vosse, one of the Beach Boys' inner circle, who was immediately beaten when he objected. As the several hundred remaining marchers barracked the officers concerned, serried ranks of riot police descended on the crowd, and mayhem ensued.

CAFF's Paul Jay Robbins witnessed the LAPD's attack on a defenceless youth: 'I saw a kid holding a sign in both hands jerk forward as though struck from behind. He fell into the path of the officers and four or five of them immediately began bludgeoning him with clubs held in one hand. I stood transfixed watching him as the officers continued beating him while he attempted to alternately protect himself and crawl forward. Finally he slumped against a wall as the officer continued to beat him.'

Sixteen people were arrested, and pictures of Sonny and Cher, dressed in fashionable Inuit furs, made the news pages. Over the following few days, Mayor Sam Yorty authorised the demolition of Pandora's Box, while, appalled at the violence, RAMCON called off the regular weekend marches. CAFF began organising a benefit concert with the Byrds and Buffalo Springfield. In the short term, the protests were muted, but politics in its rawest and most basic form – the freedom of assembly – was being discussed not just in the underground press but in the teen magazines.

The seed bed of Los Angeles pop culture was under threat just as it was reaching its apogee. On 10 December, the Beach Boys were at #1 in America with 'Good Vibrations', while Johnny Rivers, Nancy Sinatra, the Music Machine, the Association and the Mamas and Papas were all in the Top 50. The Monkees had 'Last Train to Clarksville' at #27, while their new single, 'I'm a Believer', was the highest new entry at #44. There were also recently released albums like *A Web of Sound* (the Seeds), *Da Capo* (Love) and *Buffalo Springfield*.

This being Los Angeles, the disturbances provided an extra commercial hook. In early December, two exploitation albums were recorded in Hollywood. *These Are The Hits, You Silly Savage* aimed to capture the emerging gay market, with camped-up versions of contemporary hits voiced by Teddy and Darrel, who had contributed 'Beast of the Strip' to the *Mondo Hollywood* soundtrack. In their relentless bantering and single entendres, songs like 'Wild Thing', 'Strangers in the Night' and 'Hold On, I'm Coming' took on entirely new meanings.

The Leathercoated Minds' *A Trip Down the Sunset Strip* featured the young J. J. Cale revving through tunes by the Byrds, the Count Five, the Yardbirds, Donovan and the Association, along with a couple of suitable originals – 'Sunset and Clark', 'Pot Luck' – as well as overdubbed traffic noises from the Strip. The sleeve notes proclaimed that 'The Sunset Strip is synonymous with action and excitement and certainly has become a focal point for all west coast trends. It is the hub of creativity for the teen set and young adults of Los Angeles.'

The recent publicity surrounding the Strip was too good to miss, and in December three Los Angeles performers rushed to record and release their impressions of the riot. Terry Randall's 'SOS' featured a fabulous, atmospheric opening rap – 'Sunset Strip, bright lights, pretty chicks, lotsa cars, lotsa kicks' – delivered over rapid-fire, Morse code organ stabs. Over the fade, Randall parodies the barked instructions of the LAPD as they roust the teens: 'Get up against that wall!' 'Don't gimme no backtalk!' 'Get a haircut!'

Sonny Bono's visit to the riot scene hadn't been entirely altruistic. He carried a small tape machine, and the results were released on a single towards the end of the month. 'Sunset Symphony' featured *vérité* recordings from the 10 December protest – of cops, adults and protestors alike, a confused montage of chants, loud-hailers and shrieks by the people of Sunset Strip: 'Keep your eyes on the fuzz'; 'There'll be no congregating here, let's move it off'; 'Man, I wouldn't do nothing, I can't breathe.'

'SOS' was fast teen beat and 'Sunset Symphony' bizarre reportage, but 'For What It's Worth' was a measured statement. As Stephen Stills recalled, 'The last time I had seen cops on one side of the street and a bunch of students on the other side was when I was living in Central America – the government changed three days later. The Sunset Strip riot was just a funeral for a bar. But then you had the immortal genius of the idiots that ran the LAPD, who put all of these troopers in full battle array, looking like the Macedonian army, up against a bunch of kids.'

It was the third single by Buffalo Springfield, and the first to fully capture the group's depth. Their early recordings had been trebly and tinny, but 'For What It's Worth' has a slow, measured pace – with a ringing, tremeloed guitar – that works against a sense of pervasive menace. It caught the atmosphere of the Strip at a pivotal moment: 'Paranoia strikes deep / Into your life it will creep / It starts when you're always afraid / You step out of line, the man come and take you away.'

'For What It's Worth' marked a new kind of protest. Stills had lived in Costa Rica and El Salvador as a youth, and had seen how mass youth gatherings could effect regime change, if not revolution. America's teenagers had learned well the lessons of the civil rights movement: as one young woman told Sonny Bono on the night of 10 December, 'It's history, because like maybe four years ago kids would have never done this, they never would have started rebelling for their own rights. Because they are people and they are right.'

For some observers, the riots were about the very nature of freedom in America, with the LAPD's tactics smacking of 'the Secret Police' or 'an Orwellian state'. These links were explored in a letter written by a concerned parent, Grethe Hansen, to the *Royal's World Countdown*, a new pop magazine. She remembered being a teenager in occupied Denmark, 'unable to move around Copenhagen freely without presenting [her ID] to the German soldiers'. When liberation came, 'it was like a great load was lifted. It was a very joyous thing to tear up our IDs.

'Now, having a teenage daughter of my own and living in America, I would like to ask "Who is occupying America? Who is the Enemy?" I can certainly assure you it's not my daughter and her friends, who do not wish to make enemies but would like to go out and listen to their favourite music and dance with their friends. I cannot see any reason why they should not be permitted to do this while they have their youth and can enjoy it without continuous harassment from the police, along the Sunset Boulevard where clubs exist specifically for this purpose.'

The Sunset Strip riots, for all their self-dramatisation, were a pivotal event in American youth culture. To be sure, there was folly on both sides. The police were completely out of order, while there was a lot of provocation from the protestors, with their swastika placards. Sonny Bono's tape recorder captured the burblings of one cynical young man: 'Beautiful, it's beautiful, it was great. I mean, you know if there's nothing good on the Saturday night movies, you can't beat it. Nothing like a good, clean-cut riot.'

But the LAPD were using a sledgehammer to crack a nut. What was left was an unpleasant aftertaste, a harbinger of the more serious flashpoints to come. For what it seemed to come down to was generational warfare, what Derek Taylor called 'the whole rotten issue of the Old v. the Young'. As another observer wrote that December, just after the rioting was at its height, 'The fact remains that there are two factions, two sides. One generation does

not understand or refuses to try to understand the one behind it . . .
the line has been drawn.'

* * *

'A prophetic minority creates each generation's legend. In the
1920's it was the expatriate quest for personal expression. In the
1930's it was radical social action. In the 1940's it was the heroism
of the trenches. In the 1950's it was the cultivation of the private
self. Now, halfway through the decade, it is once again the ideal of
social action that is defining a generation.'

JACK NEWFIELD, *A Prophetic Minority*, November 1966

The generation gap had long been a feature of Western life, particularly in times of rapid social change. The young of the early
1920s had defined themselves against the adults who had sent
them or their elder siblings into a catastrophic war. Just as in the
1960s, youth had been at a premium, and a self-conscious generational culture had arisen. In the 1920s, that involved hard partying,
which turned ideological in the face of adult disapproval and state
suppression. Forty years later, the same thing was happening: partying – and pop – began to become political.

The principal impetus for this came from America, where free
speech, civil rights and Vietnam were crucial organising issues. But
even more so, the post-war generation had been studied, assessed
and valued as never before, not least because of its massed purchasing power that became apparent in the mid-sixties. Those born
during the demographic bulge that peaked in 1947 – with 3.8 million births – were now reaching late adolescence. They were beginning to enter the adult world, and many of them did not like what
they saw.

'Who listens to the 25 million young Americans straining to take
over?' asked *Look* that autumn. 'Too few adults; it is time all did.'
America's young led the world in terms of a sense of entitlement
and self-recognition: brought up during the materialistic and child-
oriented 1950s and early 1960s, endlessly studied and surveyed,

they realised the power they had as a cohort. Allowed some considerable degree of self-determination thanks to a dynamic and exploratory youth culture, they began to ask the question: how could purchasing power become political?

There was a generational gulf as wide as the one that had separated the early-1920s adolescents from their elders, and it was, again, war that focused that difference and discontent. The parents of 1960s teens had been through the Second World War and had comparatively little experience of pop culture. That war had begun for America with a deadly act of aggression. This had not occurred in Vietnam but, even so, it was still a simple question of patriotism. They had fought, so why shouldn't their young? That's what good Americans did.

This belief was perfectly encapsulated in the highest new entry in the *Billboard* chart of 24 December. Debuting at #65 was the first single by the seventy-year-old Republican senator Everett Dirksen – the same man who had filibustered the 1966 Civil Rights Bill out of existence – who, over swelling strings, martial beats and a full voiced choir, recited lyrics of pride and patriotism that extolled the 'brave gallant men who have died / That others might be free / And even now, they do it still.'

But the war seemed stalled and without end – *Newsweek* called it 'cruel and chaotic' that December – and some experienced commentators were beginning to ask whether victory was indeed possible. Not that this stopped the military sucking up more and more young Americans: in November, it was announced that the draft would be extended to include half a million youths exempted because they did not pass the pre-induction mental tests. As *Time* noted, 'Intelligence tests have been lowered three times in the last year.'

In November, there were 350,000 combatants in Vietnam, with 380,000 planned for the year's end. The draft was looming large in the lives of young Americans. In a *Look* youth survey published that autumn, most of the 550 youngsters polled 'thought the war in Vietnam immoral and unjust, but 66% agree that as long as we're there, we should fight to stop the spread of communism'. Even so, there was widespread confusion: 'They shouldn't accelerate and accelerate,' said one thirteen-year-old, 'they should talk to the Vietcong instead of throwing bombs.'

In October, *KRLA Beat* hosted one of the magazine's regular 'Teen Panel' debates. One of the young participants commented, 'So much has happened in the last twenty years. It's hard for this generation to accept war because we're conditioned to a space-type age where there are so many more important things to do. I don't know how I'd have felt about war in the 1940's but this is the 1960's and war seems so simple-minded when we're about to send men to the moon. It's ridiculous really, when you think about it.'

In December, student leaders from all over America wrote a letter to the president that explained their fundamental concerns: 'Significant and growing numbers of our contemporaries are deeply troubled about the posture of their government in Viet Nam. A great many of those faced with military duty find it hard to square performance of that duty with concepts of personal integrity and conscience. Even more are torn by reluctance to participate in a war whose toll keeps escalating, but about whose purpose and value to the U.S. they remain unclear.'

Attitudes were hardening on both sides. American pop and progressive politics had flourished during Lyndon Johnson's Great Society – a dream that, by December 1966, was 'dimming'. Modernisation had been arrested, yet the ambitions of radical youth were put under the spotlight just at the moment when the backlash was set in motion. For the news magazines in late 1966 were full of the newly empowered Republican Party and its most charismatic representative, Ronald Reagan, who had been elected on a promise to sort out student radicals.

The recent history of American radicalism was summarised in a well-received book published that November: *A Prophetic Minority*, by Jack Newfield, the political editor of the *Village Voice*. Concentrating on the 250,000 or so young people who belonged to the 'New Left', Newfield exalted this 'fraction' of a generation as harbingers of a new kind of politics and a new kind of sensibility. It was they who had peopled the beat generation, the SDS and SNCC; it was they who were the consciences of their time.

The fact that many of this vanguard were middle-class, 'the first products of liberal affluence', did not denote insincerity but an even deeper critique. Yet this was only the beginning. Newfield was convinced that 'the impulse to rebel will continue to grow among marginal groups like students, Negroes, migrant farm workers, intellectuals, and white collar workers. This will happen because the generators of dissent – war, bureaucracy, guilt-producing, affluence, racism, hypocrisy, moral rot – are enduring in the fabric of modern society.'

However, his history ended with some major caveats. Newfield observed the rise of a new McCarthyism, just as the old certainties of even a couple of years before were fusing into a more general, existential revolt: 'The best of the SDS organisers are asking the same questions as Dylan in "Desolation Row", Pynchon in *V*, and Allen Ginsberg in "Howl". What is sane and what is insane? What is legal and what is illegal? What does it mean to be qualified and who decides? It is all one generation's revolt against the last one's definitions of reality.'

Student radicalism was all over the news in late 1966. Much of it centred on Berkeley, an apparent devil's den of illegal drug use and anti-war demonstrations. In early December, an estimated 6,000 students thronged Sproul Plaza to protest at on-campus recruiting by the US Navy and to call for a boycott of classes until 'an anti-draft pitch at another table at the Student Union' was allowed. There was a sit-in. The police were called, and there were ten arrests, including 'non student' and 'middle aged delinquent' Mario Savio.

The trouble had to do with freedom of assembly. After the beginnings of the Free Speech Movement, the steps of Sproul Hall had been enshrined as a site for demonstrations and for speakers of all denominations. In early 1966, Chancellor Roger Heyns had attempted to move this open site from Sproul Hall to another, more secluded part of the campus, and the issue became a running sore that continued all year, with radicals pitted against professors – and, in the background, the lurking presence of Ronald Reagan.

Reagan's solution was simple: 'No one is compelled to attend the university. Those who do attend should accept and obey the prescribed rules or get out.' Adult opinion was divided on the matter: one correspondent to *Time* stated that if Reagan's words 'were heeded, the disgraceful nonsense perpetrated by a handful of malcontents would cease'. Another disagreed: 'If boys of 18 and 19 are old enough to die for their country for a cause in which many do not believe, they are old enough to have a voice in the affairs of their country and their university.'

News of the university's continuing travails crossed the Atlantic. 'The revolution has begun afresh at Berkeley,' stated an anonymous article in the fifth issue of the *International Times*. 'The point is that this confrontation exists: whether the rebels prefer it or not Ronald Reagan has just appointed ex-CIA head, John McCone, to the California board of Regents so that he can investigate "treason and dope" in Berkeley. With the Reagan governorship, a terrible beauty is born. Choices will have to be made . . . perhaps nothing but ruin will prevail.'

In Britain, students at the London School of Economics started a sit-in in late November 1966. This was precipitated by the appointment of a new principal, Walter Adams, who had formerly been the director of University College, Rhodesia, and thus thought to be a backer of Ian Smith's apartheid regime. When the students protested, the authorities brought disciplinary proceedings against the Student Union's president David Adelstein. A sit-in ensued, with placards like 'Berkeley 1964, LSE 1966. We will bring this school to a halt, too.'

It was becoming clear that the 'prophetic minority' of the postwar generation were no longer content to be passive consumers but were prepared to tackle the power structure. In their actions and beliefs, there was a kind of certainty that unnerved adults and precluded negotiation or compromise. It was mirrored, at this stage, by the fearless experiments of the pop 'progressives', who were refusing to be bound by commercial formulae; it was as though they were, cheerfully and recklessly, chasing the impossible. And, in the spirit of the times, why not?

Yet there was a new harshness in this radical rhetoric: a confrontational, sarcastic, devil-take-the-hindmost mode of address that fused youthful obnoxiousness with post-Marxist philosophical concepts and a kind of ecstatic, negative utopianism – 'nothing means nothing any more', 'a terrible beauty is born'. The conflation of demographic/purchasing power with political power reached its apogee in the outliers of the revolutionary underground that emerged in the last quarter of 1966.

As ever, someone had to go further, and the idea arose that youth was a revolutionary class in and of itself. 'Here comes the world revolution of youth,' proclaimed *Resurgence* magazine in December 1966. 'No more laws, no more prisons. Destroy politics! Destroy Religion! Destroy the old world!' Citing the activities of China's Red Guards, the Provos and the Berkeley students, as well as the riots of Sunset Strip, Jonathan Leake called for 'a worldwide alliance of movements and groups speaking specifically about a youth revolution'.

Leake's Resurgence Youth Movement was one of a number of groups catalogued by *Black Mask*'s Ben Morea that December. In the second issue of his newsletter, he stated his intention 'to fuse factionalised struggles into a functional whole. Too long have we witnessed the weakening and eventual destruction of radical movements by their forced specialisation.' Among the groups Morea cited as reflecting this idea's 'universal presence' were Chicago's *Rebel Worker*, *Heatwave* from London and the Situationist International in Paris.

It wasn't just Vietnam, or consumerism, or even freedom of speech; it was everything, the whole rotten edifice of everyday life, that had to be transformed. In the second issue of *Heatwave*, Charles Radcliffe echoed this ambition: 'If the new revolutionary movement is to attain its ends (no less than the total overthrow of everything) – and there is little doubt that we can achieve such ends if we really want to – the first practical step is to internationalise, to interrelate the various struggles and ideas spontaneously occurring all over the world.'

From late 1966 on, simple consumerism would not be enough for the radical or even thoughtful young. Pop culture was thus caught in a cleft stick, propagating ideas and attitudes critical of materialist society at the same time as it was an integral part of that society in its rawest economic form. Together with the beginnings of youth's self-identification not just as a marketing class but as a growing social cohort, politics of all types would increasingly dominate the agenda, whether it be the Sunset Strip rioters or the students of Berkeley and the LSE.

The age of innocence – if not willed ignorance – was over.

* * *

'Everybody can go around in England with long hair a bit, and boys can wear flowered trousers and flowered shirts and things like that, but there's still the same old nonsense going on. It's just that we're all dressed up a bit different.'
JOHN LENNON, interviewed by Leonard Gross, *Look*, 23 December 1966

On 20 December, the Beatles were doorstepped on their way into Abbey Road Studios by an ITN reporter, John Edwards. It was the first interview they had done for British television since early September. Stories about their possible break-up had reached the tabloids – with headlines like 'Are the Beatles on the Way Out Now?' – and, even though they had quashed some of the rumours in their 11 November interview with the *Daily Mirror*'s Don Short, they were still lying low. Any indication of their presence was national news.

The cameras captured four young men old before their years. Each responded to being caught off-guard in different ways, although ultimately all were evasive. John Lennon arrives in a Mini Cooper. His responses are polite, albeit non-committal. Asked whether 'the songwriting team thing will keep going on', he replies: 'We'll probably carry on writing music for ever, you know – whatever else we're doing. 'Cos you just can't stop, you know. You find yourself doing it whether you want to or not.'

Paul McCartney appears on foot with the Beatles' road manager Mal Evans, and is obviously taken aback. Asked whether the group will tour again, he replies: 'It's gone downhill, performance. 'Cos we can't develop when no one can hear us, you know what I mean? So for us to perform – it's difficult. It gets difficult each time . . . more difficult.' Ringo Starr accesses his cheery, everyman persona but, again, gives little away, while George Harrison – the least keen Beatle at that point – is positively brusque, rushing into the studios with the ultimate cosmic brush-off:

Edwards: What about another word?
Harrison: (receding into the distance) There aren't any more words.

That week, *Look* published a major interview with Lennon, conducted during September at the Spanish location for *How I Won the War*. Leonard Gross found him 'rich for life at 26, yet poor still in what men of all seasons crave – full knowledge of himself. Beatling by itself, he has found, is not enough. "I feel I want to be them all – painter, writer, actor, singer, player, musician. I want to try them all, and I'm lucky enough to be able to. I want to see which one turns me on."'

Lennon talked about the group's rise to fame, only three years before, as though it had happened in the long-distant past, if not in another life and to another person. 'We weren't as open and as truthful when we didn't have the power to be. We had to take it easy. We had to shorten our hair to leave Liverpool and get jobs in London. We had to wear suits to get on TV. We had to compromise. We had to get hooked, as well, to get in and then sort of get a bit of power and say, "This is what we're like." We had to falsify a bit, even if we didn't realise it at the time.'

By that week, the Beatles were nearly a month into recording new material. One of the first reports about their return came from insider Derek Taylor, who described them in mid-November: 'Paul was abroad in a pith helmet, his score done. Lennon, slim, short, wire-spectacled, self-assured, was back from his film. Ringo was at home and George, full of tales of Bombay, was dressed in Indian clothing because that was the way he wanted to be dressed and because he looked fine dressed that way.'

Lennon had returned from Spain in early November, after the wrap of *How I Won the War*, and proceeded to resume his former life in London. On the 7th, he attended a preview of 'Unfinished Paintings', the new Yoko Ono show at Indica Gallery: Lennon always claimed that this was the first time the two met. During the next few days, he attended various shows and parties – including Brian Epstein's reception for the Four Tops – while tinkering around in his home studio with a song he had written while filming in Spain.

George Harrison had also returned from his prolonged sojourn in India by this time, grumpily telling Don Short that 'everything we've done so far has been rubbish as I see it today'. Ringo Starr had remained at home the whole time. Paul McCartney was the last to return, having taken a holiday after completing the score for the Boulting Brothers' film *The Family Way*. After driving through France and Spain, he flew out to Kenya, travelling back on the 19th. Five days later, they all met up at Abbey Road to plan their next move.

Live dates were definitely not on the agenda. As they recounted various horror stories from their summer tour, Geoff Emerick, the EMI audio engineer, noted that 'beneath the casual banter, the four Beatles were considerably more subdued, more on their guard than they had ever been before. Clearly the events of the past few months had taken their toll on them: they seemed almost robbed of their youth. No longer were they the four cuddly mop tops; now they looked and acted like seasoned musicians, weary veterans of the road.'

At Lennon's insistence, they began with the song that he had been trying out, in various permutations, for the previous couple of months. It had begun as an acoustic dirge, with the title 'It's Not Too Bad', and a rudimentary lyric. By the time he began arranging the song for electric guitar, on his return to Britain, the song had a chorus: 'Let me take you back 'cos I'm going to Strawberry Fields / Nothing is real / And nothing to get hung about.'

The next solo demo took the song at a faster lick, and then came the crucial change: 'Let me take you *down* 'cos I'm going to Strawberry Fields.' This was not to be an exercise in simple nostalgia; it wasn't 'back' but 'down' – a plunge into the subconscious. In 'She Said She Said', Lennon had begun to explore his childhood, but 'Strawberry Fields Forever' was a disturbed and disturbing creation: a deep dive into Lennon's psychology, his feelings that he was at once special and abject, his doubts about his ability to communicate and, indeed, about who he really was.

It was, as Lennon would say the next year, 'psychoanalysis set to music', the beginning of his desire to explore the innermost recesses of his soul. 'Strawberry Fields Forever' was couched in hallucinatory perception and existential riddles that echoed his favourite childhood reading, Lewis Carroll's *Alice in Wonderland*: as Alice wondered, 'Let me think, was I the same when I got up this morning? I almost think I can remember feeling a little different. But if I'm not the same, the next question is, "Who in the world am I?"'

'Strawberry Fields Forever' was at once saturated in roiling emotions and bestowed with a curious, narcotic passivity: 'It's getting hard to be someone but it all works out / It doesn't matter much to me.' It was very much a product of Lennon's thorough immersion in LSD, an experience which, as Kenneth Allsop observed that December, was not automatically benign: 'Once induced schizophrenia is accepted as a condition of LSD ecstasy, the guide lines grow hazy.'

Everything about 'Strawberry Fields Forever' was indistinct and on the edge. Lennon's LSD explorations had been framed by Leary's ideas about psychological reprogramming: 'A psychedelic experience is a journey to new realms of consciousness . . . its characteristic features are the transcendence of verbal concepts, of space–time dimensions, and of the ego or identity.' By late 1966, this was beginning to lead him into uncharted waters, and 'Strawberry Fields Forever' was, like 'Tomorrow Never Knows', an almost literal enactment of *The Psychedelic Experience*.

About the only thing that was rooted in objective reality was Strawberry Field itself, a nineteenth-century Gothic mansion converted into a Salvation Army home principally for the children of unmarried mothers. The building was only a few hundred yards from Lennon's home in Menlove Avenue, and the young boy would enter the extensive grounds either with or without permission. It was the place where he could lose himself, where he could escape. Strawberry Field had been his secret garden and, by 1966, it had become a portal into his lost childhood.

The immediate problem for the Beatles and the technicians was how to render this turbulent and contradictory creation in sound. The sessions began on 24 November, and continued well into the next month. They were as complicated as those for 'Good Vibrations', with the same density of production, the same use of unfamiliar instruments – for the theremin, substitute the mellotron, a primitive sampler based on taped presets – and the same second-guessing on the part of the song's author, as he struggled to realise the vision that he heard in his head.

The first full run-through was taken at a slow tempo, going straight into the first verse. Take 1 featured George Harrison on slide guitar and lush group harmonies in the third verse, both of which were rejected in the remake that began on 28 November and continued for a couple of days. The resulting take 7 began with Paul McCartney picking out a melody on the mellotron, set to 'flute', which then pulsed throughout the first iteration of the chorus. In the new arrangement, the song began with an invitation: 'Let me take you down.'

Geoff Emerick remembered that the song was 'deemed finished' and, on their next visit to Abbey Road, on 6 December, the Beatles began a Paul McCartney song that also looked back, but not in confusion. 'When I'm Sixty-Four' had been part of their set as far back as Hamburg, a hokey number that they could slip into as a change of pace. Inspired by the Lovin' Spoonful, and mindful of the New Vaudeville Band's success, McCartney revived the song as part of the new, loosely nostalgic concept – and to please his father, sixty-four that year.

On 8 December, the Beatles went back to remake 'Strawberry Fields Forever'. Having listened to an acetate of the 28 November version, John Lennon was still not satisfied, and he had asked George Martin to score the song for brass and string instruments. In the meantime, the Beatles recorded fifteen takes at a more manic clip, onto which backwards cymbals were overdubbed. The best of these were edited together into a new take (25), onto which lead guitar and more mellotron parts were added.

On 15 December, the brass and cellos were added. Harrison overdubbed an Indian harp called a swarmandal, and Lennon laid down his lead vocal. After yet more overdubs on 21 December, the resulting take 26 resembled nothing so much as a tone poem of madness. After two and a half minutes, it resolved into a long and chaotic outro dominated by Ringo Starr's frantically clattering drum parts, repeated harsh guitar notes and crazily looping mellotron melodies.

When ITN caught them on the 20th, the Beatles were on their way to record backing vocals for 'When I'm Sixty-Four'. They returned to 'Strawberry Fields Forever' on the 22nd. In the interim, Lennon had listened to the recent recordings and was still dissatisfied, telling producer George Martin that he preferred the opening of the first version and wanted to join that with the remake. It seemed impossible, but the tempos and the keys were fairly similar and, by speeding one up and slowing down the other, Emerick found the perfect edit, about fifty-nine seconds in.

There was, as he recalled, one final hurdle to be overcome: 'I found that I couldn't cut the tape at a normal forty-five-degree angle because the sound just kind of jumped – I was, after all, joining two completely different performances. As a result, I had to make the cut at a very shallow angle so that it was more like a crossfade than a splice.' The almost undetectable edit reconciles the song's dreamy and disturbed dualities, giving an extra agency to the word 'going' as the swerving swoop of the brass and strings takes the listener down into a very deep well.

On the next day, Friday the 23rd, Rediffusion broadcast the last-ever edition of *Ready Steady Go!*. This send-off featured song snippets and testimonials from Mick Jagger, the Who, Paul Jones, Eric Burdon, Donovan, the Small Faces and the Spencer Davis Group, among many others. The *NME*'s Keith Altham caught a decidedly unsentimental John Entwistle as the Who waited to tape their spot: questioned about the show's end, he told the reporter, 'It was getting a drag, and anyway Cathy McGowan can always do toothpaste adverts.'

Out with the old and in with the new: later that evening saw the opening of 'UFO Presents Night Tripper', the first night specifically launched from within the London underground. It was held in the Blarney Club, a basement dance hall in Tottenham Court Road run by an Irishman, Joe Gannon. Opening at 10.30 p.m., the first was run as an all-nighter and, rather than the usual drinkers, catered to the psychedelically minded, showcasing the Pink Floyd, light shows and an Akira Kurosawa film.

The brainchild of Joe Boyd and John Hopkins, the club night was an immediate success. Around 400 people turned up and the Pink Floyd improvised at length. Peter Jenner remembered that 'what had been the guitar break was becoming long waffly solos, so it seemed like the average song was about ten minutes long'. These extended, often textural explorations were an ideal soundtrack for the club. 'You'd drop acid and arrive blotto,' author Jenny Fabian recalled. 'It was like descending into a subterranean world of dreams.'

The atmosphere was electric, as the previously scattered members of the subculture found each other. 'It was a case of being in the right place at the right time,' remembers John Hopkins. 'And there was a lot of collective energy.' This was a new kind of club, one that wasn't based on speed, dancing or mods. Visiting from Tiles, Jeff Dexter was bowled over by the fact that UFO was 'totally unstructured. It was a free-for-all. There was no presentation as such, it just happened. For me, coming out of the straight world of ballroom showbiz, this was a brave new world.'

Christmas fell on a Sunday that year. In America, the eastern seaboard was covered in a blanket of snow. A two-day halt was called to military operations in Vietnam, while at home citizens spent an estimated $32 billion in the run-up to the holidays. 'Winchester Cathedral' was at #1 for the second week, with 'I'm a Believer' coming up strongly, the song being heavily promoted in each of the four December episodes of *The Monkees*. At the same time, the TV group's first LP was still firmly lodged at #1 in the album charts.

In Britain, snow fell in the north of England and Scotland. Tom Jones was still at #1 with 'Green, Green Grass of Home', and the BBC filmed him celebrating with his family in Pontypridd. *The Sound of Music* was at #1 in the album charts, with Jim Reeves, the Seekers and Val Doonican in the Top 5, and, in this season of sentimentality, the squares dominated the prime-time TV slots: *The Val Doonican Show*, *The Ken Dodd Show*, the Seekers on *Juke Box Jury*, Tom Jones on *Frankie and Bruce's Christmas Show*.

The BBC had to make a last-minute adjustment to their Christmas Day schedule. It had planned to broadcast Jonathan Miller's new version of *Alice in Wonderland* during the afternoon but, after viewing the completed film, controller Huw Wheldon announced that it was not fit for family viewing and would be shown at 9 p.m. on Wednesday 28 December. Instead, viewers were offered *Disney Time* and the pantomime *Aladdin*. The press went into overdrive, with headlines like 'Alice in Psycholand' and 'Aliceanalysis'.

It wasn't that Jonathan Miller took liberties with the text. The overt cause of the trouble lay in the treatment, which dispensed with Carroll's anthropomorphism and simply portrayed the various animals – the Mock Turtle, the White Rabbit, the Dormouse, etc. – as human beings. Here, *Alice in Wonderland* became an almost textbook depiction of various forms of psychosis. As Miller later said, 'Once you take the animal heads off, you begin to see what it's all about. A small child, surrounded by hurrying, worried people, thinking, "Is that what being grown up is like?"'

Talking to *Life*, Miller explained that *Alice* was 'a child's vision, magnified and distorted through a dream, of what it's like to be a young person in a very authoritarian Victorian household. The book, by dressing things up in animal clothes, presents a disguised – a dream-disguised – domestic charade. The Duchess is not really a Duchess. She's the new nanny looking after Alice's younger brother. The Queen is obviously Alice's mother and the King her father – these are dream forms . . . All the levels of authority and order-giving and obedience are reflected.'

Like 'Strawberry Fields Forever', Miller's *Alice in Wonderland* was at once disorienting – eliding the distinctions between dream and reality, adulthood and childhood – and psychologically acute, accurately representing the way that dreams process daily events into a parallel life that, although fantastical, has its own logic and meaning. As Alfred Hitchcock once said, 'When you dream, you dream very real. Very real. Everything seems real in a dream. You are glad to wake up, because it's so real. So, you take a dream idea – it's a nightmare – and you make it real.'

Indeed, *Alice in Wonderland* is constructed like an anxiety dream, with hostile and unpredictable adults working out their animal impulses, and a convoluted internal logic that doubles back on itself in deadly riddles and recurring loops. Miller's adaptation is full of perceptual tricks that align it firmly with the nascent psychedelic culture. Ravi Shankar's sitar weaves in and out, while the sound of insects, human breathing, animal grunts and bird calls, and the rustling of clothes is foregrounded in the mix to a hallucinatory degree.

It begins in escape: with her sister, Alice runs from her stuffy Victorian home into a grassy, unspoiled meadow – her own strawberry fields. It's the ambiguous arcadia that would soon become a prime locus of English psychedelia. 'The book itself is full of intimations about the countryside,' Miller told *Life*. 'Journeying through

England at the height of summer, I got this sudden sense of the magic lurking beneath the vegetation. It is a very old country indeed, full of gnomes and angels and apocalypses of one sort or another.'

Alice's journey into the underworld does not occur through a tunnel but in the corridors of the deserted Royal Victoria Hospital in Netley, on the south coast of England. This was a huge military hospital that, during the First World War, treated the most extreme casualties, in particular the victims of shell shock. Alice runs along an endless corridor – reported by *Life* as being '1,630 feet long . . . nearly a third of a mile' – which is lit by huge floor-to-ceiling windows, and the frayed curtains flutter around her as she passes through the echoes of madness.

The film largely avoids montage and inserts. This lack of phantasmagoric trickery only enhances the sense of unease and disturbance: as the adults behave in increasingly bizarre ways and the jarring juxtapositions impinge on her consciousness, Alice remains solid and comparatively unruffled. Miller chose an unknown teenager, Anne-Marie Mallik, to play the lead, and her lack of thespian affectations gave her portrayal the clear perception of the young faced by adult oddities, and a slight degree of understandable surliness at their impossible demands.

Madness is a constant theme. The denizens of Wonderland profess to behave in an entirely logical manner, but their actions are completely bizarre. Even Alice thinks herself immune, but she is quickly brought down to earth by the Cheshire Cat, the nearest thing in the book and the film to a voice of sanity. '"But I don't want to go among mad people," Alice remarked. "Oh you can't help that," said the Cat: "we're all mad here. I'm mad. You're mad." "How do you know I'm mad?" said Alice. "You must be," said the Cat, "or you wouldn't have come here."'

Miller was not a part of pop culture, but his Alice was saturated in Beatle references. The Duchess was played by Leo McKern, who had taken the lead dramatic role in *Help!* The Mad Hatter is played by Peter Cook; John Lennon had just made a second guest appearance on his and Dudley Moore's BBC TV show *Not Only . . . But*

Also. The White Rabbit was performed by Wilfrid Brambell, who had played Paul McCartney's grandfather in *A Hard Day's Night*, while Ravi Shankar had been George Harrison's friend and mentor during 1966.

Alice in Wonderland also caught the prevailing psychedelic wind. On the West Coast, Jefferson Airplane had recently recorded their adaptation of Lewis Carroll's book, 'White Rabbit', for their second album. Written by Grace Slick with the Great!! Society!!, she had brought it into the repertoire of her new group. The blurring of childhood and adulthood – indeed, the return to childhood idylls or traumas – accurately reproduced the possible effects of LSD, and was already a major feature in the writing of Syd Barrett and John Lennon.

Indeed, December 1966 saw yet more records with madness as a theme. It had begun with '19th Nervous Breakdown' and the summer's improbable novelty hit, Napoleon XIV's 'They're Coming to Take Me Away, Ha Ha', a rewrite of Dylan's off-kilter 'Rainy Day Women #12 and 35'. As well as Mick Softley's *Revolver*-inspired 'Am I the Red One' – chromatic riddles worthy of Alice – there was the gibbering paranoia of 'The Shadow Chasers' by the Freaks of Nature and the full-blown freak-out of the Move's 'Disturbance'.

The Association's follow-up to the harmony ballad 'Cherish' was even more bizarre. 'Pandora's Golden Heebie Jeebies' echoed the club that was at the centre of the Sunset Strip disturbances. However, it wasn't about riot but the psychological knots made into metaphor by the Greek myth: 'Freeing locks, Pandora's boxes / Devils are expended / And I'm finally free.' Penny Valentine recognised its frightening power: 'I haven't heard a record for a long time that has had me positively stunned with fear. It is a terrifyingly lonely record.'

By late 1966, it was too late: the spites had been released. At this stage, psychedelia still presented as dangerously close to psychosis. It was as though the heightened sensitivity that the hallucinogens created sucked up all the poison in society and exacerbated individual disturbance. It was becoming, all too nakedly, a mirror of the

Western world's craziness. But the other side to this chaotic tumult showed the year's secret heart: the all-pervasive but fragile sadness to be found in that season's pirate radio hit, Tim Hardin's 'How Can We Hang on to a Dream'.

'How can it, will it be, the way it seems / How can we hang on to a dream?' Hardin sang. He was in the news that autumn, after Bobby Darin's version of Hardin's 'If I Was a Carpenter' became a major hit on both sides of the Atlantic. A troubled, difficult man, labouring with a heroin problem, Hardin had the knack of matching haikus of love, loss and alienation to achingly pretty melodies. Sung to a downbeat tempo, with a jazz-inflected vibrato, his songs gained a wider audience after the July release of his first album.

'How Can We Hang on to a Dream' was his first UK single, and it hit hard. Penny Valentine announced that she had 'fallen in love with this record'. Tony Hall thought that Hardin's lyrics 'are so damn truthful, they leave everyone feeling uncomfortable and guilty. Some say that [they] contain so much truth that only the dying – or very young children – can comprehend them. I can't accept this last generalisation. Because I think that more and more teenagers are becoming aware of the truth within themselves . . . and quality pop is playing its part in bringing this about.'

British pop was fizzling out in the December end-of-year round-ups. The *Melody Maker* Pop Panel picked out 'God Only Knows', 'Along Comes Mary', 'Sunny Afternoon', 'Reach Out I'll Be There' and 'Eleanor Rigby' as '1966 singles to remember'. In *Disc and Music Echo*, Penny Valentine called 1966 a 'vintage year for new sounds', citing the Left Banke's 'Walk Away Renée', 'Out of Time', 'River Deep – Mountain High' and 'Reach Out, I'll Be There' as her records of the year, while taking side-swipes at 'cringers' like the Yardbirds' 'Happenings Ten Years Time Ago'.

Record Mirror was more scientific, going through chart placings in both Britain and America and awarding one point for a #50, going up to fifty points for a #1. In America, the best-selling record of the year was 'Ballad of the Green Berets', followed by Frank Sinatra's 'Strangers in the Night'. The best-selling artists were the

Beatles, with the Rolling Stones at #3 and the Lovin' Spoonful at #4. Richard Green noted Barry Sadler's triumph but observed that 'the follow-up, "The 'A' Team", didn't sell well enough to get into the survey. Perhaps one song was enough.'

In Britain, 'Distant Drums' was the top single, with 'Strangers in the Night' at #2 and Herb Alpert's 'Spanish Flea' at #3. Top artists were the Beach Boys, with Dave Dee, Dozy, Beaky, Mick and Tich at #2, the Kinks at #3, Ken Dodd at #4 and Dusty Springfield at #5. The Beatles were down the list at #9, no doubt suffering from a slight falling off in popularity, and the Rolling Stones were at #18. Apart from a few clunkers, the top fifty British discs were an impressive mix of the basic and the visionary, the mod and the psychedelic, West Coast and Motown.

On 29 December, Maureen Cleave entered the fray, citing as the best records of the year the Beatles' summer single and *Revolver*. She also liked 'River Deep – Mountain High', 'Substitute' by the Who and 'that perfectly extraordinary composition' by Ray Davies of the Kinks, 'Dead End Street'. '"What are we living for?" he cries in that lifeless voice of his, what indeed?'

However, the bulk of her *Evening Standard* column was devoted to ringing the death knell. As an early adopter of the Beatles, Cleave felt able to pronounce the death sentence on the British pop boom that they had inaugurated. 1966 was 'the Year that Pop Went Flat', she tolled. 'The pop singers themselves have grown old; their faces on television look old, world-weary; bored faces that have seen it all. The future is bleak – just as those pre-Beatles years were bleak – but the present, while they sort themselves out, is pretty sordid.'

Cleave reserved her full venom for the British pop elite: 'The smartest singer was, first, Mick Jagger, who had his portrait painted by Cecil Beaton, but by the end of the year it was the Beatles. They became unbearably smart. Unlike anybody else, they seemed to know what they wanted.' She ended her polemic by quoting a Beatle: 'And George Harrison said: "If we do slip, so what? Who cares? We'll be just where we were, only richer. Being a Beatle isn't the living end." Just fine as long as it lasts.'

As the *Evening Standard* hit the news-stands that Thursday afternoon, George Martin was mixing 'When I'm Sixty Four' and 'Strawberry Fields Forever'. Later in the evening, Paul McCartney started taping a new composition, 'Penny Lane'. Like 'Strawberry Fields Forever', the song was rooted in an actual location: the street called Penny Lane which, as well as giving its name to the surrounding area, crosses Allerton Road at about the halfway point between the centre of town and McCartney's childhood home at Forthlin Road.

McCartney had finally taken the plunge into LSD, and his recounting of a Liverpool childhood was, as befitted his character, upbeat and rooted in reality. 'Penny Lane' described an everyday suburban scene, with the barbers, the bank and the bus shelter. And yet there are distinct hints of sense-blurring in the lyric 'Penny Lane is in my ears and my eyes' and in the character of the pretty nurse: 'And though she feels as if she's in a play / She is anyway.'

On the 30th, McCartney added lead vocals to 'Penny Lane' before leaving the song for the new year. Later that evening, the Pink Floyd played the second show in their residency at UFO. Peter Jenner remembered 'going to one of the earlier gigs in Tottenham Court Road, and coming round the corner of Oxford Street, and noticing that there were all these people with bells round their necks, and Afghan coats. Within months, that had set in. The London Free School had hit the zeitgeist so totally. It's hard to express how quickly the underground exploded.'

In the evening of the 31st, *The Monkees* premiered on BBC TV at 6.15 p.m., following *Doctor Who*. In the new US chart, the group was at #1; at #2 was a novelty record, 'Snoopy and the Red Baron', by the Royal Guardsmen. The highest climber in the Top 10 was Aaron Neville's soulful ballad 'Tell It Like It Is', with the Temptations' equally wracked '(I Know) I'm Losing You' one place below at #8. In Britain, 'Green, Green Grass of Home' was still at the top, with Donovan's 'Sunshine Superman' at #2.

While the usual crowds thronged the cities of Britain and America, the underground had its own amusements. At 10 p.m., the

Roundhouse opened its doors for an all-nighter called 'Psychedel-icamania'. It featured the Move, the Pink Floyd and the Who, all of whom had different ideas about sensation. The Floyd lost them-selves in their sound and light show, while the Who and the Move smashed various electrical appliances – a guitar, speakers, a TV set with pictures of Hitler and Ian Smith – in the quest for 'free expres-sion'. Love or hate, which was it to be?

A few hours later, on the West Coast, the Fillmore hosted the Jefferson Airplane, the Grateful Dead and Quicksilver Messenger Service. The Family Dog held their own celebration at the Avalon, with Country Joe and the Fish and Moby Grape, who, at the show's climax, launched into a long improvisation called 'Dark Magic'. As the group snaked around each other, their guitars sounded like white-noise synthesisers and their massed harmonies ebbed and flowed like the sea. At seventeen minutes, it slowly uncoiled into a quiet resolution. The crowd roared.

By then, it was 1967.

ACKNOWLEDGEMENTS

Firstly, thanks to the professional team: editor Lee Brackstone, my agent Tony Peake, Ian Bahrami for copy-editing, and Dave Watkins, Kate Ward and Luke Bird at Faber and Faber. Thanks also to Mat Bancroft for the cover.

Thanks to the interviewees: Jeff Dexter, Steve Gibbons, Dave Godin (RIP), Tony Hall, John Hopkins (RIP), Peter Jenner, Barry Miles, Gene Sculatti, Norma Tanega, Pete Townshend, Robert Whitaker (RIP) and Vicki Wickham.

Thanks to the editors who allowed me to develop some of these ideas in print: Jenny Bulley, Steve Eriksen, Johan Kugelberg, Tim Jonze, Caspar Llewellyn-Smith and Andrew Pulver.

For providing research items and other encouragement: Jeff Gold for access to Ralph J. Gleason's archive; Terence Pepper for the loan of 1960s pop magazines and the *Dusty Springfield Bulletins*; David A. Mellor for materials and thoughts relating to Pauline Boty; for thoughts about black American dance music and its relationship to life, thanks to Naomi Elizabeth Bragin and Moncell 'ill kozby' Durden; Mark Lewisohn for taking time out from the second volume of his Beatles biography to answer several questions with accuracy and grace; Peter Doggett for information on Sandy Posey; Tom Vague for material relating to the London Free School and the Notting Hill Fayre; Ray Robinson at www.azanorak.com for allowing me access to pirate radio show audio from 1966; Gene Sculatti for material relating to California – Los Angeles and San Francisco; Peter Fowler for access to the manuscript of his autobiography; Matt Wrbican for access to the

Time Capsules at the Andy Warhol Museum and the prodigious amount of photocopying all those years ago. Thanks also to Andrew Sclanders of Beatbooks for rare material from the period, including a run of *KRLA Beat* magazine and images of *THE Global moon-edition Long Hair TIMES*.

For friendship and practical assistance beyond the call of duty: Wendy Wolf, Michael Bracewell, Amanda Brown, Adair Brouwer, Colin Fallows, Paul Fletcher, Jeff Gold and Jody Uttal, Vivienne Hamilton-Shields, Ray Hughes, Chris Jennings and Ian Davies, Johan Kugelberg, Maren Kugelberg, Johnny Marr, Neville McLennan and John Mundy, Thom Oatman, Neil Spencer, Neil Tennant, Ben Thompson, Paul Tickell, Kath Turner and John Wardle.

To my mother, who told me she missed the sixties. Too busy with me and my father.

Thanks to Maureen Cleave for permission to quote from 'Bad Joke into Social Lion?', 'How Does a Beatle Live?' and 'The Year That Pop Went Flat' – her work can be found at the Rocksbackpages website (rocksbackpages.com); to Peter Fowler for permission to quote from his autobiography *Almost Grown*, the first part of which is published by Zois Books; to William De'Ath for permission to quote from *Just Me and Nobody Else*; to Thomas Edward Shaw and Anita Klemke for permission to quote from *Black Monk Time* (Eddie currently works with the Hydraulic Pigeons, whose latest album is *Jass in Six Pieces*); to Richard Goldstein for permission to quote from 'Gear' and 'The Soul Sound from Sheepshead Bay', which appear in *Goldstein's Greatest Hits* (Prentice-Hall, 1970) (for more, see Richard Goldstein, *Another Little Piece of My Heart: My Life of Rock and Revolution in the '60s* (Bloomsbury, 2015)); to Mike Stax for permission to quote from 'A Love Supreme: The Johnny Echols Interview', *Ugly Things* #33, spring/summer 2012 (www.ugly-things.com). The extract from *Twiggy in Black and White: An Autobiography* by Twiggy Lawson is reprinted by permission of Peters, Fraser and Dunlop (www.petersfraserdunlop.com) on behalf of Twiggy Lawson.

Every effort has been made to contact copyright holders for use of quoted material. In the event of an inadvertent omission, please contact Faber & Faber.

DISCOGRAPHY

Developments in the way that people hear and consume music have, to some extent, made a conventional Discography irrelevant. It can be assumed that many readers will hear the songs mentioned in the text either through streaming, digital download, YouTube or other less legal sources – which, incidentally, while convenient, mean that the musicians and copyright holders do not get paid. CDs of the relevant songs should be easy enough to find, except in a very few cases – for instance, the Dovers' 'The Third Eye', which is officially available only on a five-year-old ten-inch compilation. Most of the major CD reissues are mentioned in the Sources for each chapter.

Bearing in mind that this is a book that celebrates the 45, this Discography will itemise the singles released during each month of 1966. Some of them are mentioned in the relevant chapters, others not. It is hoped that this list will provide a context and a way of recognising the many strong singles that are not discussed in the main text. Records are itemised, where possible, by the date of release in their country of origin. Most of them are A-sides, but there are a number of B-sides listed too. In a few cases – for instance, Otis Redding's 'I Can't Turn You Loose', November 1965 US, August 1966 UK – the release dates are different enough to be noteworthy.

Consider it a playlist that simulates the mix of music I heard on Radio Caroline South during 1966 and extends it with the intervening fifty years of knowledge. Some records – in particular, an abbreviated 'mums-and-dads' element – are in there for context and historical accuracy; others – in particular, ska records like the Rulers' 'Don't Be a Rude Boy' and 'Copasetic' – have been omitted because of the near impossibility of accurate dating. For more, go to the Rio UK and Island label discographies at 45cat.com.

A two-CD compilation of songs from the book will be released by Ace Records, and will contain around fifty of the songs mentioned below, in chronological order.

JANUARY 1966
The Ugly's, 'A Quiet Explosion', Pye
Dusty Springfield, 'Little by Little', Philips
The Supremes, 'My World Is Empty Without You', Motown
Martha and the Vandellas, 'Never Leave Your Baby's Side', Gordy

The Wheel-A-Ways, 'Bad Little Woman', Aurora
The Guys from Uncle, 'The Spy', Swan
The Poets, 'Baby Don't You Do It', Immediate
The Eyes, 'My Degeneration', Mercury
The Strangeloves, 'Night Time', Bang
The Small Faces, 'Sha-La-La-Lee', Decca
The Pretty Things, 'Midnight to Six Man', Fontana
Chris Farlowe, 'Think', Immediate
David Bowie with the Lower Third, 'Can't Help Thinking About Me', Pye
The Olympics, 'Secret Agents', Mirwood
The Ventures, 'Secret Agent Man', Dolton
Tom Jones, 'Thunderball', Decca
Cilla Black, 'Love's Just a Broken Heart', Parlophone
Bob Lind, 'Elusive Butterfly', World Pacific
Judy Collins, 'I'll Keep It with Mine', Elektra
The Van Dyke Parks, 'Number Nine', MGM
The Mindbenders, 'A Groovy Kind of Love', Fontana
Marvin Gaye, 'One More Heartache', Tamla
The Mar-Keys, 'Philly Dog', Stax
Edwin Starr, 'Stop Her on Sight (S.O.S.)', Ric Tic
Sam and Dave, 'You Don't Know Like I Know', Atlantic UK
The Spellbinders, 'Chain Reaction', Columbia
The Merseybeats, 'I Stand Accused', Fontana
Bob Dylan, 'Can You Please Crawl Out of Your Window?' CBS UK
The Byrds, 'Set You Free This Time', Columbia
Chad and Jeremy, 'Teenage Failure', CBS
The Barbarians, 'Moulty', Laurie
Crispian St Peters, 'You Were on My Mind', Decca
Slim Harpo, 'Baby Scratch My Back', Excello
The Groupies, 'Primitive', Atco
Simon & Garfunkel, 'Homeward Bound', Columbia
Nancy Sinatra, 'These Boots Are Made for Walkin'', Reprise UK
SSgt Barry Sadler, 'The Ballad of the Green Berets', RCA

FEBRUARY 1966
The Rolling Stones, '19th Nervous Breakdown', Decca
The Yardbirds, 'Shapes of Things', Columbia/EMI
The Kinks, 'Dedicated Follower of Fashion', Pye
Bob Dylan, 'One of Us Must Know', Columbia
The Seeds, 'The Other Place', GNP
The Young Rascals, 'Good Lovin'', Atlantic
Jefferson Airplane, 'Runnin' Round This World', RCA
Lyme and Cybelle, 'Follow Me', White Whale
The Walker Brothers, 'The Sun Ain't Gonna Shine Any More', Philips
Link Wray, 'Batman Theme', Swan
The Troggs, 'Lost Girl', CBS
The Monitors, 'Greetings (This Is Uncle Sam)', VIP

The Lovin' Spoonful, 'Daydream', Kama Sutra
Don Covay, 'Sookie Sookie', Atlantic
The Rising Sons, 'Candy Man', Columbia
The Great!! Society!! 'Free Advice', Northbeach Records
N. V. Groep '65, 'Pipe and You Like It', Delta Netherlands
Norma Tanega, 'Walkin' My Cat Named Dog', New Voice
The Isley Brothers, 'This Old Heart of Mine (Is Weak for You)', Tamla
Ray Sharpe, 'Help Me (Get the Feeling) Parts 1–2', Atco
Tony Jackson, 'You're My Number One', CBS
Tami Lynn, 'I'm Gonna Run Away from You', Atlantic UK
The San Remo Golden Strings, 'Festival Time', Ric Tic
The Beatles, 'Nowhere Man', US Capitol
The Hollies, 'I Can't Let Go', Parlophone
The Cryin' Shames, 'Please Stay', Decca
Frugal Sound, 'Norwegian Wood', Pye
Mouse, 'A Public Execution', Fraternity
The Woolies, 'Who Do You Love', Dunhill
Dave Dee, Dozy, Beaky, Mick and Tich, 'Hold Tight', Fontana
Four Tops, 'Shake Me, Wake Me (When It's Over)', Motown
The Temptations, 'Get Ready', Gordy
James Brown, 'I Got You (I Feel Good)', UK release, Pye Intl
The San Remo, 'Golden Strings Festival Time', Ric Tic
James Carr, 'You've Got My Mind Messed Up', Goldwax
Goldie, 'Going Back', Immediate
Wilson Pickett, '634-5789 (Soulsville U.S.A.)', Atlantic
Otis Redding, 'Satisfaction', Volt
Paul Revere and the Raiders, 'Kicks', Columbia
Q '65, 'You're the Victor', Decca Netherlands
The Animals, 'Inside Looking Out', Decca
Eddy Arnold, 'Make the World Go Away', RCA UK

MARCH 1966
The Who, 'Substitute', Reaction
Robert Parker, 'Barefootin'', Nola
The Capitols, 'Cool Jerk', Karen US
Junior Walker and the All Stars, '(I'm a) Road Runner', Soul
Sam and Dave, 'Hold On, I'm a Coming', Stax
The Mamas and the Papas, 'Monday Monday', RCA
Bobby Fuller Four, 'Love's Made a Fool of You', Mustang
The Craig, 'I Must Be Mad', Fontana
William Bell, 'Marching Off to War', Stax
The Golliwogs, 'Fight Fire', Scorpio
Fleur de Lys, 'Circles', Immediate
Thane Russal and Three, 'Security', CBS
Love, 'My Little Red Book', Elektra
The Monks, 'Oh How to Do Now', Polydor International, Germany
The Association, 'Along Comes Mary', Valiant

Brian Wilson, 'Caroline, No', Capitol
The Shangri-Las, 'He Cried', Red Bird
The Bachelors, 'The Sound of Silence', Decca
Dusty Springfield, 'You Don't Have to Say You Love Me', Philips
The Spencer Davis Group, 'Somebody Help Me', Fontana
The Flamingos, 'The Boogaloo Party', Philips US
Shadows of Knight, 'Gloria', Dunwich
The Pleasure Seekers, 'What a Way to Die', Hideout Records
Link Cromwell, 'Crazy Like a Fox', Hollywood
The Heard, 'Stop It Baby', Audition
Johnny Rivers, 'Secret Agent Man', Imperial
James Brown, 'New Breed (Part 1) (The Boo-ga-loo)', Smash
We the People, 'My Brother the Man', Hotline
Percy Sledge, 'When a Man Loves a Woman', Atlantic
Jim Reeves, 'Distant Drums', RCA US
Dionne Warwick, 'A Message to Michael', Scepter
Phil Upchurch Combo, 'You Can't Sit Down (Part 1)', Sue UK
Mitch Ryder and the Detroit Wheels, 'Little Latin Lupe Lu', New Voice
Billy Butler, 'Right Track', OKeh
Jimmy Smith, 'Got My Mojo Workin' (Part 1)', Verve
Modern Folk Quartet, 'Night Time Girl', Dunhill
The Answers, 'Just a Fear', Columbia (EMI)
The Outcasts, 'I'm in Pittsburgh and It's Raining', Askel
The Remains, 'Diddy Wah Diddy', Columbia
Captain Beefheart and His Magic Band, 'Diddy Wah Diddy', A&M
The Beach Boys, 'Sloop John B', Capitol
The Byrds, 'Eight Miles High', Columbia

APRIL 1966
The Dovers, 'The Third Eye', Miramar
Beau Brummels, 'One Too Many Mornings', Warner Bros
Bob Dylan, 'Rainy Day Women #12 & 35', Columbia
The Pretty Things, 'Come and See Me/£.s.d', Fontana
Earl Cosby, 'Land of 1000 Dances', Mirwood
Lee Dorsey, 'Confusion', Amy
The Wailers, 'Put It On', Island UK
Albert King, 'Laundromat Blues', Stax
Roy 'C', 'A Shotgun Wedding', Island, UK
The Chiffons, 'Sweet Talking Guy', Laurie
Syndicate of Sound, 'Little Girl', Bell
New Colony Six, 'At the River's Edge', Sentaur
The Troggs, 'Wild Thing', Fontana
Jamo Thomas, 'I Spy (For the FBI)', Thomas
Chris Montez, 'The More I See You', A&M
The Lovin' Spoonful, 'Did You Ever Have to Make Up Your Mind?', Kama
  Sutra
The Cyrkle, 'Red Rubber Ball', Columbia

Manfred Mann, 'Pretty Flamingo', HMV
Peter, Paul and Mary, 'The Cruel War', Warner Bros
The Bonzo Dog Doo-Dah Band, 'My Brother Makes the Noises for the
    Talkies', Parlophone
Sir Douglas Quintet, 'Quarter to Three', Tribe
Nancy Sinatra, 'How Does that Grab You Darlin'', Reprise
Danny Hutton, 'Funny How Love Can Be', MGM
The Searchers, 'Take It or Leave It', Pye
The Merseys, 'Sorrow', Fontana
Swingin' Medallions, 'A Double Shot of My Baby's Love', Smash
The Leaves, 'Hey Joe', Mira
The Bush, 'To Die Alone', Hiback
Simon & Garfunkel, 'I Am a Rock', Columbia
Maxine Brown, 'One in a Million', Wand
Edwin Starr, 'Headline News', Ric Tic
The Voice, 'The Train to Disaster', Mercury
James Brown and the Famous Flames, 'It's a Man's, Man's, Man's World',
    King
Mike Vickers and His Orchestra, 'Morgan – A Suitable Case for Treatment',
    HMV

MAY 1966
13th Floor Elevators, 'You're Gonna Miss Me', International Artists
The Small Faces, 'Hey Girl', Decca
The Rolling Stones, 'Paint It, Black', Decca
Sandie Shaw, 'Nothing Comes Easy', Pye
Them, 'Richard Cory', Decca
Mouse and the Traps, 'Maid of Sugar, Maid of Spice', Fraternity
Rex Garvin and the Mighty Cravers, 'Sock It to 'Em J.B. – Part I and Part II',
    Like Records
The Electric Prunes, 'Ain't It Hard', Reprise
Barry Fantoni, 'Little Man in a Little Box', Fontana
The Shangri-Las, 'Past, Present and Future', Red Bird
The Eyes, 'You're Too Much', Mercury
The Yardbirds, 'Over Under Sideways Down', Columbia
J. J. Cale, 'In Our Time', Liberty
J. J. Barnes, 'Day Tripper', Ric Tic
The Temptations, 'Ain't Too Proud to Beg', Gordy
Tommy James and the Shondells, 'Hanky Panky', Roulette
Four Tops, 'Loving You Is Sweeter than Ever', Motown
Twice as Much, 'Sittin' on the Fence', Immediate
Otis Redding, 'My Lover's Prayer', Volt
Billy Preston, 'Billy's Bag', Sue UK
The Dovers, 'She's Not Just Anybody', Miramar
The Turtles, 'The Grim Reaper of Love', White Whale
The Outsiders, 'Thinking about Today', Relax
Shadows of Knight, 'Oh Yeah', Dunwich

Ike and Tina Turner, 'River Deep – Mountain High', Philles
Wilson Pickett, 'Ninety-Nine and a Half (Won't Do)', Atlantic
Sam the Sham and the Pharaohs, 'Lil' Red Riding Hood', MGM
Sandy Posey, 'Born a Woman', MGM
Bobby Hebb, 'Sunny', Philips USA
Norma Tanega, 'A Street that Rhymes at 6 A.M.', New Voice
Sugar Pie deSanto, 'There's Gonna Be Trouble', Chess UK
Paddy, Klaus and Gibson, 'Quick Before They Catch Us', Pye
Keith Relf, 'Mr. Zero', Columbia

JUNE 1966

The Beatles, 'Paperback Writer'/'Rain', Parlophone
Chris Farlowe, 'Out of Time', Immediate
The Kinks, 'Sunny Afternoon'/'I'm Not Like Everybody Else', Pye
The Creation, 'Making Time', Planet
Q '65, 'Cry in the Night', Decca Netherlands/RPM
T. C. Atlantic, 'Faces', Turtle US
Love, 'Hey Joe', London American Recordings UK
Bob Dylan, 'I Want You', CBS
Jimmy Ruffin, 'What Becomes of the Brokenhearted', Soul
Wimple Winch, 'Save My Soul', Fontana
Judy Henske, 'Road to Nowhere', Reprise
The Surfaris, 'Wipe Out', DOT reissue
Los Bravos, 'Black Is Black', Decca
Herman's Hermits, 'This Door Swings Both Ways', Columbia
Dionne Warwick, 'Trains and Boats and Planes', Scepter
The Roosters, 'One of These Days', Progressive Sounds of America
We the People, 'Mirror of Your Mind', Challenge
The Tikis, 'Bye Bye Bye', Warner Bros.
The Mamas and the Papas, 'I Saw Her Again', RCA
Georgie Fame, 'Get Away', Columbia
Jefferson Airplane, 'Come Up the Years', RCA
Country Joe and the Fish, 'Section 43', Rag Baby
Ravi Shankar, 'Song from the Hills', Fontana
The Blue Things, 'Doll House', RCA
Slim Harpo, 'Shake Your Hips', Excello
The W. C. Fields Memorial Electric String Band, 'I'm Not Your Stepping
    Stone', Mercury
The Hollies, 'Bus Stop', Parlophone
Al 'TNT' Briggs, 'Earthquake', Peacock
Jackson and Smith, 'Party '66', Polydor
Dave Dee, Dozy, Beaky, Mick and Tich, 'Hideaway', Fontana
David and Jonathan, 'Lovers of the World Unite', Columbia
Chris Curtis, 'Aggravation', Pye
Jason Eddie and the Centremen, 'Singing the Blues', Parlophone
The Daily Flash, 'Jack of Diamonds', Parrot
Billy Stewart, 'Summertime', Chess

The Left Banke, 'Walk Away Renée', Smash
Darrell Banks, 'Open the Door to Your Heart', Revilot
Stevie Wonder, 'Blowin' in the Wind', Tamla
The Byrds, '5D (Fifth Dimension)', Columbia

JULY 1966
Love, '7 And 7 Is', Elektra (UK release September 2, 1966)
The Velvet Underground, 'I'll Be Your Mirror'/'All Tomorrow's Parties',
    Verve
Dusty Springfield, 'Goin' Back', Philips
The Beach Boys, 'Wouldn't It Be Nice'/'God Only Knows', Capitol
Donovan, 'Sunshine Superman'/'The Trip', Epic
The Rolling Stones, 'Mother's Little Helper'/'Lady Jane', London
Lee Dorsey, 'Working in the Coal Mine', Amy
Joe Tex, 'You'd Better Believe It, Baby', Dial
Eddie Floyd, 'Knock on Wood', Stax
Chris Clark, 'Love's Gone Bad', VIP
The Sandpipers, 'Guantanamera', A&M
James Brown and the Famous Flames, 'Money Won't Change You Part 1',
    King
The Temptations, 'Beauty Is Only Skin Deep', Gordy
Wilson Pickett, 'Land of 1000 Dances', Atlantic
Lovin' Spoonful, 'Summer in the City', Kama Sutra
Neil Diamond, 'Cherry Cherry', Bang
Tim Hardin, 'Don't Make Promises', Verve US
The Sons of Adam, 'You're a Better Man Than I', Decca US
The Seeds, 'Pushin' Too Hard', GNP Crescendo
The Turtles, 'Outside Chance', White Whale
The Pretty Things, 'House in the Country', Fontana
Robert Parker, 'Barefootin''/'Let's Go Baby (Where the Action Is)', Island UK
Carla Thomas, 'B-A-B-Y', Stax
Junior Walker and the All Stars, 'How Sweet It Is to Be Loved by You', Soul
The Supremes, 'You Can't Hurry Love', Tamla
The Troggs, 'With a Girl Like You', Fontana
Alvin Cash and the Registers, 'The Philly Freeze', Mar-v-lus
Manfred Mann, 'Just Like a Woman'/'I Wanna Be Rich', Fontana
Simon & Garfunkel, 'The Dangling Conversation', Columbia
The Mothers of Invention, 'How Could I Be Such a Fool', Verve
Napoleon XIV, 'They're Coming to Take Me Away, Ha-Haaa!', Warner Bros.

AUGUST 1966
The Tornados, 'Do You Come Here Often?', Columbia
? and the Mysterians, '96 Tears', Cameo
The Standells, 'Good Guys Don't Wear White', Tower
Count Five, 'Psychotic Reaction', Double Shot
The Beatles, 'Yellow Submarine'/'Eleanor Rigby', Parlophone
Bob Dylan, 'Just Like a Woman', Columbia

Sonics, 'You Got Your Head on Backwards', Jerden
The Small Faces, 'All or Nothing'/'Understanding', Decca
Cannibal and the Headhunters, 'Land of a Thousand Dances', Date reissue
Otis Redding, 'I Can't Turn You Loose', Atlantic UK
Tidal Waves, 'I Don't Need Love', HBR
Them, 'I Can Only Give You Everything', Parrot US
The Santells, 'So Fine', Sue UK
The Olympics, 'Baby, Do the Philly Dog', Mirwood
The Temptations, 'Beauty Is Only Skin Deep', Gordy
King Perry, 'Doctor Dick', Island UK
Nancy Sinatra, 'In Our Time', Reprise
Kathy Kirby, 'The Adam Adamant Theme', Decca
David Bowie, 'I Dig Everything', Pye
Spencer Davis Group, 'When I Come Home', Fontana
The Southern Sound, 'Just the Same as You', Columbia
Four Tops, 'Reach Out I'll Be There', Motown US
The Elgins, 'Heaven Must Have Sent You', VIP
The Del-Vetts, 'Last Time Around', Dunwich
The Shadows of Knight, 'Gospel Zone', Dunwich
The Who, 'I'm a Boy', Reaction
The Remains, 'Don't Look Back', Columbia
Buffalo Springfield, 'Do I Have to Come Right Out and Say It?', Atco
The Clarendonians, 'Rude Boy Gone Jail', Island UK
'Groove' Holmes, 'Groove's Groove', CBS UK
The New Vaudeville Band, 'Winchester Cathedral', Fontana
Jim Reeves, 'Distant Drums', RCA

SEPTEMBER 1966
The Ugly's, 'End of the Season', Pye
The Byrds, 'Mr. Spaceman'/'What's Happening?!?!', Columbia
Jacques Dutronc, 'Et Moi, Et Moi, Et Moi', Disques Vogues UK
Lorraine Ellison, 'Stay with Me', Warner Bros
Paul and Ritchie and the Cryin' Shames, 'Come on Back', Decca
Beau Brummels, 'Here We Are Again', Warner Brothers
The Kirkbys, 'It's a Crime', RCA
Little Mac and the Boss Sounds, 'In the Midnight Hour', Atlantic UK
The Velvelettes, 'These Things Will Keep Me Loving You', Soul
James and Bobby Purify, 'I'm Your Puppet', Bell
James Carr, 'Pouring Water on a Drowning Man', Goldwax
Paul Revere and the Raiders, 'The Great Airplane Strike', Columbia
The Thoughts, 'All Night Stand', Planet
Oscar, 'Join My Gang', Reaction
The Squires, 'Going All the Way', Atco
Los Bravos, 'I Don't Care', Decca
The Roaring 60s, 'We Love the Pirates', Marmalade
Nino Tempo and April Stevens, 'All Strung Out', White Whale
Dave Dee, Dozy, Beaky, Mick and Tich, 'Bend It', Fontana

The Birds, 'Daddy Daddy', Reaction
The Troggs, 'I Can't Control Myself', Page One
The Rubaiyats, 'Omar Khayyam', Sansu
Jefferson Airplane, 'Bringing Me Down', RCA
Positively Thirteen O'Clock, '13 O'Clock Theme for Psychotics', HBR
Euphoria, 'No Me Tomorrow', Mainstream
The Beau Brummels, 'Here We Are Again', Warner Bros.
Johnny Rivers, 'Poor Side of Town', Imperial
Bobby Darin, 'If I Was a Carpenter', Atlantic
Dusty Springfield, 'All I See Is You', Philips
Janis Ian, 'Society's Child', Verve
Herman's Hermits, 'No Milk Today', Columbia
Paul Stewart, 'Queen Boadicea', Philips
Dr West's Medicine Show and Junk Band, 'The Eggplant that Ate Chicago',
    Go-Go
Otis Redding, 'Fa-Fa-Fa-Fa-Fa (Sad Song)', Volt
The Vibrations, 'Soul a Go-Go', OKeh
The Chambers Brothers, 'Time Has Come Today', Columbia
Kim Fowley, 'The Trip', Island UK
Cat Stevens, 'I Love My Dog'/'Portobello Road', Deram
Beverley, 'Happy New Year', Deram
The Rolling Stones, 'Have You Seen Your Mother, Baby', Decca
James Brown, 'Tell Me that You Love Me', King

OCTOBER 1966
The Yardbirds, 'Happenings Ten Years Time Ago', Columbia
Paul Jones, 'High Time', HMV
Donovan, 'Mellow Yellow'/'Sunny South Kensington', Epic
The Other Half, 'Mr Pharmacist', GNP
Terry Knight, 'Numbers', Lucky Eleven
Q '65, 'I Despise You', Decca Netherlands
The Creation, 'Painter Man', Planet
The Standells, 'Why Pick on Me', Tower
Belfast Gypsies, 'Secret Police', Island
The Spencer Davis Group, 'Gimme Some Loving', Fontana
The Supremes, 'You Keep Me Hangin' On', Motown
The Miracles, '(Come Round Here) I'm the One You Need', Tamla
Roy Richards, 'South Vietnam', Island UK
Lee Dorsey, 'Holy Cow', Amy
Love, 'She Comes in Colors', Elektra
The Lovin' Spoonful, 'Rain on the Roof', Kama Sutra
Simon & Garfunkel, 'A Hazy Shade of Winter', Columbia
The Magic Mushrooms, 'It's-A-Happening', A&M
Manfred Mann, 'Semi-Detached, Suburban Mr James', Fontana
The Easybeats, 'Friday on My Mind', United Artists
Cream, 'Wrapping Paper', Reaction
The Hollies, 'Stop Stop Stop', Parlophone

The Bonzo Dog Doo-Dah Band, 'Alley Oop', Parlophone
John Mayer's I-J-7, 'Acka Raga', Columbia
The Charlatans, 'The Shadow Knows', Kapp
Big Brother and the Holding Company, 'Blind Man', Mainstream
The New Breed, 'Want Ad Reader', World United
The Blues Magoos, '(We Ain't Got) Nothin Yet', Mercury
Ray Charles and His Orchestra, 'I Don't Need No Doctor', ABC
The Three Caps, 'Zig-Zagging', Atlantic UK
Martha and the Vandellas, 'I'm Ready for Love', Gordy
Ike and Tina Turner, 'A Love Like Yours (Don't Come Knockin' Every Day)',
    London American UK
John's Children, 'The Love I Thought I'd Found', Columbia
The Impac, 'Too Far Out', CBS
The Sandpipers, 'Louie Louie', A&M
Val Doonican, 'What Would I Be', Decca
The Ronettes, 'I Can Hear Music', Philles
Alf Newman (MAD), 'It's a Gas', Golden 12 Germany
The Zipps, 'Kicks and Chicks'/'Hipsterism', Relax
The Bees, 'Voices Green and Purple', Liverpool
The Monocles, 'Psychedelic (That's Where It's At)', Denco
13th Floor Elevators, 'Reverbaration (Doubt)', International Artists
Tom Jones, 'Green, Green Grass of Home', Decca
The Beach Boys, 'Good Vibrations', Capitol

NOVEMBER 1966
The Kinks, 'Dead End Street'/'Big Black Smoke', Pye
The Association, 'Pandora's Golden Heebie Jeebies', Valiant
Shadows of Knight, 'I'm Gonna Make You Mine', Dunwich
Allen Pound's Get Rich, 'Searchin' in the Wilderness', Parlophone
The Blue Things, 'One Hour Cleaners', RCA Victor
Bob Dylan, 'Mixed Up Confusion', CBS Netherlands
The Outsiders, 'Touch', Relax
J. J. Cale, 'After Midnight', Liberty
The Mighty Hannibal, 'Hymn No. 5', Josie
Fleur de Lys, 'Mud in Your Eye', Polydor
Wilson Pickett, 'Mustang Sally', Atlantic
The Temptations, '(I Know) I'm Losing You', Gordy
Otis Redding, 'Try a Little Tenderness', Volt
Jimmy Ruffin, 'I've Passed This Way Before', Soul
Aaron Neville, 'Tell It Like It Is', Par Lo
Jimmy Castor, 'Hey Leroy, Your Mama's Callin' You', Smash
Buffalo Springfield, 'Burned', Atco
Keith, '98.6', Mercury
The Young Holt Trio, 'Wack Wack', Brunswick
? and the Mysterians, 'I Need Somebody', Cameo
The Spike Drivers, 'Baby Won't You Tell Me How I Lost My Mind', Reprise
The Electric Prunes, 'I Had Too Much to Dream Last Night', Reprise

Sons of Adam, 'Feathered Fish', Alamo
Butch Engle and the Styx, 'Going Home', Loma
The Truth, 'Hey Gyp (Dig the Slowness)', Deram
The Who, 'Disguises', *Ready Steady Who* EP, Reaction
Human Expression, 'Love at Psychedelic Velocity', Accent
The Sopwith Camel, 'Hello Hello', Kama Sutra
Oxford Circle, 'Foolish Woman', World United
The Tears, 'Weatherman', Scorpio
The Other Side, 'Walking Down the Road', Brent
Fred Neil, 'The Dolphins', Capitol
Sandy Posey, 'Single Girl', MGM
The Seekers, 'Morningtown Ride', Columbia
Stevie Wonder, 'A Place in the Sun', Tamla
The Monkees, 'I'm a Believer', RCA
Alvin Cash and the Registers, 'Alvin's Boo-Ga-Loo', Mar-v-lus
The Four Tops, 'Standing in the Shadows of Love', Motown

DECEMBER 1966
The Small Faces, 'My Mind's Eye', Decca
The Left Banke, 'Pretty Ballerina', Smash
The Who, 'Happy Jack', Reaction
Cream, 'I Feel Free', Reaction
Jimi Hendrix Experience, 'Hey Joe', Polydor
Marvin Gaye and Kim Weston, 'It Takes Two', Tamla
Earl Van Dyke and the Motown Brass, '6 By 6', Soul
Joe Tex, 'Papa Was Too', Dial
Georgie Fame, 'Sitting in the Park', Columbia
Dyke and the Blazers, 'Funky Broadway', Original Sound
The Skatalites, 'Guns of Navarone', Island reissue
Spike Milligan, 'Tower Bridge', Parlophone
Senator Everett McKinley Dirksen, 'Gallant Men', Capitol
The Fugs, 'Kill for Peace', ESP
Chocolate Watch Band, 'Sweet Young Thing', Tower
The Music Machine, 'Talk Talk', Original Sound
The Troggs, 'Any Way that You Want Me', Page One
The Velvet Underground, 'Sunday Morning'/'Femme Fatale', Verve
Don Covay and the Goodtimers, 'See-Saw', Atlantic UK
We the People, 'In the Past', Challenge
Freaks of Nature People, 'Let's Freak Out', Island
The Flies, 'I'm Not Your Steppin' Stone', Decca
The Misunderstood, 'I Can Take You to the Sun', Fontana
The Move, 'Night of Fear'/'Disturbance', Deram
The Seeds, 'Mr Farmer', GNP Crescendo
Rainy Daze, 'That Acapulco Gold', Chicory
Buffalo Springfield, 'For What It's Worth (Stop, Hey What's that Sound)',
    Atco
People of Sunset Strip, 'Sunset Symphony', Atco

Mick Softley with the Summer Suns, 'Am I the Red One', CBS
Terry Randall, 'S.O.S.', Valiant
David Bowie, 'The London Boys', Deram
The Marvelettes, 'The Hunter Gets Captured by the Game', Tamla
Patti Labelle and the Blue Belles, 'Take Me for a Little While', Atlantic
Tim Hardin, 'How Can We Hang on to a Dream?', Verve UK

SOURCES

For general information on single releases: www.45cat.com
For the *Billboard* Top 100 Charts (US) and the *Record Retailer* (UK) charts for
1966: www.old-charts.com
For the Radio Caroline Countdown of Sound: www.radiolondon.co.uk/
caroline/stonewashed/index.html

INTRODUCTION
'You see, there's something else . . .': Maureen Cleave, 'How Does a Beatle
    Live? John Lennon Lives Like This', *Evening Standard*, 4 March 1966
Lou Reed, 'The View from the Bandstand', and Robert Shelton, 'Orpheus
    Plugs In', both from *Aspen*, vol. 1 issue 3, the 'Fab' issue, December 1966
Bob Dylan in 1966: Sean Wilentz, *Bob Dylan in America* (Bodley Head,
    2010); C. P. Lee, *Like the Night* (Helter Skelter, 2004); Robert Shelton, *No
    Direction Home: The Life and Music of Bob Dylan* (New English Library,
    1986); Clinton Heylin, *Behind the Shades: The 20th Anniversary Edition*
    (Faber and Faber, 2011); *Bob Dylan Live 1966, The 'Royal Albert Hall'
    Concert* (Columbia, 1998); Bob Dylan, *Genuine Live 1966* (Scorpio bootleg,
    2000)

CHAPTER I
'"THE SOUND OF SILENCE" . . .: Judith Piepe, sleeve notes for *The Paul
    Simon Song Book* (CBS UK, August 1965)
Paul Williams, *The Performing Artist: The Music of Bob Dylan Volume 1,
    1960–1973* (Underwood Miller, 1990)
Adrian Henri quote from 'It Seemed Right and Still Does': John Minnion and
    Philip Bolsover (Eds), *The CND Story: The First 25 Years of CND in the
    Words of the People Involved*, Chapter 6 – 'Words, Music and Marches'
    (Allison and Busby, 1983)
Steve Gibbons quotes from author interview, January 2013
David Wells, sleeve notes to *The Quiet Explosion: The (Complete) Ugly's*
    (Sequel Records, 2004)
Norman Jopling and Peter Jones, 'New Singles Reviewed . . .', *Record Mirror*,
    22 January 1966
For a general history of the atomic arms race from the early 1950s onwards:

Norman Moss, *Men Who Play God: The Story of the Hydrogen Bomb* (Penguin, 1970)

'In the new world, the light was harsh' and the generations 'divided': Jeff Nuttall, *Bomb Culture*, Part 1 – 'Pop, II' (MacGibbon & Kee, 1968)

Paul Boyer, *By the Bomb's Early Light: American Thought and Culture at the Dawn of the Atomic Age* (Pantheon, 1985)

For the details of Sam Hinton's 'Old Man Atom' and many other Atomic records: Bill Geerhart and Ken Sitz, sleeve notes to *Atomic Platters: Cold War Music from the Golden Age of Homeland Security* (Bear Family Records, 2005)

Peggy Duff, 'CND: 1958–1965', in *Left, Left, Left: A Personal Account of Six Protest Campaigns 1945–65* (Allison & Busby, 1971)

Norman Moss, *Men Who Play God*, op. cit., Chapter 7 – 'Ban the Bomb'

John Minnion and Philip Bolsover (Eds), *The CND Story*, op. cit., Chapter 1 – 'Aldermaston and the Early Years' and Chapter 2 – 'Problems of the 1960's'

'Members of Parliament, professors and students': Peggy Duff, 'The Aldermaston Marches', 'CND: 1958–1965', in *Left, Left, Left*, op. cit.

'any moment to be blinded by the first dazzling bomb flash': Pat Arrowsmith, *Jericho*, Chapter 27 (Cresset Press, 1965)

John Charlton, *Don't You Hear the H-Bomb's Thunder?* North East Labour History (Merlin Press, 2009)

John Minnion and Philip Bolsover (Eds), *The CND Story*, op. cit., Chapter 6 – 'Words, Music and Marches'

For more on *March to Aldermaston*: www.screenonline.org.uk/film/id/533592

'A photograph from the Jeff Nuttall archive': George McKay, 'Trad Jazz in 1950s Britain – protest, pleasure, politics – interviews with some of those involved', usir.salford.ac.uk/9306/1/trad_jazz_interviews_2001-02_PDF.pdf

'owned an extensive collection . . .' and 'made his magnificent hominoids . . .': *Bomb Culture*, op. cit., Part IV – 'Sick II'

'The Colyer fans . . .': ibid., Part II – 'Protest II'

Barry Miles, author interview, October 2013

'in the square below there were many thousands . . .': Peggy Duff, 'The Direct Action Committee and the Committee of 100', 'CND: 1958–1965', in *Left, Left, Left*, op. cit.

'They have sacrificed a lot . . .': *Bomb Culture*, op. cit., Part II – 'Protest II'

For Cuba in general, the 'What does it matter how we eat?' story and the Pat Arrowsmith quote: *Men Who Play God*, op. cit., Chapter 12 – 'The Nuclear Cool'

Mike Down quote from 'We're not there yet, but we're getting there: Mike Down, 2001', *Don't You Hear the H-Bomb's Thunder*, op. cit., Addendum 1

Bob Dylan, sleeve notes to *The Freewheelin' Bob Dylan* (CBS UK, November 1963)

John Hopkins, author interview, May 2012

John Hopkins, *From the Hip: Photographs by John 'Hoppy' Hopkins 1960–66* (Damiani Editore, 2008)

'the line in the sand between the old order . . .': Colin Harper, *Dazzling*

Stranger: Bert Jansch and the British Folk and Blues Revival, Chapter 6 –
'Nineteen Sixty-Five' (Bloomsbury, 2000)

Meeting Point: Outcasts and Outsiders featured Judith Piepe talking to Tom
Salmon about her work among young people in the clubs of Soho and was
shown at 6.15 p.m. on 20 November 1966

Judith Piepe's voiceover and Al Stewart singing 'Pretty Golden Hair' can be
seen at www.youtube.com/watch?v=b4zULQipyM8

The *Top of the Pops* video that showed Dylan arriving at London Heathrow
was taken from the D. A. Pennebaker footage that later became *Don't Look
Back*. It was aired on 22 April 1965

In late 1965, the British Ember Records label released an album of early
Barry McGuire material, *Barry McGuire Sings*, with an added title insert,
'The Eve of Destruction Man', and a graphic picture of an atomic bomb
exploding

For more on Mick Softley: psychedelicbaby.blogspot.co.uk/2015/01/mick-
softley-songs-for-swingin.html

Peter Watkins, *The War Game*, BFI DVD 2003 (also includes Dr John Cook's
documentary *The War Game – The Controversy*)

For Peter Watkins's quotes: pwatkins.mnsi.net/warGame.htm

George W. Brandt (Ed.), *British Television Drama*, Chapter 9 – 'Peter
Watkins' by S. M. J. Arrowsmith (Cambridge University Press, 1981)

Mary Whitehouse added her voices to those calling for the film to be banned:
Ben Thompson (Ed.), *Ban This Filth! Letters from the Mary Whitehouse
Archive* (Faber and Faber, 2012)

Peter Watkins, *The War Game* (Sphere Books, 1967)

Tony Hall on *The War Game*: 'The Tony Hall Column', *Record Mirror*, 14
May 1966

For the Palomares incident: David Stiles, 'A Fusion Bomb over Andalucía:
U.S. Information Policy and the 1966 Palomares Incident', *Journal
of Cold War Studies*, winter 2006 (www.mitpressjournals.org/doi/
abs/10.1162/152039706775212067#.VYl5dV5UoYU). A sanitised version of
this disaster became the plot line in the Cliff Richard film *Finders Keepers*,
released in December 1966

For Love's 'Mushroom Clouds': Andrew Sandoval, notes to Love's *Love*
reissue (Elektra/WSM, 2001)

For the Wheel-A-Ways review: 'Top 100 Pick', *Cashbox*, 29 January 1966

CHAPTER 2

'Today's Princes of Pop . . .': '10 Years of Pop', *Boyfriend Book 1966*

Louise Criscone, 'The Stones Speak to the Press', *KRLA Beat*, 8 January 1966

Norman Jopling and Peter Jones, 'The Singles Reviewed', *Record Mirror*, 5
February 1966

Penny Valentine, 'Stones Stay with Dylan!', *Disc Weekly*, 5 February 1966

The *Rave* review of '19th Nervous Breakdown' is in the March 1966 issue:
'*Rave*'s Whether Chart Forecast for March'

Maureen Cleave, 'Bad Joke into Social Lion?' *Evening Standard*, 4 February
1966 (from the Rocksbackpages website: www.rocksbackpages.com)

Jennifer Harris, Sarah Hyde and Greg Smith, *1966 and All That: Design and the Consumer in Britain 1960–1969* (Trefoil Design Library, 1986)

'The Teen-Agers: What They're Really Like', *Newsweek*, 21 March 1966

'Music is the pulse and flow of teenage life . . .': Peter Laurie, *The Teenage Revolution*, Chapter 5 – 'In His Day, Shakespeare Was Almost as Pop as Presley in His' (Anthony Blond, 1965)

For record prices: Albert McCarthy, *The Gramophone Popular Record Catalogue*, September 1966

'discs which were most successful chart-wise throughout the year': Richard Green, 'Top Stars . . . and the Top Discs', *Record Mirror*, 18 December 1965

For teenage spending and saving and the youth media: *The Teenage Revolution*, op. cit., Chapter 4 – 'How Cleverly Do Adults Fleece the Young?'

Thanks to Terence Pepper for his thoughts on 1960s magazines. See also Jon Savage, 'Portraits of Pop', in Terence Pepper (Ed.), *From Beatles to Bowie: The 60s Exposed* (National Portrait Gallery); and www.theguardian.com/music/2009/sep/06/sixties-60s-pop-magazines-beatles

For details of *Top of the Pops* 3 February 1966 (and other episodes during 1966): www.tv.com/shows/top-of-the-pops-uk/3rd-february-1966-365592

For a general '1960s British Rock and Pop Chronology': www.skidmore.edu/~gthompso/britrock/60brchro/60brch66.html

For the British Top 50 and the American Top 100 in 1966: www.old-charts.com

Vicki Wickham, email correspondence with the author, May 2015

For details of *Ready Steady Go!* episodes: www.tv.com/shows/ready-steady-go/episodes

For the Rolling Stones' August 1965 performance of '(I Can't Get No) Satisfaction' on *Ready Steady Go!*: www.youtube.com/watch?v=VCtwAuoahoA

For the Radio London chart of 6 February 1966: www.radiolondon.co.uk/rl/scrap60/fabforty/65fabs/feb66/060266/fabo60266.html

For audio files on request, including the Jack Spector US Top 40 show: www.azanorak.com

For a general pirate radio history: Mike Leonard, *The Beat Fleet: The Story Behind the 60's 'Pirate' Radio Stations*, Forest Press, 2004

Tom Lodge, 'The Pirate's Den', *Music Echo*, 12 February 1966

For the three generations: *The Teenage Revolution*, op. cit., Chapter 1 – 'Fission: The Young Have Always Been One Pace Ahead, Now They Are Two'

Peter Whitehead, *Charlie Is My Darling* (DVD, ABCKO Films, 2012)

The Rolling Stones photo with Dezo Hoffman and Andrew Loog Oldham can be seen in Robert Palmer, *The Rolling Stones* (Sphere, 1983)

Andrew Loog Oldham, *2Stoned* (Secker and Warburg, 2002)

Mark Abrams, *The Teenage Consumer* (The London Press Exchange Ltd, July 1959)

'Over the average teenager hovers . . .': *The Teenage Revolution*, op. cit., chapter entitled 'How Does the Teenager See Himself in the Grown-Up World; How Do Adults Help Him to Arrive There?'

'young people are suffering from an enforced schizophrenia . . .': Wilfrid
De'Ath, 'A Short Sharp Shock', in *Just Me and Nobody Else* (Hutchinson,
1966)

Eden, 'DYLAN', *KRLA Beat*, 22 January 1966

Christopher Gibbs, author interview, June 1995

For more images from the Franklin Canyon shoot: guywebster.com

David Griffiths, 'Have Your Personalities Changed Much in the Three Years
You've Been Pop Stars? YES', *Record Mirror*, 12 February 1966

Richard Green, 'Brian Wants to Swop His Rolls for a Mini', *Record Mirror*, 12
February 1966

The *Record Mirror* reviews of '19th Nervous Breakdown', 'Shapes of Things',
'Dedicated Follower of Fashion' and 'Substitute' are contained in the issues
of 5, 19 and 26 February and 12 March 1966

'We had the Rolling Stones here last week . . .' and subsequent quotes from
Ray Davies: author interview, October 1983; published in Jon Savage, *The
Kinks: The Official Biography* (Faber and Faber, 1984)

'Just Dennis: A Boy's Angle on Boy's Fashion', *Rave*, February and March 1966

NME Kinks cover, 4 March 1966

Dawn James, 'Putting You Straight About the Kinks', *Rave*, March 1966

Eden, 'Havin' a Wild Rave-Up with Five Yardbirds', *KRLA Beat*, 29 January
1966

Dawn James, 'Five Square Yardbirds', *Rave*, December 1965

Greg Russo, *Yardbirds: The Ultimate Rave-Up* (Crossfire Publications, 2001)

The *Rave* reviews of 'Dedicated Follower of Fashion' and 'Shapes of Things'
are in the April 1966 issue

David Dalton, *The Rolling Stones: The First Twenty Years* (Thames and
Hudson, 1981)

Pete Townshend quotes from author interview, September 2011

'met a rather gaudy Mod in stripes . . .': *The Teenage Revolution*, op. cit.,
'SCENES FROM TEENAGE LIFE. SUNDAY A.M.' in Chapter 3 –
'The Importance of Ephemeral Things'

'only comprehensible if one sees them as . . .': *The Teenage Revolution*, op. cit.,
Chapter 1 – 'Fission'

For the Pete Townshend *Whole Scene Going* interview: www.youtube.com/
watch?v=oYhJ4zjYQvY

Alan Freeman, 'The Truth About Our Generation', *Rave*, February 1966

Dawn James, 'Who Knows What the Who Are Really Like?' *Rave*, March 1966

Andy Neill and Mat Kent, *Anyway Anyhow Anywhere: The Complete
Chronicle of the Who 1958–1978* (Virgin Books, 2002)

Review of 'Substitute' in *Record Mirror*, 12 March 1966

John Heilpern, 'The Who – The Prediction Business (2)', *Observer* colour
magazine, 20 March 1966

For Colin Jones and the Who photograph: www.theguardian.com/media/2011/
jul/31/five-decades-of-the-observer-magazine

'London Swings!' *Rave*, April 1966

Wilfrid De'Ath, 'Leave Me Alone' and 'You Take What You Want', *Just Me
and Nobody Else*, op. cit.

For a description of how Pharaoh came to write his *New Society* article: ibid., 'Confessions for Sale'

Neale Pharaoh, 'The Long Blunt Shock', *New Society*, 26 September 1963, cited in Stan Cohen, 'A Note on Detention Centres', from 'Approved Schools and Detention Centres', *Anarchy 101*, July 1969

Neale Pharaoh, 'He Gets Out of It', *New Society*, 20 February 1964, cited in Richard Davenport-Hines, *The Pursuit of Oblivion: A Social History of Drugs* (Orion, 2001)

For Pharaoh ('Neil') and Eric Clapton and Eel Pie Island: John Platt, 'Eel Pie Memories', *Comstock Lode*, no. 7. Go to: www.eelpie.org/comstock7.htm

Dan Van Ver Vat and Michele Whitby, *Eel Pie Island* (Francis Lincoln Limited, 1999)

'The "Mod" has been diverted to purely material channels . . .': Wilfrid De'Ath, 'You Take What You Want', *Just Me and Nobody Else*, op. cit.

'The students, especially the art students . . .': ibid., 'Confessions for Sale'

Feliz Aeppli, *The Ultimate Guide to the Rolling Stones 1962–2012*, aeppli.ch/tug.htm

Eden, 'Exclusive: BEAT Attends Closed Stones' Session', *KRLA Beat*, 16 April 1966

Mike Ledgerwood, 'JAGGER back from Paris with a gashed eye', *Disc Weekly*, 9 April 1966

Could You Walk on Water? is mentioned as the new Stones album in *Record Mirror*, 29 January 1966

Richard Green, 'The Smash LP of the Year?' *Record Mirror*, 6 April 1966

Pete Fowler, excerpted from an autobiography to be published as *Almost Grown* (Zois Books, 2015)

Piri Halasz, 'You Can Walk It Across the Grass', *Time*, 15 April 1966

Jackie Harlow, 'The British Boom – Is It Over?' *Rave*, February 1966

The *Rolling Stones Monthly* quote 'We had just done five weeks' hectic work' is reprinted in David Dalton, *The Rolling Stones: The First Twenty Years* (Random House, 1984)

Chris Curtis: Frank Allen, 'The Day the Crack-Up Came for Chris', *Disc and Music Echo*, 23 April 1966. For more on Chris Curtis, see *2Stoned*, op. cit., Chapter 12

'It was like *Morgan: A Suitable Case for Treatment*': Ray Davies, author interview 1983/4, published in *The Kinks: The Official Biography*, op. cit.

Morgan: A Suitable Case for Treatment [DVD] 2011. For more, go to www. theguardian.com/film/2011/feb/10/morgan-suitable-case-for-treatment-dvd

CHAPTER 3

For increase in US troops in Vietnam: Christian G. Appy, *Working Class War: American Combat Soldiers and Vietnam*, Chapter 5 – 'The Terms of Battle' (University of North Carolina Press, 1993)

Stanley Karnow, *Vietnam: A History*, Chapter 11 – 'LBJ Goes to War', Chapter 12 – 'Escalation' and Chapter 13 – 'Debate, Diplomacy, Doubt' (Pimlico, 1994)

For LBJ's approval rating and 43 per cent thinking he was not doing enough:

Robert Dallek, *Lyndon B. Johnson: Portrait of a President*, Chapter 10 – 'Lyndon Johnson's War' (Penguin, 2005)

For generational attitudes to war: *Working Class War: American Combat Soldiers and Vietnam*, op. cit., Chapter 2 – 'Life Before the Nam'

Carol Deck, 'Barry Sadler Sings of War Without Protest', *KRLA Beat*, 26 February 1966

Uncredited writer, 'Ballads: Of Men and Green Berets', *KRLA Beat*, 26 March 1966

Uncredited writer, 'Teen Panel Discussion: Green Berets and Barry McGuire', *KRLA Beat*, 30 April 1966

John Michaels, 'Barry Sadler: You Don't Have to Shake Dandruff', *KRLA Beat*, 9 July 1966

The president's 46 per cent approval rating: *Lyndon B. Johnson: Portrait of a President*, op. cit., Chapter 10 – 'Lyndon Johnson's War'

For a complete history of Vietnam records, for and against: the Bear Family compilation . . . *Next Stop Is Vietnam: The War on Record – 1961–2008* (13xCD, 2010)

Mario Savio's 3 December 1964 speech is quoted in the Free Speech Movement archives: www.fsm-a.org/stacks/mario/mario_speech.html

Robert Cohen and Reginald E. Zelnik (Eds), *The Free Speech Movement: Reflections on Berkeley in the 1960s*, Part 1 – 'Roots', including Mario Savio, 'Thirty Years Later: Reflections on the FSM', and Part 2 – 'Experience' (University of California Press, 2002)

Lari Blumenfeld and Fred Gardner, 'Anti-War Pickets Vow More Troop Train Demonstrations', *Berkeley Daily Gazette*, 7 August 1965

Jerry Belcher, 'Pickets Outrun Police, but Troop Train Passes', *San Francisco Examiner*, 13 August 1965

Paul Avery, 'Battle Over Train – GI's Go Through', *San Francisco Chronicle*, 13 August 1965

Three clippings from August 1965 from Ralph Gleason Archive, 'PROTESTS – Vietnam' file

For more details on Berkeley Vietnam protests: www.lib.berkeley.edu/MRC/pacificaviet.html

For a general history of Vietnam involvement and protest in 1965: www.historyplace.com/unitedstates/vietnam/index-1965.html

For the footage of the Berkeley protest on 15 October 1965: www.lib.berkeley.edu/video/catalog/Vgb7nj_e5BGtzob-WNBn1w/Ht2fLtEZ5RGysLXEKp5wiA/1435082192

For Country Joe McDonald and 'Fixin' to Die Rag': www.countryjoe.com/howrag.htm

'Why We March Against the War in Vietnam' leaflet contained in Ralph Gleason Archive, 'PROTESTS – Vietnam' file

Michael Stewart Foley, *Confronting the War Machine: Draft Resistance During the Vietnam War* (University of North Carolina Press, 2003)

There were also frequent attacks by infuriated citizens on anti-war activists, see Michael Stewart Foley, ibid., 'Pacifists' Progress, 1957–66' and 'I Fought the Law, and the Law Won', in Chapter 1 – 'A Little Band of Bold Pioneers'

For difference between the Second World War and Vietnam: *Working Class War: American Combat Soldiers and Vietnam*, op. cit., Chapter 1 – 'Working-Class War: The Vietnam Generation's Military Minority – A Statistical Profile'

For 60 per cent avoidance, 2 per cent of all draftees, graduate schools 'besieged' and 4,000 draft boards: Lawrence M. Baskir and William A. Strauss, *Chance and Circumstance: The Draft, the War, and the Vietnam Generation*, Chapter 1 – 'Vietnam Generation' (Vintage, 1978) 'predominantly older, white middle-class men . . .': ibid.

Jim Osterberg and the draft: Iggy Pop and Anne Wehrer, *I Need More* (Karz-Cohl, 1982)

Lou Reed and the draft: Peter Doggett, *Lou Reed: The Defining Years*, Chapter 4 (Omnibus, 2013)

80 per cent of all those serving in Vietnam came from working-class or poor backgrounds: *Working Class War: American Combat Soldiers and Vietnam*, op. cit., 'Introduction'

For black Americans in Vietnam: *Working Class War: American Combat Soldiers and Vietnam*, op. cit., Chapter 1 – 'Working-Class War: The Vietnam Generation's Military Minority: A Statistical Profile'; 'African Americans in the Vietnam War', www.english.illinois.edu/maps/poets/s_z/stevens/africanamer.htm; and Vietnam war statistics: www.shmoop.com/vietnam-war/statistics.html

struggle for 'the right to fight': *Working Class War: American Combat Soldiers and Vietnam*, ibid.

Student Nonviolent Coordinating Committee, Statement on Vietnam, 6 January 1966: www.crmvet.org/docs/snccviet.htm

Thomas Hauser, *Muhammad Ali*, Chapter 6 – 'Ain't Got No Quarrel' (Pan, 1997)

For more on Bobby Jameson, who died in May 2015, go to this excellent obituary by Bryan: nightflight.com/remembering-mondo-hollywoods-bobby-jameson/. This explains the almost total disappearance of 'Vietnam' when it was originally released on 45: 'He later found out that the reason he wasn't getting much airplay in his hometown of L.A. was that deejays like Reb Foster thought he was using anti-war demonstrations (like those happening on the Sunset Strip regularly) to further his career. He was told he was too "political".'

Bobby Jameson: for the recording of 'Vietnam': bobbyjameson.blogspot.co.uk/2008/03/part-28-lsd-downers-and-vietnam-new.html; for the draft story: bobbyjameson.blogspot.co.uk/2008_04_04_archive.html; Jameson and 'Mondo Hollywood': bobbyjameson.blogspot.co.uk/2008/03/part-29.html

Robert Cohen, *Mondo Hollywood* (Customflix DVD, 2006)

The Monitors, *The Complete Motown Singles Volume 6: 1966*, track-by-track annotations by Bill Dahl and Keith Hughes (Motown Records, 2006)

Thomas Edward Shaw and Anita Klemke, *Black Monk Time* (Carsonstreet Publishing, 1994). For the origin of 'Monk Time', see Chapter 23. For 'try looking angry . . .', see Chapter 24. For the GI story – 'I just got back from Vietnam you assholes! . . .' – see Chapter 27.

'I believe it's all going . . .': 'Six Faces of Youth', *Newsweek*, 21 March 1966

Harold Wilson refusing President Johnson's requests to send UK troops to Vietnam: Ben Pimlott, *Harold Wilson*, Chapter 18 – 'Super-Harold' (Harper Collins, 1992)

Ray Coleman, 'New LPs', review of Barry Sadler's 'The Ballad of the Green Berets', *Disc and Music Echo*, 9 July 1966

'A terribly sick song . . .': *Melody Maker*, 2 April 1966

'nightmarish carnival': Robert Novak and Rowland Evans, 'The Agony of Berkeley', *San Francisco Examiner*, October 1 1965; cited in Michelle Reeves, '"Obey the Rules or Get Out": Ronald Reagan's 1966 Gubernatorial Campaign and the "Trouble in Berkeley"', *Southern California Quarterly*, vol. 92, no. 3 (fall 2010)

'A Plan for Action', Ronald Reagan's Announcement of Candidacy, 4 January 1966

CHAPTER 4

'I began to turn into myself . . .': John Cashman, *The LSD Story*, Chapter 1 – 'The Third Eye' (Fawcett Publications, 1966)

For the history of the Dovers and the group members' quotes: Mike Markesich, liner notes for the Dovers compilation *We're Not Just Anybody* (Misty Lane Records, 2010)

T. Lobsang Rampa, *The Third Eye: The Autobiography of a Tibetan Lama*, Chapter VI – 'Life in the Lamasery' and Chapter VII – 'The Opening of the Third Eye' (Secker and Warburg, 1956; Corgi mass market paperback, 1966)

H. P. Blavatsky, 'Evolution of Root Races in the Fourth Round', 'The Secret Doctrine: The Synthesis of Science, Religion and Philosophy' (Theosophical University Press, 1952)

Gary Lachman, *Madame Blavatsky: The Mother of Modern Spirituality* (Penguin, 2002)

For Cyril Hoskin and T. Lobsang Rampa: hoaxes.org/archive/permalink/the_third_eye_of_t._lobsang_rampa

For the 'Psychedelic Rock' business card: Paul Drummond, *Eye Mind: The Saga of Roky Erickson and the 13th Floor Elevators*, see illustration in Chapter 4 – 'Boom (Evolutionary Not Revolutionary)' (Process, 2007)

'Acid can be a beautiful reaction . . .': quoted in Richard Alpert, Sidney Cohen and Lawrence Schiller, *LSD* (New American Library, June 1966)

George Andrews quoted in Andy Roberts, *Albion Dreaming: A Popular History of LSD in Britain* (Marshall Cavendish, 2008)

'Q: What is your concept . . .': Bob Feigel: '"Real" Teen Revolt – Byrds', *KRLA Beat*, 27 November 1965

For info on the Gamblers' 'LSD-25': diddywah.blogspot.co.uk/2009/12/lets-go-surfing.html

For Dylan and LSD: *Albion Dreaming: A Popular History of LSD in Britain*, op. cit.

John Lennon and George Harrison on LSD: 'The Dental Experience' and 'LSD', in The Beatles, *Anthology* (Cassell, 2000)

Dr John Riley was first mentioned by name in Steve Turner's *The Fab Four: The Gospel According to the Beatles* (WJK Press, 2006)

Paul Jay Robbins: quoted in Christopher Hjort, *So You Want to Be a Rock'n'Roll Star: The Byrds Day by Day 1965–1973*, entry for 23 April 1965, '1965' (Outline Press, 2008)

For the beginnings of LSD's spread and its connections to the US military, see Jay Stevens, *Storming Heaven: LSD and the American Dream* (Heinemann, 1988) and Martin A. Lee and Bruce Schlain, *Acid Dreams: The CIA, LSD and the Sixties Rebellion* (Grove Press, 1985)

Juergen Suess, Gerold Dommermuth and Hans Maier, *Beat in Liverpool* (Europäische Verlagsanstalt, 1966)

Michael Hollingshead, *The Man Who Turned on the World*, Chapter 6 – 'London on My Mind' (Blond Briggs, 1973)

Barry Miles: author interview, October 2013

Barry Miles, '101 Cromwell Road', in *In the Sixties* (Jonathan Cape, 2002)

Timothy Leary, Ralph Metzner and Richard Alpert, *The Psychedelic Experience: A Manual Based on the Tibetan Book of the Dead* (University Books, 1964)

'He envisions a society in . . .': Stephen Bello, 'Timothy Leary: Silhouette', *Harvard Crimson*, 13 October 1965

Timothy Leary, *The Politics of Ecstasy* (Paladin, 1970)

The first Acid Test: 'The Acid Test Chronicles' at www.postertrip.com/public/5572.cfm. For an index of all subsequent Acid Tests: www.postertrip.com/public/department37.cfm

Barry Miles on Indica stock: interview and email communication with author, October 2013

Titbits review of Spontaneous Underground: www.pinkfloydsound.it/1966.htm

For early Acid Tests and *Rubber Soul* as 'the soundtrack of Haight-Ashbury', see Charles A. Perry, *The Haight-Ashbury: A History*, Chapter 2 – 'The First Flash' (Vintage Books, 1985)

Glenn Povey, *'Echoes: The Complete History of Pink Floyd* (Omnibus Press, 2007)

Pink Floyd concerts in 1966: www.brain-damage.co.uk/concert-dates/1966-tour-dates-concerts.html

For details of Los Angeles clubs: Dominic Priore, 'That's the Hollywood Nightlife', in *Riot on Sunset Strip: Rock'n'Roll's Last Stand in Hollywood* (Outline Press, 2007)

Tom Wolfe, *The Electric Kool-Aid Acid Test* (Bantam, 1969)

For more on individual Acid Tests, in particular the 12 February 1966 Watts Acid Test, go to Postertrip: www.postertrip.com/public/5580.cfm

UK exposés: *Albion Dreaming: A Popular History of LSD in Britain*, op. cit.

'The colourless, odorless, tasteless substance called LSD . . .': 'LSD: The Exploding Threat of the Mind Drug that Got Out of Control', *Life*, 25 March 1966

Johnny Rogan, *The Byrds: Timeless Flight Revisited* (Rogan House, 1997)

Tony Hall, 'You Can Even Dig Indian Music!' *Record Mirror*, 22 January 1966

Byrds reviews and interviews in *So You Want to Be a Rock'n'Roll Star*, op. cit., entries from 23 February, 14 March and 28 March, in '1966' chapter

Transcript of the Byrds' March 1966 conference in sleeve notes to the Byrds' *Another Dimension* (Sundazed Records, 2005)

For the early 1966 layoff, see John Lennon's comments in 'The Lennon Interview' with Chris Hutchins, *NME*, 11 March 1966: 'It's an accident that we're not working now; we should have had just two weeks holiday after Christmas and then started on the next film, but it isn't ready and won't be for months'

All four March 1966 interviews that Maureen Cleave did with the Beatles are online at www.rocksbackpages.com/Library/Writer/maureen-cleave. John Lennon's was printed on 4 March, Ringo Starr's on the 11th, George Harrison's on the 18th and Paul McCartney's on the 25th

The *Disc and Music Echo* 'Sound of the Stars' 45 can be found at: www. youtube.com/watch?v=KaF4quazrZw

The full audio of the Tom Lodge interview can be found online, if you must

Robert Whitaker: author interview, April 2011

The Psychedelic Experience, op. cit., 'General Introduction'

'The hedonistic cults . . .': Sidney Cohen, answer to 'Q: What Is Your Estimate of the Future of Psychedelics?', in *LSD*, op. cit.

'particularly attractive to students . . .': Alan Bestic, *Turn Me on Man*, Chapter 8 (Tandem paperback, 1966)

Anne Gillie, *The Chemistry and Sociology of LSD* (Naturalism Inc., April 1966)

John Hopkins: author interview, May 2012

Barry Miles on Christopher Gibbs's party: 'THE Global moon-edition Long Hair TIMES', in *In the Sixties*, op. cit.

Michael Hollingshead on WPC bust: *The Man Who Turned on the World*, op. cit., Chapter 7 – 'The New Heresy'

Timothy Leary arrest: 'DRUGS: On and Off', *Time*, 2 May 1966

Bernard Weintraub, 'LSD: A Fascinating Drug and a Growing Problem', *New York Times*, 22 April 1966

Michael Cooper, *Blinds and Shutters* (Genesis Publications, 1990)

Marianne Faithfull and David Dalton, *Faithfull: An Autobiography* (Little Brown, 1994)

For the groups playing at Tara Browne's party, go to entry for 23 April 1966 at thebritishsound.blogspot.co.uk/2011/07/peter-bs-shotgun-express-family-tree.html

For the *Gavin Report* and Derek Taylor's response: *So You Want to Be a Rock'n'Roll Star*, op. cit., entries for 29 April 1966 and 9 May 1966 in '1966' chapter

For a detailed discussion of 'Eight Miles High' and the *Gavin Report*: Mark Teehan, 'The Byrds, "Eight Miles High"', the *Gavin Report*, and Media Censorship of Alleged "Drug Songs" in 1966: An Assessment', Popular Musicology Online: www.popular-musicology-online.com/issues/04/teehan.html

Mr Jones, 'The Future of Psychedelics', *Daily Californian*, 19 May 1966

Norman Jopling and Peter Jones, 'New Singles Reviewed . . .', *Record Mirror*, 14 May 1966

Tony Hall, 'The Tony Hall Column', *Record Mirror*, 14 May 1966

'BEATLES: WHAT A CARVE-UP!' *Disc and Music Echo*, 11 June 1966

For details of the Donovan bust: Simon Wells, *Butterfly on a Wheel: The Great Rolling Stones Drug Bust* Chapter 3 – 'Chelsea' (Omnibus, 2011)

A Boy Called Donovan has not been reissued. It was viewable for a while online but has now disappeared

Time, 'The States: The Law and LSD', 10 June 1966

Background Reading

Aldous Huxley, *The Doors of Perception and Heaven and Hell* (Penguin, 1959)

Sybille Bedford, *Aldous Huxley: A Biography. Volume 2 1939–1963* (Chatto and Windus, 1974)

Rex Boyland and Rex Lode, *The Third Eye of America* (Lyle Stuart, 1963)

Albert Hoffman, *LSD: My Problem Child* (McGraw Hill, 1980)

John Pollard, Leonard Uhr and Elizabeth Stern, *Drugs and Phantasy* (Little Brown and Company, 1965)

R. E. L. Masters and Jean Houston, *The Varieties of Psychedelic Experience* (Anthony Blond, 1966)

David Solomon (Ed.), *LSD: The Consciousness-Expanding Drug* (Putnam, 1964). The articles by Alan Harrington, Dan Wakefield and Aldous Huxley were first published in the November 1963 issue of *Playboy*

Lewis Carroll, *Alice's Adventures in Wonderland* (Macmillan and Co., 1957)

Constance A. Newland, *My Self and I* (Coward McCann, 1962)

Robert S. de Ropp, *Drugs and the Mind* (Grove Press, 1961)

Stewart Home, *Tainted Love* (Virgin, 2005)

Nicholas Murray, *Aldous Huxley: An English Intellectual* (Abacus, 2002)

CHAPTER 5

'A revolution is on the way . . .': Sue Tate, *Pauline Boty: Pop Artist and Woman*, Chapter 4 – 'Pop Artist and Woman' (Wolverhampton Art Gallery, 2013)

'Walkin' My Cat Named Dog' release details from 45 cat: www.45cat.com

Radio Caroline chart for 23 April 1966 from: radiolondon.co.uk/caroline/stonewashed/carolinecharts/034%20April%2023%201966.htm

The clip of 'Walkin' My Cat Named Dog' can be found on YouTube: www.youtube.com/watch?v=SPZVrmJ2HH8

Author interview with Norma Tanega, March 2014

'I never thought I'd see the day': 'Your Page', *Record Mirror*, 14 May 1966

'Norma Wants Music for Herself and Dog', *KRLA Beat*, 16 April 1966

Peter Jones, 'Norma Just Wants to Hide and Paint', *Record Mirror*, 9 July 1966

'Charm in the Charts', in Paul Denver (Ed.), *Radio Caroline Annual* (World Distributors, 1965)

'The freedom to lead . . .': Betty Friedan, *The Feminine Mystique*, Chapter 14 – 'A New Life Plan for Women' (Penguin Classics Edition, 2010)

Richard Mabey, *The Pop Process*, Chapter 2 – 'Survey' (Hutchinson Educational, 1969)

Susan Brownmiller, *In Our Time: Memoir of a Revolution*, Prologue (Delta paperbacks, 1999)

The March 1966 BBC programme *Six Sides of a Square* can be viewed at: www.bbc.co.uk/archive/70sfeminism/10401.shtml

Nell Dunn, *Talking to Women*, Preface (Pan Books, 1966)

Frances Chadwicke: ibid.

The Feminine Mystique, op. cit., Preface

Young wives: quoted in *The Feminine Mystique*, Chapter 1 – 'The Problem That Has No Name'

For Friedan's history of feminism: ibid., Chapter 4 – 'The Passionate Journey'

For the 1950s counter-revolution: ibid., Chapter 8 – 'The Mistaken Choice'

Simone de Beauvoir, *The Second Sex*, translated by Constance Borde and Sheila Malovany-Chevallier (Vintage Books, 2011)

Sheila Rowbotham, *Promise of a Dream: Remembering the Sixties*, Chapter 1 – '1960–61' (Verso, 2001)

Jenny Diski, *The Sixties*, Chapter 1 – 'Consuming the Sixties' (Profile Books, 2009)

Lynne Reid Banks, *The L-Shaped Room* (Vintage Classics, 2004)

For the impact of *The L-Shaped Room* and *A Taste of Honey*, see *The Sixties*, op. cit., Chapter 3 – 'Body Work'

'without a compass between the dreaded Scylla . . .': *Promise of a Dream*, op. cit., Chapter 2 – '1961–4'

Helen Gurley Brown, *Sex and the Single Girl: The Unmarried Woman's Guide to Men* (Pocket Books, 1963)

Gloria Steinem, 'I Was a Playboy Bunny', in *Outrageous Acts and Everyday Rebellions* (Holt, Rinehart and Winston, 1983)

For major feminist events in the US during the 1960s, including publications and legislation: en.wikipedia.org/wiki/Timeline_of_feminism_in_the_United_States#1960s

For a timeline of UK feminism: www.mmu.ac.uk/equality-and-diversity/doc/gender-equality-timeline.pdf

Margaret Mead and Frances Bagley Kaplan (Eds), *American Women* (Charles Scribner's Sons, 1965)

Casey Hayden and Mary King, 'Sex and Caste: A Kind of Memo'. This can be read in full at www.uic.edu/orgs/cwluherstory/CWLUArchive/memo.html

Mary King, *Freedom Song: A Personal History of the 1960s Civil Rights Movement*, Chapter 12 – 'Manifesto' (William Morrow and Company, 1987)

'The real dynamo . . .': *The Teenage Revolution*, op. cit., Chapter 10 – 'Where Have All the Young Men Gone? When There Are More of Them Than There Are Girls'

Jenny Diski, *The Sixties*, op. cit., 'Introduction'

Promise of a Dream, op. cit., Chapter 3 – '1964–6'

'It was agony, as though . . .': 'I'd Marry Anyone to Spite My Parents', in *Generation X*, op. cit.

'the present generation is going . . .': ibid., 'You Can't Enjoy Yourself in Church'

'a fifteen-year-old girl . . .': *The Teenage Revolution*, op. cit., Chapter 1 – 'Fission'

'Cathy was the face of the 1960s . . .': Vicki Wickham, email correspondence with author, May 2015

Barbara Hulanicki on Cathy McGowan: *From A to BIBA: The Autobiography of Barbara Hulanicki*, Chapter 5 (V&A Publishing, 2007); subsequent quotes re. 'heavy boned' and 'postwar babies' from same chapter

Michael Schofield, *The Sexual Behaviour of Young People* (Prentice Hall Press, 1965)

The Teenage Revolution, op. cit., Chapter 7 – 'Things That Worry Grown-Ups: Politics, Religion, Morality, Sex'

'There's a Feeling in the Air That Something Is Going to Happen', in *Generation X*, op. cit.

Richard Mabey on transvestism: *The Pop Process*, op. cit., Chapter 4 – 'Sources of Fashion: The Audience'

'from a gross inequality of sexes . . .': *The Teenage Revolution*, op. cit., Chapter 7 – 'Things That Worry Grown-Ups: Politics, Religion, Morality, Sex'

'This Is Your Life: Leaving Home?' *Rave*, May 1966

Nova details and Mary Grieve quotes: Janice Winship, *Inside Women's Magazines* (Rivers Oram Press, 1987)

Mary Grieve (Ed.), *Fifteen* (Collins, 1966)

'Can You Be a Star and Human Too?', *Boyfriend Book 1966* (Pictorial Press, 1966)

'Our own personal top girls . . .': 'Pick of the Popsies: Our Star Choices for 1966', ibid.

For a general résumé of the girl groups: Charlotte Greig, *Will You Still Love Me Tomorrow?* (Virago Press, 1989)

Faithfull, op. cit., Chapter 2 – 'As Tears Go By'

Richard Goldstein, 'The Soul Sound from Sheepshead Bay', in *Goldstein's Greatest Hits* (Prentice-Hall, 1970). For more, see Richard Goldstein, *Another Little Piece of My Heart: My Life of Rock and Revolution in the '60s* (Bloomsbury, 2015). Also go to www.richardgoldsteinonline.com.

Mary Wilson, *Dreamgirl: My Life as a Supreme* (Sidgwick and Jackson, 1987). Chaperones and Artist Development dept, Chapter 14; the Beatles story is from Chapter 16

'The Supremes: From Real Rags to Real Riches', *Look*, 3 May 1966

Dusty Springfield, author interview, March 1989; published in the *Observer*, 4 April 1989

Penny Valentine and Vicki Wickham, *Dancing with Demons: The Authorised Biography of Dusty Springfield* (Hodder Paperbacks, 2001)

For quotes from contemporary magazines, including the *Woman's Own* series, these were reprinted in Paul Howes, *The Dusty Springfield Bulletin*, issues 7–37, May 1989 on. For more info: www.cpinternet.com/~mbayly/dsb.htm and also Paul Howes, *The Complete Dusty Springfield* (Reynolds and Hearn, 2009)

For more on Dusty Springfield: Lucy O'Brien, *Dusty* (Sidgwick and Jackson, 1989); Annie J. Randall, *Dusty: Queen of the Postmods* (Oxford University Press, 2009); Penny Valentine, Dusty Springfield interview, *Disc and Music Echo*, 30 April 1966

Sue Watling and David Alan Mellor, *Pauline Boty: The Only Blonde in the World* (AM Publications, 1988)

For illustrations of the pictures mentioned and Boty's biography: *Pauline Boty: Pop Artist and Woman*, op. cit.

'Pop Goes the Easel' (BBC *Monitor* 1962) can be viewed on YouTube: www.youtube.com/watch?v=3tbVTEW7wS8

Nell Dunn, 'Pauline Boty', in *Talking to Women*, op. cit.

Twiggy Lawson, 'Twiggy: In Black and White' (Simon and Schuster, 1997)

Twiggy: A Life in Photographs (National Portrait Gallery Publications, 2009)

CHAPTER 6

For general Velvet Underground background material: Johan Kugelberg, *The Velvet Underground – New York Art* (Rizzoli, 2009); Richie Unterberger, *White Light/White Heat: The Velvet Underground Day to Day* (Jawbone, 2009); Victor Bockris and Gerard Malanga, *Up-Tight: The Velvet Underground Story* (Omnibus Press, 1983); this excellent site has full details of concerts, reviews and photographs from 1966: olivier.landemaine.free.fr/vu/live/1965-66/perf6566.html

For more general Warhol material: Stephen Shore and Lynne Tillman, *The Velvet Years: Warhol's Factory 1965–1967* (Pavilion, 1995); Wayne Koestenbaum, *Andy Warhol: A Penguin Life* (Lipper/Viking, 2001); Steven Watson, *Factory Made: Warhol and the Sixties* (Pantheon, 2003); Nat Finkelstein and David Dalton, *Edie Factory Girl* (VH1 Press, 2006); Tony Scherman and David Dalton, *POP: The Genius of Andy Warhol* (Harper Collins, 2009)

Much of the material quoted in this chapter comes from the Time Capsules contained in the Collection of the Andy Warhol Museum in Pittsburgh. Where relevant and possible, the Time Capsule in which the clipping is located is mentioned at the end of the source, i.e. TC 14, TC 5, etc.

'A Pop person is like a vacuum . . .': John L. Wasserman, 'Conjurer's Dream from Pop World,' *San Francisco Chronicle*, 23 May 1966 (TC 14)

'Let Yourself a Go Go!: POP into Channel 7's "Pop Art Theater"', press release from Phyllis Doherty, WNAC-TV, 2 June 1966 (TC 14)

Ralph J. Gleason, 'On the Town: The Sizzle that Fizzled', *San Francisco Chronicle*, 30 May 1966 (TC 14)

Joan Chatfield Taylor, 'The Lion's Sheep', *San Francisco Chronicle*, 30 May 1966 (TC 14)

'Wild New Flashy Bedlam of the Discotheque', *Life*, 27 May 1966, p. 72ff.

Nico and Warhol interview: John L. Wasserman, 'Conjurer's Dream from Pop World', op. cit.

The brief clip of Nico hosting the 'Pop Art Theater' can be seen at www.youtube.com/watch?v=r_FUijtJwr4

'Pop Art–Las Vegas Gambol . . .' and 'the Peter Pan of the current art scene': 'Let Yourself a Go Go!: POP into Channel 7's "Pop Art Theater"', op. cit.

Bob Reilly, unpublished interview with Andy Warhol, spring 1966 (TC 14)

'TV reporter: Andy . . .': Jim Paltridge, 'Andy Out West', *The Daily Californian Weekly Magazine*, vol. 3, no. 2, 10 October 1967 (TC 11). Paltridge was the Arts & Entertainment Editor for the student newspaper *The Daily Californian*, and Warhol thought that this 'was one of the best articles about him that he had ever read'. For more on Paltridge, see notes to 'Andy Out West', in *I'll Be Your Mirror: The Selected Andy Warhol Interviews*, Kenneth Goldsmith (Ed.) (Carroll and Graf, 2004)

Claude Hall, 'High-Riding MGM Sets Up Pop Artist Project Helmed by Wilson', *Billboard*, 21 May 1966

A copy of the MGM Records/Velvet Underground and Nico contract, dated 2
May 1966, is held in Time Capsule 11

The Nico/mirror story is contained in *POP: The Genius of Andy Warhol*, op.
cit., Chapter 7 – '1966'

For more about the Norman Dolph acetate, see David Fricke, sleeve note for
The Velvet Underground & Nico (45th Anniversary Super Deluxe Edition)
(UMC/Polydor, 2012)

John Wilcock, 'A "High" School of Music and Art', *The East Village Other*, 15
April–1 May 1966

John Richmond, 'In View: Towards a Definition of Soft', *Saturday Night*, July
1966 (TC 14)

Gretchen Berg, 'Andy Warhol: My True Story', *The East Village Other*, 1
November 1966

Jean Clay, 'Andy's Warhorse', *Realities*, December 1967

'Pop is trying to give people instant . . .': Richard Goldstein, 'Before or Beyond
the Slick?,' *New York*, no. 16, February 1967 (TC 11)

Jim Paltridge, 'Way Out West', op. cit.

'Three boxes in particular covered the year . . .': these are numbered as Time
Capsules 11, 14, and 47

Warhol quotes re. Pop, end of painting and Philadelphia show: Andy Warhol
and Pat Hackett, *Popism: The Warhol Sixties* (Harper Collins, 1983)

Gloria Steinem, 'The Ins and Outs of Pop Culture', *Life*, 20 August 1965

A 1963 calendar with pictures of Cliff, Elvis, etc. is contained in TC 14;
Mannlich etc. are in TC 47

John Cale with Victor Bockris, *What's Welsh for Zen?* (Bloomsbury Publishing,
1998)

The full clip of *The Making of an Underground Film from CBS Evening News
with Walter Cronkite*, broadcast on 31 December 1965, can be seen at www.
youtube.com/watch?v=DS7knWefSiQ

For more on the Piero Heliczer/Cronkite footage, including several photos and
Sterling Morrison, 'Going Back in Time to Piero Heliczer', in *The Velvet
Underground – New York Art*, op. cit.

Victor Bockris and Gerard Malanga, *Up-Tight: The Velvet Underground Story*,
Chapter 1 – 'Making Andy Warhol Uptight' (Omnibus Press, 1983)

Lou Reed, 'The View from the Bandstand', op. cit.

Jean Stein, *Edie* (Jonathan Cape, 1982)

The Leather Man catalogue, undated (TC 47)

The 3 January rehearsal can be heard, in part, on the fourth disc of *The Velvet
Underground & Nico (45th Anniversary Super Deluxe Edition)*

For a definitive account of the Screen Tests, see Callie Angell, *Andy Warhol
Screen Tests: The Films of Andy Warhol Catalogue Raisonné*, Introduction,
Chapter 2 – 'Screen Tests A–Z' and Chapter 5 – 'Background Reels: EPI
Background, Screen Test Poems, and Others' (Harry N. Abrams, 2006)

Seymour Krim, 'Andy Warhol's "Velvet Underground": Shock Treatment for
Psychiatrists', *New York Herald Tribune*, 14 January 1966; Grace Glueck,
'Syndromes Pop at Delmonico's', *New York Times*, 14 January 1966. Both
are reproduced in *The Velvet Underground – New York Art*, op. cit.

Archer Winsten, 'Andy Warhol at Cinematheque', *New York Post*, 9 February 1966 (TC 49)

John Wilcock, 'On the Road with the Exploding Plastic Inevitable', in *The Autobiography and Sex Life of Andy Warhol* (Other Scenes, 1971); reproduced in *The Velvet Underground – New York Art*, op. cit.

Morrison 'invisibility' quote and Ingrid Superstar quote about 'immature punks': *Up-Tight*, op. cit., Chapter 4 – 'On the Road with "Andy Warhol: Up-Tight"'

The interview between Ignacio Juliá and Sterling Morrison is contained in Albin Zak III, *The Velvet Underground Companion: Four Decades of Commentary*, Part 4 – 'The Velvet Warriors' (Schirmer Books, 1997) and in Ignacio Juliá (Ed.), *Feed-back: The Velvet Underground: Legend, Truth* (Ignacio Juliá, 2011)

The advert for the Dom is contained in *Village Voice*, 17 March 1966; reproduced in *The Velvet Underground – New York Art*, op. cit.

Bruce Pollock, 'Lou Reed Does Not Want Anyone to Know How He Writes His Songs', *Modern Hi-Fi and Music*, 1975. The article is available on Rocksbackpages at www.rocksbackpages.com/Library/Article/lou-reed-does-not-want-anyone-to-know-how-he-writes-his-songs

John Wilcock, 'A "High" School of Music and Art', op. cit.

The Jonas Mekas review of the Dom is contained in the *Village Voice*, 26 May 1966

'The Story of POP: What It Is and How It Came to Be', *Newsweek*, 25 April 1966 (TC 30)

There was a half-page ad for the Trip residency in *KRLA Beat*, 14 May 1966

The article about the Trip is contained in *KRLA Beat*, 26 May 1966; reproduced in *The Velvet Underground – New York Art*, op. cit.

For more details about the Trip residency, see *Andy Warhol's Screen Tests: The Films of Andy Warhol Catalogue Raisonné*, Note 365, op. cit.

'Strip's Trip Hit by 3G Pay Claim as Club Shutters', *Variety*, 17 May 1966; reproduced in *The Velvet Underground – New York Art*, op. cit.

For more on Lisa Law, see *Flashing on the Sixties* (Chronicle Books, 2007). Severn Darden was pictured in Joan Chatfield Taylor's 'The Lion's Sheep', op. cit. For more, see www.independent.co.uk/news/people/obituaries-severn-darden-1584744.html

Dominic Priore, 'There's Battle Lines Being Drawn', in *Riot on Sunset Strip*, op. cit.

Merla Zellerbach, 'My Fair City: Andy Warhol, Son of Hip', *San Francisco Chronicle*, 27 May 1966

Mary Woronov, *Swimming Underground: My Years in the Warhol Factory* (Journey Editions, 1995). The 'amphetamine and acid' quote is reproduced in Martin Torgoff, *Can't Find My Way Home: America in the Great Stoned Age, 1945–2000* (James Bennett Pty Ltd, 2004)

'TV reporter: Andy . . .': Jim Paltridge, 'Andy Out West', op. cit.

'The Story of POP', *Newsweek*, op. cit.

Bob Reilly, unpublished interview, op. cit.

Elenore Lester, 'So He Stopped Painting Brillo Boxes and Bought a Movie Camera', *New York Times*, 11 December 1966

For Danny Williams, see Esther Robinson, *A Walk into the Sea: Danny Williams and the Warhol Factory* (Arthouse, 2011)

Warhol cover is on the 'Today's Teenagers' issue, *Time*, 29 January 1965

Frances Folin, *Embodied Visions: Bridget Riley, Op Art and the Sixties* (Thames and Hudson, 2004)

'Posters by Painters', 22 June–2 August 1965, American Greetings Gallery (TC 5)

'Children's Village', *Newsweek*, 23 May 1966 (TC 14)

Ross Wetzsteon, 'Violence/Non-Violence: The Evil in Each', *Village Voice*, 14 April 1966 (TC 47)

'Trials: Addenda to De Sade', *Time*, 6 May 1966 (TC 14)

Schmid case: 'Arizona: Growing Up in Tucson', *Time*, 11 March 1966, and Robert Moser, 'He Cruised in a Golden Car, Looking for the Action', *Life*, 4 March 1966

A copy of the *Their Town* script is contained in Time Capsule 11

'attention was nailed . . .': www.warholstars.org/ronald_tavel.html

For *Batman*, see 'Pow' cover of *TV Guide*, 26 March–1 April 1966. The writers of *Batman* eventually paid homage to Warhol in the 22 March 1967 episode 'Pop Goes the Joker'

Gloria Steinem, 'The Ins and Outs of Pop Culture', op. cit.

'Letters to the Editor', *Village Voice*, 14 April 1966 (TC 47)

'Selective Panel Casts in Cold Blood', *Town & Country*, May 1966 (TC 14)

'Who Is a Hero? And Why?' *Mademoiselle*, July 1966 (TC 14)

Archer Winsten, 'Andy Warhol at Cinematheque', op. cit.

Alan Rinzler (Ed.), *Andy Warhol's Index* (Random House, 1967). The book also contains an uncredited interview, entitled 'Yes and No', in which Warhol proves himself a master of null:

> 'Do you think Pop art is . . .'
> 'No.'
> 'What?'
> 'No.'
> 'Do you think Pop art is . . .'
> 'No . . . No I don't.'

This interview was in fact by Joseph Freeman, and was published in *Bay Times*, Sheepshead High School, Brooklyn, 1 April 1966

The handwritten Nico letter is contained in Time Capsule 11

For more on the shooting and projection of *Chelsea Girls*: www.warholstars.org/chelsea_girls.html

Andy Warhol, 'CHELSEA GIRL Instructions for Split-Screen Projection', typed sheet (TC 11)

Michaela Williams, 'Warhol's Brutal Assemblage | Non-Stop Horror Show', *Chicago Daily News*, 22 June 1966

Susan Nelson, 'Pop Revue – Way Out? Very In?' *Chicago Tribune*, 24 June 1966 (TC 47)

For details of Danny Williams, Warhol and 1966, see *POP: The Genius of Andy Warhol*, op. cit., Chapter 7 – '1966'

John Cale quotes re. Paul Morrissey and Danny Williams fighting and re. amphetamine in the strobe light: Robert Greenfield, 'Shards of Velvet Afloat in London', *Rolling Stone*, 18 February 1971

'Warhol's "Exploding Show" Stirs Psychosis in Chi's Offbeat Poor Richard's', *Variety*, 29 June 1966

Ronald Nameth's *Andy Warhol's Exploding Plastic Inevitable* can be seen at vimeo.com/14888508. For more detail: www.n3krozoft.com/_xxbcf67373. TMP/tv/ronald_nameth.html

The sleeve to 'All Tomorrow's Parties' is pictured on page 132 of *The Velvet Underground – New York Art*, op. cit.

'a very apt description . . .' and 'I kept notes . . .': David Fricke, essay for *Peel Slowly and See*, Velvet Undeground box set (Polydor, 1995)

For details of Velvet Underground and Nico and Mothers of Invention singles releases: www.45cat.com

For Verve US discography: www.globaldogproductions.info

Marshall McLuhan, *The Medium Is the Massage* (Penguin Books, 1967)

CHAPTER 7

General background information: for an excellent overview of dance in America, see Ralph G. Giordano, *Social Dancing in America: A History and Reference, Volume 2: Lindy Hop to Hip Hop, 1901–2000* (Greenwood Press, 2007); Marshall and Jean Sterns, *Jazz Dance: The Story of American Vernacular Dance* (Schirmer, 1968); Michael Haralambos, *Right On: From Blues to Soul in Black America* (Causeway Press, 1994); Steven Kasher, *The Civil Rights Movement: A Photographic History, 1954–68* (Abbeville Press, 1996); also the fourteen episodes of *Eyes on the Prize: America's Civil Rights Years 1945–1965* (PBS, 1987). Transcripts of each show are also available online at www.pbs.org/wgbh/amex/eyesontheprize/about/pt.html

'To enjoy the latest new thing . . .': 'Wild New Flashy Bedlam of the Discotheque', *Life*, 27 May 1966

Peter Guralnick, *Sweet Soul Music*, Chapter 6 – 'Fame and Muscle Shoals' (Virgin, 1986)

For the history of Stax, the June 1965 *Billboard* feature and the Wexler quote: Rob Bowman, *Soulsville U.S.A.: The Story of Stax Records*, Chapter 3 – 'You Don't Miss Your Water: 1961–1963', Chapter 4 – Respect: 1964–65', Chapter 5 – 'Don't Have to Shop Around: 1965' (Schirmer Books, 1997)

'people picking cotton . . .': *Sweet Soul Music*, op. cit., Chapter 6

The Wilson Pickett/Spooner Oldham photo can be found at www.gettyimages. co.uk/detail/news-photo/singer-wilson-pickett-and-keyboardist-spooner-oldham-at-news-photo/159577348

For an excellent history of 'Land of 1000 Dances', from Chris Kenner through Cannibal and the Headhunters to Wilson Pickett: www.tsimon.com/land. htm. See also Rob Finnis's sleeve notes for *Various: Land of 1000 Dances – The Ultimate Compilation of Hit Dances 1958–1965* (Ace Records, 1999) and his sleeve notes for *Various: Land of 1000 Dances – The Ultimate Compilation of Hit Dances 1956–1966 Volume 2* (Ace Records, 2002); and Tony Rounce's sleeve notes for *Various: Land of 1000 Dances – Special Soul & Funk Edition* (Ace Records, 2004)

Naomi Elizabeth Bragin, email correspondence with author, March 2014

Moncell 'ill kozby' Durden, email correspondence with author, March 2014

For the Ertegun and Wexler quotes: Gerri Hershey, *Sweet Soul Music*, Chapter 7 – 'Broadway Fricassee' (Southbank Publishing, 2006)

'The dance floor was swaying . . .': Robert Alden, '1,000 Twisters and One Floor Swing at Venerable Palladium', *New York Times*, 4 June 1964

For the Twist and all that followed: Jim Dawson, *The Story of the Song and Dance That Changed the World* (Faber and Faber, 1995)

The Hullabaloo Discotheque Dance Book (Scholastic Book Services, 1966)

For the post-Twist dances: *Social Dancing in America*, op. cit., Chapter 5 – 'The Twist, Doing Your Own Thing, and A Go-Go: 1960–69'

For the Hollywood clubs and the new generation of pop shows: *Riot on Sunset Strip*, op. cit.

'It was an instant success, a venue whose time had come': within weeks of the Whisky a Go Go opening, Johnny Rivers recorded his set at the club. *Live at the Whisky a Go Go* became one of the most popular albums of the year and set the standard for discotheque-style recordings. The 'live' audience sound would soon be found all over new dance records, including the east LA versions of 'Land of 1000 Dances' by Cannibal and the Headhunters and Thee Midnighters, as well as a wide variety of albums: *Lloyd Thaxton Presents the Land of 1000 Dances*, Sandy Nelson's *Drum Discotheque* and *Killer Joe's International Discotheque*, which featured veteran dance instructor Killer Joe Piro.

For the suspension of the *Billboard* Rhythm and Blues charts in November 1963: Suzanne E. Smith, *Dancing in the Street: Motown and the Cultural Politics of Detroit*, Chapter 2 – 'Money (That's What I Want): Black Capitalism and Black Freedom in Detroit' (Harvard University Press, 1999)

More on the Jerk: the Jerk was an extremely popular dance and was well represented on record during the second half of 1964. Jerk songs were recorded by the Contours, the Gypsies, Jackie Ross, the Miracles ('Come on Do the Jerk') and many others, but it was the Larks' 'The Jerk' that went into the Top 10 at the end of 1964, in a chart still dominated by the Beatles and British invaders the Searchers and the Zombies. Veteran doo-wopper Don Julian wrote the song after watching kids dance to Martha and the Vandellas' 'Dancing in the Street'

For chart details, go to old-charts.com, US charts 1964 and 1965

T.A.M.I. Show (Shout DVD, 2009)

The Supremes' *Ed Sullivan* performance of 'Come See about Me' can be seen at www.youtube.com/watch?v=vWoFzANIAyk

For more Supremes videos, see *Reflections: The Definitive Performances 1964–1969* (UMG, 2006)

Suzanne E. Smith, *Dancing in the Street*, op. cit., Chapter 3 – 'Come See about Me: Black Cultural Production in Detroit'

Motown as leading seller of singles in 1965: Brian Ward, 'Just My Soul Responding', in Kingsley Abbott (Ed.), *Callin' Out Around the World: A Motown Reader* (Helter Skelter, 2001)

For the Gordy concept of Motown as the auto-production line: *Dancing in the Street*, op. cit., Introduction – 'Can't Forget the Motor City'

Bill Dahl, 'Junior Walker: Motown's Screaming Sax Star', in *Callin' Out Around the World*, op. cit.

'the ideal accompaniment for driving': David Morse, *Motown and the Arrival of Black Music* (Macmillan, 1971), quoted in *Dancing in the Street*, op. cit., Chapter 3 – 'Come See about Me: Black Cultural Production in Detroit'

More thoughts on the use of the word 'soul' in the pop and R&B contexts: it had been building for a long time, with Ray Charles's 1959 'I Believe to My Soul' and King Curtis's 1962 'Soul Twist' and follow-up 'Soul Serenade'. During 1964, the term began to take on a life of its own. In March, Berry Gordy launched a subsidiary label called Soul for the earthier, more R&B productions from his assembly line: singles by Jimmy Ruffin, Shorty Long, Earl van Dyke and Junior Walker, including 'Shotgun', the label's first big hit. Solomon Burke recorded 'Rockin' Soul' and 'More Rockin' Soul'. The pace quickened into 1965. In March, the Impressions released the #29 hit 'Woman's Got Soul'. Dave Godin thought that the term came 'about '62/'63, and *Billboard* were responsible for it. The term "R&B" came to be used because records used to be listed in the Race Chart, i.e. black records selling to black people, and *Billboard* didn't like the racist connotations of that. But by the time the sixties came along, rhythm and blues, which was meant to be a liberating term, had in fact taken on a racist flavour. For a record to be classified as R&B ghettoised it, as in, "This radio station does not play rhythm and blues." So *Billboard* decided to adopt the term "soul"' (author interview, February 1995)

Sweet Soul Music, op. cit., Chapter 7 – 'Papa's Got a Brand New Bag'

Alan Leeds, sleeve notes for *James Brown, The Singles Volume Three 1964–1965* (Polydor, 2007)

Alan Leeds, sleeve notes for *James Brown, The Singles Volume Four 1966–1967* (Polydor, 2007)

James Brown and Bruce Tucker, *James Brown: The Godfather of Soul* (Sidgwick and Jackson, 1987)

R. J. Smith, *The One: The Life and Music of James Brown* (Gotham Books, 2012)

Robert Gordon, *Respect Yourself: Stax Records and the Soul Explosion* (Bloomsbury, 2013)

For Stax falling behind Motown, Atlantic, etc., Otis Redding and the hiring of Al Bell: *Soulsville U.S.A.*, op. cit., Chapter 5 – 'Don't Have to Shop Around 1965'

Rob Bowman, sleeve notes for *Otis Redding: Otis Blue Collector's Edition* (Rhino, 2008)

Ashley Kahn, sleeve notes for Otis Redding and His Orchestra's *Live on the Sunset Strip* (Stax Records, 2011)

Tony Hall, 'The Tony Hall Column: George Harrison's Fab Forty . . .', *Record Mirror*, 25 December 1965

For the Beatles recording in Memphis: *Soulsville U.S.A.* , op. cit., Chapter 6 – 'Knock on Wood: 1966'

For the Rolling Stones recording 'I've Been Loving You Too Long', see entry for 10 May at *The Complete Works of the Rolling Stones 1962–2015*: www. nzentgraf.de/books/tcw/works1.htm

Stu Hackel, 'Heart Beat', and track-by-track rundown by Bill Dahl and Keith Hughes, edited and augmented by Harry Weinger, from *The Complete Motown Singles Volume 6: 1966*, op. cit.

'That's when the thought processes . . .': *Soulsville U.S.A.*, op. cit., Chapter 6 – 'Knock on Wood: 1966'

Mike Boone, 'Jerry-O (The Papa Chew of Detroit Soul)', 2006: chancellorofsoul.com/jerryo.html

Oliver Wang, 'Boogaloo Nights', *The Nation*, 10 January 2008

A history of the Boo-Ga-Loo can be found in *Social Dancing in America*, op. cit., Chapter 5 – 'The Twist, Doing Your Own Thing, and A Go-Go: 1960–69'

For more on Tom and Jerrio: www.dance-forums.com/threads/origins-of-the-boogaloo-dance.24944

Dave Godin, 'James Brown: The Soul of Mr. Brown', *Record Mirror*, 26 March 1966

Peter Jones, 'Brown's a Super-Spectacle: James Brown: Walthamstow Granada, London', *Record Mirror*, 9 March 1966

'Things were just getting bigger . . .': *James Brown: The Godfather of Soul*, op. cit., Chapter 24 – 'Sex Machine'

'James Brown is unprecedented . . .': *The One*, op. cit., Chapter 10 – 'The Cape Act'

'James Brown in Manhattan', *Time*, 1 April 1966

For details of James Brown on *Ed Sullivan*, 1 May 1966: www.tv.com/shows/the-ed-sullivan-show/may-1-1966-james-brown-the-supremes-nancy-ames-london-lee-ascap-salute-107879/. Part of the performance can be seen at www.youtube.com/watch?v=to8ejaQqWjY

The generally accepted quote has Dylan saying that Smokey Robinson was America's greatest poet; however, that was, in fact, a PR quote made up *c*.1967. It has some basis in truth. At the 3 December 1965 televised press conference he gave at the studios of KQED TV in San Francisco, moderator Ralph J. Gleason asked him, 'What poets do you dig?' Dylan answers: 'Rimbaud, I guess; W. C. Fields; The family, you know, the trapeze family in the circus; Smokey Robinson; Allen Ginsberg; Charlie Rich – he's a good poet.' Read more at www.rollingstone.com/music/news/bob-dylan-gives-press-conference-in-san-francisco-19671214 and njnnetwork.com/2015/02/bob-dylan-on-tracks-of-my-tears

According to R. J. Smith, 'It's a Man's Man's Man's World' was co-written by Brown with Betty Jean Newsome, who had to fight for years to get proper accreditation. *The One*, op. cit., Chapter 11 – 'Man's World'

Look, cover of 3 May 1966 issue

Aram Goudsouzian, *Down to the Crossroads: Civil Rights, Black Power, and the Meredith March Against Fear*, Chapter 1 – 'The Bible and the Gun: Memphis to Hernando June 5–6, 1966 (Farrar Strauss and Giroux, 2014)

'The Impressions' "Keep on Pushing" . . .': LeRoi Jones, 'The Changing Same

(R&B and New Black Music)', in *Black Music* (William Morrow and Sons, 1967)

The Selma footage is contained in 'Bridge to Freedom', Episode 5 of *Eyes on the Prize: America's Civil Rights Years 1945–1965* (PBS, 1987)

The Lyndon B. Johnson quotes come from the President's Special Message to the Congress: The American Promise, 15 March 1965, available in full at: www.lbjlib.utexas.edu/johnson/archives.hom/speeches.hom/650315.asp

For general histories and overviews of the civil rights movement: *Eyes on the Prize*, op. cit.; a timeline at www.infoplease.com/spot/civilrightstimeline1. html; Daniel W. Wynn, *The Black Protest Movement* (Philosophical Library Inc., 1974)

Steven Kasher, *The Civil Rights Movement: A Photographic History 1954–68*, Chapter 7 – 'Selma' (Abbeville Press, 1996)

For material on Martin Luther King, go to the Online King Records Access (OKRA) database at Stanford University: okra.stanford.edu/SearchMLKP_JP.htm

The C. T. Vivian/Clark confrontation is contained in 'Bridge to Freedom', Episode 5 of *Eyes on the Prize*, op. cit.

Death of Malcolm X: Manning Marable, *Malcolm X: A Life of Reinvention*, Chapter 15 – 'Death Comes on Time, February 14–February 21, 1965 (Allen Lane, 2011)

'The Ballot or the Bullet' speech: ibid., Chapter 11 – 'An Epiphany in the Hajj, March 12–May 21, 1964'. The full text can be found online at Social Justice Speeches, EdChange Multicultural Pavilion: www.edchange.org/multicultural/speeches/malcolm_x_ballot.html

Malcolm X's Detroit speech is covered in detail in 'Motown Music, Afro-American Dignity, and Brotherhood', *Dancing in the Street*, op. cit., Chapter 4 – 'Afro-American Music, without Apology: The Motown Sound and the Politics of Black Culture', and *Malcolm X*, op. cit., Chapter 15 – 'Death Comes on Time'. The full text of the speech is online at www.malcolm-x.org/speeches/spc_021465.htm

For SNCC's non-violent strategy: Daniel Wynn, 'The Philosophy of Nonviolent Resistance', in *The Black Protest Movement*, op. cit., Chapter 4 – 'Nonviolent Direct Action: The Montgomery Bus Boycott'

For the full text of Martin Luther King's Nobel acceptance speech: www.nobelprize.org/nobel_prizes/peace/laureates/1964/king-acceptance_en.html

For an excellent history of Los Angeles: Mike Davis, *City of Quartz: Excavating the Future in Los Angeles* (Verso, 2006)

For an account of Marquette Frye and his arrest: articles.latimes.com/1986-12-25/local/me-486_1_marquette-frye

Life quotes from 'Arson and Street War – Most Destructive Riot in U.S. History', *Life*, 27 August 1965

For more background, see Paul Bullock (Ed.), *Watts: The Aftermath, An Inside View of the Ghetto by the People of Watts*, Chapter 1 – 'Watts: Before the Riot' and Chapter 2 – 'The Riot' (Evergreen Black Cat, 1970)

Bayard Rustin, 'The Watts Manifesto and the McCone Report', *Commentary* 41, March 1966; reprinted in Bayard Rustin, *Down the Line: The Collected*

Writings of Bayard Rustin (Quadrangle Books, 1971)

Martin Luther King, 'Beyond the Los Angeles Riots', *Saturday Review*, 14
November 1965

Rob Bowman, sleeve notes for *Stax Revue: Live at the 5/4 Ballroom 7th and
8th August 1965* (Ace Records, 1991)

Rob Bowman on Stax musicians and Watts Riots: *Soulsville U.S.A.*, op. cit.,
Chapter 5 – 'Don't Have to Shop Around: 1965'

A note on the relation of black American pop and R&B to civil rights: Neither
'A Change Is Gonna Come' nor 'Keep on Pushing' refer to specific events.
They don't explode with rage or discuss tactics, but instead express a dignified
sense of hope and determination: as Curtis Mayfield sang, 'What's that I see
/ A great big stone wall / Stands there ahead of me / But I've got my pride /
And I'll move on aside / And keep on pushin''. In 1966, ESP Disk released
an album called *Movement Soul* that featured field recordings from the voter
registration campaigns in Mississippi – Selma, Greenwood, Jackson – during
1963 and 1964. Many of the songs are hymns or old spirituals, like 'Go Tell It
on the Mountain', 'Wade in the Water' and 'Ain't Scared of Your Jails', with
lyrics adapted for the demands of the moment as part of the collective process.
Other popular songs included 'Ain't Gonna Let Nobody Turn Me Around'
and 'Ninety-Nine and a Half Won't Do', which was turbocharged by Wilson
Pickett on his May 1966 single 'Ninety-Nine and a Half (Won't Do)'

The Marvin Gaye quote comes from David Ritz, *Divided Soul* (Da Capo Press,
2003), and is reproduced in 'The Many Meanings of the Motown Sound', in
Dancing in the Street, op. cit., Chapter 4 – 'Afro-American Music, without
Apology: The Motown Sound and the Politics of Black Culture'

'Mississippi Goddam': when issued on 45 in July 1964, the song was retitled
'Mississippi *%??**&%'

'Nina Simone Reveals "Mississippi Goddam" Song "Hurt My Career"', *Jet*, 24
March 1986

'an opening gunshot crack': for the 'Shotgun' discussion and the October 1965
poem by Roland Snellings, see 'The Many Meanings of the Motown Sound',
Dancing in the Street, op. cit., Chapter 4 – 'Afro-American Music, without
Apology: The Motown Sound and the Politics of Black Culture'

For the 7 January 1966 Martin Luther King quote and the Chicago campaign:
kingencyclopedia.stanford.edu/encyclopedia/encyclopedia/enc_chicago_
campaign

Peniel E. Joseph, *Stokely: A Life*, Chapter 7 – 'Lowndes County: New
Directions: April 1965–May 1966' (Basic Civitas, 2014)

'Well of course when the Black panther . . .': the Black Panther symbol is
discussed in Question 29 in the 1988 *Eyes on the Prize* interview between
Judy Richardson and Stokely Carmichael, conducted by Blackside, Inc. on
7 November 1988 for Washington University Libraries, Film and Media
Archive, Henry Hampton Collection. The full transcript can be found at
digital.wustl.edu/e/eii/eiiweb/car5427.0967.029stokleycarmichael.html

The full substance of the Student Nonviolent Coordinating Committee
Statement on Vietnam, 6 January 1966 can be found at www.crmvet.org/
docs/snccviet.htm

For the divisions at the 'To Fulfill These Rights' conference: Taylor Branch, *At Canaan's Edge: America in the King Years: 1965–68* (Simon and Schuster, 2006)

For an online account of the March Against Fear, see Richard F. Weingroff, 'The Road to Civil Rights', www.fhwa.dot.gov/highwayhistory/road/road. pdf

For a televisual history of the March Against Fear and footage of Carmichael's 16 June 1966 Black Power speech, see *Eyes on the Prize*, Episode 7 – 'The Time Has Come'; see also transcript at www.pbs.org/wgbh/amex/ eyesontheprize/about/pt_201.html

For Meredith 'fear' quotes: *Down to the Crossroads*, op. cit., Chapter 1 – 'The Bible and the Gun: Memphis to Hernando June 5–6, 1966'

Steven Kasher, *The Civil Rights Movement*, op. cit., Chapter 8 – 'Black Power and the March Against Fear'. Includes a photograph by Bob Fitch of Carmichael delivering the Black Power speech

'Negroes in South to Be Violent if Whites Continue', *Jet*, 26 May 1966

'SNCC Sees Best Chance for Local Political Control', *Jet*, 16 June 1966

For 'Black Power' speech, Peniel E. Joseph, *Stokely*, op. cit., Chapter 8 – 'The Meredith March, May 8–June 29, 1966'

Daniel W. Wynn, *The Black Protest Movement*, op. cit., Chapter 6 – 'The Black Power Movement'

Judy Richardson, 1988 interview, op. cit., Questions 51 to 55

Kalen M. A. Churcher, 'Stokely Carmichael, "Black Power"' (29 October 1966), archive.vod.umd.edu/civil/carmichael1966int.htm

For the chance encounter with Carmichael: Lyda Phillips, 'That Close', from *Mr. Touchdown* (Universe Star); reproduced at www.chapter16.org/content/ close

Pompano riot: www.mrpopculture.com/june-22-1966 and Susan Gillis, *Fort Lauderdale: The Venice of America* (Arcadia Publishing, 2004)

'This is a terrible town . . .': *Down to the Crossroads*, op. cit., Chapter 13 – 'Brotherly Love: Louise to Yazoo City; Philadelphia June 21 1966'

For the Canton riot, see *Down to the Crossroads*, op. cit., Chapter 15 – 'The Shadow of Death: Benton to Canton June 23 1966', and also *Stokely*, op. cit., Chapter 8 – 'The Meredith March, May 8–June 29, 1966'

James Brown and the Freedom Riders: *James Brown*, op. cit., Chapter 19 – 'Apollo Three, Four, Five . . .'

Involvement with issues and Meredith March of Fear: *James Brown*, op. cit., Chapter 25 – 'Getting Into It'

For a description of the Tougaloo show: *The One*, op. cit., Chapter 11 – 'Man's World'

'wheedled, shouted, moaned . . .': 'Stars Sparkle at Mississippi Benefit Show', *Jet*, 14 July 1966

Chester Higgins, 'Divided on Tactics, Leaders Agree March a Success', *Jet*, 14 July 1966

The clip from the March Against Fear that segues into 'Land of 1000 Dances' occurs at 39m 30s into *Eyes on the Prize*, Episode 7

For more on the Chicago Freedom Movement: 'Chicago activists challenge

segregation (Chicago Freedom Movement), USA, 1965–1967': nvdatabase.
swarthmore.edu/content/chicago-activists-challenge-segregation-chicago-
freedom-movement-usa-1965-1967
'We cannot wait . . .' and for more on the West Side Riots: 'Launching
the National Fair Housing Debate: A Closer Look at the 1966 Chicago
Freedom Movement', Poverty and Race Action Research Council,
www.prrac.org/full_text.php?text_id=1047&item_id=9645&newsletter_
id=0&header=Current+Projects
For the weather in Chicago that July: C. A. Bridger and L. A. Helfand,
'Mortality from Heat during July 1966 in Illinois', link.springer.com/
article/10.1007%2FBF01552978
'West Side Story', Newsweek, 25 July 1966
King on Watts in Chicago speech, March 1966: kingencyclopedia.stanford.edu/
encyclopedia/encyclopedia/enc_watts_rebellion_los_angeles_1965
'Black Power: Politics of Frustration', Newsweek, 11 July 1966
'Watts Still Seething' front cover, Life, 15 July 1966; and Jerry Cohen and
William S. Murphy, Burn, Baby, Burn! (Avon, 1967)
Stokely Carmichael, 'Black Power' speech, 28 July 1966, transcript at www.
encyclopedia.com/doc/1G2-3401804839.html
'Stokely Carmichael Speaks on Black Power in Detroit, July 30, 1966', Pan
African News Wire, panafricannews.blogspot.co.uk/2006/06/stokely-
carmichael-speaks-on-black.html

CHAPTER 8
'Johnny's radio is on . . .': John Rechy, 'Seven', Numbers (Grove Press Inc,
1967)
Weather in New York 1966: weatherspark.com/history/31081/1966/New-
York-United-States. For the August 1966 weather report for the UK: www.
metoffice.gov.uk/archive/monthly-weather-report-1960s
Uncredited writer, 'Sixth National Jazz and Blues Festival, Windsor: Jazz on a
Summer's Weekend', Melody Maker, 6 August 1966
'the ultimate in pop violence': Richard Green, 'MUD dominated the Windsor
Festival', Record Mirror, 6 August 1966
Ray Davies, author interviews late 1983 and early 1984 for The Kinks, op. cit.
'It was a strange time . . .': Jonathan Cott, 'Ray Davies Talks', Rolling Stone,
10 November 1969, available online at www.icce.rug.nl/~soundscapes/
VOLUME04/MIRROR/Ray_Davies_Rolling_Stone.html
For the wages freeze, see 'Britain at the Brink', Newsweek, 25 July 1966. For
more and the Sunday Times quote, see Jennifer Harris, Sarah Hyde and
Greg Smith, 1966 and All That: Design and the Consumer in Britain, 1960–
69, chapter entitled '1966: A Year in Focus' (Trefoil Design Library, 1986)
'The Lovin' Spoonful Captures the Feel, the Flavor, the Heartbeat of Summer
in the City', Kama Sutra advertisement, page 5, Billboard, 2 July 1966
'Charles Whitman: The Psychotic and Society', Time, 12 August 1966
King in Chicago: The Civil Rights Movement, op. cit., Chapter 9 – 'The
Eclipsing of Nonviolence, 1965–68'. Also kingencyclopedia.stanford.edu/
encyclopedia/encyclopedia/enc_chicago_campaign

East Lansing riot: www.historyorb.com/date/1966/august

George Rockwell: en.metapedia.org/wiki/Chronology_of_George_Lincoln_ Rockwell#1966

Tornados reviews by Peter Jones and Norman Jopling in *Record Mirror*, Penny Valentine in *Disc and Music Echo*, both 20 August 1966

Billy Fury, 'Blind Date', *Melody Maker*, 20 August 1966

Both 'Is This a Ship I Hear' and 'Wishing Well' featured in Radio Caroline's *Countdown of Sound*, Saturday 27 August 1966: radiolondon.co.uk/caroline/ stonewashed/carolinecharts/052%20August%2027%201966.htm

Robb Huxley's recollections of the 'Do You Come Here Often?' session are in 'The New Tornados – Part 2': www.silvertabbies.co.uk/huxley/ newtornados2.html

Richard Dyer, *The Culture of Queers*, Chapter 4 – 'It's Being So Camp as Keeps Us Going' (Routledge, 2002)

'We are undergoing presently . . .': R. E. L. Masters, *The Homosexual Revolution*, 'Foreword' (Belmont Books, 1962)

For a detailed history of gay records: www.queermusicheritage.com

For a full CAMP records discography and a history of the label: J. D. Doyle, 'The Most Outrageous (and Queerest) Record Label of the 1960's', at www. queermusicheritage.com/camp.html

For the eight laws: Patrick Higgins, *Heterosexual Dictatorship: Male Homosexuality in Post-War Britain*, Chapter 8 – 'The Operation of the Law' (Fourth Estate, 1997)

'Essay: The Homosexual in America', *Time*, Friday 21 January 1966

Randolfe Wicker, 'The Wicker Report', *Eastern Mattachine*, November– December 1965

For homophobia leading to poor self-esteem in gay men, see, for instance, Donald Cory, *The Homosexual in America*, Chapter 2 – 'Hostility and Its Hidden Sources' and Chapter 14 – 'From Handicap to Strength' (Greenberg, 1951)

John Repsch, *The Legendary Joe Meek: The Telstar Man* (Woodford House, 1989)

There are many compilations of Meek's productions but a good starting point is *Joe Meek: The RGM Legacy – Potrait of a Genius* (Sanctuary, 2008). Also *Joe Meek: The Alchemist of Pop – Home Made Hits and Rarities 1958–1966* (Sanctuary, 2008)

Oldham and Charles Blackwell re. Meek: Andrew Loog Oldham, *Stoned*, Chapter 7 (Martin Secker and Warburg, 2000)

For more on Paul, Ritchie and the Cryin' Shames: www.liverpoolbeat.com/ rocknroll/category/the-history-of-merseybeat/greatest-merseybeat-bands/the-cryin-shames

Larry Parnes, author interview, November 1985

For the Epstein importuning story: Debbie Geller, *The Brian Epstein Story*, Chapter 2 – 'A Magic World' (Faber & Faber, 2000)

'Johnny Remember Me' was featured in an episode of *Harpers West One*, a popular ATV soap opera (1961–3) that was set in a department store. John Leyton played Johnny St Cyr, a pop star promoting his new record in-store

For the Epstein John Leyton story, *The Brian Epstein Story*, op. cit., Chapter 3 – 'Prodigal Son'

'would be bigger than Elvis . . .': Mark Lewisohn, *All These Years: Tune In – Extended Special Edition*, Chapter 29 – 'A Tendency to Play Music (6 February–8 March 1962)', 'Year 5, 1962: Always Be True' (Little Brown, 2013)

Brian Epstein, *A Cellarful of Noise* (Souvenir Press, 1964)

Derek Taylor, interview with author, August 1997

Derek Taylor, *Fifty Years Adrift* (Genesis Books, 1984)

For more on the Lord Montagu witch-hunt: Patrick Higgins, *Heterosexual Dictatorship: Male Homosexuality in Post-War Britain* (Fourth Estate, 1996), as well as Peter Wildblood's classic campaigning book *Against the Law* (Weidenfeld and Nicholson, 1956)

Nat Weiss quotes from *The Brian Epstein Story*, op. cit., Chapter 8 – 'Private Lives'. The original interview was conducted by the author for the 1998 BBC *Arena* documentary 'The Brian Epstein Story'.

Le Duce: jackthatcatwasclean.blogspot.co.uk/2008/02/gay-london-at-le-duce. html

'I never worried . . .': Peter Burton, *Parallel Lives*, Chapter 1 – 'Setting the Scene' (Gay Men's Press, 1985)

'FACE IT! Revolution in Male Clothes', *Life*, 13 May 1966

Jeremy Reed, *The King of Carnaby Street: The Life of John Stephen* (Haus Publishing, 2010)

Le Duce: *Parallel Lives*, op. cit., Chapter 2 – 'Clubland', and also an excellent blog by Haydon Bridge at the Online Mod/ern/ist Archive: jackthatcatwasclean.blogspot.co.uk/2008/02/gay-london-at-le-duce.html

'Ten years in the community . . .': Dick Leitsch, 'We Are Ten', *Eastern Mattachine*, November–December 1965

For a general history of gay politics in the post-war period: Jeffrey Weeks, *Coming Out: Homosexual Politics in Britain, from the Nineteenth Century to the Present* (Quartet, 1977); Patrick Higgins, *Heterosexual Dictatorship*, op. cit.; Stephen Jeffery-Poulter, *Peers, Queers and Commons: The Struggle for Gay Law Reform from 1950 to the Present* (Routledge, 1991); Anthony Grey, *Quest for Justice: Towards Homosexual Emancipation* (Sinclair-Stevenson, 1992)

For the 63 per cent statistic and the 'irrationality' of the debates: *Peers, Queers and Commons*, op. cit., Chapter 4: 'Burbling On About Buggery: 1964–1967', 'Peers, Queers and Commons: The Struggle for Gay Law Reform from 1950 to the Present'

For a timeline of the Arran bill: *Coming Out*, op. cit., Part Four, Chapter 15 – 'Law Reform', 'Coming Out: Homosexual Politics in Britain, from the Nineteenth Century to the Present'

For Arena Three and Allan Horsfall: *Quest for Justice*, op. cit., Chapter X – 'Meanwhile, Back at the Ranch . . .'

For the HLRS's lack of influence on the legislation: ibid., Chapter VIII – 'Lords' Marathon'

For the mask as a concept, see for instance the front cover of ONE, February 1959: 'the tragedy of MASKS'

'Until we are willing to speak out . . .': *The Homosexual in America*, op. cit., Chapter 1 – 'The Unrecognized Minority'. See also 'From the First to the Second Cory Report by Donald Webster Cory', *One*, October 1963

James T. Sears, 'Section Three: MATTACHINE (1950–1953)', *Behind the Mask of the Mattachine, The Hal Call Chronicles* (Routledge, 2012)

John D'Emilio, *Sexual Politics, Sexual Communities: The Making of a Homosexual Minority in the United States* (University of Chicago, 1998)

Stuart Timmons, *The Trouble with Harry Hay: Founder of the Modern Gay Movement* (Alyson Books, 1990)

'Let's Push Homophile Marriage', *One*, June 1963

For the relation of the homophile movement to civil rights, see, for example, 'We're on the Move Now' (quoting Martin Luther King's talk to the Selma–Montgomery marchers), *Eastern Mattachine*, June 1965

Erika Hastings, 'ECHO 1965: The Homosexual Citizen in the Great Society', *The Ladder*, January 1966

For a history of physique magazines: Thomas Waugh, *Hard to Imagine: Gay Male Eroticism in Photography from Their Beginnings to Stonewall* (Columbia University Press, 1996). The sales figures, the *MANual* v. *Day* information and the 'most significant gay cultural achievement . . .' quote also come from *Hard to Imagine*, 'The Kinsey Generation: The Golden Age of Magazines and Mail Order' (1945–1963).

For a full history of the Guild Press (the publisher of *MANual*, the magazine in the 1962 test case), DSI (Directory Services Inc) et al. and their legal problems, see David K. Johnson, 'Physique Pioneers: The Politics of 1960's Gay Consumer Culture', *Journal of Social History*, summer 2010 (University of South Florida)

For more DSI history: tim1965.livejournal.com/2019638.html

Rupert Smith, *PHYSIQUE: The life of John S. Barrington* (Serpents Tail, 1997)

Rick Stokes interviewed by Paul Gabriel, San Francisco 1961–1966 (from video tape, 19 September 1996)

GLBT Historical Society: www.glbthistory.org

A sample of gay exploitation books from the period: D. Royal, *I, Homosexual* (Fleur de Lis, 1965); Don Holliday, *The Man from C.A.M.P.* (Corinth Publications, 1966); Robert Saunders, *The Gay Lords* (Unique, 1966); Carl Corley, *A Chosen World* (Pad Library, 1966); Don Holliday, *The Gay Trap* (Corinth Publications, 1966); Ed Culver, *Gay Three-Way* (PEC, 1966); Dean Hudson, *The Lavender Elves* (Corinth Publications, 1966); Lee Dorian, *The Other Men* (Viceroy, 1966); Anthony James, *America's Homosexual Underworld* (L. S. Publications, 1966); Norm Winski, *The Homosexual Explosion* (Challenge Publications, 1966)

DSI: *Tiger* no. 2 (1966); *Butch* no. 1 (1965); *Butch* no. 2 (1966); *Butch* no. 5 (1966)

By 1965/6 there were other, more explicit magazines like *Leather!* (Guild Press, 1965), *beach adonis* (YP Publications, 1966) and *Big Boys* (Guild 1966)

For a contemporary discussion of this peculiar mix of exploitation and consciousness-raising, see Warren Adkins, review of Carlson Wade, 'The Twilight Sex', *Eastern Mattachine*, March 1965

For the April 'sip-in', see David Carter, *Stonewall: The Riots That Sparked the*

Gay Revolution, Chapter 2 – Oppression, Resistance, and Everyday Life (St Martin's Press, 2004)

For Don Slater's report on the gay motorcade from *Tangent*, May 1966: www. tangentgroup.org/history/articles/motorcade.html

For Vanguard's 1966 handbill 'WE PROTEST': 'A (Brief) History of Vanguard', 2011, www.glbthistory.org/Vanguard/images%20vanguard/ vanguard-lowres.pdf

Jean Paul Marat: quoted in Laurence Tate, 'Exiles of Sin, Incorporated', *Berkeley Barb*, 11 November 1966

Adrian Ravarour, interview with Joey Plaster, San Francisco GLBT Historical Society, 2010

Joey Plaster, 'A (Brief) History of Vanguard', op. cit.

'VANGUARD is an organisation . . .': 'YOUNG Rejects Form Organization,' *Cruise News*, July 1966

Mark Forrester, 'Central City: Profile of Despair', *Vanguard*, issue 1, summer 1966

For a detailed description of hair fairies, see Adrian Ravarour: 'Billy Garrison described himself as a hair fairy – which meant that the clothing he wore was heterosexual, you know, guys clothes – jeans and a shirt – but then he had his hair ratted up and hair sprayed so it was stacked like a beehive almost. And he then had on make-up eye, brow pencil [*sic*], rouge, some lipstick, foundation, he did his nails.' www.glbthistory.org/Vanguard/ images%20vanguard/vanguard-lowres.pdf

For a general history of gay San Francisco: Nan Alamilla Boyd, *Wide Open Town: A History of Queer San Francisco to 1965* (University of California Press, 2003)

For Comptons: Mack Friedman, *Strapped for Cash: A History of American Hustler Culture*, Chapter 5 – 'City Slickers: Metropolitan Hustlers, 1950– 1970' (Alyson Books, 2003)

David Carter, *Stonewall*, op. cit., Chapter 6 – 'Dawn Is Just Breaking'

Martin Duberman, *Stonewall*, Part Four – 'The Mid-Sixties' (Plume/Penguin, 1994)

John D'Emilio, *Sexual Politics, Sexual Communities: The Making of a Homosexual Minority in the United States* (University of Chicago, 1998)

The principal researcher of this extraordinary event is Dr Susan Stryker: see 'The Compton's Cafeteria Riot of 1966', in Susan Stryker and Stephen Whittle (Eds), *The Transgender Studies Reader* (Routledge, 2006), and Victor Silverman and Susan Stryker, *Screaming Queens: The Riot at Compton's Cafeteria* (Frameline DVD, 2010)

'Young Homos Picket Compton's Restaurant', *Cruise News and World Report*, August 1966. Vanguard distributed a broadside demanding that management 'changes its policies of harassment and discrimination of the homosexuals, hustlers, etc., of the Tenderloin Area'. For more, see vanguardrevisited.blogspot.co.uk/2011_02_01_archive.html:

VANGUARD, the organization whose membership is drawn from 'kids on the street,' tested out its muscle on one of the worst offenders against human dignity in the Tenderloin area of San Francisco.

Compton's at Turk and Taylor has long treated the younger residents as if they were not at all human.

On various occasions, according to spokesmen of VANGUARD, the Rent-A-Cop (Pinkerton Men) have manhandled innocent customers because they did not drink their coffee fast enough to suit the Rent-A-Cop.

On the 18th of July VANGUARD had bout 25 persons carrying picket signs from 10 pm til 12 pm. The action was televised by ABC and a fair presentation of the cause of VANGUARD was telecast.

Specifically VANGUARD was protesting:

We of the Tenderloin are picketing and boycotting this Gene Compton Restaurant for the following reasons:

1. We of the Tenderloin are continuously subjected to physical and verbal abuse by both the management and the Pinkerton Special Officers assigned there.

2. We feel that the 25 cent 'Service' charge was put into effect to keep out those of us who have little or no money.

THEREFORE:

Until the management of this restaurant changes its policies of harassment and discrimination of the homosexuals, hustlers, etc., of the Tenderloin Area, we will boycott and picket this restaurant.

For the contemporary description of the riot, beginning with 'With that cups, saucers . . .': Guy Strait, *Cruise News and World Report*, August 1966; cited in *Strapped for Cash*, op. cit., Chapter 5 – 'City Slickers: Metropolitan Hustlers, 1950–1970'

The picture of the hair fairies cleaning up the Tenderloin can be found on page 14 of www.glbthistory.org/Vanguard/images%20vanguard/vanguard-lowres.pdf

Vanguard press release re. 'WHITE POWER' and 'BLACK POWER' is from *Vanguard*, vol. 1, issue 2, October 1966; reproduced in www.glbthistory.org/Vanguard/images%20vanguard/vanguard-lowres.pdf

'America is not too settled . . .': Derek Taylor, 'But They Shouldn't Be Here . . .', *Disc and Music Echo*, 20 August 1966

John Rechy, author interview, November 1990

Rupert Smith, 'Midnight Cowboy: John Rechy Recalls 40 Years of Hustle', *Independent*, 27 April 2008 – www.independent.co.uk/arts-entertainment/books/features/midnight-cowboy-john-rechy-recalls-40-yeas-of-hustle-815124.html

For 'number' in gay slang: Dr Albert Ellis, introduction to *The Guild Dictionary of Homosexual Terms* (Guild Press, 1965)

Charles Casillo, *Outlaw: John Rechy* (Advocate Books, 2002)

'hopped up dirges': *Numbers*, op. cit., 'Thirteen'

'Suddenly, with a blast . . ..' and 'a roster . . .': ibid., 'One'

'by an enormous craving . . .', ibid., 'Fifteen'

'RACES: Simmering Symptoms', *Time*, 12 August 1966

'CRIME: The Madman in the Tower', ibid.

'A Gun-Toting Nation', ibid.

'The Symptoms of Mass Murder', ibid.

'Under the Clock, A Sniper with 31 Minutes to Live', *Life*, 12 August 1966

David Nevin, 'Charlie Whitman: The Eagle Scout Who Grew Up with a Tortured Mind', ibid.

'A Town's Troubled Mood as . . . A War Comes Home', ibid.

Pamela Hansford Johnson, 'Who's to Blame When a Murderer Strikes?' ibid.

Shepherd's Bush murders, anonymous scrapbook with clippings, August 1966. Harry Roberts was eventually captured in November 1966 and sentenced to life in prison. He was eventually released in late 2014, forty-eight years after his conviction

'Our image was only a teeny part of us . . .': Hunter Davies, *The Beatles*, Chapter 22 – 'Beatlemania' (Heinemann, 1968)

'Beatles: What a Carve-Up!', *Disc and Music Echo*, 11 June 1966

Ray Coleman, 'Paul: Exclusive', ibid.

'Beatles' New Single – YOUR Verdict', *Disc and Music Echo*, 4 June 1966

Penny Valentine, 'Last Word by Singles Reviewer', ibid.

'was as relevant as Vietnam': Alan Walsh, 'George: More to Life than Being a Beatle', *Melody Maker*, 25 June 1966

Robert Whitaker, author interview, April 2011

Ron Tepper, 'Dear reviewer . . .', Capitol-headed letter, 14 June 1966

Ron Tepper, undated addition with '"pop art" satire' quote, Capitol-headed letter

Jo Sobeck, 'DESTRUCTION OF OLD BEATLE JACKETS (S)T2553', memo to R. L. Howe, Capitol notepaper, 28 June 1966. Capitol memos thanks to Jeff Gold

Alan Livingstone quoted in *The Brian Epstein Story*, op. cit., Chapter 11 – 'The Fire This Time'

Earl Caldwell, 'Mop Heads – or Lop Heads? Beatles Had the Wrong Groove', *New York Post*, 21 June 1966

The figure of $200,000 is from 'Cap Takes 200G Loss on Beatles Cover Experiment', *Variety*, 22 June 1966

'Beatle L.P. Cover Banned', *KRLA Beat*, 2 July 1966

'Beatles Change Erases Profit', *KRLA Beat*, 16 July 1966

'Letters to the Editor', ibid.

For the 'Paperback Writer'/'Rain' videos and for footage of the 1966 World tour, I referred to *The Beatles Film & TV Chronicle*, Discs 11–12 (bootleg DVD, 2005)

'Japanese xenophobia': see Shibly Nabhan, 'Showdown at Budokan', *Japan Times*, July 2006; online at www.japantimes.co.jp/life/2006/07/02/to-be-sorted/showdown-at-budokan/#.VZ6fkV5UoYU

For the Philippines: www.beatlesbible.com/1966/07/03/beatles-arrive-in-manila-philippines and the following pages.

The Philippines quotes cited come from Tony Barrow, *John, Paul, George, Ringo & Me* (Andrew Deutsch, 2005)

The ITN news item is contained in *The Beatles Film & TV Chronicle*, op. cit.
Brian Epstein's 25 July 1966 letter is reproduced in *Fifty Years Adrift*, op. cit.
Datebook 'Shout-Out' issue, September 1966
'I Don't Know Which Will Go First – Rock 'n' roll or Christianity!', *Datebook*,
    September 1966
For material on Tommy Charles, including a picture of Charles and Doug
    Layton ripping and breaking Beatles records: flashbak.com/god-forever-the-
    beatles-never-when-lennon-compared-the-beatles-to-jesus-in-1966-30043
Jonathan Gould, *Can't Buy Me Love: The Beatles, Britain and America*,
    Chapter 32 (Portrait, 2007)
Bob Spitz, *The Beatles: The Biography* (Little Brown and Company, 2005)
Tony Barrow, *John, Paul, George, Ringo & Me*, op. cit.
For the 6 August Brian Epstein press conference: www.beatlesbible.
    com/1966/08/06/brian-epstein-press-conference
For transcripts of the 11 and 12 August interviews: www.beatlesinterviews.org/
    db1966.0812.beatles.html
'We're just trying to move forwards . . .': www.beatlesinterviews.org/
    db1966.0811.beatles.html
James Morris, 'The Monarchs of the Beatle Empire', *Saturday Evening Post*,
    27 August 1966
For the Tommy Charles 'Beatle bonfire', see unattributed clipping from
    Gleason archive, dated 4 August 1966: 'Rock'n'Roll Disc Jockeys Ban
    Beatles'
For a day-to-day account of the American tour: www.beatlesbible.
    com/1966/08/12/live-international-amphitheatre-chicago-2 and the following
    twenty days. A day-to-day account is also given in Barry Tashian, *Ticket to
    Ride – The Extraordinary Story of the Beatles' Last Tour* (Dowling {Press
    1997). Also see the accounts by Jerry Leighton in *Disc and Music Echo*, 20
    August 1966 on, and Ren Grevatt in the *Melody Maker*
ITN, *Reporting 66: The Beatles Across America*, transmitted 24 August 1966.
    It can be viewed at www.itnsource.com/shotlist//BHC_ITN/1966/08/24/
    X24086601
A full transcript of the Beatles interview can be seen at www.beatlesinterviews.
    org/db1966.0819.beatles.html
'It was that bad': The Beatles, *Anthology*, op. cit.
'It felt like . . .': ibid.
For the audience reaction at Shea Stadium: Myles Jackson, 'Beatles' Blast at
    Shea Stadium Described by Erupting Fans', bootleg LP, 1966
Paul McCartney to Judith Sims, quoted in *Ticket to Ride*, op. cit.
'Well, that's it . . .': Tony Barrow, *John, Paul, George, Ringo & Me*, op. cit.
Mark Lewisohn in email correspondence with author, September 2014:
    'George's comment on the post-Candlestick Park flight has always been
    reported by Tony Barrow. He was saying it in interviews as early as 1972,
    so I believe it's true. In his book, Tony says George said it to him, though
    the impression I've always had is that he merely said it out loud, to anyone
    who might be listening, or even just to himself. Interpretation is the key – it
    really hinges on George's perception of the part of himself that was "George

Beatle". The line didn't mean he was leaving the group, or that the group had no future, just that one part of his persona, his public persona, was being put away.'

'It yet remains to be seen . . .': Rev. Ralph Blair, '"Op-Op": Open Panel on Problems', *Drum*, nos 18–19, September 1966

John Repsch, *The Legendary Joe Meek*, op. cit.

'a witches' stew . . .': Peter Brown and Steven Gaines, *The Love You Make*, p. 215 (McGraw-Hill, 1983)

Nat Weiss's account of the Dizz Gillespie robbery and aftermath is in *The Brian Epstein Story*, op. cit., Chapter 11 – 'The Fire This Time'

'I suddenly realised . . .': ibid., Chapter 13 – 'All You Need Is Love'

CHAPTER 9

'One of the basic factors . . .': Orlando Patterson, 'The Dance Invasion', *New Society*, 15 September 1966; reprinted in full in *The Pop Process*, op. cit., Chapter 4 – 'Sources of Fashion: The Audience'

'Home Safe and Sound', *NME*, 2 September 1966

June Harris, 'Beatle Bravery Worth More Than Money', *NME*, 2 September 1966

There was another factor in the comparative decline of British pop in autumn 1966: the question of cost, which was affected by the freeze. In the spring, the price of a 45 rpm single had increased from a basic 5/9 – 5 shillings and 9 pence – to 6/3. At the same time, tax on each purchase increased from 11 pence to 1s/11/4d, with the total price amounting to 7s/41/2d by the autumn. At a time when a factory apprentice's wage could be as low as £2.10s, even this small increase was enough to affect teenage spending and to tip the weight towards adults.

Dawn James on Brian Jones: 'The Case of the Disappearing Image', *Rave*, August 1966

Chas Chandler quote from Chris Welch: 'Group 67: Whither the Groups? Are We Seeing the End of an Era?' *Melody Maker*, 15 October 1966

Thom Keyes, *All Night Stand* (W. H. Allen, 1966)

David Griffiths, 'British Rockers Slipping in US?' *Record Mirror*, 30 July 1966

'America the Brave', *Record Mirror*, 6 August 1966

Derek Johnson, 'Is the Big British Boom Over?' *NME*, 2 September 1966

Tony Hall on West Coast groups: 'Now It's the White Groups that Are "Where It's At"', The Tony Hall Column, *Record Mirror*, 7 May 1966

The Monkees ad is in *Billboard*, 27 August 1966, page 2

Andrew Sandoval, note for 'Last Train to Clarksville', *The Monkees Music Box* (Rhino Records, 2008)

Readers polled in 'Monkees to Be TV's Beatles?' *KRLA Beat*, 8 October 1966

'A 20-year-old told me . . .': Robert de Roos, 'The Lacy Trousered Kids Are in Revolt', *San Francisco Sunday Examiner and Chronicle*, 25 September 1966

For recording information of '7 And 7 Is': Andrew Sandoval, sleeve notes to *Da Capo* (Elektra/Rhino, 2002)

The *American Bandstand* clip of 'My Little Red Book' can be seen at www.youtube.com/watch?v=ftO9ClIhFAo

The Castle: Bob Dylan and the Velvet Underground and Nico stayed there in the first few months of 1966. The Castle was owned at that point by Jack Simons and Lisa and Tom Law – see note on Lisa Law and Severn Darden in Chapter 7.

For details of Arthur Lee's life and Lee quotes: John Einarson, *Forever Changes: Arthur Lee and the Book of Love – The Authorized Biography of Arthur Lee* (Jawbone, 2010)

Anonymous, sleeve notes to issue of the American Four's 'Luci Baines' (Monster Records)

All Johnny Echols quotes from Mike Stax, 'A Love Supreme: The Johnny Echols Interview', *Ugly Things* #33, spring/summer 2012

'We were at ground zero . . .': sleeve notes to *Da Capo*, op. cit.

Rochelle Reed, 'Love: Is Love Lost?' *KRLA Beat*, 9 July 1966

'7 And 7 Is' review in 'Top 60', *Billboard*, 17 July 1966

Penny Valentine on ? and the Mysterians: 'Quick Spins', *Disc and Music Echo*, 1 October 1966

For the 'Where the Action Is' clip from October 1966: www.youtube.com/watch?v=wFZX_vzvvwI

For Mike Metrovitch and 'Hanky Panky': Miriam Linna, sleeve notes to *Mad Mike Monsters Volume 2* (Norton Records, 2008)

For the 13th Floor Elevators' 'You're Gonna Miss Me' and the definitive group histories, see Paul Drummond, sleeve notes for box set *13th Floor Elevators: Sign of the Three Eyed Men* (Charly, 2009), and Drummond, *Eye Mind: Roky Erikson and the 13th Floor Elevators* (Process, 2007)

For material about teen beat/garage bands: Lenny Kaye, *Nuggets: Original Artyfacts from the First Psychedelic Era, 1965–1968* (Elektra double LP, 1972, and the 4 CD version, Elektra/Rhino, 1998)

For the pure, unsullied teen beat aesthetic – no psychedelia, no folk rock – Tim Warren's *Back from the Grave* series is the direct source: ten LPs (vols 1–10) and six CDs on Crypt Records

Also for Greg Shaw and *Who Put the Bomp!* magazine, see Mick Farren and Suzy Shaw, *Bomp! Saving the World One Record at a Time* (AMMO books, 2007)

For the connection between the Trashmen through to the 1966 teen groups: Jon Savage, 'Introduction', in Suzy Shaw and Mike Stax (Eds), *Bomp! 2: Born in the Garage* (BOMP/UT Publishing, 2009)

For an examination of a truly American 1960s aesthetic: Miriam Linna, sleeve notes to *Mad Mike Monsters Volumes 1–3* (Norton Records, 2008)

Greg Shaw talking about his formative musical taste: 'One of my favorite phases of 60s garage was 1963, when nobody had ever heard of England, and songs like "Louie Louie" and "Surfin' Bird" were drawing on 50s R&B to create something really new. That influence was joined by the British one, but always in America there were many streams of influence, from rockabilly, rock and roll, surf, r&b, soul, British, folk, blues, and regional styles too.' Interview by Roberto Calabro, published in Italian magazine *Fun House*, issue 3

Also see issues of *Ugly Things*, Ed. Mike Stax, passim. The influence of the drive-in horror movie on sixties American teen beat was suggested by Greg Provost

See also Mike Markesich's definitive survey *Teenbeat Mayhem!* (Priceless Info Press, 2012)

Richard Goldstein, 'Gear', originally published in the *Village Voice*, summer 1966; collected in *Goldstein's Greatest Hits*, op. cit.

Carnival of Souls is at www.youtube.com/watch?v=exUFpSFblaw

Uncredited sleeve notes to *The Roosters: All Of Our Days* (Break-A-Way Records, 2011)

'a window into the future': 'California', *Look*, 25 September 1962; see also 'California', *Look*, 28 June 1966

Robert Cohen, *Mondo Hollywood* (Radical Films DVD, 2005)

Mike Fessier quoted in *Riot on Sunset Strip*, op. cit., 'Progenitors of the Broader Social Consciousness'

For the Strip as incubator of pop culture: ibid., 'TV a Go Go and the Battle of the Bands'

Also see *So You Want to Be a Rock'n'Roll Star*, op. cit., '1965' and '1966', in particular the entries for 'Friday 16–Sunday 25 1965, Ciro's Le Disc, Hollywood, CA' and Saturday 4 June 1966, which reproduces a Derek Taylor column from *Disc and Music Echo* from that date: 'The teenage rebellion is complete on the Strip. Here is total deadlock between matriarchal, middle-aged American youth and uniformed authority. There is no meeting place between young and old.'

For the Seeds: Alec Palao, sleeve notes for *The Seeds* and *A Web of Sound* (Ace Records, 2012 and 2013)

The Mothers of Invention, *Freak Out* (Verve Records double LP, June 1966) (early copies included the 'Freak Out Hot Spots' map)

Robert de Roos, 'The Lacy Trousered Kids Are in Revolt', op. cit.

'We foresee as the next logical step . . .': Jane Heil, 'A Loud and Quiet Look at the Pop Scene', *Hit Parader*, August 1966

Andrew Loog Oldham, sleeve note for *Out of Our Heads* (Decca, 1965) and *December's Children* (London Records, 1965)

Charles Radcliffe, 'Rebel Worker: 1966', in *Two Fiery Flying Rolls: The Heatwave Story 1966–1970* (Charles H. Kerr Publishing Company, 2005)

'As Jim McGuinn Sees Himself', *TeenSet*, October 1966

'California is the centre . . .': Editorial, *San Francisco Oracle*, issue 1, 20 September 1966

Nat Hentoff, 'Something's Happening and You Don't Know What It Is, Do You, Mr. Jones?' *Evergreen*, June 1966

'Albums in Review', *TeenSet*, October 1966

Richard Goldstein, 'Shango Mick Arrives', summer 1966; reprinted in *Goldstein's Greatest Hits*, op. cit.

Paul Williams, editorial, *Crawdaddy!* no. 1, 7 February 1966. The front simply contained a quote from the Fortunes in *Music Echo*, 29 January 1966: 'There is no musical paper scene out there like there is in England. The trades are strictly for the business side of the business and the only things left are the fan magazines that do mostly the "what colour socks my idol wears" bit.'

Paul Williams, 'Understanding Dylan', *Crawdaddy!* no. 4, August 1966
Paul Williams, 'Along Comes Maybe', ibid.
Paul Williams, 'The New Sounds', ibid.
Richard Farina, 'Your Own True Name', *Crawdaddy!* no. 3, March 1966
Greg Shaw and Richard Harris, 'Editorial', *Mojo Navigator*, vol. 1, no. 1, 8
    August 1966
'to do things that nobody has done before': Greg Shaw and Richard Harris,
    'The Straight Theater', *Mojo Navigator*, vol. 1, no. 2, 16 August 1966
Greg Shaw and Richard Harris, 'The Grateful Dead', *Mojo Navigator*, vol. 1,
    no. 4, 30 August 1966
Greg Shaw and Richard Harris, Velvet Underground review, 'News, Rumors,
    Gossip', *Mojo Navigator*, vol. 1 no. 6, 18 September 1966
Gene Sculatti, author interview, October 2014
For more on Tom Donohue's Autumn Records: *Autumn Records Story* (Edsel
    Records, 1999)
For more on the SF garage bands: *Good Things Are Happening* (Big Beat
    Records, 1995) and *Love Is the Song We Sing: San Francisco Nuggets 1965–
    1970* (Rhino 4 CD set, 2007)
Ralph J. Gleason, 'On the Town', undated columns March and May 1966, *San
    Francisco Chronicle*, from scrapbook provided by Gene Sculatti
The Haight-Ashbury, op. cit.
For Haight-Ashbury under threat of highway development: foundsf.org/index.
    php?title=The_Freeway_Revolt
San Francisco Oracle, issue 1, op. cit.
'a long and dismissive discussion . . .': 'Indo Rock', ibid.
I.D. 1966 Band Book, September 1966
Gene Sculatti, 'San Franciscan Bay Rock', *Crawdaddy!* no. 6, November 1966
'Three Berkeley VDC Members Subpoenaed by Un-American Activities
    Committee', *Berkeley Daily Gazette*, 5 August 1966
Associated Press, 'House Probe of Viet Dissent Opens in Furor', *San Francisco
    Chronicle*, 17 August 1966
'A Noisy Windup to House Probe', *San Francisco Chronicle*, 20 August 1966
'We denounce capitalism . . .': Roel van Duyn, 'This Is Provo', translated by
    Hugo le Comte, *Anarchy*, issue 66, 'Provo', August 1966
Bill C. Haigwood, 'Telly's Teen-Age "Hiplings" Talk of Rebellion – But Their
    Real "Scene" Is One of Boredom', *Berkeley Daily Gazette*, 16 August 1966
Michael Wall, 'Another Kind of Dutchman', *San Francisco Sunday Examiner
    and Chronicle*, 14 August 1966
Joseph Lelyveld, 'Dadaists in Politics', *New York Times Magazine*, 2 October
    1966
Richard Kempton, *PROVO: Amsterdam's Anarchist Revolt* (Autonomedia,
    2007)
For more on Provo, including illustrations of pamphlets and magazines, see Jan
    Pen, Provo Images, provo-images.info
'Appeal to the International Provotariat', *PROVO*, issue 8, April 1966;
    reprinted in *Anarchy*, issue 66, op. cit.
For the origins of Provo, see *PROVO*, op. cit., Chapter 1 – 'amsterdam, the

magic centre (1961–1965)', Chapter 2 – 'the prophet of magic amsterdam: robert jasper grootveld' and Chapter 3 – 'the birth of provo (may–july 1965)'

For the protests against the royal wedding, see Kempton, ibid., Chapter 4 – 'the state is provoked! (july 1965–march 1966)', Chapter 5 – 'the finest hour of the dutch republic (march 10, 1966)'

For the demonstrations of 13 June on, see Kempton, ibid., Chapter 6 – 'the two dimensions of police brutality: amsterdam under siege (march 19 – june 13, 1966)' and Chapter 7 – 'the monster of amsterdam (june 14, 1966)'

Charles Radcliffe, 'Day Trip to Amsterdam', *Anarchy*, issue 66, op. cit., reprinted from *Heatwave*, no. 1, July 1966

For more on Dutch youth during that spring/summer and the leading Dutch group, Q65, see Pim Scheelings, *Q65* (Ugly Things Books, 2010)

Charles Radcliffe as Ben Covington, 'Only Lovers Left Alive', *Heatwave*, no. 1, July 1966

Charles Radcliffe, 'The Seeds of Social Destruction', ibid.

'one of the few things in this society . . .': ibid.

Charles Radcliffe, 'Pop Goes the Beatle', 'Mods, Rockers and the Revolution', *Rebel Worker*, no. 1, 1965

For dissolution of Provo: *PROVO*, op. cit., Chapter 8 – 'aftermath of the battle: the gradual decline and death of provo (june 15, 1966–may 14, 1967)'

Kenneth Coutts-Smith, 'Violence in Art', *art and artists*, vol. 1, no. 5, August 1966

Gustav Metzger, untitled statement, ibid.

Charles Radcliffe, 'The Who – Crime Against the Bourgeoisie', *Rebel Worker*, no. 6, May 1966

Pete Townshend, author interview, 2011

For the Who nearly breaking up in May: entries for 'Tuesday, 3 May' and 'Friday, 20 May', in *Anyway Anyhow Anywhere*, op. cit., and entry for 'May 20 1966' in Johnny Black, *Eyewitness: The Who: The Day-by-Day Story* (Carlton Books, 2001). Keith Moon: 'It was incredibly violent for a time. It was common knowledge in England because there were a lot of people coming to see our shows and we came on with sticking plasters, bleeding. There were even fistfights on stage. Every five minutes, someone was quitting the group.'

If you can find it, there is excellent Canadian TV footage from the 9 July 1966 show at Westminster Technical College in London, which features Townshend and Moon smashing their respective instruments.

'I don't think the rebellion line . . .': Nick Jones, 'Whither the Groups?' *Melody Maker*, 15 October 1966

Norman Jopling, 'The Who: Anti Love', *Record Mirror*, 15 October 1966

'an obvious hit . . .': Norman Jopling and Peter Jones, 'New Singles Reviewed', *Record Mirror*, 2 September 1966

For an excellent history of DIAS, including Metzger quote, Ortiz story, etc.: Kristine Styles, 'The Story of the Destruction in Art Symposium and the "DIAS Effect",' in Sabina Breitweiser (Ed.), *Gustav Metzger, Geschichte Geschichte* (Generali Foundation and Hatje Cantz Verlag, 2005)

'Destruction IN art did not mean the destruction OF art': Dario Gamboni,

'Modern Art and Iconoclash: The Destruction of Art as Art', in *The Destruction of Art: Iconoclasm and Vandalism Since the French Revolution* (Reaktion Books, 1997)

For 'anal' and 'sadomasochistic' quotes: poster for the Theater of Orgies and Mysteries March 1968 performance in New York, www.vasulka.org/archive/ Artists4/Nitsch/NitschPoster.pdf

Gustav Metzger, 'Excerpts from Selected Papers Presented at the 1966 Destruction in Art Symposium', *Studio International*, December 1966

Barry Farrell, 'The Other Culture', cover story, *Life*, 17 February 1967

Allan Kaprow, *How to Make a Happening* (Mass Art LP, 1966)

'Psychedelic Art', *Life*, 9 September 1966

'Greetings and welcome Rolling Stones . . .': 'Manifesto', a single-page leaflet handed out at the *Rolling Stones* concert at the Hollywood Bowl, 25 July 1966

2Stoned, op. cit.

'some songs I write . . .': in Rochelle Reed, 'That's Tough, Mom', *KRLA Beat*, 22 October 1966

'A Great Face Job', *Melody Maker*, 24 September 1966

'the Shadow is the . . .': *The Rolling Stones: The First Twenty Years*, op. cit.

'Can you imagine . . .': Bill Harry, 'Mick the Fighter', *Record Mirror*, 10 September 1966

For Rolling Stones 1966 timeline: www.timeisonourside.com/chron1966.html and www.nzentgraf.de/books/tcw/works1.htm

Keith Richards and Mick Jagger quotes: 'A Great Face Job!', *Melody Maker*, 24 September 1966

The two separate videos for 'Have You Seen Your Mother, Baby, Standing in the Shadow?' were up on YouTube but seem to have disappeared

'came over the top . . .': Mike Ledgerwood, 'Stones Stampede', *Disc and Music Echo*, 1 October 1966

'It should be nestling . . .': 'At Home', *Record Mirror*, 24 September 1966

'Stones Slipped Disc', *Melody Maker*, 15 October 1966

'the most astounding shock . . .' and Bobby Elliot and Mike d'Abo quotes from Penny Valentine, 'Stones – What Went Wrong?' *Disc and Music Echo*, 5 November 1966

CHAPTER 10

'Reeves Tops Pop 50', *Melody Maker*, 24 September 1966

For more on Jim Reeves's life: Larry Jordan, *Jim Reeves: His Untold Story* (Page Turner Books, 2011)

Dick Tatham, sleeve notes for *Finchley Central* LP (Fontana Records, 1967)

'The Junk Shop Vaudeville Sound', *Melody Maker*, 15 October 1966

Mark Frumento, sleeve notes to the New Vaudeville Band's *Winchester Cathedral* (RPM CD, 2007)

Neil Innes interview: transatlanticmodern.com/2013/06/24/interview-neil-innes

Bonzos interview: Jeff Penczak, 'Three Bonzos and a Piano', www.terrascope. co.uk/Features/Three_Bonzos_Feature.htm

Richard Allen, sleeve notes to *Songs the Bonzo Dog Band Taught Us* (Freak Emporium CD, 2007)

Bob Kerr info: tradjazzradio.blogspot.co.uk/2007/08/making-whoopee.html
Kieron Tyler, sleeve notes to Alan Klein's *Well at Least It's British* (RPM, 2008)
Spencer Leigh interview with Alan Klein: sweetwordsofpismotality.blogspot.
    co.uk/2010/10/gnome-thoughts-13.html
'What a drag . . .': 'Zooming Up the Chart!: Hit Talk by Mindbender Bob',
    Disc and Music Echo, 1 October 1966
Chris Welch, 'Let the Good Times Roll!', *Melody Maker*, 22 October 1966
For details of 'Tell Me that You Love Me': Alan Leeds, sleeve notes to James
    Brown's *The Singles Volume 4: 1966–67* (Polydor, 2007)
For Pathé Yoko Ono footage: www.britishpathe.com/video/concept-art-on-
    show-in-london/query/Ono
Allan Kaprow, *How to Make a Happening*, op. cit.; a full transcript is available
    at primaryinformation.org/files/allan-kaprow-how-to-make-a-happening.pdf
'The Electronic Front Page', *Time*, 14 October 1966; also 'Television: The
    Most Intimate Medium', ibid.
Marshall McLuhan, 'The Invisible Environment: The Future of
    Consciousness', *Perspecta* (Yale Architectural Journal), no. 11, fall 1966
Irwin Allen's The Time Tunnel: The Complete Series (20th Century Fox DVD,
    2011)
Adam Adamant Lives! The Complete Collection (BBC DVD, 2006)
Pauline Boty in *Scene*, November 1962: quoted in *Pauline Boty: Pop Artist
    and Woman*, op. cit., Chapter 4 – 'Pop Artist and Woman'
'Aubrey Beardsley: An Exhibition of Original Drawings, Manuscripts, Books,
    Paintings, Posters Etc.' was held at the Victoria and Albert Museum
    between 19 May and 19 September 1966. It was the first major museum
    exhibition I ever went to. The catalogue was written by Brian Reade: *Aubrey
    Beardsley* (Her Majesty's Stationery Office, 1966)
Paul Flora, *Vivat Vamp!* (Dobson Books, 1965)
For I Was Lord Kitchener's Valet and the Jagger jacket: interview with Robert
    Orbach on the Victoria and Albert Museum's website – www.vam.ac.uk/
    content/articles/i/robert-orbach. 'I'm sitting there one morning and in
    walked John Lennon, Mick Jagger and Cynthia Lennon. And I didn't know
    whether I was hallucinating . . . but it was real. And Mick Jagger bought a
    red Grenadier guardsman drummer's jacket, probably for about £4–5. They
    all came from Moss Bros and British Army Surplus. In 1966 it was only fifty
    or so years from Victorian times, when we had an empire. We used to buy
    fur coats by the bale . . . we had to throw quite a lot away. So Mick Jagger
    bought this tunic and wore it on *Ready Steady Go!* when the Stones closed
    the show by performing "Paint It Black". The next morning there was a line
    of about 100 people wanting to buy this tunic . . . and we sold everything in
    the shop by lunchtime.'
For more: dandyinaspic.blogspot.co.uk/2011/09/i-was-lord-kitcheners-valet.
    html
The site dandyinaspic also has an excellent blog on the various incarnations of
    Granny Takes a Trip: dandyinaspic.blogspot.co.uk/2011/07/granny-takes-
    trip.html
'We started making clothes for men and women . . .': Sophia Satchell-

Baeza, 'Welcome Cosmic Visions: An Interview with Nigel Waymouth', sophiasbfilm.wordpress.com/2014/04/16/welcome-cosmic-visions-an-interview-with-nigel-waymouth

Max Decharne, *Kings Road: The Rise and Fall of the Hippest Street in the World* (Weidenfeld and Nicholson, 2005)

Maureen O'Grady, 'The Imperfect Pop Star', *Rave*, October 1966

Peter Watkins, *Privilege* (BFI Flipside, 2011)

The Beat Fleet, op. cit., Chapter 6 – 'Expansion and Tragedy' and Chapter 7 – 'Outlawed'

For 'We Love the Pirates' in Radio Caroline countdown: radiolondon.co.uk/caroline/stonewashed/carolinecharts/054%20September%2010%201966.htm

'They're Coming to Take Us Away', *Disc and Music Echo*, 1 October 1966

'The government makes me sick . . .': interview with Ray Coleman, *Disc and Music Echo*, 6 August 1966

'Nationalised Pop to Replace Pirates?' *Melody Maker*, 1 October 1966

For *Blow-Up* filming and Yardbirds timeline: 'Jimmy Page's Psychedelic Era' and 'Yardbirds Concert Dates' in *Yardbirds: The Ultimate Rave-Up*, op. cit.

'Antonioni and "The Blow Up"', *Continental Film Review*, September 1966

Christopher Gibbs, author interview, June 1995: 'There's this bend in the river, so you get a mile of water, and you get these amazing light effects, opposite Cheyne Walk, by the boats, what they call Turner's Reach. I was staying up all night taking acid, and entertaining quite expansively, having twenty-five people I'd never seen before, and there were piles of Moroccan things and ancient Persian carpets and tapestries hanging on the wall, and more or less no furniture. I had this backdrop place and Antonioni was brought there by Claire Peploe, who lived with Antonioni and then married Bertolucci. A lot of the people who came to the party were my friends. If I looked at it I could probably point out twenty of them, and half of them might still be alive.'

Penny Valentine, 'Penny Spins the Discs', *Disc and Music Echo*, 22 October 1966

'Mod Britain '67: Bob Farmer Reporting from Newcastle', *Disc and Music Echo*, 5 November 1966

'The new factor in U.S. race relations . . .': 'What the Negro Has – And Has Not – Gained', *Time* editorial, 28 October 1966

For the *Billboard* chart of 1 October, go to Google Books and search for the issue of that date. Almost all the issues of *Billboard* from 1966 are viewable at Google Books. For more, go to old-charts.com

Rochelle Reed, 'James Brown Says "I'm a Dynamo!"', *KRLA Beat*, 8 October 1966; also at rocksbackpages.com

James Brown and Bruce Tucker, 'Getting Into It', in *James Brown: The Godfather of Soul*, op. cit.

For the history of the Hunter's Point disturbances: Arthur E. Hippler, *Hunter's Point – A Black Ghetto* (Basic Books, 1974)

'several huddled, cowering children of preteen age': ibid., Chapter 10 – 'The "Riot"'

For 'white power' images: *The Civil Rights Movement*, op. cit., Chapter 9 – 'The Eclipsing of Nonviolence, 1965–68'

Cicero March, by Film Group Inc., can be seen at www.
movingimagearchivenews.org/the-1966-march-on-cicero-a-step-towards-equity

Mick Rogers, *Freakout on Sunset Strip*, Chapter 5 – 'Skinheads, Greasers and Surfers' (Greenleaf Classics, 1967)

Lerone Bennett, 'Stokely Carmichael: Architect of Black Power', *Ebony*, September 1966

For anti-war speeches and Atlanta disturbance: *Stokely: A Life*, op. cit., Chapter 9 – 'The Magnificent Barbarian: July–September 1966'

Defeat of 1966 Civil Rights Bill: 'Civil Rights – Ahead of Its Time', *Time*, 30 September 1966

'resistance of whites . . .' and '52% of them think . . .': 'Politics: The Turning Point', *Time*, 7 October 1966

For Reagan and Berkeley, and black Republicans: Robert Dallek, *The Right Moment*, Chapter 9 – 'The Search for Order' (Oxford University Press, 2009)

'beatniks, radicals and filthy speech advocates': 'The Morality Gap at Berkeley', speech at Cow Palace, 12 May 1966

Michelle Reeves, '"Obey the Rules or Get Out"', op. cit.

Huey P. Newton, *Revolutionary Suicide*, Chapters 14–17 (Penguin Classics, 2009)

Joshua Bloom and Waldo E. Martin, Jr, *Black Against Empire: The History and Politics of the Black Panther Party* (University of California Press, 2014)

The full Black Panther manifesto is reprinted in *Revolutionary Suicide*, op. cit., Chapter 16 – 'The Founding of the Black Panther Party'

'Amsterdam, London, San Francisco . . .': Dave Rothlop, letter to *The Psychedelic Oracle*, issue 2, October 1966

'the surrounding neighbourhood . . .': *Dark Stars and Anti-Matter: 40 Years of Loving, Leaving and Making Up with the Music of the Grateful Dead* (Rhino ebook, 2012)

Ralph J. Gleason, 'On the Town: Dance Concert Isle of Sanity', *San Francisco Chronicle*, 2 October 1966

Stephen Schneck, 'The Action', *San Francisco Oracle*, issue 2, October 1966

Diggers material from www.diggers.org – an excellent site, including www.diggers.org/ring_compilation/ring_compilation_209_263.htm; www.diggers.org/Outrageous_Pamphleteers-A_History_Of_The_Communication_Company.pdf

For the early leaflets, including 'A-Political Or, Criminal Or Victim Or Or Or . . .': www.diggers.org/digger_sheets.htm

Emmett Grogan, *Ringolevio: A Life Played for Keeps* (Little Brown, 1972)

List of 1966 SF rock shows: www.sfmuseum.org/hist1/rock.html

SF State Acid Test: www.postertrip.com/public/5587.cfm

Erik Bluhm, 'The Story of the Wildflower, San Francisco's Lost Band', *Ugly Things*, issue 29

For the nuclear attack simulation at the Awareness Festival and the Love Pageant Rally: *The Haight-Ashbury*, op. cit., Chapter 4 – 'Big Plans'

'THE TRULY INSANE ARE HELPLESS!': Schneck, 'Flex, Re-Flex', *San Francisco Oracle*, issue 2, October 1966

Digger Free Food leaflet: Dominic Cavallo, 'It's Free Because It's Yours',
www.diggers.org/cavallo_pt__1.htm, and *The Haight-Ashbury*, op. cit.,
Chapter 4 – 'Big Plans'
Mojo Navigator reviews: issue 9, 17 October 1966
Hendrik Herzberg material: deadsources.blogspot.co.uk/2014/08/october-1966-
san-francisco-sound.html. The article was finally printed in *Newsweek*, 19
December 1966
Peter Jenner, author interview, December 2014
For a full history of the Portobello Road area and Carnival: Ishmahil Blagrove,
Jr (Ed.), *Carnival* (RICENPEAS, 2014)
Grove magazine, 23 June 1966 is quoted in *Carnival*, ibid., 'Introduction'
Julian Mash, 'Pageant, Fireworks, Music, Plays and Poetry: The London
Free School and the 1966 Carnival', in *Portobello Road: Lives of a
Neighbourhood* (Frances Lincoln, 2014)
John Hopkins, author interview, May 2012
The Joe Gannon and Dave Tomlin pictures are in 'Rhuane Laslett, the Notting
Hill Festival', in *Carnival*, op. cit.
Pink Floyd concerts in 1966: www.brain-damage.co.uk/concert-dates/1966-
tour-dates-concerts.html
AMM Keith Rowe interview: www.paristransatlantic.com/magazine/
interviews/rowe.html
Mark Blake, *Pigs Might Fly: The Inside Story of the Pink Floyd* (Aurum, 2007)
Julian Palacios, *Lost in the Woods: Syd Barrett and the Pink Floyd* (Boxtree,
1998)
Barry Miles, *Pink Floyd: The Early Years* (Omnibus, 2006)
Pink Floyd 14 October set list: Rob Chapman, *Syd Barrett, A Very Irregular
Head*, Chapter 3 – 'Flicker Flicker Blam Blam Pow' (Faber & Faber, 2010)
'a spark that was magnetic . . .': 'Pink Floyd Go into Interstellar Overdrive' in
Portobello Road, op. cit.
'bring your own poison . . .': *Syd Barrett, A Very Irregular Head*, op. cit.,
Chapter 3 – 'Flicker Flicker Blam Blam Pow'
'2500 Ball at IT-Launch', *International Times*, 31 October–13 November 1966
Barry Miles, 'THE Global moon-edition Long Hair Times', 'The Pink Floyd',
'International Times', 'IT Launch at the Roundhouse', all from *In the
Sixties*, op. cit.
'resisted any whole-hearted move . . .': 'Surrogate Americans', ibid.
'You', editorial, *International Times*, 14–27 October 1966
'There seem to be many . . .': Casey Hayden and Mary King, 'Sex and Caste: A
Kind of Memo', *Liberation*, April 1966
Jacqueline Susann, *Valley of the Dolls* (Grove Press, 1966)
For details of *That Girl*: www.imdb.com/title/tt0060034/
episodes?year=1966&ref_=tt_eps_yr_1966
Peter Doggett, sleeve notes to Sandy Posey's *A Single Girl* (MGM/RPM
Records, 2002)
Craig Fenton, sleeve notes to Jefferson Airplane's *Live at the Fillmore
Auditorium 10/16/66 Grace's Debut* (Collector's Choice, 2010)
Big Brother interview from *Mojo Navigator News*, vol. 1, no. 8, 5 October 1966

'You Keep Me Hangin' On' was intended as a 'one–two punch' and 'the sound of a telegraph that you'd hear in an old movie': see track-by-track annotations by Bill Dahl and Keith Hughes, op. cit.

'the actions needed . . .', 'not just talk' and 'I knew in my gut . . .': Betty Friedan, *Life So Far*, Chapter 7 – 'Starting the Women's Movement' (Simon & Schuster, 2000)

Text of National Organisation of Women founding statement: www.feminist.org/research/chronicles/early1.html

For Stokely Carmichael 27 October pre-induction facility and partying in the Haight after the 29 October speech: *Stokely: A Life*, op. cit., Chapter 10 – 'A New Society Must Be Born'

Michelle Reeves, '"Obey the Rules or Get Out"', op. cit.

Full text of Stokely Carmichael's 'Black Power' address at Berkeley, 29 October 1966: www.americanrhetoric.com/speeches/stokelycarmichaelblackpower.html

For the context and implications: Kalen M. A. Churcher, 'Stokely Carmichael, "Black Power"' (29 October 1966): archive.vod.umd.edu/civil/carmichael1966int.htm

'to get to the bottom of the Berkeley mess': see description of 11 September 1966 *Meet the Press* appearance in *The Right Moment*, op. cit., Chapter 10 – 'Prairie Fire'

CHAPTER 11

'It is way off beam . . .': Dave Godin, 'SOUL The Reasons Why Are Explained', letter to *Record Mirror*, 26 November 1966

Penny Valentine, 'If You've Any Soul, Buy This!' *Disc* singles review, 8 October 1966

Marc Weingarten quote and disagreements: see note for Four Tops' 'Reach Out I'll Be There', Bill Dahl and Keith Hughes, op. cit.

Marc Weingarten, interview with Lamont Dozier, *Mojo*, no. 45, August 1997

'we will release nothing less . . .': in note for The Supremes' 'You Can't Hurry Love', Bill Dahl and Keith Hughes, op. cit.

'1966 will undoubtedly be recorded as . . .': DISCussion by Eden, *KRLA Beat*, 5 November 1966

Tony Hall, 'The Tony Hall Column', *Record Mirror*, 8 October 1966

Bob Farmer, 'FOUR TOPS Spin Up to the Top!' *Disc and Music Echo*, 22 October 1966

Norman Jopling, 'Here's How a Sophisticated Nightclub Act . . .', *Record Mirror*, 29 October 1966

'This is the most important record of our career . . .': Norman Jopling, 'The Tops Talk about the Songwriting Set . . .', *Record Mirror*, 19 November 1966

'Tony Hall introduced the Four Tops . . .': Penny Valentine, 'Blowing their TOPS!' *Disc and Music Echo*, 19 November 1966

Tony Hall, 'My Scene by Tony Hall', *Record Mirror*, 26 November 1966

Dusty Springfield, 'Watch Out! – The Yanks Are Winning', *Disc and Music Echo*, 26 November 1966

'a divergent culture . . .': Dave Godin, author interview, July 1997 'fabulous, neurotic sound': Penny Valentine, 'Stones Stay with Dylan!' *Disc Weekly*, 5 February 1966

'The "in" crowd always said . . .': Maureen O'Grady, 'The Soul Parade', *Rave*, November 1966

For more on the impact of black American music in the UK in autumn 1966, see K. L. Yershon, 'The R&B Phenomenon', *Record Mirror*, 29 October 1966: 'Sales of R/B records have risen so much that the appearance of several of them at a time in the National Pop Charts is now quite a regular occurrence.' A chronological list of R&B records that made the national charts between 7 May and 17 October is tabulated: 'It's a Man's World' [*sic*], 'Confusion', 'When a Man Loves a Woman', 'River Deep – Mountain High', 'Ain't Too Proud to Beg', 'Loving You Is Sweeter Than Ever', 'My Lover's Prayer', 'Tell Her I'm Not Home', 'Barefootin'', 'Warm and Tender Love', 'Headline News', 'Working in the Coalmine', 'Summertime', 'Blowin' in the Wind', 'How Sweet It Is', 'I Can't Turn You Loose', 'I Guess I'll Always Love You', 'Land of 1000 Dances', 'You Can't Hurry Love', 'Little Darlin' (I Need You)', 'Sunny', 'Beauty Is Only Skin Deep', 'Reach Out I'll Be There'

'like orphans in a storm' and 'I actually sat down . . .': Dave Godin, author interview, February 1995

For UK Stateside label details: 45cat – www.45cat.com/label/stateside

'How can kids . . .': Dave Godin, author interview, February 1995

For Count Suckle, see obituary at www.theguardian.com/music/2014/jun/04/count-suckle

Material about sixties Soul Clubs from Forum on www.soul-source.co.uk/soulforum/topic/265981-60s-soho-soul-clubs-southern-soul-era. Also sixtiescity.net/Culture/Soho1.htm

Supplemental information about clubs thanks to Ady Croasdell, email correspondence with author, 2015

Jeff Dexter, author interview, January 2014

Bill Brewster, interview with Jeff Dexter, February 1999: www.djhistory.com/interviews/jeff-dexter

'turned instantly to night . . .': Rob Finnis, sleeve notes for *The UK Sue Label Story: The World of Guy Stevens* (Ace Records, 2004)

Mike Atherton and Tony Rounce, sleeve notes for *The UK Sue Label Story Volume 2: Sue's Rock'N'Blues* (Ace Records, 2004)

'seemed incredible . . .': Geoff Green, 'LONDON: THE SCENE CLUB and SOHO', 2 September 2007, jackthatcatwasclean.blogspot.co.uk/2007/09/london-scene-club-and-soho-thanx-to.html

'The first night I did . . .' and 'I had to keep people dancing': Bill Sykes, *Listen to This: The Roger Eagle Story*, Chapter 3 – 'The Brazennose Street Twisted Wheel club (Empire Publications, 2012)

Joe Boy, sleeve notes to *Twisted Wheel: Brazennose and Whitworth Street, Manchester 1963–71* (Charly, 2013)

Island Records details: 45cat – www.45cat.com/label/island

Malcolm Imrie, 'The Secret Ska History of Stamford Hill', www.uncarved.org/blog/2011/08/the-secret-ska-history-of-stamford-hill

'a time when genres and pigeonholes . . .': Ady Croasdell, sleeve notes for *The UK Sue Label Story Volume 3: The Soul of Sue* (Ace Records, 2004)

'Out of the blue I got a five-page telegram . . .': Dave Godin, author interview, February 1995

Vicki Wickham, email correspondence, March 2015

Ready Steady Go! programme listings from www.tv.com/shows/ready-steady-go/episodes

Kingsley Abbott, 'Launching the Tamla Motown Label: Reminiscences with Derek Everett', from Kingsley Abbott (Ed.), *Calling Out All Around the World: A Motown Reader* (Helter Skelter, 2001)

'I went to Manchester Square to meet them . . .': Jeff Dexter, author interview, January 2014

Richard Williams, 'Are You Ready for a Brand New Beat? www.theguardian.com/music/2005/mar/18/popandrock

Jim Stewart, 'The UK Concerts', from *Calling Out All Around the World*, op. cit.

'I was in charge . . .': Tony Hall on 'In the Midnight Hour' and 'My Girl', author interview, March 2015

'First, the coloured artist . . .': Rob Finnis, sleeve notes, op. cit.

For John Abbey and blues and soul: www.soulmusic.com/index.asp?S=1&T=38&ART=2423

David Griffiths, 'James Brown Live', *Record Mirror*, 5 March 1966

Dave Godin, 'James Brown: The Soul of Mr. Brown', *Record Mirror*, 26 March 1966

Tom Wolfe, 'The Noonday Underground', in *The Pump House Gang* (Bantam, 1969)

'It became boring quite frankly . . .': Bill Sykes, *Listen to This*, op. cit., Chapter 4 – 'The Whitworth Street Twisted Wheel Club'

Re. this accelerated style: it's possible to fix 1966 as Ground Zero for Northern Soul. Dave Godin cited the following records as examples of the style that was in his mind when he coined the term: Billy Butler's 'The Right Track' (March 1966), Darrell Banks's 'Open the Door to Your Heart' (June 1966), the Velvelettes' 'These Things Will Keep Me Loving You 1966' (August 1966) and the Elgins' 'Heaven Must Have Sent You' (August 1966) (all US release dates)

'It was like finding freedom, really . . .': Jeff Dexter, author interview, January 2014

Orlando Patterson, 'The Dance Invasion', *New Society*, 15 September 1966: reprinted in *The Pop Process*, op. cit.

'Atlantic Making UK Take Notice with Five Hot-Selling Records', *Billboard*, 17 September 1966

Uncredited writer, 'Otis Redding: Mr Cool and the Clique from Memphis', *Melody Maker*, 17 September 1966 – sourced from rocksbackpages.com

Bill Miller, 'Otis Redding at Tiles', *Soul Music Monthly*, October 1966 – sourced from rocksbackpages.com

Tony Hall, 'Tony's Comments on TAMLA SUCCESS', *Record Mirror*, 17 October 1966

For data on EMI's Soul Supply series (on Verve, Liberty, Stateside, etc.):
www.45cat.com/45_search.php?sq=soul+supply+series&sm=se

David Griffiths, 'Rhythm & Roll' (Lee Dorsey and Marshall Seehorn talk
about their definition of soul), *Record Mirror*, 29 October 1966

Dave Godin, 'SOUL the Reason Why Explained', letter to *Record Mirror*, 26
November 1966

Bob Farmer, 'Why TAMLA'S tops with BRUM, MOD Britain '67', *Disc and
Music Echo*, 26 November 1966

'Paul Jones in Colour Bar Clash', *Disc and Music Echo*, 17 December 1966

'It was incredible. It hit . . .': Jeff Dexter, author interview, January 2014

'Aberfan was no longer a disaster . . .': Tony Austin, *Aberfan: The Story of a
Disaster*, Chapter 3 – 'Friday Afternoon' (Hutchinson and Co., 1967)

For a description of the disaster: ibid., Chapter 2 – 'Friday Morning'

'heard a noise like thunder . . .': ibid., Chapter – 'Friday Afternoon'

'Everyone just froze in their seats . . .': www.hiraeth.wales/aberfan/the-story-
of-the-disaster

For background of Aberfan: *Aberfan: The Story of a Disaster*, op. cit., Chapter
1 – 'A Village in Wales'

Details of *The Heart of Show Business* ('All-star concert and tribute to support
"The Aberfan Fund". Which followed a Welsh mining disaster in 1966 in
which both adults and children were killed'): www.imdb.com/title/tt1169937

'I wanted to write a modern-day depression song' and 'It's all about people
who weren't chic enough . . .': Ray Davies, author interviews 1983/4, from
The Kinks: The Official Biography, op. cit.

Ray Davies, *X-Ray*, Chapter 16 – 'Powerman' (Viking, 1994)

Doug Hinman, entry for October 'Friday 21st – Saturday 22nd' 1966, *The
Kinks: All Day and All of the Night – Day-by-Day Concerts, Recordings and
Broadcasts, 1961–1996* (Backbeat Books, 2004)

'It's a very London song . . .': Ray Davies, author interviews 1983/4, op. cit.

The 'Dead End Street' video can be seen at www.youtube.com/
watch?v=ioWPC-N3UYE

Penny Valentine, 'Kinks: A Hit, But What About Love?' *Disc and Music
Echo*, 19 November 1966

'There's nothing funny about old people dying . . .': '"Sick" Kink Film Banned
by "Top of the Pops"', *Disc and Music Echo*, 3 December 1966

Jeremy Sandford quotes: www.jeremysandford.org.uk. The following links
are particularly relevant: for Sandford and Nell Dunn's reverse migration:
www.jeremysandford.org.uk/jsarchive/warp-king-s-road.html. For the
origins of *Cathy Come Home*: www.jeremysandford.org.uk/jsarchive/warp-
cathy-storyline.html; www.jeremysandford.org.uk/jsarchive/warp-cathy.
html; www.jeremysandford.org.uk/jsarchive/warp-essential-tony-garnett.
html. For its political impact and press coverage: www.jeremysandford.org.
uk/jsarchive/warp-petition-to-parliament.html; www.jeremysandford.org.
uk/jsarchive/warp-press-comment-on-cathy.html; www.jeremysandford.org.
uk/jsarchive/warp-tvs-kleptocracy-1.html; www.jeremysandford.org.uk/
jsarchive/cathy-30today.html; www.jeremysandford.org.uk/jsarchive/warp-
cathy-come-home.html

Derek Paget, '"Cathy Come Home" and "Accuracy" in British Television Drama', www.reading.ac.uk/web/FILES/ftt/PagetPublications.pdf

George W. Brandt (Ed.), *British Television Drama*, Chapter 8 – 'Jeremy Sandford' by Martin Banham (Cambridge University Press, 1981)

Statement of Minister for Housing Anthony Greenwood in House of Commons, 15 December 1966: hansard.millbanksystems.com/commons/1966/dec/15/housing-subsidies-bill#S5CV0738P0_19661215_HOC_243

Ken Loach, *Cathy Come Home* (BFI Archive Television DVD, 1996)

Jeremy Sandford, *Cathy Come Home* (Pan Paperbacks, 1967)

'People are part of my music . . .': Brian Wilson, 'This Is Brian Wilson. He Is a Beach Boy. Some Say He Is More. Some Say He Is a Beach Boy and a Genius', *Go!*, July 1966; republished in Dominic Priore, *Look! Listen! Vibrate! Smile!* (Surfin' Colours Production, 1988)

Mike Love on 'Good Vibrations' in the style of James Brown: Rob Hughes, 'The Making of . . . The Beach Boys' "Good Vibrations"', *Uncut*, June 2007

For details of the 'Good Vibrations' sessions: Craig Slowinski and Alan Boyd, notes for Disc 5, 'The Beach Boys – SMiLE Sessionography', *The Beach Boys SMiLE Sessions* (Capitol 5 CD set, 2011)

Jim Delehant, 'Dennis Wilson: We Just Want to Be a Good Group', *Hit Parader*, June 1967

Derek Taylor, 'LOST: Beach Boys' Tape for Their Next Single', *Disc and Music Echo*, 1 October 1966

'Beach Boys have a giant . . .': Derek Taylor, 'Our Man in America', *Disc and Music Echo*, 22 October 1966

'The Beach Boys are lucky . . .': undated interview republished in *Look! Listen! Vibrate! Smile!*, op. cit.

'I know that in some circles . . .': ibid.

'hard work . . .': Derek Taylor, *As Time Goes By*, Chapter 4 – 'About 1965–8 – Written 1970. Leonard' (Davis-Poynter, 1973)

Tony Asher quotes re. uncontrollable anger and Wilson paranoia: Steven Gaines, *Heroes and Villains: The True Story of the Beach Boys*, Chapters 7 and 8 (New American Library, 1986)

'Brian was forever staring into the mirror . . .': Derek Taylor, *Fifty Years Adrift*, op. cit., p. 266

'The idea is simple and spiritual . . .': Dennis Wilson interview, *Rave*, January 1967

Tony Asher re. childhood memory: Dominic Priore, *SMiLE: The Story of Brian Wilson's Lost Masterpiece*, Chapter 5 – 'Good, Good, Good, Good Vibrations' (Sanctuary, 2005)

Tom Nolan, 'The Frenzied Frontier of Pop Music', *Los Angeles Times WEST* magazine, 27 November 1966

For Beach Boys cover: *Disc and Music Echo*, 5 November 1966; *Record Mirror* put them on the cover of their 19 November issue

For poll result: 'Beatles Beaten!', *Record Mirror*, 29 October 1966

'World Winners & Losers', *Record Mirror*, 5 November 1966

Derek Taylor, 'Beach Boys – Maverick Millionaires!' *Disc and Music Echo*, 22 October 1966

Ray Coleman, 'Beach Boys Blitz Britain!' *Disc and Music Echo*, 12 November 1966

Nick Jones and David Griffiths, 'On Stage? Carl Wilson Talks about the Sound Problems that Face the Beach Boys', *Record Mirror*, 12 November 1966

'a glorious, naive and spontaneous coming together . . .': *Fifty Years Adrift*, op. cit., p. 277

'They're calling out the sheriff . . .': Tandyn Almer, 'Sunset Strip Soliloquy', *KRLA Beat*, 22 October 1966

'Republican Resurgence', *Time*, 18 November 1966

'Now the President's popularity . . .': 'G.O.P '66: Back on the Map', *Newsweek*, 21 November 1966

Clay Carson, 'Election Reveals Democrats' Weakness', *Los Angeles Free Press*, 18 November 1966

Andrew E. Busch, '1966 Midterm Foreshadows Republican Era', ashbrook. org/publications/oped-busch-06-1966

'sexual misconduct': Ronald Reagan's 'The Morality Gap at Berkeley' speech at Cow Palace, 12 May 1966 – see *The Right Moment*, op. cit., Chapter 9 – 'The Search for Order', and Michelle Reeves, '"Obey the Rules or Get Out"', op. cit.

Robert Cohen, 'Mario Savio and Berkeley's "Little Free Speech Movement" of 1966', in Robert Cohen and Reginald E. Zelnik (Eds), *The Free Speech Movement*, op. cit., Part IV – 'Aftermath'

'The button had been pushed . . .': Art Kunkin, 'Daily Newspapers Distort Meaning of Youth Protest Against Police Acts', *Los Angeles Free Press*, 18 November 1966

'formed into groups and began . . .': ibid.

Terry W. Bales, 'Angry Owners of Plush Sunset Strip Clubs Hope to Prevent More Riots', unattributed clipping dated 14 November 1966 from Ralph Gleason files

'A Riot on Sunset Strip', *San Francisco Chronicle*, 14 November 1966

'In People Are Talking About . . .', *KRLA Beat*, 6 November 1966

Jules Siegel, 'Surf, Wheels & Free Souls', *Saturday Evening Post*, 19 November 1966. The 'Superlungs' reference is to a song recorded by Donovan that year; it would not be released, in a different version, until 1969

'to get them out, their parents must sign for them': Roger Vaughan, 'The Mad New Scene on Sunset Strip', *Life*, 26 August 1966

For Victory Girls: www.faqs.org/childhood/Th-W/Victory-Girls.html

For the 3 November interview: 'There's Battle Lines Bein' Drawn', in *Riot on Sunset Strip*, op. cit.

'Hollywood Division Police Commander States Views', *Los Angeles Free Press*, 18 November 1966

'two groups of businessmen fighting each other': Kunkin, op. cit.

'Gestapo Gestapo': Mike Davis, 'Riot Nights on Sunset Strip', journals.hil. unb.ca/index.php/LLT/article/viewFile/5848/6853

'seemed to be in a state of panic', 'used shocking language' and 'that it takes intelligence . . .': Kunkin, op. cit.

Jules Siegel, 'The New Sound: Tune In, Turn On, and Take Over', *Village Voice*, 17 November 1966

'Ken Kesey and the Great Pumpkin', *San Francisco Oracle*, issue 3, November 1966

'Book Raid: "Obscene Poetry" and a Big Fuss', *San Francisco Chronicle*, 16 November 1966

Donovan Bess, '"Love Book" Arrest at City Lights', *San Francisco Chronicle*, 18 November 1966

K-RON TV, 'The Psychedelic Shop Gets Raided', diva.sfsu.edu/collections/sfbatv/bundles/210733

Lenore Kandel, *The Love Book* (Stolen Paper Review Editions, San Francisco, 1966)

Ken Hunt, 'Lenore Kandel: Beat Poet Whose "The Love Book" Fell Victim to One of San Francisco's Longest Ever Court Cases', www.independent.co.uk/news/obituaries/lenore-kandel-beat-poet-whose-the-love-book-fell-victim-to-one-of-san-franciscos-longest-ever-court-cases-1837947.html

Julian Guthrie, 'Lenore Kandel – "The Love Book" Author – Dies', www.sfgate.com/bayarea/article/Lenore-Kandel-The-Love-Book-author-dies-3212680.php

Lenore Kandel, 'With Love', *San Francisco Oracle*, issue 4, 12 December 1966

Lee Meyerzone, 'Kandel and McClure: Oracles of Love', ibid.

For the CLEAN campaign: Josh A. Sides, 'Sexual Propositions: The Bedroom and the Ballot', *Boom: A Journal of California*, vol. 1, pp. 30–43, fall 2011

Brian Carr, 'Police Mobilize as Teen Unrest Continues on Strip', *Los Angeles Free Press*, 25 November 1966

'Some of the demonstrators . . .': uncredited front-page article, ibid.

'The missing element of excitement . . .': Brian Carr, op. cit.

Derek Taylor on CAFF: *As Time Goes By*, op. cit., Chapter 5 – About 1965–68 – Written 1970. New Chapter'

'New Teen Rioting on Sunset Strip', *San Francisco Sunday Examiner and Chronicle*, 20 November 1966

'there was no plan or purpose . . .' and 'Man, the kids have had it': Mike Davis, 'Riot Nights on Sunset Strip', op. cit.

For details of 'Fire' recording: Craig Slowinski and Alan Boyd, 'Sessionography, Disc 1', *The SMiLE Sessions – The Beach Boys*, op. cit.

Jules Siegel, 'Goodbye Surfing, Hello God', *Cheetah*, vol 1, no. 1, October 1967

Brian Wilson, 'Pop Think In', *Melody Maker*, 8 October 1966

'The mirrors into which Brian Wilson looks . . .': Derek Taylor, 'Paul Drops in at a BEACH BOYS Recording Session', *Disc and Music Echo*, 22 April 1967; reproduced in *Look! Listen! Vibrate! Smile!* op. cit.

'dwarf Watts to a tea party': Lawrence Lipton, 'Radio Free America', *Los Angeles Free Press*, 25 November 1966

'If this powder keg is ignored . . .': Brian Carr, op. cit.

CHAPTER 12

'It's pretty obvious . . .': Tony Hall, 'My Scene', *Record Mirror*, 3 December 1966

'happy to be photographed raiding the Carnaby Street boutiques': this continued until late 1966; see, for instance, 'Faces in Air Drama', front cover of *Disc and Music Echo*, 3 December 1966

Richard Green, 'Steve Admits What the Group REALLY Thought of '"Sha La La La Lee"', *Record Mirror*, 10 September 1966

Chris Welch on Small Faces: *Melody Maker*, 10 September 1966; reproduced in *Small Faces & Faces: The Ultimate Music Guide* (*Uncut* Ultimate Guide Series, issue 9, October 2013)

Dawn James, 'Little Stevie Wonders . . .', *Rave*, November 1966

Penny Valentine, 'Small Faces: Their Biggest Hit Yet', *Disc and Music Echo*, 12 November 1966

For the controversy about the 150-year-old hymn: 'Cheek of the Small Faces', *Disc and Music Echo*, 3 December 1966

For Don Arden and the premature release of 'My Mind's Eye': Paolo Hewitt and John Hellier, *Steve Marriott: All Too Beautiful . . .* (Helter Skelter, 2009)

For change of management etc.: 'Small Faces Bid', *Disc and Music Echo*, 10 December 1966

Nick Jones, 'Small Faces in a Tight Green Circle', *Melody Maker*, 17 December 1966

Keith Altham on Small Faces: *NME*, 16 September 1966; reproduced in *Small Faces & Faces*, op. cit.

Dawn James, 'In My Mind's Eye . . . The Pop Scene Seen by Steve Marriott', *Rave*, December 1966

'Very few people are ahead . . .': Nick Jones, 'The Folk Flavour of Today', *Melody Maker*, 3 December 1966

'Tamla – Tom Jones too Switch?', ibid.

Richard Green, 'When Rock Went Country', *Record Mirror*, 3 December 1966

'How Miner's Son Tom Struck Gold', *Disc and Music Echo*, 7 January 1967; for more info: www.tomjones.com

'It's a Square Whirl: Where Have All the Hippies Gone? Asks Pete Townshend', *Disc and Music Echo*, 3 December 1966

'Doonican – Square Route to the Top!' *Disc and Music Echo*, 26 November 1966

Nick Jones, 'The Folk Flavour of Today', op. cit.

Chris Welch, 'Progressive Pop', ibid.

'Too Old at 25', *Melody Maker*, 3 December 1966

Unemployment figures: 'Britain: Still Freezing', *Time*, 9 December 1966

Gene Farmer, 'Shrinking Pains of Mini-England', *Life* (international edition), 26 December 1966

'We hate the Swinging London scene': Dawn James, 'The Little Drummer Boy', *Rave*, December 1966

'Antonioni's Hypnotic Eye on a Frantic World', interview with Nadine Laber, *Life*, 27 January 1967

'Move Threatened', *Disc and Music Echo*, 24 December 1966

Picture of Brian Jones in SS uniform: 'Raving Reports', *Rave*, January 1967

Bob Farmer, 'Pirate Ships Shake-Up: Deejays Overboard', *Disc and Music Echo*, 10 December 1966

Ready Steady Go!: 'Another Pop Show Bites the Dust', *Disc and Music Echo*, 19 November 1966

Tony Hall, 'The Era Is Over', *Record Mirror*, 19 November 1966

For R. W. Lightup letter and responses: 'My Scene by Tony Hall', *Record Mirror*, 3, 17 and 24 December 1966

Bob Farmer, 'Mod Britain 67?: Swinging London?' *Disc and Music Echo*, 24 December 1966

Bowie review in Penny Valentine, 'Penny Spins the Singles', *Record Mirror*, 3 December 1966

Dawn James, 'A Bird's Eye View of Stevie Winwood', *Rave*, January 1967

Keith Altham, 'Ronnie Lane Interview', *NME*, 16 September 1966; reproduced in *Small Faces & Faces*, op. cit.

Zoot Money, 'This Music Is Valid', letters to *Melody Maker*, 3 December 1966

Chris Welch and Bob Dawbarn, 'Psychedelic the New In Word . . . And What It Really Adds Up to Is the Great American Comeback', *Melody Maker*, 22 October 1966

David Griffiths's review of the Misunderstood: 'Psychedelic – 15 Years Ago & Now', *Record Mirror*, 24 December 1966

Gene Sculatti on 'San Francisco Bay Rock' in *Crawdaddy!* issue 6, November 1966, and Tim Jurgens, review of *Jefferson Airplane Takes Off*, *Crawdaddy!* issue 7, January 1967

'more than the ridiculous 20 minutes . . .: 'What Goes On?' *Crawdaddy!* issue 7, January 1967

Tony Hall on Hendrix, 'Striking Visual Performer', *Record Mirror*, 10 December 1966

Peter Jones, 'Mr. Phenomenon', ibid.

For Hendrix's launch at Blaise's: jasobrecht.com/jimi-hendrix-in-london

'Superman Donovan Strikes Again!' *Disc and Music Echo*, 17 December 1966

'Rave-Elations', *Rave*, January 1967

'a long word to keep masses . . .': Letters, *Melody Maker*, 3 December 1966

Ray Davies, interview with Jon Savage, 1984

'it needs the Beatles . . . to sort things out': Penny Valentine, 'WHO Boss Attacks Beach Boys', *Disc and Music Echo*, 24 December 1966

'Young people are measuring . . .': 'Not Respectable Now Say Stones', *KRLA Beat*, 5 November 1966

David Riesman quote in 'Man of the Year', *Time*, 6 January 1967

John Wilcock, 'John Wilcock's Other Seens', *International Times*, no. 5, 12–25 December 1966

'Turned-on Way of Life', *Newsweek*, 28 November 1966

'help your professors . . .': 'Timothy Leary's Press Conference at the Fairmont Hotel, San Francisco, December 12, 1966', *San Francisco Oracle*, issue 4, 16 December 1966

Kenneth Allsop, 'Turn On, Tune In, Drop Out', *The Spectator*, 9 December 1966; reprinted in *The Pop Process*, op. cit., Chapter 4 – 'Sources of Fashion: the Audience'

For the Velvet Underground Midwest dates: olivier.landemaine.free.fr/vu/live/1965-66/perf6566.html

For the *Cashbox* review: olivier.landemaine.free.fr/vu/discog/singles/singles.html

The 4 November Valley Dale Ballroom show is on Discs 5 and 6 of *The Velvet*

Underground & Nico (45th Anniversary Super Deluxe Edition), op. cit.

'Lovin' Spoonful Scandal', *Mojo Navigator*, no. 14, April 1967

Steve Boone with Tony Moss, *Hotter Than a Match Head: Life on the Run with the Lovin' Spoonful*, Chapter 6 – 'Pow!' (ECW Press, 2014)

Paul Drummond, *Eye Mind*, op. cit., Chapter 10 – 'Psychedelic Sounds Of', and sleeve notes to *Sign of the Three Eyed Men*, op. cit.

Mick Rogers, *Freakout on Sunset Strip*, op. cit., Chapter 16 – 'Turning On'

Richard Alpert, 'Leary Press Conference', *San Francisco Oracle*, issue 4, December 1966

Bob Chamberlain, '. . . it's-the-on-ly-ra-dio-sta-tion-that's-ne-ver-off-the-air . . .', *Aspen* Fab issue, vol. 1, no. 3, December 1966

'Country Joe and the Fish Interview', *Mojo Navigator*, no. 11, 22 November 1966

'San Francisco's contribution to the music scene . . .': Letters, ibid.

Michael McCausland, 'Fillmore Billy Rides Again', *San Francisco Oracle*, issue 4, December 1966

Singles reviews in *Mojo Navigator*, no. 12, 22 December 1966

Gleason column reprinted in 'Report from San Francisco', *Crawdaddy!* no. 8, March 1967

Chet Helms/Bill Graham letters in *Mojo Navigator*, no. 11, 22 November 1966

'*Mojo* Banned from Fillmore', *Mojo Navigator*, no. 10, 8 November 1966

Joel Fort, 'Methedrine Use and Abuse in San Francisco', *San Francisco Oracle*, issue 4, December 1966

'an old cunt rag of misinformation . . .'; Letters, *San Francisco Oracle*, issue 3, 8 November 1966

George Metesky, 'The Ideology of Failure' (*Berkeley Barb*, 18 November 1966), and Zapata, 'In Search of a Frame' (*Berkeley Barb*, 25 November 1966), both at www.diggers.org/chrono_diggers.asp

'A visitor to the Diggers' Page Street garage . . .': Steve Leiper, 'At the Handle of the Kettle', *San Francisco Oracle*, issue 4, December 1966

For the 10 December Sunset Strip demonstration, the placards and the Paul Jay Robbins quote: Mike Davis, 'Riot Nights on Sunset Strip', collected in *In Praise of Barbarians* (Haymarket Books, 2007)

Sonny and Cher pictured in '16 Jailed in New Protest on "Strip"', *San Francisco Chronicle*, 12 December 1966

For Teddy and Darrel: historysdumpster.blogspot.co.uk/2012/07/teddy-darrel.html and ukjarry.blogspot.co.uk/2010/01/356-camp-comedy-cash-in-records.html

Jeff Jarema, *A Trip Down the Sunset Trip*, sleeve notes to Sundazed reissue (2006); originally released on Viva Records US/Fontana Records UK (1967)

Stephen Stills quote: *Riot on Sunset Strip*, op. cit.

'Dear Editor' letter by Mrs Grethe Hansen, *The Royal's World Countdown*, vol. 2, no. 1, December 1966

'the whole rotten issue of the Old v. the Young': *As Time Goes By*, op. cit., Chapter 5: About 1965–68 – Written 1970. New Chapter'

'The fact remains that there are two factions . . .': Jerry Hopkins, untitled column, *The Royal's World Countdown*, op. cit.

'A prophetic minority creates . . .': Jack Newfield, *A Prophetic Minority* (Anthony Blond, 1967)

For demographic bulge: 'Youth '66: The Open Generation', *Look*, 20 September 1966

The Dirksen record: 'People', *Time*, 30 December 1966

'cruel and chaotic': 'The American Way of War', *Newsweek*, 5 December 1966

'Defense: Refilling the Pool', *Time*, 11 November 1966

'They shouldn't accelerate and accelerate': Jack Shephard, '"Are You a Teen-Ager?" "Yeah I'm Afraid So"', *Look*, 20 September 1966

'Teen Panel: War: Anti-American or Anti-Hypocrisy', *KRLA Beat*, 8 October 1966

'Youth Questions the War', reprinted in 'Man of the Year', *Time*, 6 January 1967

'dimming': 'The Dimming of the Dream', *Time*, 9 December 1966

Jack Newfield, *A Prophetic Minority*, reviewed in *Newsweek*, 14 December 1966

'the first products of liberal affluence': *A Prophetic Minority*, op. cit., Chapter 1 – 'The Movement'

'the impulse to rebel will continue . . .': ibid., Chapter 9 – 'The Future'

'The best of the SDS organisers are asking . . .': ibid., Chapter 8 – 'The Generation Gap'

Robert Cohen and Reginald E. Zelnik, *The Free Speech Movement*, op. cit., Part IV – 'Aftermath', chapter entitled 'Mario Savio and Berkeley's "Little Free Speech" Movement of 1966'

'No one is compelled to attend the university . . .': 'Education: Universities: Sad Scenes at Berkeley', *Time*, 9 December 1966

'Guidelines to Berkeley', letters to *Time* magazine, 30 December 1966, by N. Donald Diebel and Henri Temianka respectively

Michelle Reeves, '"Obey the Rules or Get Out"', op. cit.

'Berkeley Explodes Again: This Time It's War', *International Times*, no. 5, 12–25 December 1966

For more student unrest: 'Aberrations at Harvard', *Time*, 18 November 1966; 'Bad Days at Berkeley', *Newsweek*, 12 December 1966; and 'Uneasy Truce at Berkeley', *Newsweek*, 19 December 1966

LSE protest: 'Berkeley-on-Thames', *Newsweek*, 5 December 1966

Jonathan Leake, 'Teen Revolt', *Resurgence Youth Movement* magazine, undated, late 1966

Benn Morea, 'The Total Revolution', *Black Mask*, no. 2, December 1966

Raoul Vaneigem, *The Totality for Kids*, translated by Christopher Gray and Philippe Vissac (Christopher Gray, July 1966)

Christopher Gray and Charles Radcliffe, 'Editorial: All or Not at All', *Heatwave*, no. 2, October 1966

For more on the Situationists and the events at Strasbourg University in November and December 1966, see Charles Radcliffe, 'Two Fiery Flying Rolls: The Heatwave Story, 1966–1970', in Charles Radcliffe and Franklin Rosemont, *Dancing in the Streets: Anarchists, IWWs, Surrealists, Situationists & Provos in the 1960s* (Charles H. Kerr, 2005);

Raoul Vaneigem, *The Revolution of Everyday Life* (Rebel Press, 1983); Guy Debord, *Society of the Spectacle* (Black and Red, 1970); Michele Bernstein's 'The Situationist International', originally published in the *Times Literary Supplement*, 2 September 1964, reproduced at www.notbored. org/the-SI.html; Stephen Canfield and Robert Peterson, 'The Return of the Durutti Column by Andre Bertrand', Eastern Illinois University, at detournementexhibition.org/durutti.php; Jean-Michel Mension, *The Tribe* (City Lights, 2001); 'De La Misere En Milieu Etudiant', A.F.G.E.S., November 1966, translated by Christopher Gray as *Ten Days That Shook the University* (Situationist International, 1967) – with 'Postscript: if you make a social revolution, do it for fun'

'Everybody can go around . . .': Leonard Gross, 'John Lennon: Beatle on His Own', *Look*, 23 December 1966

For Beatles 'door-stop' interviews and 'Are the Beatles on the Way Out Now?' headline: 'Reporting '66', ITN, transmitted 28 December 1966; footage at www.youtube.com/watch?v=ZtDwFJ8psoI

Beatles interviews transcribed on www.beatlesinterviews.org

'everything we've done so far has been rubbish . . .': 11 November 1966 Don Short interview, collected in Keith Badman, *The Beatles: Off the Record* (Omnibus Press, 2000)

Derek Taylor, 'The Beatles Are Dead? Long Live the Beatles!' *Melody Maker*, 26 November 1966

Geoff Emerick and Howard Massey, *Here, There and Everywhere: My Life Recording the Music of the Beatles*, Chapter 8 – 'It's Wonderful to Be Here, It's Certainly a Thrill: Sgt. Pepper Begins' (Gotham Books, 2007)

For the evolution of 'Strawberry Fields Forever': www.beatlesebooks.com/ strawberry-fields-forever; for day-to-day entries regarding Beatles activities: www.beatlesbible.com (for 24 November 1966 onwards); and bootlegs like *Nothing Is Real* (Op8 Music)

'psychoanalysis set to music': Lennon interview from 1970, collected in Brian Roylance, 'How I Won the War', *The Beatles Anthology* (Weidenfeld & Nicholson, 2001)

Kenneth Allsop, 'Turn On, Tune In, Drop Out', *The Spectator*, 9 December 1966; reprinted in *The Pop Process*, op. cit., Chapter 4 – 'Sources of Fashion: The Audience'

'I found that I couldn't cut the tape . . .': *Here, There and Everywhere*, op. cit., Chapter 8 – 'It's Wonderful to Be Here, It's Certainly a Thrill: Sgt. Pepper Begins'

Keith Altham, 'Who's For A Merry Xmas!', *NME*, 24 December 1966

UFO: Barry Miles, 'UFO', in *In the Sixties*, op. cit.

Julian Palacios, *Lost in the Woods*, op. cit., Stage Two – 'The Wild Wood (1966)'

Rob Chapman, *Syd Barrett*, op. cit., Chapter 3 – 'Flicker Flicker Blam Blam Pow'

'You'd drop acid and arrive blotto . . .': *Pigs Might Fly*, op. cit., Chapter 3 – 'A Strange Hobby'

Jeff Dexter quote: DJ History interview at www.djhistory.com/interviews/jeff-dexter

Author interviews with John Hopkins, May 2012, and Peter Jenner, January 2015

Time quote re. most prosperous year in US history: 'The Economy: The Year of Tight Money and Where It Will Lead', 30 December 1966

'Santa '66: Fattest of All', *Newsweek*, 5 December 1966

'Road Toll Is Mounting', *Evening Standard*, 24 December 1966

'225 Hurt on Roads at Week-End', *Scotsman*, 27 December 1966

Tom Jones clip: www.bbc.co.uk/programmes/p012gfg4

'Xmas Pop Guide to Viewing & Listening', *NME*, 24 December 1966

'BBC's "Alice" for Adults Only', *Life* (international edition), 26 December 1966

Horace Judson, 'A Study of "Classic Textbook Psychoses"', interview with Jonathan Miller, *Life* (international edition), 26 December 1966

Hitchcock quote from nofilmschool.com/2014/03/breaking-down-the-crop-duster-scene-from-hitchcocks-north-by-northwest

Lewis Carroll, *Alice in Wonderland*, Kindle edition

For both the Association and Tim Hardin reviews: Penny Valentine, 'Penny Spins the Discs', *Record Mirror*, 10 December 1966

Tony Hall on Tim Hardin: 'My Scene', *Record Mirror*, 31 December 1966

'1966 Singles to Remember', *Melody Maker*, 3 December 1966

Penny Valentine, 'Vintage Year for New Sounds', *Disc and Music Echo*, 24 December 1966

Richard Green, 'The Ups and Downs of the U.S. Charts', *Record Mirror*, 31 December 1966

Richard Green on the UK charts: 'Giants of '66', *Record Mirror*, 31 December 1966

Maureen Cleave, 'The Year Pop Went Flat', *Evening Standard*, 29 December 1966; reproduced in *The Pop Process*, op. cit., Chapter 6 – 'A Case History: Protest Music'

For details of Beatles activities on 29 and 30 December: www.beatlesbible.com

Peter Jenner, author interview January 2015

The UK launch of the Monkees: monkeestv.tripod.com/Monkees_UKTV.html

For accounts of Psychedelicamania: Julian Palacios, *Lost in the Woods*, op. cit., Stage Two – 'The Wild Wood (1966)'; www.sydbarrettpinkfloyd.com/2009/12/roundhouse-psychedelicamania-december.html; www.rocksbackpages.com/Library/Article/the-who-the-move-pink-floyd-the-roundhouse-chalk-farm-london

For 'Dark Magic': David Fricke, sleeve notes to *Moby Grape Live* (Sundazed, 2010)

INDEX